Big Data for Twenty-First-Century Economic Statistics

NBER

NATIONAL BUREAU *of*
ECONOMIC RESEARCH

Studies in Income and Wealth

Volume 79

National Bureau of Economic Research

Conference on Research in Income and Wealth

NBER
NATIONAL BUREAU *of*
ECONOMIC RESEARCH

Big Data for Twenty-First-Century Economic Statistics

Edited by **Katharine G. Abraham, Ron S. Jarmin, Brian C. Moyer, and Matthew D. Shapiro**

The University of Chicago Press

Chicago and London

The University of Chicago Press, Chicago 60637
The University of Chicago Press, Ltd., London
© 2022 by the National Bureau of Economic Research
Chapter 6, "Transforming Naturally Occurring Text Data into
Economic Statistics: The Case of Online Job Vacancy Postings," by
Arthur Turrell, Bradley Speigner, Jyldyz Djumalieva, David Copple,
and James Thurgood © Bank of England
Published 2022
Printed in the United States of America

31 30 29 28 27 26 25 24 23 22   1 2 3 4 5

ISBN-13: 978-0-226-80125-4 (cloth)
ISBN-13: 978-0-226-80139-1 (e-book)
DOI: https://doi.org/10.7208/chicago/9780226801391.001.0001

Library of Congress Cataloging-in-Publication Data

Names: Abraham, Katharine G., editor. | Jarmin, Ronald S., 1964–,
    editor. | Moyer, Brian, editor. | Shapiro, Matthew D. (Matthew
    David), editor.
Title: Big data for twenty-first-century economic statistics / edited by
    Katharine G. Abraham, Ron S. Jarmin, Brian C. Moyer, Matthew D.
    Shapiro.
Other titles: Big data for 21st century economic statistics | Studies in
    income and wealth ; v. 79.
Description: Chicago : University of Chicago Press, 2022. | Series:
    Studies in income and wealth ; volume 79
Identifiers: LCCN 2021030585 | ISBN 9780226801254 (cloth) |
    ISBN 9780226801391 (ebook)
Subjects: LCSH: Economics—Statistical methods—Data processing.
    | Big data.
Classification: LCC HB143.5 .B54 2022 | DDC 330.072/7—dc23
LC record available at https://lccn.loc.gov/2021030585

♾ This paper meets the requirements of ANSI/NISO Z39.48-1992
(Permanence of Paper).

Relation of the Directors to the Work and Publications of the NBER

1. The object of the NBER is to ascertain and present to the economics profession, and to the public more generally, important economic facts and their interpretation in a scientific manner without policy recommendations. The Board of Directors is charged with the responsibility of ensuring that the work of the NBER is carried on in strict conformity with this object.

2. The President shall establish an internal review process to ensure that book manuscripts proposed for publication DO NOT contain policy recommendations. This shall apply both to the proceedings of conferences and to manuscripts by a single author or by one or more co-authors but shall not apply to authors of comments at NBER conferences who are not NBER affiliates.

3. No book manuscript reporting research shall be published by the NBER until the President has sent to each member of the Board a notice that a manuscript is recommended for publication and that in the President's opinion it is suitable for publication in accordance with the above principles of the NBER. Such notification will include a table of contents and an abstract or summary of the manuscript's content, a list of contributors if applicable, and a response form for use by Directors who desire a copy of the manuscript for review. Each manuscript shall contain a summary drawing attention to the nature and treatment of the problem studied and the main conclusions reached.

4. No volume shall be published until forty-five days have elapsed from the above notification of intention to publish it. During this period a copy shall be sent to any Director requesting it, and if any Director objects to publication on the grounds that the manuscript contains policy recommendations, the objection will be presented to the author(s) or editor(s). In case of dispute, all members of the Board shall be notified, and the President shall appoint an ad hoc committee of the Board to decide the matter; thirty days additional shall be granted for this purpose.

5. The President shall present annually to the Board a report describing the internal manuscript review process, any objections made by Directors before publication or by anyone after publication, any disputes about such matters, and how they were handled.

6. Publications of the NBER issued for informational purposes concerning the work of the Bureau, or issued to inform the public of the activities at the Bureau, including but not limited to the NBER Digest and Reporter, shall be consistent with the object stated in paragraph 1. They shall contain a specific disclaimer noting that they have not passed through the review procedures required in this resolution. The Executive Committee of the Board is charged with the review of all such publications from time to time.

7. NBER working papers and manuscripts distributed on the Bureau's web site are not deemed to be publications for the purpose of this resolution, but they shall be consistent with the object stated in paragraph 1. Working papers shall contain a specific disclaimer noting that they have not passed through the review procedures required in this resolution. The NBER's web site shall contain a similar disclaimer. The President shall establish an internal review process to ensure that the working papers and the web site do not contain policy recommendations, and shall report annually to the Board on this process and any concerns raised in connection with it.

8. Unless otherwise determined by the Board or exempted by the terms of paragraphs 6 and 7, a copy of this resolution shall be printed in each NBER publication as described in paragraph 2 above.

Contents

Prefatory Note

This volume contains revised versions of the papers presented at the Conference on Research in Income and Wealth entitled "Big Data for 21st Century Economic Statistics," held in Washington, DC, on March 15–16, 2019.

We gratefully acknowledge the financial support for this conference provided by the Alfred P. Sloan Foundation under grant G-2018-11019. Support for the general activities of the Conference on Research in Income and Wealth is provided by the following agencies: Bureau of Economic Analysis, Bureau of Labor Statistics, the Census Bureau, the Board of Governors of the Federal Reserve System, the Statistics of Income/Internal Revenue Service, and Statistics Canada.

We thank Katharine G. Abraham, Ron S. Jarmin, Brian C. Moyer, and Matthew D. Shapiro, who served as conference organizers and as editors of the volume.

Introduction
Big Data for Twenty-First Century Economic Statistics: The Future Is Now

Katharine G. Abraham, Ron S. Jarmin, Brian C. Moyer, and Matthew D. Shapiro

The infrastructure and methods for official US economic statistics arose in large part from the federal government's need to respond to the Great Depression and Second World War. The US economy of the late 1940s was heavily goods based, with nearly a third of payroll employment in manufacturing. Although censuses of manufacturing activity had been undertaken as early as 1810, the first comprehensive quinquennial economic census was conducted in 1954. Economic census data provide the backbone for the measurement of nominal economic activity in the national income and product accounts. Surveys based on probability samples developed after World War II collect accurate statistics at lower cost than complete enumerations and make central contributions to high-frequency measurements. Administrative data, especially data on income from tax records, play an important role in the construction of the income side of the accounts and in imputing missing data on the product side.

The deflators used to construct estimates of real product were developed separately from the measurement system for nominal income and product. The earliest Consumer Price Index (CPI) was introduced in 1919 as a cost-

Katharine G. Abraham is professor of economics and survey methodology at the University of Maryland, and a research associate of the National Bureau of Economic Research.

Ron S. Jarmin is Deputy Director and Chief Operating Officer of the US Census Bureau.

Brian C. Moyer is Director of the National Center for Health Statistics.

Matthew D. Shapiro is the Lawrence R. Klein Collegiate Professor of Economics, and Director and Research Professor of the Survey Research Center, both at the University of Michigan, and a research associate of the National Bureau of Economic Research.

For acknowledgments, sources of research support, and disclosure of the authors' material financial relationships, if any, please see https://www.nber.org/books-and-chapters/big-data-21st-century-economic-statistics/introduction-big-data-21st-century-economic-statistics.

of-living index for deflating wages. The CPI and Producer Price Index programs provide the price measurements used to convert nominal measures into estimates of real product.[1]

This measurement infrastructure, established mostly in the middle part of the twentieth century, proved durable as well as valuable not only to the federal government but also to a range of other decision makers and the research community. Spread across multiple agencies with separate areas of responsibility, however, it is less than ideal for providing consistent and comprehensive measurements of prices and quantities. Moreover, as has been noted by a number of commentators, the data landscape has changed in fundamental ways since the existing infrastructure was developed. Obtaining survey responses has become increasingly difficult and response rates have fallen markedly, raising concerns about the quality of the resulting data (see, for example, Baruch and Holtom 2008; Groves 2011; and Meyer, Mok, and Sullivan 2015). At the same time, the economy has become more complex, and users are demanding ever more timely and more granular data.

In this new environment, there is increasing interest in alternative sources of data that might allow the economic statistics agencies to better address users' demands for information. As discussed by Bostic, Jarmin, and Moyer (2016), Bean (2016), Groves and Harris-Kojetin (2017), and Jarmin (2019), among others, recent years have seen a proliferation of natively digital data that have enormous potential for improving economic statistics. These include detailed transactional data from retail scanners or companies' internal systems, credit card records, bank account records, payroll records and insurance records compiled for private business purposes; data automatically recorded by sensors or mobile devices; and a growing variety of data that can be obtained from websites and social media platforms. Incorporating these nondesigned Big Data sources into the economic measurement infrastructure holds the promise of allowing the statistical agencies to produce more accurate, timelier, and more disaggregated statistics, with a lower burden for data providers and perhaps even at lower cost for the statistical agencies. The agencies already have begun to make use of novel data to augment traditional data sources. More fundamentally, the availability of new sources of data offers the opportunity to redesign the underlying architecture of official statistics.

In March 2019, with support from the Alfred P. Sloan Foundation, the Conference on Research in Income and Wealth (CRIW) convened a meeting held in Bethesda, Maryland, to explore the latest research on the deployment of Big Data to solve both existing and novel challenges in economic measurement. The papers presented at the conference demonstrate that Big

---

1. See Carson (1975) and Goldberg and Moye (1985) for discussions of the development of the existing infrastructure for the production of economic statistics.

Data together with modern data science tools can contribute significantly and systematically to our understanding of the economy.

An earlier CRIW conference on *Scanner Data and Price Indexes,* organized by Robert Feenstra and Matthew Shapiro and held in the fall of 2000 in Arlington, Virginia, explored some of these same themes. Authors at the 2000 conference examined the use of retail transaction data for price measurement. Although there was considerable interest at that time in this new source of data, many of the papers pointed to problems in implementation and performance of the resulting measures (Feenstra and Shapiro 2003). Research continued, but for a variety of reasons, innovations in official statistics to make use of the new data were slow to follow.

Twenty years on, the papers in this volume highlight applications of alternative data and new methods to a range of economic measurement topics. An important contribution to the conference was the keynote address given by then Statistics Netherlands Director General Dr. Tjark Tjin-A-Tsoi. He reported on that agency's impressive progress in supplementing and replacing traditional surveys with alternative Big Data sources for its statistical programs. Notwithstanding the issues and challenges that remain to be tackled to realize the full potential of Big Data for economic measurement at scale, there was much enthusiasm among the conference participants regarding their promise.

The message of the papers in this volume is that Big Data are ripe for incorporation into the production of official statistics. In contrast to the situation two decades ago, modern data science methods for using Big Data have advanced sufficiently to make the more systematic incorporation of these data into official statistics feasible. Indeed, considering the threats to the current measurement model arising from falling survey response rates, increased survey costs, and the growing difficulties of keeping pace with a rapidly changing economy, fundamental changes in the architecture of the statistical system will be necessary to maintain the quality and utility of official economic statistics. Statistical agencies have little choice but to engage in the hard work and significant investments necessary to incorporate the types of data and measurement approaches studied in this volume into their routine production of official economic statistics.

The COVID-19 crisis that emerged the year following the conference (and so is not addressed in any of the papers) has driven home the importance of modernizing the federal data infrastructure by incorporating these new sources of data. In a crisis, timely and reliable data are of critical importance. There has been intense interest in the high-frequency information by location and type of activity that private researchers working with Big Data have been able to produce. For example, near-real-time location data from smartphones have provided detailed insights into the response of aggregate activity to the unfolding health crisis (Google 2020; University of Maryland 2020). Based on data from a variety of private sources, Opportunity Insight's

Economic Tracker is providing decision makers with weekly indexes of employment, earnings, and consumer spending (Chetty et al. 2020). While the findings reported in the proliferation of new working papers using novel data sources have been highly valuable, for the most part, these measurement efforts have been uncoordinated and captured particular aspects of the pandemic's economic impact rather than providing a comprehensive picture.

Statistical agencies also responded nimbly to the crisis. For example, in addition to introducing two new Pulse Surveys providing important information on the response of households (Fields et al. 2020) and small businesses (Buffington et al. 2020) to the crisis, the Census Bureau released a new measure of weekly business creation based on administrative data. The Bureau of Labor Statistics (BLS) added questions to ongoing employer and household surveys to learn about how business operations were changing in response to the crisis (Beach 2020). Unfortunately, the use of Big Data by the statistical agencies for real-time granular economic measurement is in a nascent state and the infrastructure for the routine production of key official economic statistics based on robust and representative Big Data sources is not yet developed. Our hope is that, at the point when the American economy experiences any future crisis, the statistical agencies will be prepared to make use of the ongoing flow of Big Data to provide information that is both timely and comprehensive to help with guiding the important decisions that policy makers will confront.

The Promise of Big Data for Economic Measurement

As already noted, the current infrastructure for economic measurement has been largely in place since the mid-twentieth century. While organized in various ways, with some countries adopting a more centralized model (e.g., Canada) and others a more decentralized one (e.g., the United States), official economic measurement typically uses a mix of data sourced from sample surveys, government administrative records, and periodic censuses to support key statistics on output, prices, employment, productivity, and so on. For decades, as the primary collectors, processors, and curators of the raw information underlying economic statistics, government statistical offices were near monopoly providers of this information. Organizations such as the Census Bureau and the BLS collected information through household interviews or paper questionnaires completed by business survey respondents based on company records. In many cases, the information was digitized only when it was entered in the statistical agencies' computers. Today, in contrast, staggering volumes of digital information relevant to measuring and understanding the economy are generated each second by an increasing array of devices that monitor transactions and business processes as well as track the activities of workers and consumers.

The private sector is now the primary collector, processor, and curator of the vast majority of the raw information that potentially could be utilized to produce official economic statistics. For example, the information systems of most retailers permit tracking sales by detailed product and location in near real time. In some cases, although their data products are not intended to replace official measures, the private sector even is beginning to disseminate economic statistics to the public, as with ADP's monthly employment report, the Conference Board's Help Wanted Online publications, and the statistical information produced by the JPMorgan Chase Institute.

Timeliness is particularly important to many users of official economic statistics. Users of these data also commonly express a need for geographically disaggregated information. State and local agency representatives who met with members of a recent Committee on National Statistics panel reviewing the Census Bureau's annual economic surveys, for example, made clear that they find even state-level data of limited use. Ideally, they said, they would like data that could be aggregated into custom local geographies, such as a user-specified collection of counties (Abraham et al. 2018). Survey sample sizes, however, often limit what can be produced with any degree of reliability to national or perhaps state estimates.

Though often both timely and extraordinarily rich, many of the new sources of data generated in the private sector lack representativeness, covering only subpopulations such as the businesses that use a particular payroll service or customers of a particular bank. These considerations point in the direction of a blended survey–Big Data model for incorporating new sources of information into official statistics. Finding ways to do this effectively holds the promise of allowing the agencies to produce vastly more timely and detailed information.[2] To be clear, we do not suggest that official statisticians should want to produce estimates of Cheerios sold in Topeka last week. Rather, we believe it is possible to do much better than producing only aggregated national estimates at a monthly or quarterly frequency, as is the typical current practice.

Access to timely Big Data pertaining to wide swaths of economic activity also can help to reduce the revisions in official statistics. The estimates of Gross Domestic Product (GDP) produced by the Bureau of Economic Analysis (BEA) go through multiple rounds of sometimes substantial revisions, largely because the information that undergirds the initial estimates is sparse and better information arrives only with a substantial delay. These revisions can cause significant problems for users of the data. Recent research, including papers in this volume, shows that even incomplete information from private sources available on a timely basis can help with producing better initial estimates that are less subject to later revision.

Finally, new tools should make it possible to automate much of the produc-

2. Producing more granular statistics does raise challenges related to the preservation of privacy and confidentiality, challenges we discuss further below.

tion of economic statistics. To the extent that processes can be reengineered so that natively digital information flows directly from the source to the agency or organization responsible for producing the relevant economic statistics, the need for survey data can be reduced and scarce survey resources can be directed to measurement domains in which survey data are the only option. In the longer run, the use of Big Data has the potential for reducing the cost and respondent burden entailed with surveys and with enumerations such as the manual collection of prices in the CPI program.

The future is now, or so we say in this essay. Given the successes documented in the papers in the volume, we believe the time is ripe for Big Data to be incorporated systematically into the production of official statistics.

Using Big Data for Economy-Wide Economic Statistics

Major innovations in official statistics often have followed improvement in source data. The first five papers in this volume feature research using data sources that are new to economic measurement. The authors of these papers all are interested in using these new data sources to improve the timeliness and granularity of economic statistics. While the findings are encouraging, the authors are quick to point out that incorporating these new sources into routine production of economic statistics is not trivial and will require substantial investments.

In their paper, Gabriel Ehrlich, John Haltiwanger, Ron Jarmin, David Johnson, and Matthew Shapiro offer a vision of what integrated price and quantity measurement using retail transaction-level data might look like. Currently, retail prices and nominal sales are measured separately (prices by the BLS and nominal sales by the Census Bureau), using separate surveys drawn from different frames of retail businesses. Collecting prices and sales volumes separately limits how the resulting data can be used. Furthermore, the survey-based methodologies employed to collect the data limit the timeliness as well as the geographic and product specificity of the resulting estimates. Computing estimates of prices, quantities, and total retail sales directly from point-of-sale transactions data—which record both the prices and quantities of items sold at particular locations—can overcome all these issues. The trick is first to secure access to transaction-level data and second to develop the computational and analytic infrastructure to produce reliable estimates from them. Ehrlich et al. use a subset of transaction-level data from Nielson and the NPD Group to demonstrate feasible methods for accomplishing this. They describe many of the practical challenges involved in using transaction-level data for economic measurement, especially for measuring price changes. A key feature of transaction-level data is the large amount of product turnover. While the methods proposed by Ehrlich et al. show promise, the authors stress the work on methodological and data access issues that is needed before the agencies can use transaction-level data for measuring retail prices and quantities at scale.

The paper by Crystal Konny, Brendan Williams, and David Friedman in this volume examines several alternative data sources the BLS has studied for use in the CPI. First, they describe efforts to use transaction summaries from two corporate retailers, one of which is unwilling to participate in traditional BLS data collections, as a replacement for directly collected prices. An important issue encountered in the data for one of these firms was the presence of large product lifecycle price declines. Absent sufficiently rich descriptions of the products being priced, there was not a good way to deal with this. Second, Konny, Williams, and Friedman discuss how the BLS has used data obtained from several secondary sources, prioritizing product areas with reporting issues. In the case of data on new vehicle sales from JD Power, BLS has been able to field a successful experimental series and intends to introduce these data into regular CPI production. This is expected to be more cost effective than existing collection methods. Finally, the authors report on efforts to scrape data on fuel prices from a crowdsourced website (GasBuddy) and to use Application Programming Interfaces (APIs) to obtain data on airline fares. Overall, the authors describe excellent progress at the BLS on introducing new data sources into the CPI. The work to date, however, relies on idiosyncratic methods related to the specific data sources and products or services involved. This may limit the ability of the BLS to scale these approaches across additional items in the CPI basket or to expand the basket to include a larger subset of the potential universe of items.

Rebecca Hutchinson's paper describes ongoing work at the Census Bureau to obtain alternative source data for retail sales. The Census Bureau's monthly retail trade survey has experienced significant response rate declines and thus has been prioritized for modernization (Jarmin 2019). Like Ehrlich et al. (this volume), Hutchinson uses data from NPD's database, but rolled up to observations on the dollar value of sales at the product-by-store level. She examines how well the NPD numbers map to the retail sales data collected for the same companies and also how closely movements in the aggregated NPD numbers align with national-level Census estimates. Work is underway to examine how the product codes in the NPD data map to those used for the 2017 Economic Census. The results are very encouraging. Indeed, the Census Bureau has replaced monthly survey data with NPD sourced retail sales for over 20 companies and is working with NPD to increase that number. Hutchinson provides a valuable summary of the Census Bureau's process for negotiating access to and testing of the NPD data. It is instructive to see how much effort was required to implement what was, compared to other alternative data efforts, a relatively straightforward process. In addition to the explicit cash costs for third-party data acquisition, these implicit costs will need to come down through increased experience if the agencies are to scale these efforts under realistic budget assumptions.

The paper by Aditya Aladangady, Shifrah Aron-Dine, Wendy Dunn, Laura Feiveson, Paul Lengerman, and Claudia Sahm uses anonymized credit card transactions data from First Data, a large payments processor, for retail stores and restaurants. The data permit the authors to look at daily spending within tightly defined geographic regions with a lag of only a few days. The authors show that national monthly growth rates in the data track fairly well with the Census Bureau's monthly retail trade estimates, suggesting that both are capturing the same underlying reality. Then they use daily data to track the impact of shocks, such as the 2018–2019 government shutdown and natural disasters, on consumer spending. Before the data can be used for analysis, a number of filters must be applied. A key filter controls for the entry and exit of particular merchants from the database. The necessity of accounting for attributes of an alternative data source that complicates its application to economic measurement is a feature of many of the papers in this volume. Aladangady et al. demonstrate that the careful application of filters to raw Big Data sources can result in data that are fit for various measurement tasks.

The final paper in the section, by Tomaz Cajner, Leland Crane, Ryan Decker, Adrian Hamins-Puertolas, and Christopher Kurz, aims to improve real-time measurement of the labor market by combining timely private data with official statistics. Many efforts to use alternative data for economic measurement attempt to mimic some official series. Cajner et al. depart from this by bringing multiple noisy sources together to better measure the true latent phenomenon, in their case payroll employment. Thus, they model payroll employment using private data from the payroll processing firm Automatic Data Processing (ADP) together with data from the BLS Current Employment Statistics survey. Importantly for policy makers, forecasts using the authors' smooth state space estimates outperform estimates from either source separately. An attractive feature of the ADP data, which are available weekly, is their timeliness. This featured critically when the authors, in collaboration with additional coauthors from ADP and academia, recently used these data and methods to produce valuable information on employment dynamics during the COVID-19 crisis (Cajner et al. 2020).

Uses of Big Data for Classification

Many data users do not care exclusively or even primarily about aggregate measurements but also or even mostly about information by type of firm, product, or worker. Published official statistics are based on standardized classification systems developed with the goal of allowing agencies to produce disaggregated statistics that are categorized on a comparable basis. In a "designed data" world, information about industry, product category, occupation and so on is collected from the firm or worker and used to assign each observation to an appropriate category. In some cases, expense precludes collecting the information needed to produce statistics broken out in accord with a particular classification. Even when it is collected, the responses to the relevant questions may be missing or unreliable. Responses from businesses about organizational form or industry, for example, frequently are missing from surveys, and when provided, the information can be unreliable because the question asks about a construct created by the agency rather than a variable that has a natural counterpart in businesses' operations. The next three papers provide examples of how nondesigned data can be used to produce statistics broken out along dimensions relevant to users of the data or to better categorize the information already being collected by the statistical agencies.

In their paper, Arthur Turrell, Bradley Speigner, Jyldyz Djumalieva, David Copple, and James Thurgood begin by noting that the statistics on job openings available for the United Kingdom are reported by industry but are not broken out by occupation. Turrell et al. use machine learning methods in conjunction with information on job advertisements posted to a widely used recruiting website to learn about occupational vacancies. Using matching algorithms applied to term frequency vectors, the authors match the job descriptions in the recruitment advertisements to the existing Standard Occupational Classification (SOC) documentation, assigning a 3-digit SOC code to each advertisement. Turrell et al. then reweight the vacancy counts so that total vacancies by industry match the numbers in published official statistics. The result is estimates that integrate official job openings statistics designed to be fully representative with supplementary Big Data that provide a basis for further disaggregation along occupational lines.

Joseph Staudt, Yifang Wei, Lisa Singh, Shawn Klimek, Brad Jensen, and Andrew Baer address the difficult measurement question of whether an establishment is franchise affiliated. Franchise affiliation was hand-recoded in the 2007 Census, but due to resource constraints, this was not done for the 2012 Census. While commercial sources showed an increase in the rate of franchise affiliation between 2007 and 2012, the Economic Census data showed a significant decline, suggesting a problem with the Economic Census data. The authors make use of web-scraped information collected directly from franchise websites as well as data from the Yelp API to automate the recoding process. They apply a machine learning algorithm to probabilistically match franchise establishments identified in the online sources to the Census Business Register (BR), allowing them to code the matched BR establishments as franchise affiliated. This approach leads to a substantial increase in the number of establishments coded as franchise affiliated in the 2017 Economic Census.

Similar to the Staudt et al. paper, John Cuffe, Sudip Bhattacharjee, Ugochukwu Etudo, Justin Smith, Nevada Basdeo, Nathaniel Burbank, and Shawn Roberts use web-scraped data to classify establishments into an industrial taxonomy. The web-scraped information is based on text; it includes variables routinely used by statistical agencies (establishment name, address, and type) and novel information including user reviewers that bring a new dimension—customer assessment—to informing the classification of businesses. As with the previous paper, establishments identified via web scraping are matched to the BR and coded with a characteristic—in this case, a North American Industry Classification System (NAICS) industry classification. This approach yields a fairly low misclassification rate at the 2-digit NAICS level. Further work is needed to evaluate whether the general approach can be successful at providing the more granular classifications required by agencies.

Uses of Big Data for Sectoral Measurement

New types of data generated by social media and search applications provide opportunities for sectoral measurement based on the wisdom of crowds. The paper by Edward Glaeser, Hyunjin Kim, and Michael Luca is motivated by the fact that official County Business Patterns (CBP) statistics on the number of business establishments at the zip code level do not become available until roughly a year and a half, or in some cases even longer, after the end of the year to which they apply. There would be considerable value in more timely information. Glaeser, Kim, and Luca ask whether information gleaned from Yelp postings can help with estimating startups of new businesses generally, and restaurants specifically, for zip code geographies in closer to real time. Yelp was founded in 2004 to provide people with information on local businesses and the website's coverage grew substantially over the following several years. The data used by Glaeser, Kim, and Luca span a limited period (2012 through 2015) but have broad geographic coverage with more than 30,000 zip code tabulation areas. They apply both regression and machine learning methods to develop forecasts of growth in the zip-code-level CBP establishment counts. Both for all businesses and for restaurants, adding current Yelp data to models that already include lagged CBP information substantially improves the forecasts. Perhaps not surprisingly, these improvements are greatest for zip codes that are more densely populated and have higher income and education levels, all characteristics that one would expect to be associated with better Yelp coverage.

Three of the papers in the volume leverage data sources that are generated as a byproduct of how activity in a particular context is organized, taxed, or regulated. Because of the way in which foreign trade is taxed and regulated, there are detailed administrative data on the prices and quantities associated with international transactions that do not exist for domestic transactions. Because medical care typically is accompanied by insurance claims, rich data exist on health care diagnoses, treatment costs, and outcomes. State and local property taxation means that there are detailed data on the valuations and sales of residential real estate. Other regulated or previously regulated sectors (e.g., transportation, energy utilities) also have rich and often publicly available sources of data that are a byproduct of the regulatory regime. Industrial organization economists long have used these data for studying market behavior. The three papers in the volume that use such information show how these sorts of data can be used to produce meaningful statistical measures.

The paper by Don Fast and Susan Fleck looks at the feasibility of using administrative data on the unit values of traded items to calculate price indexes for imports and exports. The paper uses a fairly granular baseline definition for what constitutes a product, making use of information on each transaction's 10-digit harmonized system (HS) code. Still, the items in these categories are considerably more heterogeneous than, for example, the products used to construct traditional matched model price indexes, or the products identified by retail UPC codes in the scanner data used in other papers in this volume. This creates a risk that changes in average prices in a given 10-digit HS category could reflect changes in product mix rather than changes in the prices of individual items. Although they do not have information that allows them to track specific products, Fast and Fleck have other information that they argue lets them get closer to that goal, including the company involved in the transaction and other transaction descriptors. Fast and Fleck report that there is considerable heterogeneity in transaction prices within 10-digit HS codes but that this heterogeneity is reduced substantially when they use additional keys—that is, the other transaction descriptors available to them. Their work suggests that, by using the additional descriptors to construct sets of transactions that are more homogeneous, it may be feasible to produce import and export price indexes using the administrative data.

There have been substantial advances in recent years in the use of large-scale datasets on medical treatments for the measurement of health care. As described by Dunn, Rittmueller, and Whitmire (2015), the BEA's Health Satellite Account uses insurance claims data to implement the disease-based approach to valuing health care advocated by Cutler, McClellan, Newhouse, and Remler (1998) and Shapiro, Shapiro, and Wilcox (2001). The major advantage of health insurance claims data is that they can provide comprehensive measurements of inputs and outputs for the treatment of disease. This volume's paper by John Romley, Abe Dunn, Dana Goldman, and Neeraj Sood uses data for Medicare beneficiaries to measure multifactor productivity in the provision of care for acute diseases that require hospitalization. Output is measured by health outcomes that, in the absence of market valuations, provide a proxy for the value of healthcare (Abraham and Mackie, 2004). The authors use the Medicare claims data to make comprehensive adjustments for factors that affect health outcomes such as comorbidities and social, economic, and demographic factors, allowing them to isolate the effect of treatments on outcomes. While they find evidence for improvements in the quality of many health treatments, which would lead price indexes that do not adjust for quality change to overstate healthcare price inflation, their results imply that quality improvement is not universal. For heart failure, one of the eight diseases studied, there is evidence that over the years studied the productivity of treatment declined.

Case and Shiller (1989) introduced the idea of using repeat sales of houses to construct a constant quality measure of changes in house prices. Building on these ideas, the increasing availability of data on transaction prices from local property assessments and other sources has revolutionized the residential real estate industry. Zillow provides house price estimates based on repeat sales at the house level. Marina Gindelsky, Jeremy Moulton, and Scott Wentland explore whether and how the Zillow data might be used in the national income and product accounts. The US national accounts use a rental equivalence approach to measuring the services of owner-occupied housing. Implementing the rental equivalence approach requires imputation since, by definition, owner-occupied housing does not have a market rent. An important difficulty with this approach is that it relies on there being good data on market rents for units that are comparable to owner-occupied units. The paper discusses the challenges to the implementation of the rental equivalence approach and the steps taken by the BLS and BEA to address them.

The paper then asks whether a user cost approach facilitated by Big Data house prices is a useful alternative to the rental equivalence approach. As explained in detail in the paper, the real user cost of housing depends on the price of housing, the general price level, the real interest rate, the depreciation rate, and the real expected capital gain on housing. Many of the components of the user cost formulation, especially the real expected capital gain on housing, are difficult to measure at the level of granularity of the data used by the authors. In the paper's analysis, the empirical variation in user cost comes almost exclusively from variation in the price of housing. During the period under study, the US experienced a housing boom and bust, and the user cost estimates reported in the paper mirror this boom-and-bust cycle in housing prices. The observed fluctuation in house prices seems very unlikely to reflect a corresponding fluctuation in the value of real housing services. Hence, while the paper contains a useful exploration of housing prices derived from transaction-based data, it is difficult to imagine the method outlined in the paper being used for the National Income and Product Accounts.

Methodological Challenges and Advances

As already mentioned, one significant impediment to realizing the potential of Big Data for economic measurement is the lack of well-developed methodologies for incorporating them into the measurement infrastructure. Big Data applications in many contexts make use of supervised machine learning methods. In a typical application, the analyst possesses observations consisting of a gold-standard measure of some outcome of interest (e.g., an estimate based on survey or census data) together with Big Data she believes can be used to predict that outcome in other samples. A common approach is to divide the available observations into a training data set for estimating the Big Data models, a validation data set for model selection, and a test data set for assessing the model's out-of-sample performance. Validation and testing are important because overfitting can produce a model that works well in the training data but performs poorly when applied to other data.

The fact that Big Data suitable for the production of economic statistics have only relatively recently become available, however, means the standard machine learning approaches often cannot simply be imported and applied. That is the challenge confronted in the paper by Jeffrey Chen, Abe Dunn, Kyle Hood, Alexander Driessen, and Andrea Batch. Chen et al. seek to develop reliable forecasts of the Quarterly Services Survey (QSS) series used in constructing Personal Consumption Expenditures (PCE). Complete QSS data do not become available until about two-and-a-half months after the end of the quarter and their arrival often leads to significant PCE revisions. Chen et al. consider several types of information, including credit card and Google trends data, as potential predictors of QSS series for detailed industries to be incorporated into the early PCE estimates. They also consider multiple modeling approaches, including not only moving average forecasts and regression models but also various machine learning approaches. Because the 2010Q2 through 2018Q1 period for which they have data captures growth over just 31 quarters, splitting the available information into training, validation, and test data sets is not a feasible option. Instead, Chen et al. use data on growth over 19 quarters of data to fit a large number of models using different combinations of source data, variable selection rule, and algorithm. Then, they assess model performance by looking at predicted versus actual outcomes for all the QSS series over the following 12 quarters. The intuition behind their approach is that modeling approaches that consistently perform well are least likely to suffer from overfitting problems. Chen et al. conclude that, compared to current practice, ensemble methods such as random forests are most likely to reduce the size of PCE revisions and incorporating nontraditional data into these models can be helpful.

Rishab Guha and Serena Ng tackle a somewhat different methodological problem. Use of scanner data to measure consumer spending has been proposed as a means of providing more timely and richer information than available from surveys. A barrier to fully exploiting the potential of the scanner data, however, is the challenge of accounting for seasonal and calendar effects on weekly observations. Events that can have an important effect on consumer spending may occur in different weeks in different years. As examples, Easter may fall any time between the end of March and the end of April; the 4th of July may occur during either the 26th or the 27th week of the year; and both Thanksgiving and Christmas similarly may fall during a different numbered week depending on the year. Further, the effects of these events may differ across areas. Unless the data can be adjusted to remove such effects, movements in spending measures based on scanner data cannot be easily interpreted. Methods for removing seasonal and calendar effects from economic time series exist (Cleveland 1983), but these methods typically require a substantial time series of data. Even when data are available for a sufficiently long period, developing customized adjustment models is resource intensive and unlikely to be feasible when the number of data series is very large.

Guha and Ng work with weekly observations for 2006–2014 for each of roughly 100 expenditure categories by US county. Their modeling first removes deterministic seasonal movements in the data on a series-by-series basis and then exploits the cross-section dependence across the observations to remove common residual seasonal effects. The second of these steps allows for explanatory variables such as day of the year, day of the month, and county demographic variables to affect spending in each of the various categories. As an example, Cinco de Mayo always occurs on the same day of the year and its effects on spending may be greater in counties that are more heavily Hispanic. Applying machine learning methods, Guha and Ng remove both deterministic and common residual seasonality from the category by county spending series, leaving estimates that can be used to track the trend and cycle in consumer spending for detailed expenditure categories at a geographically disaggregated level.

Erwin Diewert and Robert Feenstra address another important issue regarding the use of scanner data for economic measurement—namely, how to construct price indexes that account appropriately for the effects on consumer welfare when commodities appear and disappear. Using data for orange juice, the paper provides an illustrative comparison of several empirical methods that have been proposed in the literature for addressing this problem. On theoretical grounds, they say, it is attractive to make use of the utility function that has been shown to be consistent with the Fisher price index. On practical grounds, however, it is much simpler to produce estimates that assume a constant elasticity of substitution (CES) utility function as proposed by Feenstra (1994) and implemented in recent work by Redding and Weinstein (2020) and Ehrlich et al. in this volume. The illustrative calculations reported by Diewert and Feenstra suggest that results based on the latter approach may dramatically overstate the gains in consumer welfare associated with the introduction of new products. A possible resolution, currently being explored by one of the authors, may be to assume a more flexible translog expenditure function that better balances accuracy with tractability.

Increasing the Use of Big Data for Economic Statistics: Challenges and Solutions

The papers in this volume document important examples of the progress thus far in incorporating Big Data into the production of official statistics. They also highlight some of the challenges that will need to be overcome to fully realize the potential of these new sources of data.

One of the lessons learned from successful current partnerships between federal agencies and private data providers is the necessity of accepting Big Data as they exist rather than requiring data providers to structure them in some predefined fashion. What that means, however, is that the agencies need to be nimble in working with data that were not originally designed for statistical analysis. As illustrated by the papers in this volume, there are several ways in which information generated for commercial or administrative purposes may not readily map into measurements that are immediately useful for statistical purposes:

- The variables generated by business and household data frequently do not correspond to the *economic and statistical concepts* embodied in official statistics. This is not to say that survey responses are always complete or correct (see, for example, Staudt et al. and Cuffe et al., this volume). Incorporating Big Data, however, will require the statistical agencies to find ways to map the imported data into desired measurement constructs. Many of the papers in this volume confront the problem of turning naturally occurring Big Data into variables that map into the paradigm of economic statistics.
- Data created for business purposes may not be coded into the *categories required* for the production of official statistics. As an example, scanner data contain product-level price information, but to meet the operational needs of the CPI program, the individual items must be mapped into the CPI publication categories (Konny, Williams, and Friedman, this volume).
- There are many complications related to the *time intervals of observations*. Weekly data on sales do not map readily to months or quarters (Guha and Ng, this volume). Payroll data, for example, refer to pay period, which may not align with the desired calendar period (Cajner et al., this volume). The BLS household and establishment surveys deal with this problem by requiring responses for a reference period, which

shifts the onus onto respondents to map their reality into an official survey, but using Big Data puts the onus for dealing with the issue back onto the statistical agency.

• Data generated as a result of internal processes may lack *longitudinal consistency*, meaning there may be discontinuities in data feeds that then require further processing by the statistical agencies. Even if the classification of observations is consistent over time, turnover of units or of products may create significant challenges for the use of Big Data (see, for example, Ehrlich et al. and Aladangady et al., this volume).

Producing nominal sales or consumption totals is conceptually simpler than producing the price indexes needed to transform those nominal figures into the real quantities of more fundamental interest. Product turnover causes particular difficulties for price index construction. The BLS has developed methods for dealing with product replacement when specific products selected for inclusion in price index samples cease to be available, but these methods are not feasible when indexes are being constructed from scanner data that may cover many thousands of unique items. As pioneered by Feenstra (1994) and advanced by Ehrlich et al. (this volume), Diewert and Feenstra (this volume), and Redding and Weinstein (2020), dealing with ongoing product turnover requires new methods that take advantage of changes in spending patterns to infer consumers' willingness to substitute across products.

Another set of issues concerns the arrangements under which data are provided to the statistical agencies. Much of the work done to date on the use of Big Data to improve economic statistics has been done on a pilot basis—to assess the feasibility of using the data, or to fill specific data gaps (see Hutchinson and Konny, Williams, and Friedman, both this volume). In several instances, the use of Big Data has been initiated when companies preferred to provide a larger data file rather than be burdened by enumeration (Konny, Williams, and Friedman, this volume). Even when data are more comprehensive, they may be provided under term-limited agreements that do not have the stability and continuity required for use in official statistics. The papers by Federal Reserve Board authors using credit card and payroll data (Aladangady et al. and Cajner et al., this volume) are examples in which this appears to be the case. Several of the papers in this volume make use of retail scanner data made available through the Kilts Center at the University of Chicago under agreements that specifically exclude their use by government agencies.

At least given the statistical agencies' current budgets, unfortunately, scaling the existing contracts at a similar unit cost would be cost-prohibitive. Some data providers may find it attractive to be able to say that their information is being used in the production of official statistics, perhaps making it easier for the agencies to negotiate a mutually agreeable contract for the continuing provision of larger amounts of data. In general, however, new models are likely to be needed. As an example, Jarmin (2019) suggests that existing laws and regulations could be changed to encourage secure access to private sector data for statistical purposes. One possible path would be to allow third-party data providers to report to the federal statistical agencies on behalf of their clients, making that a marketable service for them. For example, as part of the services small businesses receive from using a product like QuickBooks, the software provider could automatically and securely transmit data items needed for economic statistics to the appropriate agency or agencies.

In some cases, public-facing websites contain information that could be used to improve existing economic statistics. This volume's papers by Konny, Williams, and Friedman; Staudt et al.; Cuffe et al.; and Glaeser, Kim, and Luca all make use of such information. Even where data are posted publicly, however, the entities that own the data may place restrictions on how they can be used. As an example, the terms of use on one large retailer's website state "(Retailer) grants you a limited, non-exclusive, non-transferable license to access and make non-commercial use of this website. This license does not include . . . (e) any use of data mining, robots or similar data gathering and extraction tools." This typical provision would appear to mean that any statistical agency wanting to use information from this retailer's website would need to negotiate an agreement allowing that to happen. Multiplied across all the websites containing potentially useful information, obtaining these agreements could be a daunting task. In some cases, it may be possible to obtain desired information using an API provided by an organization, though this is by no means guaranteed.

One concern often cited with regard to the use of Big Data in the production of economic statistics is that the data could cease to be available or be provided in an inconsistent fashion over time, jeopardizing continuity in the production of statistical estimates. To be sure, in the face of sharply declining survey response rates and sporadic response to nonmandatory surveys, the sustainability of the statistical agencies' current business model is itself very much an open question. These recent trends suggest strongly that business as usual is simply not an option. Further, unexpected events such as the recent COVID-19 crisis can disrupt planned survey data collections and the timing of deliveries of key administrative data. In such circumstances, the flow of Big Data could be less vulnerable to interruption than the flow of data from traditional sources. Although Big Data are not produced primarily with the federal statistical agencies in mind, there often are other data users who are paying customers and rely on continuity of data provision. While not obviating the problem, this may provide some assurance that data on which an agency is relying will continue to be available. Contractual agreements also may help to ensure that a data source does not disappear without warning. As an example, agencies could enter into rolling multiyear contracts, such that an agreement for data provision is always in place for several years ahead.

A separate but related worry is that a sole-source contract with a data provider could lead to a hold-up problem. Once an agency has made the investments needed to ingest and process information from a particular data provider, that data provider would have leverage to raise the amount it charges the agency. There are limits, though, to how successful a hold-up attempt could be. Faced with unreasonable demands from a data provider on which it has come to rely, a statistical agency might have few options in the short run but could turn to alternative data sources in the longer run. This is another concern that rolling multiyear contracts could help to address, as such contracts would give a statistical agency faced with a hold-up demand some time to respond. Where possible, dividing data sourcing among two or more data providers would reduce the ability of any one data provider to hold up the statistical agency. More generally, increasing reliance on Big Data will require the development of Plan B's that could be implemented in the event incoming data are disrupted or become unaffordable.

Another concern with the use of commercial Big Data, especially from data aggregators, is that the data provider may have advanced insight into official statistics by virtue of providing major inputs into them. There are ways to address this concern. For example, data vendors' employees could be required to undergo training in the handling of confidential information and made subject to laws prohibiting them from trading based on nonpublic, prerelease information. These measures are similar to the measures currently in place to ensure that statistical agency employees do not share confidential prerelease information or benefit from their access to it. All else the same, the statistical agencies ideally would draw data from a sufficient diversity of sources that no one supplier's data have an undue influence on the published statistics, but there may be cases where this is not feasible or efficient and other approaches may be needed.

A central set of challenges for realizing the potential of Big Data for economic statistics arises from the way in which the agencies' collaborations with businesses and with each other are structured. Historically, each of the three main economic statistics agencies—the BLS, Census Bureau and BEA—has had a well-defined set of largely distinct responsibilities. Although there always has been collaboration among the agencies, survey data collections largely have been designed to collect data from businesses for specific statistical series, with each of those series produced independently. In a Big Data world, however, there are compelling reasons for agencies to adopt more integrated data collection and production processes.

The collection of transactions data from businesses is a key domain for such collaboration and coordination. At present, the Census Bureau carries out surveys to measure nominal sales by industry; the BLS carries out surveys to produce the price indexes needed to convert nominal sales into real quantity measures; and the BEA uses these separate measures as inputs to the National Income and Product Accounts. As discussed by Ehrlich et al. (this volume), however, the same underlying data could be used to produce both sales and price statistics in a much more integrated fashion. Rather than individual agencies negotiating separately with the providers of Big Data related to sales or prices, a single data use agreement could be negotiated on behalf of all the interested agencies. The development of standardized data use agreements could help to facilitate their negotiation, reducing the frictions associated with collaboration between agencies and businesses. Agency–business collaborations would be multipurpose rather than one-off solutions to particular issues, so that they would apply beyond the specific problem and could be scaled more easily. Allowing businesses to substitute data feeds for the completion of multiple burdensome surveys and enumerations could benefit them as well as the statistical agencies.

Having official statistics spread over the measurement and estimation programs of several agencies creates barriers to achieving the sort of coordination just described and realizing the full potential of Big Data. At present, the Census Bureau and BEA are located together in the Department of Commerce, whereas the BLS is part of the Department of Labor. Over the decades, there have been multiple proposals for consolidating the agencies or, absent such reorganization, for reducing legal and institutional barriers to coordinating their measurement programs. In the new Big Data world, the potential benefits of coordination or reorganization loom much larger than in the past. Absent reorganization, legal changes that will allow the agencies to coordinate their activities more effectively would advance the agenda for using Big Data to improve official statistics.

One of the most attractive features of the economic statistics that could be generated from Big Data also poses one of the biggest challenges associated with their production. Big Data offer the opportunity to produce very granular statistics. Protecting the privacy of the individuals or businesses underlying such detailed statistics, however, is inherently difficult. The fundamental challenge is that the more accurate the statistics computed from a private dataset, the more privacy is lost (Dinur and Nissim 2003). Formal methods, such as differential privacy, allow data publishers to make precise choices between privacy protection and data utility. A balance must be struck, however, between these competing objectives (Abowd and Schmutte 2019). As the controversy around the Census Bureau's adoption of differential privacy as the privacy protection methodology for products from the 2020 Census demonstrates, coming to an agreement about what is appropriate can be a difficult process. That said, the Census Bureau has also used these methods to protect privacy in products such as the Post-Secondary Employment Outcomes (PSEO) without much controversy (Foote, Machanavajjhala, and McKinney 2019). A key distinction is that there are well-established and politically sensitive use cases for decennial census data, whereas products like the PSEO are new and would be impossible to produce with sufficient accuracy and privacy protection without using modern disclosure avoidance techniques. This gives us hope that new economic statistics computed from detailed transactions, geolocation, and other sensitive sources can be released with an acceptable trade-off between utility and privacy and be broadly accepted by data users.

While not the focus of this volume, the computing infrastructure of the agencies will need to be improved for the agencies to benefit from these new data sources and tools. This is especially the case if the agencies intend to access data in new automated ways such as through APIs or taking advantage of approaches like secure multiparty computing. There has been recent progress on moving some agency computing infrastructure to the Cloud. Continued progress and investments in modern computing capabilities are necessary conditions for success in the Big Data era.

Beyond these issues related to accessing and processing new sources of Big Data, limitations in the capabilities of the existing statistical agency staff could impede the incorporation of these data into ongoing statistical production. Reflecting the needs of existing production processes, most of these staff have backgrounds in statistics or economics rather than data science. This surely will be corrected over time as staff receive training in the use of the relevant data science methods. The Census Bureau has collaborated with academia to develop a rigorous training curriculum for agency staff (see Jarmin et al. 2014). This evolved into the Coleridge Initiative, a collaboration among researchers at New York University, the University of Maryland, and the University of Chicago that is providing growing numbers of agency staff with hands-on training on data linkage and data science applications. Further, new hires increasingly will arrive with data science skills acquired as part of their college educations. That said, the statistical agencies will need to make concerted investments to build the skills required to acquire, process, and curate data sets that are larger and less structured than the surveys and administrative records on which the agencies have relied historically.

In the meantime, partnerships with those at academic and other research institutions with relevant expertise will be especially important for the agencies. The NSF-Census Research Network (NCRN) is a successful example of such collaboration across a number of universities and the Census Bureau (see Weinberg et al. 2019). The CRIW and NBER also have long been a nexus of collaboration between agencies and academics on measurement issues. This volume is a good example, with several of the papers including both agency and academic coauthors. A more recent nexus of collaboration that is directly relevant to data and methods discussed in this volume are the Tech Economics Conferences held by the National Association of Business Economists. These have featured economists and data scientists from academia, the public sector, and the private sector, especially tech and other companies that have pioneered using data in new and innovative ways.

Despite the challenges and the significant agenda for research and development they imply, the papers in the volume point strongly toward more systematic and comprehensive incorporation of Big Data to improve official economic statistics in the coming years. Indeed, the future is now.

References

Abowd, John, and Ian Schmutte. 2019. "An Economic Analysis of Privacy Protection and Statistical Accuracy as Social Choices." *American Economic Review* 109 (1): 171–202.

Abraham, Katharine G., Constance F. Citro, Glenn D. White Jr., and Nancy K. Kirkendall, eds. 2018. *Reengineering the Census Bureau's Annual Economic Surveys*. Washington, DC: National Academies Press.

Abraham, Katharine G., and Christopher Mackie, eds. 2004. *Beyond the Market: Designing Nonmarket Accounts for the United States*. Washington, DC: National Academies Press.

Baruch, Yehuda, and Brooks C. Holtom. 2008. "Survey Response Rate Levels and Trends in Organizational Research." *Human Relations* 61 (8): 1139–60.

Beach, William. 2020. "Innovations at BLS during the COVID-19 Pandemic." Commissioner's Corner blog post. Accessed December 29, 2020. https://blogs.bls.gov/blog/2020/11/24/innovations-at-bls-during-the-covid-19-pandemic/.

Bean, Charles. 2016. *Independent Review of UK Economic Statistics*. London: Cabinet Office and H.M. Treasury.

Bostic, William G., Ron S. Jarmin, and Brian Moyer. 2016. "Modernizing Federal Economic Statistics." *American Economic Review: Papers and Proceedings* 106 (5): 161–64.

Buffington, Catherine, Carrie Dennis, Emin Dinlersoz, Lucia Foster, and Shawn Klimek. 2020. "Measuring the Effect of COVID-19 on U.S. Small Businesses: The Small Business Pulse Survey." Working Paper No. 20-16, Center for Economic Studies, US Census Bureau.

Cajner, Tomaz, Leland D. Crane, Ryan A. Decker, John Grigsby, Adrian Hamins-Puertolas, Erik Hurst, Christopher Kurz, and Ahu Yildirmaz. 2020. "The U.S. Labor Market during the Beginning of the Pandemic Recession." *Brookings Papers on Economic Activity*, conference draft, June 25, 2020.

Carson, Carol. 1975. "The History of the National Income and Product Accounts: The Development of an Analytical Tool." *Review of Income and Wealth* 21 (2): 153–81.

Case, Karl E., and Robert J. Shiller. 1989, "The Efficiency of the Market for Single-Family Homes." *American Economic Review* 79 (1): 125–37.

Chetty, Raj, John Friedman, Nathaniel Hendren, and Michael Stepner. 2020. "How Did COVID-19 and Stabilization Policies Affect Spending and Employment? A New Real-Time Economic Tracker Based on Private Sector Data." NBER Working Paper No. 27431, National Bureau of Economic Research, Cambridge, MA.

Cleveland, William S. 1983. "Seasonal and Calendar Adjustment." *Handbook of Statistics*, 39–72. Amsterdam: Elsevier.

Cutler, David M., Mark McClellan, Joseph P. Newhouse, and Dahlia Remler. 1998. "Are Medical Prices Declining? Evidence from Heart Attack Treatments." *Quarterly Journal of Economics* 113 (4): 991–1024.

Dinur, Irit, and Kobbi Nissim. 2003. "Revealing Information while Preserving Privacy." *Proceedings of the 22nd ACM SIGMOD-SIGACT-SIGART Symposium on Principles of Database Systems*, 202–10. New York: Association for Computing Machinery.

Dunn, Abe, Lindsey Rittmueller, and Bryn Whitmire. 2015. "Introducing the New BEA Health Care Satellite Account." *Survey of Current Business* 95 (1): 1–21.

Feenstra, Robert C. 1994. "New Product Varieties and the Measurement of International Prices." *American Economic Review* 84 (1): 157–77.

Feenstra, Robert C., and Matthew D. Shapiro, eds. 2003. *Scanner Data and Price Indexes*. Studies in Income and Wealth, vol. 64. Chicago: University of Chicago Press.

Fields, Jason, Jennifer Hunter-Childs, Anthony Tersine, Jeffrey Sisson, Eloise Parker, Victoria Velkoff, Cassandra Logan, and Hyon Shin. 2020. "Design and Operation of the 2020 Household Pulse Survey." Unpublished paper, US Census Bureau.

Foote, Andrew, Ashwin Machanavajjhala, and Kevin McKinney. 2019. "Releasing Earnings Distributions Using Differential Privacy: Disclosure Avoidance System for Post-Secondary Employment Outcomes (PSEO)." *Journal of Privacy and Confidentiality* 9 (2).

Goldberg, Joseph P., and William T. Moye. 1985. *The First Hundred Years of the Bureau of Labor Statistics*. Washington, DC: US Department of Labor.

Google. 2020. "COVID-19 Community Mobility Reports." Accessed July 24, 2020. https://www.google.com/covid19/mobility/.

Groves, Robert M. 2011. "Three Eras of Survey Research." *Public Opinion Quarterly* 75 (5): 861–71.

Groves, Robert M., and Brian A. Harris-Kojetin, eds. 2017. *Innovations in Federal Statistics*. Washington, DC: National Academies Press.

Jarmin, Ron S. 2019. "Evolving Measurement for an Evolving Economy: Thoughts on 21st Century US Economic Statistics." *Journal of Economic Perspectives* 33 (1): 165–84.

Jarmin, Ron S., Julia Lane, Alan Marco, and Ian Foster. 2014. "Using the Classroom to Bring Big Data to Statistical Agencies." *AMSTAT News*, November, 12–13.

Meyer, Bruce D., Wallace K. C. Mok, and James X. Sullivan. 2015. "Household Surveys in Crisis." *Journal of Economic Perspectives* 29 (4): 199–226.

Redding, Stephen J., and David E. Weinstein. 2020. "Measuring Aggregate Price Indices with Taste Shocks: Theory and Evidence for CES Preferences." *Quarterly Journal of Economics* 135 (1): 503–60.

Shapiro, Irving, Matthew D. Shapiro, and David W. Wilcox. 2001. "Measuring the Value of Cataract Surgery." In *Medical Care Output and Productivity*, edited by David M. Cutler and Ernst R. Berndt. Studies in Income and Wealth, 62:411–37. Chicago: University of Chicago Press.

University of Maryland. 2020. "COVID-19 Impact Analysis Platform." Accessed July 30, 2020. https://data.covid.umd.edu/.

Weinberg, D. H., J. M. Abowd, R. F. Belli, N. Cressie, D. C. Folch, S. H. Holan, M. C. Levenstein, K. M. Olson, J. P. Reiter, M. D. Shapiro, and J. Smyth. 2019. "Effects of a Government-Academic Partnership: Has the NSF-Census Bureau Research Network Helped Secure the Future of the Federal Statistical System?" *Journal of Survey Statistics and Methodology* 7 (4): 589–619.

I

Toward Comprehensive Use of Big Data in Economic Statistics

1

Reengineering Key National Economic Indicators

Gabriel Ehrlich, John C. Haltiwanger, Ron S. Jarmin, David Johnson, and Matthew D. Shapiro

1.1 Introduction

Statistical agencies face multiple challenges in the present environment. Traditional methods of collecting data—whether asking businesses or individuals to complete surveys or gathering price data by sending enumerators

Gabriel Ehrlich is an economic forecaster at the University of Michigan, where he is the director of the University's Research Seminar in Quantitative Economics (RSQE).

John Haltiwanger is a professor of economics at the University of Maryland, and a research associate of the National Bureau of Economic Research.

Ron S. Jarmin is Deputy Director and Chief Operating Officer of the US Census Bureau.

David Johnson is the Director of the Panel Study of Income Dynamics at the Institute for Social Research, University of Michigan.

Matthew D. Shapiro is the Lawrence R. Klein Collegiate Professor of Economics, and Director and Research Professor of the Survey Research Center, both at the University of Michigan, and a research associate of the National Bureau of Economic Research.

We acknowledge financial support of the Alfred P. Sloan Foundation and the additional support of the Michigan Institute for Data Science and the Michigan Institute for Teaching and Research in Economics. The results here are in part based on researchers' own analyses calculated (or derived) based in part on data from the Nielsen Company (US), LLC and marketing databases provided through the Nielsen datasets at the Kilts Center for Marketing at the University of Chicago Booth School of Business. The conclusions drawn from the Nielsen data are those of the researchers and do not reflect the views of Nielsen. Nielsen is not responsible for, had no role in, and was not involved in analyzing and preparing the results reported herein. We also use the NPD data housed at the US Census Bureau. All results using the NPD data have been reviewed to ensure that no confidential information has been disclosed (CBDRB-FY19-122). Any opinions and conclusions expressed herein are those of the authors and do not necessarily represent the view of the US Census Bureau. We thank Katharine Abraham, Robert Cage, Robert Feenstra, David Friedman, Greg Kurtzon, Robert Martin, Stephen Redding, and David Weinstein for helpful comments. We thank Jamie Fogel, Diyue Guo, Edward Olivares, Luke Pardue, Dyanne Vaught, and Laura Zhao for superb research assistance. For acknowledgments, sources of research support, and disclosure of the authors' material financial relationships, if any, please see https://www.nber.org/books-and-chapters/big-data-21st-century-economic-statistics/re-engineering-key-national-economic-indicators.

to stores—face increasing challenges.[1] These include declining response rates to surveys, increasing costs for traditional modes of data collection and, perhaps most importantly, the difficulty of keeping pace with rapid changes in the economy. The information technology revolution is dramatically changing how and where consumers and businesses carry out their transactions. Consumers shop online, summon cars for hire with an app, watch "TV" without television stations or TVs, and "bank" without cash or checks. These technologies are leading to widespread changes in industrial structure and the organization of markets, with implications for prices and real output that the official economic statistics may fail to capture.

The good news for economic measurement is that these transactions inherently create huge amounts of data precisely because they are driven by information technology. Determining how to operate in this data-rich environment is therefore both a major challenge and a great opportunity for the statistical system. The information economy calls for more than using new technologies and new sources of data to improve on existing approaches to data collection. Instead, now is a promising time to explore reengineering the system of national statistics, specifically the National Income and Product Accounts (the NIPAs, which include GDP), productivity and consumer and producer price measurement, by collecting specific product data at source, or as close to the source as is feasible. In particular, we advocate that price and quantity be collected or aggregated simultaneously from retailers.

Before sketching how such a new infrastructure might look, we first briefly describe how the NIPAs and price indexes are currently assembled. We focus on consumer spending and prices, but similar issues apply across other components. In brief, nominal sales are collected by the Census Bureau, prices are collected by the Bureau of Labor Statistics (BLS), and real and nominal GDP are constructed by the Bureau of Economic Analysis (BEA) using these and other data sources.

A key point to understand is that prices and sales are currently based on different samples and levels of aggregation. Measurements of retail sales and the prices used to deflate them are not matched at the outlet level, let alone at the item level. A similar mismatch of price and nominal variables pervades productivity data, in which industry-level producer price indexes are used as deflators. This generates great challenges for micro productivity analysis but also is problematic for the industry-level indexes.

The information technology revolution brings huge opportunities for replacing this multilayered, multimode, multiagency methodology with a unified approach to collecting price and quantity information simultaneously at the source. Retail transactions—whether online or at brick-and-mortar stores—ubiquitously create a record of the sale at the item level.

---

1. Ehrlich et al. (2019) give a short introduction to some of the arguments and results presented in this paper.

Individual items are defined finely enough—by barcode or SKU—that price can be calculated simply by dividing the nominal value of the sale by the quantity sold. Other sectors also increasingly have digitized transaction-level data.

Transaction-level information summarized to the item level should, in principle, allow the production of greatly improved statistics. First, price and quantity could be based on the same observations. Second, the granularity of the data along multiple dimensions could be greatly increased. Statistics could be constructed at a fine level of geographical detail. Similarly, product-level detail could be greatly refined. Third, time series could, in principle, be constructed at any frequency—yearly, monthly, weekly, daily, or even hourly. The daily data would be particularly helpful for dealing with "seasonality" relating to trading days and holidays and how that seasonality interacts with pay dates. Data could, in principle, be available with a very short lag. Using all transactions rather than a sample should greatly reduce sampling error and data revisions. Additionally, improved measurement of price change and quantities would directly affect the quality and detail of measurement of productivity.

Implementing such a new architecture for measuring economic activity and price change is not, however, without considerable challenges. Our paper explores three general areas of such challenges relating to (1) measurement, (2) data access, and (3) the capabilities and mandates of the statistical agencies. First, consider the measurement challenges. Given the firehose of newly available data, the economist or official statistician is confronted quickly with a case of "be careful what you wish for." There are technical and computing challenges for dealing with the volume of data. The statistical system will need to learn from best practices in computer and data science and business to process the data at scale. Moreover, because the data are created for tracking transactions and other internal purposes, they are not organized for the convenience of official statisticians. In contrast, official statistics are often based on surveys where businesses and households are asked to fit their answers into the strictures of economists' and statistical agencies' nomenclature. That makes such designed data convenient for official statisticians, but potentially difficult and costly for respondents to prepare. With naturally occurring data, the statistical agency needs to transform the data to suit its purpose. This shift of burden from respondent to agency will be costly, but if done correctly, can improve data quality because it will reduce reliance on getting accurate responses from businesses and individuals who might lack incentives for giving accurate responses and may not understand what is being asked.

A related practical measurement and conceptual challenge is that there is enormous turnover of goods. Roughly speaking, if a good defined at the barcode or SKU level is sold today, there is only a 50 percent chance it will be sold a year from today. This turnover of goods is one of the greatest challenges of using the raw item-level data for measurement, but also is an enormous opportunity. When new goods replace old goods there is frequently a change in both price and quality. Appropriately identifying whether changing item-level prices imply changes in the cost of living or instead reflect changes in product quality is a core issue for measuring activity and inflation. The statistical agencies currently perform these judgments using a combination of direct comparisons of substitutes, adjustments, and hedonics that are very hard to scale. Hence, new techniques will be needed to implement quality adjustment at scale. Luckily, such techniques—leveraging the resource made available by Big Data—may now be coming available.

We explore and compare two proposed approaches to measuring prices and real quantities using item-level data. The first is the Unified Price Index (UPI) approach proposed by Redding and Weinstein (2018, 2020), who build on the traditional Feenstra (1994) product turnover-adjusted Sato-Vartia price index.[2] This approach requires sales and price (i.e., price and quantity data) at the individual product level. Redding and Weinstein's results suggest that traditional indexes (e.g., Paasche, Laspeyres, Sato-Vartia) typically miss important components of quality change. The second approach that we explore is the possibility of doing hedonics at scale in the spirit of, for example, Bajari and Benkard (2005). Such hedonic approaches use the attributes that are available in retailers' information systems or can be scraped from the web. These attributes can include the standard hedonic covariates (size, color) or nonstandard data such as images.

One key lesson from our explorations is that despite these methods' elegance and ingenuity, there are many practical challenges and nuances involved in implementing them at scale and in interpreting the results. We believe more research is necessary to reach consensus on many of these issues before these methods can serve as the basis of official statistics. Indeed, both of these methods are the subject of active research by the academic and statistical communities. Given that research is actively evolving, we expect new developments over the coming years. This paper both examines and advances this evolving state of the art. Digging into the details of these active research agendas helps to reveal the challenges and opportunities of working with price and quantity data in this context.

The first section of this paper reviews the existing paradigm in which

---

2. We use the terminology UPI in this paper because it is the terminology of Redding and Weinstein (2018). In their revised paper (Redding and Weinstein 2020) they denote this price index as the CUPI. This alternative naming convention reflects the CES demand structure underlying this price index. We use the UPI naming convention because our approach more closely follows that of what we will call the theoretical UPI in Redding and Weinstein (2018). Redding and Weinstein (2020) implement some changes (to a version we call the seasoned UPI based on our discussant's comments) to address issues of the slow rollout of goods post-entry and the slow exit process of goods before final exit. We are sympathetic to these issues but as discussed below we think that more research is needed to understand them. Using the theoretical UPI permits us to draw out the issues.

economic statistics are built from disparate sources—often starting with source data that are already substantially aggregated (e.g., firm-level sales) and combining price measurement from samples independent from the nominal values. It also requires substantial interpolation and extrapolation to produce higher-frequency time series benchmarked to detailed data that are collected infrequently.

Building key national indicators from item-level transactions data requires reengineering how data are collected and accessed for official statistics. A new architecture for data collection is a requisite for implementing the procedures studied in this paper at scale. The logic and logistics of building economic statistics from the ground up mandates that there be entirely new procedures for data collection that lever the information systems that already exist in business. In this paper we discuss alternative modes for capturing the data from business information systems. These include direct feeds of transactions data from businesses to agencies, the use of applications interfaces that produce business-level statistics from transactions data that are transmitted to agencies, and the use of commercial data aggregators.

Transaction-level data are sensitive commercial information. Statistical agencies are already gathering sensitive information at the establishment and firm levels on a regular basis and providing privacy and confidentiality protection for such data. Part of reengineering the data collection process will involve modifying protocols to assure the continued high level of protection of confidential information, and the confidence that information will be used for statistical purposes only and will be maintained in a modernized architecture built around digitized transactions data.

Finally, to implement this new architecture, there would have to be changes in the organization and capabilities of the statistical agencies. The simultaneous collection of price and quantity data requires combining data collection activities that are now spread over multiple agencies. The agencies are already undertaking major initiatives to use transactions data to supplement or replace data collected by surveys or enumerations. Yet, because these are largely efforts to replace data streams within the existing architecture, they do not create the improvements to measurement of economic activity envisioned in this paper.

The agencies would also need staff with the expertise to do this type of work, which lies at the intersection of data science, economics, and statistics. We recognize that this proposed new architecture for official statistics would be costly to implement. Substantial R&D would be necessary to put these innovations into action. The current system would have to run in parallel for a period of time to allow consistent time series to be published. While the agencies are already taking steps in these directions, a wholesale reengineering would take a high-level commitment to change and commensurate funding during the transition period. Given the promise of improved data quality together with the potential for lower long-run cost, it is essential to undertake these investments now. Indeed, without them, we risk deterioration of the quality of statistics as response rates continue to erode and the cost of business as usual continues to outpace agency budgets.

Our paper provides an overview of this reengineering approach, including a discussion of the issues and challenges mentioned above. We also argue, and provide evidence, that while the challenges are great, there are reasons to be optimistic that practical implementation of many components of this approach is relatively close at hand. We provide examples of the implementation of this approach using item-level data for the retail trade sector. Our examples highlight that the data are already being generated and the computational capacity to undertake this approach is readily available.

1.2   Existing Architecture

Table 1.1 summarizes the source data and statistics produced to measure real and nominal consumer spending.[3] A notable feature of the current architecture is that data collection for total retail sales (Census) and for prices (BLS) are completely independent. The consumer price index program collects prices based on (1) expenditure shares from the Consumer Expenditure Survey (BLS manages the survey and Census collects the data), (2) outlets selected based on the Telephone Point of Purchase Survey, and (3) a relatively small sample of goods at these outlets that are chosen probabilistically (via the Commodities and Services Survey). The Census Bureau collects sales data from retailers in its monthly and annual surveys. The monthly survey is voluntary and has suffered from declining response rates. In addition, the composition of the companies responding to the monthly survey can change over time, which complicates producing a consistent time series. Store-level sales data are only collected once every five years as part of the Economic Census.

Integration of nominal sales and prices by BEA is done at a high level of aggregation that is complicated by the availability of product class detail for nominal sales that is only available every five years from the Economic

3. Table 1.1 is an oversimplification of how economic statistics in general, and the NIPA in particular, are produced. The simplification that Census collects nominal sales, BLS collects prices, and BEA uses them to produce price and quantity is a useful one. This simplification is broadly accurate as a portrayal of the current architecture and conveys why it cannot accommodate the measurement innovations that this paper addresses. Nonetheless, it is important to recognize that each agency does multiple data collections that contribute to the real and nominal national accounts in complex ways (e.g., the BLS Housing Survey for rents and owner-equivalent rents that enter the NIPA). BEA collects data on prices and transactions from multiple sources to produce the NIPA. The agencies have made substantial strides in bringing in new sources of data for official statistics, a number of which are presented in papers in this volume. Nonetheless, as discussed in sections 1.5 and 1.6 of this paper, these efforts are largely aimed at improving measurement within the current paradigm and therefore do not generally lever the advantages of simultaneous collection of price and quantity as advanced in this paper.

Table 1.1   **Measuring real and nominal consumer spending—Current architecture**

Census (nominal spending)	BLS (prices)
Data collection:	Data collection:
Retail trade surveys (monthly and annual)	Consumer Expenditure survey (used for spending weights), collected under contract by Census
Economic Census (quinquennial)	Telephone Point of Purchase survey (purchase location)[a]
Consumer expenditure survey (conducted for BLS)	CPI price enumeration (Probability sampling of goods within outlets)
Published statistics:	Published statistics:
Retail trade (monthly and annual) by firm type	Consumer Price Index (monthly) by product class
Retail trade (quinquennial) by product class	

BEA (aggregation and deflation)
Data collection:
  Census and BLS data; supplemented by
    multiple other sources
  Published statistics:
  Personal consumption expenditure:
    Nominal, real, and price (monthly)
  GDP (quarterly)

Note: This table shows key elements for measurement of real and nominal consumer spending.
[a] The TPOPS will be incorporated into the CES.

Census. In the intervening periods, BEA interpolates and extrapolates based on the higher frequency annual, quarterly, and monthly surveys of nominal sales by the Census Bureau. These higher frequency surveys are typically at the firm rather than establishment level. Moreover, they classify firms by major kinds of business. For example, sales from the Census Monthly Retail Trade Survey (MRTS) reflect sales from "Grocery Stores" or "Food and Beverage Stores." Such stores (really firms) sell many items beyond food and beverages, complicating the integration of the price indexes that are available at a finer product-class detail.

This complex decentralized system implies that there is limited granularity in terms of industry or geography in key indicators such as real GDP. BEA's GDP by industry provides series for about 100 industries, with some 4-digit (NAICS) detail in sectors like manufacturing, but more commonly 3-digit and 2-digit NAICS detail. The BEA recently released county-level GDP on a special release basis, a major accomplishment. However, this achievement required BEA to integrate disparate databases at a high level of aggregation with substantial interpolation and extrapolation. Digitized transactions data offer an alternative, building up from micro data in an internally consistent manner.

1.3   Using Item-Level Transactions Data

In the results presented here, we focus on two sources of transactions data summarized to the item level. One source is Nielsen retail scanner data, which provide item-level data on expenditures and quantities at the UPC code level for over 35,000 stores, covering mostly grocery stores and some mass merchandisers.[4] Any change in product attributes yields a new UPC code so there are no changes in product attributes within the item-level data we use. The Nielsen data cover millions of products in more than 100 detailed product groups (e.g., carbonated beverages) and more than 1,000 modules within these product groups (e.g., soft drinks is a module in carbonated beverages). While the Nielsen scanner item-level data are available weekly at the store level, our analysis aggregates the item-level data to the quarterly, national level.[5] Since the weeks may split between months, we use the National Retail Federation (NRF) calendar to aggregate the weekly data to monthly data. The NRF calendar places complete weeks into months and controls for changes in the timing of holidays and the number of weekends per month, and we use the months to create the quarterly data used in this paper. For more than 650,000 products in a typical quarter, we measure nominal sales, total quantities, and unit prices at the item level. We use the Nielsen scanner data from 2006:1 to 2015:4. The NPD Group (NPD)[6] data cover more than 65,000 general merchandise stores, including online retailers, and include products that are not included in the Nielson scanner data. We currently restrict ourselves to the analysis of one detailed product module: memory cards.[7] The NPD raw data are at the item-by-store-by-month level; NPD produces the monthly data by aggregating weekly data using the NRF calendar, as we do ourselves with the Nielsen data. Again, for our analysis we aggregate the data to the quarterly, national item level. For example, the item-level data for memory cards tracks more than 12,000 item-by-quarter observations for the 2014:1 to 2016:4 sample period. As with the Nielsen data, we measure nominal sales, total quantities, and unit prices at the item-level by quarter.

Because items are defined very narrowly (i.e., the UPC level) in both datasets, dividing sales by units sold gives a good measure of unit price. In

4. Nielsen also has a scanner dataset based on household sampling frames called the Consumer Panel (Homescan). We discuss this dataset below and provide estimates based on it in the appendix. The results in the main body of the paper are based on the Nielsen retail scanner data made available through the Kilts Center of the University of Chicago.

5. The use of quarterly indexes at the national level minimizes the problem of entry and exit of goods owing to stockouts or zero sales. Redding and Weinstein (2018) use quarterly aggregation, partially for this reason. To implement these methods in the statistical agencies, monthly indexes would be required.

6. NPD, formally known as National Purchase Diary Panel Inc., collects, processes, and analyzes transactions data from retail locations.

7. The NPD data include a wide variety of product categories. The current analysis exams only one product; however, in future research we also plan to explore additional products.

Table 1.2   **Comparisons of nominal quarterly growth for food sales—Surveys vs. scanner data**

	Scanner	Census MRTS (grocery)	PCE
A. Seasonally adjusted			
Mean	0.87	0.74	0.78
Standard deviation	0.98	0.64	0.61
Correlations:			
Scanner	1.00		
Census MRTS (grocery)	0.49	1.00	
PCE	0.65	0.86	1.00
B. Not seasonally adjusted			
Standard deviation	2.87	2.70	
Correlations:			
Scanner	1.00		
Census MRTS (grocery)	0.31	1.00	

Notes: Census MRTS is for grocery stores. PCE is for food and non-alcoholic beverages, off premises. Period is 2006:2–2015:3. PCE is seasonally adjusted by BEA and MRTS by Census. Scanner seasonally adjusted in top panel using seasonal dummies.

principle, any changes in product attributes should yield a new UPC code. Both retailers and manufacturers have strong incentives to make UPC codes unique to specific products and the cost of assigning unique codes is minimal. Indeed, the ability to infer prices from unit values is a central advantage of measuring P and Q using scanner data. The unit price within a time interval is an average price for an item that will not capture within-period variation in prices that may be of interest.[8]

1.3.1   Nominal Revenue Indexes

Digitized item-level transactions data from individual retailers or data aggregators such as Nielsen and NPD can be used as an alternative source for measuring nominal expenditures. Moreover, such data permit the integration of the nominal expenditure and price measures at a highly detailed level (i.e., at the item level). This approach solves many of the data integration and aggregation issues discussed above. In addition, novel approaches to quality adjustment of prices, including capturing the improvements in quality from product turnover, are available. Quality-adjusted prices built up from the same micro-level transactions data for measuring nominal expenditures have great advantages, as discussed above.

To begin, we compare the properties of nominal expenditure measures from survey vs. item-level transactions data. Table 1.2 presents summary

8. For the Nielsen scanner data, our unit prices adjust for product size (e.g., number of ounces) so that the units within a product group are comparable.

statistics for nominal food sales from the Nielsen scanner data, nominal sales from grocery stores from the MRTS, and nominal BEA Personal Consumption Expenditure (PCE) for off-premises food and nonalcoholic beverages. The PCE data are only available seasonally adjusted, while the MRTS are available both not seasonally adjusted and seasonally adjusted. The Nielsen scanner data are not seasonally adjusted. We use a simple quarterly dummy seasonal adjustment procedure to create a seasonally adjusted series.

The top panel of table 1.2 compares seasonally adjusted statistics for all three series. Despite their completely different source data, the scanner, MRTS, and PCE have similar average growth rates. The PCE is based in part on the MRTS, so the similarity is not surprising. Consistent with this, the PCE is more highly correlated with the MRTS than with the Nielsen scanner series.

Nonetheless, there are important differences in the data sources for the series that highlight the value of item-level transactions data for measuring nominal volumes. Census monthly and annual retail sales are measured across all retail establishments within a firm. Census monthly retail sales are based on a relatively small sample of firms (13,000 for the entire retail trade sector), while the Nielsen scanner data cover about 35,000 stores for grocery stores and mass merchandisers alone.[9] Census retail sales at grocery stores include many nonfood items but can exclude sales of food at, for example, general merchandise stores. In contrast, the Nielsen scanner data, which we aggregated based on product codes, include only sales of food regardless of the type of outlet and contain information on more than 650,000 item-level products per month. Thus, one source of the differing volatility and seasonality of the scanner and the MRTS series (as exhibited in the bottom panel of table 1.2) is likely differences in the coverage of nonfood items.

Considering the estimates of PCE highlights the advantages of item-level data that yield detailed product class information. Much of the high-frequency data underlying commodities in PCE come from the MRTS, which as we have seen provides estimates by type of outlet, not by product. Every five years the Economic Census (EC) yields information on sales at the establishment level by detailed product class. In the intervening time periods, the Annual Retail Trade Survey (ARTS) and the MRTS survey firms for their total sales, classifying firms into major kind of business (e.g., grocery stores). The revenue growth and quantity indexes developed by BEA using the integrated data from Census and BLS require extrapolating the detailed EC information at the product class level with the more current information by outlet type from the ARTS and MRTS.

9. Appropriate caution is needed in comparing firm-level and store-level counts. Large national firms in retail trade have many establishments (stores). Foster et al. (2015) report that there are about 400 national firms in 2007 in Retail Trade that operate in more than 18 states. These 400 firms operate about 290,000 establishments. Our point is not that the MRTS has limited coverage of retail activity, but rather it is collected at a highly aggregated (firm-level) basis.

A related issue is that the EC uses an annual reference period, so it provides the BEA no information on the within-year composition of products sold by outlets. Thus, the EC provides no information for the BEA to produce non-seasonally-adjusted PCE at the detailed goods level at high frequencies. BEA uses within-year composition information from scanner data from a commercial aggregator, in combination with the PCE reported in table 1.1, to produce statistics on more detailed food products (e.g., poultry).[10]

This example highlights the extrapolative nature of high-frequency GDP estimation given the current architecture. Data users might not be too concerned about the fact that GDP statistics abstract from the shifting seasonal mix of goods sold by grocery stores. But the same issue will apply at business cycle frequency and for business cycle shocks, with the potential for the current system to either overstate or understate cyclical fluctuations depending on the product mix across outlets and their cyclicality sensitivity.

1.3.2   Quality- and Appeal-Adjusted Price Indexes

The promise of digitized data goes beyond the ability to produce internally consistent price and nominal revenue data. The item-level price and quantity data, which are often accompanied by information on item-level attributes, offer the prospect of novel approaches to quality adjustment. Currently, the BLS CPI implements hedonic quality adjustment on a relatively small share of consumer expenditures (about 5 percent). For the remaining items, a matched model approach is used with ad hoc quality adjustments when feasible (e.g., if a new model of an item has more features than a prior matched item, then an attempt is made to adjust the prices to account for the change in features). The sample of products in the CPI consumption basket is rotated every four years and no quality adjustment is made to prices when a new good enters the index due to product rotation.

The digitized data offer the possibility of accounting for the enormous product turnover observed in item-level transactions data. For the Nielsen scanner data, the quarterly rates of product entry and exit are 9.62 percent and 9.57 percent, respectively. By product entry and exit, we mean the entry and exit of UPCs from the data. Some of the product turnover at the UPC code level in the scanner data involves minor changes in packaging and marketing, but others represent important changes in product quality.

We consider two approaches for capturing the variation in quality in price indexes using transactions data. The first approach is based on consumer demand theory and has been developed by Redding and Weinstein (2018, 2020) who build on the earlier work by Feenstra (1994). The second

10. This use of aggregated scanner data by BEA is an example of how the statistical agencies are incorporating transactions data into the NIPA in the current architecture. Note that this use of aggregated scanner data is a patch to address a limitation of the existing architecture—that the detailed data from Census are only available once every five years for an annual reference period while the BEA is producing statistics at monthly and quarterly frequency.

approach uses hedonic methods, following the insights of Pakes (2003, 2005) and Erickson and Pakes (2011). While these hedonic approaches are already partly in use by BLS and BEA, the item-level transactions data offer the potential for implementing these approaches with continuously updated weights and with methods to avoid selection bias arising from product entry and exit and—equally importantly—at scale. Bajari et al. (2021) is an initial attempt to implement hedonics at scale using a rich set of product attributes. We draw out the many different issues that must be confronted for practical implementation of these modern methods by the statistical agencies. Since both methods are part of active research agendas, we emphasize that our discussion and analysis is exploratory rather than yielding ultimate guidance for implementation.

Redding and Weinstein (2018, 2020) use a constant elasticity of substitution (CES) demand structure at the product group level to generate the UPI. It is useful to provide a brief overview of the demand structure and the underpinnings of the derivation of the UPI because this helps draw out conceptual and implementation issues. The CES demand structure for a narrow product group yields the unit expenditure function (the exact price index) given by:

$$
(1) \qquad P_t = \left[\sum_{k \in \Omega_t} \left(\frac{p_{kt}}{\varphi_{kt}} \right)^{1-\sigma} \right]^{1/(1-\sigma)},
$$

where Ω_t is the set of goods available in time t in this product group, p_{kt} is the price of good k at time t (purchased quantities), σ is the elasticity of substitution across goods within the product group, and φ_{kt} are relative product appeal terms.[11]

The UPI implements this exact price index, which accounts for quality change and product turnover within a product group, using only observable data and an estimate for the elasticity of substitution. The UPI is given by the formula:

$$
(2) \qquad \ln(\text{UPI}) = \ln\left(\frac{P_t}{P_{t-1}} \right) = \text{RPI} + PV_{adj} + CV_{adj},
$$

where RPI is a Jevons index given by the ratio of the geometric means of the prices for continuing goods between periods $t - 1$ and t, PV_{adj} is a product variety adjustment bias term based on Feenstra (1994), and CV_{adj} is a consumer valuation bias adjustment term that is novel to the UPI. Formally, these three terms are given by:

$$
(3) \qquad \text{RPI} = \frac{1}{N_t^*} \sum_{k \in \Omega_t^*} \ln\left(\frac{p_{kt}}{p_{kt-1}} \right),
$$

11. A normalization is made so that average product appeal for a product group remains invariant over time.

(4)
$$PV_{adj} = \frac{1}{\sigma - 1} \ln\left(\frac{\lambda_t}{\lambda_{t-1}}\right), \text{ and}$$

(5)
$$CV_{adj} = \frac{1}{\sigma - 1} \frac{1}{N_t^*} \sum_{k \in \Omega_t^*} \ln\left(\frac{s_{kt}^*}{s_{kt-1}^*}\right),$$

where a * represents goods that are common in period $t-1$ and t, s_{kt}^* is good k's share of expenditures on common goods in period t, p_{kt} is the price of good k in period t, and σ is the elasticity of substitution across goods. The product variety adjustment term (PV_{adj}) depends on $\lambda_t \equiv (\sum_{k \in \Omega_t^*} p_{kt} C_{kt}) / (\sum_{k \in \Omega_t} p_{kt} C_{kt})$, where C_{kt} is the consumption of good k at time t (purchased quantities). A remarkable and attractive feature of the UPI is that given an elasticity of substitution, this price index incorporating unobservable quality adjustment factors φ_{kt} is computable using observable information on prices and expenditure shares along with information to define common entering and exiting goods.

The UPI is designed to be implemented on a narrow product group basis, which the item-level transactions data permit. Critical issues for the implementation of this approach include determining the classification of goods into narrow product groups, estimating the elasticity of substitution for each product group, and defining what constitutes entering, exiting, and common goods. We discuss these implementation issues below as we explore this method.

Before proceeding to the implementation issues, it is helpful to provide some intuition regarding the adjustment factors incorporated into the UPI. The product variety adjustment bias term depends on the relative expenditure shares of entering versus exiting goods. Following Feenstra (1994), a higher expenditure share devoted to entering goods relative to exiting goods implies improvements in quality from product turnover. Feenstra's procedure adjusts expenditure shares for differences in prices of entering and exiting goods based on a CES demand structure. In particular, Feenstra's exact CES price index adjusts the Sato-Vartia exact price index for product turnover simply by adding the PV_{adj} term defined in equation (4).[12] Feenstra's price index is thus given as:

(6)
$$\log(\text{Feenstra}) = \ln\left(\frac{P_t}{P_{t-1}}\right) = PV_{adj} + \sum_{k \in \Omega_t^*} \omega_{kt} \ln\left(\frac{p_{kt}}{p_{kt-1}}\right),$$

where the weights ω_{kt} are defined as:

(7)
$$\omega_{kt} = \frac{s_{kt}^* - s_{kt-1}^*}{\ln(s_{kt}^*) - \ln(s_{kt-1}^*)} \Big/ \sum_{k \in \Omega_t^*} \frac{s_{kt}^* - s_{kt-1}^*}{\ln(s_{kt}^*) - \ln(s_{kt-1}^*)}.$$

12. The Feenstra price index is not simply the UPI holding the CV term constant. Instead, it is an adjustment to the Sato-Vartia index. The RPI in the UPI is not the Sato-Vartia index, but the simple ratio of geometric means of prices across time periods (the Jevons index).

Consumer demand theory implies that the quantitative importance of such quality change depends on the elasticity of substitution. Product turnover of very close substitutes (large σ) yields little product variety adjustment bias; mathematically, as the elasticity of substitution σ goes to infinity in equation (4), the PV_{adj} term goes to zero regardless of the amount of product turnover, because the new products are close substitutes with the old products. With a finite elasticity of substitution, the PV_{adj} term will be negative when the expenditure share on entering products is larger than on exiting products. Conversely, the PV_{adj} term will be positive when the expenditure share on exiting products is greater. In our analysis below, we consider the Feenstra index along with the UPI.

The consumer valuation bias adjustment term applies similar logic by permitting changes in how consumers value continuing products over time. If the relative appeal of a product increases between periods $t-1$ and t, then consumer demand will shift toward that product. The relevant appeal-adjusted price should take into account consumers' substitution toward more desired products. The inclusion of the consumer valuation (CV) bias adjustment in the UPI is therefore internally consistent with consumer demand theory, which recognizes that relative product appeal can change over time, even for a given item.[13] The elasticity of substitution is again a critical factor for the quantitative relevance of the CV term.

Implementation of the UPI requires an estimate of the elasticity of substitution at the product group level. Estimation of this elasticity is based on the demand function relating expenditure shares to prices, given by:

$$(8) \qquad s_{kt} = \frac{p_{kt}c_{kt}}{\sum_l p_{lt}c_{lt}} = \frac{(p_{kt}/\varphi_{kt})^{1-\sigma}}{\sum_{l\in\Omega_t}(p_{lt}/\varphi_{lt})^{1-\sigma}} = \frac{(p_{kt}/\varphi_{kt})^{1-\sigma}}{P_t^{1-\sigma}}, \ k \in \Omega_t.$$

In practice, a common procedure is to use the Feenstra (1994) estimation approach or some related modification. Focusing on the shares of the expenditures on common goods, the expenditure share relationship can be double-differenced (differencing out time effects but also potentially specific group effects like brand, or firm effects as in Hottman, Redding, and Weinstein (2016)) to yield the relationship:

$$(9) \qquad \Delta\ln \bar{s}_{kt}^* = \beta_0 + \beta_1\Delta\bar{p}_{kt} + u_{kt}, \beta_1 = (1-\sigma)$$

(where the notation reflects the impact of double-differencing). Feenstra (1994), Hottman, Redding, and Weinstein (2016) and Redding and Wein-

---

13. Cost of living indexes are typically defined by holding utility constant, so normally do not allow for taste shocks. Redding and Weinstein note, however, that there are very large changes in demand for goods that are not accounted for by changes in price and developed the UPI to account for this fact. This churning in demand is evident from item-level transactions data, so the analytic innovation of Redding and Weinstein is motivated as an approach to accommodate such data in a price index. Note that the shocks are to relative demand within a narrow product group, not to the level of demand given income.

stein (2018, 2020) overcome the potential endogeneity bias in equation (9) by: (i) specifying and double-differencing an analogous supply curve; (ii) assuming the double-differenced demand and supply shocks are uncorrelated; and (iii) assuming heteroskedasticity across individual products in the relative variances of demand and supply shocks. The advantage of this method is that it can be implemented at scale with item-level transactions data, but the disadvantage is that it relies on these strong identifying assumptions.

Another critical issue is defining what constitutes common, entering, and exiting goods. In our analysis, we implement the UPI with an entering good in period t (quarterly) defined as a good that had no expenditures in period $t-1$ but positive expenditures in t; an exiting good as one with positive expenditures in period $t-1$ but not in t; and a common good as one that has positive expenditures in both periods. This implementation is consistent with the theory, and we denote our implementation the *theoretical UPI*.[14]

In the published version of the paper, Redding and Weinstein (2020) depart from these assumptions by defining common goods based on a much longer horizon in their baseline estimates. Specifically, their baseline calculates the UPI based on changes from the fourth quarter of year $t-1$ to the fourth quarter of year t. They define *common goods* between those two periods as follows: (i) the good must have been present in the three quarters prior to the fourth quarter of $t-1$; (ii) the good must have been present in the three quarters after the fourth quarter of t; and (iii) the good must be present cumulatively for at least six years. With this definition of common goods, *entering goods* are any goods in the fourth quarter of year t that have positive expenditures in that period but are not common goods. Likewise, *exiting goods* are any goods in the fourth quarter of year $t-1$ that have positive expenditures in that period but are not common goods.

The motivation for this alternative baseline definition of common goods is based on practical implementation concerns about the implications of the UPI that we will discuss in detail below.[15] Redding and Weinstein (2020) suggest that the slow roll-out of new goods across stores and geographic areas creates complex entry dynamics. Likewise, there is a slow process of exit along the same dimensions. Moreover, the dynamics of product entry and exit may reflect dynamic learning by consumers, along with heterogene-

14. This version is close to the implementation of Redding and Weinstein (2018), with one exception. Redding and Weinstein calculate annual price changes from the fourth quarter of one year to the fourth quarter of the next year. They define common goods as goods that are present in both of those quarters. In our implementation, we calculate price changes on a quarter-over-quarter basis and define common goods as goods that are present in those two consecutive quarters. We chain the resulting price index to calculate annual inflation. This difference does lead to quantitatively different measures of price change,

15. Technically the issue can be understood by reviewing the terms in the consumer valuation adjustment in equation (8). This term is the unweighted average of log changes in expenditure shares of common goods. Goods with very small shares can have very large log changes that dominate this term. We are grateful to our discussant Robert Feenstra for this observation.

ity in the preferences for newer goods across consumers. Since these factors are outside the scope of their theoretical model, they suggest in their 2020 paper that permitting this type of seasoning of entering and exiting goods is a practical way to abstract from these factors. Following Robert Feenstra's discussion of our paper at the conference suggesting a similar approach, we call this version the *seasoned UPI*.

We are sympathetic to these practical concerns, but given our objective of exploring key issues, in the interest of transparency we find it instructive to implement the theoretical UPI. In addition, our use of the timing conventions for entering, exiting, and common goods in the theoretical UPI closely align with the definitions of entering, exiting, and common goods used in the hedonics literature. This enables us to draw out the differences between the UPI and hedonic approaches more readily. In addition, as will become apparent, we think there are other implementation issues beyond seasoning that must be addressed, and they are easier to understand using the implementation of the theoretical UPI. Moreover, the seasoned UPI has the limitation that it could not be implemented on a timely basis at scale. One would only know whether a good is common in a period until well after that period is complete.[16] As we discuss, below there are alternative ways of implementing a common good rule, but we think that considerable research is required to develop a practical implementation.

If attribute data are available along with the price and quantity data, then an alternative approach to accounting for product turnover and quality adjustment is to use hedonics. Following Pakes (2003), Bajari and Benkard (2005), and Erickson and Pakes (2011) we estimate hedonic regressions using item-level data every period within a product group of the form

$$\ln(p_{it}) = X_i'\beta_t + \eta_{it}, \tag{10}$$

where X_i is the vector of characteristics or attributes of good i. Note that the attributes are time-invariant at the item-level in contrast to earlier hedonic approaches that examine how price changes for a broadly defined good (a car, a computer) as the attribute changes. In the approach we feature here, the goods are narrowly defined at the item level. If the attributes change, it is presumed that the good will be given a new UPC or barcode, and therefore be treated as a different good. A core challenge of implementing hedonics is measuring the relevant set of attributes. As Bajari and Benkard (2005)

---

16. This problem is even more of a challenge because the objective is to generate timely, monthly price indexes. There are also some conceptual issues with the definition of the common goods in terms of how long a good must be present to be a common good. It is important to emphasize that the common good rule approach of Redding and Weinstein (2020) blurs the distinction between entering and exiting goods. Their common goods rule implies that goods that do not satisfy the threshold are in practice put into the entry/exit category. This implies that their entry/exit category in period t includes goods that have positive sales in both $t-1$ and t.

emphasize, if only a subset of the relevant attributes is included in the regression, then this generates a bias in the hedonics-based price indexes.

A Laspeyres index quality-adjusted using hedonics at the product group level is given by

$$(11) \qquad Laspeyres\ Hedonic\ Index\ (t) = \frac{\sum_{i \in A_{it-1}} h^t(X_i) q_{it-1}}{\sum_{i \in A_{it-1}} h^{t-1}(X_i) q_{it-1}},$$

where $h^t(X_i) = X_i' \beta_t$ is the period-t estimate of the hedonic function and A_{it-1} is the set of all goods sold in period $t-1$ (including exits). Using hedonics in this manner adjusts for quality and selection bias from exiting goods by imputing the price of the exiting goods in period t using the hedonic function.[17] Transactions data permit use of item-level rather than sample weights from alternative sources. An analogous approach can be used for a Paasche index that adjusts for selection bias for entering goods. The Fisher ideal index using hedonics incorporates both adjustments. An important feature of implementation in this setting with item-level transactions data is the use of continuously updated weights (period $t-1$ weights for Laspeyres and t weights for Paasche). Bajari and Benkard (2005) observe that such chain weighting is readily feasible with item-level transactions data and that such chain weighting accommodates the incorporation of product turnover.

A practical challenge for implementing hedonics at scale is measuring attributes at scale. Machine learning approaches as in Bajari et al. (2021) could in principle be used to overcome this issue. Bajari et al. (2021) convert text and images to vectors and use dimensionality reduction techniques to estimate hedonically adjusted prices at scale for millions of products at a high frequency. They show that their approach yields high R^2 measures in the estimation of hedonic functions.

In comparing the UPI and hedonic approaches, an advantage of the UPI is that it is fully consistent with micro consumer demand theory that reconciles the relationship between expenditure shares and prices. As is apparent from equations (8) and (9), the UPI approach defines the product quality/appeal as the residual from the demand equation. This contrasts with the hedonic approach, which only uses the variation in prices that can be accounted for by observable characteristics. As already noted, omitted characteristics will bias the estimates obtained using the hedonic approach. We discuss the strengths and weaknesses of claiming the entire residual (as in the UPI) below.

These two approaches can in principle be combined. Crawford and Neary (2019) build on both approaches in developing a Feenstra (1994) product

---

17. Pakes (2003) emphasizes that this is one of the key advantages of hedonic indexes relative to standard price indexes.

variety adjustment factor for the standard hedonic approach. For this purpose, their suggested price index is analogous in form to the Feenstra-adjusted Sato-Vartia index but using characteristics in the adjustment factor and the remainder of the index is a Sato-Vartia hedonic index. We have not explored this hybrid approach ourselves, but our results below suggest this is a promising area to pursue. Our separate consideration of the UPI and hedonics does raise issues that need to be confronted by practical implementation of this hybrid approach developed by Crawford and Neary (2019).[18]

1.4 Results

We implement both the UPI and the hedonics approach and compare these quality-adjusted price indexes to standard price indexes using transaction-level data. For the Nielsen scanner data, we only implement the UPI because attribute data are less readily available. For the NPD scanner data, we have rich attribute data that permit us to implement both the UPI and hedonics approaches. We also have obtained estimates of a CPI-type index restricted to the same product groups in the Nielsen scanner data. BLS created aggregate indexes for the comparable food and nonfood items.[19] Thus, for the analysis of the Nielsen scanner data, we compare the BLS CPI to the price indexes from the transactions data.

We begin by examining prices for the Nielsen scanner data classifying the more than 100 product groups into food and nonfood items. To implement the Feenstra index and the UPI, we require estimates of the elasticity of substitution. For our initial analysis with both the Nielsen and NPD data, we use the Feenstra (1994) estimation procedure as modified by Redding and Weinstein (2018) for use with item-level transactions data. The sizes and impacts of the CV and product valuation (PV) adjustment terms depend critically on the elasticity estimates. The estimated elasticities for the 100+ product groups display considerable variation. While the median is about 8, the 10th percentile is 4 and the 90th percentile is 16.[20]

Table 1.3a provides summary statistics of alternative price indexes for the 2006–2015 period using the BLS CPI and Nielsen scanner data where the 100+ product groups have been classified into food and nonfood items. The number of item-level price quotes each month in the BLS CPI for these product groups is about 40,000, compared to the 650,000 item-level prices

18. The proposed hybrid by Crawford and Neary (2019) does not incorporate the time-varying product appeal terms that are at the core of the UPI. In many respects, this hybrid approach should be interpreted as a hybrid of the Feenstra-adjusted Sato-Vartia index and hedonics.
19. We thank the BLS for producing food and nonfood CPI indexes using the product groups in the Nielsen data. The BLS data provided should be interpreted with care because they do not meet BLS's standard publication criteria.
20. The mean is 9 and the standard deviation is 5. The median estimate of 8 is similar to that reported in Table 2 of Redding and Weinstein (2018) using the Feenstra estimator.

Table 1.3a   **Summary statistics on comparisons of quarterly price indices**

	BLS CPI	Scanner Laspeyres	Scanner Feenstra	Scanner UPI
A. Food				
Mean	0.57%	0.76%	0.16%	−2.49%
Standard deviation	0.77%	0.82%	0.82%	0.84%
Correlations:				
BLS CPI	1.00			
Scanner Laspeyres	0.91	1.00		
Scanner Feenstra	0.91	0.97	1.00	
Scanner UPI	0.63	0.72	0.66	1.00
B. Nonfood				
Mean	0.22%	−0.05%	−0.62%	−4.59%
Standard deviation	0.46%	0.36%	0.38%	0.77%
Correlations:				
BLS CPI	1.00			
Scanner Laspeyres	0.42	1.00		
Scanner Feenstra	0.37	0.90	1.00	
Scanner UPI	−0.22	0.18	0.23	1.00

Note: Nielsen scanner product groups are classified into food and nonfood items. BLS CPI is harmonized to these product groups. Quarterly series from 2006:2–2015:4 reflect the log first differences of the price indices.

in the scanner data. We first create quarterly estimates for the 2006–2015 period at the product group level. We then aggregate the quarterly estimates to food and nonfood items using Divisia expenditure share weights by product groups. Table 1.3a provides summary statistics using the quarterly food and nonfood price indexes.

The top panel of table 1.3a shows the results for the food product groups and the lower panel the nonfood product groups. Each panel displays results for quarterly price changes based on three indexes calculated from the scanner data: a Laspeyres index; the CES demand-based price index with the adjustment for product turnover proposed by Feenstra discussed above (hereafter Feenstra); and the UPI. To calculate the Laspeyres index using the item-level data, we use previous-quarter expenditure weights updated for each quarter.

For food, the average rate of price change using the BLS CPI is very similar to (albeit slightly lower than) the Laspeyres index from the scanner data, and the two price indexes track each other well (with a correlation of about 0.91). The Feenstra shows a notably lower average price change and a correlation with the CPI that is also 0.91. The UPI has a much lower average and a correlation with the CPI of 0.63. The finding that the CPI and the Laspeyres from the scanner data track each other so well is reassuring, but also not surprising given that the quality adjustments used in the CPI for food are modest, and we made similar adjustments for changes in package size in

Table 1.3b   Summary statistics on comparisons of quarterly price indices—
                    Consumer Panel [CP] data

	BLS CPI	CP Laspeyres	CP Feenstra	CP UPI
		A. Food		
Mean	0.49%	0.91%	0.01%	−1.27%
Std deviation	0.76%	0.77%	0.81%	0.86%
Correlations:				
BLS CPI	1.00			
CP Laspeyres	0.80	1.00		
CP Feenstra	0.81	0.86	1.00	
CP UPI	0.60	0.66	0.75	1.00
		B. Nonfood		
Mean	0.21%	0.51%	−0.58%	−3.31%
Std deviation	0.43%	0.42%	0.56%	0.79%
Correlations:				
BLS CPI	1.00			
CP Laspeyres	0.48	1.00		
CP Feenstra	0.50	0.64	1.00	
CP UPI	0.37	0.48	0.70	1.00

Note: This table replicates the calculations in table 1.3a using the Nielsen Consumer Panel [CP] data instead of the Nielsen retail scanner data. Data are quarterly from 2004–2016 and reflect the log first differences of the price indices.

the Nielsen data. The close relationship between the CPI and Laspeyres for food provides a benchmark to gauge the impact of the quality adjustments via Feenstra and the UPI, which like the Laspeyres use the scanner data.

The lower panel shows greater differences across price indexes for nonfood. For this category, the CPI inflation rate is slightly higher than the scanner Laspeyres rate, but their correlation is substantially weaker (0.42) than for food. The Feenstra price index has a substantially lower mean and the UPI a much lower mean. The CPI's correlation with the Feenstra is 0.37 and with the UPI is negative (−0.22). The larger gap across price indexes for nonfood than for food is consistent with the hypothesis that quality adjustments from product turnover and changes in product appeal for continuing goods (i.e., consumer valuation) are likely to be more important for nonfood. Also consistent with that hypothesis, there is a larger gap between the Feenstra and UPI than there is between the Laspeyres and Feenstra.

Results for the UPI presented here differ somewhat from the patterns presented in Redding and Weinstein (2018), who use the Nielsen Consumer (Homescan) Panel in their analysis. The latter tracks the expenditures of about 55,000 households. Households scan the bar codes from purchased items, and prices are either downloaded from the store where the item was purchased, or hand entered. Table 1.3b presents the analogous statistics to table 1.3a, comparing the BLS CPI for food and nonfood items (covering the same product groups) to the consumer panel-based price indexes.[21] Qualitatively, the patterns are similar between the retail scanner and consumer panel indexes, with some exceptions. For food, the correspondence between the BLS CPI and consumer panel Laspeyres is weaker than that between the BLS CPI and retail scanner Laspeyres. The correlation is 0.80 instead of 0.91, and the BLS CPI has a notably lower mean (0.42 percent lower) than the consumer panel Laspeyres. Additionally, the gap between the UPI and Laspeyres is much smaller for the consumer panel compared to the retail scanner data. Especially notable is that the gap between the Feenstra and UPI indexes is substantially smaller using the consumer panel compared to the retail scanner data for both food and nonfood. This implies the CV adjustment is not as large for the consumer panel compared to the retail scanner data.[22] Even more dramatic reductions in the magnitude of the CV adjustment using the consumer panel emerge by using the seasoned UPI as developed by Redding and Weinstein (2020).[23]

Taken at face value, the results suggest that the UPI captures substantially more quality adjustment than the CPI, especially for nonfood. Appropriate caution is required in drawing this inference because both the Feenstra and UPI require specification of a utility function and estimates of the elasticity of substitution parameters. Although estimating the elasticities at a product group level (e.g., carbonated beverages for food and electronic products for nonfood) allows for over 100 different elasticities within the scanner data, this level of aggregation may still be too high. While each product group contains goods that are close substitutes, many product groups also contain goods that are quite different. For product turnover and expenditure share volatility with close substitutes, the quality adjustment factors in the Feenstra and UPI indexes become very small. The procedure used in tables 1.3a and 1.3b is to assume (and estimate) the same elasticity of substitution for all products within a product group.

Turning now to the analysis using the NPD data, the detailed characteristic data allow us to consider the hedonic approach. For the analysis in this paper, we present estimates for memory cards. We have estimated a separate hedonic regression relating an item's log price (at the national quarterly level)

---

21. We estimate the elasticities of substitution separately for the Consumer Panel data.

22. It is beyond the scope of this paper to investigate the sources of discrepancies between the results using the retail scanner and consumer panel databases. We focus on the retail scanner dataset because it is arguably more comprehensive and also more suitable for the objectives of reengineering key national indicators.

23. In unreported results, we have found that we can replicate the findings in Redding and Weinstein (2020) using a "seasoned" UPI based on a simpler to implement common goods rule than their longevity rule. Specifically, if we define common goods as those with above the fifth percentile of market shares over the current and prior five quarters, we can closely approximate their findings. As we have discussed, we have not implemented a common good rule in this paper to produce a "seasoned" UPI because it is our objective to draw out the issues associated with dealing with the rich entry and exit dynamics of goods and their impact on the UPI. Imposing such a rule limits the ability to explore such issues.

to its attributes for each quarter. We use a quadratic in memory card size and speed and dummy variables capturing card types (e.g., flash cards, memory chips). At the national level, the dataset contains about 12,000 observations of product items for all quarters over the three-year period.

Memory cards have exhibited substantial improvements in quality over our short sample period. Figure 1.1 shows the sales-weighted linear trend of memory card size and speed, with both size and speed more than doubling over the sample period. Figure 1.2 shows that the marginal value of additional size and speed appears to be declining over time. Hedonic regressions

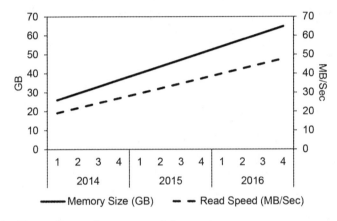

Fig. 1.1   Key attributes of memory cards by quarter
Source: NDP data.
Note: The figure shows estimated linear trends in sales-weighted national memory size and read speeds used to produce the estimates in table 1.4.

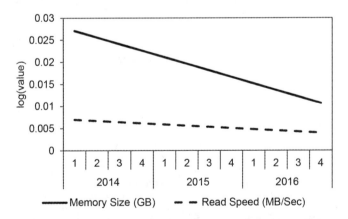

Fig. 1.2   Changing marginal value of attributes by quarter
Source: NDP data.
Note: This figure shows the changing marginal value (from linear term from table 1.4) in estimation of hedonic specification for memory cards.

Table 1.4   Means, standard deviations, and correlations of alternative price indices—Memory cards

	Laspeyres	Feenstra	Hedonic (Laspeyres)	Hedonic (Paasche)	UPI
Mean price change	−0.039	−0.059	−0.060	−0.049	−0.096
Standard deviation (price change)	0.034	0.039	0.024	0.025	0.024
Laspeyres	1.00				
Feenstra	0.89	1.00			
Hedonic (Laspeyres)	0.72	0.72	1.00		
Hedonic (Paasche)	0.61	0.72	0.77	1.00	
UPI	0.15	0.07	0.32	0.48	1.00

Note: Source is NPD data at item-level quarterly from 2014 to 2016. Price indices constructed at a quarterly frequency. Reported statistics are correlations of quarterly indices (not seasonally adjusted).

that include both size and speed and the squares of size and speed show that prices are increasing by size and speed but at a decreasing rate.[24] The R^2 is about 0.8 in each quarter, suggesting that there could be other unobserved characteristics that affect the prices.

As with the Nielsen scanner data, we also estimate a UPI using the NPD data. The elasticity of substitution (i.e., demand elasticity estimate) is about 4. We can use this method to estimate product quality levels for entering and exiting goods using the φ_{kt} in Redding and Weinstein equation (4). As expected, entering goods have substantially higher average quality (−0.28) than exiting goods (−1.23), but they also have much more dispersion in quality (standard deviation of 1.59 for entering goods compared to 1.43 for exiting). Greater dispersion at entry suggests potentially interesting post-entry dynamics that may involve selection and learning. We explore this below.[25]

Table 1.4 summarizes means, standard deviations, and correlations of the alternative price indexes for memory cards. Quality-adjusted prices are declining much more rapidly than standard price indexes indicate: the Feenstra and hedonic indexes are substantially lower than the Laspeyres index, and the UPI is even lower. Most of the series are highly correlated, except for the UPI. Interestingly, the price indexes most highly correlated with UPI are the hedonic indexes. This suggests the hedonics come the closest to capturing the quality adjustment measured in the UPI.

1.4.1   What Does the CV Term Capture, and Why Is It So Large?

Taken at face value, the UPI yields the most comprehensive quality-adjusted prices. Our analysis suggests it yields substantially more quality

24. Hedonic regressions of log(price) regressed on quadratic in size and speed along with attribute dummies (not reported) estimated by quarter from 2014 to 2016.
25. We also note that it is not feasible to implement the seasoned UPI using the very long horizons specified in Redding and Weinstein (2020) for the NPD data, since being a common good requires being present for six years.

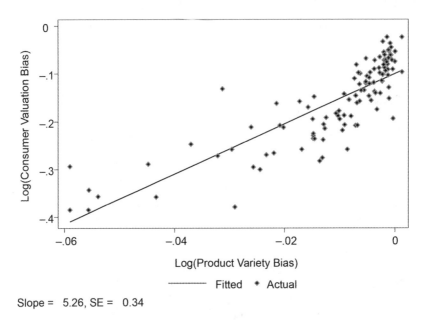

Slope = 5.26, SE = 0.34

Fig. 1.3   The relationship between product variety bias and consumer valuation bias
Source: Nielsen scanner data.
Note: Each dot represents a product group showing average PV and CV adjustment factors from quarterly measures of PV and CV. Quarterly series from 2006:2–2015:4.

adjustment than the Feenstra index and the hedonics-based indexes. The differentiating factor for the UPI is the inclusion of the CV. In principle, the hedonic approach also permits changing valuations of characteristics that could capture the variation in the CV. Even though we find that the hedonic indexes are the most highly correlated with the UPI for memory cards, it is apparent that the UPI via the CV captures quality adjustment not captured in the other indexes.

This discussion suggests it is critical to understand what the CV adjustment bias (using what we denote as the theoretical UPI) is capturing. To explore this issue, we conduct some further exploratory analysis. Figure 1.3 shows that (the logs of) PV and CV are negative on average for virtually all products in the Nielsen data (or alternatively, PV and CV in levels are below one). The figure also shows that PV and CV are positively correlated across product groups. However, CV shows much more variation than PV; log PV ranges from 0 to −.06 while CV ranges from 0 to −0.4.

Figure 1.4 shows the UPI components for two narrow product modules that highlight the variation depicted in figure 1.3. The top panel shows the (log of) UPI and its components for soft drinks (RPI, PV, and CV, in logs and, for PV and CV, multiplied by $1/(\sigma - 1)$. The bottom panel shows the analogous components for video games. Both panels show quarterly log

A. Soft Drinks

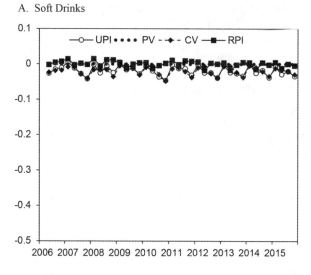

B. Video Games

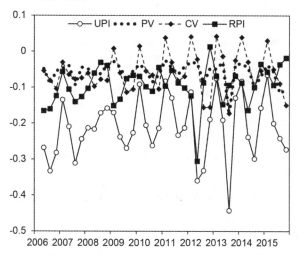

Fig. 1.4   UPI components for specific product modules

Source: Nielsen scanner data.

Note: Log differences at quarterly rate.

price changes—that is, they are not expressed as annualized values. The scales of the two figures are the same in order to highlight the dramatic differences in the respective roles of PV and CV across these product modules. Video games thus fit the pattern of figure 1.3 in that both PV and CV are large in magnitude.

The scale of figure 1.4 obscures substantial measured price declines for soft drinks. The UPI implies average price deflation of approximately 2 percent per quarter, from 2006:1 to 2015:4. Put differently, the UPI suggests that entry- and appeal-adjusted prices for soft drinks fell by more than half over a period of 10 years. Mechanically, almost all of that decline stems from the CV term.[26] The large amount of price deflation for soft drinks implied by the UPI is dwarfed by the massive deflation that is measured for video games. The UPI suggests that (appropriately measured) prices for video games fell by more than 99 percent over the same 10-year period.

These large, implied rates of quality-adjusted price declines are heavily dependent on the estimated elasticities of substitution. For soft drinks, we use the estimate of $\sigma = 6.22$, the estimate for the carbonated beverages product group using the Feenstra estimation method. If we let $\sigma = 12$, then the rate of price decline is less than 1 percent per quarter (less than half of that reported in figure 1.4). Thus, even without changing the definitions of common goods, the UPI delivers more plausible results for higher estimated elasticities of substitution. The Feenstra method for estimating the latter makes strong identifying assumptions and further research is needed in this area.

Figure 1.3 suggests that CV may reflect post-entry and pre-exit dynamics given its close relationship with PV. To explore this possibility, we conducted some small-scale simulations of product entry and exit with associated changes in product quality presented in figures 1.5, 1.6, and 1.7. In each of the simulations, we track the evolution of 14 items within a simulated product group with an assumed elasticity of substitution of five. Seven goods enter and seven goods exit; one entering good and one exiting good in each period. To focus on product quality, we keep the price for each good equal and constant across time; that is, the goods are produced competitively with a constant and equal marginal cost. To examine the quality and price changes, the average quality increases over time. Thus, all the variation in appeal shows up in appeal-adjusted prices. As a result, the constant quality index represented by the Laspeyres shows no price change, while the appeal-adjusted UPI shows a decreasing price index. In each figure, panel A shows an example of the relative quality paths for an entering and exiting good, along with the increase in average quality, and Panel B shows the implied price indexes.

In figure 1.5, new products enter at higher quality than exiting products, but there is no change in quality post-entry or pre-exit. This results in flat post-entry appeal in the example in panel A where the new good enters in the fourth period; however, average quality increases due to the higher quality new goods. Panel B of figure 1.5 shows the implied Laspeyres, Feenstra, and

---

26. For comparison, the official CPI published by the BLS for carbonated beverages yields an average quarterly price increase of 0.4 percent from 2006:1 to 2015:4, and the Sato-Vartia index for soft drinks yields a similar 0.4 percent average quarterly increase. The RPI term of the UPI for soft drinks tracks the CPI fairly well yet yields an average quarterly change of zero. The correlation coefficient between the two series is 0.75. The major differences between the UPI and the CPI therefore arise from the PV and CV terms.

A. Relative Product Quality

—□— Exiting goods   ▪●▪ Entering goods   ▪▪▪▪▪ Average

B. Implied Price Indices

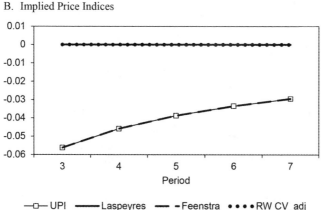

—□— UPI   ▬▬ Laspeyres   ▬ ▬ Feenstra   ●●●● RW CV_adj

Fig. 1.5   Simulated product entry and exit with quality change: No continuing good quality change

Note: These figures show the results of a simulation in which 14 goods enter and exit with constant price and changing quality. Panel A shows an example of the relative quality paths for an entering and exiting good along with the increase in average quality and panel B shows the implied price indices.

UPI log price indexes along the CV adjustment factor component of the UPI. The Laspeyres exhibits no rate of change given constant unadjusted prices. The Feenstra and UPI show substantial negative price change reflecting the product entry and exit that are identical. The CV adjustment factor component is zero because there is no change in quality for continuing goods. The latter implies that common goods expenditure shares are not changing over time.

In figure 1.6, the 14 new products exhibit post-entry dynamics as upon entry, and exiting goods exhibit pre-exit dynamics. An example of an entering and exiting good is shown in panel A, with a new good entering in period

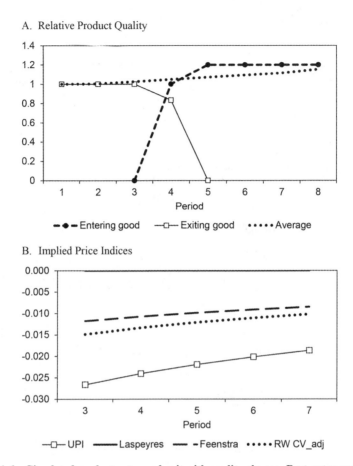

Fig. 1.6 **Simulated product entry and exit with quality change: Post-entry and pre-entry quality dynamics**

Note: These figures show the results of a simulation in which 14 goods enter and exit with constant price and changing quality. Panel A shows an example of the relative quality paths for an entering and exiting good along with the increase in average quality and panel B shows the implied price indices.

4 with a relative appeal of 1.0 and increasing in appeal to 1.2 in the next period, while the exiting good has the reverse pattern. With these entering and exiting goods in each period, panel B shows the implied Laspeyres, Feenstra and UPI log price indexes (making the same assumption of constant unadjusted prices). As with each example, the Laspeyres exhibits no rate of change given constant unadjusted prices. The Feenstra and UPI show substantial negative price change reflecting product entry and exit but there is a large gap between the UPI and the Feenstra. The CV adjustment component is large, suggesting the CV is capturing post-entry and pre-exit dynamics.

To emphasize this possibility, figure 1.7 depicts an alternative simulation

A. Relative Product Quality

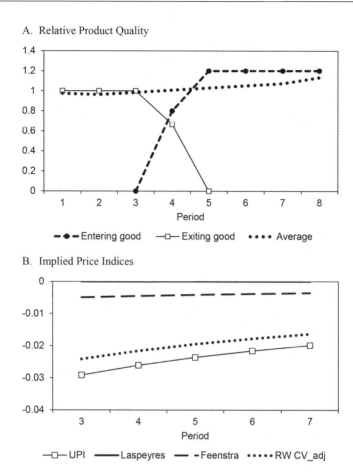

B. Implied Price Indices

Fig. 1.7   Simulated product entry and exit with quality change: Slower post-entry and pre-exit quality dynamics

where the post-entry buildup of appeal is slower. Panel A shows an example of a new good entering in period 4 with a relative appeal of 0.8 that increases to 1.2 in the next period. Alternatively, pre-exit dynamics are faster in that the initial fall in appeal, .067, is larger. As a result, panel B shows that the gap between the Feenstra price index and UPI is even larger in this case, with slower and richer post-entry dynamics. The richer post-entry dynamics generate a larger gap between the UPI and the Feenstra price indexes with the CV capturing a larger share of the dynamics.

While these are simple illustrative simulations, they highlight a potentially important driving force distinguishing the UPI from the Feenstra—namely, that the UPI captures changes in relative product appeal associated with more complex post-entry and pre-exit dynamics than permitted by the Feenstra index. The latter only captures quality differences at the exact points of product entry and exit. Instead, it may be that there are learning and other

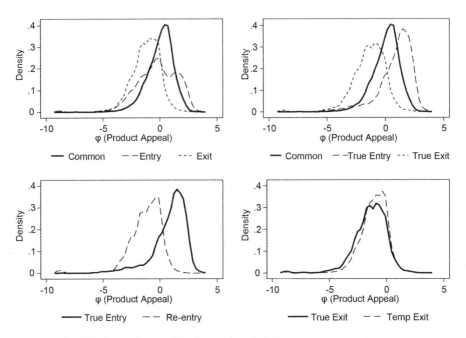

Fig. 1.8   Relative product quality by entry, exit: Video games

Source: Nielsen scanner data.

Note: True entry is the first quarter a good appears, true exit is the last period a good appears, reentry is for a good that changed from zero to positive sales in the current period but not true entry, and temp exit is for a good that changed from positive sales in the prior period to zero in the current period but the good reenters at a later period. Reported are kernel density estimates of the distributions of the demand quality/appeal residual ($\varphi\varphi_{kkkk}$).

adjustment dynamics that imply the product quality changes from product turnover take time to evolve post-entry and pre-exit. In this respect, our finding that the UPI and the CV play a significant role relative to the Feenstra index highlights the potential advantages of the UPI, but also suggests the need for care in interpreting both the CV and the UPI.

Figures 1.5 to 1.7 emphasize the potential role of post-entry and pre-exit dynamics that may be associated with the lifecycle dynamics of products. In a related fashion, a simpler and more basic relationship between the CV and PV may emerge due to measurement and timing issues. At high frequencies (e.g., weekly or monthly) it is likely that entering and exiting products exhibit some ramp-up as products become available in a diffuse manner geographically and some ramp down as the last product is sold in a specific location. Our use of quarterly, national measures mitigates these measurement and timing issues. Nonetheless, these issues remain present, underlying the gap between the theoretical and seasoned UPIs.

Figures 1.8 and 1.9 document patterns in relative product appeal among entering and exiting goods in the video game and soft drink modules, respec-

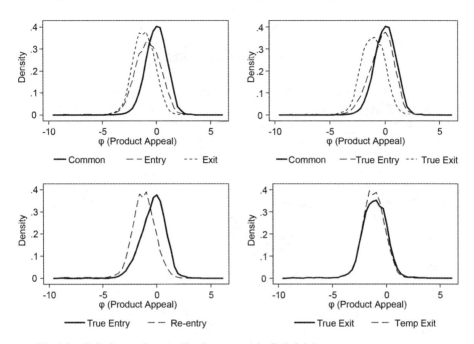

Fig. 1.9   Relative product quality by entry, exit: Soft drinks

Source: Nielsen scanner data.

Note: True entry is the first quarter a good appears, true exit is the last period a good appears, reentry is for a good that changed from zero to positive sales in the current period but not true entry, and temp exit is for a good that changed from positive sales in the prior period to zero in the current period but the good reenters at a later period. Reported are kernel density estimates of the distributions of the demand quality/appeal residual ($\varphi\varphi_{kkkk}$).

tively, of the Nielsen scanner data.[27] Both figures display the distributions of relative appeal of continuing, entering, and exiting goods. The upper-left-hand panel of figure 1.8 shows that for video games, as for memory cards, entering goods have a higher mean appeal than exiting goods but a lower mean than continuing or common goods. Entering goods also have more dispersion in relative appeal than either exiting or common goods, consistent with what we found for memory cards.

The remaining panels of the figure show, however, that this is an incomplete characterization of entry and exit. In the upper-left-hand panel, entry is defined for any item that had zero sales in the prior quarter and positive sales in the current quarter. Exit is likewise defined for any item that had positive sales in the prior quarter and zero sales in the current quarter. In many cases, these entry and exit dynamics don't represent true entry (the first quarter an item is observed) or true exit (the last period an item is observed). The remaining panels show that the mean product appeal of true entrants is

27. As with figure 1.3, this uses the estimate of φ_{kt}.

substantially higher than of re-entrants and indeed is higher than the mean for common goods. In contrast, exiting and re-exiting goods have similar means. These patterns suggest that reentering and temporarily exiting goods are likely part of the end of a product life cycle (hence the similar means between reentering, temporary exits, and true exits). Figure 1.9 shows the analogous patterns for soft drinks. Qualitatively, the patterns are similar, but they are substantially less pronounced, consistent with the notion that changes in product appeal and technological change are less rapid for soft drinks than for video games.

The post-entry and pre-exit dynamics of relative product appeal, price, and market share for video games and soft drinks are depicted in figures 1.10 and 1.11. The figures display patterns for 11 quarters after entry and 11 quarters prior to exit.[28] Statistics for post-entry are relative to the first period of entry for each good. Statistics for pre-exit are relative to 11 quarters prior to exit for each good. Both means and medians of these lifecycle dynamics are displayed.

For video games, products decline in relative product quality, market share, and price both post-entry and pre-exit, with the means and medians showing similar patterns. The magnitudes of the declines are substantial. Relative quality declines by 150 log points in the first 11 quarters post-entry, price declines by 100 log points, and market share declines by 300 log points. Similar magnitudes are present for the 11 quarters prior to exit. These patterns of substantial post-entry and pre-exit dynamics help account for the large role of the CV adjustment for video games. Recall our simulations in figures 1.5 through 1.7 show that post-entry and pre-exit dynamics that exhibit substantial changes in relative quality yield a substantial CV adjustment. To help put these patterns into context, it is useful to observe that the probability of exit increases with product age. In unreported statistics, we find that the exit rate rises from under 5 percent in the first five quarters post-entry to over 20 percent after 20 quarters.

For soft drinks, the dynamics are different, and the effects are somewhat muted. There is a hump-shaped behavior in post-entry relative appeal, price, and market share. The gap between the mean and median patterns is also substantial—consistent with the right tail driving the mean dynamics relative to the median. At the mean, relative quality rises more than 30 log points in the first five quarters, but it falls to 15 log points lower than the initial product quality after 11 quarters. Pre-exit dynamics show monotonic patterns similar to video games but are less steep. Relative product quality is 100 log points lower just before exit than 11 quarters prior to exit. This compares to the 150 log point gap for video games. Even though the magnitudes are

---

28. We restrict analysis for post-entry to goods that survive at least 11 quarters and for pre-exit for goods that are present for all 11 quarters prior to exit. Results without these restrictions show similar patterns.

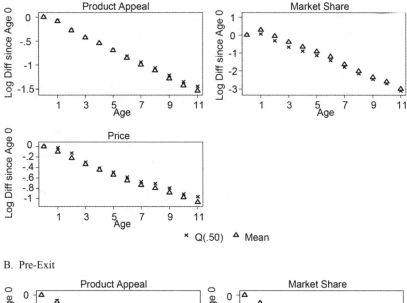

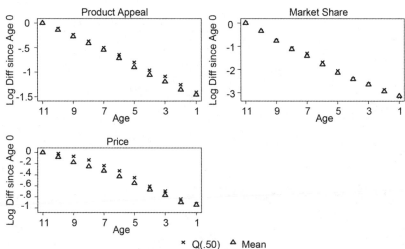

Fig. 1.10   Post-entry and pre-exit dynamics of relative product appeal, price, and market share for video games

A. Post-entry

Source: Nielsen scanner data.

Note: Age is number of quarters since entry. Reported statistics are relative to the product's value in its first quarter. Analysis is restricted to items that survive for 11 quarters.

B. Pre-exit

Source: Nielsen scanner data.

Note: Age is number of quarters prior to exit. Reported statistics are relative to the product's value 11 quarters prior to exit. Analysis is restricted to items that are present for 11 quarters prior to exit.

A. Post-Entry

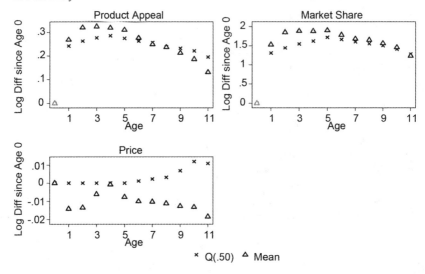

B. Pre-Exit

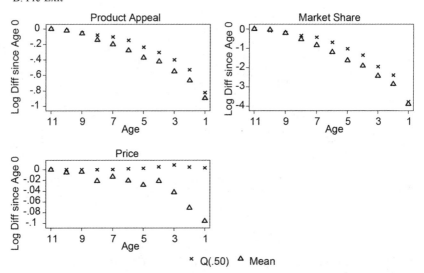

Fig. 1.11   Post-entry and pre-exit dynamics of relative product appeal, price and market share for soft drinks

A. Post-entry

Note: See notes to figure 1.10A.

B. Pre-exit

Note: See notes to figure 1.10B.

somewhat smaller, they are still substantial and help account for the nontrivial CV adjustment for soft drinks. The exit rate also rises with product age for soft drinks but again the patterns are more muted, with the rate increasing from about 4 percent shortly after entry to about 6 percent after 20 quarters.

The CV term's close connection with the PV adjustment term introduced by Feenstra (1994) complicates attempts to interpret the PV term in isolation. For instance, Diewert and Feenstra (2021) argue that the infinite reservation or choke price implied for every good under CES preferences is *a priori* unreasonable. They advocate for a rule of thumb that price indexes should reflect one half of the welfare gains implied by a CES utility function. Their setting does not allow for time-varying appeal shocks, however. As we have seen in this section, allowing for such shocks via the CV term substantially increases measured deflation via a channel that is independent of consumers' reservation prices. It may well be that when the consumer valuation channel is considered, the welfare gains from entering products are larger than is implied by the classic Feenstra (1994) approach.

All of this discussion of complex entry and exit dynamics can be used to justify the practical implementation of the seasoned UPI. However, from our vantage point, this appears to be an important area for future research. Instead of simply assuming a long horizon for seasoning,[29] we think it useful to understand the nature of the entry and exit dynamics. The discussion above suggests that the nature of those dynamics likely varies across goods. Simply assuming a common horizon for seasoning is likely to be inadequate; at the least, this topic merits further investigation.

1.4.2   Claiming φ: The Demand Residual

The large declines in the UPI, even for product categories such as soft drinks that are not obvious hotbeds of technological innovation, raise the question of whether the implied estimates are reasonable, and if so, how best to interpret them.

Redding and Weinstein (2018) take a strong view in formulating the UPI: they treat *all* of the *measured* residual demand variation not accounted for by changing prices as reflecting changes in product appeal or quality. The UPI exactly rationalizes observed prices and expenditure shares by treating the entire error in an estimated demand system as reflecting such changes. In contrast, other approaches such as hedonics or the Feenstra (1994) approach, leave an estimated residual out of the price index calculation. Although hedonic approaches can in principle capture much of the variation from changing product quality and appeal, the R^2 in period-by-period hedonic regressions is typically substantially less than one. Conceptually, therefore, although both the UPI and hedonics capture time-varying quality

---

29. Or alternatively, some threshold rule for market share for common goods in the implementation of the UPI.

and appeal valuations from both product turnover and continuing products, the UPI is arguably more general because it comprehensively captures the error term from the underlying demand system in the price index.

The debate over whether it is appropriate to treat the entire error term from an estimated consumer demand system as reflecting changes in product quality and appeal that affect the cost of living is very much in its infancy, however. The measured error term from the estimated demand system may reflect measurement or specification error from several sources. Specification error may reflect not only functional form but also a misspecified degree of nesting or level of aggregation. Presumably, those errors would ideally be excluded from the construction of a price index.

Another possible source of specification error relates to permitting richer adjustment dynamics in consumer demand behavior. Diffusion of product availability, diffusion of information about products, habit formation, and learning dynamics will show up in the error term from estimation of specifications of static CES demand models. A related but distinct possibility is that the underlying model of price and quantity determination should reflect dynamic decisions of the producing firms (through endogenous investments in intangible capital like customer base as well as related marketing, promotion, and distribution activity by firms). It is important to remember that the approaches being used to estimate the elasticity of substitution are jointly estimating the demand and supply system, so misspecification of either the demand or supply equations can yield specification error.

We are not yet able to quantify the importance of these measurement and specification issues. One area we think is especially promising is to explore a more theoretically based definition of product group classification and nesting. In the next section, we examine the UPI's sensitivity to product group classification and nesting.

1.4.3   Product Group Classification and Nesting

An inherent challenge for implementing the UPI is the definition of product groups and the associated estimation of the elasticities of substitution. In our implementation (and consistent with the approach taken in Redding and Weinstein (2018)), we have assumed all items within a product group or module defined by the data provider are equally substitutable. A review of the individual items in these groups quickly suggests this is a very strong assumption. Consider soft drinks. Presumably, some soft drinks (e.g., caffeinated, with sugar, colas) are much closer substitutes than others. Moreover, some of the item-level variation in the scanner data for soft drinks reflects changes in packaging associated with marketing during holiday seasons. Similar remarks can be made about nonfood items. For video games, essentially the same game may be released with slightly different features or complementary support products—again suggesting very close substitutes in some cases. Alternatively, vintage video games from only a few years

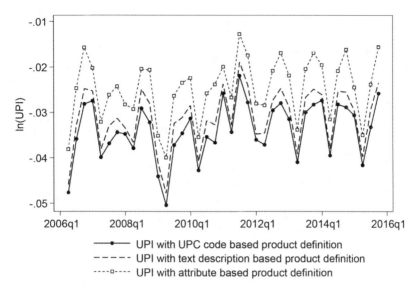

Fig. 1.12   Sensitivity of UPI to product classification
Source: Nielsen scanner data.

ago (e.g., PacMan) are quite primitive compared to the latest games with advanced graphics, animation, and audio (e.g., FIFA World Cup Soccer 2018). In spite of the likely substantial differences in the degree of substitutability among subgroups of products, the estimation of the elasticity of substitution we have considered so far pools items by cross-section and over time, yielding a single elasticity by product group.

To provide some perspective on the potential importance of this issue, figure 1.12 illustrates three different versions of the UPI calculated using the Nielsen scanner data for all product groups, but classifying groups at different levels of aggregation. The first version of the UPI is constructed using item-level (UPC code) variation. The second UPI aggregates items to common text descriptions within the Nielsen scanner data. The third UPI aggregates items based on item attributes defined in terms of product module, brand, size, and packaging.[30] For each UPI considered, all products within an aggregation (e.g., text descriptions or attributes) are treated as perfect substitutes. The UPI becomes substantially less negative using these more aggregated product definitions. Figure 1.12 demonstrates that important components of the UPI (via the PV and CV terms) depend on the methods of classifying products and reflect variation between goods

30. For this exercise, the elasticities of substitution at the product group level are based on the Feenstra estimation procedure for each product group. They are computed as usual for the first version of the UPI. For the second and third versions, we use the same elasticity for the components within the product group. Hence, the exercise highlights the effects of aggregation.

that are likely much closer substitutes than with other items in the same pre-defined grouping.

In principle, a nested CES approach can be used to construct the UPI, potentially overcoming this issue. Redding and Weinstein (2018) show in their appendix that this is feasible conceptually. There are two primary challenges for implementing a nested CES. First, what classification of goods should be used? Hottman, Redding, and Weinstein (2016) consider a nested CES using a within versus between firm classification, and they provide evidence that goods produced within a firm are more substitutable than goods produced across firms. It is unclear, though, that this is an ideal or sufficient classification approach. An alternative might be to use product attributes. This possibility raises an interesting question: could the use of product attributes to define nests lead the UPI and hedonic approaches to be more similar in implementation than they first appear in principle? Our initial analysis above already found that the price indexes that most closely approximate the UPI are the hedonic indexes; perhaps making use of the same attributes as in the hedonic approach to generate product classification and nests for the UPI will yield indexes that track each other even more closely.

A second primary challenge for implementing a nested (or even non-nested) CES utility-based index is the estimation of the elasticities of substitution. The various approaches used for estimation in the literature make strong identifying assumptions. These identification issues become that much more complex in a nested environment. For example, Hottman, Redding, and Weinstein (2016) use a nested procedure that is essentially a modified version of the Feenstra approach for the within-firm estimation (double-differencing firm and time effects) and then use an instrumental variables procedure for the higher level between-firm estimation. The instrument that emerges from the structure of the model as the firm-level price index is a UPI at the firm level with one important term being the within-firm CV adjustment term. The latter reflects changing relative product appeal shocks across goods within the firm. They argue that the latter is orthogonal to the (double-differenced) between-firm relative appeal shocks. This procedure uses strong identifying assumptions at both levels.

Finally, the approach to hedonics with item-level transactions data based on Bajari and Benkard (2005) that we pursued for memory cards has some advantage over traditional implementations of hedonic methods, but it requires further enhancements to be scalable. An advantage of using hedonics with transactions data is that the weights can be updated continuously, and in turn selection bias from exit (as in the Laspeyres approach above), entry (the Paasche approach), or both (using both Laspeyres and Paasche hedonics adjustment and computing a Fisher hedonics adjustment) is feasible. Still, the approach we used for memory cards relied on high-quality and relevant attributes (memory card size and speed) being readily available from the NPD data. Other datasets, such as the Nielsen scanner data, have less readily available information on item attributes. As noted above, the machine learning approaches of Bajari et al. (2021) show great promise in overcoming these issues.

1.5 Reengineering the Data Architecture

The opportunities created by the ubiquitous digitization of transactions can only be realized with a new architecture for data collection. The aim is for the statistical system to use all the relevant detail provided by transactions data. There are a number of issues the new data architecture would need to address (see Jarmin 2019). These include issues of privacy, confidentiality, and value of business data; cost to businesses and the statistical agencies of the new architecture; and the technical and engineering issues of building a new architecture.

There are multiple potential modes for businesses providing such data. All have advantages and disadvantages. We expect that the new architecture should support multiple approaches to providing and collecting data. The agencies will need to be flexible.

Direct feed of transaction-level data. The agencies could get transaction-level data directly from firms and do the calculations necessary to aggregate them. This approach has already been implemented by the Australian Bureau of Statistics for its retail food price index. While the agencies should be receptive to such arrangements, it is unlikely to be practical in the US context because of unwillingness of companies to provide such granular data and the difficulty for the agencies of handling the volume of data that it would entail.

Direct feed of (detailed) aggregate measures of price, quantity, and sales via APIs. Alternatively, and probably more practical in the US context, firms (e.g., retailers) could do the calculations needed to produce detailed but aggregated measures of price, quantity, and sales that could then be transmitted to the statistical agencies. Surveys and enumerations could be replaced by APIs. The agencies—in collaboration with businesses—would have to design a large, but finite, number of APIs that would mesh with the information systems of firms. As is typical for IT innovations, doing so would have a substantial fixed cost, but then provide much improved data at low marginal cost.

Third-party aggregators. Third-party aggregators are already collecting much of the relevant data from many firms (especially retailers). These third parties could do the aggregation as part of their service and provide client firms with an option of responding to statistical agency requests using their service.

Note that the choice among these modes is not just a matter of how the data are collected but carries substantive implications for producing the indexes discussed in this paper. The first option of direct feed of transactions, and perhaps the third option of third-party aggregators, potentially allow the pooling of observations at the item level across firms. In contrast, the second option would provide price, quantity, and sales measures possibly aggregated into quite detailed products, but would not allow direct pooling at the item level across businesses because the index number formulas are highly nonlinear. Hence, there is an interaction between decisions about nesting in the index number construction discussed in section 1.4.3 with the data architecture.

These approaches—whether direct data feeds, API, or third parties— would have many benefits to firms beyond improving the public good provided by official statistics. Firms could save costs by not having to transform their business data to meet the requirements of statistical agencies' surveys. This approach would reduce the current burden associated with collecting data to replace multiple survey requests from agencies. For example, this approach would replace having BLS price enumerators visit outlets. These visits take the time of store management through queries related to sampling goods and finding replacements for goods that disappear. In addition, obtaining revenue data directly from firms could replace the collection of Census's monthly retail trade survey.

Notwithstanding these potential benefits, achieving firms' participation in a new data collection paradigm will be a considerable challenge. Voluntary compliance with current data collection is far from universal, so cooperating with a new paradigm for collecting data certainly cannot be taken for granted. New approaches to data collection may require firms to incur additional costs, at least at the outset. More generally, it may require firms to rethink how and why they interact with statistical agencies. The next section of this paper and the Introduction to this volume consider some of these challenges.

1.6 Capabilities and Mandates of the Statistical Agencies

This paper envisions a new architecture for economic statistics that would build consistent measurement of price and quantity from the ground up. Currently, the collection and aggregation of data components is spread across three agencies. Implementing the new architecture we envision undoubtedly will be a challenge. Moving away from a survey-centric form of data collection for retail prices and quantities to computing statistics from detailed transaction-level data requires an approach that would have businesses providing their data in a unified way. The institutional arrangements that fundamentally separate the collection of data on prices and quantities would need to be changed. There have long been calls for reorganizing BEA, BLS, and Census to help normalize source data access, improve efficiencies, and foster innovation. Regardless of whether the agencies are realigned or reorganized, they need to review the current structure given how the production of statistics is evolving. Having one agency negotiate access to transaction-level data will be difficult enough. Having multiple agencies doing so unduly burdens both businesses and the taxpayer. Importantly, under the current statistical system structure, no agency has the mandate to collect data on both price and quantities, so implementing the data architecture to measure price and quantity simultaneously is not in scope for any agency.[31]

There are also difficult questions about the legal and policy structure needed to govern how statistical agencies access private data assets for statistical uses. For instance, a key question is whether companies would seek to charge for access to the type of data described above and, if so, whether the associated fees would be within the budgetary resources of the statistical agencies.

To further test, develop, and implement a solution such as we are proposing here, the statistical agencies must expand their general data science capabilities. Whether transaction level data are transmitted to the agencies or whether retailers provide intermediate calculations, an important point of focus for the statistical agencies will be not only the acquisition but the curation of new types of unstructured data. The ingestion, processing, and curation of these new sources introduces scalability concerns not present in most survey contexts. Also, negotiating access will require the agencies to hire more staff with the skills to initiate and manage business relationships with data providers.

Clearly, modernization requires significant investments in computer science and engineering expertise at the statistical agencies. This is a major challenge given the competition for attracting talent across other government agencies and with the private sector. Collaboration with academic experts and contracting can be part of the solution, but some internal expertise is essential.

The collective economic measurement system will need to make a number of investments. It will need to invest in building relationships across government agencies and the private sector to secure access to high-quality source data. It will need to invest in staff with the skills to acquire, process, and curate large datasets and build reliable and privacy-protected statistical products from blended data. Information systems will need to be redesigned

31. The agencies are undertaking important and innovative work using transactions data as part of their ongoing measurement programs, some of which is described in papers in this volume. The Census Bureau pays for access to limited data for experimenting with augmenting the Monthly Retail Trade Survey (Hutchinson 2019). The BLS has multiple efforts to replace or augment CPI enumerations with alternative sources (Friedman, Konny, and Williams 2019). Notably, both efforts are focused on using nonsurvey data to supplant or supplement data collections within the current architecture, so the Census effort does not measure prices and the BLS efforts do not measure quantities. The Census Bureau is, however, supporting this project by providing NPD data that do measure price and quantity simultaneously. An exception to the agencies not considering both price and quantity simultaneously when using nonsurvey data is the BEA's extensive program to address measurement of quality change in health care.

to accommodate both survey and alternative data processing. These are large challenges, but we believe they are necessary in order to build a twenty-first-century statistical system that can deliver the trusted information needed by private and public sector decision makers.

1.7   Concluding Remarks

In the introduction to the 2000 NBER/CRIW conference volume *Scanner Data and Price Indices*, Feenstra and Shapiro (2002) stated, "Scanner data and other electronic records of transactions create tremendous opportunities for improving economic measurement." Almost two decades after that conference, researchers have made progress using digitized transactions data on many dimensions, but the US statistical agencies have not yet implemented the vision of using such data for dramatic improvements in economic measurement for official statistics. Indeed, many of the papers in that conference pointed to the difficulty in using scanner data for measurement. Both push and pull factors, however, suggest the time is now ripe for full-scale implementation of using transaction-level data that will yield a significant reengineering of key national indicators. In particular, developments in economics and computer science such as the UPI and hedonics-at-scale, are innovations that address some of the difficulties with using scanner data for economic measurement under the existing architecture for economic statistics.

On the push side, declining response rates on business and household surveys yield both higher costs and lower quality of economic measurement. Relatedly, the current decentralized system imposes a substantial burden on households and businesses with a multiplicity of surveys. On the pull side, the digitization of virtually everything has been dramatic over the last two decades. Moreover, substantial progress has been made on the technical challenges for implementation. Active research using item-level transactions data has yielded development of price index methodology that captures quality changes from product turnover and changing product appeal for continuing goods. Based on our review and exploration of the methodological innovations, we conclude that integration of the alternative approaches that have been proposed is likely to be fruitful.

In particular, the UPI methodology developed by Redding and Weinstein (2018) has great promise, but it likely requires refinements that are closely connected to an alternative hedonics-based approach to quality adjustment. We suspect that a successful implementation of the UPI methodology requires a nested product classification approach based on nests defined by product attributes of individual items. Tracking item-level product attributes is at the core of the hedonics-based approach. A limitation of the latter is that implementation has involved intensive study of each product group (e.g., computers) one at a time. Advances in machine learning and other data dimensionality reduction techniques offer the prospect of implementation of either the nested UPI or the hedonics approach with attributes at scale. It remains to be seen what exact method will prove to be conceptually and practically the best approach.

Beyond the issues of developing classification of groups based on hedonics, the theoretical UPI also faces other practical implementation challenges related to the complex dynamics of entering and exiting goods. One practical implementation method is to use what we have denoted as the seasoned UPI to overcome these issues. We think it is premature to settle on this methodology. We instead suggest further investigation into the nature of the entry and exit dynamics of goods. We anticipate substantial progress will be made on this issue in future research.

Active and intensive research on these issues should be a high priority. At the same time, substantial effort needs to be made in exploring how the US statistical agencies can harvest the firehose of digital data that are increasingly available. The agencies are experimenting with alternative harvesting approaches, but a variety of challenges remain. In addition, implementing this twenty-first-century approach to using integrated price and quantity collection and measurement will require rethinking the coordination and organization of the US statistical agencies.

References

Bajari, Patrick, and C. Lanier Benkard. 2005. "Hedonic Price Indexes with Unobserved Product Characteristics, and Application to Personal Computers." *Journal of Business and Economic Statistics* 23 (1): 61–75.

Bajari, Patrick, Zhihao Cen, Manoj Manukonda, Jin Wang, Ramon Huerta, Junbo Li, Ling Leng, George Monokroussos, Suhas Vijaykunar, and Shan Wan. 2021. "Hedonic Prices and Quality Adjusted Price Indices Powered by AI." Cenmap Working Paper CWP04/21. https://www.cemmap.ac.uk/wp-content/uploads/2021/02/CWP0421-Hedonic-prices-and-quality-adjusted-price-indices-powered-by-AI-1.pdf.

Bureau of Labor Statistics. 2018. "Chapter 17: The Consumer Price Index." *Handbook of Methods*. Washington, DC: US Bureau of Labor Statistics.

Crawford, Ian, and J. Peter Neary. 2019. "New Characteristics and Hedonic Price Index Numbers." CESifo Working Paper No. 7529. https://www.cesifo.org/en/publikationen/2019/working-paper/new-characteristics-and-hedonic-price-index-numbers.

Diewert, Erwin, and Robert Feenstra. 2021. "Estimating the Benefits of New Products," in *Big Data for Twenty-First Century Statistics*, edited by Katherine G. Abraham, Ron S. Jarmin, Brian C. Moyer, and Matthew D. Shapiro. Studies in Income and Wealth, vol. 79. Chicago: University of Chicago Press.

Ehrlich, Gabriel, John Haltiwanger, Ron Jarmin, David Johnson, and Matthew D.

Shapiro. 2019. "Minding Your Ps and Qs: Going from Micro to Macro in Measuring Prices and Quantities." *AEA Papers and Proceedings* 109:438–43.

Erickson, Tim, and Ariel Pakes. 2011. "An Experimental Component Index for the CPI: From Annual Computer Data to Monthly Data on Other Goods." *American Economic Review* 101 (5): 1707–38.

Feenstra, Robert C. 1994. "New Product Varieties and the Measurement of International Prices." *American Economic Review* 84 (1): 157–77.

Feenstra, Robert C., and Matthew D. Shapiro. 2002. "Introduction." In *Scanner Data and Price Indices*, edited by Robert C. Feenstra and Matthew D. Shapiro. Studies in Income and Wealth, vol. 64. Chicago: University of Chicago Press.

FitzGerald, J., and O. Shoemaker. 2013. "Evaluating the Consumer Price Index Using Nielsen's Scanner Data." Statistics Statistical Survey Paper, US Bureau of Labor Statistics, Washington, DC. https://www.bls.gov/osmr/research-papers /2013/st130070.htm.

Foster, Lucia, John Haltiwanger, Shawn Klimek, C. J. Krizan, and Scott Ohlmacher. 2015. "The Evolution of National Retail Chains: How We Got Here." In *Handbook of Retail Trade*, edited by Emek Basker. Northampton, MA: Edward Elgar Publishing.

Friedman, David, Crystal Konny, and Brendan Williams. 2019. "Big Data in the U.S. Consumer Price Index: Experiences and Plans." Paper presented at the Conference on Research in Income and Wealth, Bethesda, MD, March 15–16, 2019.

Hottman, Colin, Stephen Redding, and David Weinstein. 2016. "Quantifying the Sources of Firm Heterogeneity." *Quarterly Journal of Economics* 131 (3): 1291–1364.

Hutchinson, Rebecca. 2019. "Using Nontraditional Data Sources to Reduce Respondent Burden in United States Census Bureau Economic Data Products." Paper presented at the Conference on Research in Income and Wealth, Bethesda, MD, March 15–16, 2019.

Jarmin, Ron. 2019. "Evolving Measurement for an Evolving Economy: Thoughts on 21st Century US Economic Statistics." *Journal of Economic Perspectives* 33 (1): 165–84.

Pakes, Ariel. 2003. "A Reconsideration of Hedonic Price Indexes with an Application to PCs." *American Economic Review* 93 (5): 1578–96.

———. 2005. "Hedonics and the Consumer Price Index." *Annales d'Economie et de Statistique* 79–80:729–49.

Redding, Stephen, and David Weinstein. 2018. "Measuring Aggregate Price Indexes with Demand Shocks: Theory and Evidence for CES Preferences." NBER Working Paper No. 22479, revised May 2018, National Bureau of Economic Research, Cambridge, MA. https://www.nber.org/papers/w22479.rev2.pdf.

———. 2020. "Measuring Aggregate Price Indexes with Demand Shocks: Theory and Evidence for CES Preferences." *Quarterly Journal of Economics* 135 (1): 503–60.

Shapiro, Matthew D., and David W. Wilcox. 1996. "Mismeasurement in the Consumer Price Index: An Evaluation." *NBER Macroeconomics Annual 1996*, vol. 11, edited by Ben S. Bernanke and Julio J. Rotemberg, 93–142. Cambridge, MA: MIT Press.

Big Data in the US Consumer Price Index
Experiences and Plans

Crystal G. Konny, Brendan K. Williams,
and David M. Friedman

2.1 Introduction

The Bureau of Labor Statistics (BLS) has generally relied on its own sample surveys to collect the price and expenditure information necessary to produce the Consumer Price Index (CPI). The burgeoning availability of Big Data could lead to methodological improvements and cost savings in the CPI. The BLS has undertaken several pilot projects in an attempt to supplement and/or replace its traditional field collection of price data with alternative sources. In addition to cost reductions, these projects have demonstrated the potential to expand sample size, reduce respondent burden, obtain transaction prices more consistently, and improve price index estimation by incorporating real-time expenditure information—a foundational component of price index theory that has not been practical until now.

Government and business compile data for their administrative and operational needs, and some of these data can potentially be used as alternatives

Crystal G. Konny is the former Chief of the Branch of Consumer Prices at the Bureau of Labor Statistics.

Brendan K. Williams is a Senior Economist in the Branch of Consumer Prices at the Bureau of Labor Statistics.

Prior to his retirement in February 2020, David M. Friedman served as the Associate Commissioner for Prices and Living Conditions at the Bureau of Labor Statistics.

Any opinions and conclusions expressed herein are those of the authors and do not necessarily represent the view of the US Bureau of Labor Statistics. We thank Matthew Shapiro, Katherine Abraham, Kate Sosnowski, Kelley Khatchadourian, Jason Ford, Lyuba Rozental, Mark Bowman, Craig Brown, Nicole Shepler, Malinda Harrell, John Bieler, Dan Wang, Brian Parker, Sarah Niedergall, Jenny FitzGerald, Paul Liegey, Phillip Board, Rob Cage, Ursula Oliver, Mindy McAllister, Bob Eddy, Karen Ransom, and Steve Paben for their contributions. For acknowledgments, sources of research support, and disclosure of the authors' material financial relationships, if any, please see https://www.nber.org/books-and-chapters/big-data-21st -century-economic-statistics/big-data-us-consumer-price-index-experiences-and-plans.

to BLS's surveyed data. We use the term alternative data to refer to any data not collected through traditional field collection procedures by CPI staff, including third-party datasets, corporate data, and data collected through web scraping or retailer Application Programming Interfaces (APIs). Alternative data sources are not entirely new for the CPI. Starting as far back as the 1980s, CPI used secondary source data for sample frames, sample comparisons, and supplementing collected data to support hedonic modeling and sampling. What is new now is the variety and volume of the data sources as well as the availability of real-time expenditures. This paper will review BLS efforts to replace elements of its traditional CPI survey with alternative data sources and discuss plans to replace and/or augment a substantial portion of CPI's data collection over the next several years.

2.2   Overview of CPI

The CPI is a measure of the average change over time in the prices paid by urban consumers for a market basket of goods and services. The CPI is a complex measure that combines economic theory with sampling and other statistical techniques and uses data from several surveys to produce a timely measure of average price change for the consumption sector of the American economy. BLS operates within a cost-of-living-index (COLI) framework when producing the CPI.

Weights used in the estimation of the CPI are derived primarily from two surveys. The Consumer Expenditure (CE) Survey furnishes data on item category purchases of households and is used to draw the CPI item sample. The Telephone Point of Purchase Survey (TPOPS) collects data on retail outlets where households purchased commodities and services and is used as the outlet frame from which BLS selects a sample of outlets.[1] Weights are derived from the reciprocal of the probabilities of selection. BLS has not had access to the expenditure information necessary to produce superlative indexes, the preferred class of index formulas for COLI estimation, for the lower-level component indexes that feed all CPI outputs. BLS currently only uses a superlative index formula to produce the Chained CPI-U at the upper level of aggregation.[2] The lower-level indexes used in CPI aggregates almost all use a geometric mean index formula, which approximates a COLI under the restrictive assumption of Cobb-Douglas utility.[3]

Pricing information in the current CPI is primarily based on two surveys.

1. BLS is currently pursuing an effort to include the collection of point-of-purchase information within the Consumer Expenditure Survey. This will replace TPOPS starting with indexes released in FY 2021.

2. See Klick, "Improving Initial Estimates of the Chained Consumer Price Index" in the February 2018 issue of the *Monthly Labor Review* for more information on changes made to the formula in calculating the *preliminary* C-CPI-U starting with the release of January 2015 data.

3. For additional detail on the construction of the CPI, see "Consumer Price Index: Calculation" in the online BLS *Handbook of Methods* (https://www.bls.gov/opub/hom/cpi/calculation.htm).

BLS data collectors, known as Economic Assistants (EAs), conduct the Commodities and Services (C&S) survey by visiting each store location or website (known as an outlet in BLS nomenclature) selected for sampling. For each item category, known as an Entry Level Item (ELI), assigned to an outlet for price collection, an EA using information from a respondent on the portion of the outlet's sales of specific items, employs a multistage probability selection technique to select a unique item from among all the items the outlet sells that fall within the ELI definition. The price of that unique item is followed over time until the item is no longer available or that price observation is rotated out of the sample. The Housing survey is used to collect rents for the Rent of Primary Residence (Rent) index and these rent data are also used to calculate changes in the rental value of owned homes for the Owners' Equivalent Rent index. While the CPI has generally used these two surveys for price and rent data, historically in several cases CPI turned to alternative data sources, including for used cars and airline fare pricing and sales tax information.[4]

Several challenges arise in calculating the CPI using traditional data collection. First, because the CPI aims to measure constant quality price change over time, when a unique item is no longer sold a replacement item must be selected, and any quality change between the original and replacement items must be estimated and removed to reflect pure price change in the index. Second, new goods entering the marketplace must be accounted for in a timely manner with the appropriate weight. Third, the CPI is based on samples, which can introduce sampling error. Lastly, the CPI may only be able to collect offer prices that might not reflect all the discounts applied to a transaction.

In terms of survey operations, the collection of data by BLS through pricing surveys is increasingly costly and more difficult. Metropolitan areas have generally increased in size, which causes a corresponding increase in travel costs. The growth in the number of chain stores has increased the time to obtain corporate approval to collect data. Response rates are declining as the result of many factors: new confidentiality requirements, increasing number of surveys, increasing distrust of government, data security concerns, and/or less confidence in the accuracy of the CPI.

2.3 Working with Alternative Data in CPI

Alternative data sources provide an opportunity to address many of the challenges encountered by the CPI over the past few decades. Adopting alternative data sources could address the challenges mentioned above as

4. See the CPI Fact Sheet on "Measuring Price Change in the CPI: Used Cars and Trucks" for more information on the use of National Automobile Dealers Association (NADA) data for used cars beginning in 1987. Airline fare pricing was previously based on prices collected from the SABRE reservation system and is now collected using web-based pricing. See the CPI Fact Sheet on "Measuring Price Change in the CPI: Airline Fares" for more information.

well as increase sample sizes, reflect consumer substitution patterns more quickly, reduce or eliminate respondent burden, help address nonresponse problems in the CPI's surveys, and reduce collection costs. In some instances, BLS receives real-time expenditure information as well. Data may be at a more granular level, for many more items than in the sample, or timelier such as daily. Initial exploration of the use of alternative data in CPI was focused on response problems and improving index accuracy in hard-to-measure product areas. In more recent years, BLS has been giving equal attention to finding new cost efficiencies in the collection process.

The CPI program classifies its alternative data sources into three main categories:

1. *Corporate-supplied data* are survey respondent-provided datasets obtained directly from corporate headquarters in lieu of CPI data collectors in respondent stores or on their websites. As the datasets are typically created for their own use, respondents define data elements and structure, and the BLS must adapt them to BLS systems. BLS receives varying levels of information about the datasets—in general, the information provided is what the companies are willing to give. Discussions with corporate data respondents often involve finding a level of aggregation that the corporation is comfortable providing to address their confidentiality concerns.

2. *Secondary source data* (third-party datasets) are compiled by a third party, contain prices for goods or services from multiple establishments, and need to be purchased by BLS or, in some limited cases, are provided free of charge from the data aggregator, who has made some effort to standardize the data elements and structure across business establishments.

3. *Web/Mobile app scraping data* are collected by BLS staff using in-house software that extracts prices and product characteristics from websites and mobile apps. Some establishments provide Application Programming Interfaces, or *APIs*, to allow partners to access pricing information. Data collection through an API is often easier and more straightforward than maintaining web scraping code over time.

BLS needs to evaluate each alternative data source, regardless of type, to ensure it meets the measurement objectives of the CPI as well as to deal with various operational considerations. In general, CPI's process for deciding whether an alternative data source is fit for CPI use currently involves the following steps for each item or establishment:

1. Determine what item or establishment to pursue (criteria taken into consideration are reflected in the appendix, in table 2A.1)
2. Evaluate alternative data source options
3. Evaluate selected data source, including definition, coverage, and other quality aspects

4. Evaluate data quality over a predefined amount of time, which will depend on the type of data
5. Determine research approach and alternative methodologies to test, including:
   a. match and replace individual prices in CPI with individual prices in the alternative source (see Wireless Telephone Services case)
   b. match and replace individual prices in CPI with an average price for a unique item or over a defined set of items (see CorpY case)
   c. replace price relatives in the CPI with estimates of price change based on new methodologies (see the CorpX and New Vehicles cases)
   d. use all establishments and items in alternative data and calculate an unweighted index (see the Crowdsourced Motor Fuels case)
6. Evaluate replacement indexes based on statistical tests and cost benefit analysis based on criteria for production use:
   a. Is the data a good fit for CPI?
   b. Is it as good as or better than current pricing methodology?
   c. Is it more cost effective or does the improvement in the index justify the additional cost?
   d. In some cases, BLS will implement a short-term solution that meets the criteria for use in production while still researching longer-term improvements (see Corp X case for example).
7. Determine the best way to incorporate the data into the CPI (e.g., transition plans, risk mitigation/contingency plans, systems considerations)

While there are numerous potential benefits to introducing new alternative data sources in the CPI as noted earlier, the CPI program has also encountered challenges that have impeded BLS from quickly incorporating alternative data into its outputs. Prior to discussing specific experiences, the paper will summarize the challenges.

2.4 Methodological Challenges

Because the CPI is designed to use its own surveyed data, BLS has encountered some challenges related to alternative data congruence with CPI methodology. The primary obstacle to dealing with transaction data in the CPI has been dealing with *product lifecycle effects*—that is, when products exhibit systematic price trends in their lifecycle. For certain goods such as apparel and new vehicles, a product is typically introduced at a high price on the market and gradually discounted over time. At the point where the good exits, the price has been discounted substantially and may be on clearance. In the CPI, a similar good is selected, and its price is compared with that of the exiting good. The price relative constructed by comparing these two items typically implies a large increase in price from the exiting good to its replacement. This large increase will offset the incremental price declines over the prior product's lifecycle. While this method works in the CPI's fixed weight index, Williams and Sager (2019) found that a price comparison between exiting and new goods in a dynamically weighted index may undercorrect in situations where an exiting item is a low-inventory item on clearance, or overcorrect in other situations, and that multilateral price index methods designed to address chain drift, specifically the rolling year Gini Elteto Köves Szulc (GEKS) index discussed in Ivancic, Diewert, and Fox (2011), did not remedy downward drift associated with product lifecycles. Greenlees and McClelland (2010) found that hedonic price indexes often exhibit the same drift as matched-model indexes. Conventional hedonic methods also do not address product lifecycle effects. Silver and Heravi (2005) found that coefficient estimates from hedonic regressions may be affected by product cycles, which they attributed to pricing strategies, including the dumping of obsolete merchandise. More generally, the implications of product lifecycles have not received much attention in the price index literature, with some exceptions such as Melser and Syed (2016) and Ehrlich et al. (this volume).

A second obstacle relates to representativeness. Many alternative data sources are constructed as "convenience" samples, based on the ease of collecting data on a certain segment of the market. When major companies, brands, or market segments are not represented in an alternative dataset, it can suffer from *loss in representativeness*, thus potentially introducing coverage error into the CPI that is based on representative samples. Comingling sampled and unsampled data can undermine the interpretation of the CPI's existing variance measurement, which in addition to providing a measure of the uncertainty in the CPI because of sampling, is used to allocate the CPI's sample across items and outlets to minimize variance as described in Sheidu (2013). An inaccurate estimate of variance could cause an inefficient allocation of sample.

The remaining methodological challenge deals with the *level of detail* provided by an alternative source. Corporate data providers and vendors may be unwilling or unable to provide the level of detail BLS economic assistants collect from observation, and resolution may require compromise and the acceptance of aggregated data that are less than ideal for price index calculation. A corporation may define a unique item differently than BLS, making it difficult to price the same item over time. Limited information on product features and unstructured item descriptions requires new approaches to matched model indexes and quality adjustment in the CPI.

Most alternative data sources also omit sales tax information and may not provide enough information to identify the tax jurisdiction that CPI needs to apply a tax rate. In general, BLS adapts methods on a case-by-case basis to address the specific issues of each alternative data source.

2.5   Operational Challenges

While *timeliness* is often listed as one of the virtues of Big Data, it can be an issue for both corporate and secondary sources—BLS needs for a monthly index are not always a high priority or even possible for data vendors and corporate headquarters. At times, BLS risks publication delays or must accept truncating observations from the end of the month. In other cases, the data are only available with a lag—this is particularly the case with medical claims data, as described in the Physicians and Hospitals Services case. To the extent that the CPI is making use of data from multiple sources that come in with varying lags, BLS may need to reconsider the CPI as a measure that is published and never revised, taking into consideration the impact that might have on use of the CPI for cost-of-living-adjustments and contract escalation.

BLS has control over all data processing of traditionally collected data and has many procedures and systems in place to control the overall *quality of the micro data* collected and used in CPI's outputs. With alternative data, BLS has to rely on others who do not always have the same data quality needs. Data cleanliness can be a risk with vendor data, descriptive data are not always collected, and data comparability over time is not guaranteed. In addition, *continuation of any vendor data source* is not guaranteed and could disappear without any warning; thus, BLS spends some time looking at these risks and how best to mitigate them. BLS creates fallback plans but recognizes that their implementation—if needed—may not be fast enough or smooth enough to prevent temporary gaps in coverage in the CPI.

In order for an alternative data source to be incorporated into the aggregate CPI measure, the data must be *mapped into CPI's item categorization and geographic structure*. This is simple when a dataset's coverage directly corresponds to a CPI item category. However, in many cases, transaction data cover a broad range of items and BLS must concord these items to the CPI structure based on the company's categorizations and item descriptions. BLS developed a machine-learning system to assist in the CorpX categorizations, which has greatly improved its ability to handle large datasets with hundreds of thousands of items.

Once BLS acquires a data source, resolves any methodological issues, and decides to incorporate it into the CPI, it must still deal with *integrating the data into current CPI information technology systems*, which assume data are structured according to the traditional survey data collection process. There are essentially two ways of doing this without completely redoing all of CPI's systems—replacing an individual price observation in the CPI or replacing a component index with an index derived from alternative data. In both cases, *transition decisions* must be specified—how to inform CPI data users, timing, addressing aggregation with other CPI components, and so on. The New Vehicles case is instructive as an example of replacing a component index with an index derived from alternative data. Replacing individual price observations works well when mixing surveyed and alternative data in item categories. For example, BLS replaces one corporate respondent's data with alternative data while using surveyed data to represent other respondents, thus keeping outlet weights constant. However, the current system is not designed to generate new price observations, so the current strategy is to match a price or price change estimate to an existing price observation that has been selected for sampling. If the alternative data include information that cannot be matched to the existing sample (for example, a combination of seller and city that has not been selected), it cannot be used under the match and replace method. Both the Residential Telecommunications Services and New Vehicles cases are good examples of the various kinds of adaptations made in this regard.

Ultimately, BLS must standardize collection and use of alternative data sources to the degree possible to avoid a proliferation of individual respondent and secondary source systems that can only handle data from one source. Longer term, BLS is considering more extensive changes to CPI IT systems to utilize alternative data more fully.

2.6   Legal, Policy, and Budgetary Challenges

BLS needs to deal with legal, policy, and budgetary challenges. For secondary sources, this usually focuses on *negotiation of contracts* that are consistent with federal laws and meet the needs of both parties, as well as making sure that costs are reasonably controllable in the longer term (there are limits to the number of option years BLS can have on a contract). Nevertheless, there is the possibility that *contract costs* can increase exponentially when it comes time for renewal, and BLS needs to plan accordingly to the extent possible. Sole source contracts are problematic for BLS, and without data continuity, the risk is having to continually change production systems to accommodate new data and formats, which could be quite costly or lead to unpublishable indexes. In the case of secondary source datasets, a condition of the contract could be that the vendor be acknowledged publicly, such as J. D. Power in the New Vehicles case. In addition, for corporate data, there could be a need to enter into a formal user agreement.

The BLS's primary obstacle to *adopting web scraping* has been legal. The Confidential Information Protection and Statistical Efficiency Act (CIPSEA) is the primary US law ensuring the *confidentiality* of BLS microdata. To ensure all alternative data used in research or production is protected under CIPSEA, BLS must provide establishments, including those whose data are collected online whether manually or automatically through scraping, a pledge of confidentiality promising to use the information for exclusively statistical purposes. Moreover, Terms of Service agreements

(TOS) for websites and APIs often have aspects that are problematic for federal agencies. Website user terms and conditions often require users to agree to accept the law in the state in which the establishment resides, rather than federal law. Some TOS restrict storage of data, which is a requirement for CPI to ensure reproducibility. Many TOS have open-ended indemnity clauses to which federal agencies cannot legally commit. Corporate legal departments sometimes find it simpler to refuse access than to negotiate exemptions or alternative terms of service.

The issues related to web scraping involving private entities need to be resolved before CPI can proceed beyond the initial research efforts. After extensive consultations with various BLS stakeholders and the DOL Solicitor, BLS recently developed a policy for web and mobile app scraped data in which BLS provides a pledge of confidentiality to potential website owners and obtains their consent to web scrape with the understanding that BLS will use best practices. TOS are negotiated to follow federal law. Similar to the New Vehicles case, there can be situations in which web scraping involves obtaining data from a third-party vendor, such as in the Crowd-sourced Motor Fuels experience, where CPI identifies the vendor.

Finally, CPI has an overall goal to make sure that the transition to alternative data sources *does not increase its overall budget*—that is, that this work remains at least budget neutral if not actually resulting in overall cost savings. The Food at Home case is a good example of how this emphasis on overall cost effectiveness can play out.

2.7   Experiences with Corporate Data Collection

Three companies provide corporate datasets to BLS; two are described in this section. The other company has been providing airline fare data for less than a year, so those data are still in the evaluation stage. Both companies described below initially started providing corporate data in reaction to their reluctance to allow continued in-store collection.

2.7.1   CorpX

In May 2016, a department store (CorpX) began supplying BLS with a monthly dataset of the average price and sales revenue for each product sold for each CorpX outlet in the geographic areas covered in the CPI. (Prior to May 2016, BLS was obtaining data that were not approved for production use, and then CorpX restructured its database and decided to provide different data to BLS.) However, the data only include limited descriptions of the items being sold. There is no structured data on product features, and the variable description is short and sometimes not descriptive at all. This lack of descriptive data prevents constructing hedonic regressions or even making informed decisions on the relative comparability of new to exiting items,

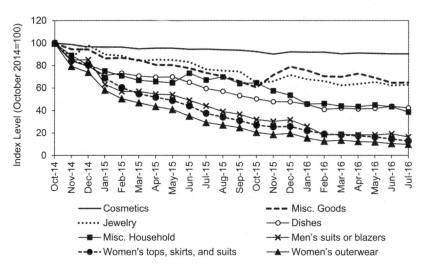

Fig. 2.1   Matched-model indexes for CorpX in Dallas
Source: CorpX data.

limiting CPI's ability to apply usual replacement and quality adjustment methods. BLS assessed the data over a period of two years for replacement of more than 1,000 price quotations used in the CPI and approved its use in production beginning with the March 2019 index.

Figure 2.1 shows Tornqvist, matched-model indexes for a selection of eight item categories in one city. Matched-model indexes drop precipitously. Several item categories show more than a 90 percent decline in less than two years. Products are introduced at a high price and discounted over time. Most indexes display the largest price decline over a period of less than two years. These findings are similar to those of Greenlees and McClelland (2010), who analyzed an earlier sample of data from the same retailer. Greenlees and McClelland also found that matched-model price indexes implied implausibly large price declines that were not remedied when treated as chain drift. They found that hedonic indexes also showed large declines unless coefficients were constrained to be a fixed value over the timespan of the estimated index.

While research continues on the best way to deal with product lifecycle effects, BLS has developed a short-term methodology that mimics current CPI procedures in order to begin incorporating data from this retailer into the CPI. The methodology selects a probability proportional to size sample from sales transactions included in the dataset provided by CorpX and calculates match-model price relatives for these selected items over the course of a year. These matched-model indexes typically display the downward trend mentioned above. After twelve months, a new sample of products from the same item category is selected and a price relative is constructed as the average price of all new products in the item category relative to the average price of products in the category 12 months ago. This ratio between the unit prices of the new and old samples is typically positive and offsets the within-year price declines because of product lifecycles. Since the item categories are broadly homogenous in terms of item characteristics and pricing strategy, BLS is assuming constant quality between the new sample items and the year-old sample. The sample selection process occurs twice a year corresponding to the seasonality of the items.

In order to incorporate data from CorpX into the CPI, BLS also developed a way of mapping item categorizations. The retailer provides short descriptions and categorization information for each item sold at its stores in the geographic areas covered in the CPI. Manually matching each of these items, on the order of hundreds of thousands, to a CPI item category was not feasible. Based on methods developed in Measure (2014) for auto-coding workplace injuries at BLS, CPI staff used machine learning to classify items by the CPI structure based on their descriptions, hand-coded classifications for a segment of the items in the corporate data to create a training dataset and used the "bag-of-words" approach based on the frequency of word occurrences in the item descriptions. A logistic regression was then used to estimate the probability of each item being classified in each category based on the word frequency categorizations in the training data. After validating the results and reviewing low confidence predictions, BLS uses this approach with each monthly dataset to categorize new items.

Figure 2.2 compares the current published apparel price index with the experimental index that incorporates CorpX transaction data using the methodology described above. The published index does not omit CorpX

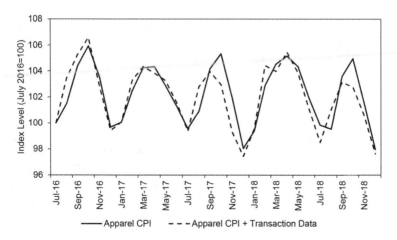

Fig. 2.2   Impact of incorporating CorpX Data
Source: CorpX data, apparel CPI.

entirely. Once EAs could no longer collect in stores, they collected prices for items on the store's website. The experimental index replaces these web-collected prices with a price index that represents the corporately supplied data and price change from the method described above. The two series show similar seasonal patterns, and the inclusion of transaction data does not significantly change the index's trend.

2.7.2   CorpY

In February 2012, another company (referred to as CorpY) refused to participate in the initiation of new prescription drug rotation samples because of the burden placed on in-store pharmacies. Discussions ensued between regional office staff and the company to obtain corporate data that are acceptable for CPI use and meet the confidentiality concerns of CorpY. Since March 2015, CorpY has been providing the CPI with a bimonthly dataset of average prices for a sample of their in-store prescription drug transactions.

With traditional collection methods, the CPI defines a unique item to track over time to include National Drug Code (NDC), prescription size, and insurance provider and plan or cash price. By holding these variables constant, the CPI can ensure that any price change is not due to changes in the drug's quality. The FDA-assigned NDC specifies a pharmaceutical molecule, manufacturer, and dosage. Since each NDC corresponds to a manufacturer, the CPI can also control for whether the pharmaceutical is a brand-name drug or a generic competitor. Economic Assistants (EAs) in the field collect prices for these quotes by recording list prices at prescription drug retailers. While EAs attempt to capture a realistic ratio of insurance to cash prices, the CPI is biased toward cash list prices. Respondents often refuse to provide insurance prices or simply cannot because of their database systems.

When brand-name drugs lose their patent protection and generics enter the marketplace, generic sales are slow to start as the result of prescriptions lasting for multiple days, weeks, or months. After approximately six months, BLS believes the generic has sufficiently penetrated the market. At this point, EAs ask pharmacists the percentage of generic versus brand-name drug sales and, based on those percentages, samples brand or generic to continue pricing. If a generic is selected, the price change between brand-name and the generic is reflected in the CPI.

Ideally, CorpY would have agreed to furnish a corporate dataset that provided a census of CorpY's monthly prescription transactions, including a complete breakdown of brand and generic transactions. Due to the company's concerns about confidentiality and reporting burden, BLS instead receives the bimonthly dataset mentioned above and whose features are described in detail in table 2.1. CorpY defines unique items using the Generic Code Number (GCN) instead of NDC. Each GCN defines a particular drug's composition, form, and dosage strength. Unlike NDC, the GCN does not specify a manufacturer, so whether the drug is brand or generic is unknown. CorpY averages prices across brand name and generic versions. As consumers substitute between brand and generic versions of a drug, the average price will change.

Table 2.1 compares the sampling and pricing methodology between CorpY and CPI traditional collection (called "In-Store") and demonstrates the tradeoffs and negotiations that can take place with establishments when discussing the corporate dataset option, including providing insight into how CPI evaluates the fit with its measurement objectives. BLS was satisfied that notwithstanding these considerations, the CorpY data are suitable for the CPI.

2.8   Experiences with Secondary Data Sources

Several vendors aggregate and sell data, both retail transaction data and offer prices. These datasets are typically used by marketers and are often constructed with a focus on category-level sales rather than providing product-level detail. Most datasets cover far more items than the CPI sample. The BLS has purchased several datasets and researched their use as replacements for production CPI components. Secondary data sources present similar issues to those found in corporate data. The data are often lacking in descriptive detail compared to information recorded by data collectors in the C&S survey. Secondary sources often lack transparency in terms of degree of willingness to fully share their methodologies with BLS. In this section, we cover CPI's experience with five secondary data sources.

2.8.1   New Vehicles

In response to respondent burden, low response rates, dealer-estimated prices, and high collection costs, the BLS has pursued an alternative to its traditional data collection for new vehicles. BLS purchases transaction-level data from J. D. Power that cover about one third of new vehicle sales in the United States. BLS analysis has shown that the market shares of vehicle makes in the CPI sample and J. D. Power's data are similar to each other and to sales data reported in industry publications, which leads to the conclusion that there is little loss of representativeness even though J. D. Power's dataset is not created through sampling. Each record contains information on the vehicle configuration, transaction price, and any financing set up by the dealer. The item identifier available in the J. D. Power dataset does not provide the same level of detail that BLS gets through conventional data collection—especially the specific options sold with a given transaction.

New vehicle sales display a product lifecycle where vehicles are introduced at a high price and then discounted through the model year until they are replaced by a successor vehicle. As a result of this pattern, matched-model

Table 2.1   CorpY trade-off

Topic	CorpY	In-store	BLS preferred approach
Sampling	Probability proportional to size (PPS) over the past year nationally by sales excluding lowest 10% of transactions	PPS based on price of the last 20 prescriptions sold	CorpY: The last 20 prescriptions was a compromise since pharmacists were limited in their time and ability to pull data from their records. Sampling over a one-year period is likely to be more representative.
Geographic level	National	Outlet Specific	In-Store: Distribution of drug sales may differ between various regions.
Price	Average price of at least 100 transactions	Single price	CorpY: Less volatility and the switch from brands to generics is shown as a unit price change.
	Insurance prices	Mostly uninsured prices	CorpY: Because most consumers pay through insurance. Ideally prices would be separated by insurance plan, and CorpY averages across insurance companies and plans.
	National price	Outlet specific price	CorpY: Averaging across all stores in the US gives a more representative price at the US level, and research showed that there was little regional price variation.
	Per pill price	Per prescription price	In-Store: Per-prescription price allows CPI to control for price differences per pill between prescription sizes such as quantity discounts.
Patent loss adjustment	Unit prices by GCN average across brand and generic	Based on analyst monitoring of patents for an NDC	CorpY: Since the GCN averages across generic and branded drugs, any patent loss will be reflected in a unit price change. Monitoring patent loss is time-consuming and difficult.
Timing	Bimonthly	Monthly and bimonthly	In-Store: CorpY only delivers data during odd months. In-store collection is done monthly or bimonthly depending on survey design.

new vehicle price indexes show steady declines because they only reflect within-year price declines and do not account for any cross-model year price change. This index behavior may suggest chain drift due to index nontransitivity, but as was the case with CorpX indexes, price index declines appeared to be the result of showing price decreases over a product's lifecycle. In the current BLS methodology, such declines are offset by showing a price comparison between the heavily discounted older model year and the new model year sold at or near full price. However, this method only offsets declines when using a fixed-weight index, and one of the advantages of the J. D. Power dataset is the ability to use real-time expenditure weight.

Based on the methodology developed in Williams and Sager (2019), BLS began monthly releases of a research New Vehicle index on May 15, 2019, and continues to release monthly indexes approximately three days after the release of the CPI. To construct this index, individual transaction records in the J. D. Power dataset are aggregated using a geometric mean into a unit price for a specific vehicle. Price comparisons are made between the old and new version one year apart with a year-over-year price relative to represent price change between similar points in a vehicle's product cycle. Vehicle configurations without an observed prior version are omitted. The twelfth root of these relatives are taken to represent monthly price changes, which are aggregated using the Törnqvist index with expenditure shares of each vehicle in the dataset in this month and one year ago. Year-over-year price measurement smooths over high-frequency fluctuations in the market. In order to restore information on the short-run behavior of the new vehicle market, BLS uses a time series filter to separate a cyclical component from trend in a monthly frequency index, which is susceptible to product cycle bias. The natural logarithm of this cyclical component is added to the natural log of the year-over-year trend and then exponentiated to create an index (YOY+Cycle) that reflects both the short- and long-term behavior of new vehicle prices. The YOY and YOY+Cycle indexes are compared to the CPI for New Vehicles in figure 2.3. The current BLS methodology for the CPI New Vehicles index reduces to a year-over-year price comparison since intermediate monthly price changes cancel in the fixed-weight CPI. The YOY+Cycle methodology used in the research index generalizes this measure to accommodate nonfixed weight indexes and, as a result, produces a similar measure of price change.

Following a period of comment and review, BLS may replace the new vehicles component index of the CPI with indexes based on J. D. Power data. For more detailed information, see the methodology fact sheet for the R-CPI-U-NV index on the BLS/CPI website. The expense of J. D. Power data is slightly less than the current cost of collecting new vehicle prices in the field, and the J. D. Power data have added benefits including a much larger sample size, transaction prices, and real-time expenditure information.

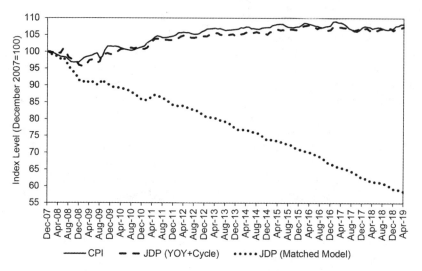

Fig. 2.3   New vehicles price indexes: CPI vs. J. D. Power
Source: JD Power, New Vehicles CPI.

2.8.2   Physicians' and Hospital Services

Currently, the medical care major group has the worst response rate of all major groups in the CPI, and of that major group, "Physicians' Services" and "Hospital Services" have the highest relative importance. There are multiple reasons for this low response, and all are very difficult to overcome, such as confidentiality concerns magnified by the Health Insurance Portability and Accountability Act (HIPAA), difficulty in determining insurance plan rates, separate physicians and billing offices, and gatekeeper issues. BLS decided to explore the feasibility of supplementing traditional data collection of cash and Medicare prices of these two items with insurance claims data, and purchased a dataset covering 2009 and 2010 medical claims data for one insurance carrier for a small sample of medical services in the Chicago metropolitan area. BLS received average prices across all transactions for the provider/medical service combination, and the number of transactions used in creating the average price. A key research objective was to analyze the effect of using lagged insurance claims data. Claims often take months to be fully adjudicated and data processing by the vendor may take additional time. Claims data are lagged, ranging from two to nine months, before they can be delivered to the CPI.

BLS calculated indexes several ways using this dataset; the one seeming to most accurately reflect CPI methodology used a two-step weighting process. Medical services are first aggregated within outlets and weighted by their monthly quantity share to get an outlet relative. Each medical service quantity share weight is updated every month. Outlet relatives are then aggregated using outlet expenditure shares from 2008. The outlet weights were fixed for the two years of research data. Outliers were removed from the data.

Results of this preliminary research are promising but not definitive. First, BLS did not identify and request all price-determining characteristics. Each medical service in Hospital Services was identified and sampled using its procedure code, the Current Procedural Terminology (CPT) for outpatient and diagnosis-related group (DRG) for inpatient. Upon examination of outliers, researchers realized that diagnosis codes—International Classification of Diseases (ICD) codes[5]—are price-determining for inpatient services in addition to the DRG. Still, price indexes created using insurance claims data tracked closely to the CPI Hospital Services index. Initial results indicate that supplementing claims data with the CPI data did not significantly change the CPI Hospital Services index values in the Chicago area, where response rates are better than average. In areas where CPI is less productive, claims data may increase accuracy.

While claims data did not significantly impact the Hospital Services index, they had a more noticeable effect on Physicians' Services. In the Chicago area, Physicians' Services price indexes combining lagged insurance claims data and CPI data for cash and Medicare prices markedly improves upon the CPI Physicians' Services index by compensating for poor response rates in surveyed data and increasing representation of insured payers. Moreover, the cost of claims data is less than traditional data collection. Future plans include expanding the research to all CPI geographic areas, using a larger sample of medical services, and experimenting with time-series modeling.

2.8.3   Wireless Telephone Services

Currently, at the request of respondents, the majority of the CPI's wireless telephone services sample is collected online using the carriers' websites. Without the assistance of a knowledgeable respondent, the CPI sample was not accurately reflecting consumer purchasing habits. The BLS prioritized the examination of alternative data for this item because of its high relative importance and online collection and has seen promising results. Beginning in February 2018, BLS researched and leveraged a secondary source of household survey data on wireless carriers to create sampling percentages for wireless telephone services to aid field economists in selecting more representative unique items.

BLS also calculated research indexes with another secondary source that contains list prices for wireless telephone service plans collected from the websites of wireless carriers. Coverage of CPI providers was over 90 percent.

---

5. The ICD is a system used by physicians and other healthcare providers to classify and code all diagnoses and symptoms. See https://www.who.int/standards/classifications/classification-of-diseases for more information.

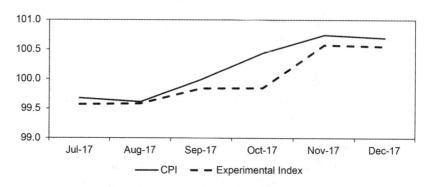

Fig. 2.4   Wireless telephone services indexes
Source: Wireless Telephone Services CPI, alternative data source.

BLS used a "match and replace" methodology to calculate indexes, whereby the service plans in CPI collection are matched to the plan descriptions in the alternative data, the prices are replaced, and indexes are recalculated using current CPI methodology and the rest of the CPI sample not covered by the data.

As reflected in figure 2.4, over the six-month period examined, the official index increased 0.69 percent while the research index rose 0.55 percent. This difference occurred in large part because CPI data collection is spread out over the month, whereas the data in the alternative dataset were collected at one point of time in the month. BLS preliminarily concludes that this data source can replicate data collected by BLS at reduced cost with at least the same level of accuracy. BLS is exploring one other data source, calculating indexes over a longer period of time, and will make a decision on production use in the next year, while continuing to explore transaction price data sources.[6]

2.8.4   Residential Telecommunications Services

Similar to Wireless Telephone Services, at the request of respondents, the majority of the CPI's Residential Telecommunications Services sample is collected online using the carriers' websites. Beginning in February 2019, based on purchased household survey data, BLS created sampling percentages for landline phone service, cable and satellite television service, and internet service to aid field economists in selecting more representative unique items.

6. On a related note, CPI started using a secondary source to assist with the process of quality adjustment for smartphones beginning with the release of January 2018 data and started directed substitution in April 2018 to bring the CPI sample more in line with what consumers are purchasing. See https://www.bls.gov/cpi/notices/2017/methodology-changes.htm and https://www.bls.gov/cpi/factsheets/telephone-hardware.htm.

BLS purchased another dataset containing list prices for Residential Tele-communications services compiled from several sales channels by a data aggregator. The data are not directly comparable to CPI prices; for example, add-on purchases like premium movie channel subscriptions or rental fees are not included, and items excluded from CPI prices such as rebates, activation, and installation are included. There is also no data on quantities or expenditures. To calculate research indexes, BLS used CPI outlet weights and distributed that weight across all items in the dataset equally, and then developed matched model indexes to replicate the CPI methodology. There were significant index differences between the CPI and research indexes, which researchers determined were due to procedures for missing data and the lack of substitution methodology in the research index series. There was also difficulty in determining a unique item to price in the alternative data. Nevertheless, preliminary results demonstrate that it is possible to calculate the CPI for Residential Telecommunications services with alternative data. With access to a broader, richer dataset, BLS can get results with as good or better quality than traditional field collection. Thus, further research is planned in addition to exploring transaction price data sources.

2.8.5   Food at Home

BLS purchased historical Nielsen Scantrack scanner data and used it to create indexes for comparison with the CPI Food at Home categories. The purchased dataset covers five years of historical data ending in 2010 at the Universal Price Code (UPC)/geographic area and includes some product descriptors and an average price for each observation. The Nielsen data that BLS purchased do not cover the full scope of outlet types covered in the CPI for Food at Home categories, omitting convenience stores, bakeries, butchers, smaller grocery stores, warehouse stores, and gas stations.[7] BLS mapped Nielsen's UPC data into the item categorization used in the CPI. About 80 percent of the UPCs could be mapped directly into a CPI category based on their Nielsen categorization, but the other 20 percent had to be matched manually (though BLS now has experience using machine learning to aid in mapping new items).

Initial research focused on comparing selected CPI Food at Home categories with the Nielsen Scantrak data and using the results to improve traditional data collection processes and procedures—for example, improving the price-determining characteristics on data collection forms to better measure quality change. Later efforts, including work documented in FitzGerald and Shoemaker (2013), turned toward exploring whether Nielsen Scantrack data could be used as replacement for certain Food at Home item categories in the CPI. The data covered around 2 million UPCs, orders of magnitude

---

7. Nielsen offers data for convenience stores, warehouse stores, and gas stations but BLS chose not to purchase those data in this initial research project.

higher than the number of items tracked in the CPI. Some item categories produced price indexes similar to corresponding CPIs. Other categories with product cycles displayed extreme downward declines similar to other transaction data indexes. Researchers dealt with this downward bias by constructing common goods indexes, where entering and exiting goods were excluded from the index. Ultimately, BLS found that it was less expensive to collect data in stores than to pay for Nielsen Scantrack real-time data and the geographic and outlet detail needed to support the monthly CPI. BLS plans to explore whether retailers would be willing to provide us corporate datasets, but unlike the examples discussed above, BLS has not yet experienced many response or collection issues in Food at Home outlets.

2.8.6   Housing

The CPI Housing Survey records rents from about 47,000 units selected to form a representative sample of the private rental market. Every six months a mix of property managers, renters, and their representatives are asked about actual transaction rent and what utilities and services are included in the rent, along with characteristic data. BLS explored a secondary dataset of housing rents and estimated rents to evaluate the potential for replacing or supplementing CPI Housing Survey data. The secondary source dataset is not designed as a representative sample or census for a geographic area, and although it included rents and estimated rents for more than 50 million housing units, the match rate to CPI units was only about 30 percent. Rents in the secondary source appeared much more volatile than those in the CPI, in part because the CPI includes ongoing and renewed leases while the secondary source estimates the current market rate for new rentals. In the final analysis, BLS decided that the differences between CPI Housing and the secondary source dataset were too significant in terms of sample coverage and differing purposes to use this secondary source in the CPI at this time. BLS is exploring alternative data sources.[8]

2.9   Experiences with Web Scraping/APIs

Currently, even when collecting information from websites, CPI data collectors manually enter data into the same data collection instrument used for in-store collection. The CPI is exploring using web scraping to automate data collection from these websites instead, given recent agreement on an acceptable approach within BLS after consultation with the DOL solici-

---

8. Although it does not involve an alternative data source, CPI management has discussed potential new modes for collecting housing data from its respondents, including what would be the first use of the BLS Internet Data Collection Facility (IDCF) to update data for a household survey. Thus, CPI is not just looking at new data sources, but at more cost-effective collection modes as well.

tor. Web scraping consists of automatically accessing a web page, parsing its contents, and recording pricing and other relevant information. Others, including MIT's Billion Prices Project (Cavallo and Rigobon 2016), have demonstrated the benefits of using web scraping to collect massive amounts of data for the purposes of price measurement. Certain online retailers provide public access to pricing data through APIs, which usually places less burden on server resources than web scraping and allows information to be collected in machine-readable format rather than parsing mark-up intended to create a human-readable webpage.

The BLS is also working on adapting its systems in order to benefit from web scraping. The BLS's current systems are highly integrated so that variance estimation, weighting, outlet sampling, and unique item selection are all intertwined. "Plug and play," simply collecting a massive dataset of prices from the web and incorporating them into CPI calculations, is not as straightforward as it might appear. The index calculation system assumes that a fixed number of observations are selected from each respondent. For example, if three unique products are selected at an outlet, only prices from these three observations will be used in calculations from that outlet. (When an observation cannot be collected, imputation is used.) If this respondent gave us a corporate dataset of thousands or millions of observations, our systems would not be able to accommodate additional observations beyond the three that had been selected for sampling. CPI will be adapting its systems in order to allow calculations when the number of prices by source varies.

We discuss two current research efforts related to web scraping—one using data from a crowdsourcing website as a potential replacement for CPI's collection of motor fuels price data and one related to making BLS collection of airline fares from the web more cost effective. CPI is also negotiating terms of service with a person-to-person sharing app business that offered BLS use of its API.

2.9.1 Crowdsourced Motor Fuels

Motor fuels are one of the easier items for EAs to collect, but the large number of motor fuel outlets in the CPI (1,332 as of December 2017) leads to a high aggregate cost in terms of travel and time. Motor fuels are also an easy to define, undifferentiated product. GasBuddy is a tech company that crowdsources fuel price collection from close to 100,000 gas stations in the US.[9] CPI obtained permission from GasBuddy to web scrape data from its website and acknowledge them as a source.

Unlike most other items in the CPI where individual item categories are sampled, all five motor fuel categories are automatically selected at any

---

9. See https://www.gasbuddy.com/ for more information.

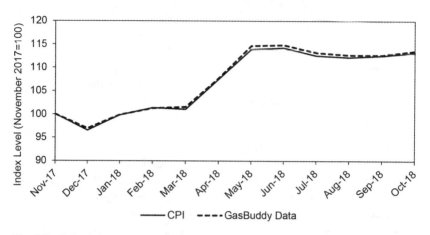

Fig. 2.5   Price indexes for regular gasoline
Source: Gasoline, unleaded regular CPI, GasBuddy.

sampled motor fuel retailer in the current C&S survey. Of the five categories of motor fuels in the CPI, GasBuddy's information can replace the collected data for the three grades of gasoline and diesel, but they do not have coverage of alternative fuels. Currently, few gas stations actually offer alternative motor fuels (such as electrical charging, ethanol, E85, or biodiesel), so observations for motor fuel alternatives can be collected conventionally and comingled with the web-scraped data. CPI data collectors record certain features of gasoline that may affect pricing, including the payment type (e.g., any cash discount or cash pricing) and whether the gasoline is ethanol free, both characteristics not available from GasBuddy.

GasBuddy does not provide any means of weighting their price information. In incorporating GasBuddy price information into a price index, CPI had the choice of matching prices to the weighting information in the TPOPS survey or simply calculating an index with equal weighting for the price relatives within an area. BLS constructed indexes using the latter method and found that unweighted Jevon's price indexes based on GasBuddy data are very similar to the CPI's gasoline components, despite the fact that the CPI uses TPOPS to weight gas stations. Figure 2.5 shows results from one of the gasoline indexes. The CPI showed a 13.221 percent increase in the price of unleaded regular gasoline over the 11 months ending in October 2018, while the GasBuddy index showed an increase of 13.595 percent—a difference of 0.374 percentage points. Preliminary results show that average prices and price indexes based on GasBuddy and CPI data behave very similarly, which suggests that any quality bias is not systematically large. BLS is calculating average prices and indexes over a longer period of time and will evaluate results and make a decision on production use in the next year.

2.9.2   Airline Fares

Current pricing procedures for airline fares involve EAs in the Washington office collecting prices from respondents' websites. Web-based pricing enables the CPI to track a defined trip month-to-month, one-way or roundtrip fare, originating and destination cities, departure and return dates, and fare class of the ticket. Each month the same advance reservation specification (designated by number of weeks) and day of the week specification will be used to collect a price. For example, a quote with a "seven-week" advance reservation specification and "Tuesday" as the day of the week specification will always be priced as if the consumer booked airfare in the current month for departure seven weeks in advance on a Tuesday.

BLS is negotiating with respondents for corporately reported data, permission to use their APIs, or permission to web scrape their sites, which is CPI's order of preference. BLS prefers corporate data for transaction prices and possibly weights, as well as many more price observations, but will accept the mode the company is willing to provide. BLS received permission to web scrape from one company and has also been receiving corporate data since October 2018 from another respondent.

In the short term, research is focusing on a match and replace methodology, meaning collection of prices for each of the quotes currently in the CPI sample based on the quote's specifications. Long term, research will focus on increasing the sample size used for the calculation of price change for each respondent. BLS has not yet collected enough data to analyze the automatically collected data and associated research indexes. The plan is to introduce automatic collection or corporate collection for respondents over time as each one is approved for production use.

2.10   A Few Words about Future Plans and Conclusions

For over a century, the CPI has been constructed primarily using data collected by BLS staff. Big Data can provide information on real-time weighting, the missing fundamental piece from official price statistics for years. New alternative data sources have the potential to address many of the problems faced in recent years, including lower response rates and higher collection costs. After several years of work on various alternative data sources, BLS now has a goal to replace a significant portion of CPI direct collection with alternative data sources by 2024. BLS will prioritize alternative data for item categories and outlets based on a number of factors including the relative importance of the item, the number of quotes replaced, the cost of collection, the cost of alternative data, the accuracy of the current item index, respondent relationship with BLS, ease of implementation, response rates, and the concentration of the sample for a given item. For example, 15 establishments each account for more than 1,000 price quotations apiece. BLS will prioritize gaining cooperation for corporate data collection from large establishments such as these, as well as respondents in specific highly concentrated markets, and will also explore alternative data for item categories that may benefit in terms of accuracy and/or efficiency. In addition to agency-specific efforts, the BLS is working with our partner statistical agencies to collaborate on acquiring new data sources and exploring new uses for existing administrative and survey datasets. BLS is also sponsoring a new National Academy of Sciences Committee on National Statistics (CNSTAT) panel, comprised of academic and other experts, to investigate three key methodological issues, including how BLS should modify current CPI methodology to deal with the challenges presented by blending traditionally collected data with alternative data.[10]

As reflected in table 2A.1 at the end of this paper, there are numerous items to pursue, balancing index accuracy and operating costs. The table is organized in parallel to the CPI-U news release tables, with item categories aggregated to the highest level at which alternative data can be pursued. The legend at the end of the table provides information on the contents of each column. This is the current plan and will change as progress is made and experience gained. As of now, table 2A.1 indicates that the CPI has either current or potential planned "experience" in item categories to some degree, representing about 30 percent of the relative importance in the CPI-U.

While alternative data usage may result in a variety of methodological improvements, research to date demonstrates fundamental issues that require resolution. Simple techniques such as matched-model price indexes do not necessarily produce tenable results, and current CPI methods may not translate well to transaction data. BLS has developed ways of addressing product lifecycle with the research new vehicles indexes, and a short-term solution that allows us to replace manual collection of price data from the CorpX website with a corporate transaction dataset. BLS continues to review the academic literature for the latest transaction data price index methods, while developing new methods and procedures for taking advantage of alternative data and the challenges presented by this important opportunity. BLS will continue to introduce alternative data incrementally in the CPI, while being mindful of core CPI measurement objectives and meeting the needs of the program's broad base of data users.

10. See https://www.nationalacademies.org/our-work/improving-cost-of-living-indexes -and-consumer-inflation-statistics-in-the-digital-age for more information, including links to the materials from the two public meetings on October 7 and October 30, 2020, regarding uses of alternative data for consumer price indexes at BLS and elsewhere.

Appendix

Table 2A.1   Preliminary CPI alternative data plans

Item	RI	# Quotes	Concentration	Issues	Priority	Source of data	Experience	% sample
All items	100.000 0	128,282 2	L					
Food at home	7.256	32,546	M	L	M			
Food away from home:	5.979	5,586	L	L				
Full-service meals and snacks	2.969	1,844	L	L				
Limited-service meals and snacks	2.542	2,808	M	L	M	corp	pursue	
Food at employee sites and schools	0.181	462	L	L				
Food from vending machines & mobile vendors	0.091	300	L	L				
Other food away from home	0.196	172	M	L				
Energy:	8.031	7,777	L	L				
Fuel oil and other fuels	0.193	359	M	L				
Gasoline (all types)	4.344	3,778	M	L	H	scrape	20/21	100
Other motor fuels	0.094	830	M	L	H	scrape	20/21	90
Electricity	2.655	1,406	M	M	H		seek	
Utility (piped) gas service	0.747	1,404	M	M	H		seek	
Household furnishings and supplies:	3.336	8,479	M	L				
Window and floor coverings and other linens	0.258	916	H	L				
Furniture and bedding	0.883	1,881	L	L				
Appliances	0.216	610	H	L				
Other household equipment and furnishings	0.491	1,872	M	L				
Tools, hardware, outdoor equipment & supplies	0.659	1,436	H	L	M			
Housekeeping supplies	0.829	1,764	H	L	M			

(*continued*)

Table 2A.1 (cont.)

Item	RI	# Quotes	Concentration	Issues	Priority	Source of data	Experience	% sample
Apparel:								
Men's apparel	3.114	21,919	M	L	M	corp	some	
Boys' apparel	0.593	4,468	M	L		corp	some	
Women's apparel	1.103	8,853	M	L	M	corp	some	
Girls' apparel	0.185	2,904	M	L		corp	some	
Men's footwear	0.217	674	M	L		corp	some	
Boys' and girls' footwear	0.161	937	M	L		corp	some	
Women's footwear	0.295	1,774	M	L		corp	some	
Infants' and toddlers' apparel	0.140	580	H	L		corp	some	
Watches	0.099	303	M	L		corp	some	
Jewelry	0.152	408	M	L		corp	some	
Transportation commodities less motor fuel:	6.514	7,145						
New vehicles	3.695	1,900	L	H	H	sec	20/21	100
Used cars and trucks	2.329	4,537	H	H	H	sec	prod	100
Motor vehicle parts and equipment	0.378	708	M	L				
Medical care commodities:	1.710	5,860	H					
Prescription drugs	1.316	4,641	H	H	H	corp	some	
Nonprescription drugs	0.336	863	H	L				
Medical equipment and supplies	0.057	356	H	L				
Recreation commodities:	1.792	5,835	M					
Video and audio products	0.231	1,113	H					
Pets and pet products	0.600	1,311	M	L				
Sporting goods	0.488	1,016	M					
Photographic equipment and supplies	0.033	272	H					
Newspapers and magazines	0.069	395	L	L				
Recreational books	0.044	316	H	L				
Toys	0.256	958	H	L				
Sewing machines, fabric and supplies	0.023	240	H	L				
Music instruments and accessories	0.036	214	M	L				

Item								
Education and communication commodities:	0.546	1,192	M	L				
Educational books and supplies	0.131	245	M	L				
Personal computers & peripherals	0.315	368	H	L				
Computer software and accessories	0.024	294	H	L				
Telephone hardware, calculators, and other consumer information items	0.076	285	H	M				
Alcoholic beverages:	0.963	1,243	L					
Other goods:	1.545	3,341	M					
Tobacco and smoking products	0.647	1,027	M					
Hair, dental, shaving, and miscellaneous personal care products	0.381	987	H	L				
Cosmetics, perfume, bath, nail preparations and implements	0.301	734	M	L				
Miscellaneous personal goods	0.210	593	H	L				
Shelter:	32.893	896	M					
Rent of primary residence	7.825	N/A						
Housing at school, excluding board	0.114	214	L	L				
Other lodging away from home, including hotels and motels	0.858	499	M	L				
Owners' equivalent rent of residences	23.723	N/A						
Tenants' and household insurance	0.374	183	H	L				
Water and sewer and trash collection services:	1.079	985	L					
Water and sewerage maintenance	0.815	624	L	L				
Garbage and trash collection	0.265	361	M	L				
Household operations	0.870	605	M					
Medical care services:	6.883	5,704	L					
Physicians' services	1.728	1,993	L	H	H	sec	20/21	75
Dental services	0.780	396	L	M	M			
Eyeglasses and eye care	0.316	421	L	M	M			
Services by other medical professionals	0.415	254	L	M	M			
Hospital services	2.312	2,123	L	H	H	sec	20/21	85
Nursing homes and adult day services	0.191	345	L	L				
Care of invalids and elderly at home	0.087	172	L	M	M			
Health insurance	1.053	N/A			M	sec	prod	100

(continued)

Table 2A.1   (cont.)

Item	RI	# Quotes	Concentration	Issues	Priority	Source of data	Experience	% sample
Transportation services:	5.945	5,385	M					
Leased cars and trucks	0.655	265	L	H	M	sec	research	100
Car and truck rental	0.118	515	H	M	M			
Motor vehicle maintenance and repair	1.117	1,097	L	L				
Motor vehicle insurance	2.382	517	H	M	M			
Motor vehicle fees	0.539	562	L	L				
Airline fares	0.683	1,745	H	L	M	scrape, corp	research	
Other intercity transportation	0.166	451	M	L				
Intracity transportation	0.277	233	M	L				
Recreation services:	3.850	6,338	L					
Cable and satellite television service	1.501	1,906	H	H	H	sec	20/21	95
Video discs and other media, including rental of video	0.086	411	H	M	M			
Pet services, including veterinary	0.413	265	L	L				
Photographers and photo processing	0.038	166	M	L				
Club membership for shopping clubs, fraternal, or other organizations. . . fees	0.666	1,226	L	L				
Admissions	0.655	2,141	L	M	M			
Fees for lessons or instructions	0.217	223	L	L				
Education and communication services:	6.062	5,953	M					
Tuition, other school fees, and childcare	2.900	2,566	L	L				
Postage	0.094	230	H	L		sec	prod	
Delivery services	0.014	231	H	L		corp	pursue	
Wireless telephone services	1.693	1,279	H	H	H	sec	20/21	98
Land-line telephone services	0.572	874	H	H	H	sec	20/21	95
Internet services & electronic info providers	0.780	773	H	H	H	sec	20/21	95
Other personal services:	1.632	1,493	L					
Personal care services	0.623	495	L	L				
Miscellaneous personal services	1.009	998	L					

Notes:

RI: Relative importance as of September 2018, Consumer Price Index for All Urban Consumers: US city average. Subcategories may not add up to the RI at the category level because of unsampled items not displayed on this table.

quotes: The number of quotes in CPI sample as of August 2018 (monthly, bimonthly odd and even)

Concentration: Percent of CPI item sample in the top ten establishments where data is collected.

- L: Less than 33% of CPI sample is in top ten establishments
- M: 33% to 66%
- H: 66% to 100%

Issues: Index quality issues—High, Medium, and Low based on a number of factors, such as response rate, collection of list prices rather than transaction prices, collecting prices on websites due to respondent request, restricted pricing at certain times of year, difficult collection methodology, costly collection, difficult item descriptions, and the degree of subjectivity in specification descriptions. An "H" means that BLS could substantially improve index accuracy and/or cost efficiency with alternative data.

Priority: Priority in seeking alternative data based on factors such as index quality issues, relative importance, size of sample, alternative data source availability. An "H" means these items will be BLS priority to pursue, 'M' is next to pursue as resources are available, and a blank means BLS currently has no plans to pursue alternative collection.

Source of data: The type of alternative data initially pursued for that item category. Scrape: web scraping or API; Corp: corporately collected data; Sec: secondary source data

Experience: The status of BLS alternative data progress.

- Pursue: actively pursuing one or more establishments or secondary sources
- 20/21: Items where initial research is complete and with results so far, BLS is expecting research to be approved for production with implementation in 2020 or 2021
- Prod: in production
- Research: actively researching alternative data
- Seek: examining alternative sources
- Some: alt data account for some percent of sample in production

% of sample: % of sample replaced either in production or based on research. Corporate blank due to disclosure protection.

References

Bureau of Labor Statistics. 2020. "Consumer Price Index." In *Handbook of Methods.* https://www.bls.gov/opub/hom/cpi.

Cavallo, Alberto, and Ricardo Rigobon. 2016. "The Billion Prices Project: Using Online Prices for Measurement and Research." *Journal of Economic Perspectives* 30 (2): 151–78.

FitzGerald, Jenny, and Owen Shoemaker. 2013. "Evaluating the Consumer Price Index Using Nielsen's Scanner Data." Paper presented at the Joint Statistical Meetings 2013—Government Statistics Section, Montreal, Canada, October 2013. https://www.bls.gov/osmr/research-papers/2013/pdf/st130070.pdf.

Greenlees, J., and R. McClelland. 2010. "Superlative and Regression-Based Consumer Price Indexes for Apparel Using U.S. Scanner Data." Paper presented at the Conference of the International Association for Research in Income and Wealth, St. Gallen, Switzerland, August 27, 2010.

Ivancic, Lorraine, W. Erwin Diewert, and Kevin J. Fox. 2011. "Scanner Data, Time Aggregation and the Construction of Price Indexes." *Journal of Econometrics* 161 (1): 24–35. https://doi.org/10.1016/j.jeconom.2010.09.003.

Kellar, Jeffrey H. 1988. "New Methodology Reduces Importance of Used Cars in the Revised CPI." *Monthly Labor Review* 111 (12): 34–36. http://www.jstor.org/stable/41843067.

Klick, Joshua. 2018. "Improving Initial Estimates of the Chained Consumer Price Index." *Monthly Labor Review* (February). https://doi.org/10.21916/mlr.2018.6.

Measure, Alexander. 2014. "Automated Coding of Worker Injury Narrative." Paper presented at the Joint Statistical Meetings 2014—Government Statistics Section, Boston, MA, August 2014. https://www.bls.gov/osmr/research-papers/2014/pdf/st140040.pdf.

Melser, Daniel, and Iqbal A. Syed. 2016. "Life Cycle Price Trends and Product Replacement: Implications for the Measurement of Inflation." *Review of Income and Wealth* 62 (3): 509–33. https://doi.org/10.1111/roiw.12166.

Sheidu, Onimissi. 2013. "Description of the Revised Commodities and Services Optimal Sample Design." Paper presented at the Joint Statistical Meetings 2013—Government Statistics Section, Montreal, Canada, October 2013. https://www.bls.gov/osmr/research-papers/2013/pdf/st130060.pdf.

Silver, Mick, and Saeed Heravi. 2005. "A Failure in the Measurement of Inflation: Results from a Hedonic and Matched Experiment Using Scanner Data." *Journal of Business and Economic Statistics* 23 (3): 269–81. www.jstor.org/stable/27638820.

Williams, Brendan, and Erick Sager. 2019. "A New Vehicles Transaction Price Index: Offsetting the Effects of Price Discrimination and Product Cycle Bias with a Year-over-Year Index." Bureau of Labor Statistics Working Papers, No. 514. https://www.bls.gov/osmr/research-papers/2019/pdf/ec190040.pdf.

Improving Retail Trade Data Products Using Alternative Data Sources

Rebecca J. Hutchinson

3.1 Introduction

The US Census Bureau has long produced high-quality official statistics for the retail trade sector.[1] These data are obtained through traditional survey data collection and are a critical input to the calculation of the Gross Domestic Product (GDP), of which retail trade made up nearly 25 percent of the 2019 estimate (Bureau of Economic Analysis 2020). The retail data are also critical to Census Bureau data users because they analyze the current state of a retail sector facing store closures, industry disrupters, and e-commerce growth. To continue to meet this need for high-quality official statistics while also exploring opportunities for improvement, the Census Bureau's retail trade survey program is exploring the use of alternative data sources to produce higher-frequency and more geographically detailed data

Rebecca J. Hutchinson is the Big Data Lead in the Economic Indicator Division of the US Census Bureau.

The author would like to thank Catherine Buffington, William Davie, Nicole Davis, Lucia Foster, Xijian Liu, Javier Miranda, Nick Orsini, Scott Scheleur, Stephanie Studds, and Deanna Weidenhamer, as well as the CRIW committee of Katharine Abraham, Ron Jarmin, Brian Moyer, and Matthew Shapiro for their thoughtful comments on previous versions of this paper. The Census Bureau has reviewed this data product for unauthorized disclosure of confidential information and has approved the disclosure avoidance practices applied (Approval ID: CBDRB-FY19-EID-B00001). Disclaimer: Any views expressed are those of the author and not necessarily those of the United States Census Bureau. For acknowledgments, sources of research support, and disclosure of the author's material financial relationships, if any, please see https://www.nber.org/books-and-chapters/big-data-21st-century-economic-statistics /improving-retail-trade-data-products-using-alternative-data-sources.

1. The production of quality statistics is the principal goal of the US Census Bureau. The Commerce Department (2014) lists the criteria government statistics must meet: comprehensive, consistent, confidential, credible, and relevant. The Census Bureau strives to meet these criteria.

products, to supplement traditional survey data collection, to ease respondent burden, and to assist with declining response rates (US Census Bureau 2018). Alternative data sources for retail may include point-of-sale data, credit card data, and payment processor data. In 2016, the Census Bureau conducted a pilot project to test if retailer point-of-sale data from The NPD Group, Inc. (NPD) could be used in place of the data reported by retailers to the monthly and annual retail surveys (Hutchinson 2020). The positive results of that project led to the acquisition of more third-party data. Here I expand that initial work by examining the viability of using point-of-sale data as a replacement for retail survey data more broadly. During the pilot project and in preliminary analysis, I used data for five retailers. During this expanded effort, I review a larger purchase of this third-party retailer data for quality issues and explore additional uses. I document the use of point-of-sale data for a small number of retailers in the production of the Monthly Retail Trade Survey (MRTS) estimates (US Census Bureau 2019).

The rest of the paper proceeds as follows. Section 3.2 provides background on the Census Bureau's retail survey programs as well as modernization efforts currently underway. Section 3.3 discusses point-of-sale data broadly and provides details on the point-of-sale data from NPD used in this project. Section 3.4 discusses the results from a review of the point-of-sale data, including visual and regression analysis conducted at national and store levels. Section 3.5 provides an overview on the product category mapping exercise done between NPD and the Census Bureau's Economic Census product categories. Section 3.6 provides a discussion of the challenges and costs of using these data in official government statistics. Section 3.7 lays out the next steps for this project.

3.2   Retail Data Collection and Modernization Efforts

Retail trade is currently measured by the Census Bureau through monthly and annual surveys, as well as through a quinquennial Economic Census, and covers retail companies as defined by the North American Industry Classification System (NAICS). Retail businesses (NAICS Sector 44-45) may be chain retailers with many store locations, retailers with only one store location, or retailers operating solely online as e-commerce businesses. The retail businesses represented may or may not have paid employees. Table 3.1 provides a summary of the Census Bureau's retail trade programs. In years ending in "2" and "7," the Economic Census collects detailed sales and product-level information as well as employment, payroll, and business characteristics for each physical store location that a retailer operates. Data collected by the Economic Census is used to update the sampling frame for the annual and monthly retail trade surveys. Each year, the Annual Retail Trade Survey (ARTS) collects annual sales, e-commerce sales, inventories, and expenses data as well as some retailer characteristics at the retailer

Table 3.1   **Overview of the Census Bureau's retail trade programs**

	Economic Census	Annual Retail Trade Survey (ARTS)	Monthly Retail Trade Survey (MRTS)	Advance Monthly Retail Trade Survey (MARTS)
Frequency	Conducted every five years in years ending in '2' and '7'	Conducted annually	Conducted monthly	Conducted monthly
Response	Required by law	Required by law	Voluntary	Voluntary
Sample source	N/A	Sampled from frame created by the Economic Census	Subsampled from the Annual Retail Trade Survey	Subsampled from the Monthly Retail Trade Survey
Data collection level	Individual store location	Total retailer by NAICS	Total retailer by NAICS	Total retailer by NAICS
Data items captured	• Business characteristics • Employment and payroll • Detailed product-level sales	• Business characteristics • E-commerce sales • Sales • Inventories • Expenses	• Limited business characteristics • Sales • Inventories • E-commerce sales	• Limited business characteristics • Sales • E-commerce sales

level nationally by NAICS. The MRTS—a subsample of the ARTS—is a voluntary monthly survey done at the retailer level and collects sales and inventories. The timeliest measurement of the retail economy is the Advance Monthly Retail Trade Survey (MARTS), a subsample of the MRTS. This survey's estimates are published approximately two weeks after month's end and measure only sales.

In recent years, the Census Bureau has placed a growing emphasis on the use of nontraditional means to collect and obtain data (Jarmin 2019). These nontraditional means have the potential to help the Census Bureau continue producing high-quality data while also addressing data user demands for higher-frequency and more granular data. They can also address both declines in survey response and increases in the cost of traditional survey operations. Alternative data sources are one such nontraditional avenue of exploration. Data sources of interest to the retail programs include high-frequency and near real-time data that can be used to measure retail sales, including point-of-sale retailer data. Additionally, system-to-system data collection and web scraping are two alternative data collection methods that could be utilized to collect and obtain data (Dumbacher and Hanna 2017). These alternative data sources and collection methods could be used in conjunction with existing survey and administrative data to create new data products while improving the efficiency and quality of the survey lifecycle.

The improvements and benefits that may be achieved through these alternative data sources and collection methods are coupled with concerns. These concerns include the transparency in the methodology as well as issues related to the quality, consistency, and confidentiality of the data. The Census Bureau strives to be transparent in its methodologies and it is unclear how adopting third-party data use will impact that transparency. A study done by the National Academy of Sciences recommends that federal statistical agencies explore the benefits of using third-party data sources but remain mindful of both the unknowns in determining the quality of these data sources and the challenges when combining data sources (Groves and Harris-Kojetin 2017).

3.3   Point-of-Sale Data

Point-of-sale data, also known as scanner data, are detailed sales data for consumer goods that are obtained by scanning the barcodes or other readable codes on the products at electronic points-of-sale both in physical store locations and online (Organisation for Economic Co-operation and Development 2005). Point-of-sale data offer important advantages relative to other types of third-party data. Point-of-sale data can provide information about quantities, product types, prices, and the total value of goods sold for all cash and card transactions in a store. These data are available at the retailer, store, and product levels. By contrast, credit card data or payment processor data are often only available at an aggregated level; due to confidentiality agreements, information about the retailer composition of these data is rarely available. Additionally, cash sales are excluded from both credit card data and payment processor data but are included in point-of-sale data.

Much work has been done on the use of point-of-sale data in producing price indices. Feenstra and Shapiro (2003) highlight the benefits of point-of-sale data including the comprehensiveness of the data and capturing all products over a continuous period. Point-of-sale data also capture new product offerings faster than traditional price collection methods. The United States Bureau of Labor Statistics has researched using point-of-sale data to supplement the Consumer Price Index (CPI) calculations (Horrigan 2013).

This paper explores the use of point-of-sale data with a focus on the sales value rather than the prices. The working hypothesis is that if all items that a retailer sells are captured in a point-of-sale data feed, then the sum of those sales across products and store locations over a month or over a year should equal the total retail sales for a retailer for that same period. If the hypothesis holds, the sales figure from the point-of-sale data should be comparable to what is provided by a retailer to Census Bureau retail surveys. When used for this purpose, a point-of-sale dataset needs to identify the data by retailer name, provide product-level sales for each retail store location, and have data available by month.

Retailer point-of-sale data feeds can be obtained either directly from a retailer or through a third-party vendor. While the raw data from either source should be identical, there are advantages and disadvantages to both (Boettcher 2014). A third-party vendor will clean and curate the data in a consistent format to meet its data users' needs, but often at a high cost. These high costs pose a major challenge to the scalability of the effort as it can be difficult to find a third-party data source that both covers the scope of a survey program and can be obtained under budget constraints (Jarmin 2019). Though potentially cheaper in terms of data costs, obtaining point-of-sale data directly from a retailer can require extensive IT and staffing resources to store, clean, and process. The Census Bureau is interested in obtaining data feeds directly from retailers in the future but point-of-sale data from a third party are the more reasonable option from a resource perspective at this time.

Point-of-sale data for this project were provided by NPD.[2] NPD is a private market research company that captures point-of-sale data for retailers around the world and creates market analysis reports at detailed product levels for its retail and manufacturing partners.[3] NPD currently has data that

2. The NPD Group, Inc. was selected as the vendor for this project through the official government acquisitions process.
3. By providing the data to NPD, retailers have access to NPD-prepared reports that help retailers measure and forecast brand and product performance as well as identify areas for improved sales opportunities.

are potentially useful for this project for over 500 retailers. In comparison, the 2017 Economic Census identified over 600,000 retail firms. Thus, the NPD dataset is not scalable to the entire retail sector.

NPD receives, processes, edits, and analyzes weekly or monthly data feeds containing aggregated transactions by product for each individual store location of its retailers.[4] These data feeds include a product identifier, the number of units sold, product sales in dollars, and the week ending date.[5] Sales tax and shipping fees are excluded. Any price reductions or redeemed coupon values are adjusted for prior to the retailer sending the feed to NPD, so the sales figures in the feed reflect the final amount that customers paid. Data from NPD are limited to stores located in the continental United States.

Because its market analysis reports are done at the product level, NPD's processing is driven by its product categories. NPD processes data for many product categories including apparel, small appliances, automotive, beauty, fashion accessories, consumer electronics, footwear, office supplies, toys, and jewelry and watches. NPD only classifies data for those products in the product categories listed above and sales from any items that do not belong in these categories are allocated to an unclassified category. For example, NPD currently does not provide market research on food items; all food sales data are tabulated as unclassified.

As part of the acquisition process, the Census Bureau provided dataset requirements to NPD and NPD curated datasets from their data feeds based on these requirements. Retailer datasets received by the Census Bureau from NPD contain monthly data at the store and product levels with monthly sales available for each product, store location, and retailer combination. The datasets include values for the following variables: time period (month/year), retailer name, store number, zip code of store location, channel type (brick-and-mortar or e-commerce), product classification categories, and sales figures. One observation for each month and each store location is the total sales value of the unclassified data.

The Census Bureau and NPD work together to onboard retailers to the project. From a list of retailers that provide data feeds to NPD, the Census Bureau selects retailers whose data would be most useful to this project. Retailers that consistently report to the MRTS, the ARTS, or the 2012 and/or 2017 Economic Census are useful for baseline comparisons. Priority is also given to selecting MRTS nonrespondents because this voluntary survey is the timeliest measure of retail sales and response is critical to survey quality.[6] High-burden retailers are also considered a priority.[7]

4. Some retailers do not provide individual store location feeds to NPD and just provide one national feed.
5. NPD does not receive information about individual transactions or purchasers.
6. Response rates to the Monthly Retail Trade Survey have fallen from 74.6 percent in 2013 to 66.5 percent in 2017.
7. High-burden retailers are those retailers that receive a large number of survey forms from survey programs across the Census Bureau, including the Annual and Monthly Retail Trade Surveys.

NPD needs to obtain signed agreements with retailers to share data with the Census Bureau. NPD utilizes its retailer client contacts to reach out to retailers. The Census Bureau provides a letter to the retailers detailing the goals of the project, including reducing respondent burden and improving data accuracy. The letter informs retailers that any data obtained from NPD is protected by United States Code Title 13, such that it is kept confidential and used only for statistical purposes.[8] Retailer participation in this effort is voluntary and some retailers do decline to participate. Declining retailers cited a variety of reasons including legal and privacy concerns; others stated that completing Census Bureau surveys is not burdensome.

Once a retailer agrees to share data, NPD delivers a historical data set of monthly data for the retailer back to 2012, or the earliest subsequent year available, within 30 days from when the retailer, the Census Bureau, and NPD all sign the agreement of participation.[9] Subsequent monthly deliveries of retailer data are made 10 to 20 days after month's end. NPD datasets do not require much cleaning as the file formats, variables, and contents were specified in detail in the terms of the contract. Upon delivery, the Census Bureau first verifies contractual requirements are met. This process verifies that the product categories, store locations, retailer channels, and other categorical variables have remained consistent over time.[10]

3.4 Data Quality Review

The quality review process focuses on determining how well the NPD data align with data collected or imputed by the Census Bureau's retail trade programs. National-level NPD sales for each retailer are compared against what the retailer reports to the MRTS and the ARTS. NPD store-level retail sales for each retailer are compared against the retailer's reported store-level sales in the Economic Census. NPD product-level sales for each retailer are compared to the retailer's reported product-level sales in the Economic Census. There are currently no official or standardized quality measures in place to deem a retail third-party data source's quality acceptable, so developing a quality review process for third-party data sources is an important

8. To uphold both the confidentiality and privacy laws that guide Census Bureau activities, a small number of NPD staff working on this project completed background investigations and were granted Special Sworn Status. These NPD staff are sworn to uphold the data stewardship practices and confidentiality laws put in place by United States Codes 13 and 26 for their lifetimes.

9. NPD will sometimes acquire data from other data providers. When these acquisitions occur, there is no guarantee that the full time series for the retailer will be available to NPD to process and share. In these scenarios, NPD provides data beginning with the earliest year available after 2012.

10. In this early part of the review, the imputation rate of the NPD data is also checked. For the vast majority of months, the imputation rate is zero for retailers. However, NPD will impute a small amount of data if the retailer could not provide all values in its data feed for a given month. The average imputation rate for the data provided by NPD across all retailers and all months is 0.15 percent.

research goal. To date, the decision to use or not to use a retailer's data has relied heavily on retail subject matter expertise.

The review of a retailer's data begins with a simple visual review of the time series properties of the data, plotting the monthly NPD data against the MRTS data.[11] Issues with both the NPD and the MRTS data have been identified during this visual review. To date, the issues identified were unique to the individual retailer and each issue required specific research. As this project grows, a process including automated algorithms must be developed so these types of issues can be identified in a timely manner and then resolved efficiently by both NPD and Census Bureau staff.

With the project expansion, the need for more definitive quality metrics has grown more urgent. The long-term goal is to develop quality review profiles for each individual retailer that can dictate the decision to use the NPD data and allow a retailer to stop reporting sales to Census Bureau retail surveys. This profile might include metrics that show variation in levels and month-to-month changes between the NPD point-of-sale data and Census Bureau survey data. Included in this profile will be an algorithm that identifies cases for analyst review based on the size of the anomalies detected.

In developing these metrics, a method to identify discrepancies between NPD and Census data is needed. Here we summarize differences through the use of regression models that show how much of the variation in the MRTS data is explained by the NPD data. The models are run for aggregated national and store levels, individual retailers, and groupings of retailers.

Sections 3.4.1 and 3.4.2 detail the results of this initial data quality review for data at the national level and at the store level. The review includes breakouts of the brick-and-mortar sales, e-commerce sales, and the sum of these two sales figures, also known as whole store sales. New retailers agree to share their NPD data with the Census Bureau on a regular basis. To create a consistent base for the analysis, I report results for 10 retailers. These retailers represent a mix of different types of retail businesses. Most have an e-commerce component to their MRTS data. Six of the retailers are consistent reporters to the MRTS. The remaining four are sporadic reporters or nonreporters to the survey. Starting dates for NPD data vary between 2012 and 2015. The analysis end point for each retailer's time series is October 2018.[12]

3.4.1 National-Level Data

Visual inspections of time series plots of the NPD and MRTS data are a good way to identify issues early and develop intuition about the type of issues that might arise. Figure 3.1 displays whole store sales aggregated for

11. Comparisons are done to the MRTS due to the large number of data points available (currently 60–84 monthly data points per retailer versus 5–7 annual data points).
12. Because most retailers operate on a fiscal calendar that runs from February to January, any annualized NPD figures referenced below are for that fiscal year.

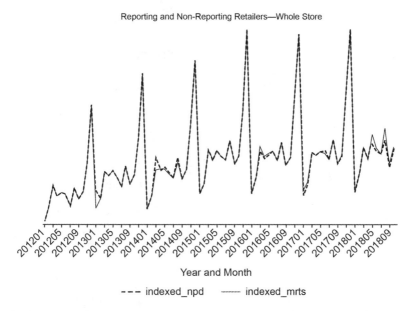

Fig. 3.1   Indexed whole store sales comparisons between NPD data and MRTS data for 10 retailers
Source: NPD and MRTS data.
Note: January 2012 = 1.000.

all 10 retailers. Overall, the data align well between the NPD and MRTS data. The most notable deviation is in March 2014, where the NPD sales are higher than the MRTS sales; this data point has been investigated but a cause has not been identified. Given the volume of data ingested, some data issues—particularly data points near the beginning of the time series—may be too far removed to be resolved. This is one challenge with committing to third-party data to replace a Census collection: determining its accuracy may not always be obvious from the exploration of time series properties.

Another important use of the NPD data is to validate Census Bureau tabulated data. Figure 3.2 displays the comparisons for two groups: consistent reporters to the MRTS and the sporadic or nonreporters whose data are imputed by the Census Bureau. The consistent reporters are responsible for the tight alignment observed in figure 3.1. MRTS nonreporters drive the deviations between the NPD data and the imputed MRTS data over the time series.

Imputation methodology for the MRTS reflects a retailer's past information as well as industry behavior from reporting companies each month. Thus, survey imputation will not be successful in capturing idiosyncratic retailer activity outside of industry trends and seasonal patterns.

Good Reporters–Whole Store

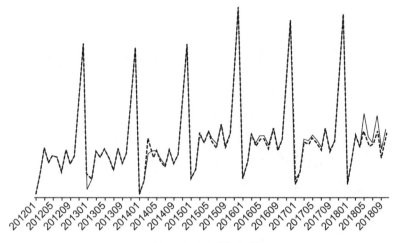

Nonreporters–Whole Store

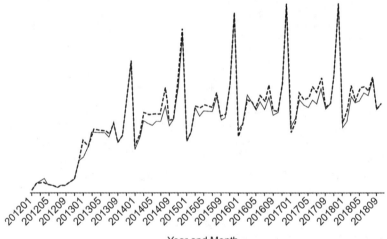

Year and Month

---- indexed_npd ——— indexed_mrts

Fig. 3.2   Indexed whole store sales comparisons between NPD data and MRTS data for six consistent reporters (top) and four nonreporters (bottom) to the MRTS for January 2012–October 2018

Source: NPD and MRTS data.

Note: January 2012 = 1.000. MRTS data for nonreporters are imputed values.

Point-of-sale data will capture firm-specific movements so differences between the NPD data and imputed MRTS data are expected.

As part of this project, work has begun on establishing more sophisticated quality metrics for the NPD data. The first attempt at this utilizes an ordinary least squares regression with the natural log of the NPD monthly sales data as an independent variable and the natural log of the MRTS sales data as the dependent variable. A coefficient of one suggests that a change in the NPD data results in an equal change in the MRTS data. The R^2 value from this regression indicates how well the change in a retailer's NPD data can explain the change in variation in the retailer's MRTS data. A higher R^2 value could be one statistical diagnostic to determine whether the NPD data are good enough to use in place of MRTS data.

Figure 3.2, however, indicates that because the NPD data for nonreporters may not align as well with the imputed MRTS data, the use of R^2 to evaluate the quality of the NPD data may be less useful for retailers who do not report to the MRTS. If future data feeds include a large enough number of retailers such that there are other retailers with similar characteristics (e.g., kind of retail business, size) to the nonreporting retailers, more sophisticated models that include local, industry, and time-specific shocks could be used to evaluate the use of NPD data for nonreporters. At this time, the Census Bureau is not receiving enough retailer data to fully explore this idea and determine what other diagnostic values should be established but some initial work has been done. Table 3.2 presents results from regressions performed using data from the 10 retailers. This specification explains over 99.3 percent of the variation in the MRTS data. The model for e-commerce sales for MRTS nonreporters has the lowest R^2 of 24.0 percent. One possible explanation for this is the current imputation methodology for e-commerce sales. The e-commerce component of retailers with a separate online division is captured in a NAICS code (NAICS 4541, Nonstore Retailers) that is different from their brick-and-mortar sales NAICS code. The current imputation methodology estimates e-commerce sales for nonrespondents within this nonstore retailer grouping with no differentiation among the primary types of business conducted. That is, e-commerce sales for sporting goods stores, department stores, clothing stores, etc. within the nonstore retailer component are imputed using the same imputation ratio. Research is planned to determine if this imputation should consider the primary kind of retail business.

3.4.2   Store-Level Data

The store-level data in the NPD dataset has the potential to reduce respondent burden in the Economic Census where the reporting unit is the establishment or store location. The inclusion of a retailer-provided store number in the NPD datasets allows for a direct match to the Economic Census database, which also includes the same retailer-provided store

Table 3.2 Ordinary least squares regression results for regression of MRTS sales data on NPD sales data

Dependent variable: Natural log of monthly retail trade sales

	(Whole store)			(E-commerce)			(Brick and mortar)		
	All retailers (A)	Consistent reporters (B)	Non-reporters (C)	All retailers (D)	Consistent reporters (E)	Non-reporters (F)	All retailers (G)	Consistent reporters (H)	Non-reporters (I)
Natural log NPD monthly sales	1.008***	1.008***	1.005***	0.984***	1.047***	0.335***	0.999***	1.002***	0.992***
	(0.003)	(0.002)	(0.008)	(0.015)	(0.009)	(0.049)	(0.003)	(0.002)	(0.010)
Constant	-0.180	-0.166	-0.149	0.306	-0.828	11.844	-0.016	-0.036	0.119
Observations	748	456	292	491	342	149	748	456	292
R^2	0.993	0.998	0.982	0.898	0.978	0.240	0.992	0.998	0.974

Source: NPD and MRTS data. Standard errors in parentheses.

Notes: An F-test for the null hypothesis that the coefficient for the natural log of NPD monthly sales is equal to 1 is not rejected for columns C, D, G, H, and I. Coefficients are statistically different from 1 otherwise. *** $p < 0.01$, ** $p < 0.05$, * $p < 0.1$.

Table 3.3   **Ordinary least squares regression results for regression of 2012 Economic Census store sales on NPD annualized 2012 store sales**

Dependent variable:
Natural log of 2012 economic sales by store location

Natural log annualized 2012	0.871***
NPD sales by store location	(0.007)
Constant	2.075
	(0.126)
Observations	2,601
R^2	0.984

Source: NPD and 2012 Economic Census data. Standard errors in parentheses.
Notes: Firm effects are included for each retailer but not displayed. *** $p < 0.01$, ** $p < 0.05$, * $p < 0.1$

number variable in each store location record. As a result, store-level sales data comparisons are possible.

Of the 10 retailers considered in this paper, seven reported store-level information to the 2012 Economic Census and had 2012 NPD data available.[13] The store-location match rate between the two data sets was over 98 percent. Potential causes for mismatches include store number differences and store openings and closures that are captured by one source but not the other. The ratio of the natural log of 2012 NPD sales to the natural log of 2012 Economic Census sales for each matched store location were plotted.[14] In this plot, there is a large cluster of values around the 45-degree angle line, indicating that the 2012 NPD data for a store location is close to the sales data that the retailer reported to the 2012 Economic Census for that particular store location. There are also some outliers. Store-level data can be more burdensome for retailers to report and retailers may report estimates rather than actual figures. Store openings and closures may also affect the precision of the data. Thus, store-level data can be noisier than the national-level data where small differences across store sales may cancel out.

Store-level regression analysis is done for retailers using an ordinary least squares regression similar to the national-level regressions in section 3.4.1 but with the natural log of the NPD annualized sales for each store as an independent variable and the natural log of 2012 Economic Census store sales as the dependent variable. At the individual store locations for retailers that reported to the 2012 Economic Census and had NPD data available for 2012, this specification explains over 98 percent of the variation in the store sales figures tabulated in the 2012 Economic Census (table 3.3).

13. A complete analysis of the data in the 2017 Economic Census is underway. For the purposes of this paper, the focus is on the 2012 Economic Census store-level data.
14. This graphic could not be displayed due to disclosure concerns.

3.5   Product Data

The Economic Census collects detailed product-line sales information from all large retailers and a sample of smaller retailers. Product-level reports are made available to the public approximately three years after the end of the Economic Census year. Alternative product-level data sources could help with not only reducing respondent burden but also creating more timely and higher-frequency product reports.

Point-of-sale data from NPD is collected at the stock-keeping unit level (SKU), which allows retailers to track product inventories. NPD assigns detailed product attributes to each of these SKUs and assigns them to product categories including but not limited to apparel, small appliances, and toys. These categories are defined differently than the Census Bureau's product-level categories. For this reason, the NPD product-line research focuses on whether a mapping between the NPD product lines and the Census Bureau product lines is feasible. The 2017 Economic Census was the first Economic Census to use the North American Product Classification System (NAPCS), a demand-based, hierarchical product classification system. With assistance from Census Bureau classification staff and NPD product-line experts, a NAPCS code has been assigned to each item in the NPD product catalog.

With this mapping successfully completed, sales in the NPD dataset can be tabulated by NAPCS code. Work is underway to compare the NPD product-level data and the 2017 Economic Census data by NAPCS code.

3.6   Challenges

While the findings of this project have been promising, there are several challenges. There are substantial upfront costs associated with a third-party data source like NPD. These costs cover the overhead expenses of working with retailers to obtain consent to share NPD data with the Census Bureau and curating the retailer datasets. This process becomes more streamlined over time and costs may diminish. Any arrangement that would reduce Census Bureau costs while still benefiting the Census Bureau, NPD, and the retailers would likely require a change in government policy regarding third-party vendors' ability to collect fees from retailers and provide the data to official statistical agencies (Jarmin 2019).

Another challenge is that only sales data are currently available through the NPD data feeds. The retail surveys collect other items including inventories and expenses. NPD is exploring the feasibility of collecting other data items through its data feeds. Other third-party data sources that capture business operations data may be able to provide additional data items.

There are several risks associated with the use of third-party data. Concerns with transparency and coverage were highlighted earlier in the paper. Other risks include a vendor going out of business or being acquired by another entity, a decline in the vendor's share of the market, or an increase in the price of the data. Additionally, a third-party vendor could create its own data product comparable to an existing Census Bureau data product, reverse engineer Census Bureau estimates for financial benefit, or recover confidential information about other nonparticipating retailers. Mitigating these risks requires careful selection of a diversified pool of data sources.

3.7   Next Steps

This project has demonstrated potential for the use of point-of-sale data not only to reduce respondent burden and supplement existing Census Bureau retail surveys but also to create new data products. Currently, a conservative approach is being taken to use the data in survey estimates based on a case-by-case review of the differences between the NPD and MRTS data by retail subject matter experts. Beginning with the October 2018 MRTS estimates, NPD data for a small number of retailers who do not report to the survey were included in the estimates (US Census Bureau 2019). NPD data for the consistent reporters is used to verify reported survey data and we are developing retailer quality review profiles to guide the decision to use the NPD data and allow a retailer to stop reporting sales on Census Bureau retail surveys. We continue to analyze the data at the store and product levels, comparing against the newly collected 2017 Economic Census data. The NPD data provide an opportunity not only to help with respondent burden and survey nonresponse but also to help produce more timely and more granular estimates. Of particular interest are the product-level data. The Census Bureau currently only publishes product-level data every five years, making use of data collected in the Economic Census. The NPD data have monthly product-level information that could be utilized to create timelier product-level data products. Additionally, the monthly NPD datasets include store-level information that can identify store openings and closures more quickly than current Census Bureau survey operations. Developing a pipeline to use these data to create a more up-to-date picture of retail economic turnover would be valuable both at the national level and at more granular geographies. Exploratory work on these concepts is currently underway.

References

Boettcher, Ingolf. 2014. "One Size Fits All? The Need to Cope with Different Levels of Scanner Data Quality for CPI Computation." Paper presented at the UNECE Expert Group Meeting on CPI, Geneva, Switzerland, May 26–28, 2014. https://www.unece.org/fileadmin/DAM/stats/documents/ece/ces/ge.22/2014/WS4/WS4_04_One_size_fits_all.pdf.

Bureau of Economic Analysis. 2020. Gross Domestic Product, Third Quarter 2020 (Second Estimate), table 3, November 25, 2020. https://www.bea.gov/sites/default /files/2020-11/gdp3q20_2nd_0.xlsx.
Department of Commerce. 2014. "Federal Innovation, Creating Jobs, Driving Better Decisions: The Value of Government Data." July 2014. Washington, DC. https://www.commerce.gov/sites/default/files/migrated/reports/revisedfostering innovationcreatingjobsdrivingbetterdecisions-thevalueofgovernmentdata.pdf.
Dumbacher, Brian Arthur, and Demetria Hanna. 2017. "Using Passive Data Collection, System-to-System Data Collection, and Machine Learning to Improve Economic Surveys." Paper presented at the 2017 Joint Statistical Meetings, Baltimore, MD. http://ww2.amstat.org/meetings/jsm/2017/onlineprogram/AbstractDetails .cfm?abstractid=322018.
Feenstra, R. C., and M. D. Shapiro. 2003. Introduction to *Scanner Data and Price Indexes*, edited by Robert C. Feenstra and Matthew D. Shapiro, 1–14. Chicago: University of Chicago Press.
Groves, Robert M., and Brian A. Harris-Kojetin, eds. 2017. *Innovation in Federal Statistics*. Washington, DC: National Academies Press.
Horrigan, Michael. 2013. *Big Data and Official Statistics*. Washington, DC: Author. https://www.bls.gov/osmr/symp2013_horrigan.pdf.
Hutchinson, Rebecca J. 2020. "Investigating Alternative Data Sources to Reduce Respondent Burden in United States Census Bureau Retail Economic Data Products." In *Big Data Meets Survey Science: A Collection of Innovative Methods*, edited by Craig A. Hill, Paul P. Biemer, Trent D. Buskirk, Lilli Japec, Antje Kirchner, Stas Kolenikov, and Lars E. Lyberg, 359–85. Hoboken, NJ: John Wiley and Sons.
Jarmin, Ron S. 2019. "Evolving Measurement for an Evolving Economy: Thoughts on 21st Century US Economic Statistics." *Journal of Economic Perspectives* 33 (1): 165–84.
Organisation for Economic Co-operation and Development. 2005. OECD Glossary of Statistical Terms. January 11. https://stats.oecd.org/glossary/detail.asp ?ID=5755.
US Census Bureau. 2018. *U.S. Census Bureau Strategic Plan—Fiscal Year 2018 through Fiscal Year 2022*. Washington, DC: US Census Bureau. https://www2 .census.gov/about/budget/strategicplan18-22.pdf.
———. 2019. "U.S. Census Bureau Streamlines Reporting for Retailers." Press release, February 5. https://www.census.gov/newsroom/press-releases/2019/retailers.html.

4

From Transaction Data to Economic Statistics
Constructing Real-Time, High-Frequency, Geographic Measures of Consumer Spending

Aditya Aladangady, Shifrah Aron-Dine, Wendy Dunn, Laura Feiveson, Paul Lengermann, and Claudia Sahm

4.1 Introduction

Access to timely, high-quality data is crucial for the ability of policymakers to monitor macroeconomic developments and assess the health of the economy. Consumer spending—70 percent of overall GDP—is key in policy deliberations about the economy. Existing official statistics on consumer spending are extremely useful, but they have limitations. For instance, the official retail sales data from the Census Bureau's surveys are only published

Aditya Aladangady is a principal economist in the Microeconomic Surveys Section of the Board of Governors of the Federal Reserve System.

Shifrah Aron-Dine is a graduate student in the Department of Economics at Stanford University.

Wendy Dunn is an adviser of the Program Direction Section of the Board of Governors of the Federal Reserve System.

Laura Feiveson is chief of the Household and Business Spending Section of the Board of Governors of the Federal Reserve System.

Paul Lengermann is assistant director of the Program Direction Section of the Board of Governors of the Federal Reserve System.

Claudia Sahm is a senior fellow at the Jain Family Institute. She is currently a contributing writer for *New York Times Opinion* and *Bloomberg Opinion*, and founder of Stay-At-Home-Macro Consulting.

We especially thank Dan Moulton, Aaron Jaffe, Felix Galbis-Reig, and Kelsey O'Flaherty for extensive work and conversations in constructing these new spending indexes. We also thank Zak Kirstein, Tommy Peeples, Gal Wachtel, Chris Pozzi, Dan Williams, and their colleagues at Palantir who have been integrally involved in implementation. The views expressed here are those of the authors and not necessarily those of other members of the Federal Reserve System. For acknowledgments, sources of research support, and disclosure of the authors' material financial relationships, if any, please see https://www.nber.org/books-and-chapters/big-data -21st-century-economic-statistics/transactions-data-economic-statistics-constructing-real -time-high-frequency-geographic-measures.

for the nation as a whole and only at a monthly frequency.[1] The monthly figures are available two weeks after the end of the month and are subject to substantial revisions. Until recently, for analysis of regional shocks, researchers and policymakers had to rely on other data sources, such as the quarterly regional accounts from the Bureau of Economic Analysis (BEA), or household expenditure surveys like the Consumer Expenditure Survey. These more detailed data sources have limited sample sizes at smaller geographies and are only available a year or two after the fact. Our new real-time geographic data on spending data allow for better monitoring of shocks at the regional level and have the potential to serve as an early warning system to policymakers. Indeed, research on the Great Recession, such as Mian, Sufi, and Rao (2013), has shown that consumption declines were larger and appeared sooner in areas with subsequent collapses in house prices. Our prior research shows other examples of how real-time geographic data are useful for studying economic events, such as Hurricane Matthew, sales tax holidays, and legislative hold on disbursement of Earned Income Tax Credit (EITC) in Aladangady et al. (2016, 2017, 2019, respectively).

The question motivating our research is whether alternative data sources can provide a timelier and more granular—but still reliable—picture of consumer spending. A promising new source of information on retail spending is the massive volume of data generated by consumers using credit and debit cards and other electronic payments.[2] Industry analysts and market researchers have long tapped into such transaction data to observe retail shopping behavior and market trends. Recently, economic researchers have also begun to use these and other nontraditional data, such as scanner data or online financial websites, in empirical studies of consumption.[3] These new data can offer timely and extremely detailed information on the buyers, sellers, and items purchased, yet they also pose myriad challenges, including protecting the privacy of individuals and businesses, ensuring the quality of the data, and adjusting for nonrepresentative samples.

In this project, we develop a comprehensive research dataset of spending activity using transaction data from First Data Merchant Services LLC (First Data, now Fiserv), a global payment technology company that processes $2 trillion dollars in annual card transaction volumes. We filter, aggre-

1. In September 2020, the Census Bureau began publishing 12-month percent changes (not seasonally adjusted) in state-level retail sales estimates. They used existing Census surveys as well as private Big Data sources. See for more details: https://www.census.gov/retail/state _retail_sales.html. The Bureau of Economic Analysis, the Bureau of Labor Statistics, and other statistical agencies have also begun using private data sources. Many of those efforts are detailed in this volume.

2. Moreover, cards—as we use in our new series—are now the prevailing method of payment for most retail purchases in the United States. Survey data from financial institutions indicate that total card payments were $6.5 trillion in 2017 (Federal Reserve Board 2018).

3. Some recent examples are Mian, Rao, and Sufi (2013) using credit card company data, Farrell and Grieg (2015) using accounts from a large bank, as well as Baker (2018) and Gelman et al. (2014) using data from apps used by households.

gate, and transform the card transactions into economic statistics. To protect the anonymity of all merchants and customers, we are restricted from accessing the transaction-level data. Instead, we worked with Palantir Technologies from 2016 to 2019—First Data's technology business partner—to build the new, fully-anonymized series to our specifications.[4] We currently have created estimates of daily retail spending from 2010 to the present for several industry categories, at the national, state, and metropolitan statistical area (MSA) level.

Our merchant-centric data on spending is, in some ways, conceptually similar to the Census Bureau's Monthly Retail Trade Survey (MRTS). As with the Census survey, our transaction data are organized by the classification of the merchant making the sale. We adopt the same industry categories as the MRTS, which allows us to compare the national estimates from our new dataset to the corresponding Census estimates. However, an important difference in our approach is how we construct our sample. The Census Bureau uses a statistical sampling and survey design of tax records to select its sample of about 13,000 employer firms that own or control one or more retail establishments. The survey is used to produce estimates that are representative of all retail activity in the United States.[5] In contrast, First Data's client merchants that we use are not necessarily representative of all retailers, and some First Data client merchants do not permit us access to their data. In this paper, we describe the multi-stage process we developed to obtain high-quality, representative estimates of spending that are used for economic analysis at the Federal Reserve.

Despite being constructed from very different underlying raw data sources and methods, our new spending series and the Census retail sales data exhibit remarkably similar time-series patterns. The strong correlation of our new national series with the official statistics validates the soundness of our methodology and the reliability of our estimates. It showed that our new series was of high enough quality to use in policy analysis.

In this paper, we present two examples of how our new series could have been used to inform policy. First, we show how our series provided valuable insights on economic activity during the 2019 government shutdown, when the publication of official statistics was delayed. During a time of heightened uncertainty and financial market turbulence, it was crucial for policymakers to fill this information gap. Months before the Census data became available, we were able to see that spending slowed sharply early in the shutdown

4. Specifically, Palantir suppresses any spending estimate based on fewer than 10 merchants or where a single merchant comprises over 20 percent of the total transaction volume. In addition, some merchants also have "opt out" agreements with First Data, and their transaction data are not used in any of the analyses.

5. For more details on the survey construction, see the Census Bureau's "Monthly Retail Trade Survey Methodology," https://www.census.gov/retail/mrts/how_surveys_are_collected.html. wNote also that a merchant in First Data is similar conceptually to an establishment in Census.

but rebounded soon after, implying that the imprint of the shutdown on economic activity was largely transitory.

Second, we describe how we used the geographic detail in our daily data to track the effects of Hurricanes Irma and Harvey on spending. We showed that the hurricanes significantly reduced—not just delayed—consumer spending in the affected states in the third quarter of 2017. Although the level of spending quickly returned to normal after the storms, very little of the lost activity during the storm was made up in the subsequent weeks. Thus, on net over the span of several weeks, the hurricanes reduced spending. This episode was an example of how it is possible to create reliable estimates of the effects of a natural disaster in real time.

The remainder of this paper is organized as follows. In section 4.2, we describe the transaction data from First Data. Section 4.3 details the methodology we use to construct our spending series from the raw transaction data. In section 4.4, we compare our new series with official estimates from the Census Bureau as a data validation exercise. Finally, in section 4.5 we show how we used the transaction data to track consumer spending during the government shutdown in early 2019 and in the weeks surrounding Hurricanes Harvey and Irma in 2017. Section 4.6 concludes.

4.2   Description of the Transaction Data

Our daily estimates are built up from millions of card swipes or electronic payments by customers at merchants that work with First Data. The total dollar amount of the purchase and when and where it occurred are recorded.[6] Only card or electronic transactions at merchants that work with First Data (or one of their subsidiaries) are included in our data. Cash payments as well as card payments at First Data merchant clients that do not allow further use of their data are also omitted. Geography of spending is determined by the location of the merchant, which may differ from the location of the purchaser.

First Data (now Fiserv) is a global payment technology company and one of the largest electronic payment processors in the United States. As of 2016, First Data processed approximately $2 trillion in card payments a year. First Data serves multiple roles in the electronic payments market. As a merchant acquirer, First Data sells card terminals to merchants and signs them onto First Data's transaction processing network. As a payments processor, First Data provides the "plumbing" to help credit card terminals process payment authorization requests and settlements (irrespective of whether they are on First Data card terminals). Transactions at both types of merchant-clients are included in our data.

---

6. The name and zip code of the merchant are in the raw data. Bank Identification Numbers (BINs) can be mapped to the card numbers and in some cases we have a flag as to whether the card was present for the transaction (in store) or not (online). While these data are initially recorded by First Data, they are only available to us in an aggregated and anonymized form.

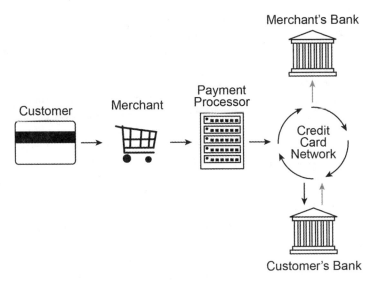

Fig. 4.1   The role of payment processors in credit card transactions

Figure 4.1 illustrates the role of payment processors in a credit card trans-action. When a consumer makes a purchase at a First Data merchant, First Data serves as the intermediary between the merchant and the various credit card networks. When a consumer swipes a card at a merchant's point-of-sale system, the processor sends the transaction information through the credit card network to the consumer's bank, which then decides whether to authorize the transaction. That information is then relayed back to the point-of-sale system and the transaction is either approved or denied. When the transaction is settled, the final transaction amount (for example, including tip) is transferred from the customer's account to the merchant's account. There may be a lag of several days between authorization and settlement due to individual bank procedures. These two dates and the transaction amounts at authorization and settlement are in our data.[7]

7. For January 2012 to the present, First Data reports both authorization and settlement dates and amounts. The authorization date should be the same as the purchase date. Thus, the most accurate representation of a purchase is the authorization timestamp and the settlement amount. The settlement amount is more accurate than the authorization amount because it would include tips, which are typically not in the authorization amount. When available, we combine data from both authorizations and settlements to characterize each transaction. The date of the transaction is the timestamp of the authorization request (when the credit card was swiped) and value of the transaction is the settlement amount (so as to include tip, or any revision in the original authorization amount). When a valid authorization time stamp is not available, we use both the time stamp and value of the settlement. From January 2010 until January 2012, First Data only reports transaction settlement dates and amounts. Due to batch processing by consumers' banks, the settlement date can be days after the actual purchase data. We used the older database to extend our time series back to 2010 by adjusting the timing of transactions with only settlement data according to the average difference in timing between settlement and authorization.

First Data has details about every card transaction including the authorization and settlement amount and date, merchant address, merchant name, and merchant category code (MCC).[8] Even though First Data only covers a portion of purchases made with cards, the number of consumer spending transactions we observe with these data is quite large. According to the 2017 Diary of Consumer Payment Choice, consumers use credit and debit cards for 30.3 percent of their payments, in dollar value, while they use cash for just 8.5 percent of dollars paid (Greene and Stavins 2018). For the categories that we focus on—retail goods and restaurant meals—the card share of transactions is even higher. For example, it is nearly twice as high among groceries. (Cohen and Rysman 2013).

In this paper, we focus on a subset of First Data transactions at retailers and restaurants, which we refer to as the "retail sales group." The retail sales group is a key aggregate from the Census Bureau that the Federal Reserve and other macroeconomic forecasters track closely, because these data inform the estimates for about one third of personal consumption expenditures.[9] To create a comparable subset in our data, we map the available MCCs to 3-digit North American Industry Classification System (NAICS) categories in the Census data. We use a mapping tool developed by staff at the Census Bureau and the Bureau of Economic Analysis, shown in appendix A.

Because First Data has business relationships with merchants, not consumers, our data provide a merchant-centric view of spending. While technically a customer initiates a transaction and the data have an anonymized identifier for each credit and debit card, we do not observe the purchases that individuals make at merchants who are not in the First Data network. Moreover, we have information on merchants, not customers. Our merchant-centric orientation is the same as Census Retail Sales, which surveys firms. In contrast, other data sources on spending like the Consumer Expenditure Survey are household-centric. Both have advantages and disadvantages.

---

8. First Data client merchants decide their own MCC identification. MCC is an industry standard, but the accuracy of MCC assignments is not integral to the payment processing. Palantir staff have found cases when the assigned MCC is inconsistent with the type of business that the merchant does (based on the name of the merchant). A client merchant can also have multiple MCCs—for example, a grocery store with an affiliated gas station could have one MCC for terminals in the grocery and one for terminals at the gas pumps.

9. The retail sales group is the subset of retail and food service industries in the Census retail sales survey that are also used to estimate approximately one third of aggregate personal consumption expenditures in the National Income and Product Accounts. It includes the following NAICS categories: 4413—Auto Parts, Accessories, and Tire Stores, 442—Furniture and Home Furnishings Stores, 443—Electronics and Appliance Stores, 445—Food and Beverage Stores, 446—Health and Personal Care Stores, 448—Clothing and Clothing Accessories Stores, 451—Sporting Goods, Hobby, Book, and Music Stores, 452—General Merchandise Stores, 453—Miscellaneous Store Retailers, 454—Non-store Retailers, 722—Food Services and Drinking Places. It is worth noting that First Data also has ample coverage of several other NAICS categories not included in the retail sales group: 444—Building Material and Garden Equipment and Supplies Dealers, 447—Gasoline Stations, 721—Accommodation, 713—Amusement, gambling, and recreation industries.

4.3   Methodology

In this section, we describe the methodology we instructed Palantir to use to filter, aggregate, and transform the raw transaction data into daily spending indexes for different industries and geographies. One of the major challenges with using nontraditional data like these for economic analysis is that we do not have a statistical sample frame. Our set of merchants is not representative of all US merchants, and it does not come with a well-established method to statistically reweight the sample, as in the Census survey. We had to develop new procedures that would yield usable statistics.

4.3.1   Filtering with 14-Month Constant-Merchant Samples

First Data's unfiltered universe of merchant clients and their associated payment transactions are not suitable, on their own, as economic statistics of retail spending. In the absence of a statistical sampling frame, the filtering of transactions is an important first step in the analysis of these nontraditional data. The filtering strategy is necessary to remove movements in the data resulting from changes in the First Data client portfolio, rather than those driven by changes in economic activity.

As shown in figure 4.2, there are vast divergences in year-over-year changes in the unfiltered sum of retail sales group transactions and in the equivalent Census series. The huge swings in the First Data series in 2014 and 2015 reflect their business acquisitions of other payment processing platforms. The unfiltered index of all merchants and all transactions includes the true birth and death of merchants; however, it also reflects choices by individual merchants to start, end, or continue their contract with First Data as their payment processor.

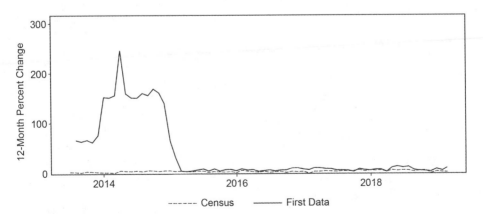

Fig. 4.2   Unfiltered sum of retail sales group transactions
Source: First Data and Census, authors' calculations.
Note: Not seasonally adjusted.

The first challenge for our filter is the considerable entry and exit of merchants in the transaction data. Some instances of this so-called merchant churn are to be expected and reflect economic conditions. For example, the decision to open a new business or to close an existing one is a normal occurrence that should be reflected in our statistics. In fact, the Census Bureau has adopted formal statistical procedures to capture these "economic births and deaths" in its monthly estimates of retail sales. Our unfiltered data include merchant churn based on those economic decisions; however, the data also include a large amount of merchant churn related to First-Data-specific business decisions, which should be excluded from our spending measures. Specifically, the decision of a merchant to contract with First Data as their payment processor should not be included in economic statistics. Given the rapid expansion of First Data over the past decade, client merchant churn is a big problem in the unfiltered data and must be effectively filtered from our spending series. To address this phenomenon, we developed a "constant-merchant" sample that restricts the sample to a subset of First Data merchants that exhibit a steady flow of transactions over a specific time period. Our method is aggressive in that it filters out economic births and deaths over that period, along with the First Data client churn. A future extension of our work is to create a statistical adjustment for economic births and deaths, but even without it, our current filter delivers sensible economic dynamics. Given the rapid expansion in First Data's business, and the economic growth in the retail sector overall, it would be far too restrictive to select merchants that transact in the full data set from 2010 onward. At the other extreme, using very short windows for the constant-merchant approach, such as comparing transactions one day to the next or even one month to the next, would also be problematic because of strong seasonal and day-of-week patterns in retail spending.

To balance these tradeoffs, we combine a set of 14-month windows of constant-merchant samples. Each sample is restricted to include only those merchants that were "well-attached" to First Data (criteria described below) over the 14 months ending in the reference month of a given spending estimate. We need only 13 months to calculate a 12-month percent change but including an additional month at the start of the filtering window ensures that merchants who begin to register First Data transactions in the middle of a month do not enter the 12-month percent change calculations. We do not include a 15th month at the end of each window because it would delay our spending estimates for the most recent month and defeat a key purpose of making timely economic statistics available.

To give a concrete example—shown in the first row of figure 4.3—the constant-merchant sample of January 2017 is the subset of well-attached client merchants that transacted in each month from December 2015 to January 2017. The sample for December 2016—in the second row—is based on transactions from November 2015 to December 2016. The same merchant

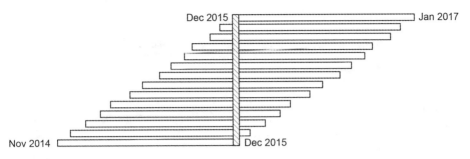

Fig. 4.3   Illustration of overlapping of 14-month constant-merchant samples

may appear in multiple overlapping monthly samples, but it will depend on the merchant's transaction behavior within each 14-month window.

An implication of this method of constructing 14-month constant-merchant samples is that, for any calendar month, we have multiple samples from which to estimate spending in a given reference month. For instance, the shaded area in figure 4.3 shows the 14 different merchant samples that we use to estimate spending in December 2015. The reference months for the constant-merchant samples shown in figure 4.3 range from December 2015 to January 2017. We discuss below how we combine the estimates across the separate merchant samples into a single time series. This overlapping sample methodology is applied independently to each 3-digit NAICS category and geography.

4.3.2   Additional Criteria for Selecting "Well-Attached" Merchants

We applied several other filtering criteria for selection into each 14-month constant-merchant sample:[10]

1. *Misclassified MCCs to NAICS mapping:* Some merchants were determined by Palantir to be paired with inaccurate MCCs and were subsequently dropped from our analysis. For example, MCC code 5962 (Merchandising Machine Operators) was found to contain many merchants that should be classified as Travel Vendors.

2. *Batch processors:* Merchants cannot have more than 40 percent of their transaction volume concentrated in one day in a month. This cutoff is well above the typical transaction distribution for extreme days such as Black Fridays and the days before Christmas. The goal of this filter is to remove merchants who batch their transactions over several days for processing.

10. The underlying raw sample (before filtering) excludes merchants that have opted out of having their data shared. We also control for the introduction of new payment processing platforms by imposing a three-month lag before merchants on the new platform can appear in the sample because merchants often exhibit volatile behavior in the data when a new platform comes online. Three small platforms with several data quality issues are dropped from our sample.

Table 4.1   **Filtering steps—14-month window ending January 2017**

Filter criteria applied in the step	Cumulative dollar volumes remaining (percent of raw sample)	Cumulative merchants remaining (percent of raw sample)
Misclassified MCCs to NAICS mapping	86.7	89.5
Batch processors	85.2	81.5
Minimum monthly spending/transaction days	85.2	80.2
14-month constant-merchant sample	52.7	29.1
Growth outliers	51.4	29.1

Note: Table shows fraction of merchants and associated transaction volumes that meet each successive filtering criterion in the 14-month window from December 2015 to January 2017.

3. *Minimum monthly spending/transaction days:* Merchants must transact more than four days and clear at least 20 dollars in every month of the sampling window. This filter removes merchants who effectively leave the First Data platform but still send in occasional transactions to avoid inactivity/early termination fees. It also removes any merchants that may be batching transactions at a lower frequency that were not captured above.

4. *Growth outliers:* The 12-month percent change in each merchant's sales must be within the inner 99.99 percent of the distribution of growth rates of merchants at that NAICS 3-digit industry and geography combination.

Table 4.1 shows how our filtering techniques affect the number of First Data merchants and transactions in our series. Specifically, we report the fraction of spending removed from our sample in each filtering step for the 14-month window for January 2017. The denominator throughout is the unfiltered set of merchants in the retail sales group that do not have opt-out agreements with First Data. Our final, filtered sample, shown in the last row of the table, accounts for a little over half of the dollar transaction volume in the unfiltered data, but it reflects a set of merchants with a stable attachment to First Data, and for whom sales growth appears well-measured by the data.

4.3.3   Combining Constant-Merchant Samples

After applying the filtering methods described above, we combine our adjusted 14-month constant-merchant samples to produce a daily index of spending growth and then monthly estimates of growth for each NAICS 3-digit industry and geography. The technical details here will be of interest to researchers who are applying our techniques to other data. For others, much of this section can be skipped. Since the transaction data at a specific merchant in our 14-month constant-merchant sample are daily, we cannot simply back out an index by cumulating the average monthly growth rates from our 14-month samples. That approach would have been the most natural if we were using monthly transaction data. Instead, for a given day we take a weighted average of the *level* across the 14-month samples that include that day. The weights remove level differences across the samples due to client-merchant churn. The result is a single, continuous daily index for each NAICS 3-digit industry and geography.

More precisely, we scale each successive 14-month sample by a factor, f_t, such that the average of spending over the first thirteen months of the series is equal to the average spending of those same thirteen months in the preceding, and already scaled, 14-month sample.[11] These factors are multiplicative; $f_t = \prod_{s=0}^{t-1} q_{t-s}$ where $q_t = (\sum_{k=1}^{13} \sum_{i \in t-k} a_{it-k}^t) / (\sum_{k=1}^{13} \sum_{i \in t-k} a_{it-k}^{t-1})$ and a_{it}^{t+j} denotes the estimate of daily sales on day i of month t from the 14-month sample series ending in month $t + j$. Then, we average together the 14 indexes that cover each day's spending to get our daily spending series:[12]

$$x_{it} = \frac{1}{14} \sum_{j=0}^{13} f_{t+j} a_{it}^{t+j}.$$

We obtain estimates of monthly growth from our daily indexes. See also appendix C.

In our method, each month's estimate relies on multiple constant-merchant samples, so the most recent month's estimate will revise as additional samples are added over time. Figure 4.4 shows the magnitudes of the revisions between the first growth estimate for a month (vintage 0) and its final estimate (vintage 13) when all the merchant samples are available. The dots and bars reflect the average revision at each vintage and its 90 percent confidence intervals. The revision is the final estimate of a month's growth rate (at vintage 14) minus the growth estimate at a specific vintage (from 1 to 13). The figure covers the period from April 2011 to December 2017. The range of revisions, particularly for the first few vintages, is high, with a 90 percent confidence interval of around plus or minus 0.8 percentage point. The average revision is near zero, so early estimates are not biased. It is worth noting that the preliminary estimates of monthly retail sales growth from Census have roughly comparable standard errors to our estimates.[13] As we make further refinements to our data estimation methods, we anticipate that the revision standard errors will shrink (for further details, see appendix).

In the final step, we create dollar-value estimates. Benchmarking is an important step when using a nonrepresentative sample and incomplete data. If some industries are over- or underrepresented among First Data merchants relative to all US merchants, or if use of noncard payments for spend-

11. Prior to this step, and as described in appendix B, we make a statistical adjustment to the first and final month of each 14-month sample. The adjustment attempts to correct bias due to our inability to perfectly filter new and dying merchants at the beginning and end of the sample. The notation for variable a in the equation above reflects the series after the correction has been applied.

12. For days in the months at the start or end of the existing data span, we average together whatever indexes are available for that period, which will be less than 14.

13. The standard deviation of the revisions to the preliminary Census monthly growth rate is 0.4 percentage point, as compared to 0.5 percentage point in the First Data.

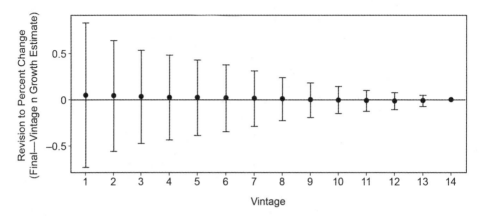

Fig. 4.4   **Revision properties of First Data retail sales group monthly growth rates**
Source: First Data, authors' calculations.
Note: Black dots show the mean revision to monthly seasonally adjusted growth rates, and bars show the 90% confidence interval; that is, 1.65 times the standard deviation.

ing differs across industries, a simple aggregation of our industry indexes would not accurately reflect overall growth.

The Economic Census—conducted every five years—is the only source of retail sales data with sufficient industry and geographic detail to serve as our benchmark. The most recent census available is from 2012. With each of our industry indexes for a specific geography, we set the average level in 2012 equal to the level in the Economic Census for that industry and geography.[14] We then use our daily indexes from First Data transactions to extrapolate spending from the Census level in 2012. Our final spending series in nominal dollars reflects the Census levels, on average, in 2012 and the First Data growth rates at all other times. This approach provides spending indexes in which the nominal shares of each industry are comparable to those across all US merchants, not just First Data clients. Then, to construct total spending indexes for the Retail Sales Group, or any other grouping of retail industries, we simply sum over the benchmarked industry indexes that compose the desired aggregate. We use this benchmarking procedure to create levels indexes for national-, state-, and MSA-level spending.

Prior to benchmarking, the Economic Census also allows us to check how well the First Data indexes cover the universe of sales in the country. For each year, the "coverage ratio" of each index is computed by dividing

14. For those geography-NAICS code pairs for which the 3-digit NAICS code is suppressed in the Economic Census, we impute them using the number of firms in that industry and region. When the First Data index is suppressed for 2012, we instead normalize the first full year of the First Data index to the Economic Census level for that region-industry that is grown out using the national growth rates for the 3-digit NAICS.

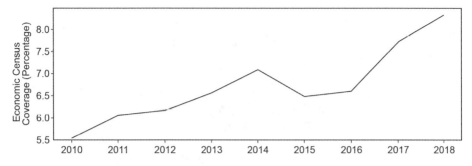

Fig. 4.5   First Data coverage of national retail sales group sales
Source: First Data and Census, authors' calculations.

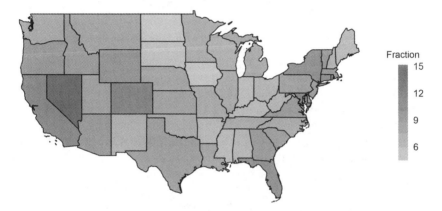

Fig. 4.6   First Data coverage of Economic Census retail sales group sales by state, 2018
Source: First Data and Census, authors' calculations.

the total First Data sales that are used in the creation of the index by the total estimated sales in the region.[15] Figure 4.5 shows that the coverage ratio of the national retail sales group has increased from roughly 5.5 percent in 2010 to 8.3 percent in 2018. However, the coverage is not uniform across the country. Figure 4.6 plots the coverage ratio of the retail sales group in each state in 2018. Some states, such as North Dakota and Iowa, both have low coverage at 3.7 percent, while others have higher coverage such as Nevada with 15.1 percent and Alaska (not shown) with 11.6 percent.

15. For years other than 2012, estimates from Economic Census for a specific industry and geography are grown out using national growth estimates for that industry from the Census Monthly Retail Trade Survey.

4.3.4   Seasonal Adjustment

In order to use our monthly spending indexes for time-series analysis, we also need to filter the indexes to remove regular variation related to week-days, holidays, and other calendar effects. After exploring several alternative strategies, we have taken a parsimonious approach: We seasonally adjust the data by summing the daily transactions by calendar month and running the monthly series through the X-12 ARIMA program maintained by the Census Bureau. An advantage of this method is that it is also used to seasonally adjust the Census retail sales data, which we use for comparison with our own monthly estimates. We do not seasonally adjust our daily estimates; instead, we include day of the week and holiday controls when using them in analysis.[16]

4.4   Comparing Our Spending Measures with Official Statistics

An important step in the development of our new spending indexes has been making comparisons to official Census estimates of retail sales. Because the Census survey is administered to firms with at least one retail establishment, it is a useful benchmark against which to compare the indexes that we derive from aggregating the First Data merchant-level data. The Census surveys roughly 13,000 firms monthly, with the full sample being reselected every five years.[17] Firm births and deaths are incorporated quarterly.

Even if we have isolated the true signal for economic activity from First Data transactions, we would not expect a perfect correlation with the Census series. In reality, the First Transaction data offer an independent, albeit noisy, signal of economic activity. Moreover, the Census estimates are also subject to measurement error, such as sampling error. Figure 4.7 shows the 12-month percent change in the national retail sales group from the First Data indexes and Census retail sales. Our spending indexes and the Census

16. Seasonal adjustment of the daily data is more challenging, partly because the methods for estimating daily adjustment factors are not as well established. That said, working with daily data offers some potential advantages in this regard. As pointed out by Leamer (2014), with daily data we can directly observe the distribution of spending across days of the week, and this allows for a relatively precise estimation of weekday adjustment factors. Indeed, we find that retail transaction volumes vary markedly by the day of the week—the highest spending days appear to be Thursday, Friday, and Saturday, and the lowest spending day by far is Sunday. Interestingly, there also appears to be a slow shift in the composition of spending by day of week, toward Fridays and Saturdays and away from Mondays and Tuesdays. This pattern is likely capturing trends in the timing of shopping activity, though it may also be partly due to an unobserved change in the composition of merchants represented in our sample.

17. The Census Bureau's initial estimate of retail sales for a month comes from the "Advance" Monthly Retail Trade Survey, which has a smaller sample of firms, roughly 5,000. The results from the Advance survey are released for a specific month about two weeks after the month end. The MRTS for that same month is released one month later. Because firms are often delayed in their responses, the MRTS can undergo major revisions as additional firms report sales in subsequent months or in the annual retail sales survey, released each March.

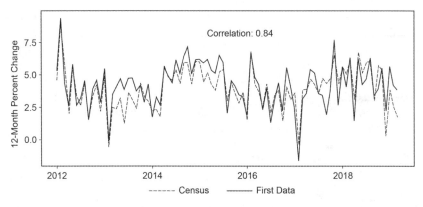

Fig. 4.7   National retail sales group (12-month percent change)
Source: First Data and Census, authors' calculations.
Note: Not seasonally adjusted.

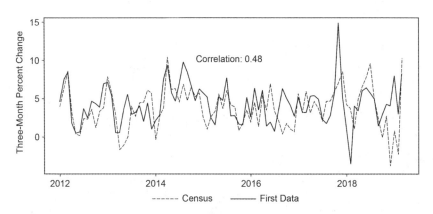

Fig. 4.8   National retail sales group (3-month percent change)
Source: First Data and Census, authors' calculations.
Note: Seasonally adjusted, annualized growth rate.

estimates clearly share the same broad contours, as one would expect from two noisy estimates of the same underlying phenomenon.

Figure 4.8 shows three-month percent changes in seasonally adjusted versions of both Census and First Data series. While the co-movement between the series is certainly weaker than the 12-month NSA changes in figure 4.7, the broad contour of growth in the two series remains quite correlated even at a higher frequency. The standard deviation of the growth rates is also similar.

The results in this section have made us confident that we are, in fact, measuring monthly growth in consumer spending well. Furthermore, the signal derived from the First Data series provides a read on spending that is timelier than the official statistics. For any particular month, the initial reading on retail spending from First Data comes only three days after the completion of the month, while the Census's initial read lags by two weeks. Moreover, while the First Data series provides an independent read on retail spending, it also enhances our ability to forecast the final growth estimates published by Census, even when controlling for the preliminary estimates from Census. A regression of the final three-month Census retail sales group growth rate on the preliminary three-month Census growth rate has an adjusted R^2 of 0.48, while the addition of the preliminary First Data series raises the adjusted R^2 to 0.55. While the incremental improvement in forecasting revisions is small, the First Data estimates are particularly helpful as an independent signal when Census preliminary estimates show an unusually large change in sales. This timeliness and incremental signal content allow policymakers, such as the members of the Federal Open Market Committee deciding monetary policy—to base their decisions on a more accurate assessment of the current cyclical state of the economy.

4.5   Applications: Real-Time Tracking of Consumer Spending

The First Data indexes developed in this paper can improve the information set of policymakers, including at the Federal Reserve. In this section, we discuss how our First Data indexes helped policymakers during the partial government shutdown in 2019 and in the wake of Hurricanes Harvey and Irma in 2017.

4.5.1   The Partial Government Shutdown in 2019

In December 2018 and January 2019, heightened turmoil in global financial markets raised concerns about the pace of economic activity; as a result, policymakers were acutely focused on the incoming economic data to inform their decisions. Unfortunately, a government shutdown delayed the publication of many official statistics, including December retail sales—ordinarily one of the timeliest indicators of consumer spending—leaving policymakers with less information to assess current economic conditions.

The First Data spending index remained available during the shutdown. In contrast to the worrying signs in financial markets, the December reading from First Data indicated only a modest decline in retail spending, as shown in figure 4.9.

When the shutdown ended and Census published its first estimate of December retail sales (on February 14, a month later than usual), it showed an exceptionally large decline. At that point, however, the January First Data reading was also available, and it pointed to a solid rebound in spending. Indeed, the first Census reading for January also popped back up when it was eventually published on March 11.

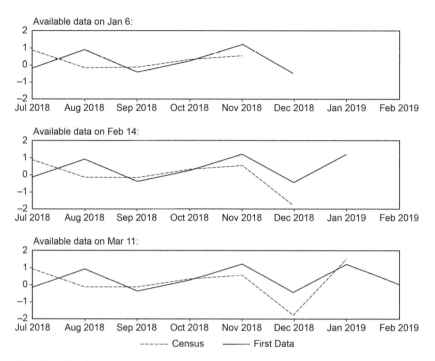

Fig. 4.9   Retail sales data releases during 2019 government shutdown
Source: First Data and Census, authors' calculations.
Note: Monthly growth rates of latest vintage available.

4.5.2   Hurricanes Harvey and Irma in 2017

Another useful application of our data is for assessing the impact of severe weather events, like hurricanes. The disruptions to spending during a storm are often severe but localized and short-lived, so that the lost spending is hard to quantify with monthly national statistics where the sampling frame may be inadequate to capture geographic shocks. Moreover, policymakers ultimately care about the extent to which swings in aggregate spending reflect the effect of a large, short-run disruption like a hurricane versus a change in the underlying trend in spending.

The 2017 Atlantic hurricane season was unusually active, with 17 named storms over a three-month period. Two of these hurricanes—Harvey and Irma—were especially large and severe. On August 28, Hurricane Harvey made landfall in Texas. Historic rainfall and widespread flooding severely disrupted life in Houston, the fifth largest metropolitan area in the United States. Less than two weeks later, Hurricane Irma made landfall in South Florida after causing mass destruction in Puerto Rico, and then proceeded to track up the western coast of the state, bringing heavy rain, storm surge, and flooding to a large swath of Florida and some areas of Georgia and South Carolina. By Monday, September 11, 2017, more than 7 million US residents of Puerto Rico, Florida, Georgia, and South Carolina were without power.[18] In figure 4.10, panel A depicts the path of the two hurricanes and panel B the Google search intensity during the two storms.

Using daily, state, and MSA-level indexes, we examined the pattern of activity in the days surrounding the landfalls of Hurricanes Harvey and Irma. To quantify the size of the hurricane's effect, we estimated the following regression specification for each affected state:

$$\ln(Spending_t) = \sum_{i=-7}^{i=14} \beta_i * H_{t-i} + \sum_{w=Mon}^{w=Sun} \delta_w * I(Day_t = w)$$

$$+ \sum_{m=July}^{m=Nov} \delta_m * I(Month_t = m) + T_t + \varepsilon_t.$$

The state-specific hurricane effects are captured by the coefficients on the indicator variables, H_{t-i}, which equal one if the hurricane occurred on day $t-i$, and zero otherwise. The regression also controls for variation in spending due to the day of week, the month of year, and a linear time trend (T_t). The coefficient β_0 is thus the estimated effect on (log) spending in that state on the day the hurricane struck.

Figure 4.11 illustrates the results of the regression for Hurricanes Harvey and Irma effects on national daily retail sales group spending. For this broad category of retail spending, there is little evidence of spending in advance of the storm. In the days following the landfall of Hurricane Harvey, daily retail sales group was about 3 percent lower than what normally would have occurred without a hurricane. In the case of Hurricane Irma, the disruption in spending was larger, reducing national retail sales group spending by more than 7 percent in the day after landfall. However, the level of spending rebounded quickly after both hurricanes and within a week of landfall was back to normal levels. On balance, these data suggest that little of the reduced spending associated with Hurricanes Harvey and Irma was offset by higher spending in the days before or just after the storms.

It is a useful exercise to translate the daily effects on national spending to quarterly GDP growth. To roughly gauge the direct reduction in GDP, we first sum the percentage deviation from baseline in daily retail group spending from both hurricanes, shown in figure 4.11. We then divide this total by the 92 days in the quarter and scale the effects by the retail sales group's share of GDP (about 0.25). By this measure, we find that together both hurricanes reduced GDP growth by almost ½ percentage point (annual rate) in the third quarter of 2017. The gradual makeup, unlike the sharp drop on impact, is

18. Because our data do not cover Puerto Rico, we could not conduct a comparable analysis of Hurricane Maria, which devastated Puerto Rico several weeks later.

Panel A. Paths of Hurricanes Harvey and Irma

Panel B: Hurricane Timelines and Google Search Intensity

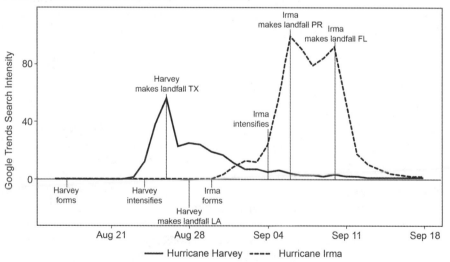

Fig. 4.10 Path and timing of Hurricanes Harvey and Irma
Panel A. Paths of Hurricanes Harvey and Irma
Source: National Oceanic and Atmospheric Administration.
Panel B. Hurricane timelines and Google search intensity
Source: Google Trends search intensity for the terms "Hurricane Harvey" and "Hurricane Irma."

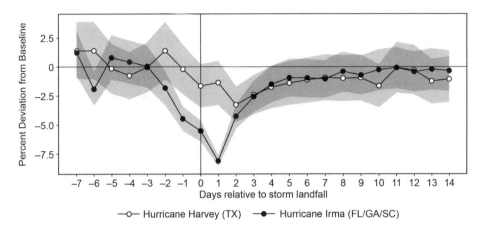

Fig. 4.11   Effects of hurricanes on national retail sales group spending
Source: First Data, authors' calculations.

difficult to distinguish from the usual variability in daily spending, so our direct estimate may overstate the negative effect of the hurricanes. In addition, this estimate is derived only from behavior in retail sales group spending and therefore excludes other consumption, like recreation services, or unplanned inventory accumulation or other production disruptions (see also Bayard, Decker, and Gilbert 2017). Our spending indexes, albeit incomplete, may still be able to capture the GDP effects better than official statistics on retail sales. The national sampling frame of such survey measures may not measure localized shocks well.

In addition to tracking the effects of hurricanes on national spending, our new dataset allows us to study local effects. As seen in figure 4.12, in both Texas (panel A) and Florida (panel B), the hurricanes brought spending in their direct path to a near halt. Daily geographic data can trace out the economic effects of the hurricanes, and specific circumstances such as evacuation orders, power outages, or flooding, with greater clarity than the national monthly statistics. With these data it would also be possible to explore possible shifts in spending to nearby areas and other spending categories, such as sales at gasoline stations or hotel accommodations, which are not included in the retail sales group.

To further unpack our results, we also estimated the same regression using more detailed categories of spending in Hurricane Irma in Florida (figure 4.13). Interestingly, responses around the day of Hurricane Irma varied noticeably among these categories. Spending at building materials stores actually ramped up before the hurricane and rebounded afterwards, such that the net effect for this category is positive (12 percent for the month). Spending at grocery stores also ramped up before the hurricane but did not rebound afterwards, so that the net effect was negative (–3.5 percent for the month). By adjusting the timing of purchases, consumers smoothed out

Panel A: Houston and Texas Metros

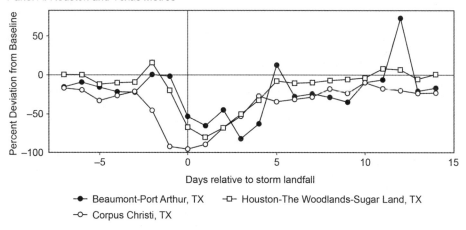

--•-- Beaumont-Port Arthur, TX   --□-- Houston-The Woodlands-Sugar Land, TX
--○-- Corpus Christi, TX

Panel B: Miami and Other Florida Metros

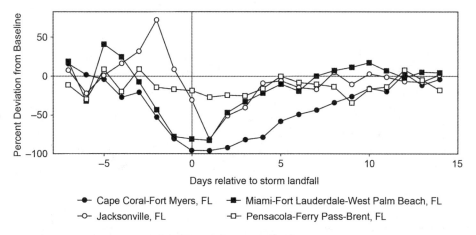

--•-- Cape Coral-Fort Myers, FL   --■-- Miami-Fort Lauderdale-West Palm Beach, FL
--○-- Jacksonville, FL   --□-- Pensacola-Ferry Pass-Brent, FL

Fig. 4.12   Effects on local retail sales group spending
Source: First Data, authors' calculations.

the temporary disruption of the hurricane, with little effect on their overall grocery spending.

However, other retail categories look quite different, showing no evidence of a ramp-up in spending prior to the storm or a quick make-up in spending afterwards. In these cases, the spending lost during the storm appears to be largely forgone, at least in the near term. For example, our estimates indicate net reductions in spending in October due to the hurricane at restaurants (–9.5 percent) and clothing stores (–21 percent).

One possible explanation for the lack of a quick reversal in spending is that some purchases are tied together with time use. For example, going out to eat requires time spent at a restaurant. If the storm makes it more

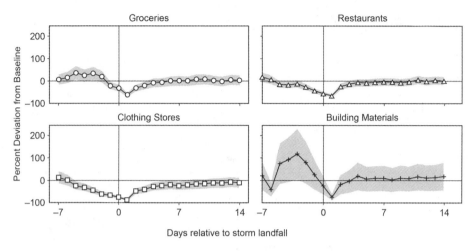

Fig. 4.13   Effect of Hurricane Irma on selected components of spending in Florida
Source: First Data, authors' calculations.

difficult to spend time on such activities, then individuals are likely to cut back on restaurant spending, and some may substitute to alternatives such as buying groceries to eat at home. In addition, purchases that are directly tied to an experience, such as an afternoon out with friends, may be forgone or postponed for some time. See also our related discussion of Hurricane Matthew in Aladangady et al. (2016).

Another potential explanation for the apparent lack of make-up spending is that some portion of spending is "impulse purchases" that arise from a mood or temptation in the moment.[19] If bad weather disrupts a shopping trip or dampens the mood of consumers, then these impulse purchases may never happen. Such psychological factors seem like a plausible explanation for the lack of make-up spending in several types of purchases, like clothing.

Of course, we cannot rule out that the make-up in spending was gradual enough that the estimated effects in the days following the storm cannot be statistically distinguished from zero.[20] Furthermore, we cannot observe whether consumers make up spending in online sales rather than brick-and-mortar establishments. Even so, the transaction aggregates provide suggestive evidence that temporary disruptions like hurricanes can have persistent effects on some types of spending.

19. As some examples of related research, Busse et al. (2015) find that weather has a psychological effect on car purchases and Spies, Hesse, and Loesch (1997) argue that mood can influence purchases.

20. We also tested specifications that allowed for hurricane effects more than seven days after the storm. The longer window did not materially change the results, and estimated coefficients for 7 to 21 days after the storm were not statistically different from zero.

4.6   Conclusion

In this paper, we present our methodology for transforming transaction data from a large payment processing company into new statistics of consumer spending. Raw payment transaction volumes are clearly not suitable and transforming payments data into sensible measures required us to address a host of thorny measurement issues. The steps we took to address these challenges can be improved upon; nevertheless, the spending series we developed have already proven to be a timely and independent signal about the cyclical position of the economy.

Our spending estimates at the daily frequency and at detailed geographies can be used to examine several economic questions. In this paper, we considered the high-frequency spending responses to Hurricanes Harvey and Irma. In other work, we used our series to study sales-tax holidays and delays in EITC refund payments.[21]

Looking ahead, we plan to refine our methodology. We would like to produce estimates for more detailed geographies, such as counties. With a longer time series, we will also be able to improve the seasonal adjustment of our spending series. Another significant improvement to our current methodology would be to account for establishment births and deaths (see appendix D).

To conclude with a broader perspective, we believe that nontraditional data can be used successfully to produce new economic statistics. In fact, several statistical agencies, including Census Bureau, the Bureau of Economic Analysis, and the Bureau of Labor Statistics are now using private Big Data to improve existing data series and expand their data offering. The collaborative efforts in our project—and by many other agencies detailed in this volume—with researchers focusing on the economic statistics, software engineers handling the computations with the raw data, and a private firm allowing controlled access to its data could be a useful model for other Big Data projects going forward.

Finally, we would note that the project discussed in this paper represents our third attempt over several years to obtain promising new data sources and use them to create spending statistics. Through earlier false starts, we learned valuable lessons about the many challenges that must be overcome to convert proprietary Big Data into functional economic statistics. This paper details the ingredients for our eventual success, including a private company supportive of our statistical efforts, skilled staff from a technology company to process the raw data, and rich data structured in a way that we could map to Census retail sales.

---

21. See Aladangady et al. (2016) and Aladangady et al. (2018).

Appendix A

Table 4A.1   Mapping of MCC to NAICS for retail stores and restaurants

MCC	MCC description	NAICS2	NAICS3	NAICS	NAICS description
5533	Automotive parts, accessories stores	44	441	441310	Automotive parts and accessories stores
5531	Automobile supply stores	44	441	441310	Automotive parts and accessories stores
5996	Swimming pools: sales, service, and supplies	45	45	45	#N/A
5997	Electric razor stores: sales and service	45	45	45	#N/A
5998	Tent and awning shops	45	45	45	#N/A
5940	Bicycle shops: Sales and service	45	451	451110	Sporting goods stores
5941	Sporting goods stores	45	451	451110	Sporting goods stores
5970	Artist's supply and craft shops	45	451	451120	Hobby, toy, and game stores
5945	Hobby, toy, and game shops	45	451	451120	Hobby, toy, and game stores
5949	Sewing, needle, fabric, and piece goods stores	45	451	451130	Sewing, needlework, and piece goods stores
5733	Music stores, musical instruments, piano sheet music	45	451	451140	Musical instrument and supplies stores
5942	Book stores	45	451	451211	Book stores
5994	News dealers and newsstands	45	451	451212	News dealers and newsstands
5735	Record shops	45	451	451220	#N/A
10	#N/A	45	452	452111	Department stores (except discount stores)
5311	Department stores	45	452	452111	Department stores (except discount stores)
5310	Discount stores	45	452	452112	Discount department stores
5300	Wholesale clubs	45	452	452910	Warehouse clubs and supercenters
5331	Variety stores	45	452	452990	All other general merchandise stores
5399	Misc. general merchandise	45	452	452990	All other general merchandise stores
5992	Florists	45	453	453110	Florists
5978	Typewriter stores: sales, rental, service	45	453	453210	Office supplies and stationery stores
5943	Stationery stores, office and school supply stores	45	453	453210	Office supplies and stationery stores
5947	Card shops, gift, novelty, and souvenir shops	45	453	453220	Gift, novelty, and souvenir stores
5932	Antique shops	45	453	453310	Used merchandise stores
5931	Used merchandise and secondhand stores	45	453	453310	Used merchandise stores

5937	Antique reproductions	45	453	453310	Used merchandise stores
5995	Pet shops, pet foods, and supplies stores	45	453	453910	Pet and pet supplies stores
5971	Art dealers and galleries	45	453	453920	Art dealers
9	#N/A	45	453	453930	Manufactured (mobile) home dealers
5271	Mobile home dealers	45	453	453930	Manufactured (mobile) home dealers
5993	Cigar stores and stands	45	453	453991	Tobacco stores
5972	Stamp and coin stores: Philatelic and numismatic supplies	45	453	453998	All other miscellaneous store retailers
5974	#N/A	45	453	453998	All other miscellaneous store retailers
5973	Religious goods stores	45	453	453998	All other miscellaneous store retailers
5999	Miscellaneous and specialty retail stores	45	453	453998	All other miscellaneous store retailers
5961	Mail order houses including catalog order stores, book/record clubs	45	454	454113	Mail-order houses
5983	Fuel: fuel oil, wood, coal, liquefied petroleum	45	454	454311	#N/A
5960	Direct marketing–Insurance service	45	454	454390	Other direct selling establishments
5962	Direct marketing: Travel related arrangements services	45	454	454390	Other direct selling establishments
5967	Direct marketing: Inbound teleservices merchant	45	454	454390	Other direct selling establishments
5969	Direct marketing: Not elsewhere classified	45	454	454390	Other direct selling establishments
5422	Meat provisioners: Freezer and locker	45	454	454390	Other direct selling establishments
5963	Door-to-door sales	45	454	454390	Other direct selling establishments
4815	VisaPhone	45	454	454390	Other direct selling establishments
5966	Direct marketing–Outbound telemarketing merchant	45	454	454390	Other direct selling establishments
5964	Direct marketing: Catalog merchant	45	454	454390	Other direct selling establishments
5965	Direct marketing: Catalog and catalog and retail merchant	45	454	454390	Other direct selling establishments
5968	Direct marketing: Continuity/subscription merchant	45	454	454390	Other direct selling establishments
5812	Eating places and restaurants	72	722	722110	#N/A
5814	Fast food restaurants	72	722	722211	#N/A
5811	Caterers	72	722	722320	Caterers
5813	Drinking places (alcoholic beverages), bars, taverns, cocktail lounges, nightclubs and discotheques	72	722	722410	Drinking places (alcoholic beverages)

Source: Staff at the CENSUS Bureau and the Bureau of Economic Analysis developed this mapping from MCC to NAICs.

Note: Other MCC/NAICs outside of retail stores and restaurants not shown here.

Appendix B

Adjustments to the First and Last Month of the Constant-Merchant Sample

Before we combine information from the overlapping 14-month merchant samples, we need to correct for a bias at the beginning and end of the samples. For each month in the dataset (excepting the first 13 months and the most recent 13 months), there are exactly fourteen 14-month samples that have a sales estimate for that month, and thirteen 14-month samples that have a monthly sales *growth* estimate for that month (which requires that months t and $t-1$ be in the sample). Although the monthly level of sales in each sample is highly dependent on the merchant births, deaths, and business acquisitions between overlapping 14-month merchant samples, we find that the estimates of monthly growth in different samples are, on average, similar, with two notable exceptions: The first monthly growth estimate from a 14-month merchant sample is biased upwards, and the last monthly growth estimate is biased downwards. To make things more explicit, call g_t^{t+j} the estimate of monthly growth in time t that comes from the 14-month sample ending in month $t+j$. For each month t, we construct the average growth rate, $\underline{g}_t$ using all 14-month samples that include an estimate of the growth rate in t:

$$\underline{g}_t = \frac{1}{13} \sum_{j=0}^{12} g_t^{t+j}.$$

Next, we calculate the deviation of the growth estimate t from a merchant sample $t+j$ relative to the average across all samples:

$$\textit{deviation from mean } (j,t) = g_t^{t+j} - \underline{g}_t.$$

In figure 4B.1, we plot the distribution of deviations in all calendar months in the dataset, based on where the growth estimate falls in the merchant sample window (the index j).[22] The upward bias at the beginning of the 14-month sample—that is, the growth rate at time t for the sample that runs from $t-1$ through $t+12$—comes from a "birthing" bias due to firms that were just born and who are therefore ramping up sales. Equivalently, the downward bias at the end of a sample—the growth rate that runs from $t-13$ through t—is from the fact that firms that are about to die (say in time $t+1$, just after the sample ends) tend to have falling sales.

To address this issue, we apply a simple correction model to fix the first and last month's estimate based on the mean growth rates from other sample estimation windows. Assuming that the size of the bias varies by month

---

22. Figure 4B.1 shows the results for the national retail sales group, although the picture is similar for other NAICS codes and geographies.

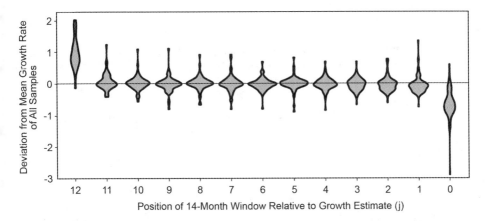

Fig. 4B.1   Deviation from mean growth in each month of the 14-month sample
Source: First Data.

of the year (m), we estimate a separate correction factor β_m^j for each month of the year, for both the 14-month sample ending in $t + 12$ ($j = 12$), and the sample ending in $t(j = 0)$, as:

$$\underline{g}_{t,m} = \beta_m^j g_{t,m}^{t+j} + \varepsilon_t.$$

The β_m^j applies a correction that results in adjusting up the growth estimates from the end of a 14-month sample and adjusting down the growth estimates from the beginning of a 14-month sample. We run these regressions separately for every NAICS code and geography.

To apply this fix to the daily values within the first and last month, we assume that the magnitude of the last-month bias increases and the first-month bias decreases over the course of the month. If Δ is defined as the dollar value of the adjustment for a particular month's estimate, the daily dollar adjustment amount for day d in a month of length D is:

$$\frac{2\Delta d}{D^2 + D}.$$

This correction is particularly important to achieve unbiased readings of spending for the most recent months of the data output. The index that covers recent months will necessarily only depend on the 14-month samples that end with those months (since the subsequent 14-months samples do not yet exist), their growth rates would be severely biased downward without this correction.

Appendix C

Decomposing Monthly Growth Rates of the Series into a Weighted Average of the Monthly Growth Rates from the Contributing 14-Month Samples

Given the daily series, x_{it}, the monthly growth rates for the months in the middle of our sample can be derived as shown in the equation below:

$$1 + g_t = \frac{\sum_{i \in t} x_{it}}{\sum_{i \in t-1} x_{it-1}} = \frac{\sum_{j=0}^{13} f_{t+j} \sum_{i \in t} a_{it}^{t+j}}{\sum_{j=0}^{13} f_{t-1+j} \sum_{i \in t-1} a_{it-1}^{t-1+j}}.$$

Define a_t^j to be the total sales in a 14-month sample j in month t, such that $a_t^j = \sum_{i \in t} a_{it}^j$. Furthermore, as in appendix B, define g_t^{t+k} to be the average monthly growth in time t within the 14-month series ending in $t + k$ for $k \geq 0$, such that $g_t^{t+k} = [(f_{t+k} a_t^{t+k})/(f_{t+k} a_{t-1}^{t+k})] - 1$. For $k = -1$, we define $g_t^{t-1} = [(f_{t+13} a_t^{t+13})/(f_{t-1} a_{t-1}^{t-1})] - 1$, which is the monthly growth rate achieved from using the normalized monthly value for month t from the 14-month sample ending in time $t + 13$ and the normalized monthly value for month $t - 1$ from the 14-month sample ending in time $t - 1$. We can then rearrange the above equation to show the monthly growth rate of our series is a weighted average of these monthly growth rates:[23]

$$g_t = \sum_{k=0}^{13} g_t^{t+k-1} * \frac{f_{t+k} a_{t-1}^{t+k-1}}{\sum_{j=0}^{13} f_{t+j-1} a_{t-1}^{t+j-1}}.$$

The equation above is instructive as it shows us that the monthly growth rates derived from our daily index can be naturally interpreted as a weighted average of monthly growth rates for each constant-merchant sample that contains those months (in addition to one final "faux" monthly growth rate using the first and last 14-month samples that contain those months).

Appendix D

Mathematical Derivation of Birth and Death Bias

The main disadvantage of the constant-merchant methodology described above is that we cannot capture true economic births and deaths. To show

23. For the 13 months at the beginning of our index and the 13 months at the end of our index, this equation will be slightly modified to account for the fact that there are fewer than 14 14-month samples that cover those months. The modified growth equations for these months can still be written as a weighted average of the growth estimates from the available 14-month estimates.

the bias that may result, we introduce some notation. In a given month t let x_t be the total consumer spending in that month so that the true monthly growth rate of consumer spending is simply:

$$g_t = \frac{x_t}{x_{t-1}} - 1.$$

Some set of firms transact in both period t and $t - 1$ and we can call the spending at these firms in time t, s_t^- (where the minus denotes that these are the firms that existed in both that period and the previous one, so t and $t - 1$) and, in time $t - 1$, s_{t-1}^+ (where the plus denotes the firms that existed in both that period and the following one, so $t - 1$ and t). The growth rate of spending for merchants who transact in both periods, what we will refer to as "constant-merchant" growth, is simply:

$$\hat{g}_t = \frac{s_t^-}{s_{t-1}^+} - 1.$$

However, we know that in every period new establishments are born, and we assume that they make up some fraction b_t of the sales in the previous period so that their total sales in the current period t are $b_2 x_{t-1}$. Similarly, some fraction, d_t, of total sales are by firms that die at the end of the period such that total sales in period $t - 1$ can be expressed as:

$$x_{t-1} = \frac{s_{t-1}^+}{(1 - d_{t-1})}.$$

And sales in period t can be written as:

$$x_t = s_t^- + b_t \frac{s_{t-1}^+}{(1 - d_{t-1})}.$$

Assuming that births and deaths are a small fraction of the total spending in our sample we derive an approximate expression for total growth:

$$g_t = \left(s_t^- + b_t \frac{s_{t-1}^+}{(1 - d_{t-1})} \right) \left(\frac{s_{t-1}^+}{(1 - d_{t-1})} \right) - 1.$$

In simplifying this equation, we see that growth is approximately equal to "constant-merchant" growth plus the rate of births minus the rate of deaths.

$$g_t = \left(\frac{s_t^-}{s_{t-1}^+} (1 - d_{t-1}) + b_t \right) - 1$$

$$g_t \approx \hat{g}_t + b_t - d_{t-1}.$$

The constant-merchant methodology described in the previous sections yields an estimate of $\hat{g}_t$, using the constant-merchants within the First Data platform. Thus, if we assume that the First Data merchant sample is close to representative, we see that "true" growth is approximately equal to the growth rate derived from the First Data, $\hat{g}_t^{FD}$, plus the true birth rate minus the true death rate.

$$g_t \approx \hat{g}_t^{FD} + b_t - d_{t-1}.$$

Thus, the cost of the constant-merchant methodology is that we are necessarily missing true births and deaths, but as long as they are small and/or roughly offsetting, the constant-merchant growth rate would do well at approximating total growth. One particular concern is that shifts in $b - d$ may occur at turning points.

References

Aladangady, Aditya, Shifrah Aron-Dine, David Cashin, Wendy Dunn, Laura Feiveson, Paul Lengermann, Katherine Richard, and Claudia Sahm. 2018. "High-Frequency Spending Responses to the Earned Income Tax Credit." FEDS Notes, June 21. Washington, DC: Board of Governors of the Federal Reserve System. https://doi.org/10.17016/2380-7172.2199.
Aladangady, Aditya, Shifrah Aron-Dine, Wendy Dunn, Laura Feiveson, Paul Lengermann, and Claudia Sahm. 2016. "The Effect of Hurricane Matthew on Consumer Spending." FEDS Notes, December 2. Washington, DC: Board of Governors of the Federal Reserve System. https://doi.org/10.17016/2380-7172.1888.
———. 2017. "The Effect of Sales-Tax Holidays on Consumer Spending." FEDS Notes, March 24. Washington, DC: Board of Governors of the Federal Reserve System. https://doi.org/10.170162380-7172.1941.
Baker, Scott. 2018. "Debt and the Response to Household Income Shocks: Validation and Application of Linked Financial Account Data." *Journal of Political Economy* 126 (4): 1504–57.
Bayard, Kimberly, Ryan Decker, and Charles Gilbert. 2017. "Natural Disasters and the Measurement of Industrial Production: Hurricane Harvey, a Case Study." FEDS Notes, October 11. Washington, DC: Board of Governors of the Federal Reserve System. https://doi.org/10.17016/2380-7172.2086.
Busse, Meghan R., Devin G. Pope, Jaren C. Pope, and Jorge Silva-Risso. 2015. "The Psychological Effect of Weather on Car Purchases." *Quarterly Journal of Economics* 130 (1): 371–414.
Cohen, Michael, and Marc Rysman. 2013. "Payment Choice with Consumer Panel Data." Research Department Working Paper Series No. 13–6, Federal Reserve Bank of Boston.
Farrell, Diana, and Fiona Greig. 2015. *Weathering Volatility: Big Data on the Financial Ups and Downs of U.S. Individuals.* Washington, DC: JPMorgan Chase & Co. Institute. https://www.jpmorganchase.com/content/dam/jpmc/jpmorgan-chase-and-co/institute/pdf/54918-jpmc-institute-report-2015-aw5.pdf.
First Data. n.d. *First Data Retail Volume Aggregates.* https://www.firstdata.com/en_us/home.html.
Gelman, Michael, Shachar Kariv, Matthew D. Shapiro, Daniel Silverman, and Steven Tadelis. 2014. "Harnessing Naturally Occurring Data to Measure the Response of Spending to Income." *Science* 345 (6193): 212–15.

Greene, Claire, and Joanne Stavins. 2018. "The 2017 Diary of Consumer Payment Choice." *Federal Bank of Atlanta Research Data Reports*, No. 18-5. https://www .atlantafed.org/banking-and-payments/consumer-payments/research-data -reports/2018/the-2017-diary-of-consumer-payment-choice.

Leamer, Edward. 2014. "Workday, Holiday and Calendar Adjustment: Monthly Aggregates from Daily Diesel Fuel Purchases." *Journal of Economic and Social Measurement* (1–2): 1–29. https://EconPapers.repec.org/RePEc:ris:iosjes:0005.

Mian, Atif, Kamalesh Rao, and Amir Sufi. 2013. "Household Balance Sheets, Consumption, and the Economic Slump." *Quarterly Journal of Economics* 128 (4): 1687–1726.

Spies, Kordelia, Friedrich Hesse, and Kerstin Loesch. 1997. "Store Atmosphere, Mood and Purchasing Behavior." *International Journal of Research in Marketing* 14 (1): 1–17.

Improving the Accuracy of Economic Measurement with Multiple Data Sources
The Case of Payroll Employment Data

Tomaz Cajner, Leland D. Crane, Ryan A. Decker,
Adrian Hamins-Puertolas, and Christopher Kurz

5.1 Introduction

Economists and statisticians are increasingly confronted with new data sources, often produced by private companies as part of their business operations, which may be useful for economic research and measurement. These new data hold promise for advancing economic measurement and understanding, but their use raises many questions. How are new, alternative data different from traditional surveys and censuses? How are we to assess

Tomaz Cajner is a group manager in the Industrial Output Section at the Board of Governors of the Federal Reserve System.

Leland D. Crane is a senior economist in the Industrial Output Section at the Board of Governors of the Federal Reserve System.

Ryan A. Decker is a senior economist in the Industrial Output Section at the Board of Governors of the Federal Reserve System.

Adrian Hamins-Puertolas is a technology analyst at the Board of Governors of the Federal Reserve System.

Christopher Kurz is chief of the Industrial Output Section at the Board of Governors of the Federal Reserve System.

We thank ADP for access to and help with the payroll microdata that underlie the work described by this paper. In particular, this work would not have been possible without the support of Jan Siegmund, Ahu Yildirmaz, and Sinem Buber. We are grateful for discussions with Katharine Abraham, Borağan Aruoba, Simon Freyaldenhoven, Erik Hurst, Gray Kimbrough, Alan Krueger, Norman Morin, Matthew Shapiro, John Stevens, David Wilcox, Mark Zandi, and seminar participants at the Federal Reserve Board, the Federal Reserve Bank of Cleveland, ESCoE Conference on Economic Measurement, BLS, NBER CRIW meetings, the Bank of England, and the 2018 ASSA meetings. The analysis and conclusions set forth herein are those of the authors and do not indicate concurrence by other members of the research staff or the Board of Governors. For acknowledgments, sources of research support, and disclosure of the authors' material financial relationships, if any, please see https://www.nber.org/books-and-chapters/big-data-21st-century-economic-statistics/improving-accuracy-economic-measurement-multiple-data-sources-case-payroll-employment-data.

their reliability? How should multiple disparate data sources be synthesized to produce the best possible estimates?

We seek to answer these questions in the context of measuring payroll employment. In particular, we use data from a private payroll provider—ADP—to build an index of US private payroll employment, similar in spirit to the Current Employment Statistics (CES) survey. While the CES survey is carefully conducted and uses an extremely large sample, it still suffers from significant sampling error and nonresponse issues. The ADP-derived employment indexes are based on a sample that is roughly the same size as the CES sample, so it is plausible that pooling the information from ADP with that from CES would reduce sampling error and increase our understanding of the state of the labor market at a given time.

Previous work by Cajner et al. (2018) describes the construction of weekly and monthly aggregate employment series based on ADP's weekly payroll microdata. Their aggregate series (referred to as ADP-FRB) are designed to be an independent signal about labor market conditions rather than solely an attempt to forecast monthly Bureau of Labor Statistics (BLS) employment figures. However, Cajner et al. (2018) do indeed find that the timeliness and frequency of the ADP payroll microdata improves forecast accuracy for both current-month employment and revisions to the BLS CES data.

In this paper we further compare the ADP-FRB index to existing, high-quality government estimates and find encouraging results. The ADP-FRB index, and state-space estimates derived from it, provide information about future CES estimates in real time, including at the start of the Great Recession. In addition, we integrate benchmark employment data and compare the ADP-FRB benchmark revisions with the CES benchmark revisions. While the CES and ADP-FRB series are both prone to significant sampling and nonsampling error, the BLS Quarterly Census of Employment and Wages (QCEW) is generally considered the "final word" for annual employment growth because of its comprehensive administrative source data. Consequently, we benchmark the ADP-based series to the QCEW on an *annual* basis. The benchmarking procedure is similar to CES benchmarking and ensures that year-to-year changes in ADP-FRB are governed by the QCEW, while higher-frequency changes, and the period after the most recent benchmark, are mostly a function of the ADP data.[1]

Existing work on using nontraditional data sources for economic measurement typically takes official government data as the source of truth, at all frequencies. For example, the monthly National Employment Report (ADP-NER) series published by ADP are constructed with the goal of predicting the fully revised CES data.[2] In this paper we take a different approach, rec-

---

1. Benchmarking illustrates an essential role that government statistics play even when there is significant value in nontraditional data sources.

2. Mastercard's SpendingPulse, which attempts to forecast US retail sales, is another example.

ognizing that both CES and ADP-FRB employment are subject to nonnegligible measurement error and using the Kalman filter to extract estimates of unobserved "true" employment growth from observations of both series.

Our baseline model assumes that true US employment growth follows a persistent, latent process and that both the CES and ADP-FRB estimates are noisy signals of this underlying process. Standard state-space tools allow us to estimate the latent process and the observation error associated with each series. We find that the optimal predictor of the unobserved state, using only contemporaneous information, puts approximately equal weight on the CES and ADP-FRB series. This finding is not necessarily surprising, as the ADP sample covers a roughly similar fraction of private nonfarm US employment as the CES sample, so the sampling errors ought to be of roughly similar magnitudes. We also show that the smoothed state estimate, as constructed in real time, helps forecast future values of CES. Throughout, we focus on the role of these privately generated data as a complement to existing official statistics. While there is no substitute for official statistics in terms of consistency, transparency, and scientific collection methods, official numbers do have limitations that alternative data sources can address.

The paper proceeds as follows. Section 5.2 reviews the related literature. Section 5.3 describes the process of creating ADP-based employment indexes and lays out the strengths and the inherent limitations of measuring nationwide payroll employment with ADP data. In section 5.4 we compare the annual ADP-FRB employment estimates to the official benchmarks, discuss the role of the birth-death model in the official estimates, present a case study of the usefulness of alternative employment data during the Great Recession, and show the efficacy of the ADP-FRB estimates in predicting fully revised CES payroll employment numbers. Section 5.5 introduces the state-space model that combines the information from both the ADP-FRB and CES-based estimates and provides evidence that the combined state improves our understanding of current and future payroll gains. Section 5.6 concludes.

5.2 Related Literature

Ours is not the first paper to make use of ADP payroll data. Several papers study the National Employment Report (NER), ADP's publicly available monthly estimate of US payroll gains constructed jointly with Moody's Analytics. Importantly, NER estimates are derived from a model including not only ADP microdata but also other contemporaneous and lagged indicators of US economic activity. The existing literature finds that the NER moves closely with CES (Phillips and Slijk 2015) and has some ability to forecast CES, though it does not appear to improve forecasts based on other available information, such as existing consensus forecasts (Gregory and Zhu 2014; Hatzius et al. 2016).

As noted above, we do not use the NER but instead focus on the ADP microdata. A number of recent papers explore these data. Cajner et al. (2018) analyze the representativeness of ADP microdata (relative to CES and QCEW) and construct an ADP payroll index that can improve forecasts of CES; we employ that index in the present paper. Ozimek, DeAntonio and Zandi (2017) use ADP's linked employer-employee microdata to study the negative effect of workforce aging on aggregate productivity growth. Grigsby, Hurst, and Yildirmaz (2021) study wage rigidity in the same data, finding that the high-frequency microdata can be useful for shedding light on a key business cycle question. Cho (2018) uses ADP microdata to study the employment and wage effects of the 2009 American Recovery and Reinvestment Act.

Our approach in the present paper is different from those above in that we explicitly investigate the usefulness of ADP as a supplement to CES data for tracking the underlying state of the labor market. In this respect, our work is inspired by Aruoba et al. (2016), who note difficulties in assessing the growth of aggregate output in real time given limitations on the comprehensiveness and timeliness of GDP measures. Two independent measures of GDP exist—the commonly reported expenditure-side approach and the income-based approach—and both are prone to measurement errors arising from various sources. Aruoba et al. (2016) combine the two measures using a state-space framework, recovering an underlying state of output growth which they label "gross domestic output." We follow this general approach with a focus on employment rather than output.

5.3   Data

This paper primarily uses three data sources: ADP microdata, the CES survey, and the QCEW. Before turning to the ADP microdata in section 5.3.1, it is useful to briefly lay out the relevant features of the CES and the QCEW.

The CES is the main source of monthly employment information in the United States. It is published by BLS a few days after each reference month and is based on a stratified sample survey, which includes about 500,000 private establishments covering about 24 percent of all US private employees.[3] However, the CES survey response rate—the share of eligible units that respond by the final reading—is only about 60 percent, which implies that CES data contain information for about 15 percent of US private employment.[4] The CES asks each respondent for the count of employees

3. See BLS (2019). Note that the CES contains data for total nonfarm payroll employment, but here we focus only on private payroll employment, excluding government employment to be consistent with the reliable scope of ADP.
4. For CES response rates, see: https://www.bls.gov/osmr/response-rates/.

who worked or received pay for any part of the pay period including the 12th of the reference month. Aggregate CES employment growth is a (weighted) average of the growth reported by units that respond for two or more consecutive months, plus a residual adjustment for establishment birth and death.

While the CES is a very large survey, it is still based on a sample and subject to sampling and nonsampling error (as discussed further below). In contrast, the QCEW, also maintained by BLS, is a near-census of employment covered by unemployment insurance and serves as the sampling frame for much of the CES as well as the target for the annual benchmark of the CES. The employment concept for the QCEW is the number of workers who worked or received pay for any part of the pay period including the 12th of the reference month (even though the firm may have been paying UI insurance for other workers at other times during the month). The main drawback of the QCEW is that the data are collected quarterly and published with a lag of two quarters. Thus, while the QCEW has negligible sampling error, it is of limited use to real-time decision makers. In addition, the QCEW is subject to various sources of nonsampling error.[5] Nevertheless, we follow CES in using the QCEW for reweighting the ADP microdata and as a benchmark target.

5.3.1   Structure of the ADP Microdata

ADP provides human capital management services to firms, including payroll processing. Processing payroll for a client firm involves many tasks, including maintaining worker records, calculating taxes, and issuing paychecks. ADP processes payroll for about 26 million US workers each month (about 20 percent of total US private employment). The structure of the microdata is determined by the business needs of ADP. ADP maintains records at the level of payroll account controls (PAC), which often correspond to business establishments (but may sometimes correspond to firms) as defined by the Census Bureau and BLS. Each PAC updates their records at the end of each pay period. The records consist of the date payroll was processed, employment information for the pay period, and many time-invariant PAC characteristics (such as an anonymized PAC identifier, NAICS industry code, zip code, etc.). PAC records include both the number of individuals employed ("active employees") and the number of individuals issued a paycheck in a given pay period ("paid employees"). Active employees include wage earners with no hours in the pay period, workers on unpaid leave, and the like. Paid employees include any wage or salary workers issued regular paychecks during the pay period as well as those issued bonus checks and payroll corrections. In this paper we focus exclusively on active employment, having found that it is substantially less volatile, more closely resembles officially published aggregates, and performs better

---

5. For a detailed analysis of measurement challenges in CES and QCEW, see Groen (2012).

in forecasting exercises, though we plan to further investigate the active/paid distinction in the future.[6]

The data begin in July 1999.[7] In terms of frequency, the files we use are weekly snapshots of individual PAC records, taken every Saturday since July 2009 (snapshots were taken semimonthly between May 2006 and June 2009 and monthly before May 2006). Each snapshot contains the most recent pay date for each PAC, the relevant employment counts, and the other information described above. As few firms regularly process payroll more than once per week, the weekly snapshots provide a comprehensive history of PAC-level employment dynamics.[8]

We can compare ADP payroll microdata to the QCEW and CES data in terms of pay frequency, region, establishment size, and industry composition. Most notably, ADP has significantly more employment in midsized units than does CES, with a distribution that looks reasonably similar to QCEW.[9]

5.3.2   Series Construction

The process of transforming the raw data to usable aggregate series is complex. Here we provide a brief, simplified explanation of the process. The interested reader may refer to Cajner et al. (2018) for details.

Each week, we calculate the weighted average growth of employment at PACs appearing in the data for two consecutive weeks. The restriction to "continuers" allows us to abstract from changes in the size of ADP's client base. For example, if ADP suddenly gains a large number of clients, this expansion does not directly affect our estimated level of employment. Rather, the growth rate of the businesses once they enter the sample is what matters. As long as business growth is independent of entering or exiting the ADP sample, the growth rate of continuers will be a valid estimate of aggregate growth (of continuers).[10]

Growth rates are weighted by PAC employment and further weighted

---

6. One topic for further investigation is exactly *why* active employment performs better than paid employment. It is possible that double counting due to the inclusion of payroll corrections, reimbursements, and bonuses adds noise to paid employment as measured in the ADP data. See Cajner et al. (2018) for further discussion.

7. When accessing the microdata, we follow a number of procedures to ensure confidentiality. Business names are not present in the data we access.

8. While ADP microdata generally do not revise over time, our employment indexes do revise in a way analogous to CES data. First, our real-time readings for a particular month revise as we incorporate information for additional weeks and businesses that pay at lower pay frequency. Second, we revise our data annually by benchmarking it to QCEW.

9. For more detail, see Cajner et al. (2018).

10. This assumption will inevitably be violated in practice, as firms that are growing fast or shrinking quickly will make different operational choices with respect to their payroll systems. However, we are not aware of any clear evidence on the direction of these biases or any indication that their magnitudes are economically significant.

for representativeness by size and industry. We use QCEW employment counts by establishment size and two-digit NAICS as the target population. Formally, let $w_{j,t}$ be the ratio of QCEW employment in a size-industry cell j to ADP employment in cell j in week t, let $C(j)$ be the set of ADP businesses in cell j, let $e_{i,t}$ be the employment of the i'th business, and let $g_{i,t} = (e_{i,t} - e_{i,t-1})/e_{i,t-1}$ be the weekly growth rate of business i.[11] Aggregate growth is estimated as:

$$g_t = \frac{\sum_{j=1}^{J} w_{j,t-1} \sum_{i \in C(j)} e_{i,t-1} g_{i,t}}{\sum_{j=1}^{J} w_{j,t-1} \sum_{i \in C(j)} e_{i,t-1}}.$$

Cumulating the weekly growth rates across time yields a weekly index level for employment. Our focus in this paper is on monthly estimates. We calculate the monthly index as the average of the weekly index for each month, weighting by days to account for partial weeks in each month.[12] Monthly averaging smooths through the weekly volatility, and the results in Cajner et al. (2018) suggest that averaging improves performance relative to point-in-time methods more similar to the CES. The monthly index is seasonally adjusted at the aggregate level using the X-12 algorithm.[13]

Figure 5.1 displays the seasonally adjusted ADP-FRB series (black thick line) along with the indexed CES estimate (gray thin line). Importantly, the growth rate of the (weighted) ADP-FRB series is very similar to the CES, and the business-cycle frequency fluctuations are very closely aligned. Moreover, this ADP-FRB series does not incorporate any of the benchmarking discussed below, so nothing forces it to resemble CES. It is also evident that the ADP-FRB series is volatile, and much of the month-to-month variation does not appear to be related to the monthly swings in the CES data. We interpret this finding as evidence that both series are contaminated with measurement error, which can plausibly be attenuated by modeling the series jointly. For reference, figure 5.1 also shows the ADP-FRB unweighted series, which does not correct the ADP size-industry distribution. Clearly, the unweighted series has a markedly different trend growth rate, though it shares the qualitative business-cycle frequency behavior of the others.[14]

---

11. For weighting, we use March QCEW employment values for each year. For years where the March QCEW has not been released, we use the last available March QCEW. While we could allow QCEW values to vary quarterly or monthly, the shares are slow moving and thus this change would not significantly alter the results.

12. For example, if a calendar week has four days in January and three days in February, our weighting by days procedure proportionally attributes the weekly employment to both months.

13. BLS seasonally adjusts the CES data with X-13ARIMA-SEATS at the 3-digit NAICS level and then aggregates those seasonally adjusted series.

14. While we do not directly use the weekly ADP-FRB series in this paper, we view these high-frequency measurements as a promising topic for future research on, for example, natural disasters. The weekly series are discussed in more detail in Cajner et al. (2018).

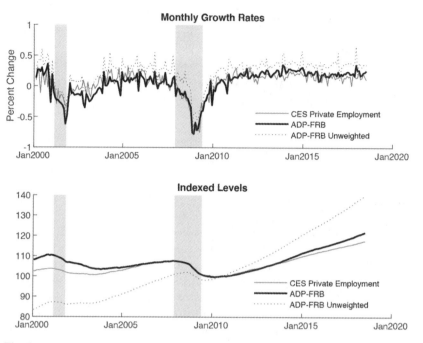

Fig. 5.1   Monthly growth rates and indexed levels
Source: ADP, CES, authors' calculations. CES series is benchmarked; ADP-FRB is not.
Note: Monthly data (current vintage), normalized to 100 in 2010.

5.3.3   Strengths and Weaknesses of Different Types of Payroll Employment Data

Perhaps the most important issue when analyzing the quality of a dataset is its representativeness. Obviously, the QCEW data have a clear advantage here because these data represent population counts.[15] In contrast, CES and ADP estimates are sample based. As with CES, our ADP samples are adjusted with weights that are meant to make the estimates representative of the United States, but the weighting does not solve all issues. In the case of ADP, an important sample selection issue exists because only the firms that hire ADP to manage their payrolls show up in the ADP data. In the case of CES, the data are based on a probability sample of establishments, but because the response rates are only about 60 percent as argued above, this can introduce a potential sample selection issue as well (Kratzke 2013).

Both the ADP and the CES data are subject to dynamic selection issues related to establishment entry and exit. In the United States, young firms

15. Note, though, that there is a small scope discrepancy between QCEW on the one hand and CES/ADP on the other hand: about 3 percent of jobs that are within scope for CES/ADP estimates are exempt from UI tax law. For more detail, see https://www.bls.gov/news.release/cewqtr.tn.htm.

account for a disproportionate share of employment growth (Haltiwanger, Jarmin, and Miranda 2013); indeed, mean and median net employment growth rates of firms above age five tend to be around zero (Decker et al. 2014). A critical limitation of the CES sample is its lack of coverage of new firms and establishments.[16] In addition, the CES does not directly measure establishment deaths. BLS attempts to correct for these shortcomings using an establishment birth/death estimation methodology; for most of the time period we study (up to early 2020), this estimation involved a two-step approach. In the first step, employment losses from known business deaths are excluded from the sample to offset the missing employment gains from new business births. Thus, dead establishments (i.e., those reporting zero employment) and nonrespondents (suspected dead establishments) are implicitly given the same growth rate as the continuing establishments in the CES survey under the assumption that employment at establishment births exceeds employment at establishment deaths by an amount equal to the growth of continuing establishments. In the second step, an ARIMA model based on historical QCEW data estimates the birth/death residual: employment at newly formed establishments less employment at exiting establishments. This estimate is added to the estimates from the CES establishment sample to generate the final CES estimate. In many months, the model's contribution to headline employment estimates is sizable.[17] For example, since 2009 the net birth-death adjustment has added a nontrivial average of 800,000 jobs to a particular year's employment gains, or roughly 40 percent. Actual new firms do not affect CES monthly estimates until the sample is rotated (though births will be captured at an annual frequency when annual benchmarks are released, as we describe below).[18]

Even after an annual benchmark revision, the *monthly* CES data never truly account for the birth and death of establishments. When a benchmark revision occurs, with the January CES release each year, the previous year's March level of the CES data is set to the March level of QCEW employment. The monthly sample-based estimates for the 11 months preceding the March

16. The CES sample is redrawn only once a year (BLS 2019).

17. See a discussion of the model and its recent contributions here: https://www.bls.gov/web/empsit/cesbd.htm. Importantly, this method was tweaked—possibly temporarily—early in the COVID-19 pandemic period to allow for establishment shutdown and nonresponse to affect death estimates more materially and allow current continuers' growth patterns to affect estimates of the birth/death residual.

18. The sampling frame is based on QCEW source data (state unemployment insurance (UI) records), which lag several months. It might be wondered if the UI records pick up new establishments quickly; this is apparently the case. Employers must file UI taxes if they have paid (cumulatively) $1,500 or more in payroll, so most new employers would appear in the UI records very quickly; see https://oui.doleta.gov/unemploy/pdf/uilawcompar/2018/coverage.pdf. However, note that even after a business birth appears in the UI records, there is also time required for sampling, contacting, and soliciting cooperation from the firm as well as verifying the initial data provided. In practice, CES cannot sample and begin to collect data from new firms until they are at least a year old (BLS 2019).

benchmark are revised with a "wedge-back" procedure, where a linear fraction of the benchmark revision is added to the CES level each month (BLS 2019). The wedging-back procedure results in a constant being added to the monthly change in employment each year. So, while the year-to-year change in the post-benchmark CES data will capture the within-QCEW-scope dynamics of entry and exit at the annual frequency, the monthly numbers will never reflect the true monthly pattern of employment.

ADP data are subject to a related limitation in that we do not know the age composition of ADP clients, nor do we observe firm or establishment age in the ADP microdata. However, new and young firms may enter the ADP data immediately upon engaging ADP for payroll services. While the number of young firms in ADP data is unknown, any number could be a useful supplement to the CES data, in which young firms are absent until the sample rotation.

As discussed above, the ADP data consist of weekly snapshots (since July 2009). In contrast, the QCEW and CES data contain information for only the pay period that includes the 12th day of the month. As a result, the CES and QCEW data cannot measure employment activity over the entire month, which can be especially problematic in the case of temporary distorting events during the reference period. For example, an unusually large weather event (e.g., a hurricane or snowstorm) that reduced employment during the reference period but left the rest of the month unaffected would result in a CES employment report that understates the strength of the labor market throughout the month. In the weekly ADP data we can, in principle, observe both the shock and the recovery. In any case, averaging the level of employment for the month attenuates the impact of such short-lived events.

Finally, the QCEW and ADP data are both essentially administrative data and thus arguably somewhat less prone to reporting errors and nonresponse, which are often significant problems with survey data such as the CES.

5.4   Comparing ADP-FRB to Official Data

5.4.1   Predicting Annual Benchmarks

In this section we evaluate the ability of ADP-FRB and CES to forecast the QCEW, which can plausibly be treated as "truth." We restrict attention to annual changes (March-to-March) to avoid complications related to seasonality and seam effects in the QCEW.

We follow the CES in benchmarking the level of our ADP-FRB indexes to the QCEW each year. Our procedure closely follows that of the CES: we iteratively force each March value of ADP-FRB to match the corresponding QCEW value, and we linearly wedge back the pre/post benchmark revision. The wedge reaches zero at the previous (already benchmarked) March. At

Table 5.1   **Level differences between private employment benchmarks and estimates**

	2008	2009	2010	2011	2012	2013	2014	2015	2016	2017
ADP-FRB	-173	-451	12	709	283	-230	-1,030	-853	-322	-623
CES	-137	-933	-391	229	481	340	105	-259	-151	136
CES No BD	645	-216	-55	561	972	975	874	638	737	1,066

Source: https://www.bls.gov/web/empsit/cesbmart.pdf, authors' calculations.

Notes: Units: Thousands of jobs. CES revisions are the post-benchmark (QCEW-based) March estimate less the pre-benchmark estimate. ADP-FRB revisions are calculated analogously. CES no BD are the CES benchmark revisions that would have occurred excluding net birth-death adjustment.

the time of writing of this paper, the data are benchmarked through March 2017.

Throughout the paper, we use our monthly ADP-FRB index starting in 2007. For the purpose of annual benchmarking, this means we begin annual benchmark comparisons with the 2008 benchmark year, which measures the change in private nonfarm employment from April 2007 through March 2008. In the 10 years starting from 2008, the pre-benchmark ADP-FRB estimates were closer to the eventually published population counts in four years, while the pre-benchmark CES estimates were more accurate in six years (see table 5.1). Overall, the root-mean-squared benchmark revision is 0.49 percent for the ADP-FRB data and 0.36 percent for the CES data from 2008 onward. Interestingly, the ADP-FRB estimates markedly outperformed the CES estimates during the Great Recession (2008–2010). Specifically, from 2008 to 2010 the ADP-FRB absolute revisions averaged 200,000 per year, whereas the BLS-CES absolute revisions averaged 490,000 per year. In contrast, between 2013 and 2017 the pre-benchmark ADP-FRB estimates consistently overpredicted employment growth.

An evaluation of the CES benchmark misses should also take the net birth-death model into account, as the net birth-death adjustment adds roughly 40 percent to a particular year's employment change. As a result, a comparison of the benchmark misses of ADP-FRB series to the CES data is not exactly direct, as the ADP-FRB data would likely only capture a portion of the contribution of employment births. The third row in table 5.1 presents the benchmark miss of the CES data without the inclusion of the net birth-death adjustment. That is, the "CES no BD" row reflects the growth to the level of employment solely due to the sample of businesses for which the CES data are collected.[19]

19. Even this comparison is not exactly direct since, as noted above, ADP data may capture some birth and death. Note that for our formal ADP-FRB series, we apply a "forward benchmark" procedure that is a rough version of a birth-death model for adjusting sample-based estimates to account for biases resulting from birth, death, or other issues; this approach is similar to the bias adjustment method used by BLS prior to the introduction of the birth/death model.

As can be seen in the table, the benchmark misses for CES excluding the net birth-death adjustment are substantially larger (with a root-mean-squared revision of 0.65 percent on average since 2008). Since 2008, the misses have also been almost always positive, reflecting a positive effect of establishments' births on the level of employment. The negative revisions in 2009 and 2010 point toward the autoregressive nature of the birth-death adjustment carrying inertia forward from previous years' employment changes. That is, because new business formation falls in recessionary years, the net effect of the birth-death framework overpredicts the actual birth-death contribution to employment growth, and thus CES benchmark misses were larger than benchmark misses of CES data with no birth-death adjustment.

We more formally test the performance of ADP-FRB and CES in predicting annual benchmarked employment growth by running the following regressions. The dependent variable is the annual change in employment from March of year $t-1$ to March of year t as known upon the release of the CES benchmark revision in February of year $t+1$. We consider three different independent variables, with each annual observation specified as the econometrician observed them at the time of the CES jobs report for March of year t: (1) annual employment change from March of $t-1$ to March of t as estimated by monthly CES data; (2) estimated annual employment change from March of $t-1$ to March of t as estimated by monthly CES data in which the contributions of the birth-death model have been removed; and (3) annual employment change from March of $t-1$ to March of t as observed in the ADP-FRB ("active") employment index.[20] The purpose of the exercise is to evaluate the ability of an analyst to estimate "true" (i.e., benchmarked) employment gains for the past year, observed at the time of the CES March employment report (in early April). At that time, the analyst has in hand CES data for the first release of March of year t (which includes the second release of February of year t and the third release of January of year t and all prior months). The analyst also has in hand the past year's ADP-FRB data up through the third week of March of year t. That is, we estimate the following:

$$\Delta EMP_t^B = \alpha + \beta \Delta EMP_t^{March} + \varepsilon_t,$$

where ΔEMP_t is the change in private nonfarm employment from March of year $t-1$ to March of t, the B superscript indicates the benchmark revision vintage of the series, the *March* superscript indicates the vintage of the series that is released with the March jobs report in year t (where we construct the annual estimate by summing all non-seasonally-adjusted monthly estimates through the year), and ΔEMP_t^{March} can be the March vintage of CES, CES without birth-death model contributions, or ADP-FRB ("active") employment.

---

20. We use non-seasonally-adjusted data for all variables used.

Table 5.2   **Forecasting annual employment changes**

	(1)	(2)	(3)	(4)	(5)
CES	1.126***			1.104***	
	(0.0316)			(0.142)	
CES excluding birth-death		1.154***			0.927***
		(0.0235)			(0.0847)
ADP-FRB			0.976***	0.0197	0.199**
			(0.0543)	(0.121)	(0.0818)
Constant	−163.7*	604.5***	−135.1	−163.6*	452.5***
	(76.93)	(75.29)	(172.8)	(82.61)	(79.37)
RMSE	299.2	243.3	535.9	319.7	224.2

Notes: Dependent variable is benchmarked annual change in private nonfarm employment, March to March. Years 2008–2017. *, **, and *** indicate statistical significance at the 10%, 5%, and 1% levels, respectively. Robust standard errors in parentheses.

Table 5.2 reports results from this annual forecasting exercise. While we believe there is value in reporting this formal test, given the extremely small sample size the results are suggestive at best and should be treated with caution. That said, we find that the best predictor of benchmarked employment growth, according to both adjusted R^2 and RMSE, is the CES series that excludes birth-death model contributions (column 2). That is, the birth-death model does not appear to improve estimates of annual employment growth beyond the inclusion of a simple regression constant (compare columns 1 and 2). The ADP-FRB series (column 3) has predictive content but is outperformed by both CES series. However, we do find that adding the ADP-FRB series to the CES series that excludes birth-death contributions does improve forecasts (column 5).[21]

While the regression results in table 5.2 are interesting, it is difficult to draw conclusions from such small-sample exercises. Moreover, ADP-FRB data are most valuable to policy makers if they increase our ability to understand recessions in real time; the predictive power of ADP-FRB during periods of steady, modest job growth is much less useful. We illustrate the point with a simple case study from the only recession in our ADP sample.[22]

Consider the beginning of the Great Recession. The NBER business cycle dating committee identified December 2007 as the business cycle peak, but throughout 2008 economic data sent somewhat mixed signals about the deterioration of labor market conditions. CES data releases from throughout 2008 were revised substantially with the 2009 QCEW benchmark.

The left panel of figure 5.2 reports real-time CES estimates along with

21. In unreported exercises, we find that the results are highly sensitive to the specific time period included.
22. ADP began taking snapshots on a semimonthly basis starting in May 2006.

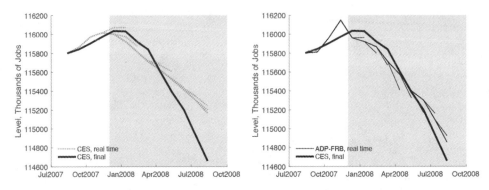

Fig. 5.2   Real-time vs. current vintage estimates

Source: ADP, CES, authors' calculations.

Note: Monthly data. NBER recession is shaded in gray. Real-time lines show each successive vintage as a connected line, with the endpoint at the first-print value for that month. All series have been normalized to match the current vintage CES estimate in August 2007.

the final (current vintage) CES estimate. The thick black line is the final CES estimate, which shows employment losses of about 1.4 million jobs by August 2008. The dotted gray lines show each real-time vintage CES estimate for 2008: each end point represents a first-print estimate, and the thicker central line represents the estimate after a few monthly revisions (but before the benchmark revision). That is, following the line back from an endpoint in month *t*, the line reflects the path of employment as it would have been known to observers in month *t* (including revisions up to that date). In the right panel, we show real-time estimates for the ADP-FRB index alongside the final CES estimate for reference.[23]

As is apparent from figure 5.2, in real time the ADP-FRB series was typically more accurate in tracking the true pace of labor market deterioration during the first year of the recession. By August, real-time CES estimates showed job losses totaling about 750,000, while ADP-FRB was at approximately 1.0 million (both numbers should be compared with the current vintage estimate of 1.4 million jobs lost). Better knowledge of this deterioration would have been useful to policy makers as the critical fourth quarter of 2008 approached. In future cyclical downturns, ADP data may again prove useful in previewing the eventual revisions to CES data.

5.4.2   Predicting Monthly Employment

While annual forecasts of the benchmark revisions are important, the CES is a monthly measure of employment that revises over several releases as both more data and benchmarks become available. In this section we evaluate the ability of the ADP-FRB employment indexes to improve fore-

---

23. All the real-time series have been normalized to equal the CES current vintage estimates in August 2008 to remove a level shift due to benchmark revisions.

Table 5.3   **Forecasting monthly employment changes**

	(1)	(2)	(3)	(4)	(5)
ADP-FRB active employment			0.29**	0.39***	0.16**
			(0.11)	(0.11)	(0.07)
Lagged private CES employment	0.82***	−0.13	−0.21	0.51***	
	(0.07)	(0.15)	(0.14)	(0.12)	
Lagged UR change	−156.73**	−45.66	−43.05	−123.09**	
	(61.56)	(52.17)	(46.84)	(58.02)	
Unemployment expectations	39.17***	30.95***	14.08	16.55	15.21
	(11.82)	(11.01)	(12.29)	(12.74)	(10.88)
Initial UI claims	−3.10***	−0.91	−0.79	−2.52***	−0.56
	(0.74)	(0.71)	(0.72)	(0.83)	(0.52)
CES employment expectations		1.15***	0.98***		
		(0.16)	(0.15)		
Private CES employment					0.97***
					(0.07)
UR change					33.12
					(36.03)
Constant	4.87	−17.77*	−24.39**	−7.48	−17.85**
	(9.36)	(10.40)	(11.58)	(10.77)	(8.98)
RMSE	99	84	80	92	58

Notes: Dependent variable is final print of CES private employment. ADP-FRB series are real-time vintage, as of five weeks after the start of the month (i.e., the week before or week of the Employment Situation release). Unemployment expectations are from the Michigan survey. CES employment expectations are eve-of-release median markets expectations. Lagged private CES employment refers to pre-Employment Situation release. Robust standard errors in parentheses. RSMEs are calculated in-sample. * $p < 0.10$, ** $p < 0.05$, *** $p < 0.01$. Estimation period: 2007m1–2018m9.

casts of CES data in real time and in conjunction with other real-time indicators. Table 5.3 reports forecasting models described in Cajner et al. (2018) using real-time ADP indexes and other variables to predict the final print of CES (i.e., after all the revisions). In particular, we estimated the following regression model:

$$(1) \quad \Delta EMP_t^{CES,final} = \alpha + \beta_1 \Delta EMP_t^{ADP\text{-}FRB,RT5} + \beta_2 \Delta EMP_{t-1}^{CES,RT} + \beta X_t + \omega_t.$$

The explanatory variables include current-month real-time (five weeks after the start of the month, which corresponds to the week before or the week of the Employment Situation release) ADP-FRB data, previous-month real-time (first print) CES private employment, as well as initial unemployment insurance claims, Michigan Survey unemployment expectations, the lagged (previous-month) unemployment rate change, and Bloomberg market CES payroll employment expectations. In addition, $\omega_t = \varepsilon_t + \rho\varepsilon_{t-1}$ is an MA(1) error term.[24]

24. The MA error term corrects for serial correlation in the errors when estimating equations of the change in employment. The results for a similar specification using OLS are qualitatively similar, despite the existence of serial correlation.

Cajner et al. (2018) discuss similar results in more detail; here we simply note that the ADP-FRB indexes for active employment make statistically significant contributions to the model and generate modest improvements to forecasting accuracy. Column (1) of table 5.3 reports the baseline forecasting model without the ADP-FRB data or market expectations. Adding market expectations in column (2) improves the forecast notably, as can be seen from the 15,000-job reduction in RMSE. In column (3) we add the ADP-FRB index and find that RMSE declines and the ADP-FRB coefficient is statistically significant; that is, the inclusion of the ADP-FRB index provides further marginal forecasting improvement beyond the inclusion of market expectations, in contrast to the Gregory and Zhu (2014) results using ADP-NER. In column (4) we report a model including ADP-FRB but omitting market expectations, which reduces RMSE by 7,000 jobs relative to the baseline. Finally, column (5) indicates that even when the first print of CES data is available, the real-time ADP-FRB data provide an additional signal about the final or "true" BLS measure of employment change.

The forecasting success of the ADP-FRB indexes should not be overstated. Cajner et al. (2018) show that the improvements in forecasting due to ADP data are statistically significant, though they are not particularly dramatic in magnitude. However, we should not expect dramatic improvement because the sampling variance of the CES estimate is large relative to the RMSE of our forecasts. For example, from 2013 until 2017 (which omits the Great Recession period of large forecast errors), the out-of-sample RMSE for predicting monthly payroll employment using the ADP-FRB data (along with other predictors) is 70,700 jobs, whereas the (sampling) standard error of the CES estimate is 65,000 (BLS 2019). To the extent that sampling error is i.i.d., the sampling error provides a lower bound on the forecasting error for CES estimates. Practically, it should be nearly impossible to reduce the RSME of a forecast below 65,000, and any forecast that achieved better performance would be forecasting sampling error, not actual changes in employment.

The fact that forecasting errors are already close to the 65,000 lower bound, even without ADP-FRB, suggests that the main value of the ADP data is not in forecasting CES. Instead, the ADP data can be used to obtain estimates that are timelier, more granular, and higher frequency. In addition, the ADP data may be combined with the CES to reduce measurement error.

On net, the ADP-FRB index adds to our understanding of annual and monthly employment changes and has some predictive power for benchmark revisions. Importantly, we find that during the Great Recession the ADP-FRB index provided a more accurate measure of employment declines. With these findings in mind, we now turn to a methodology that combines the information from both the CES and the ADP-FRB series.

5.5   State-Space Model of Employment

Payroll employment growth is one of the most reliable business cycle indicators. Each postwar recession in the United States has been characterized by a year-on-year drop in payroll employment as measured by CES and, outside of these recessionary declines, the year-on-year payroll employment growth has always been positive. Thus, if one knew the "true" underlying payroll employment growth, this would help enormously in assessing the state of the economy in real time. In this section, we present results from a state-space model to infer the "true" underlying payroll employment growth.[25]

Let ΔEMP_t^U denote the unobserved "true" change in private payroll employment (in thousands of jobs), which is assumed to follow an AR(1) process:

$$\Delta EMP_t^U = \alpha + \rho \Delta EMP_{t-1}^U + \varepsilon_t^U.$$

ΔEMP_t^U is a latent variable for which we have two observable noisy measures, that is CES (ΔEMP_t^{CES}) and ADP-FRB ($\Delta EMP_t^{ADP-FRB}$). Both are monthly changes in thousands of jobs. The observed values of CES and ADP-FRB employment gains are a function of the underlying state according to the following measurement equations:

$$\begin{bmatrix} \Delta EMP_t^{ADP-FRB} \\ \Delta EMP_t^{CES} \end{bmatrix} = \begin{bmatrix} \beta_{ADP-FRB} \\ \beta_{CES} \end{bmatrix} \Delta EMP_t^U + \begin{bmatrix} \varepsilon_t^{ADP-FRB} \\ \varepsilon_t^{CES} \end{bmatrix}.$$

Without loss of generality, we can assume that $\beta_{CES} = 1$. This assumption only normalizes the unobserved state variable to move one-for-one (on average) with CES. We make the assumption in our baseline specification but leave $\beta_{ADP-FRB}$ unrestricted.[26]

We assume that all shocks are Gaussian and that ε_t^U is orthogonal to the observation errors ($\varepsilon_t^{ADP-FRB}$, ε_t^{CES}). However, we do allow the observation errors ($\varepsilon_t^{ADP-FRB}$, ε_t^{CES}) to be contemporaneously correlated, with variance-covariance matrix Σ:

$$\Sigma = \begin{bmatrix} \sigma_{ADP-FRB}^2 & \sigma_{ADP-FRB,CES}^2 \\ \sigma_{ADP-FRB,CES}^2 & \sigma_{CES}^2 \end{bmatrix}.$$

Both the CES and ADP-FRB estimates can be regarded approximately as sample means, with the samples drawn from the same population. As such, both CES and ADP-FRB are (approximately) truth plus mean-zero

---

25. Aruoba et al. (2016) use a similar approach to provide a better measure of output.

26. The approach is in contrast to Aruoba et al. (2013), who assume that both the observation variables in their paper (GDP and GDI) have unit loadings on the unobserved state variable. While those authors' assumption is justifiable given their use of the two well-understood (and conceptually equivalent) measures of output, given the relatively untested nature of the ADP-FRB data we feel it is better to let the model choose the loading.

sampling error. This sampling error is captured by the Kalman filter in the observation noise terms.[27]

5.5.1   Characterization of the State

The estimates for the model above are collected in the first column of table 5.4. Interestingly, the estimate of $\beta_{\text{ADP-FRB}}$ is precise and not statistically different from unity. Somewhat surprisingly, the covariance of the observation errors $\sigma^2_{\text{ADP-FRB,CES}}$ is negative, though it is not statistically different from zero. Specification 2 further generalizes the model, allowing for the ADP-FRB observation equation to have its own intercept $\alpha_{\text{ADP-FRB}}$. This modification makes little difference, and the point estimates are essentially unchanged from the baseline. Specification 3 imposes a unit factor loading in the ADP-FRB equation and a diagonal Σ. Again, these alterations do not significantly change the point estimates, though the variances of the observation errors are inflated somewhat. Finally, specification 4 assumes that the unobserved state follows a random walk. All the qualitative features of specification 1 carry through to this model as well.

As discussed above, BLS produces estimates of the sampling error of CES. These estimates are based on the observed cross-sectional variation in employment growth and knowledge of the stratified sampling scheme. The estimated standard error for the change in private CES employment is about 65,000 jobs, which is remarkably close to our estimates of σ_{CES}; the square root of σ^2_{CES} reported in table 5.4 ranges between 61,000 and 69,000 jobs. In our state-space model, σ_{CES} captures all sampling and nonsampling error in the CES series, so it is reassuring that our error estimates align so closely with those of BLS.

Given that both the CES and the ADP-FRB series have been benchmarked to the QCEW, it may not be surprising that the model tends to treat them symmetrically. It is possible that most of the identification is coming from year-over-year variation, which would be dominated by the QCEW. We address this concern in specification 5, which uses an unbenchmarked ADP-FRB series. The results are remarkably similar to the other specifications, indicating that the QCEW benchmark is not, in fact, dominating our estimates.

Taken together, the results in table 5.4 suggest that is it reasonable to think of ADP-FRB and CES as two symmetric measurement series, each with approximately the same relation to the unobserved state (i.e., the same

---

27. A critical assumption for our setup is that this noise is i.i.d. over time, which would be exactly true if CES and ADP-FRB redrew their samples every month, but there is, in fact, much overlap in the units from one month to the next. Thus, any persistence in idiosyncratic establishment-level growth can propagate to persistence in the sampling error. Fortunately, the available evidence suggests that there is very low, or even negative, persistence in short-run establishment growth (Cooper, Haltiwanger, and Willis 2015), which in turn implies nearly i.i.d. sampling error and justifies the Kalman filter.

Table 5.4   Kalman filter parameter estimates

Parameter	(1)	(2)	(3)	(4)	(5)
$\rho\rho$	0.96***	0.96***	0.96***	1.00	0.96***
	(0.02)	(0.02)	(0.02)		(0.02)
$\alpha\alpha$	4.39	4.31	4.21	0.88	4.31
	(4.84)	(4.84)	(4.69)	(5.03)	(4.58)
$\beta\beta_{CCCCCC}$	1.00	1.00	1.00	1.00	1.00
$\beta\beta_{AAAAAA}$	1.03***	1.03***	1.00	1.03***	1.06***
	(0.03)	(0.03)		(0.03)	(0.04)
$\sigma\sigma^2_{UU}$	3765.41***	3786.13***	3609.16***	3698.76***	3290.51***
	(827.64)	(832.95)	(678.03)	(805.89)	(733.10)
$\sigma\sigma^2_{CCCCCC}$	3796.51***	3779.60***	3984.78***	3860.32***	4727.96***
	(721.96)	(721.17)	(642.11)	(713.98)	(853.74)
$\sigma\sigma^2_{CCCCCC,AAAAAA}$	−393.91	−388.67		−315.56	−869.32
	(573.61)	(573.63)		(563.56)	(560.55)
$\sigma\sigma^2_{AAAAAA}$	3758.90***	3773.01***	4171.35***	3852.70***	3517.13***
	(792.63)	(793.08)	(680.98)	(782.16)	(761.84)
$\alpha\alpha_{AAAAAA}$		4.10			
		(8.15)			

Notes: Maximum likelihood parameter estimates. Measurement series are the monthly change in the number of jobs according to CES and ADP-FRB, in thousands of jobs. *, **, and *** indicate statistical significance at the 10%, 5%, and 1% levels, respectively. Standard errors are in parentheses. Specification 2 allows for a nonzero intercept in the ADP-FRB observation equation. Specification 3 restricts both observation equation loadings to unity and assumes that the observation errors are uncorrelated. Specification 4 imposes a random walk on the unobserved state. Specification 5 uses an unbenchmarked version of the ADP-FRB series. Estimation period: 2006m5–2018m8.

loading and intercept) and with approximately equal degrees of uncorrelated measurement error.

With these estimates in hand, we can extract estimates of the unobserved state process. Figure 5.3 shows the smoothed (two-sided) estimate of the state (the heavy black line), along with 90 percent confidence intervals (the gray shaded area). Naturally, the state estimate is less volatile than either observation series. The standard error of the state estimate is about 34,000 jobs, about half of the CES estimated standard error of 65,000.

A simpler exercise is also instructive. Following Mankiw, Runkle, and Shapiro (1984) and Aruoba et al. (2013), we seek to approximate the state estimate using only contemporaneous observations of CES and ADP-FRB. In particular, let the estimator be:

$$\Delta EMP_t^C = \lambda \Delta EMP_t^{\text{ADP-FRB}} + (1 - \lambda)\Delta EMP_t^{\text{CES}},$$

where λ is the weighting parameter to be chosen. We minimize the distance between the state estimate and the weighted average:

$$\min_{\lambda}\left\{\sum_{t=1}^{T}\left(\widehat{\Delta EMP_t^U} - \Delta EMP_t^C\right)^2\right\},$$

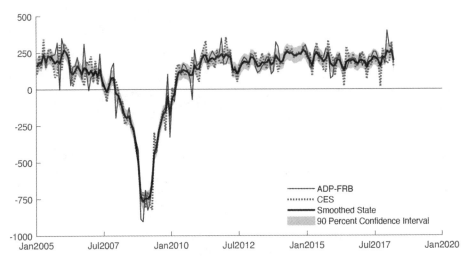

Fig. 5.3   Smoothed state estimate

Source: ADP, CES, authors' calculations.

Note: Monthly data, change of employment in thousands. Both CES and ADP-FRB are current vintage and benchmarked to QCEW. Smoothed state estimate is calculated from specification 1.

where $\widehat{\Delta EMP_t^U}$ is the state estimate from the Kalman smoother. This exercise is particularly simple under the assumptions of specification 3, where both series are just truth plus uncorrelated noise. In that case, we can plug in the estimated parameters and solve for λ as:

$$\lambda^* = \frac{\widehat{\sigma^2_{CES}}}{\widehat{\sigma^2_{ADP\text{-}FRB}} + \widehat{\sigma^2_{CES}}},$$

where $\widehat{\sigma^2_{CES}}$ is the estimated variance of the observation error in CES, and similarly for $\widehat{\sigma^2_{ADP\text{-}FRB}}$. Using the values from Specification 3 yields $\lambda^* = 0.49$, so the optimal contemporaneous estimator puts nearly equal weight on the two series.[28] Relatedly, the Kalman gains for the two series (not shown) are also very similar.

Placing roughly equal weight on CES and ADP-FRB employment gains might seem counterintuitive. However, both data sets cover roughly a similar share of private US payroll employment and thus the sampling error could plausibly be of similar magnitude. Additionally, while BLS eventually benchmarks CES payroll employment to the QCEW as discussed earlier, the month-to-month changes are largely unaffected by benchmarking due to the linear wedging-back procedure. Thus, if in a particular month the

---

28. Note that the linear combination of the ADP-FRB and CES series is nearly identical to the smoothed two-sided state estimate from the Kalman filter.

CES sample estimate of payroll employment gain is distorted because of the sampling error, it is likely that the error will survive even the subsequent revisions. As the ADP data rely on a (mostly) different sample, it should be unsurprising that taking a Kalman filter estimate of underlying gains based on both observed measures should give a more precise estimate of the current pace of employment growth, with weights being roughly similar because of the similar sample size.[29]

5.5.2   Evaluating the Estimated State's Predictive Content

The fact that the CES and ADP-FRB series receive roughly equal weight when extracting the common signal supports the idea that combining the signal from both series can contribute to our understanding of "true" employment growth. It is of interest to know how useful the state estimate is for forecasting applications, so in this section we evaluate the ability of the real-time state estimate to forecast the fully revised CES. Even though CES is only a noisy estimate of true employment growth, it is widely tracked as an indicator of the labor market, and success in forecasting it can help bolster the case that the state estimate is picking up usable signal.

For the forecasting exercises, we employ a framework similar to that found in equation (1), without the additional controls. The dependent variable is the current vintage of the CES estimate. As independent variables we include various combinations of the ADP-FRB employment estimate, the CES employment estimate, the smoothed state as estimated using both ADP-FRB and CES, and the smoothed state as estimated by CES only. This final variable is included to distinguish the time-averaging effect of the state-space model from the additional information included in ADP-FRB. If the ADP-FRB series has no information, then CES and the smoothed state based on CES alone ought to be the only relevant predictors. Importantly, all the independent variables are real-time estimates, which means that the state-space estimates include no future information.

The results of this exercise can be found in table 5.5. The first two columns include the $t + 1$ current vintage CES employment value as its dependent variable. The second column adds the CES state as an additional explanatory variable. The third column contains the average employment growth over $t + 1, t + 2, t + 3$—i.e., the average growth rate of the next three months of employment. Estimated together, the only variable that is statistically significant across all three specifications is the ADP-CES state.[30] The horserace

29. In another exercise, we replace the ADP-FRB series with the change in employment calculated from the Current Population Survey (CPS), adjusted to the CES scope of private employment. We find that the optimal weighting only puts 4 percent of the weight on the CPS series, showing that near-equal weighting scheme for CES and ADP-FRB series was not an inevitable result.

30. In unreported results, we find that estimating each equation using only one of the explanatory variables indicates that each variable is independently significant. In addition, the horserace results are qualitatively similar when using first-print CES values as the dependent variable.

Table 5.5   Forecasting monthly employment changes using state-space estimates

	CES Emp. (1)	CES Emp. (2)	3-month av. CES Emp. (3)
ADP-CES Emp. State	1.43***	1.50***	1.69***
	(0.49)	(0.55)	(0.44)
ADP-FRB Emp.	−0.18	−0.19	−0.30**
	(0.15)	(0.16)	(0.15)
CES Emp.	−0.18	−0.11	−0.41
	(0.34)	(0.55)	(0.31)
CES Emp. State		−0.12	−0.04
		(0.68)	(0.42)
Constant	−28.14	−28.52	−17.05
	(19.43)	(18.78)	(20.35)

Notes: The dependent variable in columns 1 and 2 is the fully revised change in CES private employment at time $tt + 1$; in column 3 the dependent variable is the average of the fully revised change in CES private employment for $tt + 1$, $tt + 2$ and $tt + 3$. ADP-FRB series are real-time vintage, as of five weeks after the start of the month. CES series appearing as independent variable or in state-space estimates are real-time vintage. Robust standard errors in parentheses. * $p < 0.10$, ** $p < 0.05$, *** $p < 0.01$. Estimation period: 2007m1–2018m9.

results indicate that when comparing employment-based indicators of future CES readings of employment gains, the combination of the ADP-FRB series and the past CES gains provides the most information about future employment.

5.6   Conclusion

In this paper we asked whether additional information on payroll employment could improve the accuracy of employment estimates. The answer is yes. At the monthly frequency, this question is not straightforward, as benchmarking levels *annually* implies there is no "true" measure of *monthly* employment gains.[31] With this in mind, the combination of the ADP-FRB and CES employment series should provide a more accurate representation of the actual changes in employment than the CES alone, as the sample size has increased substantially. Indeed, we find that the monthly ADP-FRB estimates outperformed CES in tracking the rapid employment decline during the Great Recession and can help predict revisions to the first prints of the CES data. In addition, the pooled estimate performs better than either ADP-FRB or the CES data in forecasting near-term employment growth. At the annual frequency, the results are somewhat less remarkable. The offi-

31. As discussed above, the QCEW is more comprehensive than either CES or ADP-FRB and serves as the annual benchmark for CES. However, the QCEW has measurement error and is not used as a time series by BLS. See Groen (2012), Krueger and Fortson (2003), and Hiles (2016).

cial CES data best predict benchmark revisions, though the sample is small. That said, the ADP-FRB data were closer to the QCEW levels in four out of the past 10 years.

Could BLS make use of data from payroll processors to supplement the CES? Our understanding is that payroll processors almost never report any client firm employment numbers to BLS. The only exceptions are isolated cases where the client firm explicitly directs payroll processors to submit their information for the CES survey. Importantly, we believe the CES sample and the ADP sample are collected largely independently. To be sure, an environment in which BLS works directly with payroll processors to process real-time labor aggregates is likely a way off.

A first step in this direction would be to link a subset of the ADP microdata to BLS databases on secure Census or BLS computer systems. If such an undertaking were possible, the project would allow for much better weighting and evaluation of the ADP sample, improving the quality of any estimates. In particular, it would be possible to evaluate what types of sample selection bias are present in the ADP sample by comparing ADP businesses to control groups or comparing businesses before and after enrollment with ADP. In addition, we could better evaluate the differences between paid employment and active employment if we had BLS employment measures available. Finally, linking would also provide a check on BLS data, which can be subject to misreporting and other issues. Crosschecking employment counts, industry codes, and multiunit status would be informative for all parties.

The results in this paper lay the foundation for future work employing private payroll microdata. We plan on testing the estimated state-space results against other measures of employment, including state- and national-level measures of employment from the QCEW. We also plan on further exploring the geographic and industry detail to improve employment estimates. Importantly, there is additional information in the measure of ADP paid employment and at the weekly frequency that we have not fully leveraged in our current research.

References

Aruoba, S. Borağan, Francis X. Diebold, Jeremy Nalewaik, Frank Schorfheide, and Dongho Song. 2013. "Improving U.S. GDP Measurement: A Forecast Combination Perspective." In *Recent Advances and Future Directions in Causality, Prediction, and Specification Analysis: Essays in Honor of Halbert L. White Jr.*, edited by Xiaohong Chen and Norman R. Swanson, 1–25. New York: Springer.
———. 2016. "Improving GDP Measurement: A Measurement-Error Perspective." *Journal of Econometrics* 191 (2): 384–97.
Bureau of Labor Statistics. 2019. "Technical Notes for the Current Employment Sta-

tistics Survey." U.S. Bureau of Labor Statistics. https://www.bls.gov/web/empsit /cestn.htm.

Cajner, Tomaz, Leland Crane, Ryan A. Decker, Adrian Hamins-Puertolas, Christopher Kurz, and Tyler Radler. 2018. "Using Payroll Processor Microdata to Measure Aggregate Labor Market Activity." FEDS Working Paper 2018-005, Board of Governors of the Federal Reserve System, Washington, DC.

Cho, David. 2018. "The Labor Market Effects of Demand Shocks: Firm-Level Evidence from the Recovery Act." Unpublished paper. https://scholar.princeton.edu /sites/default/files/davidcho/files/jmp-david-cho.pdf.

Cooper, Russell, John Haltiwanger, and Jonathan L. Willis. 2015. "Dynamics of Labor Demand: Evidence from Plant-Level Observations and Aggregate Implications." *Research in Economics* 69 (1): 37–50.

Decker, Ryan, John Haltiwanger, Ron Jarmin, and Javier Miranda. 2014. "The Role of Entrepreneurship in US Job Creation and Economic Dynamism." *Journal of Economic Perspectives* 28 (3): 3–24.

Gregory, Allan W., and Hui Zhu. 2014. "Testing the Value of Lead Information in Forecasting Monthly Changes in Employment from the Bureau of Labor Statistics." *Applied Financial Economics* 24 (7): 505–14.

Grigsby, John, Erik Hurst, and Ahu Yildirmaz. 2021. "Aggregate Nominal Wage Adjustments: New Evidence from Administrative Payroll Data." *American Economic Review* 111(2): 428–71.

Groen, Jeffrey. 2012. "Sources of Error in Survey and Administrative Data: The Importance of Reporting Procedures." *Journal of Official Statistics* 28:173–98.

Haltiwanger, John, Ron S. Jarmin, and Javier Miranda. 2013. "Who Creates Jobs? Small versus Large versus Young." *Review of Economics and Statistics* 95 (2): 347–61.

Hatzius, Jan, Zach Pandl, Alex Phillips, David Mericle, Elad Pashtan, Dann Struyven, Karen Reichgott, and Avisha Thakkar. 2016. "The ADP Employment Report: Pay Attention to Large Surprises." *Goldman Sachs Economics Research US Daily*, September 30.

Hiles, David. 2016. "QCEW Update: Acceleration Test and NAICS 2017." Presentation at AUBER Conference, Fayetteville, AR, October 24, 2016. https://slideplayer .com/slide/11685689/.

Kratzke, Diem-Tran. 2013. "Nonresponse Bias Analysis of Average Weekly Earnings in the Current Employment Statistics Survey." US Bureau of Labor Statistics. https://www.bls.gov/osmr/research-papers/2013/st130160.htm.

Krueger, Alan B., and Kenneth N. Fortson. 2003. "Do Markets Respond More to More Reliable Labor Market Data? A Test of Market Rationality." *Journal of the European Economic Association* 1 (4): 931–57.

Mankiw, N. Gregory, David E. Runkle, and Matthew D. Shapiro. 1984. "Are Preliminary Announcements of the Money Stock Rational Forecasts?" *Journal of Monetary Economics* 14 (1): 15–27.

Ozimek, Adam, Dante DeAntonio, and Mark Zandi. 2017. "Aging and the Productivity Puzzle." Moody's Analytics: Economic View Real Time. https://www.economy.com/economicview/analysis/300374/Aging-and-the-Productivity-Puzzle.

Phillips, Keith R., and Christopher Slijk. 2015. "ADP Payroll Processing Data Can Provide Early Look at Texas Job Growth." *Southwest Economy* (Second Quarter): 10–13. https://dallasfed.frswebservices.org/~/media/documents/research/ swe/2015/swe1502d.pdf.

II

Uses of Big Data for Classification

6

Transforming Naturally Occurring Text Data into Economic Statistics
The Case of Online Job Vacancy Postings

Arthur Turrell, Bradley Speigner, Jyldyz Djumalieva, David Copple, and James Thurgood

6.1 Introduction

This paper presents an example of converting naturally occurring[1] data into economic statistics for use in research and analysis. The raw data consist of millions of individual job advertisements as posted online by firms and recruitment agencies on the website Reed.co.uk in the United Kingdom. The objective is to process, clean, reweight, and use these data as a measure of job vacancies by occupation and region over time, and according to existing official statistical classifications. The methods developed for this purpose could be applied to other naturally occurring datasets. The issues

Arthur Turrell is a research economist at the Bank of England.
Bradley Speigner is a senior manager at the Bank of England.
Jyldyz Djumalieva is the Head of Open Jobs Data at Nesta.
David Copple is Policy Manager of Digital Currencies at the Bank of England.
James Thurgood is a data engineer at the Royal Bank of Scotland.
The views in this work are those of the authors and do not represent the views of the Bank of England or its policy committees. This work was carried out while all the authors were employed by the Bank of England. We are grateful to Katharine Abraham, James Barker, David Bholat, Emmet Cassidy, Matthew Corder, Daniel Durling, Rodrigo Guimarães, Frances Hill, Tomas Key, Graham Logan, Michaela Morris, Michael Osbourne, Kate Reinold, Paul Robinson, Ayşegül Şahin, Ben Sole, Vincent Sterk, anonymous reviewers, and conference and seminar participants at the European Economic Association meeting, the American Economic Association meeting, the Royal Statistical Society meeting, the NBER Conference on Big Data in the 21st Century, the Federal Reserve Board of Governors, the ONS, and the University of Oxford for their comments. We would especially like to thank William Abel and David Bradnum for their help throughout the project. For acknowledgments, sources of research support, and disclosure of the authors' material financial relationships, if any, please see https://www.nber.org/books-and-chapters/big-data-21st-century-economic-statistics/transforming-naturally-occurring-text-data-economic-statistics-case-online-job-vacancy-postings.

1. As opposed to data collected for the express purpose of constructing statistics, these data are a side-product of other economic activity.

of bias that we explore apply to most vacancy data derived from online job advertisements. There have been no UK official statistics on vacancies by region and occupation since the JobCentre Plus data were discontinued and we show how these data can fill an important gap in our understanding of labor market demand.

One of the major benefits of using individual online job postings is that they are a direct measure of the economic activity associated with trying to hire workers. Another is the sheer volume they offer—of the order of 10^5 individual vacancies at any point in time for the UK. These large numbers allow for very granular analysis.

As well as demonstrating the creation of new economic statistics on vacancies, we make a major contribution in the method we use to transform the text of job ads into time series data labeled by official classifications (here the UK Office for National Statistics', or ONS's, Standard Occupational Classification, or SOC, codes). Our algorithm draws on methods from computer science and natural language processing and makes use of both the job title and job description.[2] It could be adapted and applied to the SOC classifications of other countries or regions, or to other types of text and classifications. It could also be used by employers to check what occupation their job advertisements fall under, to better target their ads or adjust compensation.

The newly created vacancy time series, split by occupation, are compared to existing data on UK job vacancies, namely the ONS Vacancy Survey and JobCentre Plus data. We consider the likely biases of the Reed-derived vacancy time series. To demonstrate the utility of processing the text of these data we use them to estimate Beveridge curves by occupation and to calculate the rate of mismatch unemployment (by occupation) for the UK, using the mismatch framework of Şahin et al. (2014).

The structure of the paper is as follows: section 6.2 sets out previous literature relevant to vacancy statistics, section 6.3 describes the online job vacancies data in the context of other data on vacancies, section 6.4 describes the algorithm we developed to assign vacancies to official statistical classifications, section 6.5 describes the processed data, section 6.6 explores some uses of these data in economic analysis, and section 6.7 concludes.

6.2 Literature

Vacancy data have long been collected via surveys; Abraham (1983) reviews a number of regional surveys that began this in the 1960s to 1980s, before national survey data on vacancies began to be widely collected. In the UK and US, there are now designated national statistics measuring job vacancies using surveys: the ONS Vacancy Survey and the JOLTS (Job Openings and Labor Turnover Survey), respectively.

2. Computer code available at http://github.com/aeturrell/occupationcoder.

The ONS Vacancy Survey was introduced in 2001 and each month surveys around 6,000 firms on their total number of open vacancies (Machin 2003)—a measure of the stock of vacancies. The firm-level data collection allows for cross-sectional data by both firm size and industry. Data are collected on the Friday between the second and eighth of each month and are thereafter available at monthly frequency with a 40-day lag. No breakdown of vacancies by region or occupation is available. These dimensions are especially difficult for survey data to collect because firms may not be familiar with occupational codes and asking them to submit, instead of a single number, up to 368 numbers reflecting each of the 4-digit UK occupational codes would be a significant change in the administrative burden imposed by the survey. Similarly, regional data are difficult to collect via this method as it is more cost effective and potentially more accurate to contact only a firm's head office for vacancy numbers. Due to the sample being drawn from a business register, new firms are underrepresented, though this bias is only estimated to create errors of ±20,000 for vacancy levels in the hundreds of thousands. Although the scale and quality of vacancy data collection have changed substantially since the 1960s, the methodology has not. Collecting survey data is expensive, has a relatively long lag, and is ill-suited to providing occupational or regional information.

Administrative data are an alternative source of information on job vacancies that is acknowledged to be "cheap and relatively easy to produce" (Bentley 2005). These are most often vacancies notified to government employment service offices. In the UK, the main source of these data are JobCentre Plus (JCP) vacancies. They were discontinued in 2012 and underwent significant changes in 2006 so that the longest recent usable continuous time series runs from July 2006 to November 2012. The JCP had aggregate coverage of around a third of UK vacancies prior to 2003 (Machin 2003) but with large variation between regions, between sectors, and over time depending on the point in the business cycle and the policies of JCP offices. Burgess and Profit (2001) note that these vacancies have a disproportionate share of low-skilled, manual jobs and are more likely to be matched to the long-term unemployed, while Patterson et al. (2016), looking at more recent data than Machin (2003), find that they over-represent some sectors. Problems with JCP data included that a significant percentage of the entire vacancy stock was not always updated when filled or withdrawn by employers. This had the effect of biasing the stock upward by numbers as high as the multiple tens of thousands out of vacancies in the few hundreds of thousands. These data have been used in several other studies; namely Coles and Smith (1996), Smith (2012), and Manning and Petrongolo (2017). These data were not included in the ONS's labor market statistics releases between 2005 and their discontinuation because of concerns over their appropriateness as a labor market indicator (Bentley 2005). The number of ways for firms to communicate to JCP offices increased at that time, leading to structural breaks in the series, and the reliance on firms to notify JCP offices when vacancies were filled or withdrawn made the outflow series, and therefore the stock, vulnerable to bias. Indeed, the onus was on JCP offices to follow up with employers and, as this did not happen consistently or for every position, a large amount of what has been described as "vacancy deadwood" built up.

We use job advertisements that have been generated as a result of firms attempting to hire workers, but from a privately run website, Reed.co.uk, rather than from a government-run employment office. This will have implications for the nature of the jobs advertised. The ads are run at a cost to the posting party so that concerns about an ever-growing stock of vacancies that have, in reality, been filled or withdrawn do not apply. Other job advertisement website data have been used for the analysis of vacancy statistics, including Deming and Kahn (2017) with Burning Glass data, Marinescu (2017) using data from CareerBuilder.com, and Mamertino and Sinclair (2016) using data from Indeed.com. As explained by Cajner and Ratner (2016), there have been significant discrepancies between the stock of vacancies implied by two US series, the JOLTS and the Conference Board Help Wanted Online, which may be caused by changes in the price charged to employers to post online job vacancies.

Previous work has found that online job vacancy postings can give a good indication of the trends in aggregate vacancies (Hershbein and Kahn 2018). There has been a secular trend increase in the number of vacancies that are posted online, as evidenced by the replacement in the US of the Help Wanted Index of print advertisements with the Help Wanted Online Series. Although they may not offer full coverage, online vacancy statistics can powerfully complement official statistics on vacancies, which tend to be based on surveys of firms.

Our paper adds to a growing literature on the analysis of text in job vacancies. Marinescu and Wolthoff (2016) show that job titles explain more of the wage variance in US job vacancies in 2011 than SOC codes alone do. Deming and Kahn (2017) use job vacancy descriptions that have been processed into keywords to define general skills that have explanatory power for both pay and firm performance beyond the usual labor market classifications. Azar et al. (2018) leverage online job vacancies, with job title text cleaned and standardized, to estimate the labor market concentration according to the Herfindahl-Hirchman index. And Hershbein and Kahn (2018) ask whether the within-occupation skills demanded in job vacancy text accelerate during recessions.

We show how online job advertisement text can be used to generate occupational labels. Until recently, methods that existed to label vacancy text with official classifications were proprietary, limited in the number of searches, or did not make use of the job description field. While writing up our results we became aware of similar approaches being developed for the US (Atalay et al. 2017), Germany (Gweon et al. 2017) and for the International Labour Organisation occupational classification (Boselli et al. 2017, 2018).

For demonstrating the usefulness of the data, we use the search and matching theory of the labor market (Mortensen and Pissarides 1994) in which job vacancies represent the demand for labor. Labor market tightness, $\theta = V/U$, where V is the stock of job vacancies and U is the unemployment level, is an important parameter in this framework. At the centre of theories of mismatch is the matching function $h(U, V)$ that matches vacancies and unemployed workers to give the number of new jobs per unit time as described in Petrongolo and Pissarides (2001). In the applications part of the paper, we use econometric estimates of the Reed data that are published in full in Turrell et al. (2018).

6.3   Data

Our raw data are approximately 15,242,000 individual jobs posted at daily frequency from January 2008 to December 2016 on Reed.co.uk, a job advertisement website. The site facilitates matching between firms and jobseekers. Firms who wish to hire workers, or recruitment agencies acting on their behalf, pay Reed to take out advertisements on the site. As of February 2019, the cost of a single job ad to be posted any time in the next 12 months and remain live for 6 weeks is £150 + tax.[3] Reed has a direct business relationship with the firm or recruitment agency that posts the advertisement.

The fields in the raw data that are typically available include a job posted date, an offered nominal wage, a sectoral classification (similar to the ONS sectoral section classification), the latitude and longitude of the job, a job title, and a job description. Our data are unusual compared to the recent literature in that they come from a job advertisement and employee recruitment firm (a recruiter) rather than from an aggregator or a survey. There are two different kinds of websites that post job advertisements. Aggregators use so-called "spiders" to crawl the internet looking at webpages, such as firm recruitment sites that host job vacancies, and then record those job vacancies.[4] In contrast, firms post vacancies directly with recruiters. Recruiters may have access to private information about the job vacancy that an aggregator would not. In our case, an example of such information is the offered salary field. Additionally, the likelihood of duplicates is lower in a recruitment firm dataset because jobs are only added to the site as the result of direct contact with a firm. Aggregators are more likely to pick up the same job multiple times from different ad sites though they expend considerable effort in removing duplicate listings.

3. Unfortunately, we do not have a time series of advertisement posting costs.
4. Examples of research using datasets from aggregators include Deming and Kahn (2017) (Burning Glass), Marinescu (2017) (CareerBuilder.com), and Mamertino and Sinclair (2016) (Indeed.com).

A feature of all datasets collected online is that they tend to contain super-fluous information, at least relative to survey data and, similarly to survey data, may have entries that are incomplete or erroneous. However, perhaps because of the cost of posting, there are very few incomplete entries in the Reed data. The most frequently encountered erroneous information is in the form of offered wages (not always shown to jobseekers) that appear too low (not compliant with the minimum wage law) or unrealistically high. We do not use the wage data for the creation of occupational labels.

The sectoral field of each vacancy has strong similarities to ONS Standard Industrial Classification (SIC) sections, and we constructed a manual mapping from the Reed sectors to the SIC sections. The data contain fields for latitude and longitude, which are used to map each vacancy into regions given by Nomenclature of Territorial Units for Statistics (NUTS) codes. As the data are for the UK, the NUTS characters are counted only after the "UK" designation. An example 3-character NUTS code would be "UKF13," where the "F1" designates Derbyshire and Nottinghamshire (UK counties), and "F13" South and West Derbyshire.

We also use a number of other datasets from the ONS, including the *Labour Force Survey* (LFS) (Office for National Statistics 2017), the afore-mentioned *Vacancy Survey*, and sectoral productivity measures.

6.3.1   The Stock of Vacancies and Its Potential Bias

We consider how to estimate a stock of vacancies from the Reed job advertisements and what biases might affect this estimate. We want to turn the Reed job advertisements into a measure of job vacancies that are as close to the US JOLTS (Job Openings and Labor Turnover Survey) definition of vacancies as possible. JOLTS defines job vacancies as all positions that are open (not filled) on the last business day of the month. A job is vacant only if it meets all the following conditions:

1. A specific position exists and there is work available for that position. The position can be full-time or part-time, and it can be permanent, short-term, or seasonal; and

2. The job could start within 30 days, whether or not the establishment finds a suitable candidate during that time; and

3. There is active recruiting for workers from outside the establishment location that has the opening.

The ONS Vacancy Survey uses a similar definition but without the stipulation that the job could start within 30 days (Machin 2003). Both definitions are of job vacancies as a stock—that is all jobs that are open at a particular time, rather than newly opened within a particular time window.

The Reed job advertisements constitute a flow of new vacancies, arriving in daily time periods. In order to satisfy the JOLTS definition, we need to transform this flow of vacancies into a stock and ensure that all three conditions are met. We can be fairly certain that the first JOLTS condition is satisfied. As posting a vacancy incurs a cost, it seems unlikely that firms or recruitment agencies would post vacancies for which there is not an available position, at least on any large scale.

We cannot be sure about Reed advertisements satisfying the second JOLTS condition but it seems reasonable to assume that, once filled, most positions could start within 30 days because the advertisements do not have a start date field. This suggests an implicit start date of as soon as the position is filled. Typically, for job-to-job flows, the limiting factor in a new firm-worker match is the workers' notice period.

The third JOLTS condition is satisfied by the posting of the vacancy on a third-party website. It seems very likely that most job advertisements posted on Reed will satisfy these three conditions.

Now we must consider how to transform the job advertisements, which are a flow in units of ads per day, into a stock of vacancies. As entries are removed from the site after being live for six weeks, the stock is simply the number of vacancies that were posted in the last six weeks or less. More explicitly, in discrete time, let the flow of advertisements be $\dot{V}_d$ with d referring to a day. To retrieve stocks, the data are transformed as follows (where the time index refers to monthly frequency):

$$(1) \qquad V_m = V_{m-1} + \sum_{d \in m} (\dot{V}_d - \dot{V}_{d-6\times7}).$$

Note that this implicitly assumes that job advertisements are filled or withdrawn by the employer after six weeks. There is no information on whether positions are filled within the Reed job advertisement data. This is typical of online vacancy data that are not matched with data on recruitment and most survey data: we cannot properly distinguish between ad outflows (that is, job advertisements that are removed from the site) that are due to employers who have decided to stop trying to recruit and those that are due to a position being filled. In the Reed case, when an ad is not reposted after six weeks, it could be for either of these two reasons. This is an outflow-type identification problem. However, because we will later work with data at the occupational level that is matched to survey data on hires also at the occupational level, we will be able to distinguish between the two cases.

Similarly, if an advertisement is reposted it could be because either the position was not filled or the firm has decided to hire additional employees. However, in this case and with all else equal, we would see whether the number of vacancies had increased or not. As with the outflow identification, it will not matter at the occupational level for which we have data on hires from surveys.

At the occupational level, then, we need not be concerned that econometric estimates of the effect of vacancies on hires estimated on Reed data will be biased by the inability to distinguish between types of outflow or inflow.

However, the JOLTS definition requires jobs to be unfilled to be a vacancy, as does the definition used in many other analyses of vacancies (Abraham 1983), which describe them as being current, unfilled job openings that are immediately available for occupancy by workers outside a firm and for which a firm is actively seeking such workers (for full-time, part-time, permanent, temporary, seasonal, and short-term work). Therefore, our assumption, enforced by the data, that the stock of vacancies is built up from equation (1) could lead to some biases in this measure of the stock.

Let us consider these stock-flow biases. The first is that posted job ads are filled before the six weeks are up, which would bias the vacancy stock derived from the Reed data upward. This is an aggregate outflow bias. The extent of this bias overall depends on the average duration of a vacancy, which is known to vary across the business cycle (Abraham 1983, 1987). The discontinued DHI-DFH Mean Vacancy Duration Measure[5] for the USA fell markedly during recessions, to two to three weeks, and increased to over four weeks in mid-2018 (FRED 2019). If we were to assume that vacancies were to endure for the two to four weeks implied by the US data, it would mean that our aggregate vacancy stock is biased upward. Evidence from one US firm that posts online job vacancies that require technical skills (Davis and Samaniego de la Parra 2017) implies much shorter timescales; the mean post duration is nine days and most of the attention paid by job seekers to ads occurs within the first 96 hours of an advertisement going live. However, as we will shortly adjust the mean level of vacancies in the Reed data to match the ONS's measure of overall vacancies, this aggregate upward bias will be corrected.

Vacancy durations also vary by occupation (Abraham 1983, 1987), and this poses more of a problem because it means that the stock of vacancies will be differentially biased by occupation. This is a differential outflow bias. Those occupations with short vacancy durations will have vacancy stocks that are biased upward. Despite its noted issues, we can look at the vacancy duration of the JobCentre Plus data to get an estimate of durations by occupation for the UK. The 2006 to 2012 median vacancy duration by 1-digit SOC code is shown in figure 6.1. The mean of medians is 5.5 ± 1.0 weeks, suggesting that the cross-occupational differences are relatively small for the UK and that a six-week estimate for vacancy duration may not be inappropriate.

We will shortly reweight the Reed data using the fact that sectoral counts are available in both the ONS's measures of vacancies and the Reed data. By doing so, we will eliminate bias that exists across sectors. This will reduce

5. This is a series that quantifies the average number of working days taken to fill vacant job positions. It had been provided by a private firm, Delivering Hire Insights (DHI), before its discontinuation. It is based on the work of Davis, Faberman, and Haltiwanger (DFH) (Davis, Faberman, and Haltiwanger 2013).

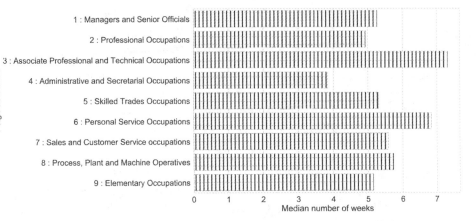

Fig. 6.1   Median JobCentre Plus vacancy durations by 1-digit SOC code based on data from 2006 to 2012

Source: National Online Manpower Information System (NOMIS).

some of the biases by occupation but, unfortunately, these biases cannot be eliminated entirely because there is no one-for-one relationship between occupation and sector. This is likely to be a problem for aggregator job advertisement sites too; if their data ultimately come from sites like Reed, who have a fixed period when a job is live, they similarly do not know if and when the vacancy was filled within that period. We also cannot exclude the possibility that some firms' hiring strategies are adapted to the method by which they post the vacancy. If they have paid for an advertisement with a duration of six weeks, they may decide to only review applications to select a preferred match once that time has expired. This strategy is typical of graduate schemes, for example.

In steady state, the aggregate vacancy inflow and the aggregate job separation rate should be approximately equal. Without any reallocation across occupations, the same should be true at the disaggregate level. In principle, these could be used as sense checks on the biases in the stocks. However, our data do not cover multiple complete business cycles and are dominated by a severe downturn followed by a weak recovery. We should therefore not necessarily expect these to match. Using the *Labour Force Survey*, we computed the aggregate combined employment to unemployment, job to job, and employment to out-of-the-workforce separation flow and found that it was, on average, 1.3 times higher than the reweighted[6] vacancy inflow. Given this disparity even in the case where the (aggregate) stock matches

6. This reweighting will be applied in the next section and ensures that the aggregate Reed vacancy stock matches the ONS Vacancy Survey.

the ONS's measure, it seems likely that the vacancy flows and job separations at the disaggregate level would be an imperfect indicator of the level of vacancy stocks.

Unfortunately, the differential outflow bias by occupation could also create bias in estimates of matching efficiency. Upward biases in the stocks of some occupations will bias the matching efficiency of those occupations downward. We consider which occupations may be affected by this: the DHI-DFH Mean Vacancy Duration Measure (FRED 2019) for the US offers a sectoral split which shows that more highly skilled vacancies, for example in financial services and business and professional services, have longer vacancy durations on average than leisure and hospitality and construction. This makes intuitive sense in the context of specialization. So, an important caveat of our results is that heterogeneous vacancy durations are likely to bias the matching efficiency of low-skill occupations downward. The reweighting we apply in the next section will reduce, but not eliminate, this bias.

6.3.2   Coverage and Representativeness Biases

We now examine bias with respect to coverage and representativeness for the Reed vacancies, as well as describing the steps we take to reduce these biases.

These two types of bias exist at the aggregate level. Vacancies posted online are unlikely to cover 100 percent of vacancies advertised in the economy, and the Reed stock of vacancies, obtained from equation (1), has aggregate coverage of around 40 percent relative to the ONS Vacancy Survey. In addition, the composition of the vacancies that are posted online is likely to be quite different from reality. These problems of bias and coverage exist for all job vacancy data based on job advertisements, including the widely used JobCentre Plus data, and have long existed in the empirical literature on job vacancies. Prior to the advent of national vacancy statistics, most previous empirical work was based on the use of vacancies advertised at job centers, which have the same problems though for different reasons.

Additionally, vacancies as posted online do not have some of the problems that data collected by surveys have. Surveys are likely to have non- or incomplete-response bias, overestimation of the vacancies posted by large firms, underestimation of vacancies from recently created firms and, when comparing vacancies and unemployment, could be biased by frequency mismatch between surveys (Abraham 1983). Nonresponse bias is not relevant for job advertisements posted online; differentials due to firm size may exist but are more likely to be caused by the ability to advertise positions (rather than size itself), and as postings are typically at daily frequency there can be no large role for frequency mismatch. The cost of posting advertisements online with a recruiter means that the problem of phantom vacancies, for which no job ever existed, is likely to be small.

There are many factors that affect the coverage of online job vacancies.

Technological diffusion is one; given that no vacancies were posted on the World Wide Web before 1990, and that newspaper circulations have fallen substantially since the 1980s, there has been a drift in job vacancies from ads in newspapers to ads placed online. Over time, the coverage of online vacancies has improved. Barnichon (2010) shows that this drift in coverage closely follows the S-shape typical of technological diffusion for the US, and that it also closely follows the similarly S-shaped fraction of internet users in that country. At the start of the period we study, 78 percent of the UK population were internet users, suggesting that the equivalent transition in the UK was already well under way by 2008.[7] Another reason why there are coverage differences for online ads posted with a recruiter versus surveys is the cost of posting vacancies online. Cajner and Ratner (2016) find that changes in the cost of posting vacancies online had a significant influence on the aggregate stock of vacancies as represented by online sources versus other sources. The (time-dependent) reweighting we will use will correct for both of these biases.[8]

The extent to which the composition of job advertisements posted online is biased relative to the composition of all vacancies in the economy is a more difficult issue to resolve. As there is a nontrivial cost to posting a job advertisement online, at least with a recruiter, those that are posted will need to have an expected return for the firm greater than that cost. Additionally, some job vacancies may get a better response if posted via other media (e.g., newspaper or shop window). There may be other pressures that determine whether vacancies appear online or not; for instance, the quality of alternative channels for matching between jobseekers and firms.

Because of being online, having a posting cost, and other factors, it is likely that Reed job advertisements are biased to overrepresent middle- and higher-skilled vacancies. This is a differential representativeness bias. The bias may not matter much for the uses demonstrated here, as long as it is reasonably fixed over time. Bias that is changing over time is the most detrimental to any analysis because (cross-section) fixed effects cannot absorb the bias effect. A fixed bias would imply that the stock of vacancies expressed as a ratio relative to the Vacancy Survey stock was also fixed over time. In figure 6.2, we show the percentage deviations of both the JobCentre Plus and Reed stocks of vacancies from their mean ratio relative to the Vacancy Survey stock of vacancies. The figure shows that neither is fixed over time and both likely suffer from a changing level of bias. On the basis of the simple measure shown in figure 6.2, bias does not seem to be more of a problem for the Reed data than for the widely used JobCentre Plus vacancy data but it nonetheless does exist.

---

7. World Bank series: Individuals using the Internet (% of population) International Telecommunication Union, World Telecommunication/ICT Development Report and database.
8. The cost of posting vacancies with Reed is not differentiated by sector or occupation.

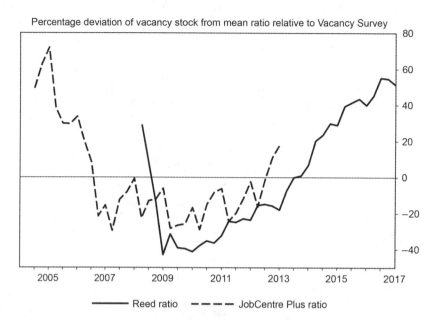

Percentage deviation of vacancy stock from mean ratio relative to Vacancy Survey

———— Reed ratio   — — — — JobCentre Plus ratio

Fig. 6.2   The percentage deviations of both the JobCentre Plus and Reed stocks of vacancies from their mean ratio relative to the Vacancy Survey stock of vacancies
Source: Reed, ONS, National Online Manpower Information System (NOMIS).

We can examine how much this bias is a problem at a more disaggregated level by taking advantage of the appearance of sectoral fields in both the Vacancy Survey and the Reed data. The mean annual ratios of the Reed to the Vacancy Survey stock of vacancies by sector are shown in figure 6.3. The annual coverage ratios of the sectoral vacancy counts of the Reed data relative to the Vacancy Survey data are closer to unity for some sectors than for others; for example, professional, scientific, and technical activities have a higher average coverage ratio than human health and social work activities. Such biases inevitably affect the stock of vacancies in the (unweighted) Reed data. For professional and scientific activities, information and communication, and administration, the Reed data are of comparable magnitude to the ONS estimates of vacancies. This could be because those sectors are well represented by the Reed data, but there could also be measurement differences that mean that the composition is different. Around 64 percent of vacancies have an annual ratio relative to the ONS survey with a median of greater than 20 percent. All are below unity, as would be expected if they were representative of the ONS equivalent sectoral counts.[9] The largest differences in magnitude between vacancies by sector in the Reed data and

9. If the Vacancy Survey is taken to be a true benchmark, values above unity would mean that there was duplication or misclassification in the Reed data.

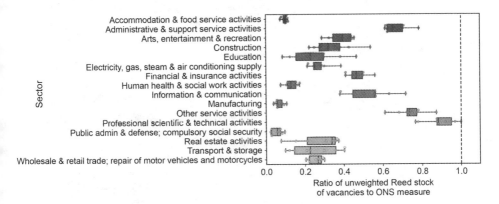

Fig. 6.3   Mean annual ratios of the Reed to Vacancy Survey stock of vacancies by sector give an indication of where the Reed data have higher coverage (first moment close to unity) and where the bias remains relatively static over time (small second moment)

Source: Reed, ONS.

the ONS data are for public administration and manufacturing. Together, these account for around 9 percent of vacancies in the last quarter of 2016 according to the Vacancy Survey.

As noted, fixed biases can be absorbed by cross-section fixed effects. This does mean that there is potential for matching efficiencies calculated from these data to be biased. The Reed stock of vacancies is likely to be biased downward for lower-skill occupations, making the matching efficiencies of these occupations biased upward. This contrasts with the differential out-flow bias noted earlier, which biases the same occupations' matching efficiencies downward. We do not know which dominates.

Some of these representativeness biases may be overcome or mitigated by reweighting the Reed stocks of vacancies by sector. We do this by using the monthly sectoral (Standard Industrial Classification) disaggregation of the Vacancy Survey and the fact that the Reed monthly stock of vacancies also has a sectoral breakdown. Their ratios are used as weights. Reweighting can almost completely eliminate any aggregate vacancy stock bias. It will reduce the online representativeness bias and the differential occupational representativeness bias only to the extent that sectoral differences are correlated with these other compositional differences. Both online and occupational representativeness are likely to be strongly correlated with skill level, and skill level and sector are also strongly correlated. So, we expect that reweighting by sector has a substantial effect on these two biases and the differential outflow bias of section 6.3.1 but cannot be sure of the quantitative extent of it. These biases, and others discussed in section 6.2, exist in the widely used JobCentre Plus data too.

In the reweighting, the stock weight of an individual vacancy v in sector i and month m is given by

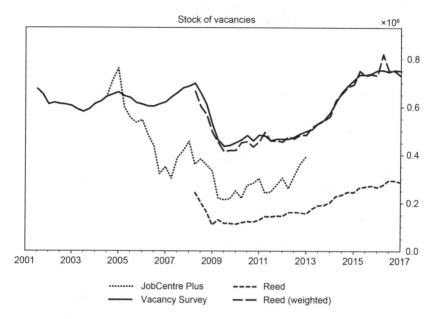

Fig. 6.4   **The aggregate stock of vacancies from three data sources**
Source: Reed, ONS, National Online Manpower Information System (NOMIS).

$$\omega_{i,m} = V_{i,m}^{vs} / V_{i,m},$$

with $V_{i,m}^{vs}$ the monthly stock of vacancies by sector according to the Vacancy Survey, and $V_{i,m}$ the stock of vacancies from the Reed data. Note that the correlation of the reweighted Reed data with the aggregate Vacancy Survey is just smaller than unity. This is because of small differences between the ONS's sectoral vacancy stocks and its aggregate measure of vacancies due to rounding and seasonal adjustments. In subsequent sections, we use the weighted Reed data.

The aggregate time series of the Vacancy Survey, raw Reed stock of vacancies, and JobCentre Plus vacancies are shown in figure 6.4. Neither of the latter two have the same overall level of vacancies as the official statistics. The weighted Reed data, with lower bias, has increased variance relative to the unweighted series but provides a good fit to the Vacancy Survey data. The correlations between the series, shown in table 6.1, show that the aggregate, unweighted Reed vacancy time series is better correlated with the Vacancy Survey measure than the JobCentre Plus data.

6.4   Matching Job Vacancy Text to Occupational Classifications

We wish to apply occupational labels to the job vacancies by making use of the text of the job title, job description, and job sector. Using the text of

Table 6.1   Correlation matrix of aggregate vacancy data

	JobCentre Plus	Vacancy Survey	Reed	Reed (weighted)
JobCentre Plus	1	0.71	0.68	0.69
Vacancy Survey	—	1	0.93	0.98
Reed	—	—	1	0.90
Reed (weighted)	—	—	—	1

Sources: Reed, ONS, National Online Manpower Information System (NOMIS).

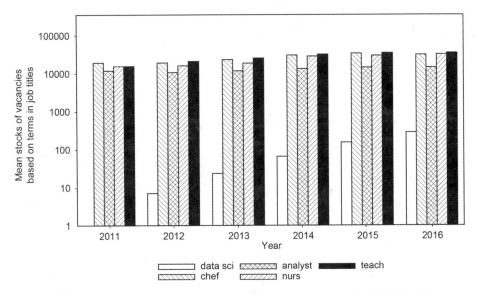

Fig. 6.5   Counts of terms in job vacancy text designed to capture the job titles of "data scientist," "analyst," "chef," "nurse," and "teacher" (note the logarithmic scale)
Source: Reed, LFS.

the vacancies can be a powerful method to capture the stocks of different kinds of vacancies, as can be demonstrated with a simple count, by year, of the roots of the words "data scientist," "analyst," "chef," "nurse," and "teacher." Figure 6.5 shows the results of this count and documents the rise of data science as a distinct job from 2011 to 2016. From this figure, we cannot know whether data scientist is rising due to new demand, extra terms in existing occupations, or because of substitution away from other roles (e.g., statistician). However, it would be prohibitively laborious to create a list of all possible job titles and search them individually. Ideally, we would want to count according to a well-defined and comprehensive classification that would put jobs into buckets according to a taxonomy. As long as the level of granularity is not too fine, this would put jobs like data scientist into buckets

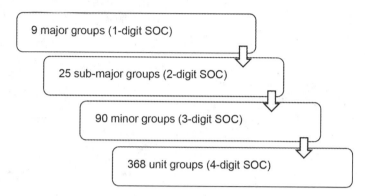

Fig. 6.6   Schematic of SOC code hierarchy

with jobs that require very similar skills and produce meaningful counts at the level of occupations. We develop and use an automated method for applying standardized occupational labels to job text. In order to use the Reed data most effectively for economic statistics, we label them with these standard classifications because they also exist in other official data—for example, on unemployment.

6.4.1   Matching Algorithm

In this section we describe the steps required to match job advertisements in the Reed data to official Standard Occupational Classification (SOC) codes. We use the job title, job sector, and job description text as the inputs into an algorithm that outputs a 3-digit SOC code. We choose the 3-digit level rather than more granular levels because there is a trade-off between more granularity and greater accuracy in classifying jobs according to the correct SOC codes. As the SOC system is hierarchical and nested, with four levels as shown in figure 6.6, generating SOC codes at the 3-digit level also delivers vacancies labeled by 1- and 2-digit codes.

In order to perform matches, we need reference information about all 3-digit SOC codes. We compile all publicly available text data, consisting of all known possible job titles and a short official description, for each SOC code and create a single text string from it. We use term frequency-inverse document frequency (tf-idf) vectors to represent these SOC code strings with a matrix with dimension $T \times D$ where t is a term from the text associated with a SOC code.[10] Our terms are comprised of all 1–3-grams[11] of salient words; that is, words that are likely to have a useful meaning in a job vacancy context (we will define this formally below). For example, the phrase "must

---

10. We use the scikit-learn Python package to do this.
11. An *n*-gram is all combinations of words with *n* words, so all 1–3-grams consist of all combinations of words with a length less than or equal to three words.

know how to cook Italian recipes" might reduce to a salient-words-only phrase "cook Italian recipes". This has 2-grams "cook Italian" and "Italian recipes" as well as 1-grams "cook," "Italian," and "recipes." The term frequency vector of this phrase would have entries equal to zero apart from the columns representing these five terms.

Rather than term frequency, which is defined as the pure count of the number of times a term appears, we use tf-idf to represent SOC codes. The "idf" part of tf-idf down-weights words that are common across the corpus and so less useful in distinguishing one vector from another. As an example, the word "work" may be salient as part of some n-grams but, as a single word, could also be very common in job advertisements. Let d be a document (in this case a text string corresponding to a 3-digit SOC code) with D documents (the number of unique 3-digit SOC codes) in total. The specific form of tf-idf we use is then given by

$$\text{tf-idf}(t,d) = \text{tf}(t) \times \text{idf}(t,d) = \text{tf}(t) \times \left[\ln\left(\frac{1+D}{1+\text{df}(t,d)} \right) + 1 \right],$$

where the document frequency, $\text{df}(t,d)$, is the number of documents in the corpus that contain term t and term frequency, $\text{tf}(t)$, is the frequency of t. Each document can be represented as a vector of tf-idf scores, $\vec{v}_d$. These are normalized via the Euclidean norm so that $\hat{\vec{v}}_d = (\vec{v}_d / \|v_d\|)$.

The algorithm has four main stages: cleaning of vacancy text, exact matching on titles, identification of similar SOC codes, and fuzzy matching. The full flow of the algorithm is shown in figure 6A.1 of the appendix. In more detail, the steps to match each vacancy in the dataset are:

- clean and combine the text of the job vacancy title, sector, and description, expanding any recognized acronyms in the process
- check whether the job title matches any known 3-digit SOC code titles (if so, use this as an exact match)
- express the given vacancy as a vector using tf-idf
- identify the five 3-digit SOC code vectors "closest" to the vacancy vector by cosine similarity
- choose from among these five the best fuzzy match between the vacancy job title and all known 3-digit SOC code job titles

The cleaning process for text converts plural forms to singular forms (with some exceptions), expands abbreviations, removes stop words[12] and non-salient words, and removes digits, punctuation, and extra spaces.

Real job vacancies are represented in the vector space by calculating their tf-idf score in the space of terms from the original corpus of SOC code descriptions and titles. A job vacancy is expressed as $\hat{\vec{v}}'$. In our algorithm,

---

12. Words that are not informative, typically conjunctions such as "and."

an arbitrary 3-digit SOC code is represented by $\hat{\bar{v}}_d$. To calculate which SOC codes are closest to $\hat{\bar{v}}'$, we solve

$$\arg \max_d \{\hat{\bar{v}}' \cdot \hat{\bar{v}}_d\}$$

for the top five documents. This process allows us to estimate how "close" a given posted job vacancy is to the "golden image" jobs defined by each 3-digit SOC code string. Of the top five matches found in this way, the known title with the closest fuzzy match is chosen. This is implemented via the Python package fuzzywuzzy, which is based on Levenshtein distance (Levenshtein 1966). We experimented with just taking the closest SOC code match by cosine similarity but using the Levenshtein distance to select among the five closest SOC code vectors provided better performance. We did not experiment with alternatives to Levenshtein distance.

In order to implement the algorithm, it was necessary to create three look-up dictionaries. The *known titles dictionary* represents known job titles and their associated SOC codes as tf-idf vectors and is also used to identify any exact job title matches, and for fuzzy matching. The text that is used to create the vectors for each 3-digit SOC code combines all the known possible job titles for that SOC code in addition to a short official job description of it. The job titles are drawn from a set of around 10^4 possible titles covering all SOC codes. Publicly available ONS resources were used to generate this dictionary; the ONS Standard Occupational Classification, an extract from which may be seen in table 6.2, and the Standard Occupational Classification 2010 Index, an extract from which is shown in table 6.3. As shown in figure 6.6, the ONS Standard Occupational Classification system is a hierarchical structure with four levels, and includes descriptions of each job. The Stan-

Table 6.2   **An extract from the ONS occupational classification structure that forms the basis of our *known titles dictionary***

Major group	Submajor group	Minor group	Unit group	Group title
3				Associate professional and technical occupations
	31			Science, engineering and technology associate professionals
		311		Science, engineering and production technicians
			3111	Laboratory technicians
			3112	Electrical and electronics technicians
			3113	Engineering technicians
			3114	Building and civil engineering technicians
			3115	Quality assurance technicians
			3116	Planning, process and production technicians
			3119	Science, engineering and production technicians n.e.c.
		312		Draughtspersons and related architectural technicians
			3121	Architectural and town planning technicians
			3122	Draughtspersons

Table 6.3   **An extract from Standard Occupational Classification Index 2010 that forms part of our *known titles dictionary***

SOC 2010	INDEXOCC	IND	ADD
1221	Manager, centre, holiday		
1225	Manager, centre, leisure		
1139	Manager, centre, mail	(postal distribution services)	
1181	Manager, centre, postgraduate	(health authority: hospital service)	
1251	Manager, centre, shopping		
1259	Manager, centre, skills		
1225	Manager, centre, sports		
1251	Manager, centre, town		
1259	Manager, centre, training		
1133	Manager, chain, supply		
2424	Manager, change, business		
2134	Manager, change, IT		
2134	Manager, change		(computing)
2134	Manager, change	(telecommunications)	
2424	Manager, change		
3545	Manager, channel		
1139	Manager, charity		
7130	Manager, check-out		
1225	Manager, cinema		
1225	Manager, circuit		(entertainment)
1190	Manager, circulation		
1225	Manager, circus		
3538	Manager, claims		
6240	Manager, cleaning		
1255	Manager, cleansing		
3545	Manager, client		(marketing)
3538	Manager, client	(bank)	
2462	Manager, client	(British Standards Institute)	
3538	Manager, client	(financial services)	

dard Occupational Classification Index 2010 extends the ONS occupational classification to capture around 30,000 alternative job titles across all unit groups. The *known titles dictionary* combines descriptions and all known titles from both sources to act as a reference list to match "raw" job vacancy titles against. Example entries are given in table 6.4.

We compiled an *acronym expansion dictionary* for processing the raw job title and job sector. It takes common within-occupation acronyms and expands them for clarity and to improve the quality of matches to the *known titles dictionary*. An example is the expansion of "rgn" to "registered general nurse." The abbreviations were drawn from those commonly found in the job vacancies. The dictionary consists of a list of 219 abbreviations. Replacing acronyms with their expansions increases the likelihood of an exact match or a strong fuzzy match. The abbreviations were initially collected from a

Table 6.4   **An extract from the *known titles dictionary***

SOC code	Titles
214	conservation and environment professionals conservation professionals environment professionals conservation adviser countryside adviser environmental chemist marine conservationist coastal nature conservationist conservationist ecological consultant environmental consultant ecologist environmental engineer geoenvironmental engineer contaminated land engineer landfill engineer . . .
215	research and development managers research and development managers head research and development analytics manager creative manager research and development design manager process development manager manufacturing development manager research and development information manager research and development consumer insights manager insights manager laboratory manager passenger link manager government product manager . . .

Table 6.5   **An extract from the *acronym expansion dictionary***

Term	Replace with
rgn	registered general nurse
ifa	independent financial adviser
nqt	newly qualified teacher
flt	fork lift truck
ce	community employment
rmn	registered mental nurse
eyfs	early years foundation stage teacher

sample of 100,000 postings, where the set of words used in that sample was compared to the set of words in the official classification reference corpus. The abbreviations were detected by checking for words that existed in the raw job postings but were not present in the set of the official classification words. Those that occurred at least five times were investigated by searching for likely elaborations based upon the raw job titles and descriptions. Table 6.5 shows an extract from the *acronym expansion dictionary*.

We also created a *known words dictionary* that contains all words present in the ONS reference corpus (official and alternative ONS job titles and job descriptions). It is used to remove extraneous information from the titles of job vacancies; any term that is not in the dictionary is treated as a custom stop word and removed from the job vacancy titles before matching. This defines what we mean by salient terms. If a term does not exist in our ONS reference corpus, then we cannot use it for exact or fuzzy job title matching. This means that the term does not help in matching and may hinder it by preventing the detection of an exact title match or strong fuzzy title match. This dictionary is generated from the known titles dictionary but excludes official minor and unit group descriptions. These descriptions were excluded because they tend to contain more general words that might be irrelevant to a job. While descriptions are used when calculating cosine similarities, for exact and fuzzy job title matching it was decided to use a stricter list of stop words in order to increase the quality of the matches. Several additional words are deleted from the dictionary (and therefore from the job vacancy titles during matching). These words are "mini," "x," "London," "nh," "for," "in," "at," "apprentice," "graduate," "senior," "junior," and "trainee." There were two reasons for this. First, words that only qualify the level of seniority, but do not change the occupation, may inhibit matching; so we wished to have "senior financial analyst" classified in the same way as "financial analyst." Second, there are words that are not common stop words and also exist in the official ONS titles but that do occur very frequently in job titles and so are not particularly informative. These were identified via our exploratory analysis.

6.4.2   Evaluating the Performance of the Occupation Coding Algorithm

There is no perfect metric against which to score the quality of SOC code assignment by our algorithm. Official classifications can be applied inconsistently. Schierholz et al. (2018) survey disagreements amongst those who code job titles into occupational classes, finding that the agreement overlap between coders is around 90 percent at the first digit of the code (the highest level, for instance "Managers, Directors and Senior Officials") but reduces to 70–80 percent at the 3-digit level that we work with for SOC codes (for instance, "Managers and proprietors in agriculture related services"). Automated approaches that use job title alone have even lower levels of agreement; Belloni et al. (2014) showed that algorithms that use job title alone agree on only 60 percent of records even at the top, 1-digit level of the International Standard Classification of Occupations. Other evidence of poor consistency in coding comes from Mellow and Sider (1983), who find an agreement level of only 57.6 percent for 3-digit occupational classifications, and Mathiowetz (1992). Additionally, not all job titles can be unambiguously assigned to an occupation. The algorithm that we contribute to match job vacancies (using both title and description) to SOC codes appears to reach at least the same level of agreement as do human coders.

To evaluate the quality of the labeling algorithm we developed, we asked the ONS to code a randomly chosen subset of our data using their proprietary algorithm. This algorithm is designed to process the responses to survey questions. The naturally occurring vacancy data contain job titles that often have superfluous information (for instance, "must be willing to travel"), which can confuse a naive algorithm. Proprietary algorithms and algorithms used by national statistical offices are typically designed for survey data, in which job title entries tend to be easier to parse and there is less extraneous information. Our algorithm must cope with a more challenging environment. We submitted 2×10^5 example vacancies to the ONS to run

Table 6.6   Summary of evaluation of SOC coding algorithm against ONS coding
                   (3-digit level)

	Manually assigned	Proprietary algorithm
Sample size	330	67,900
Accuracy	76%	91%

Source: ONS.

through their automated SOC code labeling process. Due to superfluous or missing information in the job title of the kind that would be unlikely to occur in survey data, their algorithm could only confidently produce a label for around 34 percent of these. Note that our algorithm similarly uses the job title to determine the SOC code to apply, but that it additionally uses the job description. Of the 34 percent that the ONS's approach could confidently give labels to, our method of coding based on job title and job description found the same label for 91 percent of the vacancies.

We also performed a smaller evaluation with manually assigned SOC codes. Volunteers, some associated with the project, were given parts of a list of 330 randomly chosen job titles from vacancies posted in 2016. Job titles were manually entered into the ONS online occupation coding tool, which returns a short list of the most relevant SOC codes, and volunteers then make a subjective selection of the most relevant SOC code. This is then compared with the output of our algorithm, with only a match at the 3-digit level being counted as accurate. The results from both are shown in table 6.6. The results are similar to the levels of agreement seen between human coders. This algorithm is used in all applications of SOC codes to the Reed data.

In creating the algorithm, several areas of possible future improvement became clear. It always assigns a SOC code, but it could instead assign a probability or confidence level to each SOC code and so allow for a manual coder to judge marginal cases. Historical data on vacancies and employment might also be used in marginal cases. We also found that occupations often come with both a level (e.g., manager) and a role (e.g., physicist). Better SOC assignment might result from explicitly extracting these two different types of information, and perhaps distinguishing between the higher and lower levels using offered salaries.

In interpreting the results based upon our SOC coding algorithm, it is useful to note that the less granular levels of classification are likely to have fewer incorrect classifications. There is a trade-off, as going to more aggregate classifications loses some of the rich heterogeneity that we find in the data.

Since we developed our approach, we became aware of several recent similar approaches. Atalay et al. (2017) label job vacancy advertisements appearing in US newspapers with SOC codes. Their approach shares some similarities with ours, including the use of cosine similarity, but is also different in several respects: our model is created from the official job category descriptions, while theirs is created from the vacancy text; while we use tf-idf to create a vector space, they use continuous-bag-of-words; and finally, they match to US SOC codes, while we match to UK SOC codes. We think that one advantage of creating the vector space from the official descriptions of SOC codes is that it only retains words or terms that are relevant to solving the problem of finding the right SOC code and discards all other words. This is not true when the vector space is created from the vacancy text. The vector space created the former way is inherently limited by the cardinality of SOC codes, which is a benefit, rather than potentially growing indefinitely as more job advertisements are added in the latter approach. Working with self-reported job title data from the German General Social Survey, Gweon et al. (2017) develop three different statistical approaches to apply occupational classifications. Boselli et al. (2017, 2018) take a different approach and manually label around 30,000 vacancies to then use a supervised machine learning algorithm to classify a further 6 million vacancies using ISCO (International Standard Classification of Occupations) codes. We believe that the use of supervised machine learning to train a model could potentially produce more accuracy in matching (where accuracy is measured relative to the labels that a human coder would select). However, the maintenance cost of the supervised approach is higher; if the SOC code standard changes, our approach would be trivial to update with the new master descriptions of each SOC code, but a supervised machine learning approach would need to be retrained with presumably 30,000 more vacancies labeled by humans. Similarly, applying the same approach in different countries would require model retraining. Future work could usefully compare or combine all these methods on the same SOC matching problem.

6.5   Analysis of Processed Data

Once labeled with both regional NUTS codes and occupational SOC codes, the data allow for an entirely new perspective on the heterogeneity of labor demand within the UK. In this section, we report assorted summary statistics that illustrate this. Figure 6.7 shows the labor market tightness, $\theta = v/u$, by 2-character NUTS code. Unemployment data come from the *Labour Force Survey*. The picture reflects regional incomes, with the South East having higher tightness than Northern Ireland. However, there are isolated regions of tightness outside of the South East.

We can also look at changes in tightness that occur at an extremely disaggregated level, although some caution should be taken in inferring too much from changes at the lowest possible levels of disaggregation given that the data have been reweighted from a biased source. In figure 6.8 we plot the rolling two-quarter means of the three highest mean tightnesses

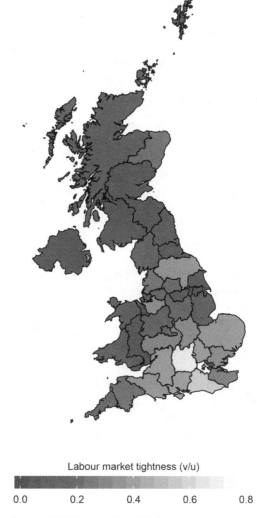

Labour market tightness (v/u)

0.0   0.2   0.4   0.6   0.8

Fig. 6.7   Map of mean UK labor market tightness

Note: θ = *u*/*u* by 2-character NUTS code over the period 2008Q1–2016Q4. Some of the NUTS classifications are different in the ONS data relative to the NUTS2010 standard (EUROSTAT 2011). This causes problems for London (UKI). We map UKI1 to UKI3 and UKI2 to UKI5. This neglects the UKI6 and UKI7 categories in NUTS2010. These are shown as white in the plot.

for 3-digit SOC codes. The appearance of nurses and welfare professionals in the three most tight occupations is consistent with the UK government's "Shortage Occupation List." Not shown are the bottom three occupations, which were elementary sales occupations, process operatives, and elementary agricultural occupations. While these are likely to have low tightnesses

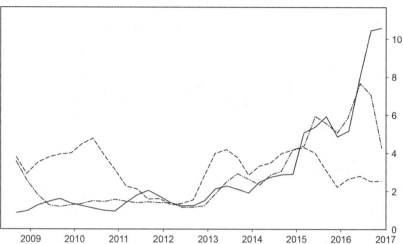

Tightness (ratio of vacancies to unemployment)

The 3 Occupations with the Highest Mean Tightness
- - - Welfare Professionals (244)   ——— Nursing and Midwifery Professionals (223)
—·—·— Customer Service Managers and Supervisors (722)

Fig. 6.8   The 3-digit SOC codes with the three highest mean tightnesses over the full time period
Source: Reed, LFS.

in part due to genuinely low demand, it is also likely that these jobs are not commonly posted online by firms.

Another useful check on the newly compiled vacancy data is that they satisfy similar stylized facts to the official data produced by the ONS. One such stylized fact is that the monthly sectoral vacancy stocks follow a Taylor power law (Taylor 1961). Firm sizes have also been shown to satisfy this law (Gaffeo et al. 2012). Let i represent a region, occupation, or sector with $\bar{V}_t = (1/I)\sum_i V_{t,i}$. Then the monthly mean and monthly variance, σ_t^2, are related to each other as

$$\sigma_t^2 = a\bar{V}_t^b,$$

where the power, b, is sometimes called the index of aggregation.[13] The ONS vacancies by sector strongly follow a Taylor power law with $R^2 = 0.857$ and $b = 2.037 \pm 0.061$. We show, in figures 6.9 and 6.10, that the breakdowns by NUTS and SOC respectively do both strongly follow Taylor power laws, giv-

---

13. $1 < b < 2$ indicates that the variation falls with increasing size of region, occupation, or sector relative to what would be expected from a relationship with constant per vacancy variability, which is $b = 2$ (Kilpatrick and Ives 2003).

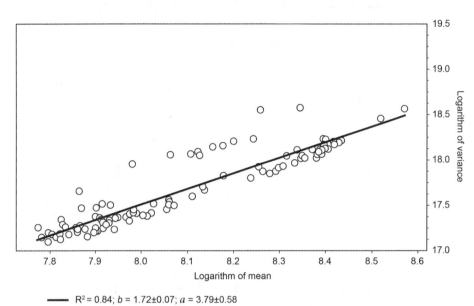

R² = 0.84; *b* = 1.72±0.07; *a* = 3.79±0.58

O   Monthly vacancy stocks; mean and variance of aggregation by 3-character NUTS code

Fig. 6.9   Monthly vacancy stocks, when aggregated by region into mean and variance, show a clear Taylor power law relationship

Source: Reed.

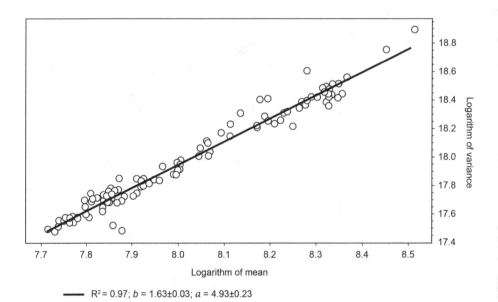

R² = 0.97; *b* = 1.63±0.03; *a* = 4.93±0.23

O   Monthly vacancy stocks; mean and variance of aggregation by 3-digit SOC code

Fig. 6.10   Monthly vacancy stocks, when aggregated by occupation into mean and variance, show a clear Taylor power law relationship

Source: Reed.

ing confidence in the methods used to produce these statistics. We also highlight the existence of these Taylor power laws in vacancy data as they could be useful for the calibration of heterogeneous models of the labor market.

The descriptive statistics of the Reed data at the disaggregated level seem to provide a plausible representation of vacancies by both occupation and region.

6.6   Use of Reed Vacancy Data

We demonstrate potential uses of these new economic statistics.

By combining Reed vacancy data labeled by occupation with data on unemployment and hires from the *Labour Force Survey*, we are able to estimate Beveridge curves.[14] These track the relationship between unemployment and vacancies over time. By utilizing vacancy data labeled by the text analysis technique developed, we are able to create Beveridge curves at the occupational level.

At the aggregate level, we assume a matching function M that takes the level of vacancies and unemployment in discrete time as inputs and outputs the number of hires (per unit time) as in the comprehensive survey by Petrongolo and Pissarides (2001). Define the aggregate number of hires, h, and matching function, M, with constant returns to scale (homogeneous of degree 1) as

$$h(U,V) = \phi M(U,V) = \phi U^{1-\alpha}V^{\alpha},$$

where ϕ is the matching efficiency and α is the vacancy elasticity of matching. These are structural parameters. Matches and new hires from unemployment are equivalent. At the disaggregated level, hires are given by h_i. Hires based upon the theoretical matching function and a segment-specific matching efficiency are given by

$$(2) \qquad\qquad h_i = \phi_i M(U_i,V_i) = \phi_i U_i^{1-\alpha}V_i^{\alpha}.$$

The key structural parameters are the scale parameter of the matching function, ϕ, and the vacancy elasticity parameter, $\alpha = (V/M)(\partial M/\partial V)$. The scale parameter is often interpreted as an indicator of the level of efficiency of the matching process; hence we refer to it as the "matching efficiency." The elasticity parameter contains information about the severity of the congestion externalities that searchers on either side of the labor market impose on each other. Econometric estimates are reported in full in Turrell et al. (2018). When the number of hires is equal to the job destruction rate and $dU/dt = 0$, the combinations of possible U and V values for a given set of matching parameters trace out a locus of points in $U - V$ space. This is the Beveridge curve, and its empirical counterpart may be seen by plotting observed U and V values against one another.

---

14. See Elsby, Michaels, and Ratner (2015) for a comprehensive review.

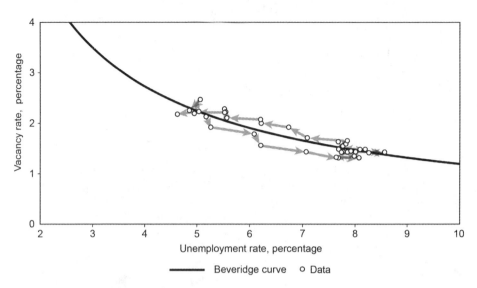

Fig. 6.11   Beveridge curve (line) vs. aggregate *uu–vv* data at quarterly frequency
Source: Reed, ONS.

Figure 6.11 shows an aggregate fitted Beveridge curve against aggregate vacancy-unemployment points at quarterly frequency for 2008 to 2017.[15] The aggregate matching efficiency is $\phi = \exp\{0.554 \pm .037\}$ (significant to 1 percent). Arrows indicate movements over time, and a shift toward higher unemployment during the Great Recession is evident, as is the high tightness in the last quarter of 2016.

Figure 6.12 shows the disaggregated equivalent of figure 6.11, with Beveridge curves and quarterly u-v points for each 1-digit SOC code. The submarket-level Beveridge curves show that a single, aggregate Beveridge curve hides a great deal of important variation in u-v space across SOC codes. There are significant differences between the apparent curves as separated by skill, with the curve for associate professional and technical occupations shifted up relative to other occupations. There are also differences in spread. The driver of the spread varies by occupation; for the Caring, Leisure and Other Service occupation (1-digit SOC code 6), it is largely driven by vacancies, while what variation there is for Managers, Directors and Senior Officials (1-digit SOC code 1) is driven by unemployment. We do not allow matching efficiency or job destruction rates to vary over the time period here so that the Beveridge curve is fixed. In practice there are shifts in

15. In the LFS data, there are discrepancies between the stocks implied by the flows in the longitudinal data and the stocks in the cross-sectional data. Due to this, we calibrate the job destruction rate in the Beveridge curves to give the best fit to the data.

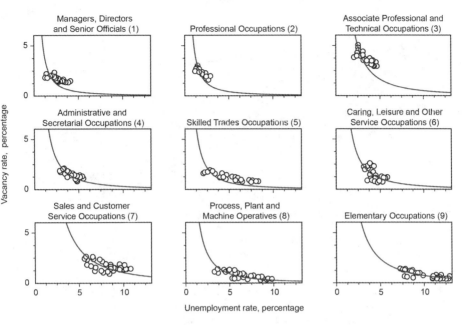

Fig. 6.12   Beveridge curves (lines), estimated with Reed data, and Reed data (points) in *uu–vv* space for each 1-digit SOC code at quarterly frequency
Source: Reed, ONS.

Beveridge curves, certainly at the aggregate level, and these are documented for the US in Barnichon et al. (2012). They find that a break in the hires per vacancy shifted the curve so that the implied unemployment rate was 2.8 percentage points lower than the actual unemployment rate. Our short time series makes a similar analysis difficult here but the estimated Beveridge curves at the occupational level provide a good fit for the entire period.

The patterns shown here could be affected by the biases discussed in sections 3.1 and 3.2. The vacancy stocks of higher numbered occupations are subject to both an upward bias, due to the likelihood of having vacancy durations shorter than the average across occupations and the six weeks assumed for the Reed data, and a downward bias, due to their being underrepresented amongst online vacancies posted at cost.

We now turn to the mismatch framework of Şahin et al. (2014) which, for heterogeneous labor markets, can determine the extent of unemployment that arises due to mismatch between jobseekers and job vacancies. Mismatch arises when there are barriers to mobility across distinct parts of the labor market, which we refer to as submarkets or market segments. Mismatch lowers the overall efficiency of the labor market; given the aggregate level of unemployment and vacancies, it lowers the rate of job finding. The mismatch

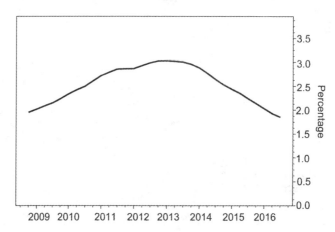

Fig. 6.13   Mismatch unemployment, $uu-vv^*$ (seasonally adjusted)
Source: ONS, Reed.

framework is also used by Smith (2012), Patterson et al. (2016), and Turrell et al. (2018)—from which the econometric estimates used here are drawn.

The Şahin et al. (2014) model provides counterfactuals due to a social planner who allocates the unemployed to search in submarkets so as to optimize output. The social planner takes into account the matching efficiency and tightness of each submarket. Mismatch unemployment is defined as the gap between actual unemployment, u, and counterfactual unemployment, u^*. We compute this mismatch unemployment rate in figure 6.13 using 1-digit SOC codes. The biases that affect the stock of vacancies also affect estimates of the matching efficiency, producing a bias both upward and downward for occupations with short vacancy durations and low online representation, respectively. Upward and downward bias in matching efficiency make mismatch unemployment seem lower or higher, respectively. While these biases mean that the level of mismatch unemployment could be shifted relative to its true level, they are likely to be less important for following the trend in mismatch unemployment as they are relatively fixed over the period under consideration. Following the recession caused by the Great Financial Crisis, mismatch unemployment gradually rose. The maximum inflection point at the end of 2012 coincides with the UK's last negative quarter-on-quarter GDP growth within the time period under consideration; mismatch unemployment subsequently falls more steeply during the recovery. Mismatch between jobseekers and firms has been implicated as one driver of the UK's productivity puzzle (Patterson et al. 2016) but the trend in mismatch unemployment seen here suggests that, while that could have been a factor up until 2013, the role it has played fell substantially between 2013 and 2017.

6.7   Conclusion

We mapped naturally occurring vacancy data into official occupational classifications in order to construct new economic statistics. The algorithm we have developed is especially useful for firms, recruitment agencies, and other researchers seeking to apply consistent occupational labels to freeform job descriptions. The tools and processes developed can be deployed on other vacancy data but could also be adapted to other types of naturally occurring text data.

We have considered the limitations due to bias and coverage in the Reed vacancy data presented. While there is undoubtedly bias in the data, we have provided a qualitative description of it and how it might affect the estimates of the stock of vacancies. We also quantified the biases by sector and reweighted the data in order to reduce the overall bias and increase the effective coverage of the data. The bias we find is no worse than in other widely used UK vacancy microdata. Example applications demonstrate the utility of these data for analysis.

These datasets are a complement, not a replacement, for existing survey-based approaches to constructing economic statistics because those existing statistics are required to assess the extent of bias and coverage in new datasets, and to create weighting schemes. We have shown that the Reed data, transformed by text analysis, can augment existing official statistics because they can give estimates of vacancies by occupation and region that survey data do not, and because of their vast scale. That scale permits very disaggregated analysis that can substantially benefit labor market research.

Detailed Occupation-Coding Algorithm Flow Diagram

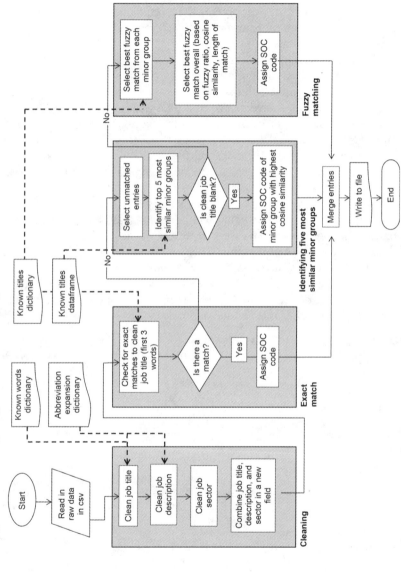

Fig. 6A.1   A more detailed overview of the algorithm that matches job vacancies to SOC codes at the minor group level (3-digit SOC code)

References

Abraham, Katharine G. 1983. "Structural/Frictional vs. Deficient Demand Unemployment: Some New Evidence." *American Economic Review* 73 (4): 708–24.
———. 1987. "Help-Wanted Advertising, Job Vacancies, and Unemployment." *Brookings Papers on Economic Activity* 1987 (1): 207–48.
Atalay, Enghin, Phai Phongthiengtham, Sebastian Sotelo, and Daniel Tannenbaum. 2017. "The Evolving US Occupational Structure." Discussion paper. https://www.econ.iastate.edu/files/events/files/skills.pdf.
Azar, José A., Ioana Marinescu, Marshall I. Steinbaum, and Bledi Taska. 2018. "Concentration in US Labor Markets: Evidence from Online Vacancy Data." National Bureau of Economic Research, Cambridge, MA. https://www.nber.org/papers/w24395.
Barnichon, Regis. 2010. "Building a Composite Help-Wanted Index." *Economics Letters* 109 (3): 175–78.
Barnichon, Regis, Michael Elsby, Bart Hobijn, and Aysegul Sahin. 2012. "Which Industries Are Shifting the Beveridge Curve?" *Monthly Labor Review* 135:25.
Belloni, Michele, Agar Brugiavini, Elena Maschi, and Kea Tijdens. 2014. "Measurement Error in Occupational Coding: An Analysis on SHARE Data." Department of Economics, University of Venice "Ca' Foscari" Working Papers 2014:24.
Bentley, R. 2005. "Publication of JobCentre Plus Vacancy Statistics." UK Office for National Statistics, *Labour Market Trends* 113 (6): 253–59.
Boselli, Roberto, Mirko Cesarini, Stefania Marrara, Fabio Mercorio, Mario Mezzanzanica, Gabriella Pasi, and Marco Viviani. 2018. "WoLMIS: A Labor Market Intelligence System for Classifying Web Job Vacancies." *Journal of Intelligent Information Systems* 51: 477–502.
Boselli, Roberto, Mirko Cesarini, Fabio Mercorio, and Mario Mezzanzanica. 2017. "Using Machine Learning for Labour Market Intelligence." In *Machine Learning and Knowledge Discovery in Databases*, Part 3, edited by Yasemin Altun, Kamalika Das, Taneli Mielikäinen, Donato Malerba, Jerzy Stefanowski, Jesse Read, Marinka Žitnik, Michelangelo Ceci, and Sašo Džeroski, 330–42. New York: Springer.
Burgess, Simon, and Stefan Profit. 2001. "Externalities in the Matching of Workers and Firms in Britain." *Labour Economics* 8 (3): 313–33.
Cajner, Tomaz, and David Ratner. 2016. "A Cautionary Note on the Help Wanted Online Data." FEDS Notes, June 23. Washington, DC: Board of Governors of the Federal Reserve System. https://www.federalreserve.gov/econresdata/notes/feds-notes/2016/a-cautionary-note-on-the-help-wanted-online-data-20160623.html.
Coles, Melvyn G., and Eric Smith. 1996. "Cross-Section Estimation of the Matching Function: Evidence from England and Wales." *Economica* 63(252): 589–97.
Davis, Steven J., R. Jason Faberman, and John C. Haltiwanger. 2013. "The Establishment-Level Behavior of Vacancies and Hiring." *Quarterly Journal of Economics* 128 (2): 581–622.
Davis, Steven J., and Brenda Samaniego de la Parra. 2017. "Application Flows." Preliminary draft. https://static1.squarespace.com/static/5e2ea3a8097ed30c779bd707/t/5e304aefdd0bc0219db0bdf1/1580223223518/Application+Flows+7+March+2017.pdf.
Deming, David, and Lisa B. Kahn. 2017. "Skill Requirements across Firms and Labor Markets: Evidence from Job Postings for Professionals." National Bureau of Economic Research, Cambridge, MA. https://www.nber.org/papers/w23328.
Elsby, Michael W. L., Ryan Michaels, and David Ratner. 2015. "The Beveridge Curve: A Survey." *Journal of Economic Literature* 53 (3): 571–630.

EUROSTAT. 2011. "Regions in the European Union: Nomenclature of Territorial Units for Statistics." NUTS 2010/EU-27. Luxembourg: Publications Office of the European Union.

FRED, Federal Reserve Bank of St. Louis. 2019. "DHI-DFH Mean Vacancy Duration Measure." https://fred.stlouisfed.org/series/DHIDFHMVDM.

Gaffeo, Edoardo, Corrado Di Guilmi, Mauro Gallegati, and Alberto Russo. 2012. "On the Mean/Variance Relationship of the Firm Size Distribution: Evidence and Some Theory." *Ecological Complexity* 11:109–17.

Gweon, Hyukjun, Matthias Schonlau, Lars Kaczmirek, Michael Blohm, and Stefan Steiner. 2017. "Three Methods for Occupation Coding Based on Statistical Learning." *Journal of Official Statistics* 33 (1): 101–22.

Hershbein, Brad, and Lisa B. Kahn. 2018. "Do Recessions Accelerate Routine-Biased Technological Change? Evidence from Vacancy Postings." *American Economic Review* 108 (7): 1737–72.

Kilpatrick, A. M., and A. R. Ives. 2003. "Species Interactions Can Explain Taylor's Power Law for Ecological Time Series." *Nature* 422 (6927): 65.

Levenshtein, Vladimir I. 1966. "Binary Codes Capable of Correcting Deletions, Insertions, and Reversals." *Soviet Physics Doklady* 10:707–10.

Machin, Andrew. 2003. "The Vacancy Survey: A New Series of National Statistics." UK Office for National Statistics, *Labour Market Trends* 111(7): 349–62.

Mamertino, Mariano, and Tara M. Sinclair. 2016. "Online Job Search and Migration Intentions across EU Member States." Institute for International Economic Policy Working Paper Series, George Washington University, Washington, DC.

Manning, Alan, and Barbara Petrongolo. 2017. "How Local Are Labor Markets? Evidence from a Spatial Job Search Model." *American Economic Review* 107 (10): 2877–2907.

Marinescu, Ioana. 2017. "The General Equilibrium Impacts of Unemployment Insurance: Evidence from a Large Online Job Board." *Journal of Public Economics* 150:14–29.

Marinescu, Ioana, and Ronald Wolthoff. 2016. "Opening the Black Box of the Matching Function: The Power of Words." National Bureau of Economic Research, Cambridge, MA. https://www.nber.org/papers/w22508.

Mathiowetz, Nancy A. 1992. "Errors in Reports of Occupation." *Public Opinion Quarterly* 56 (3): 352–55.

Mellow, Wesley, and Hal Sider. 1983. "Accuracy of Response in Labor Market Surveys: Evidence and Implications." *Journal of Labor Economics* 1 (4): 331–44.

Mortensen, Dale T., and Christopher A. Pissarides. 1994. "Job Creation and Job Destruction in the Theory of Unemployment." *Review of Economic Studies* 61 (3): 397–415.

Office for National Statistics. 2017. "Quarterly Labour Force Survey, 1992–2017: Secure Access. [data collection]." 10th ed. Social Survey Division, Northern Ireland Statistics and Research Agency, Central Survey Unit. http: //dx.doi.org/10 .5255/UKDA-SN-6727-11.

Patterson, Christina, Ayşegül Şahin, Giorgio Topa, and Giovanni L Violante. 2016. "Working Hard in the Wrong Place: A Mismatch-Based Explanation to the UK Productivity Puzzle." *European Economic Review* 84:42–56.

Petrongolo, Barbara, and Christopher A. Pissarides. 2001. "Looking into the Black Box: A Survey of the Matching Function." *Journal of Economic Literature* 39 (2): 390–431.

Şahin, Ayşegül, Joseph Song, Giorgio Topa, and Giovanni L. Violante. 2014. "Mismatch Unemployment." *American Economic Review* 104 (11): 3529–64.

Schierholz, Malte, Miriam Gensicke, Nikolai Tschersich, and Frauke Kreuter. 2018.

"Occupation Coding during the Interview." *Journal of the Royal Statistical Society: Series A (Statistics in Society)* 181 (2): 379–407.

Smith, Jennifer C. 2012. "Unemployment and Mismatch in the UK." Unpublished manuscript. https://warwick.ac.uk/fac/soc/economics/staff/jcsmith/uk_unemployment_dynamics_during_the_financial_crisis.pdf.

Taylor, L. R. 1961. "Aggregation, Variance and the Mean." *Nature* 189 (4766): 732–35.

Turrell, Arthur, Bradley Speigner, Jyldyz Djumalieva, David Copple, and James Thurgood. 2018. "Using Job Vacancies to Understand the Effects of Labour Market Mismatch on UK Output and Productivity." Bank of England Staff Working Paper 737, London.

7

Automating Response Evaluation for Franchising Questions on the 2017 Economic Census

Joseph Staudt, Yifang Wei, Lisa Singh, Shawn Klimek, J. Bradford Jensen, and Andrew Baer

7.1 Introduction

The Economic Census (EC) is the most comprehensive collection of business activity data conducted by the US Census Bureau. Every five years (those ending in 2 and 7), businesses are mandated to provide information including total sales, product sales, payroll, employment, and industry classification for each establishment that they operate. In addition, businesses are asked to identify whether they are affiliated with a franchise, and if

Joseph Staudt is an economist at the Center for Economic Studies and the Center for Big Data Research and Applications at the US Census Bureau.

Yifang Wei is a postdoctoral researcher in the Department of Computer Science at Georgetown University.

Lisa Singh is a professor in the Department of Computer Science at Georgetown University.

Shawn Klimek is Assistant Center Chief for Business Research at the Center for Economic Studies at the US Census Bureau.

J. Bradford Jensen is McCrane/Shaker Chair in international business and professor of economics and international business at the McDonough School of Business at Georgetown University, and a research associate of the National Bureau of Economic Research.

Andrew Baer is currently a senior economist at the International Monetary Fund, but he was the Assistant Division Chief of the Services Sectors in the Economy-Wide Statistics Division at the US Census Bureau when this chapter was written.

We thank John Cuffe for help with the matching software. Thanks also to Emek Basker, Lucia Foster, Cathy Buffington, Ron Jarmin, and seminar participants at the CRIW Pre-Conference: Big Data for 21st Century Economic Statistics for their useful comments. All remaining errors and omissions are those of the authors. The analysis, thoughts, opinions, and any errors presented here are solely those of the authors and do not necessarily reflect any official position of the US Census Bureau or the International Monetary Fund (IMF). All results have been reviewed to ensure that no confidential information is disclosed. The Disclosure Review Board release number is DRB #7961. For acknowledgments, sources of research support, and disclosure of the authors' material financial relationships, if any, please see https://www.nber.org/books -and-chapters/big-data-21st-century-economic-statistics/automating-response-evaluation -franchising-questions-2017-economic-census.

so, whether they are a franchisor or franchisee. Data from the 2007 and 2012 Censuses indicated that, between the two time periods, the number of franchise-affiliated business establishments declined from 453,326 to 409,104, a 9.8 percent decrease. In contrast, comparable data derived from franchise license agreements and produced by FRANdata, a research and advisory company and the strategic research partner of the International Franchise Association (IFA), showed a 4 percent *increase* in the number of franchise-affiliated establishments during this period.

One reason for this discrepancy was the decline, between 2007 and 2012, in resources the Census Bureau was able to dedicate to the manual evaluation of survey responses in the franchise section of the EC. After the 2007 EC, Census Bureau staff compared survey responses to FRANdata and followed up with respondents over the phone. Through this process, a significant number of establishments that were not originally designated as franchise affiliated based on their EC responses were recoded as franchise affiliated. Unfortunately, in 2012, comparable resources were not available to conduct this extensive manual editing, contributing to the *measured* decline in franchise-affiliated establishments.[1]

The differences between the 2007 and 2012 Censuses show that, in order to ensure an accurate count of franchise-affiliated establishments, the quality of respondents' answers on the EC survey form must be evaluated after collection. However, limited resources make it difficult to manually conduct such an evaluation. In this paper, we examine the potential of partially automating this process for the 2017 EC. Specifically, we combine external data collected from the web with new machine learning algorithms designed for fuzzy name and address matching to quickly and accurately predict which establishments in the 2017 EC are likely to be franchise affiliated and then compare our prediction to the responses (or nonresponses) for these establishments on the franchise section of the survey.[2]

To implement our procedure, we first obtain external data on franchise-affiliated establishments from two sources. First, we scrape information directly from franchise websites. This approach has the advantage of providing highly accurate and up-to-date information on a particular franchise's establishments. However, it also requires custom scraping scripts to deal with the idiosyncrasies of each website. Second, we harvest data by querying Yelp's application programming interface (API).[3] This approach has

1. Another reason for the discrepancy, as discussed in section 7.2.6, was a growth in categories of franchise-affiliated establishments that were captured by FRANdata, but often missing from the EC data.

2. The Economic Census (EC) is conducted at the firm level, not the establishment level. However, a surveyed firm gives information about each of its establishments. Thus, while a survey response may refer to a particular establishment, no one located at that establishment necessarily filled out the survey form.

3. Yelp is a search service that publishes crowdsourced reviews of local business establishments. In addition to providing information on its website (yelp.com) and mobile app, Yelp provides information through an application programming interface (API).

the advantage of scalability—only a single script needs to be written and maintained. In addition, Yelp's API provides information not typically available elsewhere, such as establishment-level average customer ratings. Unfortunately, data harvested from Yelp's API is not always complete or timely.

After collecting the external data, we use new record-linking software developed at the US Census Bureau (Cuffe and Goldschlag 2018) to link external establishments (both web-scraped and Yelp-queried) to the US Census Bureau Business Register (BR), a comprehensive list of all US business establishments. The software—Multiple Algorithm Matching for Better Analytics (MAMBA)—constructs predictive features using name and address information, and feeds these features into a random forest, generating predicted probabilities of matches. In our case, for each external establishment MAMBA identifies the establishments in the BR that are most likely to be a positive match, and thus likely to be franchise affiliated. Finally, we link these matched establishments to the 2017 EC and compare MAMBA's predictions of franchise affiliation to respondents' answers on the franchise section of the survey form.

Overall, we find that approximately 70–80 percent (depending on the source of external data) of establishments that MAMBA predicts to be franchise affiliated and are in the 2017 EC (with processed forms) are identified as franchise affiliated on the survey form—that is, MAMBA's prediction and the form responses are consistent. However, this implies that for 20–30 percent of establishments, MAMBA predicts them to be franchise affiliated, but they are not identified as such on the survey form—that is, there is a discrepancy between MAMBA's prediction and form responses. Manual investigation of these discrepancies reveals that in most cases the establishments are, indeed, franchise affiliated. That is, the MAMBA prediction is correct, and the respondent mistakenly filled out the EC form.[4] Thus, we are able to identify, with a high degree of accuracy and minimal manual investigation, franchise-affiliated establishments that are mistakenly labeled as not being franchise affiliated in the 2017 EC. Recoding these establishments increases the unweighted number of franchise-affiliated establishments in the 2017 EC by 22–42 percent.

In sum, our approach of leveraging external data in combination with machine learning provides a way to reap the benefits of manually investigating the quality of 2017 EC responses to franchise questions, but in a mostly automated and cost-effective way. In particular, it allows us to identify a large set of establishments that are likely franchise affiliated but will not be counted as such if their 2017 EC survey forms are taken at face value. Thus, for the 2017 EC, our approach should prove useful in avoiding the undercounting of franchise-affiliated establishments that occurred in the 2012

---

4. In this context, a franchise-affiliated respondent can "mistakenly" fill out the EC form in two ways. First, they may not respond to the franchise section of the survey—a nonresponse mistake. Second, they may respond to the franchise section of the survey but claim not to be franchise affiliated—an incorrect response mistake.

EC and was only avoided in the 2007 EC by the dedication of substantial resources to manual curation.

The rest of this paper is organized as follows. The next section discusses the data—both external and restricted use—that we use in our analyses. We also discuss possible alternative sources of external data on franchise-affiliated establishments that may overcome some of the shortcomings of the web-scraped and Yelp-queried data. Section 7.3 discusses the linking of web-scraped and Yelp-queried establishments to the 2017 BR and the 2017 EC. Section 7.4 compares the MAMBA predictions of franchise affiliation to survey form responses on the franchise section of the 2017 EC. Section 7.5 concludes.

7.2   Data

This project uses external data on franchise-affiliated establishments from two sources: (1) scraped directly from franchise websites ("web-scraped establishments") and (2) harvested from Yelp's API ("Yelp-queried establishments"). We also use franchise-level information from the *FranchiseTimes Top 200+* list and restricted-use data maintained by the US Census Bureau, including the 2017 BR and the 2017 EC.

7.2.1   FranchiseTimes

The *FranchiseTimes* is a trade publication that publishes news and data about franchising in the United States. Since 1999, it has published information on the largest US-based franchises, and in recent years it has published information on the largest 500 franchises in its "Top 200+" list. Among other information, the list reports the number of US establishments for each franchise. We use the Top 200+ list as a frame for franchises when querying Yelp's API (see section 7.2.3) and as an independent source to validate the establishment counts obtained using external data (see section 7.2.4).

7.2.2   Franchise Websites

We scrape establishment-level data directly from the websites of 12 franchises: 7-Eleven, Ace Hardware, Burger King, Dunkin' Donuts, Great Clips, KFC, Marco's Pizza, McDonald's, Midas, Pizza Hut, Subway, and Wendy's. We refer to these 12 franchises as our "core" set of franchises. Though the list, like franchising generally, is restaurant heavy, we made efforts to collect several nonrestaurant franchises. Throughout 2017—the reference period for the 2017 EC—scripts were written and run to scrape establishment-level data using the "Find a Location" feature available on most franchise websites.[5] For a given franchise website, the script uses a zip code to submit

---

5. All scripts were run from outside the Census Bureau's IT system and the data were then transferred to Census. However, the goal is to formalize this process for the 2022 EC and run all scripts from within the Census Bureau's IT system.

a query for locations. By iteratively submitting a query for all US zip codes, we are able to obtain an exhaustive list of establishments affiliated with the franchise. This process yielded information on 90,225 franchise-affiliated establishments.[6] Crucially for linking to the BR, this information always includes the address of each establishment.

Obtaining establishment-level information directly from franchise websites has several advantages. First, it yields data close to "ground truth"—since a franchise has a strong incentive to maintain a complete and up-to-date list of locations on its website, we are unlikely to find a more accurate source of information about the existence of individual franchise establishments. Second, there is no ambiguity regarding the franchise with which an establishment is affiliated—if an establishment is returned from a query of franchise A's website, we can be confident that the establishment is, in fact, affiliated with franchise A (as noted below, this is not always true for Yelp-queried establishments).

Lack of scalability is a disadvantage of obtaining information directly from franchise websites. Since each website has its own peculiarities, a custom script must be written and maintained for each franchise. Moreover, franchise websites often change, making the task of maintaining working scripts more difficult.

Another disadvantage is ambiguity regarding the *terms of use* for franchise websites (as noted below, no such ambiguity exists for Yelp's API). One franchise website explicitly allows accessing the site as long as scripts do not do so in a "manner that sends more request messages to the . . . servers in a given period of time than a human can reasonably produce in the same period by using a conventional online Web browser." We scraped the data using Python's *selenium* package—this allows a script to interact with a website in a point-and-click fashion, which significantly reduces the load on servers hosting franchise websites and which we initially believed was consistent with the *terms of use* for these websites. However, further review of the core franchise websites indicates that there is typically standard language prohibiting data collection without caveat. A representative example of prohibited activity includes "Use or launch any unauthorized technology or automated system to access the online services or extract content from the online services, including but not limited to spiders, robots, screen scrapers, or offline readers. . . ." In the future, the Census Bureau can follow the lead of the Bureau of Labor Statistics, which obtains permission from each company to scrape their websites for price data. This would increase the cost of collecting location information directly from franchise websites, but the high quality of the data may make this extra cost worthwhile.

---

6. For this paper, we collected a one-time snapshot of 2017 establishments. We did not continuously scrape information from franchise websites over the course of the year.

7.2.3   Yelp API

Yelp is a search service that publishes crowdsourced reviews of local business establishments. In addition to providing information on its website (yelp.com) and mobile app, Yelp provides information through an application programming interface (API). We obtained the Yelp data by repeatedly querying its API using the names of the 500 franchises listed in the 2017 *FranchiseTimes Top 200+* and approximately 3,000 county names.[7] This process took place in 2017 and resulted in a harvest of 220,064 establishments affiliated with at least one of the 500 queried franchises and 63,395 establishments affiliated with one of the 12 franchises for which we have web-scraped data (again, we refer to these 12 as "core" franchises). From the list of 500 franchises, 496 have at least one establishment in Yelp.

The primary advantage of using the Yelp API is scalability—a single script can be used to obtain establishment-level data on any franchise. Another advantage is the uniformity of the Yelp data across all establishments, and thus its comparability across franchises. In particular, all establishments across all franchises have address information—which, as noted, is crucial for linking to the BR.

The main disadvantage is that Yelp data are generated through user reviews and are inevitably incomplete. For a given franchise, this incompleteness likely decreases the number of establishments in the BR that we can identify as being affiliated with the franchise. In addition, Yelp may be slow to expunge establishments that no longer exist. A second disadvantage is ambiguity regarding the franchise with which an establishment is affiliated. When a franchise name is used to query Yelp's API, not all harvested establishments are actually affiliated with the queried franchise. For instance, a query for "franchise A" might yield several establishments affiliated with that franchise but might also yield other nearby establishments affiliated with "franchise B" (or nearby establishments not affiliated with any franchise). Thus, it is crucial to identify which establishments harvested from a query for a franchise are actually affiliated with that franchise. We are able

---

7. Here is the section of the Yelp API *terms of use* that allows for the bulk download of data for noncommercial use: "You agree that you will not, and will not assist or enable others to: a) cache, record, pre-fetch, or otherwise store any portion of the Yelp Content for a period longer than twenty-four (24) hours from receipt of the Yelp Content, or attempt or provide a means to execute any 'bulk download' operations, *with the exception of using the Yelp Content to perform non-commercial analysis* [our emphasis] (as further explained below) or storing Yelp business IDs which you may use solely for back-end matching purposes . . . Notwithstanding the foregoing, you may use the Yelp Content to perform certain analysis for non-commercial uses only, such as creating rich visualizations or exploring trends and correlations over time, so long as the underlying Yelp Content is only displayed in the aggregate as an analytical output, and not individually . . . 'Non-commercial use' means any use of the Yelp Content which does not generate promotional or monetary value for the creator or the user, or such use does not gain economic value from the use of our content for the creator or user, i.e. you." See: https://www.yelp.com/developers/api_terms.

Table 7.1   **Establishment counts for external data**

Franchise	Web-scraped	Yelp-queried	*FranchiseTimes*
Subway	27,085	13,556	26,741
McDonald's	14,153	12,060	14,153
Burger King	7,139	6,223	7,156
Pizza Hut	6,022	6,116	7,667
Wendy's	5,721	5,535	5,739
Marco's Pizza	838	789	770
KFC	4,193	3,871	4,167
Dunkin' Donuts	8,839	4,697	8,431
7-Eleven	7,624	4,067	7,008
Great Clips	3,702	3,163	3,945
Midas	1,081	1,258	1,125
Ace Hardware	3,816	2,060	4,461
Other (488 non-Core)	.	156,669	284,716
Total (12 Core)	90,213	63,395	91,363
Total (All 500)	90,213	220,064	376,079

Notes: We used the *FranchiseTimes* list to avoid disclosure risk from using confidential Census Bureau or IRS data. All external data were harvested from outside the Census Bureau's IT system.

to effectively address this issue by taking advantage of the structure of Yelp URLs, which typically contain franchise name information (see appendix A for details).

7.2.4   Comparing External Data

In this section, we compare establishment counts from the *FranchiseTimes* and our two sources of external data. We display these counts in table 7.1. As noted, across the 12 core franchises we harvested 90,213 web-scraped establishments and 63,395 Yelp-queried establishments. The *FranchiseTimes* indicates that there are 91,363 establishments affiliated with these 12 franchises. There are an additional 156,669 Yelp-queried establishments affiliated with the other 488 (noncore) franchises. The *FranchiseTimes* indicates that there are 284,716 establishments affiliated with these other franchises.

Overall, these counts make it clear that the Yelp-queried data are usually less comprehensive than the web-scraped data—they do not contain all establishments for all franchises. Indeed, for all but two franchises (Pizza Hut and Midas), the number of web-scraped establishments exceeds the number of Yelp-queried establishments.

7.2.5   Business Register (BR)

The BR is a comprehensive list of US businesses, containing information on approximately 1.8 million establishments affiliated with 160,000 multiunit firms, 5 million single-unit firms, and 21 million nonemployer firms (DeSalvo, Limehouse, and Klimek 2016). It is updated continuously and serves as the frame for most business surveys conducted at the Census Bureau—including the EC. Since we scraped data from franchise websites and queried Yelp during 2017, we linked these external establishments to the 2017 BR.

The BR contains a wide range of information on each establishment, including industry, legal form of organization, payroll, and employment. Crucially for linking to our external data, it also contains information on the name and address of each establishment.

7.2.6   Economic Census

The EC is a quinquennial survey (conducted in years ending in 2 and 7) and is the most comprehensive collection of business activity data conducted by the US Census Bureau. Businesses are mandated to provide information including total sales, product sales, payroll, employment, and industry classification for each establishment that they operate.[8] In addition, businesses are asked whether they are affiliated with a franchise, and if so, whether they are a franchisor or franchisee.[9] Prior to the 2007 EC, franchise status was collected only for restaurants. In the 2007 and 2012 Censuses, businesses across 295 North American Industrial Classification System (NAICS) industries were asked whether any of their establishments operated under a trademark authorized by a franchisor. In an attempt to reduce underreporting, the 2017 EC franchise status question was modified to ask whether an establishment operates under a trademark *or brand* authorized by a franchisor.

As noted in the introduction, FRANdata, a research/advisory company and the strategic research partner of the International Franchise Association (IFA), uses active franchise license agreements to construct a database on franchise-affiliated establishments. In contrast to EC data, which indicates a decline from 453,326 to 409,104 in the number of franchise-affiliated establishments between 2007 and 2012, comparable FRANdata indicates a 4 percent increase in franchise-affiliated establishments. After the release of the 2012 EC, Census Bureau staff, in collaboration with representatives from IFA and FRANdata, set out to identify the reasons for this discrepancy.

The first main reason for the discrepancy was a growth in categories of franchise-affiliated establishments that were captured by FRANdata but were often missing from the EC data. For instance, franchise-affiliated establishments located in another retail outlet, such as a big-box store, are often not counted as a separate business establishment in the EC. In addi-

8. An establishment is defined as the smallest operating unit for which businesses maintain distinct records about inputs, such as payroll and operating expenses. In practice, establishments are typically individual business locations. See: https://www.census.gov/eos/www/naics/2017NAICS/2017_NAICS_Manual.pdf, page 19.

9. Franchise data were also collected as part of the Survey of Business Owners (SBO) and the Annual Survey of Entrepreneurs (ASE).

tion, multiple franchises are often operated out of a single location, such as a travel plaza. However, as the entity that fills out the EC survey form, the travel plaza only counts as a single franchise-affiliated establishment. Finally, some franchises are owned by institutions that are out of scope to the EC, such as colleges and universities and government agencies.

The second main reason for the discrepancy is that in 2007, a Census Bureau staff member spent approximately three months evaluating EC survey responses, comparing them to FRANdata and following up with respondents over the phone. Through this process, a significant number of establishments owned by firms that did not fill out the franchise section on the EC form (i.e., item nonresponse) were recoded to franchise affiliated. In addition, a smaller number of establishments owned by firms that claimed not to be franchise affiliated were recoded as franchise affiliated (i.e., incorrect response). In 2012, comparable resources were not available to conduct this extensive manual editing, contributing to a *measured* decrease in the number of franchise-affiliated establishments. The substantial number of labor hours needed to fully validate and correct the franchise section on the EC form served as motivation in this paper to pursue alternative methods that could be used to quickly and accurately identify (and when necessary, reclassify) franchise-affiliated establishments in the 2017 EC.

7.2.7   Other Possible Sources of External Data

Though franchise websites are an attractive source for harvesting establishment-level franchise data, as noted earlier, this approach has some serious disadvantages. In particular, it is difficult to scale—both because many scraping scripts must be written and maintained and because prohibitions on scraping in websites' *terms of use* requires obtaining permission from each company. The use of Yelp's API is more promising with regard to *terms of use*, but as noted, coverage is incomplete. In this section, we discuss two alternative sources of establishment-level data on franchises that may allow us to achieve comprehensive coverage without violating websites' *terms of use*.

7.2.7.1   *Search Engine Location Services*

One possible alternative approach relies on location services provided by search engine companies. For example, Google provides the Google Places API and Microsoft's Bing provides the Bing Maps Locations API. A user can submit a franchise name and location information (e.g., the zip code or a county/city/state combination) and addresses of the franchise-affiliated establishments in that location are returned. The main advantages of this approach are that Google and Bing continually curate and maintain an up-to-date list of business addresses, ensuring high-quality and timely data, and that only a single script needs to be written to query an API, ensuring scalability. The main disadvantage of this approach is cost. For instance, to ensure comprehensive coverage of 500 franchises across 3,141 counties, we would need to submit over 1.5 million queries to an API, which would cost over $7,500 using Google and over $4,500 using Bing.

7.2.7.2   State Government Websites

The offer and sale of a franchise requires compliance with federal and state franchise laws. While federal law provides a franchise regulatory framework, some states have enacted supplemental franchise laws. In particular, 14 states known as "franchise registration states" require the registration of franchisors' Franchise Disclosure Documents (FDDs), which are another possible source of establishment-level franchise data.[10] One major advantage of this source is the avoidance of *terms of use* violations. Indeed, Census Bureau policy currently allows the scraping of government websites, and the Scraping Assisted by Learning (SABLE) software (Dumbacher and Diamond 2018), which has built-in checks to ensure compliance with a website's *terms of use*, is already used for this purpose. An additional advantage is that FDDs list franchisees, allowing us to distinguish between franchisee- and franchisor-owned establishments within each brand.

7.3   Linking the Data

We link the external establishments scraped from franchise websites and queried from Yelp's API to the 2017 EC in two steps. First, we use MAMBA to link the external establishments to establishments in the 2017 BR. Second, the subset of external establishments that are successfully matched to the BR are then linked to establishments in the 2017 EC. These steps are described in detail in the rest of this section.

7.3.1   Linking External Establishments to BR Establishments

MAMBA, developed by Cuffe and Goldschlag (2018), is specialized software designed to link business establishments from external data sources to establishments in the BR. It does this by constructing predictive features using name and address information, and then feeding these features into a random forest, which generates predicted probabilities of matches. In our case, for each external establishment (web-scraped or Yelp-queried), MAMBA identifies the establishments in the BR that are most likely to be positive matches. In this context, because all our external establishments are affiliated with a franchise, MAMBA essentially identifies a subset of BR establishments that are likely to be franchise affiliated.

10. These states include California, Hawaii, Illinois, Indiana, Maryland, Michigan, Minnesota, New York, North Dakota, Rhode Island, South Dakota, Virginia, Washington, and Wisconsin. On 3/11/2019, a review of active FDDs for Wisconsin suggested the existence of 1,401 active franchises—well in excess of the 500 contained in the *FranchiseTimes Top 200+*. See https://www.wdfi.org/apps/franchiseefiling/activeFilings.aspx for the current list.

Table 7.2   **Match of external establishments to Business Register (BR)**

	Web-scraped	Yelp (Core)	Yelp (non-Core)
External establishments	90,213	63,395	156,669
Any match	65,000	47,500	93,000
1-to-1 match	57,500	44,500	89,000

Notes: The counts in the "External establishments" row are exact and the counts in the "Any match" and "1-to-1 match" rows are rounded. All counts are unweighted.

The results of this linking exercise are displayed in table 7.2.[11] The row titled "External Estabs" shows that, as discussed, there are 90,213 web-scraped establishments, 63,395 core Yelp-queried establishments, and 156,669 non-core Yelp-queried establishments. The row titled "Any Match" shows that approximately 65,000 (72 percent), 47,500 (75 percent), and 93,000 (59 percent) of these are matched to a BR establishment. Thus, it is clear that establishments affiliated with a core franchise are much more likely than those affiliated with a noncore franchise to match to a BR establishment.

Note that in the "Any Match" row, a given BR establishment may be matched to more than one external establishment.[12] The next row, titled "1-to-1 Match," shows that approximately 57,500 (64 percent) web-scraped, 44,500 (70 percent) core Yelp-queried, and 89,000 (57 percent) noncore Yelp-queried establishments are 1-to-1 matches with a BR establishment—that is, an external establishment uniquely matches to a BR establishment and the BR establishment matches uniquely back to the external establishment. Since we know external establishments are affiliated with a franchise, these 1-to-1 matches can be treated as BR establishments that MAMBA predicts to be franchise affiliated.

7.3.2   Linking 1-to-1 Matches to the Economic Census

Our next step is to link the BR establishments that MAMBA predicts as being franchise affiliated (i.e., external establishments that are 1-to-1 matches with a BR establishment) to the 2017 EC.[13] This allows us to examine whether MAMBA's predictions are consistent with whether an establishment is characterized as franchise affiliated on their EC form.

---

11. Since core Yelp-queried establishments are affiliated with the same 12 franchises as the web-scraped establishments, there is substantial overlap between the two data sources (see appendix B), and so combining them will create duplicate establishments. To prevent this, web-scraped and Yelp-queried establishments are separately matched to the BR (though core and noncore Yelp-queried establishments are matched at the same time).

12. Since web-scraped and Yelp-queried establishments are separately matched to the BR, these multiple matches are not driven by the fact that some web-scraped establishments correspond with establishments in the Yelp-queried data and vice versa. Indeed, these multiple matches occur even *within* each source of external data—that is a BR establishment may match to multiple web-scraped establishments or multiple Yelp-queried establishments.

13. We use EC files captured in May 2019.

Table 7.3   Match of 1-to-1 establishments to Economic Census (EC)

	Web-scraped	Yelp (Core)	Yelp (non-Core)
1-to-1 match with BR	57,500	44,500	89,000
Surveyed in 2017 EC	52,500	40,500	78,500
EC form processed	29,000	21,500	41,000

Note: All counts are rounded and all are unweighted.

Once an external establishment is linked to the BR, it is straightforward to link it to the EC using an internal establishment identifier. Table 7.3 summarizes this link. The row labeled "1-to-1 Match with BR" shows that, as in table 7.2, there are approximately 57,500 web-scraped, 44,500 core Yelp-queried, and 89,000 noncore Yelp-queried establishments that MAMBA identifies as 1-to-1 matches with a BR establishment. The row labeled "Surveyed in 2017 EC" shows that approximately 52,500 (91 percent), 40,500 (91 percent), and 78,500 (88 percent) of these are included in the 2017 EC. Since the processing of the 2017 EC is still ongoing, the row labeled "2017 EC Form Processed" reports the number of 1-to-1 matches that are included in the 2017 EC whose forms have been processed—approximately 29,000 (55 percent) web-scraped, 21,500 (53 percent) core Yelp-queried, and 41,000 (52 percent) noncore Yelp-queried establishments.

For most of the remainder of the paper, we focus on these 29,000 web-scraped and 62,500 Yelp-queried (21,500 core and 41,000 noncore) establishments. These are the subset of establishments that MAMBA predicts to be franchise affiliated, for whom we can also examine survey responses (or nonresponses) about their franchise status on the 2017 EC form.

7.4   Evaluating Responses on the 2017 Economic Census

As noted in the previous section, we have 29,000 web-scraped, 21,500 core Yelp-queried, and 41,000 noncore Yelp-queried establishments that are both predicted to be franchise affiliated by MAMBA and have had their survey forms processed for the 2017 EC. This gives us a unique opportunity to examine whether survey responses about the establishments are consistent with MAMBA's predictions, and if they are inconsistent, examine which is correct.

Table 7.4 examines these responses to the 2017 EC survey form. The row titled "Franchisor or Franchisee" shows the number of establishments that respondents claim to be franchise affiliated. As the row name suggests, an establishment is classified as franchise-affiliated if the respondent claimed to be either a franchisor or franchisee on its EC survey form. We see that 21,500 (74 percent) web-scraped, 16,500 (77 percent) core Yelp-queried, and 28,500 (70 percent) noncore Yelp-queried establishments are identified as franchise

Table 7.4   **Responses to franchise questions for 1-to-1 establishments with processed forms**

	Web-scraped	Yelp (Core)	Yelp (non-Core)
EC form processed	29,000	21,500	41,000
Franchisor or franchisee	21,500	16,500	28,500
Not affiliated or not answered	7,400	5,000	12,500

Note: All counts are rounded and all are unweighted.

affiliated by respondents, consistent with MAMBA's prediction. Thus, for a majority of establishments, the MAMBA prediction and EC form agree that the establishment is franchise affiliated, with somewhat higher proportions for establishments affiliated with our 12 core franchises. However, the row labeled "Not Affiliated or Not Answered" shows that this leaves a substantial number of establishments—7,400 (26 percent), 5,000 (23 percent), and 12,500 (30 percent)—that respondents claim not to be franchise affiliated, contradicting MAMBA's prediction. An establishment is classified as not being franchise affiliated if the respondent either did not fill out the franchise portion of its EC survey form or did fill it out but claimed that the establishment was not franchise affiliated. Both these groups are classified as not being franchise affiliated because they would be classified as such if their EC forms were taken at face value. Overall, table 7.4 shows that a substantial portion of establishments have conflicting information.

These conflicts raise a crucial question: for how many establishments is MAMBA's prediction correct and for how many establishments is the EC survey form correct? To the extent that MAMBA correctly identifies franchise-affiliated establishments that respondents mistakenly label as not being franchise affiliated, this information can be used to recode incorrect EC forms and improve the accuracy of the count of franchise-affiliated establishments in the 2017 EC.

We answer this question by taking random samples of the 7,400 web-scraped and 17,500 Yelp-queried establishments for which the MAMBA prediction and EC form are inconsistent, manually comparing the name and address information from the BR to the franchise name and address information from the external data, and determining whether the establishments are, in fact, true matches. Note that this is the only manual part of our process. The results of this manual validation are displayed in table 7.5.

As in table 7.4, there are approximately 7,400 web-scraped, 5,000 core Yelp-queried, and 12,500 noncore Yelp-queried establishments that EC respondents report are *not* franchise affiliated, but that MAMBA predicts to be franchise affiliated. Manual investigation reveals that in most cases, MAMBA's prediction of franchise-affiliation is correct. Indeed, we estimate that 98.4 percent of web-scraped establishments whose survey form con-

Table 7.5   MAMBA's predictions vs. EC form responses

	Web-scraped	Yelp (Core)	Yelp (non-Core)
Not affiliated or not answered	7,400	5,000	12,500
MAMBA prediction correct (est.)	98.4%	95.5%	93.5%

Notes: All counts are rounded and all are unweighted. The estimates for the percent of establishments that MAMBA correctly predicts to be franchise-affiliated is based on random samples of size 300 from each category.

tradicts MAMBA's prediction are, in fact, franchise affiliated. Similarly, we estimate that the percentages are 95.5 percent and 93.5 percent for core and noncore Yelp-queried establishments. Thus, it appears that, as was also found in the 2007 EC, a substantial fraction of respondents either incorrectly filled out the franchise section on their 2017 EC survey form or did not fill it out at all.

These results suggest that we can conservatively recode the responses of 90 percent or more of establishments that MAMBA predicts are franchise affiliated but that respondents report are *not* franchise affiliated. In our data, this translates into an additional 7,282 web-scraped, 4,755 core Yelp-queried, and 11,688 noncore Yelp-queried franchise-affiliated establishments,[14] which is an increase of 34 percent, 29 percent, and 41 percent, respectively, relative to the counts obtained from the 2017 EC form alone.[15]

As noted above, 26 percent of web-scraped, 23 percent of core Yelp-queried and 30 percent of noncore Yelp-queried establishments whose 2017 EC forms have been processed are classified by respondents as not being franchise affiliated (see table 7.4). If these proportions hold, once all 52,500 web-scraped, 40,500 core Yelp-queried, and 78,500 noncore Yelp-queried establishments' EC survey forms are processed (see table 7.3), we can expect 13,650 (= 52,500 * 0.26), 9,315 (= 40,500 * 0.23), and 23,550 (= 78,500 * 0.30) to be classified as not being franchise affiliated on the basis of their EC form. If we conservatively reclassified 90 percent of these as franchise affiliated, we would obtain an extra 12,285 web-scraped, 8,384 core Yelp-queried, and 21,195 noncore Yelp-queried franchise-affiliated establishments than would be suggested by the EC form alone.

7.5 Conclusion

In this paper, we develop a method to mostly automate the evaluation of responses to the franchise section of the 2017 EC. The method combines external data on franchise-affiliated establishments with machine learning

14. These were computed using information in table 7.5: 7282 = 7400 * 0.984, 4755 = 5000 * 0.955, and 11688 = 12500 * 0.935.
15. These were computed using information from tables 7.4 and 7.5: 0.339 = 7282/21500, 0.288 = 4755/16500, and 0.410 = 11688/28500.

algorithms to predict which establishments in the BR are franchise affiliated, links these establishments to the 2017 EC, and then examines whether respondents also characterize the establishment as franchise affiliated.

We find that, while the predictions and survey forms agree for a majority of establishments, there are a substantial minority of cases in which an establishment is predicted to be franchise affiliated, but the survey form does not characterize the establishment as such. The only manual part of our approach is the examination of a random sample of these discrepancies, which reveals that the predictions of franchise affiliation are typically correct, and the form is filled out incorrectly. Recoding these establishments substantially increases the count of franchise-affiliated establishments in the 2017 EC. Thus, we find that our method provides a cost-effective way to evaluate responses to the franchise section of the 2017 EC and, in turn, to potentially improve the count of franchise-affiliated establishments in the US.

If a version of our process is used to augment the production of official franchising statistics, several improvements can be made. First, since we only collect data on 12 core and 488 noncore franchises, it will be crucial to obtain a much more comprehensive external list of franchise-affiliated establishments. We believe the most promising sources for this comprehensive data are search engine location services and franchise disclosure documents from state government websites, both of which are discussed in section 7.2.7. Our process allowed us to reclassify enough establishments to increase (relative to taking the EC form at face value) the franchise-affiliated count by 34 percent (web-scraped) and 29 percent (Yelp-queried) for the 12 core franchises and by 41 percent (Yelp-queried) for the 488 noncore franchises. Since additional franchises from an expanded list are likely to more closely resemble the 488 noncore franchises, we may expect a higher reclassification *rate* for EC establishments matched to establishments affiliated with the newly acquired franchises. However, since the newly acquired franchises will tend to have fewer affiliated establishments, the impact of adding these franchises to the total *count* of reclassified establishments may be modest.

Second, it will be important to improve MAMBA's predictions. More comprehensive data will help with this. In addition, MAMBA enables users to manually create bespoke training data tailored for a specific use case. Though the creation of these training data will require extensive manual labeling of true and false matches, the probability of significantly improving match rates between the external data and the BR is likely to make it worthwhile.

Finally, in this paper we only manually examine discrepancy cases in which MAMBA predicts that an establishment is franchise affiliated, but its EC form indicates otherwise. It will also be crucial to examine discrepancy cases in which an establishment's EC form indicates it is franchise affiliated, but MAMBA fails to predict it as such. To get a truly accurate franchise count, some of these establishments may need to be reclassified as not franchise affiliated.

Appendix A
Identifying Franchise-Affiliated Yelp-Queried Establishments

One of the disadvantages of the Yelp-queried data is ambiguity regarding the franchise with which an establishment is affiliated. Unfortunately, when a franchise name is used to query Yelp's API, not all harvested establishments are actually affiliated with the queried franchise. For instance, a query for "franchise A" might yield several establishments affiliated with that franchise but might also yield other nearby establishments affiliated with "franchise B" (or nearby establishments not affiliated with any franchise). Thus, it is crucial to identify which establishments harvested from a query for a franchise are actually affiliated with that franchise.

We address this issue by taking advantage of the fact that Yelp URLs typically embed the name of the franchise with which each establishment is affiliated. Moreover, each URL is augmented with information that distinguishes the establishment from other establishments affiliated with the same franchise. This allows us to identify, with a fairly high level of confidence, all establishments in the Yelp database that are affiliated with a given franchise. To illustrate, consider the Yelp URLs listed below.

- https://www.yelp.com/biz/**franchise-a-**-*boston-downtown-seaport-boston-2*
- https://www.yelp.com/biz/**franchise-a-**-*boston-back-bay-fenway-boston*
- https://www.yelp.com/biz/**franchise-b-**-*atlanta-ne-atlanta-2*
- https://www.yelp.com/biz/**franchise-b-**-*austin-austin*
- https://www.yelp.com/biz/**nonfranchise-establishment-1-**-*boulder-longmont*
- https://www.yelp.com/biz/**nonfranchise-establishment-2-**-*brooklyn-queens-queens*

The bold fragments of each URL indicate the name of the establishment. The italicized fragments give information on the location of the establishment, which differentiates URLs affiliated with different establishments but the same franchise. For instance, the bold fragment of the first two URLs suggests that the establishments are affiliated with franchise A, and the italicized fragment suggests the establishments are located in different neighborhoods in Boston. The bold fragment of the second two URLs suggests that the establishments are affiliated with franchise B, and the italicized fragment suggests that one establishment is located Atlanta and the other in Austin.

Finally, the bold fragment of the last two URLs suggests that the establishments are not affiliated with any franchise on the *FranchiseTimes 200+* list.

Appendix B
Linking Web-Scraped Establishments to Yelp-Queried Establishments

In this section, we use franchise names and establishment addresses to link web-scraped establishments to Yelp-queried establishments, which allows us to examine the extent of overlap between the two data sources. To do this, we use a deterministic rule-based algorithm to link establishments, which we show to be highly accurate in this context—less than 1 percent of matches are false positives.

The deterministic rule-based algorithm we use to link web-scraped and Yelp-queried establishments can be broken down into two broad steps—a preprocessing and a matching step—along with a series of sub-steps:[16]

Web-Scraped / Yelp-queried (W-Y) Establishment Matching Algorithm

- Step 1: Address and Name Preprocessing
  - –A: Clean and standardize franchise names and addresses in both the web-scraped and Yelp-queried data.
  - –B: Parse addresses into component parts.
- Step 2: Matching
  - –A: Exact match using street number, zip code, and franchise name.
  - –B: Fuzzy match on street name.

W-Y Step 1 involves preparing the web-scraped and Yelp-queried data for matching. W-Y Step 1A involves organizing the data scraped from the 12 franchise websites and data scraped from Yelp into the same format. It also involves standardization operations such as trimming of whitespace, converting all text to lowercase, eliminating nonalphanumeric characters, etc. Step 1B enables matching separately on different address components (e.g., zip code, street number, street name), rather than matching based on the entire unparsed address string.

W-Y Step 2 implements the matching process using the standardized data produced in the previous step. In W-Y Step 2A, we identify all pairwise combinations of web-scraped and Yelp-queried establishments that are affiliated with the same franchise, located in the same zip code, and have the

---

16. For this linking exercise, since we scrape data from 12 franchise websites, we only retain Yelp-queried establishments belonging to these same 12 franchises. When we link scraped establishments to the BR, we use Yelp-queried establishments from all 496 franchises in the *FranchiseTimes 200+* list.

Table 7A.1   Match of web-scraped establishments to Yelp-queried establishments

	Web-to-Yelp	Yelp-to-web
External establishments	90,213	63,395
Any match	51,144	51,642
1-to-1 match	50,255	50,255

same street number. Notice that the street name plays no role in the match process at Step 2A. However, at W-Y Step 2B the street address is used to narrow the number of possible matches. Specifically, we use 26 different string comparators to compute 26 similarity scores between the street names for each pairwise combination of establishments identified in the previous step.[17] We then compute the mean similarity score and identify the subset of establishment combinations that have the highest score.

Table 7A.1 gives an overview of the results this algorithm produces. The column titled "Web-to-Yelp" examines links of web-scraped establishments to Yelp-queried establishments. The column titled "Yelp-to-Web" examines the results for matching in the reverse direction—Yelp-queried establishments to web-scraped establishments. As also shown in table 7.1, there are a total of 90,213 web-scraped and 63,395 Yelp-queried establishments across the 12 core franchises.

The row titled "Any" indicates the count of establishments from one source that match to at least one establishment from the other source. We see that 51,144 (56.7 percent) web-scraped establishments match to a Yelp-queried establishment and 51,642 (81.4 percent) Yelp-queried establishments match to a web-scraped establishment. The row titled "1-to-1 Match" indicates the count of establishments from one source that are uniquely matched to an establishment in the other source and vice versa. By definition, this count must be the same whether we are matching Web-to-Yelp or Yelp-to-Web. We see that 50,225 external establishments are uniquely matched across the two data sources, which is 55.7 percent of web-scraped establishments and 79.3 percent of Yelp-queried establishments.

In sum, there is a large number of web-scraped establishments (43.3 percent) that are unmatched to a Yelp-queried establishment and substantially fewer Yelp-queried establishments (18.5 percent) that are unmatched to a web-scraped establishment. Conversely, about 79.3 percent of Yelp-queried establishments are 1-to-1 matches with a web-scraped establishment, but only 55.7 percent of web-scraped establishments are 1-to-1 matches with a Yelp-queried establishment. These patterns reflect the less comprehensive coverage of the Yelp data.

It is important to note that just because a web-scraped establishment and

17. We use Stata's *matchit* command to compute the similarity scores.

a Yelp-queried establishment are designated as a 1-to-1 match does not mean the match is correct. Thus, to examine the accuracy of the deterministic rule-based algorithm, we manually examine random samples of the 50,225 1-to-1 matches. This exercise leads us to conclude that the algorithm is highly accurate in this context—indeed, we estimate a false positive match rate of less than 1 percent.

References

Cuffe, John, and Nathan Goldschlag. 2018. "Squeezing More Out of Your Data: Business Record Linkage with Python." Center for Economic Studies Working Paper 18-46, US Census Bureau, Washington, DC.
DeSalvo, Bethany, Frank F. Limehouse, and Shawn D. Klimek. 2016. "Documenting the Business Register and Related Economic Business Data." Center for Economic Studies Working Paper 16-17, US Census Bureau, Washington, DC.
Dumbacher, Brian, and Cavan Capps. 2016. "Big Data Methods for Scraping Government Tax Revenue from the Web." In *Proceedings of the American Statistical Association*, Section on Statistical Learning and Data Science, 2940–54. Alexandria, VA: American Statistical Association.
Dumbacher, Brian, and L. K. Diamond. 2018. "SABLE: Tools for Web Crawling, Web Scraping, and Text Classification." Federal Committee on Statistical Methodology Research Conference, March 7, 2018. https://nces.ed.gov/FCSM/2018_ResearchPolicyConference.asp.

8

Using Public Data to Generate Industrial Classification Codes

John Cuffe, Sudip Bhattacharjee, Ugochukwu Etudo,
Justin C. Smith, Nevada Basdeo, Nathaniel Burbank,
and Shawn R. Roberts

8.1 Introduction

Statistical agencies face increasing costs, lower response rates, and increased demands for timely and accurate statistical data. These increased demands on agency resources reveal the need for alternative data sources, ideally data that are cheaper than current surveys and available within a short time frame. Textual data available on public-facing websites present an ideal data source for certain US Census Bureau (henceforth Census) statistical products. In this paper, we identify such data sources and argue that these sources may be particularly well suited for classification tasks such as industrial or occupational coding. Using these sources of data provides the

John Cuffe is a statistician on the MOJO Development Team at the US Census Bureau.

Sudip Bhattacharjee is a professor in the School of Business at the University of Connecticut, and chief of the Center for Big Data Research at the US Census Bureau.

Ugochukwu Etudo is an assistant professor in operations and information management at the University of Connecticut.

Justin C. Smith is currently a senior data scientist at Optum. He was a data scientist in the Center for Optimization and Data Science at the US Census Bureau when this chapter was written.

Nevada Basdeo is a data scientist in the Center for Optimization and Data Science at the US Census Bureau.

Nathaniel Burbank is a forecasting economist data scientist at Wayfair.

Shawn R. Roberts is the founder of Akari Technologies.

Any opinions and conclusions expressed herein are those of the authors and do not necessarily represent the views of the US Census Bureau. All results have been reviewed to ensure that no confidential information is disclosed, DRB approval CBDRB-FY19-191. We thank Catherine Buffington, Lucia Foster, Javier Miranda, and the participants of the CRIW conference for their comments and suggestions. For acknowledgments, sources of research support, and disclosure of the authors' material financial relationships, if any, please see https://www.nber.org/books-and-chapters/big-data-21st-century-economic-statistics/using-public-data-generate-industrial-classification-codes.

opportunity for statistical agencies to provide more accurate, timelier data for lower costs and lower respondent burden compared to traditional survey methods, while opening the door for new and innovative statistical products.

In this paper, we explore how public data can improve the production of federal statistics, using the specific case of website text and user reviews, gathered from Google Places API, to generate North American Industrial Classification System (NAICS) codes for approximately 120,000 single-unit employer establishments. Our approach shows that public data are a useful tool for generating NAICS codes. We also find challenges and provide suggestions for agencies implementing such a system for production purposes. The paper proceeds as follows: first, we highlight the business issues with current methods, before discussing new methods being used to generate industrial and occupational classifications in statistical agencies in several countries. Then we discuss our approach, combining web scraping with modern machine learning techniques to provide a low-cost alternative to current methods. Finally, we discuss our findings in the context of the Census Bureau's current capabilities and limitations.

8.1.1   The Case for NAICS Codes

The NAICS is the system by which multiple federal and international statistical agencies assign business establishments to industrial sectors or classes. Economic statistics, such as the Business Dynamics Statistics (Halti-wanger, Jarmin, and Miranda 2008), and survey sampling frames rely on timely and accurate industrial classification data. Currently, NAICS codes are produced by multiple statistical agencies: The Census produces classifications through multiple surveys, most notably the Economic Census (EC). The Bureau of Labor Statistics (BLS) generates and uses NAICS codes in its surveys, and the Social Security Administration (SSA) produces codes for newly established businesses via information on the SS4 Application for Employee Identification Number (EIN) form. NAICS classification provides an ideal testbed for use of public data—more accurate, timely, and consistent NAICS codes would save Census considerable effort, and improve statistical quality and timeliness. For example, the EC uses "classification cards," which are forms sent to a business prior to the EC in an attempt to identify its correct NAICS code, which enables the correct EC electronic survey path for that business. Filling out such an additional "classification card" form adds substantial burden to respondents, increases survey costs, and may also suffer from lower response rates. Our proposed methodology has the potential to allow Census to avoid such costly classification procedures and deliver better data products at a faster rate. Another compelling reason to develop NAICS codes from public data sources is that laws that govern data sharing between agencies prevent reconciliation between agency codes. A standardized set of assigned classifications would allow agencies

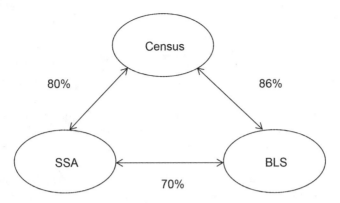

Fig. 8.1   Agreement on NAICS sectors between Census, BLS, and SSA
Source: 2012 Business Register Single Unit Businesses.
Note: Figure shows the percentage of BR establishments that share a common 2-digit NAICS sector when present in each respective data source.

to coordinate their lists and ensure all establishments receive the same code. Figure 8.1 shows the percentage of agreement, at the 2-digit level, between NAICS codes produced by the 2012 EC, BLS, and SSA for the same set of single-unit establishments active in 2012. It shows that the Census and BLS, when coding the same cases, agree on the NAICS *sector* in approximately 86 percent of cases, whereas the BLS and SSA concur in around 70 percent of cases.

Several statistical agencies have attempted to use textual data as a means for classification. Much of the work has focused on generating occupational classifications based on write-in survey responses (for example, Fairman et al. 2012; Gweon et al. 2017; Jung et al. 2008). There are also attempts to generate classifications of businesses. The British Office for National Statistics has attempted to use public textual information on companies to generate unsupervised classifications of industries (Office for National Statistics, 2018), identifying industrial clusters using a combination of Doc2Vec and Singular Value Decomposition (SVD) models. The data were fit on a "relatively small" number of observations, leaving the usefulness of the method at much more fine-grained levels unknown (Office for National Statistics 2018). Researchers from National Statistics Netherlands explored how to generate industrial classifications similar to NAICS codes using Term Frequency-Inverse Document Frequency (TF-IDF) and dictionary-based feature selections via Naive Bayes, Support Vector Machine, and Random Forest classifiers, finding three main complicating factors for classification: the size of the business, the source of the industrial code, and the complexity of the business website (Roelands, van Delden, and Windmeijer 2017). Finally, the Australian Bureau of Statistics implemented a system that generates classifications based on placing short, free-text responses into classification hierarchies using a bag of words, one-hot encoding approach. This approach has the advantage of simplicity—for each word in the vocabulary, a record receives a "1" if its response contains that word, and a zero otherwise. However, this approach also ignores the context of words, a possible issue when seeking to distinguish closely related industries (Tarnow-Mordi 2017). In the US statistical system, Kearney and Kornbau (2005) produced the SSA's "Autocoder," a system that uses word dictionaries and predicts NAICS codes based on open-response text on Internal Revenue Service (IRS) Form SS4, the application for a new EIN. The Autocoder, developed in the early 2000s, remains in service and relies on a combination of logistic regression and subject-matter experts for quality assurance and manual coding tasks. Other work has sought to apply similar methods as ours to coding occupational injuries and occupational types (Bertke et al. 2016; Gweon et al. 2017; Ikudo et al. 2018; Measure 2014).

We seek to build on previous work by generating 2-digit NAICS sectors for a sample of single-unit employer businesses active in 2015 to 2016. Our approach combines web scraping of company websites, company names, and user reviews to generate a corpus of text associated with each business. We then apply Doc2Vec methods to reduce dimensionality of the data in a similar manner to previous attempts (Roelands, van Delden, and Windmeijer 2017; Tarnow-Mordi 2017). Finally, we use the outputs of this textual analysis as inputs into a Random Forest classifier, seeking to identify 2-digit NAICS codes.

8.2   Data and Methods

Our approach includes collecting publicly available data from company websites and user-generated reviews of businesses and combining them with Census protected information on individual business establishments. We utilize public APIs to collect a target sample of approximately 1.3 million business establishments, match those records to the Business Register (BR) by name and address, perform textual preprocessing on available text in user reviews, company websites, and company name, and finally use these outputs as features (independent variables) in a Random Forest classifier to predict 2-digit NAICS codes. We first provide a brief overview of each stage of our approach, then compare our dataset sample to the universe of single-unit employer businesses.

8.2.1   Data from APIs and Web Scraping

An Application Program Interface (API) is a set of procedures that allows users to access information or other services from a provider. For example, Google Places API (used to collect our data) allows access to business information such as name, address, rating, user reviews, website URL,[1] contact information, and Google Types[2] tags. We leverage this information in two ways. First, public user reviews provide a rich source of contextual information about a business. For example, products users describe in their reviews—multiple reviews on the quality of steak from an establishment—increases the likelihood the business is a restaurant versus a manufacturing plant. Second, we visit the website (when available) and "scrape" its visible textual information. The working assumption is that a company website provides clear and direct information about products or services it offers. Next, we use Google Types, which vary in usefulness, with less useful words like "establishment" and "point of interest," but also words such as "hotel," "bar," or even "Hindu Temple," which would greatly aid a model in classifying a business. Finally, we use the name of the company, as company names often indicate the type of products on offer (e.g., Krusty Burger). Together, these four elements—all sourced from publicly gathered data—provide us with the type of information needed to describe a business, what products it may sell, and how its customers use or perceive those products (Jabine 1984).

To generate our sample of businesses, we conducted a grid search on both Yelp and Google Places APIs, based on a combination of lat/long coordinates and keywords. We identified the geographic center of each Core-Based Statistical Area (CBSA) and each county therein to serve as the starting point for our search.[3] To identify keywords, we found all words contained in the titles of all two-digit NAICS sectors.[4] We then executed an API search for each keyword in 50 random locations for each CBSA and county, around the centroids provided above, with a set search radius of 10km. This resulted in 1,272,000 records, with approximately 70 percent of those coming from Yelp API. Next, we performed a search for each of those businesses on Google Places API, retrieving website URL, user reviews, and Google Types. The website URL was then visited and text was scraped using an internally developed procedure.

For this study, we eliminated records that did not have a website and user reviews, to have the best sample to determine the overall utility of both sources of data jointly. This restriction reduced the number of available records from 1,272,000 to approximately 290,000. Future research can attempt to generate NAICS codes for establishments that lack either a website or user reviews.

---

1. URL: Uniform Resource Locator, or website address.
2. A list of over 100 different classification tags assigned by Google to describe a place.
3. This geographical search pattern will certainly mean that businesses not residing in a CBSA, or any industries that are more common in rural areas, may be undersampled. As discussed below, industries more common in rural areas (e.g., farming, mining) are heavily undersampled when we match to the BR. Further research is seeking to rectify this bias.
4. https://www.census.gov/eos/www/naics/.

8.2.2   Matching Collected Data to the Business Register

The Business Register (BR) is the Census Bureau's comprehensive data-base of US business establishments and companies, covering all employer and nonemployer businesses.[5] To identify if our 290,000 records appear in the BR, we utilized the Multiple Algorithm Matching for Better Analytics (MAMBA) software (Cuffe and Goldschlag 2018). This software utilizes machine learning techniques to link records based on name and address and provides high-quality matches. It also provides us with match metrics so we may identify quality matches over more tenuous linkages. In order to reduce the possibility of spurious linkages, we required that any matched pair must have either a 5-digit zip code, or city name, or 3-digit zip code in common—in order of importance. We ran two particular matches—the first matching on both name and address, and then a residual matching by only business name.

After matching the Google API data with the BR, we focus on the 120,000 *single-unit* (SU)[6] establishments that have both website and review text and are employer-based businesses. This accounts for 43.44 percent of the records. This seemingly low match rate is the result of three circumstances: First, we only use *single-unit employer* businesses for a cleaner analysis. *Multiunit* (MU) firms sometimes have a complicated nature of assigned industrial codes. For example, large retail companies may have storefronts (NAICS 42), warehouses (48–49), and corporate headquarters (55), all pointing to the same website with similar user reviews, making identification using our methods problematic. Additionally, the restriction to *employer* businesses may eliminate many nonemployer business matches. Second, Google records may not exist in the 2016 version of the BR. The Census Bureau estimated that approximately 350,000 businesses would form after 2016Q3 (before we initiated our search), meaning any of these businesses may appear in Google but would not appear as an employer business in the Census data (Bayard et al. 2018a, 2018b),[7] or the Google records may be falsified, and hence cannot be matched (Copeland and Bindley 2019). Finally, the initial scraping occurred in December 2017/January 2018, whereas the BR data are from 2015/2016. Thus, in some cases the BR data are almost two years older than the Google data. In some industries, this is a substantial issue: studies have found that approximately 19 percent of all service-providing businesses (e.g.,

---

5. https://www.census.gov/econ/overview/mu0600.html.

6. A single-unit (SU) establishment is a standalone business, whereas an "establishment" is defined as a particular location. A multiunit (MU) establishment in a given location is part of a larger business which operates in many locations. Our sample includes only employer-based businesses.

7. The Business Register defines a business as an employer business if it has payroll on March 12 of a given year. By measuring from 2016Q3, we account for any formations after this period. Figure sourced by taking the number of expected business formations for 2016Q3, 2016Q4, 2017Q1, and then multiplying 2017Qs 2–4 by the proportion of quarters remaining in the year.

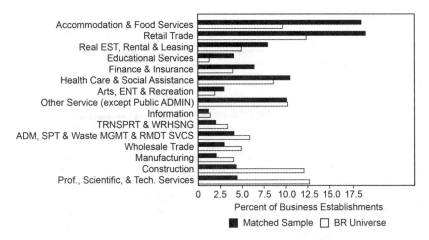

Fig. 8.2   NAICS code sample representation vs. Business Register
Source: Business Register, 2015–2016. Google Places API.
Note: Figure shows the percentage of single-unit establishments in each sector on the 2015/2016 (pool) BR (black, bottom) and the percentage of establishments in our matched sample (gray, top).

NAICS code 41 or higher) fail within their first year of operation (Luo and Stark, 2014, 11), meaning that many BR businesses may no longer exist, or appear as prominent search results, in the Google database.

8.2.3   Matched Data Quality

Figure 8.2 shows the percentage comparison for each NAICS sector between our sample (upper bar) and the BR single-unit employer universe (lower bar). It reveals that our sample heavily oversamples NAICS 44/45 (Retail Trade) and 72 (Accommodation and Food Services). Approximately 12.28 percent of all BR single-unit employers fall into the Retail Trade sector; however, this sector makes up almost 19 percent of our sample. This is expected, as approximately two thirds of our sample was sourced from Yelp, which is dominated by food services. In general, Google Places and Yelp both target public-facing industries in their APIs. On the other hand, our approach *undersamples* NAICS code 54, Professional, Scientific, and Technical Services, which is about 12.6 percent of all businesses, but only 4.36 percent in our sample. Our sample also undersamples Construction and Mining sectors relative to their size in the Business Register.

8.2.4   Textual Data

We analyzed our sample (120,000 records) to see how many unique words were used within the user reviews and website text for each NAICS sector. This provides a measure of signal to noise (textual information) for a given sector, which helps in classification accuracy of that sector. A model will

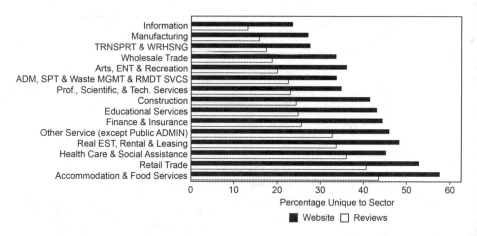

Fig. 8.3   Uniqueness of word corpora by NAICS code

Sources: Business Register, 2015–2016. Google Places API.

Note: Figure shows the percentage of words appearing in website (top, gray) and review (bottom, black) that are unique to the particular NAICS sector.

have the easiest time identifying a NAICS sector if *all* the words used in the reviews or website are unique to that sector. Figure 8.3 shows the proportion of words found in website and review text that are unique to that sector. The larger the proportion of unique words, the simpler the classification decision for a model should be. Two clear trends emerge. First, there is a great deal of heterogeneity between NAICS sectors. For example, the Information sector contains only 22 percent of words used on websites that are unique to that sector, compared to almost 58 percent in Accommodation and Food Services. Second, website text always contains a greater proportion of words that are unique to the sector compared to user reviews across all sectors. This may provide early indications that website text may provide a clearer way to identify NAICS codes; however, more sophisticated Natural Language Processing techniques are required for verification.[8]

8.2.5   Natural Language Processing

Natural Language Processing (NLP) is a suite of analysis tools that gives mathematical meaning to words and phrases, converting words and phrases to a numerical format based on their semantic and contextual occurrence within a corpus of documents. For this research, we require this approach to convert website and review text into sensible dimensions, which we can then use in a model to classify companies into NAICS sectors. The most

---

8. Another possibility here is insufficient HTML parsing. We used standardized software (BeautifulSoup4, https://www.crummy.com/software/BeautifulSoup/) for our parsing; however, it is possible many words in the HTML text are insufficiently parsed fragments.

basic form of NLP appears as "one-hot encoding," demonstrated in Matrix 1. Although this method can be used for many classifiers (e.g., Naive Bayes), it has some major disadvantages—namely, that it does not account for the context of words. For example, when identifying if the word "club" is associated with either a restaurant or a golf course, we would need to know if the word "club," when used in context, appears near to the words "sandwich" or "golf."

Matrix 1: Demonstration of one-hot encoding in a sentence

$$
(1) \quad
\begin{pmatrix} Do \\ Or \\ Do \\ Not \\ There \\ Is \\ No \\ Try \end{pmatrix}
=
\begin{pmatrix}
1 & 0 & 0 & 0 & 0 & 0 & 0 \\
0 & 1 & 0 & 0 & 0 & 0 & 0 \\
1 & 0 & 0 & 0 & 0 & 0 & 0 \\
0 & 0 & 1 & 0 & 0 & 0 & 0 \\
0 & 0 & 0 & 1 & 0 & 0 & 0 \\
0 & 0 & 0 & 0 & 1 & 0 & 0 \\
0 & 0 & 0 & 0 & 0 & 1 & 0 \\
0 & 0 & 0 & 0 & 0 & 0 & 1
\end{pmatrix} .
$$

As an alternative to contextless approaches, Word2Vec methods were first developed by Mikolov et al. (2013) to more adequately capture context in words. Word2Vec models operate by calculating the likelihood of a word appearing, *given the words surrounding it*. In this "skip-gram" model, a neural network is used to identify a latent layer of relationships between words by assessing how likely different words are to appear near each other in sets of text. Figure 8.4 shows a basic illustration, where the model seeks to identify the probability of any of the listed words appearing given the word "burger" appears nearby. In our case, we should expect to see more mentions of the words "burger," "salad," "pork," and "pizza" near one another in reviews and websites belonging to businesses in the Accommodation and Food services NAICS code, whereas we may see words like "oil," "gas," and "mine" from reviews in Construction or Mining industries. Thus, a model will be able to identify these patterns and classify businesses based on the words used in our dataset. The key output of the Word2Vec model is not the output probabilities. It is the "hidden layer"—in effect a latent variable similar to factor loadings in factor analysis, which reduces the dimensionality of the data and can be used as predictors in a classification model.

The Word2Vec model provides us with the ability to distinguish how *likely* words are to appear given their context, however it only provides the information for individual words. On the other hand, our data have paragraphs of text for each observation. To solve this issue, we use Doc2Vec models (Mikolov et al. 2013), which function in the same way to Word2Vec, but return

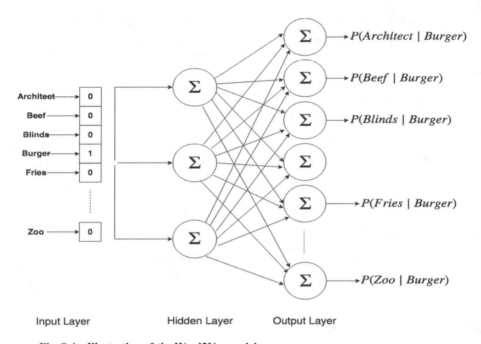

Fig. 8.4   Illustration of the Word2Vec model
Source: Adapted from http://mccornickml.com/assets/word2vec.

a hidden layer of factor loadings *for an entire document* of text. In a Doc2Vec model, a value on a hidden layer *i* for document *k* can be considered the average loading of document *k* on *i*. The Doc2Vec model returns a series of values for each establishment, accounting for the context of the words used, averaged across all the sentences in a document. In this case, user reviews and websites for businesses in different NAICS sectors should have different contexts, and this method should allow us to evaluate how user reviews for restaurants and hotels differ from those for educational establishments.

8.2.6   Machine Learning

The vector outputs from Doc2Vec models lend themselves well to unsupervised classification techniques such as clustering. They can also function as features (independent variables) in supervised machine learning algorithms. After matching our data to the BR, we get the actual NAICS sector codes for each establishment matched, which we use as our dependent variable. We build a Random Forest model–based classifier to predict the NAICS sector of each establishment, where the independent variables are the generated vectors for business name, user reviews, and websites, as well as a series of binary variables indicating the Google Type tag for each establishment. Random Forests are a method of classification techniques derived from Decision Tree classifiers but are relatively immune to overfitting that often impacts Decision Trees. In some cases, Random Forests outperform more common approaches such as logistic regression in class-imbalanced circumstances (Muchlinski et al. 2016). The 120,000 records are split into 80 percent training and 20 percent validation set for model training and evaluation.

In order to ensure our model selection is both replicable and maximizes accuracy, we performed an analysis of 1,000 different model configurations. We randomly alter the number of vectors a Doc2Vec model produces, as well as how many, and how deep, the trees are in the Random Forest model. We then tested how those different model configurations altered the accuracy and repeat this process. Minimum log-loss is chosen as the model comparison criteria, as log-loss is a penalizing function that allows us to weigh the trade-off between the prediction and its certainty. Log-loss penalizes incorrect predictions with high predicted probabilities but does not penalize less certain incorrect assumptions. For our purposes, this is an ideal trade-off, as the comparable SSA Autocoder does not assign NAICS codes if the predicted probability is less than 0.638 (Kearney and Kornbau 2005). Hence, any system based on our model will need to be sensitive to the need to prevent assigning incorrect codes without high levels of certainty.

8.3 Results

8.3.1 Model Evaluation

Figure 8.5 shows the predicted log loss (bold line) and 95 percent confidence interval (shaded area) across a range of number of vectors used in our

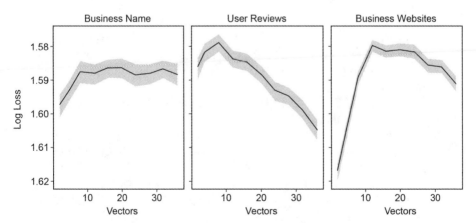

Fig. 8.5 Model performance across parameter space
Notes: Figure shows the mean and 95% confidence interval for a model using the number of vectors for the respective text source. Y-axis inverted to ease interpretation.

analysis. The goal of our grid search analysis was to minimize log loss. Lower scores on the y-axis indicate superior fit (y-axis is inverted in figure 8.5 to ease interpretation). The figure highlights one major outcome of this experimentation: in general, a relatively small number of vectors (around 10) produce better results for user reviews and websites, while it takes approximately 20 vectors for business name. These findings are slightly counterintuitive: Doc2Vec models can be fit with up to 1,000 vectors, and one would assume that a complex task such as generating NAICS codes would require more, not fewer vectors. It is possible that given our sample is tiny compared to the normal training data for Doc2Vec models, we may be simply unable to generate sufficiently predictive vectors with our current sample.

8.3.2   Predictive Accuracy

The findings here discuss our best fitting model, which utilizes 119 trees in the Random Forest, with 20 vectors for business name, 8 for user reviews, and 16 for websites. Overall, across all NAICS sectors, and for SU establishments only, our model predicts approximately 59 percent of cases accurately. This places our model substantially below the current autocoding methods used by the SSA; however, it is at a similar level to initial match rates for the SSA method, and shows comparable performance to similar exercises in other countries (Kearney and Kornbau 2005; Roelands, van Delden, and Windmeijer 2017). The model also exhibits considerable variation, with some NAICS codes (Information, Manufacturing) seeing fewer than 5 percent of observations correctly predicted, while Accommodation and Food Services has approximately 83 percent of establishments correctly predicted into their NAICS sector. Given the unbalanced nature of our sample, evaluating strictly on accuracy may be misleading—it would encourage a model to overfit to only large NAICS codes. Instead, we use the F1 score to evaluate our model.[9]

Figure 8.6 shows a scatter plot of the average number of words *unique to the NAICS sector* in our data (from figure 8.3) on the x-axis, and the F1 Score for each NAICS sector on the y-axis. Clearly, Accommodation and Food Services, and Retail Trade have the highest F1 scores, and corresponding *highest percentage of unique words*. Similarly, F1 scores for Information, Wholesale Trade, and Manufacturing sectors are exceedingly low and also have the *least percentage of unique words* appearing in those NAICS codes. This clear relationship demonstrates encouraging signs of this modeling and approach—words that are unique to a certain NAICS code represent a better signal for a model to use as a classifier. Therefore, we argue that our model performance will improve with additional data from undersampled

---

9. The F1 score is the harmonic mean of the Precision and Sensitivity. For each NAICS code k, precision measures the total number of correctly identified cases in k divided by the total number of cases identified as k by the model. Recall, or sensitivity, measures the proportion of cases in NAICS code k accurately predicted.

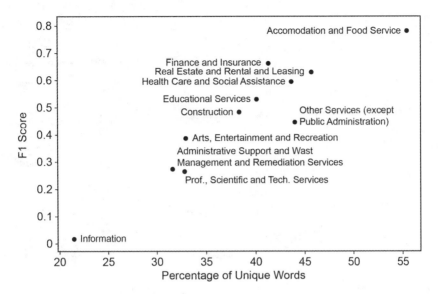

Fig. 8.6 Model performance by NAICS sector

Note: Figure shows the (averaged) percentage of words used in website and review text for each NAICS sector that is unique to that sector (x-axis) and F1 score from our model (y-axis).

sectors. Although the increase in number of unique words may not be linear compared to the number of observations, our findings point directly to our model not able to correctly predict businesses in a sector from a relatively small number of unique words, which may be ameliorated with a broader search.

8.3.3   Misclassification Analysis

One advantage of our multinomial classification approach is that we can evaluate the difficulty in distinguishing between two NAICS codes, one of which is the correct one. Figure 8.7 shows the confusion matrix between actual (y-axis) and predicted NAICS codes (x-axis), excluding correctly predicted observations. This enables us to evaluate model errors and biases.

Encouragingly, in every NAICS code, our model assigns the highest average predicted probability to correct predictions. However, it also assigns Retail Trade (NAICS 44–45) as the second most likely NAICS code for each sector. This has a particularly large impact on Wholesale Trade (NAICS sector 42). Logically, this outcome is expected—the key difference between Wholesale and Retail Trade may not often be the actual goods, but the customers. Wholesale traders sell merchandise to other businesses and not directly to the public, but the types of words used on websites and in user reviews will often be similar. This pattern may also appear across other NAICS sectors—for example, the term "golf clubs" may appear in Manu-

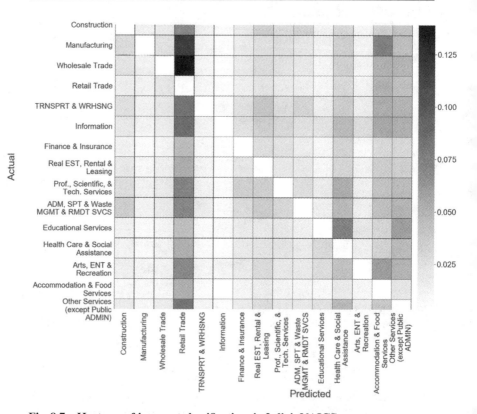

Fig. 8.7   Heatmap of incorrect classifications in 2-digit NAICS sectors
Note: Figure shows the proportion of incorrectly predicted businesses in each NAICS sector.

facturing, Wholesale Trade, Retail Trade, and "Arts, Entertainment and Recreation" sectors. In such cases, when words have similar loadings, our model tends to select the NAICS code with the largest number of observations because this reduces the impurity of the decision tree. This difficulty highlights the need for further investigation on methods and models to overcome these weaknesses.

8.4   Discussion

This paper presented a new approach for Census and other statistical agencies to gather and generate industrial classification codes, using publicly available textual data and machine learning techniques. The approach shows significant promise—in NAICS sectors where more data are available (with high signal-to-noise ratio) to train classification models, the accuracy goes up to 83 percent, with negligible fine-tuning of models. On the other hand, in sectors where little data are available, or where there are less unique words describing a sector, accuracy lowers to 5 percent. Subsequent research has demonstrated that larger datasets and alternative modeling approaches do indeed increase accuracy. Hence, further development of this approach and framework promises to improve NAICS coding at the 2-, 4-, and 6-digit levels, using publicly available data sources, in a timely and efficient manner.

Our findings indicate that these methods may eventually serve as the basis for a statistical product, once accuracy, bias, reliability, and replicability of the techniques are further researched and proven. This paper has shown that using text as data to generate NAICS codes requires data from a sufficiently large number of establishments in each NAICS sector to identify distinct signals from each NAICS code. Further, other types of predictive algorithms (e.g., logistic regression, gradient boosting, and deep learning) should be tested to find their efficacy in solving this problem. In addition, well-known methods of feature engineering, which adds derived variables from the data, have also been shown to improve model accuracy (Chakraborty et al. 2019; Forman 2003; Liao et al. 2017; Xu et al. 2012). Even with advanced methods, it is possible to still struggle to disentangle NAICS codes with similar corpora of words, such as for Retail and Wholesale Trade. This may need clerical or other approaches for a coordinated solution.

We can also identify additional possibilities where our approach can enhance current products. First, current autocoding methods rely on dictionaries of words first gathered from EIN applications between 2002 and 2004 and updated periodically. The new textual corpus could be used to update these dictionaries in an efficient, cost-effective manner. This would provide immediate added value to the Census and the SSA and could be compared to previous dictionaries for QA purposes. Second, our approach could be used for targeted searches of samples of BR data where current methods are unable to automatically assign a NAICS code. In this circumstance, Census staff could leverage our approach as opposed to hand review, reducing the cost and time investment required to produce accurate NAICS codes.

Statistical production processes require steady access to source data and computational resources, but face constraints on budget. Web scraping of company websites is substantially cheaper than survey collection, even considering the computation resources needed. However, surveys may gather additional information not available on websites. In addition, access to APIs for data collection is not free, and grid searches across geographies on the scale needed would require substantial computing effort in order to effectively generate enough data. Also, APIs are specifically designed to prevent users from replicating databases, and only provide users information based on proprietary algorithms. Practically, this may necessitate enterprise-level agreements between Census and data providers (e.g., Google) in order to gain access to the entirety of the data available. If the data are sourced from a single provider, it introduces risk because the data format, availability, or even the underlying measurement criteria in the data might change. The provider may even discontinue the data collection or show monopolistic behavior. These factors need to be carefully addressed for production purposes of statistical products from public or restricted data sources.

The prospect of web scraping public sources of data may present two risks. First, a *perceptual risk* may be that data are being gathered without consent, although the data are in the public domain. This risk could be addressed if the US Census Bureau were transparent and announced its intent to publicly gather such information to improve national statistics, reduce respondent burden, save organizations time and resources, and reduce cost.[10] Second, large-scale directed search efforts using data that are protected by Titles 13 and 26 is complicated, and *risks* not being scalable and repeatable. Such protected data need to be mixed with heavy "salting" with external data before searching can occur, to avoid fact of filing disclosures. Such an approach, while ensuring data privacy and confidentiality, complicates the identification of larger samples of BR records because there are fewer "salting" records available from external sources (i.e., other APIs).

We are excited that our approach can yield useful statistical products. Policies could be developed to reduce the risk and enhance the usability of such approaches for production purposes. This would provide a clear advantage if Census operations can utilize our approach of alternative data sources and modern machine learning techniques to help Census accomplish its mission more effectively.

References

Bayard, K., E. Dinlersoz, T. Dunne, J. Haltiwanger, J. Miranda, and J. Stevens. 2018a. Business Formation Statistics. https://www.census.gov/programs-surveys/bfs/data/datasets.html.

Bayard, K., E. Dinlersoz, T. Dunne, J. Haltiwanger, J. Miranda, and J. Stevens. 2018b. "Early-Stage Business Formation: An Analysis of Applications for Employer Identification Numbers." NBER Working Paper No. 24364, National Bureau of Economic Research, Cambridge, MA.

Bertke, S., A. Meyers, S. Wurzelbacher, A. Measure, M. Lampl, and D. Robins. 2016. "Comparison of Methods for Auto-Coding Causation of Injury Narratives." *Accident Analysis Prevention* 88:117–23.

Chakraborty, A., S. Bhattacharjee, and T. S. Raghu. 2019. "Data Privacy and Security for US Consumers: Assessing Legislative Success of Data Protection through Feature Engineering and Prediction." Working paper, University of Connecticut. Unavailable to the general public.

Copeland, R., and K. Bindley. 2019. "Millions of Business Listings on Google Maps Are Fake—and Google Profits." *Wall Street Journal*, June 20.

10. See, for example Statistics Canada web scraping explanation at: https://www.statcan.gc.ca/eng/our-data/where/web-scraping.

Cuffe, J., and N. Goldschlag. 2018. "Squeezing More Out of Your Data: Business Record Linkage with Python." Working Paper Series 18-46, Center for Economic Studies, US Census Bureau. https://www2.census.gov/ces/wp/2018/CES-WP-18 -46.pdf.

Fairman, K., L. Foster, C. Krizan, and I. Rucker. 2012. "An Analysis of Key Differences in Micro Data: Results from the Business List Comparison Project." Working Paper Series 08-28, Center for Economic Studies, US Census Bureau. https://www.census.gov/library/working-papers/2008/adrm/ces-wp-08-28.html.

Forman, G. 2003. "An Extensive Empirical Study of Feature Selection Metrics for Text Classification." *Journal of Machine Learning Research* 3 (March): 1289–1305.

Gweon, H., M. Schonlau, L. Kaczmirek, M. Blohm, and S. Steiner. 2017. "Three Methods for Occupation Coding Based on Statistical Learning." *Journal of Official Statistics* 33 (1): 101–22.

Haltiwanger, J., R. Jarmin, and J. Miranda. 2008. *Business Dynamics Statistics Briefing: Jobs Created from Business Startups in the United States.* US Census Bureau. https://www2.census.gov/library/working-papers/2008/adrm/bds_statbrief1 _jobs_created.pdf.

Ikudo, A., J. Lane, J. Staudt, and B. Weinberg. 2018. "Occupational Classifications: A Machine Learning Approach." NBER Working Paper No. 24951. Accessed July 30, 2019. https://www.nber.org/papers/w24951.pdf.

Jabine, Thomas B. 1984. *The Comparability and Accuracy of Industry Codes in Different Data Systems.* Washington, DC: National Academies Press.

Jung, Y., J. Yoo, S.-H. Myaeng, and D.-C. Han. 2008. "A Web-Based Automated System for Industry and Occupation Coding." In *Web Information Systems Engineering—WISE 2008*, edited by J. Bailey, D. Maier, K.-D. Schewe, B. Thalheim, and X. S. Wang, 443–57. Berlin: Springer Berlin Heidelberg.

Kearney, A. T., and M. E. Kornbau. 2005. "An Automated Industry Coding Application for New US Business Establishments." In *Proceedings of the American Statistical Association.* http://www.asasrms.org/Proceedings/y2005/files/JSM2005 -000318.pdf.

Liao, W., K. Al-Kofahi, and I. Moulinier. 2017. Thomson Reuters Global Resources ULC, 2017. *Feature Engineering and User Behavior Analysis.* US Patent 9,552,420.

Luo, T., and P. Stark. 2014. "Only the Bad Die Young: Restaurant Mortality in the Western US." Accessed July 30, 2019. https://arxiv.org/abs/1410.8603.

Measure, A. 2014. "Automated Coding of Worker Injury Narratives." https://www .bls.gov/osmr/research-papers/2014/pdf/st140040.pdf.

Mikolov, T., K. Chen, G. Corrado, and J. Dean. 2013. "Efficient Estimation of Word Representations in Vector Space." Accessed July 30, 2019. https://arxiv.org/abs /1301.3781.

Muchlinski, D., D. Siroky, J. He, and M. Kocher. 2016. "Comparing Random Forest with Logistic Regression for Predicting Class-Imbalanced Civil War Onset Data." *Political Analysis* 24 (1): 87–103.

Office for National Statistics. 2018. "Unsupervised Document Clustering with Cluster Topic Identification." Office for National Statistics Working Paper Series No. 14. https://cy.ons.gov.uk/methodology/methodologicalpublications /generalmethodology/onsworkingpaperseries/onsworkingpaperseriesnumber 14unsuperviseddocumentclusteringwithclustertopicidentification.

Roelands, M., A. van Delden, and D. Windmeijer. 2017. "Classifying Businesses by Economic Activity Using Web-Based Text Mining." Centraal Bureau voor de Statistiek (Statistics Netherlands). https://www.cbs.nl/en-gb/background/2017/47 /classifying-businesses-by-economic-activity.

Tarnow-Mordi, R. 2017. "The Intelligent Coder: Developing a Machine Learning

Classification System." In *Methodological News 3*. Australian Bureau of Statistics. https://www.abs.gov.au/ausstats/abs@.nsf/Previousproducts/1504.0Main%20Features5Sep%202017?opendocument&tabname=Summary&prodno=1504.0&issue=Sep%202017&num=&view=.

Xu, Y., K. Hong, J. Tsujii, and E. I. C. Chang. 2012. "Feature Engineering Combined with Machine Learning and Rule-Based Methods for Structured Information Extraction from Narrative Clinical Discharge Summaries." *Journal of the American Medical Informatics Association* 19 (5): 824–32.

III

Uses of Big Data for Sectoral Measurement

9

Nowcasting the Local Economy
Using Yelp Data to Measure
Economic Activity

Edward L. Glaeser, Hyunjin Kim, and Michael Luca

9.1 Introduction

Public statistics on local economic activity, provided by the US Census Bureau's County Business Patterns (CBP), the Bureau of Economic Analysis (BEA), the Federal Reserve System (FRS), and state agencies, provide invaluable guidance to local and national policy makers. Whereas national statistics, such as the Bureau of Labor Statistics' (BLS) monthly job report, are reported in a timely manner, local datasets are often published only after long lags. These datasets are also aggregated to coarse geographic areas, which impose practical limitations on their value. For example, as of August 2017, the latest available CBP data were from 2015, aggregated to the zip code level, and much of the zip code data were suppressed for confidentiality reasons. Similarly, the BEA's metropolitan area statistics have limited value to the leaders of smaller communities within a large metropolitan area.

Data from online platforms such as Yelp, Google, and LinkedIn raise the possibility of enabling researchers and policy makers to supplement official

Edward L. Glaeser is the Fred and Eleanor Glimp Professor of Economics at Harvard University, and a research associate and director of the working group on urban economics at the National Bureau of Economic Research.

Hyunjin Kim is an assistant professor of strategy at INSEAD.

Michael Luca is the Lee J. Styslinger III Associate Professor of Business Administration at Harvard Business School, and a faculty research fellow of the National Bureau of Economic Research.

Byron Perpetua and Louis Maiden provided excellent research assistance. Glaeser thanks the Taubman Center for financial support. Kim and Luca have done consulting for tech companies including Yelp, but their compensation and ability to publish are not tied to the results of this paper. All remaining errors are our own. For acknowledgments, sources of research support, and disclosure of the authors' material financial relationships, if any, please see https://www.nber.org/books-and-chapters/big-data-21st-century-economic-statistics/nowcasting-local-economy-using-yelp-data-measure-economic-activity.

government statistics with crowdsourced data at the granular level provided years before official statistics become available. A growing body of research has demonstrated the potential of digital exhaust to predict economic outcomes of interest (e.g., Cavallo 2018; Choi and Varian 2012; Einav and Levin 2014; Goel et al. 2010; Guzman and Stern 2016; Kang et al. 2013; Wu and Brynjolfsson 2015). Online data sources also make it possible to measure new outcomes that were never included in traditional data sources (Glaeser et al. 2018).

In this paper, we explore the potential for crowdsourced data from Yelp to measure the local economy. Relative to the existing literature on various forecasting activities, our key contribution is to evaluate whether online data can forecast government statistics that provide traditional measures of economic activity, at geographic scale. Previous related work has been less focused on how predictions perform relative to traditional data sources, especially for core local datasets like the CBP (Goel et al. 2010). We particularly focus on whether Yelp data predict more accurately in some places than in others.

By the end of 2016, Yelp listed over 3.7 million businesses with 65.4 million recommended reviews.[1] These data are available on a daily basis and with addresses for each business, raising the possibility of measuring economic activity day-by-day and block-by-block. At the same time, it is a priori unclear whether crowdsourced data will accurately measure the local economy at scale, since changes in the number of businesses reflect both changes in the economy and the popularity of a given platform. Moreover, to the extent that Yelp does have predictive power, it is important to understand the conditions under which Yelp is an accurate guide to the local economy.

To shed light on these questions, we test the ability of Yelp data to predict changes in the number of active businesses as measured by the CBP. We find that changes in the number of businesses and restaurants reviewed on Yelp can help to predict changes in the number of overall establishments and restaurants in the CBP, and that predictive power increases with zip code level population density, wealth, and education level.

In section 9.2, we discuss the data. We use the entire set of businesses and reviews on Yelp, which we merged with CBP data on the number of businesses open in a given zip code and year. We first assess the completeness of Yelp data relative to the CBP, beginning with the restaurant industry where Yelp has significant coverage. In 2015, the CBP listed 542,029 restaurants in 24,790 zip codes, and Yelp listed 576,233 restaurants in 22,719 zip codes. Yelp includes restaurants without paid employees that may be overlooked by the US Census Bureau's Business Register. We find that there are 4,355

---

1. Yelp algorithmically classifies reviews, flagging reviews that appear to be fake, biased, unhelpful, or posted by less-established users as "not recommended." Recommended reviews represent about three quarters of all reviews, and the remaining reviews are accessible from a link at the bottom of each business's page, but do not factor into a business's overall star rating or review count.

zip codes with restaurants in the CBP that do not have any restaurants in Yelp. Similarly, there are 2,284 zip codes with Yelp restaurants and no CBP restaurants.

We find that regional variation in Yelp coverage is strongly associated with the underlying variation in population density. For example, there are more Yelp restaurants than CBP restaurants in New York City, while rural areas like New Madison, Ohio have limited Yelp coverage. In 2015, 95 percent of the US population lived in zip codes in which Yelp counted at least 50 percent of the number of restaurants that the CBP recorded. This cross-sectional analysis suggests that Yelp data are likely to be more useful for policy analyses in areas with higher population density.

In section 9.3, we turn to the predictive power of Yelp for overall zip code–level economies across all industries and geographies. We look both at restaurants and, more importantly, establishments across all industries. Lagged and contemporaneous Yelp measures appear to predict annual changes in the CBP's number of establishments, even when controlling for prior CBP measures. We find similar results when restricting the analysis to the restaurant sector.

To assess the overall predictive power of Yelp, we use a random forest algorithm to predict the growth in CBP establishments. We start by predicting the change in CBP establishments with the two lags of changes in CBP establishments, as well as zip code and year fixed effects. We then work with the residual quantity. We find that contemporaneous and lagged Yelp data can generate an algorithm that is able to explain 21.4 percent of the variance of residual quantity using an out-of-bag estimate in the training sample, which represents 75 percent of the data. In a testing sample not used to generate the algorithm, our prediction is able to explain 29.2 percent of the variance of this residual quantity. We repeat this exercise using Yelp and CBP data at the restaurant level. In this case, Yelp data can explain 21.2 percent of variance out of the training sample using an out-of-bag estimate, and 26.4 percent of the variance in the testing sample.

In section 9.4, we look at the conditions under which Yelp is most effective at predicting local economic change. First, we examine the interaction between growth in Yelp and the characteristics of the locale, including population density, income, and education. We find that Yelp has more predictive power in denser, wealthier, and more educated areas. Second, we examine whether Yelp is more predictive in some industries than others, using a regression framework. We find that Yelp is more predictive in retail, leisure, and hospitality industries, as well as professional and business services industries. We then reproduce our random forest approach using geographic and industry subgroups. Overall, this suggests that Yelp can help to complement more traditional data sources, especially in more urban areas and in industries with better coverage.

Our results highlight the potential for using Yelp data to complement CBP data by nowcasting—in other words, by shedding light on recent changes in the local economy that have not yet appeared in official statistics due to long reporting lags. A second potential use of crowdsourced data is to measure the economy at a more granular level than can be done in public-facing government statistics. For example, it has the potential to shed light on variation in economic growth within a metropolitan area.

Section 9.5 concludes that Yelp data can provide a useful complement to government surveys by measuring economic activity in close to real time, at a granular level, and with data such as prices and reputation that are not contained in government surveys. Yelp's value for nowcasting is greatest in higher-density, higher-income, and higher-educated areas and in the retail and professional services industry. However, data from online platforms such as Yelp are not substitutes for official government statistics. To truly understand the local economy, it would be better to have timelier and geographically finer official data, but as long as those data do not exist, Yelp data can complement government statistics by providing data that are more up to date, granular, and broader in metrics than would otherwise be available.

9.2 Data

The County Business Patterns (CBP) is a program of the US Census Bureau that publishes annual statistics for businesses with paid employees within the United States, Puerto Rico, and Island Areas (US Census Bureau 2017). These statistics include the number of businesses, employment during the week of March 12, first-quarter payroll, and annual payroll, and are available by state, county, metropolitan area, zip code, and congressional district levels. It has been published annually since 1964 and covers most North American Industry Classification System (NAICS) industries, excluding a few categories.[2] The CBP's data are extracted from the Business Register, a database of all known single- and multi-establishment employer companies maintained by the US Census Bureau; the annual Company Organization Survey; and various US Census Bureau Programs including the Economic Census, Annual Survey of Manufacturers, and Current Business Surveys. County-level statistics for a given year are available approximately 18 months later, and slightly later for zip code–level data.

As an online platform that publishes crowdsourced reviews about local businesses, Yelp provides a quasi-real-time snapshot of retail businesses that are open (see figure 9.1 for a screenshot example of the Yelp website). As of spring 2017, Yelp has been operating in over 30 countries, with over 127 million reviews written and 84 million unique desktop visitors on a monthly

---

2. Excluded categories include crop and animal production; rail transportation; National Postal Service; pension, health, welfare, and vacation funds; trusts, estates, and agency accounts; private households; and public administration. CBP also excludes most establishments reporting government employees.

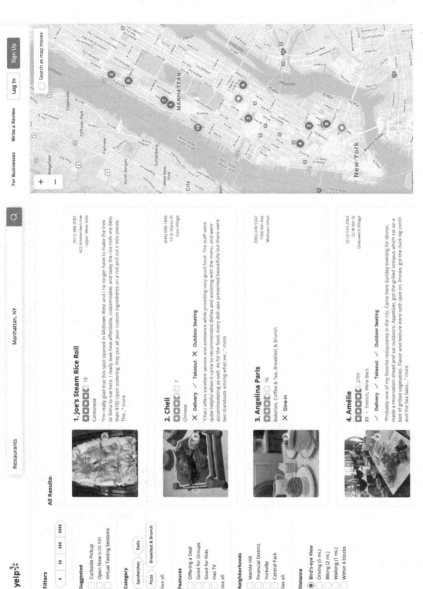

Fig. 9.1 Example of a Yelp restaurant listing

Note: This figure shows a screenshot of a search of restaurants in New York City on the Yelp platform.

average basis (Yelp 2017). Business listings on Yelp are continually sourced from Yelp's internal team, user submissions, business owner reports of their own business, and partner acquisitions, and then checked by an internal data quality team. Businesses on Yelp span many categories beyond restaurants, including shopping, home services, beauty, and fitness. Each business listing reports various attributes to the extent that they are available, including location, business category, price level, opening and closure dates, hours, and user ratings and reviews. The data begin in 2004 when Yelp was founded, which enables US business listings to be aggregated at the zip code, city, county, state, and country level for any given time period post-2004.

For our analysis, we merge these two sources of data at the zip code level from 2004 to 2015. We create two datasets: one on the total number of businesses listed in a given zip code and year, and another focusing on the total number of restaurants listed in a given zip code and year. For the latter, we use the following NAICS codes to construct the CBP number of restaurants, in order to pull as close a match as possible to Yelp's restaurant category: 722511 (full-service restaurants), 722513 (limited-service restaurants), 722514 (cafeterias, grill buffets, and buffets), and 722515 (snack and nonalcoholic beverage bars).[3]

The resulting dataset shows that in 2015, Yelp listed a total number of 1,436,442 US businesses across 25,820 unique zip codes, representing approximately 18.7 percent of the CBP's 7,663,938 listings across 38,748 zip codes.[4] In terms of restaurants, the CBP listed 542,029 restaurants in 24,790 zip codes, and Yelp listed 576,233 restaurants in 22,719 zip codes, for an overall Yelp coverage of 106.3 percent. Across the US, 33,120 zip code tabulation areas (ZCTAs) were reported by the 2010 Census, and over 42,000 zip codes are currently reported to exist, some of which encompass nonpopulated areas.

Yelp data also have limitations that may reduce their ability to provide a meaningful signal of CBP measures. First, while the CBP covers nearly all NAICS industries, Yelp focuses on local businesses. Since retail is a small piece of the business landscape, the extent to which Yelp data relate to the overall numbers of CBP businesses or growth rates in other industries depends on the broader relationship between retail and the overall economy. Even a comparison to the restaurant-only CBP data has challenges because the CBP's industry classification is derived from the Economic Census or other Census surveys. In contrast, Yelp's classification is assigned through user and business owner reports, as well as Yelp's internal quality checks. As a result, some businesses may not be categorized equivalently across the two datasets (e.g., a bar that serves snack food may be classified as a "drinking

3. Some notable exclusions are 722330 (mobile food services), 722410 (drinking places), and all markets and convenience stores.
4. These numbers exclude any businesses in Yelp that are missing a zip code, price range, or any recommended reviews.

place" in the CBP, while Yelp may classify it as both a bar and a restaurant), and Yelp includes restaurants with no employees, while the CBP does not count them. Second, the extent of Yelp coverage also depends on the number of Yelp users, which has grown over time as the company gained popularity. In areas with thicker user bases, one might expect business openings and closings to be more quickly reported by users, allowing Yelp to maintain a fairly real-time snapshot of the local economy. However, in areas with low adoption rates, businesses may take longer to be flagged as closed or open, adding noise to the true number of businesses currently open in the economy. Third, businesses with no reviews may receive less attention from users, and therefore may be less likely to be flagged as open or marked as closed even after they close, since this relies on user contributions.

To account for these limitations, we only count businesses as open if they have received at least one recommended Yelp review. In the zip codes covered by both the CBP and Yelp, Yelp's mean and median number of restaurants has steadily increased over the past 10 years (see figure 9.2). Much of this

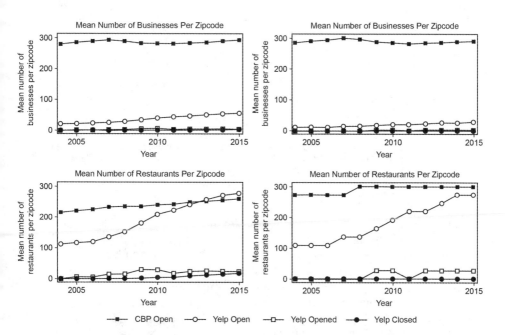

Fig. 9.2 Number of businesses and restaurants recorded by CBP vs. Yelp, 2004–2015

Notes: These figures compare the mean and median number of businesses (top) and restaurants (bottom) per zip code as recorded by Yelp and the CBP between 2004 (when Yelp was founded) to 2015, in all zip codes covered by both sources. "Yelp Opened" shows the mean and median number of restaurants opened that year per zip code, as recorded by Yelp. "Yelp Closed" represents the mean and median number of restaurants closed that year per zip code, as recorded by Yelp.

Table 9.1   Summary statistics

	Businesses		Restaurants	
	Number	Annual Growth	Number	Annual Growth
CBP number of open establishments	317.920	1.717	27.723	0.484
	(432.933)	(14.503)	(34.026)	(2.852)
Yelp number of open businesses	52.274	4.071	26.679	1.811
	(99.450)	(9.159)	(38.880)	(3.571)
Yelp number of closed businesses	1.534	0.476	1.076	0.294
	(4.878)	(2.221)	(2.745)	(1.622)
Number of Yelp reviews	272.051	69.266	247.470	63.386
	(1218.273)	(260.433)	(984.581)	(214.393)
Average Yelp rating	3.000	0.162	3.104	0.144
	(1.547)	(1.560)	(1.350)	(1.405)
Yelp number of businesses that	0.038	–0.268	0.032	–0.140
closed within 1 year	(0.235)	(8.157)	(0.204)	(3.386)
Yelp number of opened businesses	5.497	0.012	2.831	0.010
	(11.697)	(0.271)	(4.831)	(0.252)
Observations	*159,369*	*136,602*	*127,176*	*109,008*
Population density per sq. mile	1756.609		2034.598	
	(5634.997)		(6035.183)	
% bachelor's degree or higher	26.556		27.686	
	(16.249)		(16.438)	
Median household income in past	56533.953		57271.358	
12 months (in 2015 dollars)	(23725.879)		(24219.673)	
Observations	*145,425*		*122,976*	

Notes: Means and standard deviations (in parentheses) are displayed for each variable, for absolute numbers and annual changes of both businesses and restaurants. Each observation is at the zip code–year level, across years 2009–2015. Population density estimates are from the 2010 Census. Percent with a bachelor's degree or higher and median household income are from the 2015 American Community Survey five-year estimates.

increase reflects a rise in Yelp usage. We limit our sample to after 2009, because the mean number of restaurants per zip code between the CBP and Yelp becomes comparable around 2009. The mean number of restaurants in Yelp actually surpassed the mean number of restaurants in CBP in 2013, which may be explained by differences in accounting, such as industry category designations and Yelp's counts of businesses with no employees. Finally, we limit our analysis to zip codes with at least one business in the CBP and Yelp in 2009, and examine a balanced sample of zip codes from 2009 to 2015. Table 9.1 shows the summary statistics of all variables in our dataset across this time period.

In the sections that follow, we use this dataset to describe Yelp's coverage over time and geography in greater detail, as well as the findings of our analyses.

9.2.1   Comparing Restaurant Coverage on Yelp and the County
        Business Patterns

We first compare Yelp and CBP restaurant numbers to paint a more detailed picture of Yelp coverage across geography. In 2015 (the last year of CBP data available), 27,074 zip codes out of 33,120 ZCTAs listed in the US in 2010 had at least one restaurant in either the CBP or Yelp.[5] The CBP listed 542,029 restaurants in 24,790 zip codes, and Yelp listed 576,233 restaurants in 22,719 zip codes. There were 2,284 zip codes with at least one Yelp restaurant but no CBP restaurants, and 4,355 zip codes with at least one CBP restaurant and no Yelp restaurants.

We focus on Yelp coverage ratios, which are defined as the ratio of Yelp restaurants to CBP restaurants. Since we match the data by geography and not by establishment, there is no guarantee that the same establishments are being counted in the two data sources. Nationwide, the Yelp coverage ratio is 106.3 percent, meaning that Yelp captures more establishments, presumably disproportionately smaller ones, than it misses.[6] Approximately 95 percent of the population in our sample live in zip codes where the number of Yelp restaurants is at least 50 percent of the number of CBP restaurants, and over 50 percent of the population in our zip code sample live in zip codes with more Yelp restaurants than CBP restaurants (see figure 9.3).

Yelp coverage of CBP restaurants is strongly correlated with population density. In the 1,000 most sparsely populated zip codes covered by the CBP, mean Yelp coverage is 88 percent (median coverage = 67 percent), while in the 1,000 densest zip codes, mean coverage is 126 percent (median coverage = 123 percent). Figure 9.4 shows the relationship between Yelp coverage of CBP restaurants and population density across all zip codes covered by the CBP, plotting the average Yelp/CBP ratio for each equal-sized bin of population density. The relationship is at first negative and then positive for population density levels above 50 people per square mile.

The nonmonotonicity may simply reflect a nonmonotonicity in the share of restaurants with no employees, which in turn reflects offsetting supply and demand side effects. In zip codes with fewer than 50 people per square mile, Yelp tends to report one or two restaurants in many of these areas whereas the CBP reports none. Extremely low-density levels imply limited restaurant demand, which may only be able to support one or two small establishments. High-density levels generate robust demand for both large and small establishments, but higher-density areas may also have a disproportionately abundant supply of small-scale, often immigrant entrepreneurs.

---

5. We note that ZCTAs are only revised for the decennial census.
6. These ratios refer to the total counts of CBP and Yelp restaurants; we can make no claims about whether the two sources are counting the same businesses.

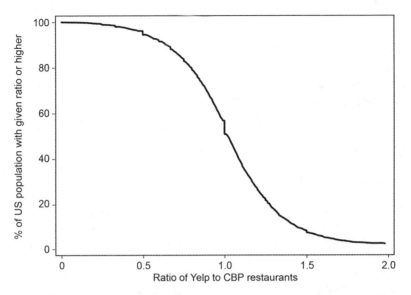

Fig. 9.3   Distribution of Yelp coverage across zip codes (weighted by population)

Note: This figure shows the cumulative density function of Yelp coverage weighted by population, across all zip codes that the CBP covers. For each ratio of Yelp to CBP restaurants, this figure shows the percentage of zip codes that has that ratio or higher. This figure has been truncated at Yelp/CBP ratio = 2.

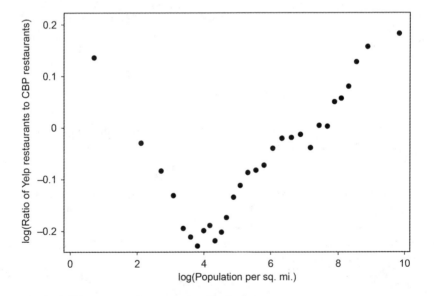

Fig. 9.4   Yelp coverage by population density

Note: This figure shows the conditional expectation function of the ratio of Yelp to CBP restaurants on population density across all zip codes covered by the CBP, plotting the average Yelp/CBP ratio for each equal-sized bin of population density.

High-density levels may also have greater Yelp usage, which helps explain the upward-sloping part of the curve.

As illustrative examples, zip code 93634 in Lakeshore, California, exemplifies low-density America, with a total population of 33 people over an area of 1,185 square miles that is mountainous. Yelp lists two restaurants in this zip code, while the CBP lists zero. The two restaurants are associated with a resort that may be counted as part of lodging establishments in the CBP. Zip code 45346 in New Madison, Ohio, is near the threshold of 50 people per square mile. This large rural area includes 42 square miles and a small village with 2,293 people. Both Yelp and the CBP track exactly one restaurant, which is a snack shop in the Yelp data. A very dense zip code like 10128 in Manhattan, New York City's Upper East Side, with a population of 60,453 in an area of 0.471 square miles, lists 177 Yelp restaurants and 137 CBP restaurants, for a Yelp coverage ratio of 129 percent. While this neighborhood contains many large eating establishments, it also contains an abundance of smaller eateries, including food trucks, that are unlikely to be included in the CBP.

9.3   Nowcasting the CBP

We now evaluate the potential for Yelp data to provide informative measures of the local economy by exploring its relationship with CBP measures, first using regression analysis and then turning to a more flexible forecasting exercise.

9.3.1   Regression Analysis

Table 9.2 shows results from regressing changes in CBP business numbers on prior CBP and Yelp measures. Column (1) regresses changes in the CBP's number of businesses in year t on two lags of the CBP. The addition of one CBP establishment in the previous year is associated with an increase of 0.27 businesses in year t, showing that there is positive serial correlation in the growth of businesses at the zip code level. The correlation is also strongly positive with a two-year lag of CBP business openings. Together, the two lags of changes in CBP establishments explain 14.8 percent of the variance (as measured by adjusted R^2).

Column 2 of table 9.2 regresses changes in CBP business numbers in year t on two lags of the CBP and the contemporaneous change in Yelp business numbers. Adding contemporaneous Yelp business numbers increases the variance explained to 22.5 percent. A one-unit change in the number of Yelp businesses in the same year is associated with an increase in the number of CBP businesses of 0.6. This coefficient is fairly precisely estimated, so that with 99 percent confidence, a one-unit increase in the number of Yelp establishments is associated with an increase between 0.55 and 0.66 in CBP establishments in the same year, holding two years of lagged CBP establishment growth constant.

Table 9.2   Predicting CBP establishment growth using regression analysis

	CBP establishment growth (1)	CBP establishment growth (2)	CBP establishment growth (3)	CBP establishment growth (4)
CBP establishment growth (lag1)	0.271*** (0.018)	0.197*** (0.017)	0.189*** (0.017)	0.188*** (0.017)
CBP establishment growth (lag2)	0.219*** (0.010)	0.190*** (0.011)	0.185*** (0.011)	0.184*** (0.011)
Yelp business growth		0.605*** (0.023)	0.443*** (0.029)	0.495*** (0.029)
Yelp business growth (lag1)			0.194*** (0.025)	0.169*** (0.025)
Yelp growth in closed businesses				−0.264*** (0.048)
Yelp reviews growth (divided by 100)				0.094 (0.081)
Constant	4.542*** (0.127)	1.782*** (0.148)	1.854*** (0.149)	1.822*** (0.144)
Year FE	Yes	Yes	Yes	Yes
Observations	91,068	91,068	91,068	91,068
Adjusted R^2	0.148	0.225	0.228	0.229

Note: All regressions include a full set of calendar-year dummies and cluster standard errors at the zip code level. * $p < 0.10$, ** $p < 0.05$, *** $p < 0.01$.

The prediction of a purely accounting model of establishments is that the coefficient should equal one, but there are at least two reasons why that prediction will fail. First, if there is measurement error in the Yelp variable, that will push the coefficient below one due to attenuation bias. Second, Yelp does not include many CBP establishments, especially in industries other than retail. If growth in retail is associated with growth in other industries, then the coefficient could be greater than one, which we term spillover bias and expect to be positive. The estimated coefficient of 0.61 presumably reflects a combination of attenuation and spillover bias, with spillover bias dominating.

Columns 3 and 4 of table 9.2 show that lagged Yelp data, as well as other Yelp variables including the number of closures and reviews, are only mildly informative in explaining the variance of CBP business number growth. Growth in CBP establishments is positively associated with a one-year lag in the growth in the number of Yelp establishments, and including that variable causes the coefficient on contemporary establishment growth to drop to 0.44. Regression (4) also shows that increases in the number of Yelp closings are negatively correlated with growth in the number of CBP establishments, and that the number of Yelp reviews is not correlated with growth in the number of CBP establishments. Some of these extra Yelp variables are

Table 9.3   **Predicting CBP restaurant growth using regression analysis**

	CBP restaurant growth (1)	CBP restaurant growth (2)	CBP restaurant growth (3)	CBP restaurant growth (4)
CBP restaurant growth (lag1)	-0.049***	-0.127***	-0.157***	-0.165***
	(0.010)	(0.009)	(0.009)	(0.009)
CBP restaurant growth (lag2)	0.059***	-0.012	-0.034***	-0.048***
	(0.008	(0.007)	(0.007)	(0.007)
Yelp restaurant growth		0.319***	0.257***	0.274***
		(0.008)	(0.008)	(0.009)
Yelp restaurant growth (lag1)			0.132***	0.088***
			(0.009)	(0.009)
Yelp growth in closed restaurants				-0.119***
				(0.013)
Yelp reviews growth (divided by 100)				0.164***
Constant	0.783***	0.160***	0.099***	(0.020)
				0.166***
	(0.025)	(0.024)	(0.025)	(0.024)
Year FE	Yes	Yes	Yes	Yes
Observations	72,672	72,672	72,672	72,672
Adjusted R^2	0.009	0.110	0.123	0.139

Note: All regressions include a full set of calendar-year dummies and cluster standard errors at the zip code level.
* $p < 0.10$, ** $p < 0.05$, *** $p < 0.01$.

statistically significant, but they add little to overall explanatory power. The adjusted R^2 only rises from 0.225 to 0.229 between regression (2) and regression (4). The real improvement in predictive power comes from the inclusion of contemporaneous Yelp openings, not from the more complex specification. This suggests that simply looking at current changes in the number of Yelp establishments may be enough for most local policy makers who are interested in assessing the current economic path of a neighborhood.

Table 9.3 replicates the analysis above for changes in the number of restaurants in a given zip code and year. The first specification suggests that there is little serial correlation in CBP restaurant openings and consequently, past changes in CBP do little to predict current changes. The second regression shows a strong correlation between changes in the number of CBP restaurant openings and contemporaneous Yelp restaurant openings. The R^2 of 0.11 is lower in this specification than in the comparable regression (2) in table 9.2 ($R^2 = 0.23$), but this is perhaps unsurprising given the much lower baseline R^2. The improvement in R^2 from adding contemporaneous Yelp data to the restaurant predictions is larger both in absolute and relative terms.

Perhaps more oddly, the coefficient on Yelp openings is 0.32, which is smaller for the restaurant data than for overall data. We would perhaps expect the measurement bias problem to be smaller for this industrial subgroup, and that would presumably lead us to expect a larger coefficient in table 9.3. The exclusion of other industries, however, reduces the scope for spillover bias, which probably explains the lower coefficient. This shift implies that both attenuation and spillover biases are likely to be large, which pushes against any structural interpretation of the coefficient.

Regression (3) includes a one-year lag of Yelp openings, which also has a positive coefficient. Including this lag causes the coefficient on lagged CBP openings to become even more negative. One explanation for this shift could be that actual restaurant openings display mean reversion, but restaurants appear in Yelp before they appear in the CBP. Consequently, last year's growth in Yelp restaurants predicts this year's growth in CBP restaurants. Including this lag improves the R^2 to 0.12.

In regression (4), we also include our measure of closures in the Yelp data and the number of Yelp reviews. The coefficients for both variables are statistically significant and have the expected signs. More Yelp closures are associated with less growth in CBP restaurants, while more Yelp reviews imply more restaurant openings, perhaps because more reviews are associated with more demand for restaurants. Including these extra variables improves the R^2 to 0.14. These regressions suggest that there is more advantage in using a more complicated Yelp-based model to assess the time-series of restaurants than to assess the overall changes in the number of establishments.

While these results suggest that Yelp data have the potential to serve as a useful complement to official data sources, these regression analyses are hardly a comparison of best possible predictors. To provide a more robust evaluation of the potential for Yelp data to provide informative measures of the local economy, we now turn to out-of-sample forecasting of CBP measures using a more sophisticated prediction algorithm.

9.3.2   Forecasting with a Random Forest Algorithm

We leverage a random forest algorithm to evaluate whether Yelp measures can provide gains in nowcasting CBP measures before the release of official statistics. We are interested in the ability of Yelp to predict changes in overall CBP establishments and restaurants over and above the prediction power generated by lagged CBP data. Consequently, we begin our prediction task by regressing the change in CBP establishments on the two lags of changes in CBP establishments and zip code and year fixed effects. We then work with the residual quantity. Given the two lags of the CBP, our sample spans years 2012 to 2015. We use a relatively simple first stage regression because we have a limited number of years, and because modest increases in complexity add little predictive power.

We assign the last year of our dataset (2015) to the test set, which represents 25 percent of our sample, and the rest to the training set. We then examine the ability of lagged and contemporaneous Yelp data to predict residual changes in CBP number of establishments in a given zip code and year. We include the following Yelp measures in the feature set: contemporaneous and lagged changes in, and absolute count of, the total number of open, opened, and closed businesses; aggregate review counts; and the average rating of businesses, all in terms of total numbers and broken down by lowest and highest price level, along with the year and total number of businesses that closed within one year. The number of trees in the forest is set to 300, and the gains to increasing this number are marginal, yielding very similar results. Using an off-the-shelf random forest algorithm on models with limited feature sets, our analyses represent basic exercises to evaluate the usefulness of Yelp data, rather than to provide the most precise forecasts.

Table 9.4 shows the prediction results. The first column shows our results for CBP establishments overall, while the second column shows the results for restaurants. We evaluate the predictive power of our model in two ways. Using the 2012–2014 data, we use an "out-of-bag" estimate of the prediction accuracy. We also use the 2015 data as a distinct testing sample.

The first row shows that the model has an R^2 of 0.29 for predicting the 2014–2015 CBP openings for all businesses and an R^2 of 0.26 for restaurants. Since the baseline data were already orthogonalized with respect to year, this implies that the Yelp-based model can explain between one-quarter and one-third of the variation across zip codes in the residualized CBP data.

The second row shows the out-of-bag estimates of R^2, based on the training data. In this case, the R^2 is 0.21 for both data samples. The lower R^2

Table 9.4   **Predicting CBP establishment and restaurant growth using a random forest algorithm**

	Establishments	Restaurants
R^2	0.292	0.264
Out-of-bag R^2	0.214	0.212
Mean absolute error	7.989	1.713
Mean squared error	222.067	7.200
Median absolute error	3.871	1.062
Mean CBP growth	3.393	0.539
St. dev CBP growth	15.078	2.913
Observations	91,068	72,672

Notes: All analyses predict residual variance in the change in CBP establishments after regressing two lags of changes in CBP establishments with zip code and year fixed effects. Features include year and the change in and absolute number of total open, opened, and closed businesses as recorded by Yelp, as well as an aggregate review count and average rating, and broken down by lowest and highest business price level. The sample covers the period 2012–2015, and all observations for 2015 are assigned to the test set, and the rest to training. The number of trees in the forest is set to 300. The number of observations, means, and standard deviations of CBP Growth are reported using the full set of observations across both training and test sets.

is not surprising given that out-of-bag estimates can often understate the predictive power of models. Nonetheless, it is useful to know that the fit of the model is not particular to anything about 2015.

There appears to be a wide range of predictive ability—but on average bounded within approximately half a standard deviation for businesses, with 8.0 mean absolute error (MAE) and 3.9 median absolute error, compared to a mean of 3.4 and a standard deviation of 15.1. The mean and median absolute errors for restaurants are substantially smaller than for businesses, at 1.7 and 1.1, respectively, but the mean and standard deviation for restaurant growth are also substantially lower than for businesses, at 0.54 and 2.9, respectively.

Yelp's predictive power is far from perfect, but it does provide significant improvement in our knowledge about the path of local economies. Adding Yelp data can help marginally improve predictions compared to using only prior CBP data.

9.4   The Limits to Nowcasting by Geographic Area and Industry

We now examine where Yelp data are better or worse at predicting local economic change, looking across geographic traits and industry categories. As discussed earlier, we believe that Yelp is likely to be more accurate when population densities are higher and when the use of Yelp is more frequent. We are less sure why Yelp should have more predictive power in some industries than in others, but we still test for that possibility. We first use a regression framework to examine the interaction between Yelp changes and local economic statistics on population density, median household income, and education. We then run separate regression analyses by industry categories. Finally, we reproduce our random forest approach for geographic and industrial subgroups.

9.4.1   Table 9.5: Interactions with Area Attributes

Table 9.5 shows results from regressions where changes in Yelp's open business numbers are interacted with indicators for geographic characteristics. We use indicator variables that take on a value of one if the area has greater than the median level of population density, income, and education, and zero otherwise. Population density estimates are from the 2010 Census, while measures of median household income and percentage with a bachelor's degree are from the 2015 American Community Survey five-year estimates. We present results just for total establishments and begin with the simple specification of regression (2) in table 9.2.

In this first regression, we find that all three interaction terms are positive and statistically significant. The interaction with high population density is 0.14, while the interaction with high income is 0.30, and the interaction with high education is 0.09. Together, these interactions imply that the coeffi-

Table 9.5   Predicting CBP establishment growth by area attributes using regression analysis

	CBP establishment growth (1)	CBP establishment growth (2)	CBP establishment growth (3)
CBP establishment growth (lag1)	0.188***	0.179***	0.179***
	(0.018)	(0.018)	(0.017)
CBP establishment growth (lag2)	0.182***	0.177***	0.175***
	(0.011)	(0.011)	(0.011)
Yelp business growth	0.195***	0.302***	0.339***
	(0.047)	(0.060)	(0.060)
High density * Yelp business growth	0.144**	0.016	0.021
	(0.047)	(0.065)	(0.065)
High income * Yelp business growth	0.295***	0.222**	0.224**
	(0.037)	(0.072)	(0.072)
High education * Yelp business growth	0.092**	–0.022	–0.004
	(0.035)	(0.068)	(0.067)
Yelp business growth (lag1)		–0.106*	–0.112*
		(0.047)	(0.047)
High density * Yelp business growth (lag1)		0.139**	0.136**
		(0.047)	(0.047)
High income * Yelp business growth (lag1)		0.086	0.084
		(0.073)	(0.073)
High education * Yelp business growth (lag1)		0.125*	0.115
		(0.062)	(0.061)
Yelp growth in closed businesses			–0.281***
			(0.048)
Yelp reviews growth (divided by 100)			0.056
			(0.074)
Constant	2.066***	2.095***	2.038***
	(0.154)	(0.156)	(0.153)
Year FE	Yes	Yes	Yes
Observations	83,100	83,100	83,100
Adjusted R^2	0.230	0.233	0.235

Notes: All regressions include a full set of calendar-year dummies and cluster standard errors at the zip code level. Indicators High density, High income, and High education equal 1 if a zip code is above the median across all zip codes in population density, median household income, and percent with a bachelor's degree, respectively. * $p < 0.10$, ** $p < 0.05$, *** $p < 0.01$.

cient on contemporaneous Yelp openings is 0.2 in a low-density, low-income and low-education zip code, and 0.73 in a high-density, high-income, and high-education zip code. This is an extremely large shift in coefficient size, perhaps best explained by far greater usage of Yelp in places with higher density, higher income, and higher education. If higher usage leads to more accuracy, this should cause the attenuation bias to fall and the estimated coefficient to increase.

In the second regression, we also add lagged Yelp openings. In this case, the baseline coefficient is negative, but again all three interactions are positive. Consequently, the estimated coefficient on lagged Yelp openings is −0.1 in low-density, low-income, and low-education locales, but 0.24 in high-density, high-income, and high-education areas. Again, decreased attenuation bias is one possible interpretation of this change. The third regression includes changes in Yelp closings and the number of Yelp reviews.

These interactions suggest that the predictive power of Yelp is likely to be higher in places with more density, education, and income. However, it is not true that adding interactions significantly improves the overall R^2. There is also little increase in R^2 from adding the lag of Yelp openings or the other Yelp variables, just as in table 9.2. While contemporaneous Yelp openings is the primary source of explanatory power, if policy makers want to use Yelp openings to predict changes in establishments, they should recognize that the mapping between contemporaneous Yelp openings and CBP openings is different in different places.

9.4.2   Table 9.6: The Predictive Power of Yelp and Area Attributes

Table 9.5 examines how the coefficient on Yelp openings changed with area attributes. Table 9.6 examines whether the predictive power of Yelp differs with the same attributes. To test this hypothesis, we replicate table

Table 9.6   Predicting CBP establishment growth by area attributes using a random forest algorithm

	Population density		Income		Education	
	High	*Low*	*High*	*Low*	*High*	*Low*
R^2	0.244	0.056	0.328	0.149	0.291	0.064
Out-of-bag R^2	0.194	0.029	0.256	0.075	0.234	0.023
Mean absolute error	12.731	3.922	9.806	6.997	11.111	5.593
Mean squared error	427.918	42.065	292.104	186.273	363.237	110.182
Median absolute error	7.966	2.492	5.0785	3.476	6.030	3.034
Mean CBP growth	6.799	0.494	6.106	1.370	6.453	0.900
St. dev CBP growth	20.484	6.485	17.654	13.011	19.137	10.153
Observations	42,644	42,648	41,548	41,552	42,224	42,568

Notes: Broken down by subsamples of the data based on population density, median household income, and percent with a bachelor's degree, all analyses predict residual variance in the change in CBP establishments after regressing two lags of changes in CBP establishments with zip code and year fixed effects. Features include year and the change in and absolute number of total open, opened, and closed businesses as recorded by Yelp, as well as an aggregate review count and average rating, and broken down by lowest and highest business price level. The sample covers the time period 2012–2015, and all observations for 2015 have been assigned to the test set, and the rest to training. The number of trees in the forest is set to 300. Each column indicates which subsample of the data was analyzed. The number of observations, means, and standard deviations of CBP growth are reported for each column using the full set of observations across both training and test sets.

9.4 on different subsamples of the data. We split the data into two groups based first on density, then income, and then education. The split is taken at the sample median. For each split, we replicate our previous analysis using a random forest algorithm. Once again, we omit the 2015 data in our training sample and use those data to test the model's predictive power.

The first panel of table 9.6 shows the split based on density. Our two primary measures of goodness of fit are the R^2 for the 2014–2015 CBP openings and the out-of-bag R^2 estimated for the earlier data. In the high-density sample, the R^2 for the out-of-sample data is 0.24, while in the low-density sample, the R^2 is 0.06. The out-of-bag R^2 is 0.19 in the high-density sample and 0.03 in the low-density sample. As the earlier interactions suggest, Yelp openings have far more predictive power in high-density zip codes than in low-density zip codes. One natural interpretation of this finding is that there is much more Yelp usage in higher-density areas and consequently, Yelp provides a more accurate picture of the local economy when density is high.

The mean and median absolute errors are higher in high-density zip codes than in low-density zip codes. Yet, the mean and standard deviation of CBP establishment growth are also much higher in such areas. Relative to the mean and standard deviation of CBP openings, the standard errors are smaller in higher-density locations. The mean and median absolute errors are 12.7 and 8.0 in the high-density sample, compared to a mean CBP growth of 7.0 and standard deviation of 20.5. In the low-density locations, the mean and median absolute errors are 3.9 and 2.5, compared to a mean CBP growth of 0.5 and standard deviation of 6.5.

In the second panel, we split based on income. In the higher-income sample, the R^2 for the 2014–2015 data is 0.33 and the out-of-bag R^2 is 0.26. In the lower-income sample, the R^2 for these data is 0.15 and the out-of-bag R^2 is 0.08. Once again, in higher-income areas where Yelp usage is more common, Yelp provides better predictions. In higher-income areas, the median absolute error (5.1) is lower than the mean CBP growth (6.1), compared to lower-income areas where the median absolute error at 3.5 is two and a half times the mean CBP growth of 1.4.

In the final panel, we split based on education and the results are again similar. The R^2 using the 2014–2015 data is 0.29 in the high-education sample and 0.06 in the low-education sample. The out-of-bag R^2 is 0.23 in the high-education sample and 0.02 in the low-education sample. Similar to the density split, the mean and median absolute errors are much higher in high-education zip codes than in low-education zip codes, but smaller relative to the mean and standard deviation of CBP establishment growth. The median absolute error in high-education zip codes is 6.0, slightly lower than the mean CBP growth of 6.5 and approximately a third of the standard deviation of CBP growth (19.1). In low-education zip codes, the median absolute error is 3.0, more than three times the mean CBP growth (0.9) and approximately a third of the standard deviation (10.2).

Table 9.6 shows that the predictive power of Yelp is much lower in lower-education or lower-density locations. Yelp does a bit better in lower-income areas. This suggests that using Yelp to understand the local economy makes more sense in richer coastal cities than in poorer places.

Yelp appears to complement population density, income, and education, perhaps because higher-density areas have more restaurant options. Consequently, Yelp is a better source for data in these areas and may be able to do more to improve local policy making. This provides yet another example of a setting where new technology favors areas with initial advantages.

9.4.3 Tables 9.7, 9.8, and 9.9: Cross-Industry Variation

We now examine whether Yelp is more predictive in some industries than others. We define industry categories loosely based on NAICS supersectors, creating six industry categories described in table 9.7. These sectors include "retail, leisure and hospitality," which is the sector that has the most overlap with Yelp coverage, "goods production," "transportation and wholesale trade," "information and financial activities," "professional and business services," and "public services."

We expect that Yelp's predictive power will be higher in those industries where Yelp has more coverage. Yelp covers local restaurants and service businesses, including hospitality, real estate, home services, and automotive

Table 9.7   **Industry Category Definitions**

Category	NAICS sectors	Description
Retail, leisure, and hospitality	44, 45, 71, 72	Retail stores and dealers, arts, entertainment, recreation, accommodation, and food services
Goods production	11, 21, 22, 23, 31, 32, 33	Agriculture, forestry, fishing, hunting, mining, quarrying, oil and gas extraction, utilities, construction, and manufacturing
Transportation and wholesale trade	42, 48, 49	Wholesale traders, markets, and agents; transportation and support activities; postal and delivery services; and warehousing
Information and financial activities	51, 52, 53	Publishing, media production, telecommunications, finance, insurance, real estate, and leasing
Professional and business services	54, 55, 56, 81	Professional, scientific, technical, administrative, and support services; management of companies; waste management; repair and maintenance; personal and laundry services; religious and other organizations
Public services	61, 62, 92, 99	Education, health care, social assistance, public administration, and government

Note: All CBP establishments are classified by NAICS codes, and each NAICS code was categorized into an industry category, based loosely on NAICS supersectors.

repair, as well as local landmarks including museums and religious buildings. These industries mostly fall into two of our industry categories—"retail, leisure, and hospitality," and "professional and business services"; with "real estate and leasing" falling into the "information and financial activities" category.

For each industrial supersector, we regress changes in CBP business numbers in year t on two lags of the CBP in that industry group, contemporaneous and lagged changes in Yelp business numbers, and changes in business closures and aggregate review counts in Yelp. We include the CBP lags in each specific industry, but we do not try to distinguish Yelp listings by industry, primarily because Yelp coverage in most of these industries is modest.

The first regression in table 9.8 shows that the coefficients for the retail, leisure, and hospitality industries are relatively large. A one-unit contemporaneous change in the number of Yelp businesses is associated with a 0.21 change in the number of CBP businesses in that sector. The coefficients on Yelp closings and total Yelp reviews are also significant. As in table 9.3, lagged CBP establishment openings are statistically insignificant in this sector.

The coefficient on contemporary Yelp openings for all the other five industrial supersectors can essentially be grouped into two sets. For professional and business services and for information and finance, the coefficient is close to 0.1, and the other Yelp variables are strongly significant as well. For the other three supersectors, the coefficient on the Yelp variables is much smaller. The R^2 mirrors the coefficient sizes. In retail, leisure, and hospitality and professional and business services categories, we can explain 8.5 to 10.2 percent of the variation in CBP measures using lagged CBP and Yelp data, compared to 0.9 to 8.2 percent in the other industry categories. These results suggest that Yelp is most likely to be useful for retail and professional services industries and less likely for public services, goods manufacturing, or transportation and wholesale trade.

Finally, table 9.9 replicates our random forest approach for each of the industrial supersectors. Again, we follow the same two-stage structure of first orthogonalizing with respect to zip code, year, and past CBP changes. We again exclude the 2014–2015 CBP data from the training data. We again calculate both the out-of-sample R^2 for that later year and we calculate the out-of-bag R^2 based on earlier data.

The cross-industry pattern here is similar to the pattern seen in the regressions. Yelp has the greatest predictive power for hospitality and leisure, professional and business services, and information and finance. Among this group, however, Yelp data have the greatest ability to predict movement in professional and business services, perhaps because that sector is less volatile than restaurants. In this group, the R^2 for 2014–2015 data ranges from 0.11 for information and finance to 0.17 for professional and business services. The out-of-bag R^2 values range from 0.08 to 0.16.

Goods production and public services show less predictability from Yelp

Table 9.8   Predicting CBP establishment growth by industry category using regression analysis

	Retail, leisure, and hospitality (1)	Goods production (2)	Transportation and wholesale trade (3)	Information and financial activities (4)	Professional and business services (5)	Public services (6)
CBP establishment growth (own industry, lag1)	-0.077	-0.010	0.006	-0.065	0.068***	0.180***
	(0.055)	(0.007)	(0.018)	(0.067)	(0.014)	(0.043)
CBP establishment growth (own industry, lag2)	0.003	0.044***	0.039*	0.038*	0.103***	0.095***
	(0.060)	(0.006)	(0.015)	(0.019)	(0.013)	(0.028)
Yelp business growth	0.214***	0.015**	0.035***	0.090***	0.112***	0.039***
	(0.016)	(0.006)	(0.007)	(0.010)	(0.013)	(0.009)
Yelp business growth (lag1)	0.025	0.034***	-0.007	0.068***	0.102***	0.054***
	(0.013)	(0.005)	(0.006)	(0.011)	(0.012)	(0.010)
Yelp growth in closed businesses	-0.112***	-0.018	-0.038***	-0.055***	-0.041*	-0.037*
	(0.030)	(0.010)	(0.011)	(0.016)	(0.020)	(0.018)
Yelp reviews growth (divided by 100)	0.086**	0.035**	0.013	-0.039	0.083*	0.084***
	(0.030)	(0.011)	(0.017)	(0.033)	(0.033)	(0.019)
Constant	-0.139	-0.139***	0.397***	0.151*	0.461***	0.034
	(0.102)	(0.029)	(0.030)	(0.071)	(0.048)	(0.033)
Year FE	Yes	Yes	Yes	Yes	Yes	Yes
Observations	91,068	91,068	91,068	91,068	91,068	91068
Adjusted R^2	0.085	0.020	0.009	0.051	0.102	0.082

Notes: All regressions include a full set of calendar-year dummies and cluster standard errors at the zip code level. * $p < 0.10$, ** $p < 0.05$, *** $p < 0.01$.

Table 9.9   Predicting CBP establishment growth by industry category using a random forest algorithm

	Retail, leisure, and hospitality	Goods production	Transportation and wholesale trade	Information and financial activities	Professional and business services	Public services
R^2	0.131	0.066	0.014	0.109	0.172	0.072
Out-of-bag R^2	0.147	0.004	0.007	0.079	0.158	0.034
Mean absolute error	3.161	2.315	1.759	2.205	3.437	2.448
Mean squared error	36.203	13.300	10.468	17.752	38.502	36.945
Median absolute error	1.616	1.392	0.967	0.982	1.659	1.161
Mean CBP growth	0.648	0.280	0.193	0.469	1.030	0.774
St. dev CBP growth	5.755	3.585	3.231	4.498	6.303	5.097
Observations	91,068	91,068	91,068	91,068	91,068	91,068

Notes: Broken down by subsamples of the data based on industry categories, all analyses predict residual variance in the change in CBP establishments after regressing two lags of changes in CBP establishments with zip code and year fixed effects. Features include year and the contemporaneous and lagged change in and absolute number of total open, opened, and closed businesses as recorded by Yelp, as well as an aggregate review count and average rating, and broken down by lowest and highest business price level. The sample covers the time period 2012–2015, and all observations for 2015 have been assigned to the test set, and the rest to training. The number of trees in the forest is set to 300. Each column indicates which subsample of the data was analyzed. The number of observations, means, and standard deviations of CBP growth are reported for each column using the full set of observations across both training and test set.

data. The 2014–2015 R^2 for both these two groups is approximately 0.07. The out-of-bag R^2 is less than 0.01 for goods production and 0.03 for public services. Finally, Yelp shows little ability to predict transportation and wholesale trade.

Our overall conclusion from this exercise is that Yelp does better at predicting overall changes in the number of establishments than in predicting changes within any one industry. The safest industries to focus on relatively fall within either hospitality or business services. For manufacturing and wholesale trade, Yelp does not seem to offer much predictive power.

9.5   Conclusion

Recent years have witnessed ongoing discussions about how to update or replace the national census across many countries. For example, the United Kingdom considered replacing the census with administrative data as well as third-party data from search engines like Google (Hope 2010; Sanghani 2013). One of the areas that the US Census Bureau has been considering in its new plan to pare $5.2 billion dollars from its cost of $20 billion for the decennial census is to utilize administrative records and third-party data (Mervis 2017; US Census Bureau 2015a, 2015b).

Our analyses of one possible data source, Yelp, suggests that such new data sources can be a useful complement to official government data. Yelp can help predict contemporaneous changes in the local economy and also provide a snapshot of economic change at the local level. It thus provides a useful addition to the data tools that local policy makers can access.

In particular, we see three main ways in which new data sources like Yelp may potentially help improve official business statistics. First, they can improve forecasting at the margin for official Census products such as the County Business Patterns (CBP) and the Business Dynamics Statistics that measure the number of businesses. While these products provide invaluable guidance across the economy, there can be a considerable lag in how they get information about new businesses and business deaths. Data sources like Yelp may be able to help identify these events earlier or provide a basis for making real-time adjustments to the statistics. Second, these data sources can help provide a cross-check for the microdata underlying these statistics and help reconcile missing or inconsistent data. For example, it may take the Census time to classify businesses correctly, especially for small and new businesses that they undersample due to respondent burden, and new data sources can provide a source of validation. Lastly, these data sources can provide new measures of how the business landscape changes across neighborhoods, such as prices, reputations, and granular business types that may not be contained in government surveys (Glaeser, Kim, and Luca 2018).

Yet our analysis also highlights challenges to the idea of replacing the Census altogether at any point in the near future. Government statistical agencies invest heavily in developing relatively complete coverage for a wide set of metrics. The variation in coverage inherent in data from online platforms makes it difficult to replace the role of providing official statistics that government data sources play.

Data from platforms like Yelp—combined with official government statistics—can provide valuable complementary datasets that will ultimately allow for more timely and granular forecasts and policy analyses, with a wider set of variables and more complete view of the local economy.

References

Cavallo, A. 2018. "Scraped Data and Sticky Prices." *Review of Economics and Statistics* 100(1): 105–19. https://doi.org/10.1162/REST_a_00652.
Choi, H., and H. Varian. 2012. "Predicting the Present with Google Trends." *Economic Record* 88:2–9. https://doi.org/10.1111/j.1475-4932.2012.00809.x.

Einav, L., and J. Levin. 2014. "The Data Revolution and Economic Analysis." *Innovation Policy and the Economy* 14:1–24. https://doi.org/10.1086/674019.

Glaeser, E. L., H. Kim, and M. Luca. 2018. "Nowcasting Gentrification: Using Yelp Data to Quantify Neighborhood Change." *AEA Papers and Proceedings* 108:77–82.

Glaeser, E. L., S. D. Kominers, M. Luca, and N. Naik. 2018. "Big Data and Big Cities: The Promises and Limitations of Improved Measures of Urban Life." *Economic Inquiry* 56 (1): 114–37. https://doi.org/10.1111/ecin.12364.

Goel, S., J. M. Hofman, S. Lahaie, D. M. Pennock, and D. J. Watts. 2010. "Predicting Consumer Behavior with Web Search." *Proceedings of the National Academy of Sciences* 107 (41): 17486–90. https://www.pnas.org/content/pnas/107/41/17486.full.pdf.

Guzman, J., and S. Stern. 2016. "Nowcasting and Placecasting Entrepreneurial Quality and Performance." In *Measuring Entrepreneurial Businesses: Current Knowledge and Challenges*, Studies in Income and Wealth, vol. 75, edited by John Haltiwanger, Erik Hurst, Javier Miranda, and Antoinette Schoar, 63–109. Chicago: University of Chicago Press. https://www.nber.org/system/files/chapters/c13493/c13493.pdf.

Hope, C. 2010. "National Census to Be Axed after 200 Years." *The Telegraph* (London), July 9, 2010. Accessed July 6, 2017. http://www.telegraph.co.uk/news/politics/7882774/National-census-to-be-axed-after-200-years.html.

Kang, J. S., P. Kuznetsova, M. Luca, and Y. Choi. 2013. "Where Not to Eat? Improving Public Policy by Predicting Hygiene Inspections Using Online Reviews." In *Proceedings of the 2013 Conference on Empirical Methods in Natural Language Processing*, 1443–48. Seattle, WA: Association for Computational Linguistics.

Mervis, J. 2017. "Scientists Fear Pending Attack on Federal Statistics Collection." *Science Magazine*, January 3. http://www.sciencemag.org/news/2017/01/scientists-fear-pending-attack-federal-statistics-collection.

Sanghani, R. 2013. "Google Could Replace National Census." *The Telegraph* (London), June 26. Accessed July 6, 2017. http://www.telegraph.co.uk/technology/google/10142641/Google-could-replace-national-census.html.

US Census Bureau. 2015a. *2020 Census Operational Plan Overview and Operational Areas*. Accessed July 6, 2017. https://censusproject.files.wordpress.com/2015/12/2020-census-opplan-conference-call_the-census-project_10-21-15_final-1.pdf.

US Census Bureau. 2015b. *Potential Data Sources to Replace or Enhance the Question on Condominium Status on the American Community Survey*. Accessed July 6, 2017. https://www.census.gov/content/dam/Census/library/working-papers/2015/acs/2015_Flanagan_Doyle_01.pdf.

US Census Bureau. 2017. *About the Bureau*. https://www.census.gov/about/what.html.

Wu, L., and E. Brynjolfsson. 2015. "The Future of Prediction: How Google Searches Foreshadow Housing Prices and Sales." In *Economic Analysis of the Digital Economy*, edited by Avi Goldfarb, Shane M. Greenstein, and Catherine E. Tucker, 89–118. Chicago: University of Chicago Press. https://doi.org/10.7208/chicago/9780226206981.003.0003.

Yelp. 2017. "Yelp to Participate in the J. P. Morgan Global Technology, Media and Telecom Conference." *BusinessWire*, May 24. https://www.businesswire.com/news/home/20170511006257/en/Yelp-Participate-J.P.-Morgan-Global-Technology-Media.

Unit Values for Import and Export Price Indexes
A Proof of Concept

Don A. Fast and Susan E. Fleck

10.1 Introduction

The US Bureau of Labor Statistics (BLS) Import and Export Price Indexes (MXPI) track price changes in internationally traded merchandise goods. The indexes underpin inflation adjustment of US net exports and trade balances from current to constant dollars. The quality of the indexes is founded on the matched model and implemented through an establishment survey. The matched model records same-good price differences at the item level and aggregates price changes weighted by product, company, and trade dollar value shares to all-goods import and export price indexes. For the past twenty years, 20,000 to 25,000 prices of unique items from thousands of companies have been collected monthly to calculate detailed and all-goods price indexes. Trade has grown and sample size has been constant

Don A. Fast is a senior economist at the US Bureau of Labor Statistics (BLS).

Susan E. Fleck is the assistant commissioner of the International Price Program at BLS.

We particularly thank Christina Qiu and Daryl Slusher for their extensive contributions to the final chapter. We recognize and thank these BLS staff for their research and data support: Jeff Blaha, Antonio Caraballo, Jenny Fitzgerald, David Friedman, Michael Havlin, Ara Khatchadourian, Laurence Lang, Robert Martin, Helen McCulley, Steven Paben, Sudha Polumatla, Tamar Schmidt, Aric Schneider, Ilmo Sung, and Praveenkumar Yerramareddy. We gratefully acknowledge the conference organizers and Jon Samuels for feedback and advice. We have benefited from comments by Ana Aizcorbe, Alberto Cavallo, John Haltiwanger, Marshall Reinsdorf, and our discussants, Carol Corrado and Susan Houseman, on earlier versions of this research. Use of the export trade data is subject to Agreement No. 2067-2018-001, Memorandum of Understanding (MOU) between the US Census Bureau and BLS. The BLS has received prior approval from the US Census Bureau, which affirms that the research results do not present disclosure risks and approves the publication of the results. For acknowledgments, sources of research support, and disclosure of the authors' material financial relationships, if any, please see https://www.nber.org/books-and-chapters/big-data-21st-century-economic-statistics/unit-values-import-and-export-price-indexes-proof-concept.

and—more recently—reduced. Both trends result in thinner item coverage, directly reducing the number of detailed indexes of publishable quality. While the top-level MXPI—principal federal economic indicators—are of consistently high quality, measures for detailed price indexes are at risk. Symptomatic of this trend is the fact that BLS publishes only one half of the most detailed Bureau of Economic Analysis (BEA) End Use goods price indexes for both imports and exports.

There exists an extensive source of administrative trade data that—up until now—has been used only as the sample frame for the international price establishment survey. The price and quantity information from these administrative records results in an average price or unit value—that is, the total dollar value of the shipment divided by the quantity shipped. The 2.9 million monthly export records dwarf the approximately 24,000 export and import items currently in the directly collected international price survey. The question analyzed here is whether and which unit values can be used on a large scale to track price change to bolster the number and improve the quality of published detailed price indexes and, by extension, the top-level indexes.

Incorporating unit values on a large scale into a BLS price index is a major methodological change to existing practices, given that the BLS program was founded in response to critiques of unit value measures. The BLS established the international price program to directly collect price data, following significant research conducted by the National Bureau of Economic Research in the 1960s. The Stigler Commission (Price Statistics Review Committee 1961), a historical series of import and export price indexes for 11 commodity groups (Lipsey 1963), and an extensive study on the measurement and calculation of price measures for international trade (Kravis and Lipsey 1971), described how unit values captured compositional effects of changes in product mix and different quality of goods and did not mimic price changes. Unit value indexes at that time were calculated from average values for customs declarations that included value and quantity. The records were often incomplete, and thus unit values covered no more than a third of finished manufactured trade and slightly more than half of commodity trade (Kravis and Lipsey 1971). The ability to determine US competitiveness was hampered because of the poor quality of these measures. The Census monthly unit value export and import indexes, published from July 1933 through 1990, were calculated for five broad economic commodity categories (crude materials, crude foodstuffs, manufactured foodstuffs and beverages, semimanufactures, and finished manufactures). The first BLS import and export price indexes based on an establishment survey were published in 1973 as a consequence of this high-profile research to replace the Census unit value indexes, which BLS also deemed as having substantial unit-value bias due to lack of detail and the inclusion of heterogeneous products (Alterman 1991).

Since that time, some experts have proposed that unit values for homogeneous goods may track prices (Mead 2014; Silver 2010). More than twenty years ago, Feenstra and Diewert (1997) proposed that BLS analyze the detailed administrative trade data that are the subject of this chapter, given the improvements in coverage, detail, and availability at that time. However, BLS had less capacity than today to address the complexity of the data and the lag in its receipt, and so did not pursue the project. More recently, Nakamura et al. (2015) set out both historic precedence and mathematical formulas to incorporate unit values into official price indexes as a viable alternative to address substitution and other biases.

The proof that unit values could be used in price indexes is in the doing, and BLS has begun research on exports to evaluate the aforementioned administrative trade transactions. The administrative trade data are reported by type of export product per exporter per vessel per day, based on the detailed Harmonized System (HS) classification with more than 5,000 merchandise good categories. The transaction records include dozens of data fields. The data provide the opportunity to evaluate whether and which grouped transactions with a range of price differences are homogeneous, essentially addressing Nakamura et al.'s "impediment 2" to the adoption of unit values—"the question of if and when auxiliary product unit attributes should be used in forming index basket product definitions" (Nakamura et al. 2015, 54).

The basic questions are (1) whether the data source can be used to calculate unit values and (2) how to select and group the attributes of these transactions into homogeneous products. The first question is more easily answered than the second. The approach we use allows for multiple transactions per product at multiple prices to calculate a unit value with current prices and quantities per time period. The second question is how to differentiate heterogeneous from homogeneous product categories—and thus unit values—with the attributes in the trade data in addition to the detailed HS product category (called here 10-digit HS). Many researchers use the trade data to calculate their own price or price index comparisons. For example, unit values are calculated for cross-country comparisons, using 10-digit HS product categories (Feenstra et al. 2009; Feenstra and Romalis 2014). Impacts of import prices on welfare in the United States group the 10-digit HS with one or two data characteristics to calculate more detailed unit values. For example, Broda and Weinstein (2006) estimate the impact of product variety changes on prices and welfares by including country of origin in their import indexes. Hottman and Monarch (2018) create an import price index that includes the foreign supplier ID and map out the welfare impacts of import price changes on select consumer profiles. Kamal and Monarch (2017) analyze the reliability of the trade data in the context of US–foreign supplier relations. These one-time research projects show the potential to calculate unit values and to group transactions into products. But we know of no work that evaluates the reliability of, bias in, or homogeneity of unit values calculated from the trade data. To consider the trade data as a source in official statistics, these topics must be addressed.

There is limited precedent using unit values as prices in the import price index in the international price program. A crude petroleum import price index is currently calculated using unit values derived from the US Department of Energy (DOE) petroleum transaction import records.[1] The DOE administrative data source is more reliable than survey data in the face of low company response rates and the price volatility of this heavily traded product. Furthermore, crude petroleum import records provide fairly detailed product information. In contrast, the administrative trade transaction records do not have consistently similar product and transaction information across the thousands of categories, in part because of the regulatory nature of trade. Many of the 10-digit HS product categories are composed of differentiated goods, which means that unit values grouped only by HS product are likely to be heterogeneous and not track product price trends. In the face of the uneven detail of administrative trade data, is it possible to move beyond a "special case" use of unit values, such as in crude petroleum, to a more comprehensive approach?

Key to the decision of whether and how to use unit values from the administrative trade data is having sound criteria for deciding when and how they can be applied. BLS requires a consistent and transparent approach to evaluate (1) whether a product category is homogeneous and, relatedly, (2) to what degree unit value bias exists in the entry level item and the published index level. The potential to use unit values for the MXPI statistics faces two hurdles. The first—evaluating and establishing a proof of concept to select homogeneous categories and calculate indexes accurately—is the focus of this paper. The second—whether there is a way to integrate the lagged administrative data into official monthly production—is not insignificant but will not be addressed here.

In this paper, we outline both concepts and methods for using administrative trade data to produce unit values and unit value indexes. Using 2015–2016 export transaction records for dairy and vegetables, we test six different ways to group characteristics in the administrative records into entry-level items (ELIs). Entry-level items are the products in the index basket for which prices are tracked across time periods, and which form the base unit of price change for price indexes. Unit values for these ELIs are described and analyzed. Prices and price changes (short-term ratios, or STRs) are tested for unit value bias within and across months to identify the groupings—or item keys—that result in the least bias. ELI prices then are aggregated using a Tornqvist index formula to produce the 10-digit HS price indexes that are

1. Import crude petroleum prices are derived from the administrative records of crude petroleum imports collected by the US Department of Energy. Detailed product categories are grouped by product and transaction characteristics (i.e., gravity, crude stream, and country of origin) and average weighted prices are incorporated into the price index.

the building blocks for the official product price indexes (Harmonized and BEA End Use) and industry price indexes for imports and exports.

For this research, applying a modified Laspeyres index formula, we use the 10-digit HS unit value price indexes to form 5-digit BEA End Use indexes, and then compare those indexes to existing BLS official price indexes as benchmarks for quality. A natural question is how our indexes compare to BLS's published BEA End Use export price indexes. Those published price indexes are used to deflate imports and exports in GDP, meaning that differences in index values would result in revisions to GDP if the unit value indexes were adopted. The comparative analysis of the unit value indexes and the benchmark indexes leads us to propose a prototype unit value index approach. The promising first results we obtain provide a road map for comprehensively evaluating all import and export price indexes for homogeneous categories.

10.2   The Research Approach

Maintaining the standard for Principal Federal Economic Indicators when considering new concepts or methodology requires thoughtful and thorough review. This research evaluates which 10-digit HS categories are homogeneous and whether a more detailed grouping of attributes is necessary to mitigate compositional effects of shipping contents on the resulting unit value. The simplest case is one in which all or some 10-digit HS unit values provide as good a measure of price change as the published import and export price indexes.

Two principles guide the methodological approaches in this research—to evaluate item homogeneity, and to improve the index where possible. The research develops and evaluates new methods to identify homogeneous products and to calculate unit value prices and indexes with administrative trade data, using a small subset of export data for two years (2015–2016) for two product areas—dairy and eggs (BEA End Use Classification 00310), and vegetables, vegetable preparations, and juices (BEA End Use Classification 00330).[2] We selected these two product categories for two reasons—because the 10-digit HS product groups that comprise each BEA End Use product area appear relatively homogeneous and because these indexes historically had been of uneven quality. The issues generally have stemmed from an insufficient number of representative businesses voluntarily participating in the survey, resulting in an insufficient number of prices, incomplete representation of sampled products, or inadvertent exclusion of large traders. Precisely because of the quality issues, the official XPI for these product

2. The administrative trade data are collected through an electronic interface that exporters and importers use to directly enter data on trade transactions. The US Census Bureau collects and cleans the export data to calculate official international trade measures, after which the data are transferred to the BLS.

categories may be an imperfect benchmark to validate the consistency and quality of the pilot index measures.

10.2.1   Defining Homogeneity

Moving from a matched model price to homogeneous product unit values requires consistency of definition of product attributes, sufficient transactions to group by similar product attributes, and persistence over time of transactions with those same attributes.

Before using a homogeneous unit value in a price index, it is necessary to define what a homogeneous product is. Nakamura et al. (2015) consider primary attributes of products as the only necessary characteristics to define a unit value. However, in the administrative trade data, many 10-digit HS product categories include a mix of different products. Given that international trade transactions are more logistically complex and depend on well-defined sales contracts in order to be backed by a letter of credit from a financial institution (Amiti and Weinstein 2009), we expect that the nonprice characteristics in the administrative records can provide additional information to define products. That is, similarity of the transaction characteristics that define a sale are expected to signal similarity of products and purchasers.

Transactions should be grouped to minimize differences in product attributes and also maximize substitutability among the products in the included set. Price-setting research tells us that the prices of homogeneous products vary over time. In studies of exchange rate pass-through spanning nearly 100,000 goods in the international price survey from 1994 to 2005, Gopinath and Itskhoki (2010) and Gopinath and Rigobon (2008) demonstrate that homogeneous goods experience both more frequent and larger price changes than differentiated goods. They attribute these differences to larger elasticities of demand by consumers contributing to greater costs of price stickiness for producers. Thus, in the case of homogeneous goods, unit values allow for substitutability among similar products with different prices. As Nakamura et al. (2015) propose, such unit values may more accurately represent import and export prices than a single price observation for the product from one sampled establishment. Additionally, the unit value indexes calculated from the unit values are expected not to demonstrate the "product replacement bias" of matched models delineated in Nakamura and Steinsson (2012), where frequent product turnover results in no price changes across months for 40 percent of imported items.

What are the shared attributes that help define homogeneity? Rauch (2001) notes that business networks linking country of origin and country of destination play an important role in market share, price, and trade volume of goods. Furthermore, Clausing (2003) describes how intra-firm trade and country impact price setting. This research leads us to suspect that 10-digit HS product categories on their own are likely to be too broad for unit value indexes to demonstrate the characteristics of homogeneous products. To group transactions with a greater level of specificity than the 10-digit HS product categories, we take into account price and nonprice trade characteristics that separate goods into unique bins or groups of substitutable products. Given the high frequency of transactions in trade data, each bin is likely to have more than one transaction. In other words, we aim to increase what we call intra-item substitutability by grouping transactions by as many attributes that define the purchaser-seller relationship while assuring persistence over time of transactions with those same attributes. To objectively evaluate the different groupings of products and their price dispersion, we use the coefficient of variation (described below) to compare the different product groupings.

10.2.2   Better Measures

Mismeasurement of trade impacts other indicators such as real GDP and productivity. The matched model has been criticized for measuring price changes of the same good only, and missing prices for new goods and different quality goods (Feldstein 2017). Nakamura et al. (2015) and Bridgman (2015) also describe sourcing substitution and trade cost biases, especially for import price indexes, arguing that official price indexes are upwardly biased.

The ability to account for new products and disappearing products and product varieties is a benefit of the new method because the current values for all items are available and can be integrated into a superlative unit value index. More specifically, the Tornqvist index is known to adequately address substitution bias and can be implemented with the proposed unit value indexes (Diewert 1976). It is important to note that the lag in collection of new goods and the lack of current weights to account for changing tastes and trading patterns are not inherent in the matched model method but are related instead to the resources available for timely data collection. The administrative data expand the ability to account for new goods, to exclude products that are no longer traded, and to use current weights in a superlative index to account for substitution. Furthermore, the use of multiple transactions at multiple prices addresses the criticism of Nakamura et al. (2015) that single items may not be representative of a product when multiple prices are present in a population.

The prices and indexes calculated and presented here are based on the two principles described above. They are tested and evaluated for the degree of homogeneity and the existence of unit value bias. Basic parameters are established as a result of this research to (1) define homogeneous unit values and items, (2) test item homogeneity, (3) identify appropriate BLS price indexes as benchmarks for comparison, and (4) propose the concepts and methods to use for survey production. These parameters provide the roadmap to systemically evaluate homogeneity at the item and index levels.

10.3 Unit Values and Unit Value Bias

10.3.1 Defining Unit Values

The point of departure for the research is to establish the 10-digit HS product category as the starting point for evaluating unit values. This level of detail is naturally occurring in the administrative trade data, as records are HS-specific.[3] Given the fact that the 10-digit HS are also the strata from which MXPI indexes are sampled and calculated, this level of detail provides the most convenient entry point to blend the unit values into the statistical production process. Our research tests the premise that the 10-digit HS product categories are homogeneous, and products grouped with more attributes are more homogeneous, thus establishing a range of homogeneity from fewer products with fewer attributes to more products with more attributes. Unit values are then calculated for this range of products within each 10-digit HS product, in which each entry-level item is actually a product group, and each entry-level item price is a unit value.

Whereas the simplest case occurs when the item key—the list of price-determining characteristics that defines the item—contains only the 10-digit HS code (H), other item keys include additional attributes that are similar to price-determining characteristics in the international price survey. The attributes used in the item keys are: HS commodity classification, EIN (establishment ID number) for the exporting company, zip code, state of origin, domestic port of export, country of destination, related or arms-length trade,[4] and unit of measure. The data fields for HS, EIN, and zip code correspond with the sampling unit (multistage sampling for the directly collected international price survey allocates price quotes across establishments at the 10-digit HS product category level). The data fields for state of origin, port of export, country of destination, and related or arms-length transaction correspond to production and/or market relations between exporter and foreign consumer. Most of these descriptors also are collected in the survey as price-determining characteristics. For measurement consistency, the unit of measure (e.g., gross, piece, ton) also is included. Each item key specification results in a different set of unique items, or ELIs, with the same attributes grouped by the same shared characteristics.

The unit value is calculated at the level of the transaction. The unit value can be represented as a transaction i of a unique item j in month t, where j

3. For a given shipment, each company must submit an individual record for each product as defined by the 10-digit HS classification (Schedule B for exports, and HTSUSA for imports). Thus, each record pertains to only one Employer Identification Number (EIN) and one shipment. The record includes total dollar value, quantity, company, transportation, and geographic information on provenance and destination of goods and shipper.
4. Related trade is an intra-firm transaction that takes place between a parent and an affiliate.

is composed of a 10-digit HS code H, and is further defined by an array of price characteristics, item key K. Transaction i involves the trade of z actual items, where z is the number of actual items traded in transaction i. The unit value price of a transaction i is the average of prices for actual items traded in i, or

$$(1) \qquad p_{K_i}^{(j,t),H} = \frac{\sum_{z \in i} p_{K_{i,z}}^{(j,t),H}}{z},$$

where z can alternatively be represented as $q_{K_i}^{(j,t),H}$.

For all like transactions of a given K that comprise the unique item j, the price of item j is represented as a weighted geometric mean of unit value transaction prices, which yields

$$(2) \qquad p_{(j,t)}^{H} = \exp \left(\frac{\sum_{i \in j} [w_{K_i}^{(j,t),H} \ln(p_{K_i}^{(j,t),H})]}{\sum_{i \in K} w_{K_i}^{(j,t),H}} \right),$$

where normalized transaction-level weights are represented as

$$w_{K_i}^{(j,t),H} = \sum_{z \in i} p_{K_{i,z}}^{(j,t),H}.$$

The quantity of item j is represented as a sum of transaction quantities:

$$(3) \qquad q_{(j,t)}^{H} = \sum_{i \in K} q_{K_i}^{(j,t),H}.$$

Taking an experimental approach to test different specifications of items supports the objective to identify the best unit value measure. For the unit value tests, we use the price changes of actual transactions based on attributes for six item key specifications.

10.3.2   Testing Unit Value Bias

To test for unit value bias, one must consider the price characteristics of a homogeneous item. Homogeneous items are close, if not perfect, substitutes. Thus, in a competitive market, they would be expected to have similar price levels and be affected by the same market conditions over time. For multiple transactions of one product, we call this condition intra-item substitutability. If there is no supply or demand shock or large exchange rate fluctuation, one would expect a homogeneous product's within-month prices to group close to a mean, and its cross-month prices to show smoothness. For an item that faces a market shock, prices may cluster around more than one mean price. Although some HS 10-digit product categories experience more variable prices both within and across months, the large majority of items display little price change between months. Efforts to define homogeneity in a consistent way lead us to apply three types of test to the prices and price changes of items for the six item key specifications. Of these tests—the price dispersion test, an across-month item percentage change test, and two price clustering tests—the first shows the most promise.

The price dispersion test was conducted on the actual unit values for dairy and vegetables transactions. The coefficient of variation (CV) is the ratio of the weighted standard deviation of prices within a month to the weighted mean; lower percentages indicate less variability in the ELI. Even though findings from the trade literature report price variability in homogeneous products, we assume there is a degree of within-month price variability for an item beyond which an item is not homogeneous. The CV test allows us to identify a frontier of price variability beyond which a group of transactions comprising an item should not be considered homogeneous. This test fits with findings from the trade literature that similar products from a producer are priced similarly. The intra-month intra-item unit values for each of the six item keys were evaluated for all 24 months. Results are shown for dairy unit values only, as vegetables trend similarly. The bins in figure 10.1 specify ranges of CVs. The least detailed item keys that exclude the company identifier (EIN, or "E" in the legend) result in a concave cumulative distribution, in which the vast majority of ELIs present with high variability of within-month prices, which implies poor intra-item substitutability. About 60 percent of dairy products had a CV of less than 52.5 percent for the two item keys that exclude EIN. When the company identifier is added to the

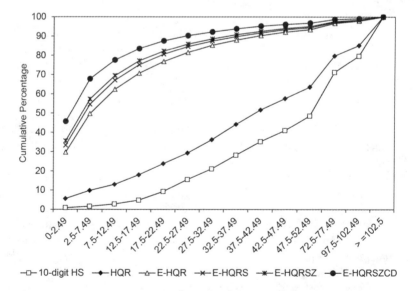

Fig. 10.1 Coefficient of variation test, dairy products and eggs, 2015–2016

Note: Letters correspond to these nonprice transaction characteristics: EIN (E), 10-digit HS (H), unit of measure (Q), related transaction (R), state of origin (S), zip code of shipper (Z), country of destination (C), domestic port code (D).

ELI specification, prices cluster closer to the mean—60 percent of the ELIs that include the company identifier had a CV less than 12.5 percent. Furthermore, the most detailed item key, which includes company identifier and country of destination, experiences the least price dispersion for each good. The wide dispersion and variability shown in the item keys that exclude the EIN demonstrate more unit value bias than for the item keys that include that characteristic.

Another test of homogeneity looks at the month-over-month percentage change in price. Monthly price changes are grouped into price variability bins for all months. Following on past price-setting research that price variability across months is not expected to be large, any such price change across months for item keys could indicate that the ELI may not represent the same good. Looking at the cumulative results for dairy and vegetables, both show 75–85 percent of ELIs with less than 22.5 percent monthly price changes. These results do not reveal intra-item substitutability improvements with additional item key attributes and are not informative for item key selection or unit value bias.

Two types of price cluster tests are applied to the price data for the ELIs. The first method minimizes the variance in the price cluster created (Ward Minimum Variance Method) and the second method minimizes the distance in the price clusters created (SAS Clustering Method 1). Assuming no price shocks and no unit value bias, the optimal number of clusters for each ELI should be one, as the item's unit price should reflect intra-item substitutability. The Ward Minimum Variance Method was applied to price clusters for all ELI that had 100 or more transactions during the two-year period. The clustering results show that all item keys for both vegetables and dairy saw around 80 percent of their ELIs falling within one cluster. When using SAS Clustering Method 1, results are sensitive to price cluster distance. When EIN is included in the item key, the ELIs fall in one cluster around 60–63 percent of the time, compared to 31–40 percent of the time when it is excluded. These results suggest that including EIN in the item key increases intra-item substitutability. Yet when outliers are removed at the second standard deviation from the mean, ELIs had one cluster around 78–91 percent of the time, demonstrating no definitive difference from the simplest case of 10-digit HS unit values.

The results of the coefficient of variation test align with the expectation of intra-item substitutability, showing that the more detailed ELIs have more similar within-month unit values. This test has strong explanatory power and is used to evaluate item homogeneity.

10.4   Benchmarking Unit Value Indexes with BLS Price Indexes

Having selected ELIs that have intra-item substitutability and established an index methodology, we consider the options for calculating the least biased unit value indexes and then compare the resulting indexes to existing BLS price indexes. As set out in the introduction, we compare the unit value indexes for 5-digit BEA End Use categories to appropriate price index benchmarks in order to evaluate the potential impact of their adoption on GDP revisions. The data we analyze are voluminous and many choices must be made in producing the unit value indexes. We apply different assumptions for index calculation, imputations, and outliers to produce a wide range of results, then compare the resulting unit value indexes for dairy and vegetables with official benchmarks. The most obvious benchmarks for the unit value indexes would be the official export price indexes based on the BEA End Use classification, but we have selected two product areas whose official export price indexes are not of the highest quality. For this reason, we consider other benchmarks.

10.4.1 Unit Value Index Calculation Methods

Unit value indexes are calculated at the level of 10-digit HS strata. This procedure generally provides an opportunity to incorporate current weights. The problem of missing prices is addressed both for the regular continuation of an ELI in the index and also as it relates to consistency of establishments' trade. The likely problem of outliers that arises with high-frequency, low-detail data is also addressed.

Tornqvist index formula. The long-term relative (LTR) of the 10-digit HS stratum is the entry point for blending data. For official price indexes, company weights are used to aggregate ELI price changes to the 10-digit HS product category, and then trade dollar weights for 10-digit HS categories, lagged two years, are used to aggregate the LTRs and map them into the BEA End Use price index and other classifications. Because current period weights are available in the administrative trade data, the unit value ELIs can be aggregated into their corresponding 10-digit strata. The 10-digit HS unit value Tornqvist indexes then are aggregated into the BEA 5-digit index using official estimation procedures. The Tornqvist index is superior to a Laspeyres index because it accounts for the introduction of new goods, disappearing goods, and changes in trade volumes (Diewert 1976; Triplett 1992). The baseline case is to use the 10-digit HS stratum unit value as the entry level item.

Using the current period weights, the 10-digit HS stratum is represented by a Tornqvist index comprising all unique items j:

$$(4) \qquad R_{H,t} = \prod_{j\in H}\left(\frac{p_{(j,t)}^H}{p_{(j,t-1)}^H}\right)^{(W_{(j,t-1)}^H+W_{(j,t)}^H)/2},$$

where $W_{(j,t)}^H = (p_{(j,t)}^H q_{(j,t)}^H)/(\sum_{j\in H} p_{(j,t)}^H q_{(j,t)}^H)$.

These calculations differ from existing methodology, not only because we are using unit values, but also in the use of current weights to account for item turnover. The opportunity to apply the Tornqvist index to the unit values addresses a common criticism of the official indexes—that they do not sufficiently account for substitution of new items.[5]

Missing prices, consistency of trade and outliers. In order to evaluate the unit value indexes, methods must be adopted to address the problems of missing prices, inconsistent trading, and outlier observations.

Index calculation requires two months of actual prices to establish an item in the index. Once an item is established, imputation fills in the gaps when the item is not traded or its price is of questionable quality.[6] Even though 80 percent of the dairy and vegetable establishments in the two-year dataset are traded every month at the 5-digit BEA product level, the items traded each month vary considerably, resulting in many missing prices. Missing prices become even more prevalent as attributes are added to the item key, because each ELI has fewer transactions and experiences more turnover. Imputation is used to maintain items in the index, but there is a point at which imputation negatively impacts index quality. To minimize the negative impact that continuing imputed prices over time has on the indexes for the 10-digit HS strata, imputation is suspended for items that have no transaction recorded after three months. Beyond that point, the price imputations overwhelmed the count of unit values calculated directly from transaction records by more than two to one.

Establishments with inconsistent trade are excluded from the sample for the official MXPI to focus on respondents that can provide monthly prices. Inconsistent trade manifests itself in the administrative trade data in the form of a trade-off at the item level between defining the item more precisely and experiencing more missing prices. The decision whether to include inconsistently traded items in the 10-digit HS unit value indexes has implications for index quality. Including inconsistently traded items increases the use of imputation but excluding items that are not consistently traded could bias unit values by not accounting for new goods. Thus, two variations are tested for the unit value calculations—retain all items regardless of consistency of trade and exclude items that are traded less than half the year. Both approaches preserve the three-month imputation rule set above.

The decision whether to eliminate outliers is of particular importance for unit value index calculation. In the official MXPI, an outlier price is flagged to evaluate the validity of monthly price change, but an outlier in the unit value of the transaction cannot be evaluated in the same way. It may represent an error, or a different product being traded. Three unit value index

5. BLS research has previously proposed using the Tornqvist index to blend secondary data sources with the matched model where current period weights are available (Fitzgerald 2017).

6. Missing item price values are imputed by applying the percent change of the item's parent 10-digit stratum to the item's price in the previous month. However, the actual month-to-month price percent change for an item may not be the same as the month-to-month price percent change for its parent classification level, which is an estimation error associated with imputation.

calculations are considered—retain the outlier; recalculate the unit value with an imputed price when the price change falls outside the two-standard-deviation band; or recalculate the unit value with an imputed price when the price change falls outside the three-standard-deviation band.

We nest outlier treatment within the two conditions of restrictions on consistent trade. Combined, these variations create six alternatives to calculating unit value indexes. Table 10.1 shows the index calculation methods from the least constrained to most constrained options regarding truncation of ELIs, and the statistical comparison of these alternative indexes against BLS price indexes. All methods use the Tornqvist index formula and impute missing prices for up to three months. The first three calculation methods include all items, and the last three calculation methods exclude items that are not consistently traded.

10.4.2   Benchmark Comparisons

The comparison of the unit value indexes against BLS official price indexes as benchmarks helps narrow down the proof of concept—of six different item keys that define the ELI and six different methodological approaches to calculate the unit value indexes—to a prototype. The 5-digit BEA End Use unit value indexes for dairy and vegetables are calculated from the 10-digit HS strata with the methods used for the official MXPI, and these indexes are then compared with a BLS price index as a benchmark. Holding all else equal, the company identifier significantly improves the correlation and reduces the root mean squared error. More detailed item keys show a closer fit than the baseline case of the 10-digit HS ELI. The differences between the index calculation methods of including or excluding consistent trade and treatment of outliers are not as clear cut.

Because the two product groups were chosen due to quality concerns, the XPI for dairy and vegetables for this time period were respectively unpublished and had low coverage. Thus, the best benchmark against which to measure the unit value indexes was not necessarily the XPI. Export Price Indexes, spot prices, the relevant Consumer Price Indexes for all urban consumers, and the relevant Producer Price Indexes (PPI) were considered as possible benchmarks for unit value indexes. The unpublished XPI was chosen as a benchmark for dairy—even though the index was unpublished due to insufficient company representativeness, there were a sufficient number of prices in the index. Although consumer prices are systematically different from export prices, meaning that the CPI is generally not the best comparative benchmark, it was chosen as the benchmark for vegetables due to seasonal weighting concerns with the official vegetable XPI.

Correlation coefficient comparison. Correlation coefficients assess how closely indexes calculated from administrative data track changes in benchmark price indexes, where an estimate of 1 suggests perfect alignment. We apply the six variations of the unit value index calculations for each of the six selected item keys. The benefits of unit value indexes are realized with more detailed item key specifications than the 10-digit HS level, but there is a possibility that item key specifications with too much detail may be "overfitted"—understating intra-item substitution and missing price changes of high-volume or price-variable products. Additionally, truncating outliers may introduce bias if outliers represent real price shocks.

Generally, correlation coefficients for dairy unit value indexes are higher than correlation coefficients for vegetable unit value indexes—that is, dairy unit value indexes do a better job of tracking the price trends in the benchmark index. For dairy, correlation coefficients remain consistent across different treatments of outliers and trade consistency. Correlation coefficients vary more for vegetables, pointing to a less consistent time series. Dairy correlation coefficients significantly improve after including company identifier in the item keys, with correlation coefficients being on average 0.090 higher than correlation coefficients of indexes excluding the company identifier, or EIN. Adding other attributes to define products resulted in correlation coefficients that were 0.002 lower on average. The large increase in dairy correlation coefficients in item keys that include the EIN implies that product differentiation may occur at the firm level for items in the dairy category. This pattern, however, is not reflected for vegetables. Comparing vegetable products with item keys that include and exclude the EIN, the correlation coefficients are on average 0.012 *lower* than correlation coefficients excluding the EIN. This statistic is of a smaller magnitude than the average 0.020 correlation coefficient increase with the addition of non-EIN attributes in vegetable item keys.

Our assessment of the impact of index calculation methods on the correlation coefficient is less informative. Dairy unit value indexes mirror the unpublished XPI benchmark, no matter the index calculation method, when the EIN attribute becomes part of the item key. The vegetable unit value indexes do not track the CPI benchmark to any large degree.

Root mean squared error/mean absolute error comparison. Root mean squared error and mean absolute error measure differences between calculated and benchmark price indexes. We interpret these measures as an indication of accuracy. Large differences are more heavily weighted in root mean squared error than in mean absolute error. An error value of 0 implies perfect similarity between unit value and benchmark price indexes. As can be seen in table 10.1, across index calculation variations the dairy unit value indexes display larger error than the vegetable unit value indexes compared to their respective benchmarks. For both indexes, error measures trend downward as item keys become more detailed, implying that accuracy increases when more attributes are used to create items, regardless of index calculation methods.

Similar to correlation coefficient trends, error decreases most significantly for dairy when EIN is added into the item key, a trend that is not observed

Table 10.1   Unit value index comparison to BLS price indexes, dairy and vegetables, 2015–2016

	Exclude company identifier		Include company identifier (EIN)			
	10-digit HS	+ transfer price + unit of measure	+ company identifier	+ state of origin	+ zip code of shipper	+ country of destination + U.S. port
Dairy U.V. index						
Correlation coefficient						
Tornqvist index w/3-month imputation	0.48	0.5	0.58	0.6	0.59	0.61
+ exclude outliers 3rd std.	0.5	0.51	0.6	0.62	0.6	0.59
+ exclude outliers 2nd std.	0.5	0.52	0.57	0.6	0.6	0.57
Tornqvist index w/3-month imputation + consistent trade	0.48	0.5	0.61	0.6	0.58	0.59
+ exclude outliers 3rd std.	0.5	0.53	0.62	0.58	0.57	0.57
+ exclude outliers 2nd std.	0.5	0.52	0.64	0.6	0.53	0.57
Root mean squared errors/Mean absolute errors						
Tornqvist index w/3-month imputation	2.71/2.16	2.61/2.07	2.00/1.57	1.91/1.45	1.90/1.35	1.82/1.44
+ exclude outliers 3rd std.	2.61/2.10	2.55/2.06	2.02/1.50	1.90/1.43	1.96/1.50	1.88/1.50
+ exclude outliers 2nd std.	2.61/2.10	2.58/2.09	2.07/1.53	2.00/1.47	1.97/1.50	1.96/1.60
Tornqvist index w/3-month imputation + consistent trade	2.72/2.18	2.59/2.10	1.99/1.53	2.04/1.52	2.03/1.48	1.96/1.54
+ exclude outliers 3rd std.	2.61/2.11	2.56/2.11	2.05/1.53	2.08/1.63	2.08/1.67	2.07/1.58
+ exclude outliers 2nd std.	2.61/2.11	2.56/2.10	1.99/1.52	2.07/1.52	2.22/1.65	2.04/1.57
Vegetable U.V. index						
Correlation coefficient						
Tornqvist index w/3-month imputation	0.37	0.48	0.24	0.23	0.29	0.35
+ exclude outliers 3rd std.	0.32	0.30	0.35	0.34	0.40	0.39
+ exclude outliers 2nd std.	0.32	0.31	0.35	0.37	0.35	0.39
Tornqvist index w/3-month imputation + consistent trade	0.26	0.37	0.32	0.35	0.37	0.33
+ exclude outliers 3rd Std.	0.33	0.32	0.38	0.38	0.43	0.41
+ exclude outliers 2nd Std.	0.33	0.33	0.40	0.45	0.46	0.47
Root mean squared errors/Mean absolute errors						
Tornqvist index w/3-month imputation	2.37/1.94	1.92/1.51	2.07/1.67	2.13/1.68	2.02/1.60	1.86/1.34
+ exclude outliers 3rd std.	2.02/1.56	2.02/1.49	1.82/1.41	1.86/1.49	1.79/1.42	1.82/1.39
+ exclude outliers 2nd std.	2.02/1.56	2.03/1.50	1.82/1.45	1.82/1.45	1.84/1.41	1.79/1.34
Tornqvist index w/3-month imputation + consistent trade	2.50/2.04	2.07/1.57	1.92/1.53	1.84/1.40	1.79/1.4	1.92/1.43
+ exclude outliers 3rd std.	2.00/1.55	1.98/1.46	1.83/1.45	1.82/1.42	1.75/1.42	1.84/1.44
+ exclude outliers 2nd std.	2.00/1.55	1.99/1.47	1.79/1.44	1.73/1.40	1.67/1.31	1.69/1.33

for vegetables. Mirroring the previous correlation coefficient analysis, root mean squared error decreases by 0.555 points on average after inclusion of EIN into the dairy item key, compared to a decrease of 0.029 points on average for inclusion of a non-EIN attribute. For vegetables, root mean squared error decreases on average by 0.126 points after EIN inclusion into item keys, compared to a decrease of 0.047 points on average for inclusion of a non-EIN characteristic. For dairy, the lowest level of error is found using the most detailed item key with the least restrictive index calculation method; for vegetables, the lowest level of error is found using the most detailed key with the most constrained index calculation method. Both findings corroborate those based on the correlation coefficient analyses.

Though the unit value dairy index tracks the benchmark index better than the unit value vegetable index tracks its benchmark, the vegetable index comparison has smaller errors, indicating greater accuracy. Both correlation coefficient and error analysis point to similar methodologies to optimize accuracy and mirroring of benchmarks; most especially, for both indexes, the inclusion of EIN in the item key but also the stronger treatment of outliers for the vegetable index.

10.5   An Initial Prototype for Unit Values and Unit Value Indexes

Coefficient of variation, correlation coefficient, and error analysis yield a prototype for unit value specification and unit value index calculation. Regarding the best specification for the ELI, the most prominent result is the importance of company identifier in the item key. The coefficient of variation results show the product prices based on the most detailed item key are the least variable in price and the most homogeneous. Results including the EIN but not necessarily other attributes were robust across the correlation coefficient, root mean squared error, and mean absolute error analyses.

Regarding the index calculation methods, results are not as clear cut. Because neither of the benchmark indexes was a published export price index, it is possible that results are not consistent when unit value indexes are compared to the benchmarks. Whereas the least constrained index method calculation—retaining outliers and not truncating ELIs that are inconsistently traded—provides a best fit for dairy, vegetables require a more rigorous treatment of outliers and consistency in trade. It is possible that the differing success of particular methods reflects differing market forces for the two cases. In particular, price and quantity changes are more variable with seasonal items like vegetables, making price outliers less informative of general price trends (see table 10.2).

To proceed with a prototype index calculation method, we make two strong assumptions in order to test other BEA 5-digit export indexes composed of homogeneous products that also have published XPI benchmarks. First, we assume that the three-month imputation rule sufficiently addresses

Table 10.2   Unit value index comparison to published export price indexes, 2016

BEA end use export classification	Correlation coefficient	RMSE	MAE
Meat, poultry, and other edible animal products	0.1657	1.677	1.128
Soybeans and soybean byproducts	0.9116	2.927	2.349
Animal feeds	0.9519	0.918	0.744

any inconsistencies in trade, and thus do not impose limits on ELIs that are inconsistently traded. Second, though dairy unit value indexes are most accurate without elimination of outliers, we proceed on the basis that it is prudent to treat price outliers, assuming that they likely are due to differences in product mix in the shipment or incorrect transaction records. Thus, we apply the Tornqvist index to a dataset with no more than three months' imputation for missing prices and additionally replace outlier prices outside the third standard deviation band with imputed values.

We apply the prototype ELI—the most detailed item key—to evaluate homogeneity of all 5-digit BEA End Use export product categories, based on the homogeneity of their ELIs. We then calculate select unit value indexes with the prototype calculation method and compare then with published XPI benchmarks. Homogeneity is evaluated as the level of intra-item substitutability, where less price dispersion indicates more homogeneity. Price dispersion is calculated through the coefficient of variation test. To limit the presence of problematic outliers, we use the coefficient of variation for prototype vegetable unit values as an upper bound on the coefficient of variation for a homogeneous category. Using this criterion, we identify 50 export and 52 import 5-digit BEA End Use unit value indexes as homogeneous. We calculate three 5-digit BEA end use export indexes—meat, soybeans, and animal feed—based on the prototype and evaluate the results against published XPIs with extensive price quotes. The indexes for soybeans and animal feed show a high degree of accuracy when assessed using correlation coefficients, and the indexes for meat and animal feed closely track published XPI benchmark indexes.

10.6   Conclusion

Our findings hold the promise that it may be possible to blend unit value indexes with directly collected survey data to calculate MXPI. Defining homogeneity and addressing unit value bias are essential to this approach. We establish that the best approach to defining homogeneous items involves adding attributes to the 10-digit HS product grouping to create more detailed items and limiting the price dispersion allowable for an item to be considered homogeneous. We identified an inverse relationship between the number of attributes used to define an item and the price variability among the transactions that comprise the item's unit value. While having more attributes and less price variability means that items are more homogeneous, it also means that there is a greater risk of the items not being traded consistently, as the number of transactions that comprise that item's unit value for a month is lower and the prevalence of missing prices across months is greater.

Establishing an index methodology that works with unit values also is essential to blending unit value indexes into the MXPI. The availability of prices and quantities allowed us to use a Tornqvist index to address substitution bias. We established imputation to account for missing prices and addressed outliers. These new methods were tested by comparing the unit value indexes against benchmark price indexes to evaluate their similarities and differences. The three tests we conducted to determine unit value index accuracy and tracking of benchmarks with 36 variations of item key and index calculation method show that EIN and other nonprice characteristics more precisely define a homogeneous good. The most detailed item key shows the least price dispersion, most accuracy, and best benchmark tracking. There was no clear result for which index formula provided the most comparable index, but the groundwork has been laid for the next round of comparisons.

Future research will assess unit value indexes from 2012 to 2017 for all 50 export and 52 import 5-digit BEA End Use categories that have sufficiently low within-category price dispersion as to be considered homogeneous. The results will be used to validate a prototype for ELI specification and index calculation that consistently provides strong results. As part of this research, options for systematically identifying overfitted and underfitted indexes will be explored. Indexes' impact on net trade and GDP, as well as on top-level price indexes, also will be evaluated. Much work remains to be done, but we are encouraged by the results obtained thus far.

References

Alterman, W. 1991. "Price Trends in U.S. Trade: New Data, New Insights." In *International Economic Transactions: Issues in Measurement and Empirical Research*, Studies in Income and Wealth, vol. 55, edited by P. Hooper and J. D. Richardson, 109–43. Chicago: University of Chicago Press.

Amiti, M., and D. E. Weinstein. 2009. "Exports and Financial Shocks." NBER Working Paper No. 15556, National Bureau of Economic Research, Cambridge, MA. http://www.nber.org/papers/w15556.

Bridgman, B. 2015. "Specific Trade Costs, Quality, and Import Prices." In *Measuring Globalization: Better Trade Statistics for Better Policy*, vol. 1, *Biases to Price, Output, and Productivity Statistics from Trade*, edited by S. N. Houseman and M. J. Mandel, 121–48. https://www.jstor.org/stable/j.ctvh4zfcn.7?seq=1#metadata_info_tab _contents.

Broda, C., and D. Weinstein. 2006. "Globalization and the Gains from Variety." *Quarterly Journal of Economics* 121 (2). https://doi.org/10.1162/qjec.2006.121.2.541.

Clausing, K. A. 2003. "Tax-Motivated Transfer Pricing and US Intrafirm Trade Prices." *Journal of Public Economics* 87 (9–10): 2207–23. https://doi.org/10.1016/S0047-2727(02)00015-4.

Diewert, W. E. 1976. "Exact and Superlative Index Numbers." *Journal of Econometrics* 4 (2): 115–45.

Feenstra, R. C., and W. E. Diewert. 1997. "Contract Report on the Methodology for the U.S. Export and Import Price Indexes." Unpublished paper, US Bureau of Labor Statistics, Washington, DC.

Feenstra, R. C., A. Heston, P. M. Timmer, and H. Deng. 2009. "Estimating Real Production and Expenditures across Nations: A Proposal for Improving the Penn World Tables." *Review of Economics and Statistics* 91 (1): 201–12. http://dx.doi.org/10.1162/rest.91.1.201.

Feenstra, R. C., and J. Romalis. 2014. "International Prices and Endogenous Quality." *Quarterly Journal of Economics* 129 (2): 477–527. https://doi.org/10.1093/qje/qju001.

Feldstein, M. 2017. "Underestimating the Real Growth of GDP, Personal Income, and Productivity." *Journal of Economic Perspectives* 31 (2): 145–64. http://dx.doi.org/10.1257/jep.31.2.145.

Fitzgerald, J. 2017. "Assessing Product Downsizing, Upsizing, and Product Churn Using Nielsen Scanner Data." Paper presented at the 2017 Joint Statistical Meetings, Session on Measuring the Economy: Economic and Workforce Statistics, Government Statistics Section, Baltimore, MD, July 30, 2017.

Gopinath, G., and O. Itskhoki. 2010. "Frequency of Price Adjustment and Pass-Through." *Quarterly Journal of Economics* 125 (2): 675–727. http://www.jstor.org/stable/27867493.

Gopinath, G., and R. Rigobon. 2008. "Sticky Borders." *Quarterly Journal of Economics* 123 (2): 531–75. https://www.jstor.org/stable/25098909.

Hottman, C. J., and R. Monarch. 2018. "Estimating Unequal Gains across US Consumers with Supplier Trade Data." Federal Reserve Issue Paper 1220, January 17. https://www.federalreserve.gov/econres/ifdp/files/ifdp1220.pdf.

Kamal, Fariha, and Ryan Monarch. 2017. "Identifying Foreign Suppliers in U.S. Import Data." International Finance Discussion Paper 1142r. https://doi.org/10.17016/IFDP.2017.1142r.

Kravis, I. B., and R. E. Lipsey. 1971. "Wholesale Prices and Unit Values as Measures of International Price Competitiveness." In *Price Competitiveness in World Trade*. New York: Columbia University Press.

Lipsey, R. E. 1963. *Price and Quantity Trends in the Foreign Trade of the United States*. Princeton, NJ: Princeton University Press. https://www.nber.org/books/lips63-1.

Mead, D. 2014. "Analyzing Alternatives to Export Price Indexes." *Beyond the Numbers: Global Economy* 3 (27). US Bureau of Labor Statistics, November 2014. https://www.bls.gov/opub/btn/volume-3/analyzing-alternatives-to-export-price-indexes.htm.

Nakamura, A. O., W. E. Diewert, J. S. Greenlees, L. I. Nakamura, and M. B. Reinsdorf. 2015. "Sourcing Substitution and Related Price Index Biases." In *Measuring Globalization: Better Trade Statistics for Better Policy*, edited by S. N. Houseman and M. J. Mandel, 21–89. https://research.upjohn.org/cgi/viewcontent.cgi?article=1250&context=up_press.

Nakamura, E., and J. Steinsson. 2012. "Lost in Transit: Product Replacement Bias and Pricing to Market." *American Economic Review* 102 (7): 3277–316. https://doi.org/10.1257/aer.102.7.3277.

Price Statistics Review Committee. 1961. Appendix A, "Export and Import Indexes," in *The Price Statistics of the Federal Government*. Cambridge, MA: National Bureau of Economic Research. https://www.nber.org/chapters/c6487.

Rauch, J. E. 2001. "Business and Social Networks in International Trade." *Journal of Economic Literature* 39 (4): 1177–203.

Silver, M. 2010. "The Wrongs and Rights of Unit Value Indices." *Review of Income and Wealth*, Series 56, Special Issue 1 (June): 206–23. https://doi.org/10.1111/j.1475-4991.2010.00391.x.

Triplett, J. E. 1992. "Economic Theory and BEA's Alternative Quantity and Price Indexes." *Survey of Current Business* (April): 49–52. https://apps.bea.gov/scb/pdf/national/nipa/1992/0492trip.pdf.

Quantifying Productivity Growth in the Delivery of Important Episodes of Care within the Medicare Program Using Insurance Claims and Administrative Data

John A. Romley, Abe Dunn, Dana Goldman, and Neeraj Sood

11.1 Introduction

Multifactor productivity (MFP) growth is the ultimate source of gains in living standards, and growth appears to have slowed in the United States since the turn of the century (Byrne, Oliner, and Sichel 2013; Fernald 2015). One view of the current situation is that the technological progress of earlier eras is unlikely to be matched in the future, notwithstanding the ongoing information revolution and foreseeable developments (Gordon 2016). An alternative view is that government economic statistics have systematically mismeasured MFP improvement, in fact understating it (Feldstein 2017).

John A. Romley is an associate professor in the Price School of Public Policy at the University of Southern California (USC), an economist at the Schaeffer Center for Health Policy and Economics, and an adjunct economist at the RAND Corporation.

Abe Dunn is assistant chief economist at the Bureau of Economic Analysis.

Dana Goldman is the interim dean at the USC Sol Price School of Public Policy, as well as the Leonard D. Schaeffer Chair and Distinguished Professor of Pharmacy, Public Policy, and Economics at the University of Southern California, and a research associate of the National Bureau of Economic Research.

Neeraj Sood is professor and vice dean for research at the USC Price School of Public Policy and a founding member the USC Schaeffer Center at the University of Southern California, and a research associate of the National Bureau of Economic Research.

We thank Helen Levy, Matthew Shapiro, Katharine Abraham, Ron Jarmin, Brian Moyer, an anonymous reviewer, and participants in the NBER-CRIW conference on Big Data for 21st Century Economic Statistics for helpful comments. Andrea Batch, Tommy Chiou, and Peter Shieh provided excellent research assistance. The views expressed in this paper are solely those of the authors and do not necessarily reflect the views of the Bureau of Economic Analysis. John Romley has a consulting relationship with the Bureau. For acknowledgments, sources of research support, and disclosure of the authors' material financial relationships, if any, please see https://www.nber.org/books-and-chapters/big-data-21st-century-economic-statistics /quantifying-productivity-growth-delivery-important-episodes-care-within-medicare -program-using.

Recent assessments cast some doubt on this alternative view as a convincing account of the apparent slowdown in productivity growth (Byrne, Fernald, and Reinsdorf 2016; Syverson 2017).

These assessments, while informative, have not squarely addressed the issue of productivity growth in health care. This sector accounted for 17.9 percent of GDP in 2017 (Martin et al. 2018). As health spending has grown, so have better treatments become available (Newhouse 1992). Quality change is a well-known challenge for measuring prices, and the mismeasurement of health care inflation was a key concern of the Boskin Commission (Boskin et al. 1998). Indeed, taking account of improved outcomes, the price of heart attack treatment has actually declined markedly over time (Cutler et al. 1998).

With respect to MFP, there is a longstanding hypothesis that health care and other services suffer from a "cost disease," by which a comparatively meager flow of labor-saving efficiencies drives production costs higher and higher (Baumol and Bowen 1965; Baumol et al. 2012; Newhouse 1992). The Medicare Board of Trustees has adopted this position in its long-term financial projections, through an assumption that MFP within the health care sector will grow more slowly than MFP outside of health care (OASDI Board of Trustees 2018). More starkly, the Bureau of Labor Statistics (BLS) has estimated that hospitals and nursing and residential care facilities experienced negative MFP growth from 1987 through 2006 (Harper et al. 2010). If productivity is truly declining in our health care system, efforts to contain cost, improve quality, or both, become even more difficult.

While the BLS measures MFP by applying a rigorous and consistent framework across industries, it is plausible that its measurement framework does not adequately reflect quality change in health care[1] (Cylus and Dickensheets 2007; Groshen et al. 2017; Matsumoto 2019). Another challenge in this context is that production is joint between the firm and the consumer in the sense that patients present themselves to providers for care with good, bad, or middling health. Providers who face sicker patients may use more (or fewer) resources in treatment. In a prior study, we found that US hospitals substantially improved their productivity from 2002 through 2011, but only after we accounted for trends in patient severity and treatment outcomes. Improvement in patient outcomes was largely responsible (Romley, Goldman, and Sood 2015).

Yet the treatment of heart attacks and other conditions does not end with discharge from the hospital. We need to understand productivity in the treatment of complete episodes of care, including, for example, rehab services and follow-up doctor visits. Even if individual providers are pro-

---

1. Similarly, the National Income and Product Accounts and the Centers for Medicare and Medicaid Services both track *spending* on health care without adjustment for quality (Sensenig and Wilcox 2001).

ductive, there is widespread concern about poor coordination of care, due to problems of information and incentives across providers (Davis 2007). Accordingly, public and private decision makers are assessing and paying with respect to performance on episodes of care.[2] For example, the Centers for Medicare and Medicaid Services (CMS) recently expanded its innovation portfolio to include a Bundled Payments for Care Improvement Advanced Model (Centers for Medicare and Medicaid Services 2019a).

While the complexity of health care makes productivity assessment challenging, at the same time there are voluminous data to work with. In this study, we use insurance claims and administrative data to quantify trends in the productivity of treatment of acute episodes of care among elderly Americans. Specifically, we assess a wide range of important conditions and procedures over a reasonably long timeframe (in the last year studied, 2014, the total cost of providing these episodes is estimated to be $38 billion, measured in 2014 dollars). To our knowledge, this is the first study that analyzes productivity change in delivering acute episodes, including services received after the initial hospital stay.

Previewing our key findings, productivity improved for a majority of the episode types studied, in some cases at an annualized rate in excess of 1 percent. For the episode types that experienced productivity improvement, patient outcomes also improved, sometimes substantially.

11.2   Approach

The starting point for our analysis is CMS's Inpatient Files (Research Data Assistance Center 2019). Our version of the Inpatient Files includes a random 20 percent sample of Medicare beneficiaries. As table 11.1 shows, there were 29,841,183 stays at 6,353 short-term acute-care hospitals over the period 2002–2014. The Inpatient File is actually a claim-level file, and multiple claims may be associated with the same stay. While the Medicare Provider Analysis and Review File reports at the stay level, we use the Inpatient File in order to implement a complex algorithm developed by CMS for the purpose of identifying unplanned hospital readmissions (Yale New Haven Health Services Corporation/Center for Outcomes Research & Evaluation (YNHHSC/CORE) 2014). Appendix figure 11A.1 provides an overview of the CMS algorithm. Publicly available code produces a stay-level dataset by combining associated claims.

One of the episode types we study is acute myocardial infarction (AMI), or heart attack. Table 11.1 shows that 811,517 stays at 5,510 hospitals were

---

2. There is general agreement among experts that *price* measures in the health care sector should focus on the entire episode of care, rather than the prices of individual service inputs (National Research Council 2010; World Health Organization 2011). Researchers at the BLS and the Bureau of Economic Analysis have recently focused on price measurement based on an episode of care.

Table 11.1   Sample construction for AMI (heart attack) episodes

Stays/episodes	Beneficiaries	Hospitals	Description
29,841,183	7,880,612	6,353	All Medicare FFS stays in short-term acute-care hospitals, 2002–2014, based on random 20% sample of beneficiaries
811,517	635,380	5,510	Heart attack (acute myocardial infarction, i.e., AMI) stays
798,414	625,301	5,505	Excluding stays in fourth quarter of 2014 (incomplete follow up as index stays)
558,999	501,940	5,290	Stays/episodes meeting CMS readmission measure criteria
476,892	432,606	4,852	Excluding episodes with any missing cost-to-charge ratios
463,770	421,133	4,769	Episodes meeting AHRQ IQI risk measure criteria
461,830	419,531	4,739	Excluding index hospital-years with no Census sociodemographic data available
413,636	376,129	3,869	Excluding index hospital-years that did not match to teaching status (residents per bed) data in CMS Impact Files
402,778	366,645	3,560	Excluding index hospital-years with a zero rate for any favorable health outcome

for patients with a principal diagnosis of AMI. The first three digits of these diagnoses were *410*, per the International Classification of Diseases, Ninth Revision, Clinical Modification (ICD-9) (National Center for Health Statistics). The other episodes include congestive heart failure, pneumonia, gastrointestinal hemorrhage ("GI bleed"), hip fracture, stroke, "lower extremity" joint (hip and knee) replacement (LEJR), and chronic obstructive pulmonary disease (COPD). These episodes are also identified on the basis of validated ICD-9 (diagnosis and procedure) codes (Agency for Healthcare Research and Quality 2019).

We define episodes of care as beginning with admission to a short-term acute-care hospital and ending either 90 days after discharge from the initial (i.e., "index") stay or with death, whichever came first. CMS's hospital-based bundled-payment models have almost invariably used 90-day post-discharge windows (Centers for Medicare and Medicaid Services 2017). Because we do not have access to Medicare service utilization in 2015, we exclude episodes that started in the fourth quarter of 2014 (see table 11.1). Death dates are available from the research-identifiable version of CMS's Beneficiary Summary Files (specifically, the A/B segments that report Medicare enrollment and other beneficiary attributes). We treat a beneficiary as having died only if her reported date was flagged as having been validated by the Social Security Administration or Railroad Retirement Board. Under our Data Use Agreement, our CMS data also include uniquely encrypted beneficiary identifiers; these IDs are used to link the Beneficiary Summary Files to the Inpatient Files (and other claims files noted below).

To quantify productivity in delivering episodes of care, we estimate the following relationship for each episode type:

$$\ln(Y_{ht}/C_{ht}) = \alpha + S_{ht}\beta_S + O_{ht}\beta_O + g(t) + \varepsilon_{ht},$$

in which Y_{ht} is the total output of episodes initiated with an admission to index hospital h during year t, C_{ht} is the total cost (including post-discharge care) of providing these episodes, S_{ht} is severity factors for the patients in these episodes, and O_{ht} is other elements of hospital production. The left-hand side of this equation is the ratio of output to inputs, or more colloquially "bang for the buck." This metric is commonly used in economic assessments of health system performance (Gu et al. 2019; Romley, Goldman, and Sood 2015; Romley et al. 2019; Sheiner and Malinovskaya 2016).

On the right-hand side of the equation, our object of interest is the function $g(t)$, a common-across-hospitals but year-specific residual between measured determinants of production and measured output. As is standard, we will interpret this residual as MFP and changes in the residual over time as productivity improvement (or decline). As is well understood, the validity of this interpretation depends on the validity of the measurement of production determinants and output.

We measure output in each index hospital-year based on the quantity as well as quality of episodes. Under this framework, the health care system receives less credit (in terms of output) for a relatively low-quality episode yet is still responsible for the cost of scarce resources in delivering the episode. In prior studies, we have defined output as the *number* of inpatient stays that met a quality threshold explained below (Romley, Goldman, and Sood 2015; Romley et al. 2019). While this definition has a natural interpretation, its implication is that the elasticity of substitution between quantity and quality is equal to −1. Evidence on the trade-off between quantity and quality in health care is remarkably scarce. Grieco and McDevitt (2016) recently investigated the provision of kidney dialysis services, and their findings imply an elasticity of quantity with respect to quality of −1.4, which is an estimate consistent with higher quality being costly to produce.[3] We apply this estimate as our baseline value, while also considering our previously used value.

In prior studies, we defined quality by a composite rate of favorable health outcomes. For hospitals, we used survival for at least 30 days beyond the admission, and avoidance of an unplanned readmission within 30 days

---

3. Grieco and McDevitt (2016) report a semi-elasticity of quality with respect to quantity of −0.016 percent, where quality is measured based on the rate of infection. To obtain the elasticity of quality with respect to quantity, we multiply this value with the mean success rate of no infections of 87.5 percent calculated from the paper to obtain an estimated elasticity of −1.4.

of discharge. Both these outcomes correspond to quality-of-care metrics publicly reported by CMS and used in Medicare hospital reimbursement (Centers for Medicare and Medicaid Services 2019c; Centers for Medicare and Medicaid Services 2019e; Centers for Medicare and Medicaid Services 2019f). Specifically, mortality has been a metric for six of the episode types we study (LEJR and COPD are the exceptions), while readmission has been a metric for all our episode types. In this study, we continue to use these outcomes. For example, as table 11.1 reports, 558,999 AMI stays at 5,290 hospitals met all the inclusion/exclusion requirements of the CMS readmission algorithm.

Some potential episodes were inconsistent with the algorithm because the corresponding admission was a readmission that occurred within an episode already in progress.[4] In addition, patients must have been 65 years old or older at admission and continuously enrolled in "traditional" fee-for-service Medicare (Parts A and B) to be included, and a candidate index stay is excluded if the patient was discharged "against medical advice."[5] Age and enrollment are determined from the Beneficiary Summary Files, while type of discharge is reported in the Inpatient Files. To maximize sample size, we do not include the optional requirement of 12 months of continuous enrollment prior to the index stay.

In this study, our quality composite is not limited to survival without an unplanned readmission, but also incorporates whether a patient "returns to the community" rather than remaining institutionalized. Under the Improving Medicare Post-Acute Care Transformation Act of 2014, discharge to the community was adopted as an interim quality metric (Centers for Medicare and Medicaid Services 2019g). We require discharge to the community during the episode window for the last claim from an institutional setting that began during the window (Inpatient, Skilled Nursing Facility and Hospice Files).[6]

In prior studies, our composite rate of favorable outcomes specified that every outcome be favorable. Thus, a patient who died experienced an unfavorable outcome, and a patient with an unplanned readmission also experienced an unfavorable outcome, and to an equal degree. This specification, while simple, is unrealistic. There is a large body of evidence on how health relates to quality of life (for example, with limb amputation for a person with diabetes), yet we have not been able to find estimates of the "decrement" to quality of life that results from institutionalization for health reasons. To assess this impact, we build on an approach developed by Cutler and Richardson (1997).

4. The version of the readmission algorithm we use requires a 30-day gap between index stays. Because our episodes last 90 days after discharge from the index stay, we modify the SAS algorithm accordingly.
5. For its purposes, CMS excludes candidate stays in which the patient dies before discharge. We modify the SAS code so as not to exclude these episodes.
6. For examples of high-quality treatment outcomes in other contexts, see Shapiro, Shapiro, and Wilcox (2001) for cataract surgery and Berndt et al. (2002) for medical treatment of depression.

In particular, we use self-reported health outcomes to calculate a quality-adjusted life year (QALY) measure for being in an institutionalized setting. A QALY is a measure of health from 0 to 1 where 1 indicates a year of life in perfect health and 0 is death; this metric has been suggested as an approach to quality adjustment in assessments of health care productivity. To create a QALY metric for our purposes, we use the Medicare Current Beneficiary Survey (MCBS) for the years 1999–2013, which contains information on a sample of over 10,000 Medicare beneficiaries each year with information on self-reported health (i.e., excellent, very good, good, fair, and poor) and whether they reside in an institutionalized setting. We assume that individuals respond to the self-reported health question using latent information about their true health. We relate this latent health information to covariates by estimating an ordered probit of self-reported health on covariates of age, sex, and whether individuals reside in an institution. We find that being in an institution has a large negative impact on self-reported health. To obtain a QALY estimate, the cut points in the ordered probit are used to rescale the coefficient to a QALY scale, where it is assumed that the cut point for "excellent" health corresponds to a QALY of 1 and the cut point for "poor" corresponds to a QALY of 0, which is equivalent to death. Based on these estimates we find that being in an institution has a QALY measure of 0.68. That is, the quality-of-life decrement from institutionalization is 0.32.[7]

There is some uncertainty regarding this estimate as strong assumptions are made, such as relating self-reported health to the quality of life. Moreover, the MCBS survey is based on a random sample of all Medicare beneficiaries, but the movement from being at home to an institutionalized setting after the acute events that we are studying may signal a declining health trajectory. That is, the relevant comparison may not be between poor and excellent health, but rather between poor and something less than excellent health. "Very good" health would imply a QALY of 0.52 for institutionalization; that is, a larger decrement in quality of life. Merely "good" health would imply an even lower QALY value, and an even larger quality of life decrement. In view of the uncertainty, we use a quality-of-life decrement (0.66) that lies halfway between the smallest decrement just discussed (0.32 = 1.0 − QALY of 0.68 based on excellent health cut point) and the value used in our prior studies (1.0) and consider the sensitivity of our finding to these extreme alternatives.

Our framework for incorporating quality is a version of what has been called the "redefine the good" approach,[8] in contrast with the "cost of living"

---

7. Our baseline specification of output is therefore $\ln Y_{ht} = \ln N_{ht} + 1.4 \ln(A_{ht}\{G|A_{ht} + 0.68[1 - G|A_{ht}]\})$, in which N_{ht} is the number of episodes initiated at hospital h in year t, A_{ht} is the rate/proportion of episodes in which the patient is alive 90 days after discharge from the index stay, and $G|A_{ht}$ is the proportion of episodes with otherwise good outcomes (i.e., avoidance of an unplanned readmission *and* return to community) among those who are alive at the end of the episode window.

8. When the elasticity of quantity with respect to quality is specified to −1.4, our version places extra weight on quality, based on the evidence described above, in comparison to the

approach (Sheiner and Malinovskaya 2016). The latter was used to develop the heart attack inflation measure referenced previously (Cutler et al. 1998). These two approaches are closely related but not identical. The cost-of-living approach determines the compensating variation associated with improved outcomes from treatment. Dauda, Dunn, and Hall (2019) show that a cost-of-living index indicates greater improvement than our approach here when the value of the health improvement exceeds its incremental cost,[9] as can and sometimes does happen in health care (Cutler and McClellan 2001). While the cost-of-living approach reflects consumer welfare, Sheiner and Malinovskaya (2016) note that the rate of productivity change is the relevant metric for assessing whether providers could deliver the same number of episodes of the same quality when their reimbursement rates are reduced, as the Affordable Care Act mandates according to the rate of productivity growth outside the heath care sector. As with the BLS conceptualization of productivity (Harper et al. 2010), our focus is on producers/firms.

Turning to production inputs, the comparative returns to capital, labor, and other factors are not of interest here, and so we combine the resources used in providing care (see, e.g., Chandra and Staiger 2007; Chandra et al. 2016; Doyle 2011; Skinner and Staiger 2015), aggregating all episodes of each type at each index hospital-year. To do so, we identify claims that overlapped with each episode, including inpatient (short-term acute-care hospitals but also long-term care hospitals and inpatient rehabilitation facilities), outpatient facilities, professional (e.g., a claim submitted by a doctor for an inpatient surgery or an office visit), skilled nursing facilities (SNFs), home health, durable medical equipment, and hospice. The Carrier File of professional claims was the largest of these; in the 2014 File, the 20 percent sample included 178 million claims, with 24.6 million of these corresponding to Medicare beneficiaries experiencing a heart attack episode over 2002–2014 and 5.3 million falling within a heart attack episode window. Where a claim in any file did not fall entirely within the episode timeframe, we allocate costs based on the proportion of days with overlap.

CMS claims do not directly report costs, but instead provide a measure of resource use. For example, total charges are reported for hospital stays. To estimate costs, we use the financial reports that institutional providers participating in Medicare are required to submit to CMS (Centers for Medicare and Medicaid Services 2019d). Hospitals, for example, report not only their actual costs, but the ratio of their charges to their costs (CCRs). So,

standard version of the redefine-the-good approach. In addition, while the approach typically defines success dichotomously, we allow success to be polychotomous according to the quality of life associated with distinct patient outcomes (see above).

9. That is, consider improved health outcomes stemming from an increase in multifactor productivity. Then the absolute value of the magnitude of the price decrease under the cost-of-living approach exceeds the magnitude of the productivity increase under the condition noted by Dauda, Dunn, and Hall (2019).

a hospital's cost for a claim is measured by linking reported charges on the claim to the hospital's reported CCR based on Medicare provider number and then multiplying the former by the latter, as is commonly done in the literature (Cutler and Huckman 2003). SNF cost reports include revenue-to-cost ratios, and so we multiply these ratios by claim-reported revenues to measure the cost of the claim.[10]

CCRs are sometimes unavailable, and our primary analysis excludes episodes for which any CCR is missing. As table 11.1 shows, this criterion excludes about 15 percent of heart attack episodes. In a sensitivity analysis, we also include episodes with one or more institutional claims that could not be matched to cost data, and whose payments for claims with missing cost data as a share of total payments for the episode type were less than or equal to the median for the episode type.[11] We then inflate total measured costs of these episodes, according payments for claims with missing costs as a share of total payments for all episodes of the same type that initiated within the same calendar year.

Professional claims report Relative Value Units (RVUs), a measure of the resources required to provide a particular service (Medicare Payment and Advisory Committee 2018). The reimbursement received by a professional is equal to the number of RVUs multiplied by a dollar-denominated "conversion factor" (CF) specified annually in CMS's Medicare Physician Fee Schedule Final Rule, adjusted for geographic differences in the cost of care (Medicare Payment and Advisory Committee 2018). One objective in setting the CF is to ensure that professional providers offer accessible care to beneficiaries, yet federal policy makers have intervened in the CF-setting process to postpone reductions in professional payments mandated by statute for the purpose of controlling cost growth (Guterman 2014). We assume that the CF in 2002 equated aggregate professional revenues with aggregate costs in that year, before the interventions began. We do not include prescription drug costs due to data limitations during the first five years of our analytic period (Medicare Part D was introduced in 2006).

We wish to measure the real cost of treating episodes. As an input into its reimbursement policy making, CMS constructs and reports "market basket indices" and the Medicare Economic Index (MEI). The Inpatient Hospital market basket index, for example, measures changes in the cost of providing inpatient hospital care. We use this index and those for other institutional settings to deflate nominal costs into real 2014 dollars. The MEI is used for professional payment, and measures inflation in the cost of providing professional services, less an adjustment for productivity growth in the economy at large (2012 Medicare Economic Index Technical Advisory Panel 2012).

---

10. Charges are not in general equal to payments in health care—due, for example, to contractual discounts off list price for commercial insurers as well as administrative pricing for Medicare and other public payers (Reinhardt 2006).

11. We include payments from all sources.

We inflation-adjust professional costs by reversing the productivity adjustments to the MEI; durable medical equipment costs are similarly deflated.

Turning to patient severity (S_{ht}), a key measure comes from the Agency for Healthcare Research and Quality's Inpatient Quality Indicators (IQIs) (Agency for Healthcare Research and Quality 2019). The IQIs were developed for the purpose of assessing the quality of care across hospitals and over time using standard administrative data (specifically, patient discharge records, which typically lack post-discharge outcomes, including mortality). The IQIs include inpatient mortality for a variety of conditions, including the six episode types for which CMS reports mortality. In order to reliably assess mortality performance, teams of clinical experts developed risk adjustment models that can be applied to individual hospitalizations (including patients who actually died during their stays). For each episode type, we use the average predicted likelihood of survival through the end of hospitalization, derived from these models, averaged across all episodes (including patients who died during stays) initiated at an index hospital in a year. Table 11.1 reports that predicted survival was not available for some episodes that are consistent with the CMS readmission algorithm. For heart attack, the IQI excludes cases whose status as the first or subsequent heart attack was not coded, while the readmission algorithm does not. For the six episode types with IQI risk models, we limit our analytic sample to episodes with predicted inpatient mortality for the sake of clinical specificity. Details of the IQI inclusion/exclusion criteria for heart attack episodes are shown in table 11A.1.

An important element of these risk models is the All Patients Refined Diagnosis Related Group (APR-DRG)—in particular, its risk of mortality scale. While the inputs into the APR-DRGs are known (e.g., diagnosis and procedure codes), a limitation of our approach is that the logic of the APR-DRG "grouper" methodology is proprietary to 3M, and so is not transparent to end users. There is a limited-license version released by AHRQ for the purpose of implementing the IQIs. We apply version 6.0 of the IQIs, the last refinement developed for use with ICD-9 coding (CMS transitioned to ICD-10 beginning in fiscal year 2015). Details on the AMI risk model are shown in table 11A.2.

In addition, for all episode types (including the two for which IQI risk models were not available), we exploit diagnostic information in our data by measuring the proportion of episodes with different numbers of Charlson-Deyo comorbidities (such as dementia) recorded in the index inpatient record. These comorbidities have been demonstrated to usefully predict death within 12 months (Charlson et al. 1987; Quan et al. 2005). For heart attack episodes, we also characterize the type based on the location within the heart, using the fourth digit of the ICD-9 code (Romley, Goldman, and Sood 2015). The type of heart attack relates to prognosis; for example, survival is relatively favorable for a "non-STEMI" heart-attack (ICD-9 of 410.7x for subendocardial infarction), at least in the near term (Cantor et al. 2005; Cox et al. 2006). The maximum number of diagnoses recorded on inpatient claims increased from 10 to 25 in 2010, so we limit ourselves to the first 10.

In addition, we use the proportion of patients who were female and of various races, as reported in the Beneficiary Summary Files. These files also report the zip code in which each beneficiary resides, which we link to zip code–level data from the 2000 Census on a variety of community sociodemographic characteristics used as proxies for patient severity in prior literature (Fisher et al. 2003a; Fisher et al. 2003b; Romley, Goldman, and Sood 2015; Romley, Jena, and Goldman 2011); examples include the poverty rate and the proportion of elderly residents with self-care limitations. As table 11.1 shows, about 1,900 of 463,800 episodes initiated at hospitals for whom *none* of the patient zip codes matched to the Census data; all other episodes could be matched. Finally, we use the proportion of discharges in each quarter, as there may be seasonality in severity and fourth-quarter discharges had to be excluded in 2014 (due to incomplete follow up).

Turning to other elements of hospital production, we account for medical education. This activity may complement AMI care or draw resources from it, and it is possible that patients with particular episodes became more (or less) likely to be treated at an academic hospital over time. We address this possibility using indicator variables for intervals of the number of medical residents per bed specified in prior literature (Volpp et al. 2007); these data are available from the Impact Files released annually by CMS in support of its inpatient prospective payment system (Centers for Medicare and Medicaid Services 2019b). Small and largely rural hospitals are not paid under this system, and so episodes initiated at these hospitals are excluded from the analytic sample (see table 11.1).

Our regressions clustered standard errors at the level of the index hospital. Because of our logarithmic specification, hospital-years with a zero rate for a favorable health outcome are excluded from the analysis; table 11.1 shows that 2.7 percent of AMI episodes treated at 8.0 percent of hospitals are excluded on this basis. For representativeness, our regressions weighted hospital-year observations by their number of episodes. In further sensitivity analysis, we include fixed effects for the hospitals at which episodes were initiated. This specification aims to deal with the possibility that unmeasured heterogeneity between providers (including MFP differences) was systematically related to patient severity or teaching status, leading to bias in our estimates of the trajectory of MFP over time.

Finally, in order to develop some insight into aggregate productivity growth in the delivery of acute episodes of care, we create a composite that combines all episode types. To do so, we weight the annualized growth rate for each episode type by the episode's share of total cost in various base years.

11.3   Findings

Before reviewing our regression results, we first describe the episodes studied, with a focus on AMI—that is, heart attack. Table 11.2 reports sample statistics for the heart attack analysis. Across 28,635 index hospital-years, the average date of the initial admission is mid-2007. The average cost per episode is $37,200 in 2014 dollars. Of elderly Medicare beneficiaries admitted to a hospital with a heart attack, 79.4 percent survived at least 90 days beyond the initial discharge. The AHRQ AMI IQI predicts that 92.2 percent would have survived beyond the initial hospital stay (though not necessarily 90 days beyond discharge). Among 90-day survivors, 85.1 percent avoided an unplanned readmission within 30 days of initial discharge. Among survivors without a readmission, 81.6 percent were discharged home from their final institutional encounter.

In terms of severity, roughly two thirds of episodes involved a non-STEMI heart attack. All episodes involved at least one Charlson-Deyo comorbidity, as a heart attack is such a comorbidity. More than 7 in 10 episodes involved additional comorbidities. The average age of beneficiaries was 78.8 years, slightly less than half were female, and almost 9 in 10 were white. Median household incomes in beneficiaries' zip codes averaged $42,600 in the 2000 Census. In terms of index hospital characteristics, slightly more than 4 in 10 episodes took place at facilities with no medical residents, while about 3 in 20 took place at a major teaching hospital (> 0.25 residents per bed).

A simple albeit limited measure of productivity is the cost of a heart attack episode, irrespective of patient severity or outcomes (Ashby, Guterman, and Greene 2000). Figure 11.1 shows this measure over 2002–2014. The cost of an episode was $34,500 in 2002, measured in 2014 dollars. The cost was reasonably flat thereafter but did increase to $35,700 by 2014. The top panel of figure 11.2 shows that average cost increased for every episode type except LEJR. Hip fracture increased the most in absolute terms ($5,100), while GI bleed increased the most in relative terms (20.0 percent).

In 2014, the total cost of all of these episodes was $38.3 billion, measured in 2014 dollars.[12] Focusing on the three episode types from our prior study (heart attack, heart failure, and pneumonia), the total cost was $16.9 billion in 2014. Limiting ourselves to the cost of the initial hospital stays (as in the prior study), the total for these three episode types was $7.8 billion. For heart attack alone, the total cost of initial hospital stays in 2014 was $2.8 billion.

---

12. Total costs in our analytic sample were multiplied by a factor of five, because we had access to a 20 percent sample of beneficiaries. In 2014, incomplete follow up (due to lack of 2015 data) required that episodes be initiated before October. Accordingly, we inflated 2014 costs by the ratio of the number of January–December episodes to the number of January–September episodes over 2002–2013. Finally, we eliminated duplicates in cases that corresponded to multiple episode types (for example, some patients with hip fracture underwent LEJR).

Table 11.2   **Sample statistics for AMI episodes**

Variable	Mean (SE)
Episodes, *n*	402,778
Hospitals, *n*	3,560
Hospital-years, *n*	28,635
Year of admission	2007.3 (3.7)
Cost per episode (000s of 2014 dollars)	$37.2 ($14.1)
Survival of episode	79.4% (12.6%)
No unplanned readmissions (30 day) among survivors	85.1% (12.0%)
Discharge home among survivors without readmissions	81.6% (15.9%)
AHRQ predicted inpatient survival	92.2% (3.8%)
Location of heart attack: Anterolateral (410.0x)	2.1% (3.7%)
Location of heart attack: Other anterior wall (410.1x)	8.1% (7.6%)
Location of heart attack: Inferolateral wall (410.2x)	1.7% (3.4%)
Location of heart attack: Inferoposterior wall (410.3x)	1.2% (2.7%)
Location of heart attack: Other inferior wall (410.4x)	9.9% (8.2%)
Location of heart attack: Other lateral wall (410.5x)	1.2% (2.8%)
Location of heart attack: True posterior wall (410.6x)	0.3% (1.5%)
Location of heart attack: Sub-endocardial (410.7x)	68.3% (16.8%)
Location of heart attack: Other specified sites (410.8x)	1.4% (4.6%)
Location of heart attack: Unspecified site (410.9x)	5.9% (9.5%)
No Charlson-Deyo comorbidity	0.0% (0.0%)
1 Charlson-Deyo comorbidity	27.7% (13.1%)
2 Charlson-Deyo comorbidities	32.3% (12.7%)
3 Charlson-Deyo comorbidities	21.0% (11.5%)
4 Charlson-Deyo comorbidities	11.2% (9.3%)
5+ Charlson-Deyo comorbidities	7.8% (8.5%)
Age	78.8 (3.1)

Table 11.2   **(cont.)**

Variable	Mean (SE)
Female	49.0%
	(14.6%)
White	88.0%
	(15.6%)
African American	7.7%
	(12.8%)
Hispanic	1.8%
	(5.9%)
Other race	2.5%
	(6.9%)
Patient zip code characteristics	
Median household income ($000)	$42.6
	($10.1)
Social Security income ($000)	$11.3
	($0.9)
Poor	12.0%
	(4.9%)
Employed	94.3%
	(2.0%)
Less than high school education	20.0%
	(6.7%)
Urban	70.3%
	(21.9%)
Hispanic	8.7%
	(12.3%)
Single	41.7%
	(4.6%)
Elderly in an institution	5.5%
	(2.4%)
Noninstitutionalized elderly with physical disability	29.3%
	(4.7%)
Mental disability	11.0%
	(2.9%)
Sensory disability among elderly	14.6%
	(2.6%)
Self-care disability	9.7%
	(2.6%)
Difficulty going-outside-the-home disability	20.5%
	(3.6%)
Index hospital characteristics	
No residents	43.2%
	(49.5%)
Residents per bed > 0 and ≤ 0.25	41.2%
	(49.2%)
Residents per bed > 0.25 and ≤ 0.6	10.7%
	(30.9%)
Residents per bed > 0.6	5.0%
	(21.7%)

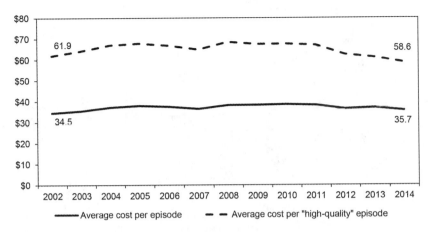

Fig. 11.1   Cost of heart-attack episodes (000s of 2014 dollars)

Notes: In this figure, a "high-quality" episode means that the patient survived through the end of the episode, avoided an unplanned readmission within 30 days of the initial discharge, and was discharged home from the last facility claim. This definition corresponds to a quality of life decrement for institutionalization of –1.0. Regression analyses considered alternative decrements, with the intermediate value of –0.66 as the baseline. Under this baseline, an episode in which the patient survived but was institutionalized is counted as 34% of an episode with survival without institutionalization.

The simple measures shown in the top panel of figure 11.2 ignore the quality of the health outcomes delivered to patients. Figure 11.3 shows that survival improved for heart attack patients, rising from a rate of 77.8 percent in 2002 to a rate of 82.8 percent in 2014. Among survivors, the rate of avoidance of unplanned readmission within 30 days of initial discharge improved from 83.5 percent to 86.8 percent. The rate of discharge to home from the last facility claim declined somewhat, from 84.4 percent in 2002 to 83.4 percent in 2014.

Defining a high-quality episode as survival without institutionalization (whether an unplanned readmission or a discharge to another facility), figure 11.3 shows that the rate of high-quality episodes increased from 55.7 percent in 2002 to 60.8 percent in 2014 for heart attack patients. The middle panel of figure 11.2 shows the rate of high-quality episodes for all episode types. This rate improved for six of the eight episode types; the increase was greatest in absolute terms for hip fracture (5.8 percentage points) and in relative terms for LEJR (18.7 percent). The rate of high-quality stays declined by 3.6 percentage points for heart failure episodes. Among these patients, avoidance of readmission improved, but survival and home discharge rates worsened.

Figure 11.1 shows that the improvement in patient outcomes dominated the modest rise in costs for heart attack patients. The cost of a high-quality heart attack episode decreased from $61,900 in 2002 to $58,600 in 2014.

A. Average Cost (000s of 2014 dollars)

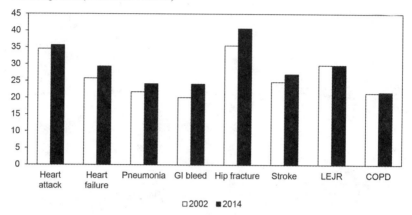

B. Rate of "High-Quality" Episodes

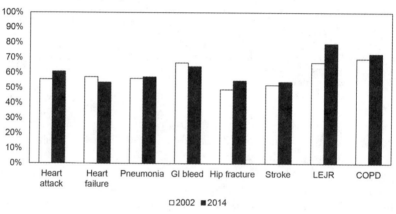

C. Average Cost per "High-Quality" Episode (000s of 2014 Dollars)

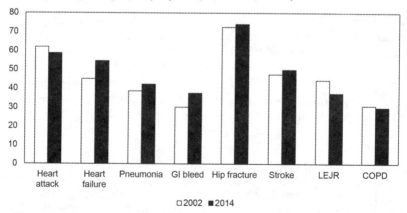

Fig. 11.2   Episode cost and quality

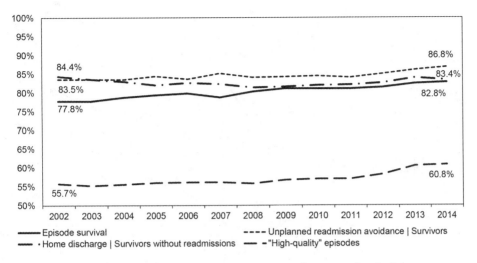

Fig. 11.3   Rates of favorable patient outcomes among heart-attack episodes

Notes: In this figure, a "high-quality" episode means that the patient survived through the end of the episode, avoided an unplanned readmission within 30 days of the initial discharge, and was discharged home from the last facility claim. This definition corresponds to a quality of life decrement for institutionalization of –1.0. Regression analyses considered alternative decrements, with the intermediate value of –0.66 as the baseline. Under this baseline, an episode in which the patient survived but was institutionalized is counted as 34% of an episode with survival without institutionalization.

Figure 11.2 shows the cost of high-quality episodes for all episode types. This cost increased for five episodes—namely, heart failure, pneumonia, GI bleed, hip fracture, and stroke. For heart failure, costs increased as quality decreased, and this episode type experienced the largest absolute increase in the cost of a high-quality episode ($9,600). GI bleed had the largest relative increase (24.6 percent). The higher costs for pneumonia, hip fracture, and stroke outweighed their quality improvements. The cost of a high-quality episode decreased for LEJR and COPD in addition to heart attack. This decrease was largest in both absolute and relative terms for LEJR (–$7,000 and –15.8 percent, respectively).

These changes in the cost of a high-quality episode may have reflected trends in the severity of patients treated. Figure 11.4 shows that the age of a heart attack patient at index admission was 78.6 years in 2002, and then rose steadily to a maximum of 79.0 years in 2008, before declining to its starting value of 78.6 years in 2014. The number of Charlson-Deyo comorbidities recorded on the index inpatient record of a heart attack patient increased substantially over time, from 2.27 in 2002 to 2.61 in 2014. The predicted likelihood of inpatient survival from the AHRQ IQI risk model decreased from 93.3 percent to 92.8 percent over the period.

Using all our patient severity measure and the results of our primary

A. Average Age at Admission

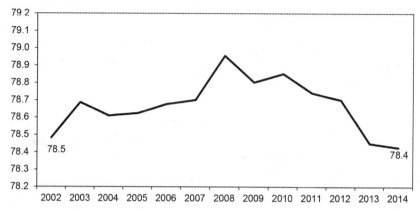

B. Number of Charlson-Deyo Comorbidities on Index Inpatient Record

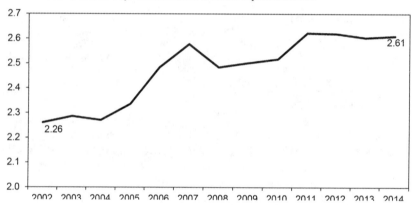

C. Predicted Inpatient Survival from AHRQ Inpatient Quality Indicator Risk Model

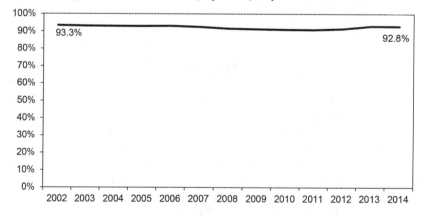

Fig. 11.4   Select patient severity measures for heart-attack episodes

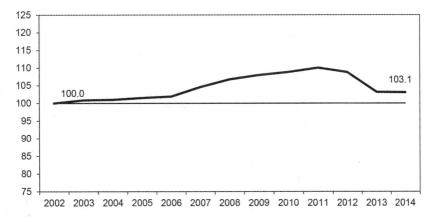

Fig. 11.5   Patient severity index among heart-attack episodes

Note: We construct the patient severity index by exponentiating $-\bar{S}_{ht}\hat{\beta}_S$, obtaining $\hat{\beta}_S$ from the regression results corresponding to Figures 16 and 17 and normalizing the index to a value of 100 in 2002.

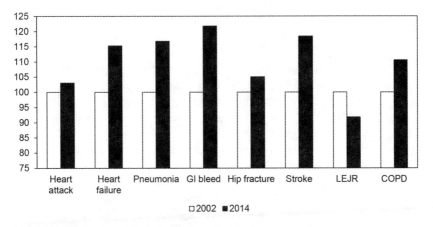

Fig. 11.6   Patient severity index among all episodes

Note: We construct the patient severity index by exponentiating $-\bar{S}_{ht}\hat{\beta}_S$, obtaining $\hat{\beta}_S$ from the regression results corresponding to Figures 16 and 17 and normalizing the index to a value of 100 in 2002.

regressions, we can construct a patient severity index.[13] For heart attack episodes, figure 11.5 shows that severity increased from its baseline value of 100 in 2002, started to rise more rapidly in 2007 and reached a peak of 110.0 in 2010, then settled at 103.1 in 2014. This pattern means that the heart attack patients treated in 2014 would have required 3.1 percent higher costs to enjoy the same outcomes as patients in 2002. Figure 11.6 shows the

---

13. The construction of the index is described in the note to figure 11.5.

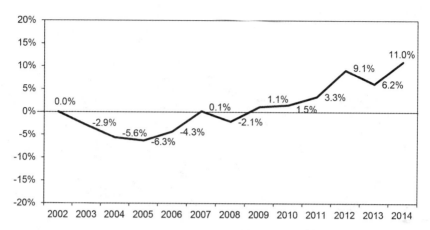

Fig. 11.7   Cumulative change in productivity since 2002 in treating heart-attack episodes

patient severity index for all episode types. LEJR experienced a decline in severity even as its cost of a high-quality episode decreased. Severity rose for all other episode types. GI bleed saw the largest increase, with an index value of 121.8 in 2014.

In addition to the severity index, we can construct an index for other hospital production—specifically, the effect (whether positive or negative) of medical education on the delivery of our acute episodes. As appendix figure 11A.2 shows for heart attack episodes, teaching status played little role in changes in productivity in treating these episodes.

Focusing on our regression analyses, the trajectory of estimated productivity for heart attack episodes appears in figure 11.7. Productivity declined at first, reaching a trough of –6.3 percent cumulative growth since 2002, before beginning to improve fairly consistently, reaching a maximum of 11.0 percent improvement (over 2002) by 2014. A similar pattern was observed in our prior studies of hospital and nursing home stays (Romley, Goldman, and Sood 2015; Gu et al. 2019). The productivity trajectories for all episode types are shown in appendix figure 11A.3; complete regression results are reported in appendix table 11A.3.[14]

14. In general, the regression coefficients have the expected signs. For the six episode types for which IQI risk models are available, a higher predicted probability of surviving beyond the initial hospital stay is associated with better outcomes or lower costs. For example, a 1 percent increase (relative, not absolute) in the average survival probability of stroke patients is associated with 4.1 percent more stays or better outcomes (given costs), or 4.1 percent lower costs (given the number of episodes and their quality). Likewise, having fewer Charlson-Deyo comorbidities recorded on the initial hospital record is associated with greater output or lower costs. For LEJR, for example, if all patients had only one comorbidity, output would be roughly 12 percent greater, or costs 12 percent lower. Finally, for all episode types except heart attack,

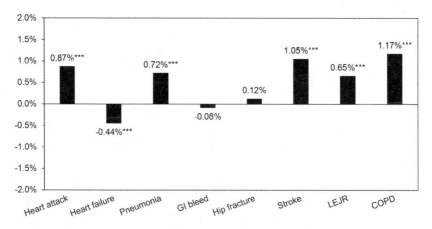

Fig. 11.8   Annualized rate of productivity growth, 2002–2014

Notes: Rates calculated according to the formula $\exp(\hat{b}_{2014}\,/\,12) - 1$, in which $\hat{b}_{2014}$ is the regression coefficient corresponding to episodes starting in 2014, relative to 2002. *, **, and *** denote statistical significance at the 10%, 5%, and 1% levels, respectively.

On an annualized basis, productivity for heart attack episodes grew by 0.87 percent on average between 2002 and 2014. Figure 11.8 shows somewhat slower growth for pneumonia and LEJR, but even greater improvement (in excess of 1.0 percent per year) for stroke and COPD. Productivity change for GI bleed and hip fracture was indistinguishable from zero. For heart failure episodes, productivity is estimated to have decreased by 0.44 percent per year on average.

Figure 11.9 shows the impact of adjustments for patient severity and outcome quality on the estimates just reported. As noted previously, severity increased for all episode types except LEJR. Consequently, estimated productivity growth is lower when we adjust for patient severity than when we do not (0.65 percent versus 1.37 percent per year). Among the episode types experiencing greater severity, the sign of estimated productivity growth changes from positive to negative for pneumonia and stroke when we ignore severity. Severity adjustment plays a relatively limited role for heart attack (+0.87 percent with versus +0.62 percent without).

Ignoring quality, the point estimates for annual productivity growth are negative for every episode type except COPD. Even in the latter case, estimated productivity improvement is 0.51 percent per year when quality is ignored, versus 1.17 percent per year otherwise. For heart failure, quality

---

a younger patient population is associated with more output or lower costs. For pneumonia, for example, a 1 percent decrease in average age is associated with 2.1 percent more output or lower costs.

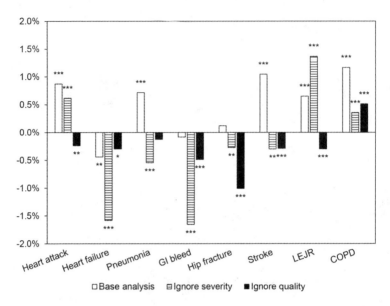

Fig. 11.9   Impacts of adjustment for outcome quality and patient severity on annualized productivity growth estimates

Note: *, **, and *** denote statistical significance at the 10%, 5%, and 1% levels, respectively.

adjustment results in somewhat more negative growth (−0.44 percent per year versus −0.30 percent per year), because quality declined in the aggregate.

The results thus far assume that institutionalization (whether unplanned readmission or discharge to another facility) causes a decrease in quality of life of −0.66. That is, survival with institutionalization is 34 percent as good as survival without institutionalization. As noted previously, there is substantial uncertainty about the impact of institutionalization on quality of life. Figure 11.10 considers two alternatives spanning our baseline value; namely, −0.32 and −1.0. Where trends in institutionalization rates are favorable, a smaller (in absolute magnitude) decrement implies that measured productivity growth will be slower. For example, with a decrement of 0.32, productivity growth for heart attack episodes is 0.72 percent per year, instead of 0.87 percent with the baseline intermediate value. With a decrement of 1.0, growth is higher; namely, 1.06 percent per year. For hip fracture, the baseline estimate is an insignificant +0.12 percent per year, but significant at +0.78 percent and −0.23 percent per year with decrements of 1.0 and 0.32, respectively. Productivity growth for LEJR episodes is also sensitive in magnitude (if not the positive direction) to the decrement value.

For the elasticity of quantity with respect to quality, our baseline value is

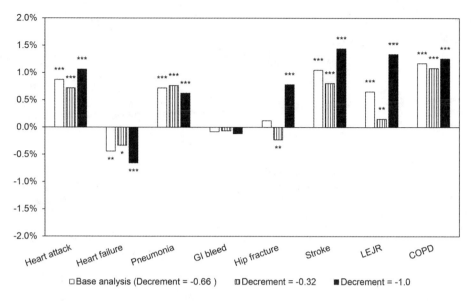

Fig. 11.10   Sensitivity of annualized productivity growth estimates to quality of life decrement for institutionalization

Note: *, **, and *** denote statistical significance at the 10%, 5%, and 1% levels, respectively.

−1.4, based on our view of the best evidence (discussed previously). We also consider a value of −1.0, consistent with prior studies (Romley, Goldman, and Sood 2015; Gu et al. 2019; Romley et al. 2019). With this alternative value, a 10 percent improvement in quality requires a 10 percent decrease in the number of episodes, instead of 14 percent according to the baseline value. Consequently, measured productivity growth, given a favorable quality trend, is slower under this alternative value. Figure 11.11 is consistent with this observation, but further shows that estimated growth is not particularly sensitive to this alternative value for the elasticity. For hip fracture, insignificant growth of +0.12 percent per year becomes a marginally significant decline of 0.20 percent per year.

As noted previously, cost data are unavailable for some facility claims (15 percent of heart attack episodes had at least one such claim). We assess the sensitivity of estimated productivity growth rates to the inclusion of episodes with some (but relatively limited) missingness, with their measured total costs inflated according to payments on claims with missing costs in comparison to total payments for such episodes in each year. Figure 11.12 shows that the changes to our estimates are negligible.

Finally, we assess the sensitivity of our estimates to the inclusion of fixed effects for hospitals. As figure 11.13 shows, measured productivity growth

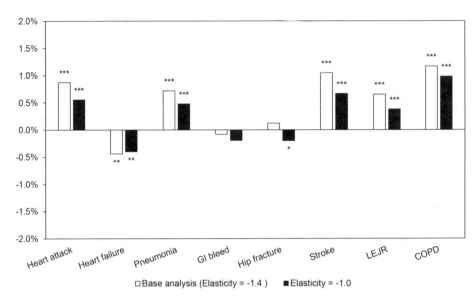

Fig. 11.11 **Sensitivity of annualized productivity growth estimates to elasticity of episode quality with respect to quantity**

Note: *, **, and *** denote statistical significance at the 10%, 5%, and 1% levels, respectively.

becomes faster for every episode type. Indeed, growth for heart failure is no longer significantly negative, and the rate for hip fracture is now significantly positive, at +0.40 percent per year.

Based on our baseline results, composite productivity growth, aggregated across all episode types, is shown in figure 11.14. The growth rate is +0.44 percent per year on average over 2002–2014 when productivity is aggregated based on cost shares using 2002 shares as the base, and +0.45 percent and +0.44 percent when using cost shares from 2008 and 2014, respectively.

11.4   Conclusion

There is widespread concern about poor coordination in US health care. Even if hospitals or doctors improve their productivity over time, information and incentive problems across providers could result in stagnant performance with respect to episodes of care. Policy makers and health practitioners are increasingly scrutinizing the performance of the health care system in delivering episodes of care.

To our knowledge this is the first study that assesses productivity growth— from the producer perspective, consistent with the focus of BLS—in the provision of acute episodes of care. We consider eight types of episodes delivered to Medicare fee-for-service beneficiaries over 2002–2014. Drawing

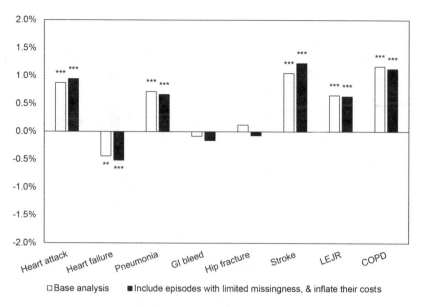

Fig. 11.12   Sensitivity of annualized productivity growth estimates to treatment of missing episode costs

Notes: "Limited" missingness refers to episodes with (a) one or more institutional claims that could not be matched to cost data, and (b) whose payments for claims with missing cost data as a share of total payments for the episode was at or below the median for the episode type. Total measured costs for these episodes were inflated according to payments for claims with missing costs as a share of total payments for all episodes of the same type that initiated in the same calendar year. *, **, and *** denote statistical significance at the 10%, 5%, and 1% levels, respectively.

on insurance claims and administrative data, we find positive multifactor productivity growth for a majority of the episode types. For stroke and chronic obstructive pulmonary disease, our baseline estimates of the rate of productivity growth over this period exceed 1 percent per year. There is, however, some evidence of negative productivity growth for heart failure. Our findings for the various episode types are fairly robust to alternative assumptions.

To develop some insight into aggregate productivity growth for these episodes, we constructed a composite measure, and found an annual growth rate of roughly 0.45 percent. The cost of care provided under Medicare Parts A and B for these episodes totaled $38 billion in 2014, measured in 2014 dollars, compared to overall program spending of $367 billion (Cubanski, Neuman, and Freed 2019). While this total is substantial, there is clearly an opportunity to address productivity in health care delivery more broadly. One potentially worthwhile direction would be to assess multifactor productivity in the treatment of various chronic conditions. Berndt et al. (2002) have already considered depression, while Eggleston et al. (2011) have addressed

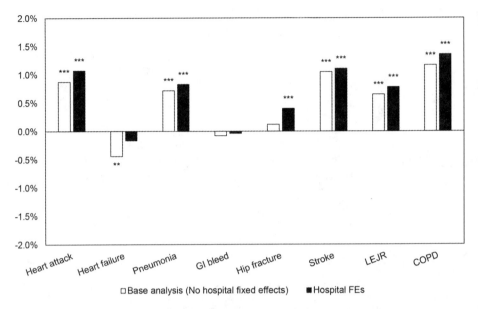

Fig. 11.13 Sensitivity of annualized productivity growth estimates to inclusion of hospital fixed effects

Note: *, **, and *** denote statistical significance at the 10%, 5%, and 1% levels, respectively.

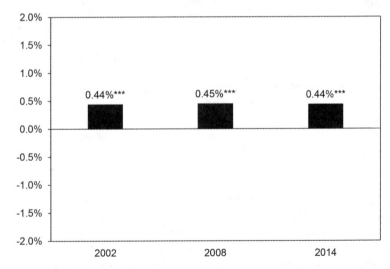

Fig. 11.14 Annualized growth of composite (all-episode-type) productivity according to base year

Note: *, **, and *** denote statistical significance at the 10%, 5%, and 1% levels, respectively.

productivity in diabetes, but from the consumer welfare perspective. In our view, and with these studies as motivating examples, such analyses will be most credible when well informed by clinical science, as well as economic practice.

For the episodes studied here, the reasonably favorable picture that emerges stems in substantial part from our efforts to account for the quality of the health outcomes experienced by patients. We measure quality based on patient survival, avoidance of unplanned readmission, and discharge to the community. The latter is of relevance to recent federal policy concerning post-acute care, and we found in auxiliary analysis that continued institutionalization rather than community discharge entails a substantial decrement to a patient's quality of life. For most episode types, these outcomes improved over time, substantially impacting measured productivity growth. For example, productivity growth for stroke is estimated to be $+1.05$ percent per year when we account for quality of care, but -0.29 percent per year if we ignore it. The importance of quality adjustment has long been recognized in the measurement of health care price indices that focus on consumer welfare (Cutler et al. 1998).

There is general agreement among experts that the output of the health care sector should be measured based on the treatments of the conditions, rather than the individual services (e.g., physician visit), which are inputs to those treatments (National Research Council 2010; World Health Organization 2011; Moulton 2018). To improve national economic measurement of the health care sector, the Bureau of Economic Analysis has recently developed a Health Care Satellite Account that tracks spending for 261 conditions (Dunn, Rittmueller, and Whitmire 2016; Dunn et al. 2018). However, this new account does not address quality of care at present. Our study strongly suggests that quality is a critical element for properly measuring output of the health care sector and our approach may point in a useful and practical direction. In addition, improved measurement of multifactor productivity in the health care system should contribute to a better understanding of the drivers, in terms of economics and policy, of system performance.

Appendix

Table 11A.1   **AHRQ inpatient quality indicator for AMI**

AHRQ Quality Indicators™ (AHRQ QI™) ICD-9-CM Specification Version 6.0 Inpatient Quality Indicator 15 (IQI 15) Acute Myocardial Infarction Mortality Rate March 2017

Provider-Level Indicator Type of Score: Rate

Prepared by:

Agency for Healthcare Research and Quality

U.S. Department of Health and Human Services www.qualityindicators.ahrq.gov

Description

In-hospital deaths per 1,000 hospital discharges with acute myocardial infarction (AMI) as a principal diagnosis for patients ages 18 years and older. Excludes obstetric discharges and transfers to another hospital.

[NOTE: The software provides the rate per hospital discharge. However, common practice reports the measure as per 1,000 discharges. The user must multiply the rate obtained from the software by 1,000 to report in-hospital deaths per 1,000 hospital discharges.]

Numerator

Number of deaths (DISP=20) among cases meeting the inclusion and exclusion rules for the denominator.

Denominator

Discharges, for patients ages 18 years and older, with a principal ICD-9-CM diagnosis code for AMI.

AMI diagnosis codes: (MRTAMID)

41000 AMI ANTEROLATERAL, UNSPEC	41050 AMI LATERAL NEC, UNSPEC
41001 AMI ANTEROLATERAL, INIT	41051 AMI LATERAL NEC, INITIAL
41010 AMI ANTERIOR WALL, UNSPEC	41060 TRUE POST INFARCT, UNSPEC
41011 AMI ANTERIOR WALL, INIT	41061 TRUE POST INFARCT, INIT
41020 AMI INFEROLATERAL, UNSPEC	41070 SUBENDO INFARCT, UNSPEC
41021 AMI INFEROLATERAL, INIT	41071 SUBENDO INFARCT, INITIAL
41030 AMI INFEROPOST, UNSPEC	41080 AMI NEC, UNSPECIFIED
41031 AMI INFEROPOST, INITIAL	41081 AMI NEC, INITIAL
41040 AMI INFERIOR WALL, UNSPEC	41090 AMI NOS, UNSPECIFIED
41041 AMI INFERIOR WALL, INIT	41091 AMI NOS, INITIAL

Denominator exclusions

Exclude cases:
- transferring to another short-term hospital (DISP=2)
- MDC 14 (pregnancy, childbirth, and puerperium
- with missing discharge disposition (DISP=missing), gender (SEX=missing), age (AGE=missing), quarter (DQTR=missing), year (YEAR=missing), or principal diagnosis (DX1=missing)

Sources: AHRQ Quality Indicators™ Program; Agency for Healthcare Research and Quality (2017a). https://www.qualityindicators.ahrq.gov/Downloads/Modules/IQI/V60/TechSpecs /IQI_15_Acute_Myocardial_Infarction (AMI)_Mortality_Rate.pdf.

Table 11A.2   **AMI inpatient mortality risk model**

Parameter	Label	Estimate	Standard error	Wald chi-square	Pr > chi-square
Intercept	Intercept	−3.6765	0.4222	75.8134	<.0001
M_AgeCat_6	Male | Age < 55	−0.2537	0.0397	40.8156	<.0001
M_AgeCat_8	Male | Age < 65	0.0759	0.035	4.697	0.0302
M_AgeCat_9	Male | Age >= 65	0.0768	0.0328	5.4625	0.0194
M_AgeCat_11	Male | Age >= 75	0.1591	0.0282	31.798	<.0001
M_AgeCat_13	Male | Age >= 85	0.1453	0.0348	17.4855	<.0001
M_AgeCat_14	Male | Age >= 90	0.1218	0.0448	7.3979	0.0065
F_AgeCat_6	Female | Age < 55	−0.1659	0.0597	7.7307	0.0054
F_AgeCat_8	Female | Age < 65	−0.0325	0.0431	0.5659	0.4519
F_AgeCat_11	Female | Age >= 75	0.1075	0.0335	10.3035	0.0013
F_AgeCat_13	Female | Age >= 85	0.1112	0.0346	10.3116	0.0013
F_AgeCat_14	Female | Age >= 90	0.2911	0.0377	59.7157	<.0001
MDC_5	MDC 5: DISEASES & DISORDERS OF THE CIRCULATORY SYSTEM	2.1557	0.4199	26.3579	<.0001
ADX161_0001	DRG 161: Cardiac defibrillator & heart assist implant	−1.6775	0.5909	8.058	0.0045
ADX161_0002	DRG 161: Cardiac defibrillator & heart assist implant	−1.7192	0.2372	52.5474	<.0001
ADX161_0003	DRG 161: Cardiac defibrillator & heart assist implant	−1.512	0.129	137.3374	<.0001
ADX161_0004	DRG 161: Cardiac defibrillator & heart assist implant	0.5553	0.0607	83.5733	<.0001
ADX162_0003	DRG 162: Cardiac valve procedures w cardiac catheterization	−1.9697	0.2068	90.7299	<.0001
ADX162_0012	DRG 162: Cardiac valve procedures w cardiac catheterization	−3.5914	0.5804	38.2825	<.0001
ADX163_0003	DRG 163: Cardiac valve procedures w/o cardiac catheterization	−2.286	0.4544	25.3048	<.0001
ADX163_0012	DRG 163: Cardiac valve procedures w/o cardiac catheterization	−2.357	0.5852	16.2216	<.0001
ADX165_0003	DRG 165: Coronary bypass w cardiac cath or percutaneous cardiac procedure	−2.7485	0.0899	934.1475	<.0001
ADX165_0004	DRG 165: Coronary bypass w cardiac cath or percutaneous cardiac procedure	−0.7461	0.0585	162.5885	<.0001
ADX165_0012	DRG 165: Coronary bypass w cardiac cath or percutaneous cardiac procedure	−4.5302	0.1782	646.075	<.0001
ADX166_0003	DRG 166: Coronary bypass w/o cardiac cath or percutaneous cardiac procedure	−2.9037	0.1974	216.3155	<.0001
ADX166_0004	DRG 166: Coronary bypass w/o cardiac cath or percutaneous cardiac procedure	−0.5389	0.1036	27.0435	<.0001
ADX166_0012	DRG 166: Coronary bypass w/o cardiac cath or percutaneous cardiac procedure	−5.2789	0.5018	110.6855	<.0001
ADX167_0004	DRG 167: Other cardiothoracic procedures	0.8715	0.296	8.6713	0.0032
ADX167_0123	DRG 167: Other cardiothoracic procedures	−0.9615	0.4683	4.2156	0.0401
ADX169_0002	DRG 169: Major thoracic & abdominal vascular procedures	−2.3345	1.0119	5.322	0.0211
ADX169_0003	DRG 169: Major thoracic & abdominal vascular procedures	−1.6476	0.5915	7.7588	0.0053
ADX169_0004	DRG 169: Major thoracic & abdominal vascular procedures	0.8006	0.226	12.5455	0.0004
ADX170_0003	DRG 170: Permanent cardiac pacemaker implant w AMI heart failure or shock	−2.4126	0.2732	77.9654	<.0001

(*continued*)

Table 11A.2   (cont.)

Parameter	Label	Estimate	Standard error	Wald chi-square	Pr > chi-square
ADX173_0003	DRG 173: Other vascular procedures	−1.599	0.2082	58.9771	<.0001
ADX173_0004	DRG 173: Other vascular procedures	0.6323	0.1469	18.5311	<.0001
ADX173_0012	DRG 173: Other vascular procedures	−1.7646	0.5897	8.9546	0.0028
ADX174_0001	DRG 174: Percutaneous cardiovascular procedures w AMI	−5.4385	0.1131	2313.699	<.0001
ADX174_0002	DRG 174: Percutaneous cardiovascular procedures w AMI	−4.1135	0.0717	3291.108	<.0001
ADX174_0003	DRG 174: Percutaneous cardiovascular procedures w AMI	−2.288	0.0532	1847.254	<.0001
ADX174_0004	DRG 174: Percutaneous cardiovascular procedures w AMI	0.2224	0.0405	30.1245	<.0001
ADX175_0001	DRG 175: Percutaneous cardiovascular procedures w/o AMI	−4.6469	1.0018	21.5166	<.0001
ADX175_0002	DRG 175: Percutaneous cardiovascular procedures w/o AMI	−2.7821	0.5828	22.7908	<.0001
ADX175_0003	DRG 175: Percutaneous cardiovascular procedures w/o AMI	−1.3744	0.3915	12.3253	0.0004
ADX176_0034	DRG 176: Cardiac pacemaker & defibrillator device replacement	−1.727	0.7246	5.6799	0.0172
ADX180_0003	DRG 180: Other circulatory system procedures	−1.2703	0.3138	16.3888	<.0001
ADX180_0012	DRG 180: Other circulatory system procedures	−2.3913	0.7158	11.1597	0.0008
ADX190_0001	DRG 190: Acute myocardial infarction	−4.2908	0.1255	1168.52	<.0001
ADX190_0002	DRG 190: Acute myocardial infarction	−2.8623	0.0588	2367.434	<.0001
ADX190_0003	DRG 190: Acute myocardial infarction	−1.3875	0.0403	1185.963	<.0001
ADX190_0004	DRG 190: Acute myocardial infarction	0.7259	0.0393	340.8797	<.0001
ADX191_0001	DRG 191: Cardiac catheterization w circ disord exc ischemic heart disease	−3.1417	1.0053	9.7658	0.0018
ADX191_0002	DRG 191: Cardiac catheterization w circ disord exc ischemic heart disease	−3.2554	1.0052	10.4873	0.0012
ADX198_0001	DRG 198: Angina pectoris & coronary atherosclerosis	−1.2529	0.3681	11.5852	0.0007
ADX198_0002	DRG 198: Angina pectoris & coronary atherosclerosis	−1.0658	0.2262	22.1947	<.0001
ADX198_0003	DRG 198: Angina pectoris & coronary atherosclerosis	−0.4057	0.1769	5.2596	0.0218
TRNSFER	Transfer Status	0.0294	0.0211	1.9368	0.164

Sources: AHRQ Quality Indicators™ Program; Agency for Healthcare Research and Quality (2017b, p. 19–21). https://www.qualityindicators.ahrq.gov/Downloads/Modules/IQI/V60/Parameter_Estimates_IQI_6.0_ICD-9-CM.pdf

Table 11A.3   **Complete results from baseline regressions**

Episode type	Heart attack	Heart failure	Pneumonia	GI bleed
Coefficient (standard error)				
Constant	−8.618***	−1.571**	5.581***	2.195***
	(0.628)	(0.701)	(0.653)	(0.600)
2003 episode	−0.030***	−0.045***	−0.003	−0.035***
	(0.011)	(0.010)	(0.010)	(0.013)
2004 episode	−0.058***	−0.098***	−0.023**	−0.053***
	(0.012)	(0.010)	(0.010)	(0.012)
2005 episode	−0.065***	−0.132***	−0.023**	−0.065***
	(0.012)	(0.011)	(0.010)	(0.013)
2006 episode	−0.044***	−0.116***	−0.015	−0.063***
	(0.013)	(0.011)	(0.010)	(0.013)
2007 episode	0.001	−0.104***	0.001	−0.033**
	(0.013)	(0.013)	(0.011)	(0.014)
2008 episode	−0.021	−0.166***	−0.044***	−0.115***
	(0.013)	(0.015)	(0.012)	(0.014)
2009 episode	0.011	−0.151***	−0.030**	−0.072***
	(0.013)	(0.017)	(0.012)	(0.014)
2010 episode	0.015	−0.172***	−0.036***	−0.093***
	(0.013)	(0.018)	(0.012)	(0.014)
2011 episode	0.033**	−0.139***	−0.002	−0.060***
	(0.014)	(0.019)	(0.012)	(0.015)
2012 episode	0.088***	−0.095***	0.042***	−0.037**
	(0.014)	(0.020)	(0.013)	(0.015)
2013 episode	0.060***	−0.121***	0.038***	−0.073***
	(0.014)	(0.020)	(0.013)	(0.014)
2014 episode	0.104***	−0.053**	0.086***	−0.010
	(0.017)	(0.023)	(0.015)	(0.017)
AHRQ predicted inpatient survival, logged	3.043***	8.184***	6.968***	7.215***
	(0.089)	(0.317)	(0.175)	(0.185)
Location of heart attack: Anterolateral (410.0x)	−0.416***	—	—	—
	(0.082)			
Location of heart attack: Other anterior wall (410.1x)	−0.354***	—	—	—
	(0.052)			
Location of heart attack: Inferolateral wall (410.2x)	−0.083	—	—	—
	(0.084)			
Location of heart attack: Inferoposterior wall (410.3x)	−0.505***	—	—	—
	(0.103)			
Location of heart attack: Other inferior wall (410.4x)	−0.350***	—	—	—
	(0.051)			
Location of heart attack: Other lateral wall (410.5x)	−0.205**	—	—	—
	(0.095)			
Location of heart attack: True posterior wall (410.6x)	−0.508***	—	—	—
	(0.184)			
Location of heart attack: Sub–endocardial (410.7x)	−0.164***	—	—	—
	(0.037)			
Location of heart attack: Other specified sites (410.8x)	−0.273***	—	—	—
	(0.080)			
Location of heart attack: Unspecified site (410.9x)	—	—	—	—

(*continued*)

Table 11A.3   **(cont.)**

Episode type	Heart attack	Heart failure	Pneumonia	GI bleed
No Charlson-Deyo comorbidities	—	—	—	—
1 Charlson-Deyo comorbidity	0.369***	0.101	–0.126***	–0.167***
	(0.041)	(0.179)	(0.031)	(0.026)
2 Charlson-Deyo comorbidities	0.198***	–0.018	–0.338***	–0.464***
	(0.039)	(0.183)	(0.031)	(0.029)
3 Charlson-Deyo comorbidities	0.086**	–0.129	–0.524***	–0.601***
	(0.042)	(0.182)	(0.040)	(0.037)
4 Charlson-Deyo comorbidities	0.027	–0.245	–0.578***	–0.722***
	(0.047)	(0.184)	(0.055)	(0.046)
5+ Charlson-Deyo comorbidities	—	–0.325*	–1.032***	–1.059***
		(0.185)	(0.062)	(0.051)
Age, logged	0.734***	-0.356***	–2.007***	–1.208***
	(0.105)	(0.123)	(0.110)	(0.102)
Female	0.037*	–0.038	–0.092***	–0.043**
	(0.022)	(0.024)	(0.022)	(0.021)
White	0.176***	0.258***	0.140**	0.121**
	(0.061)	(0.063)	(0.059)	(0.048)
African American	0.146**	0.243***	–0.117*	–0.088
	(0.068)	(0.066)	(0.068)	(0.055)
Hispanic	0.678***	0.771***	0.516***	0.399***
	(0.105)	(0.114)	(0.114)	(0.093)
Other race	—	—	—	—
1st quarter of year episode	—	—	—	—
2nd quarter of year episode	0.033	–0.013	0.006	0.034
	(0.028)	(0.031)	(0.028)	(0.026)
3rd quarter of year episode	0.014	–0.074**	–0.137***	–0.022
	(0.030)	(0.031)	(0.030)	(0.026)
4th quarter of year episode	–0.009	–0.006	–0.021	–0.036
	(0.030)	(0.032)	(0.030)	(0.026)
Patient zip code characteristics				
Median household income ($000)	–0.006***	–0.010***	–0.007***	–0.007***
	(0.001)	(0.001)	(0.001)	(0.001)
Social Security income ($000)	–0.006	–0.018*	–0.019**	–0.022***
	(0.009)	(0.010)	(0.009)	(0.008)
Poor	0.569**	–0.459*	0.293	0.239
	(0.252)	(0.242)	(0.226)	(0.226)
Employed	2.105***	0.573*	1.179***	1.228***
	(0.397)	(0.345)	(0.371)	(0.336)
Less than high school education	–0.004	–0.188	–0.604***	–0.453***
	(0.155)	(0.143)	(0.130)	(0.126)
Urban	–0.086**	–0.123***	–0.138***	–0.141***
	(0.036)	(0.035)	(0.030)	(0.032)
Hispanic	–0.581***	–0.593***	–0.574***	–0.517***
	(0.062)	(0.065)	(0.059)	(0.057)
Single	–0.757***	–0.702***	–0.530***	–0.732***
	(0.158)	(0.154)	(0.149)	(0.150)
Elderly in an institution	–0.034	0.547***	–0.173	0.206
	(0.200)	(0.209)	(0.189)	(0.166)

Table 11A.3   (cont.)

Episode type	Heart attack	Heart failure	Pneumonia	GI bleed
Noninstitutionalized elderly with physical disability	0.385*	0.236	−0.137	−0.077
	(0.221)	(0.239)	(0.219)	(0.200)
Mental disability	−0.494	−0.731**	−0.345	−0.049
	(0.338)	(0.325)	(0.308)	(0.279)
Sensory disability among elderly	0.056	−0.008	0.537*	−0.095
	(0.296)	(0.332)	(0.296)	(0.276)
Self-care disability	−0.214	0.445	0.375	0.020
	(0.393)	(0.364)	(0.369)	(0.360)
Difficulty going-outside-the-home disability	−0.124	−0.353	−0.760***	−0.267
	(0.271)	(0.269)	(0.257)	(0.253)
Index hospital characteristics				
Residents per bed = 0	—	—	—	—
Residents per bed > 0 and ≤ 0.25	−0.077***	−0.071***	−0.009	−0.049***
	(0.011)	(0.011)	(0.010)	(0.010)
Residents per bed > 0.25 and ≤ 0.6	−0.158***	−0.173***	−0.087***	−0.167***
	(0.020)	(0.022)	(0.021)	(0.021)
Residents per bed > 0.6	−0.181***	−0.211***	−0.055*	−0.188***
	(0.027)	(0.027)	(0.033)	(0.035)
Other statistics				
Hospital-years, *n*	28,635	39,650	40,735	36,804
R^2	0.191	0.227	0.268	0.243

Episode type	Hip fracture	Stroke	LEJR	COPD
Coefficient (standard error)				
Constant	4.473***	5.085***	2.131***	0.337
	(0.565)	(0.585)	(0.703)	(0.599)
2003 episode	−0.010	−0.012	−0.014*	0.008
	(0.012)	(0.015)	(0.008)	(0.012)
2004 episode	−0.033***	−0.039***	−0.024***	0.011
	(0.012)	(0.015)	(0.008)	(0.012)
2005 episode	−0.032***	−0.043***	−0.019**	0.015
	(0.012)	(0.015)	(0.008)	(0.012)
2006 episode	−0.069***	−0.032**	−0.022***	0.011
	(0.012)	(0.015)	(0.008)	(0.012)
2007 episode	−0.116***	−0.061***	−0.028***	0.038***
	(0.014)	(0.015)	(0.009)	(0.013)
2008 episode	−0.102***	−0.038**	−0.044***	−0.051***
	(0.012)	(0.015)	(0.009)	(0.013)
2009 episode	−0.099***	−0.023	−0.036***	−0.040***
	(0.012)	(0.016)	(0.009)	(0.013)
2010 episode	−0.111***	−0.023	−0.050***	−0.033**
	(0.013)	(0.015)	(0.009)	(0.013)
2011 episode	−0.096***	0.002	−0.030***	−0.010
	(0.012)	(0.015)	(0.009)	(0.013)
2012 episode	−0.045***	0.075***	0.004	0.054***
	(0.013)	(0.015)	(0.009)	(0.013)

(*continued*)

Table 11A.3   (cont.)

Episode type	Hip fracture	Stroke	LEJR	COPD
2013 episode	−0.010	0.062***	0.051***	0.092***
	(0.013)	(0.015)	(0.009)	(0.013)
2014 episode	0.014	0.125***	0.078***	0.139***
	(0.015)	(0.018)	(0.011)	(0.015)
AHRQ predicted inpatient survival, logged	3.266***	4.141***	—	—
	(0.141)	(0.123)		
Location of heart attack: Anterolateral (410.0x)	—	—	—	—
Location of heart attack: Other anterior wall (410.1x)	—	—	—	—
Location of heart attack: Inferolateral wall (410.2x)	—	—	—	—
Location of heart attack: Inferoposterior wall (410.3x)	—	—	—	—
Location of heart attack: Other inferior wall (410.4x)	—	—	—	—
Location of heart attack: Other lateral wall (410.5x)	—	—	—	—
Location of heart attack: True posterior wall (410.6x)	—	—	—	—
Location of heart attack: Sub-endocardial (410.7x)	—	—	—	—
Location of heart attack: Other specified sites (410.8x)	—	—	—	—
Location of heart attack: Unspecified site (410.9x)	—	—	—	—
No Charlson-Deyo comorbidities	—	—	—	—
1 Charlson-Deyo comorbidity	−0.171***	0.788***	−0.122***	0.696***
	(0.018)	(0.036)	(0.018)	(0.051)
2 Charlson-Deyo comorbidities	−0.283***	0.621***	−0.294***	0.437***
	(0.023)	(0.037)	(0.029)	(0.052)
3 Charlson-Deyo comorbidities	−0.389***	0.318***	−0.406***	0.289***
	(0.033)	(0.037)	(0.047)	(0.055)
4 Charlson-Deyo comorbidities	−0.454***	0.159***	−0.545***	0.180***
	(0.054)	(0.040)	(0.075)	(0.062)
5+ Charlson-Deyo comorbidities	−0.418***	—	—	—
	(0.061)			
Age, logged	−1.819***	−1.970***	−1.667***	−0.909***
	(0.084)	(0.101)	(0.103)	(0.108)
Female	0.043**	−0.133***	−0.062***	−0.115***
	(0.018)	(0.020)	(0.018)	(0.020)
White	0.116**	0.278***	0.199***	0.225***
	(0.047)	(0.056)	(0.054)	(0.055)
African American	−0.079	0.072	−0.006	0.086
	(0.060)	(0.062)	(0.068)	(0.062)
Hispanic	0.531***	0.823***	0.508***	0.613***
	(0.084)	(0.110)	(0.126)	(0.102)
Other race	—	—	—	—
1st quarter of year episode	—	—	—	—
2nd quarter of year episode	0.015	0.013	−0.020	−0.029
	(0.022)	(0.027)	(0.021)	(0.024)

Table 11A.3   (cont.)

Episode type	Hip fracture	Stroke	LEJR	COPD
3rd quarter of year episode	-0.001	0.025	-0.053**	-0.098***
	(0.020)	(0.027)	(0.020)	(0.028)
4th quarter of year episode	-0.018	0.006	-0.048**	-0.006
	(0.022)	(0.028)	(0.022)	(0.026)
Patient zip code characteristics				
Median household income ($000)	-0.005***	-0.005***	-0.007***	-0.010***
	(0.001)	(0.001)	(0.001)	(0.001)
Social Security income ($000)	-0.009	-0.014	0.004	-0.022**
	(0.007)	(0.009)	(0.009)	(0.009)
Poor	0.552***	0.072	0.639***	-0.109
	(0.180)	(0.248)	(0.227)	(0.216)
Employed	-0.125	0.207	0.472	1.062***
	(0.287)	(0.353)	(0.363)	(0.340)
Less than high school education	-0.424***	-0.322**	-0.571***	-0.186
	(0.113)	(0.144)	(0.130)	(0.139)
Urban	-0.150***	-0.155***	-0.050	-0.115***
	(0.026)	(0.035)	(0.034)	(0.031)
Hispanic	-0.552***	-0.654***	-0.482***	-0.677***
	(0.048)	(0.062)	(0.065)	(0.066)
Single	-0.483***	-0.698***	-0.804***	-0.695***
	(0.111)	(0.154)	(0.151)	(0.156)
Elderly in an institution	-0.172	0.093	0.375**	0.203
	(0.133)	(0.164)	(0.171)	(0.172)
Noninstitutionalized elderly with physical disability	-0.134	-0.015	-0.236	0.282
	(0.163)	(0.213)	(0.192)	(0.221)
Mental disability	-0.325	0.013	0.046	-0.781***
	(0.235)	(0.317)	(0.265)	(0.296)
Sensory disability among elderly	0.204	-0.070	0.045	0.152
	(0.200)	(0.264)	(0.233)	(0.288)
Self-care disability	0.319	-0.510	0.157	-0.130
	(0.271)	(0.360)	(0.312)	(0.340)
Difficulty going-outside-the-home disability	-0.268	0.001	0.124	-0.352
	(0.191)	(0.251)	(0.234)	(0.258)
Index hospital characteristics				
Residents per bed = 0	—	—	—	—
Residents per bed > 0 and ≤ 0.25	-0.021**	-0.068***	0.017*	-0.047***
	(0.009)	(0.011)	(0.010)	(0.011)
Residents per bed > 0.25 and ≤ 0.6	-0.057***	-0.154***	0.003	-0.124***
	(0.018)	(0.022)	(0.019)	(0.022)
Residents per bed > 0.6	-0.055*	-0.211***	-0.041	-0.092***
	(0.030)	(0.027)	(0.026)	(0.033)
Other statistics				
Hospital-years, *n*	29,800	32,006	34,073	39,478
R^2	0.170	0.248	0.326	0.166

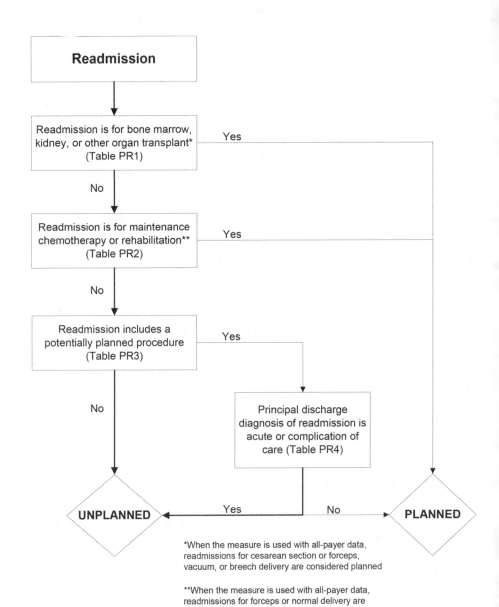

Fig. 11A.1   Overview of CMS unplanned readmission algorithm

Source: Yale New Haven Health Services Corporation/Center for Outcomes Research & Evaluation (YNHHSC/CORE 2014, 64).

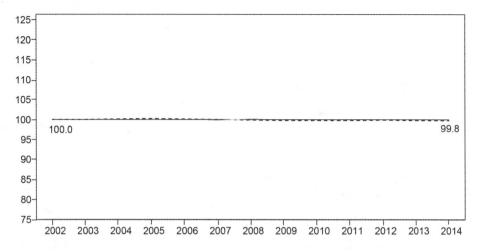

Fig. 11A.2   Other hospital production index among heart-attack episodes

Note: We construct the patient severity index by exponentiating $-\bar{O}_{ht}\hat{\beta}_O$, obtaining $\hat{\beta}_O$ from the regression results corresponding to Figures 16 and 17 and normalizing the index to a value of 100 in 2002.

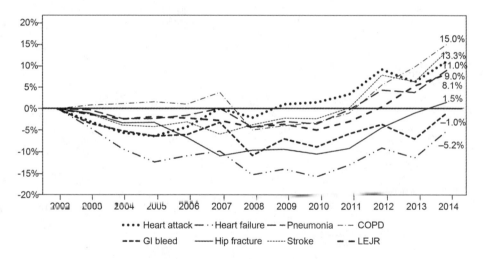

Fig. 11A.3   Cumulative change in productivity since 2002

References

2012 Medicare Economic Index Technical Advisory Panel. 2012. Report to the HHS Secretary: Review of the Medicare Economic Index.

Agency for Healthcare Research and Quality. 2017a. "Inpatient Quality Indicator (IQI 15)—Acute Myocardial Infarction (AMI) Mortality Rate." AHRQ QI™ Version 6.0 (ICD-9). March. Rockville, MD: Agency for Healthcare Research and Quality. https://www.qualityindicators.ahrq.gov/Downloads/Modules/IQI /V60/TechSpecs/IQI_15_Acute_Myocardial_Infarction_(AMI)_Mortality _Rate.pdf.

———. 2017b. "Table 11: Risk Adjustment Coefficients for IQI 15—Acute Myocardial Infarction (AMI) Mortality." Inpatient Quality Indicators (IQI) Parameter Estimates ICD-9-CM Version 6.0." March. Rockville, MD: Agency for Healthcare Research and Quality. https://www.qualityindicators.ahrq.gov/Downloads /Modules/IQI/V60/Parameter_Estimates_IQI_6.0_ICD-9-CM.pdf.

———. 2019. "Inpatient Quality Indicators Overview." https://www.qualityindicators .ahrq.gov/modules/iqi_resources.aspx.

Ashby, J., S. Guterman, and T. Greene. 2000. "An Analysis of Hospital Productivity and Product Change." *Health Affairs* 19 (5): 197–205.

Baumol, W. J., and W. G. Bowen. 1965. "On the Performing Arts: The Anatomy of Their Economic Problems." *American Economic Review* 55 (1/2): 495–502.

Baumol, W. J., D. de Ferranti, M. Malach, A. Pablos-Méndez, H. Tabish, and L. G. Wu. 2012. *The Cost Disease: Why Computers Get Cheaper and Health Care Doesn't*. New Haven, CT: Yale University Press.

Berndt, E. R., A. Bir, S. H. Busch, R. G. Frank, and S.-L. T. Normand. 2002. "The Medical Treatment of Depression, 1991–1996: Productive Inefficiency, Expected Outcome Variations, and Price Indexes." *Journal of Health Economics* 21 (3): 373–96.

Boskin, M. J., E. L. Dulberger, R. J. Gordon, Z. Griliches, and D. W. Jorgenson. 1998. "Consumer Prices, the Consumer Price Index, and the Cost of Living." *Journal of Economic Perspectives* 12 (1): 3–26.

Byrne, D. M., J. G. Fernald, and M. B. Reinsdorf. 2016. "Does the United States Have a Productivity Slowdown or a Measurement Problem?" *Brookings Papers on Economic Activity*: 109–57.

Byrne, D. M., S. D. Oliner, and D. E. Sichel. 2013. "Is the Information Technology Revolution Over?" *International Productivity Monitor* 33: 20–36.

Cantor, W. J., S. G. Goodman, C. P. Cannon, S. A. Murphy, A. Charlesworth, E. Braunwauld, and A. Langer (2005). "Early Cardiac Catheterization Is Associated with Lower Mortality Only among High-Risk Patients with ST- and Non–ST-Elevation Acute Coronary Syndromes: Observations from the OPUS-TIMI 16 trial." *American Heart Journal* 149 (2): 275–83.

Centers for Medicare and Medicaid Services. 2017. *CMS Bundled Payments for Care Improvement Initiative Models 2–4: Year 3 Evaluation & Monitoring Annual Report*. https://downloads.cms.gov/files/cmmi/bpci-models2-4yr3evalrpt.pdf.

———. 2019a. "BPCI Advanced." https://innovation.cms.gov/initiatives/bpci -advanced.

———. 2019b. "Historical Impact Files for FY 1994 through Present." https://www .cms.gov/Medicare/Medicare-Fee-for-Service-Payment/AcuteInpatientPPS /Historical-Impact-Files-for-FY-1994-through-Present.html.

———. 2019c. "Hospital Compare." https://www.medicare.gov/care-compare /?providerType=Hospital&redirect=true.

————. 2019d. "Hospital Cost Report Public Use File." https://www.cms.gov
/Research-Statistics-Data-and-Systems/Statistics-Trends-and-Reports/Medicare
-Provider-Cost-Report/HospitalCostPUF.html.

————. 2019e. "Hospital Readmissions Reduction Program." https://www.cms.gov
/medicare/medicare-fee-for-service-payment/acuteinpatientpps/readmissions
-reduction-program.html.

————. 2019f. "The Hospital Value-Based Purchasing (VBP) Program." https://
www.cms.gov/medicare/quality-initiatives-patient-assessment-instruments
/value-based-programs/hvbp/hospital-value-based-purchasing.html.

————. 2019g. "IMPACT Act of 2014 Data Standardization & Cross Setting Measures." https://www.cms.gov/Medicare/Quality-Initiatives-Patient
-Assessment-Instruments/Post-Acute-Care-Quality-Initiatives/IMPACT-Act-of
-2014/IMPACT-Act-of-2014-Data-Standardization-and-Cross-Setting-Measures
.html.

Chandra, A., A. Finkelstein, A. Sacarny, and C. Syverson. 2016. "Health Care
Exceptionalism? Performance and Allocation in the US Health Care Sector."
American Economic Review 106 (8): 2110–44.

Chandra, A., and D. O. Staiger. 2007. "Productivity Spillovers in Health Care: Evidence from the Treatment of Heart Attacks." *Journal of Political Economy* 115
(1): 103–40.

Charlson, M. E., P. Pompei, K. L. Ales, and C. R. MacKenzie. 1987. "A New Method
of Classifying Prognostic Comorbidity in Longitudinal Studies: Development and
Validation." *Journal of Chronic Diseases* 40 (5): 373–83.

Cox, D. A., G. W. Stone, C. L. Grines, T. Stuckey, P. J. Zimetbaum, J. E. Tcheng,
M. Turco, E. Garcia, G. Guagliumi, R. S. Iwaoka, R. Mehran, W. W. O'Neill,
A. J. Lansky, and J. J. Griffin. 2006. "Comparative Early and Late Outcomes
after Primary Percutaneous Coronary Intervention in ST-Segment Elevation and
Non–ST-Segment Elevation Acute Myocardial Infarction (from the CADILLAC
Trial)." *American Journal of Cardiology* 98 (3): 331–37.

Cubanski, J., T. Neuman, and M. Freed. 2019. "The Facts on Medicare Spending
and Financing." Kaiser Family Foundation. https://www.kff.org/medicare/issue
-brief/the-facts-on-medicare-spending-and-financing/.

Cutler, D. M., and R. S. Huckman. 2003. "Technological Development and Medical
Productivity: The Diffusion of Angioplasty in New York State." *Journal of Health
Economics* 22 (2): 187–217.

Cutler, D. M., and M. McClellan. 2001. "Is Technological Change in Medicine
Worth It?" *Health Affairs* (Millwood) 20 (5): 11–29.

Cutler, D. M., M. McClellan, J. P. Newhouse, and D. Remler. 1998. "Are Medical
Prices Declining? Evidence from Heart Attack Treatments." *Quarterly Journal of
Economics* 113 (4): 991–1024.

Cutler, D. M., and E. Richardson. 1997. "Measuring the Health of the US Population." *Brookings Papers on Economic Activity*: 217–82.

Cylus, J. D., and B. A. Dickensheets. 2007. "Hospital Multifactor Productivity:
A Presentation and Analysis of Two Methodologies." *Health Care Financing
Review* 29 (2): 49–64.

Dauda, S., A. Dunn, and A. Hall. 2019. "Are Medical Care Prices Still Declining?
A Systematic Examination of Quality-Adjusted Price Index Alternatives for Medical
Care." https://www.bea.gov/research/papers/2019/are-medical-care-prices-still
-declining-systematic-examination-quality#:~:text=Prices%20Still%20Declining
%3F-,A%20Systematic%20Examination%20of%20Quality%2DAdjusted
%20Price%20Index%20Alternatives%20for,when%20appropriately%20adjusted
%20for%20quality.

Davis, K. 2007. "Paying for Care Episodes and Care Coordination." *New England Journal of Medicine* 356 (11): 1166–68.

Doyle, J. J. 2011. "Returns to Local-Area Health Care Spending: Evidence from Health Shocks to Patients Far from Home." *American Economic Journal: Applied Economics* 3 (3): 221–43.

Dunn, A., L. Rittmueller, and B. Whitmire. 2016. "Health Care Spending Slowdown from 2000 to 2010 Was Driven by Lower Growth in Cost Per Case, According to a New Data Source." *Health Affairs* 35 (1): 132–40.

Dunn, A., B. Whitmire, A. Batch, L. Fernando, and L. Rittmueller. 2018. "High Spending Growth Rates for Key Diseases in 2000–14 Were Driven by Technology and Demographic Factors." *Health Affairs* 37 (6): 915–24.

Eggleston, K. N., N. D. Shah, S. A. Smith, E. R. Berndt, and J. P. Newhouse. 2011. "Quality Adjustment for Health Care Spending on Chronic Disease: Evidence from Diabetes Treatment, 1999–2009." *American Economic Review* 101 (3): 206–11.

Feldstein, M. 2017. "Underestimating the Real Growth of GDP, Personal Income, and Productivity." *Journal of Economic Perspectives* 31 (2): 145–64.

Fernald, J. G. 2015. "Productivity and Potential Output before, during, and after the Great Recession." *NBER Macroeconomics Annual* 29 (1): 1–51.

Fisher, E. S., D. E. Wennberg, T. A. Stukel, D. J. Gottlieb, F. L. Lucas, and E. L. Pinder. 2003a. "The Implications of Regional Variations in Medicare Spending, Part 1: The Content, Quality, and Accessibility of Care." *Annals of Internal Medicine* 138 (4): 273–87.

———. 2003b. "The Implications of Regional Variations in Medicare Spending, Part 2: Health Outcomes and Satisfaction with Care." *Annals of Internal Medicine* 138 (4): 288–98.

Gordon, R. J. (2016). *The Rise and Fall of American Growth: The U.S. Standard of Living since the Civil War*. Princeton, NJ: Princeton University Press.

Grieco, P. L. E., and R. C. McDevitt. 2016. "Productivity and Quality in Health Care: Evidence from the Dialysis Industry." *Review of Economic Studies* 84 (3): 1071–105.

Groshen, E. L., B. C. Moyer, A. M. Aizcorbe, R. Bradley, and D. M. Friedman. 2017. "How Government Statistics Adjust for Potential Biases from Quality Change and New Goods in an Age of Digital Technologies: A View from the Trenches." *Journal of Economic Perspectives* 31 (2): 187–210.

Gu, J., N. Sood, A. Dunn, and J. Romley. 2019. "Productivity Growth of Skilled Nursing Facilities in the Treatment of Post-Acute-Care-Intensive Conditions." *PLOS ONE* 14 (4): e0215876.

Guterman, S. 2014. "The 'Doc Fix'—Another Missed Opportunity." *New England Journal of Medicine* 370 (24): 2261–63.

Harper, M., B. Khandrika, R. Kinoshita, and S. Rosenthal. 2010. "Nonmanufacturing Industry Contributions to Multifactor Productivity, 1987–2006." *Monthly Labor Review* (June): 16–31.

Martin, A. B., M. Hartman, B. Washington, A. Catlin, and T.N.H.E.A. Team. 2018. "National Health Care Spending in 2017: Growth Slows to Post–Great Recession Rates; Share of GDP Stabilizes." *Health Affairs* 38 (1). https://doi.org/10.1377/hlthaff.2018.05085.

Matsumoto, B. 2019. "Producing Quality Adjusted Hospital Price Indexes." https://ashecon.confex.com/ashecon/2019/webprogram/Paper7866.html.

Medicare Payment and Advisory Committee. 2018. "Physician and Other Health Professional Payment System." http://medpac.gov/docs/default-source/payment-basics/medpac_payment_basics_16_physician_final.pdf?sfvrsn=0.

Moulton, B. 2018. "The Measurement of Output, Prices, and Productivity: What's Changed since the Boskin Commission?" Brookings Institution. https://www.brookings.edu/research/the-measurement-of-output-prices-and-productivity.

National Center for Health Statistics. "International Classification of Diseases, Ninth Revision, Clinical Modification (ICD-9-CM)." https://www.cdc.gov/nchs/icd/icd9cm.htm.

National Research Council. 2010. "Accounting for Health and Health Care: Approaches to Measuring the Sources and Costs of Their Improvement." https://www.nap.edu/catalog/12938/accounting-for-health-and-health-care-approaches-to-measuring-the.

Newhouse, J. P. 1992. "Medical Care Costs: How Much Welfare Loss?" *Journal of Economic Perspectives* 6 (3): 3–21.

OASDI Board of Trustees. 2018. *The 2018 Annual Report of the Boards of Trustees of the Federal Hospital Insurance Trust Fund and the Federal Supplementary Medical Insurance Trust Fund.* https://www.cms.gov/Research-Statistics-Data-and-Systems/Statistics-Trends-and-Reports/ReportsTrustFunds/Downloads/TR2018.pdf.

Quan, H., V. Sundararajan, P. Halfon, A. Fong, B. Burnand, J.-C. Luthi, L. D. Saunders, C. A. Beck, T. E. Feasby, and W. A. Ghali. 2005. "Coding Algorithms for Defining Comorbidities in ICD-9-CM and ICD-10 Administrative Data." *Medical Care* 43 (11): 1130–39.

Reinhardt, U. 2006. "The Pricing of U.S. Hospital Services: Chaos behind a Veil of Secrecy." *Health Affairs* 25 (1): 57–69.

Research Data Assistance Center. 2019. "Inpatient (Fee-for-Service)." https://www.resdac.org/cms-data/files/ip-ffs.

Romley, J., E. Trish, D. Goldman, M. Beeuwkes Buntin, Y. He, and P. Ginsburg. 2019. "Geographic Variation in the Delivery of High-Value Inpatient Care." *PLOS ONE* 14 (3): e0213647.

Romley, J. A., D. P. Goldman, and N. Sood. 2015. "US Hospitals Experienced Substantial Productivity Growth during 2002–11." *Health Affairs* (Millwood) 34 (3): 511–18.

Romley, J. A., A. B. Jena, and D. P. Goldman. 2011. "Hospital Spending and Inpatient Mortality: Evidence from California; An Observational Study." *Annals of Internal Medicine* 154 (3): 160–67.

Sensenig, A., and E. Wilcox. 2001. "National Health Accounts/National Income and Product Accounts Reconciliation: Hospital Care and Physician Services." In *Medical Care Output and Productivity*, edited by E. Berndt and D. M. Cutler. Chicago: University of Chicago Press.

Shapiro, I., M. D. Shapiro, and D. W. Wilcox. 2001. "Measuring the Value of Cataract Surgery." *Medical Care Output and Productivity* 62: 411–37.

Sheiner, L., and A. Malinovskaya. 2016. "Measuring Productivity Growth in Healthcare: An Analysis of the Literature." Brookings Institution. https://www.brookings.edu/wp-content/uploads/2016/08/hp-lit-review_final.pdf.

Skinner, J., and D. Staiger. 2015. "Technology Diffusion and Productivity Growth in Health Care." *Review of Economics and Statistics* 97 (5): 951–64.

Syverson, C. 2017. "Challenges to Mismeasurement Explanations for the US Productivity Slowdown." *Journal of Economic Perspectives* 31 (2): 165–86.

Volpp, K. G., A. K. Rosen, P. R. Rosenbaum, P. S. Romano, O. Even-Shoshan, A. Canamucio, L. Bellini, T. Behringer, and J. H. Silber. 2007. "Mortality among Patients in VA Hospitals in the First 2 Years following ACGME Resident Duty Hour Reform." *Journal of the American Medical Association* 298 (9): 984–92.

World Health Organization. 2011. "A System of Health Accounts." https://www.who
    .int/health-accounts/methodology/sha2011.pdf.
Yale New Haven Health Services Corporation/Center for Outcomes Research &
    Evaluation (YNHHSC/CORE). 2014. "2014 Measure Updates and Specifications
    Report: Hospital-Wide All-Cause Unplanned Readmission—Version 3.0." July.
    Prepared for Center for Medicare & Medicaid Services (CMS). https://altarum
    .org/sites/default/files/uploaded-publication-files/Rdmsn_Msr_Updts_HWR
    _0714_0.pdf.

12 Valuing Housing Services in the Era of Big Data
A User Cost Approach Leveraging Zillow Microdata

Marina Gindelsky, Jeremy G. Moulton,
and Scott A. Wentland

12.1 Introduction

Housing is an important part of the economy and the national economic accounts. As part of the tabulation of Personal Consumption Expenditures (PCE) within Gross Domestic Product (GDP), the Bureau of Economic Analysis (BEA) estimates aggregate expenditure on housing, measuring what households in the United States spend on housing services. Because a house is generally a long-lasting asset and the flow of its services is not consumed in its entirety in a single year, housing is not measured like many other consumption expenditures as simply the aggregate of home prices and

Marina Gindelsky is a research economist in the Office of the Chief Economist at the Bureau of Economic Analysis.

Jeremy G. Moulton is an associate professor of public policy at the University of North Carolina at Chapel Hill.

Scott A. Wentland is a research economist in the Office of the Chief Economist at the Bureau of Economic Analysis.

We would like to thank the organizing committee and participants of the 2018 NBER-CRIW Pre-Conference and corresponding 2019 Conference on Big Data for 21st Century Economic Statistics, as well as the following individuals for their valuable input: Katharine Abraham, Erwin Diewert, Dennis Fixler, Kyle Hood, Kurt Kunze, Han Liu, Raven Molloy, Brent Moulton, Mick Silver, Dylan Rassier, Matthew Shapiro, Brian Smith, and Randal Verbrugge for their helpful comments. All errors are our own. Any views expressed here are those of the authors and not necessarily those of the Bureau of Economic Analysis or the US Department of Commerce. Data provided by Zillow through the Zillow Transaction and Assessment Dataset (ZTRAX). More information on accessing the data can be found at http://www.zillow.com/ztrax. The results and opinions are those of the authors and do not reflect the position of Zillow Group. For acknowledgments, sources of research support, and disclosure of the authors' material financial relationships, if any, please see https://www.nber.org/books-and-chapters/big-data-21st-century-economic-statistics/valuing-housing-services-era-big-data-user-cost-approach-leveraging-zillow-microdata.

quantities.[1] The flow of housing services in GDP is, as a result, measured as conceptually most similar to rent for these services in a given period. For renters (tenant-occupied housing), this tabulation is straightforward, both intuitively and from an economic measurement standpoint because it amounts to the aggregate sum of rents paid for all residential units over a given period. The analogous calculation for homeowners imputes market rents (also called "space rent") for the owner-occupied housing stock as if owners "rent" to themselves. The 2008 System of National Accounts (SNA) recommends this imputation for owner-occupied housing so that the estimate of housing services is not arbitrarily distorted based on the decision to rent versus own a home, which can vary substantially across time and space.[2] Historically, both tenant- and owner-occupied housing have accounted for a substantial proportion of overall consumer expenditures and the economy more generally (approximately 16 percent of PCE, or about 10 percent of GDP final expenditures), and have been relatively stable over recent decades, as shown in figure 12.1 below.

The PCE housing series has risen steadily over the last couple of decades, congruent with other official series like the Consumer Price Index (CPI) Rent Index and the CPI Owners' Equivalent Rent Index, both depicted in figure 12.2 below. A common element among these statistics is that they rely on reported rents from survey data, as the BEA's current method follows a rental-equivalence approach leveraging survey data. Moreover, the BEA's housing estimates were adjusted over this time period using the owner-occupied rent series directly (for reasons we discuss in more depth in the next section). Recently, however, the academic literature has begun to reexamine the rental market over this period using "Big Data" sources, finding that using alternative data and methods reveals a different picture. For example, when rents are measured using different data, as shown by the Ambrose-Coulson-Yoshida (ACY) Repeat Rent Index (also depicted in figure 12.2) using market transaction data from Experian RentBureau, a conflicting story emerges as rents flatten out earlier than the CPI series and even fall in absolute terms in 2008–2009.[3] This drop in rents, while less dra-

---

1. Housing is included in both consumption and investment expenditures in GDP statistics, where new construction is accounted for in Residential Fixed Investment. The focus of this paper is on Housing Services within Personal Consumption Expenditures.

2. Specifically, the 2008 SNA states: "The production of housing services for their own final consumption by owner occupiers has always been included within the production boundary in national accounts, although it constitutes an exception to the general exclusion of own-account service production. The ratio of owner-occupied to rented dwellings can vary significantly between countries, between regions of a country and even over short periods of time within a single country or region, so that both international and inter-temporal comparisons of the production and consumption of housing services could be distorted if no imputation were made for the value of own-account housing services" (United Nations et al. 2010, 99).

3. This index is derived from Ambrose, Coulson, and Yoshida's (2015) recent work constructing a rent index more similar to Case-Shiller's repeat sales method using Big Data, although the series only goes through 2010 at the time of this publication.

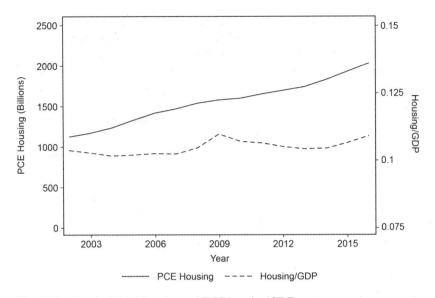

Fig. 12.1   Nominal PCE housing and PCE housing/GDP

Source: US Bureau of Economic Analysis, "Table 2.5.5: Personal Consumption Expenditures (PCE) by Function," bea.gov.

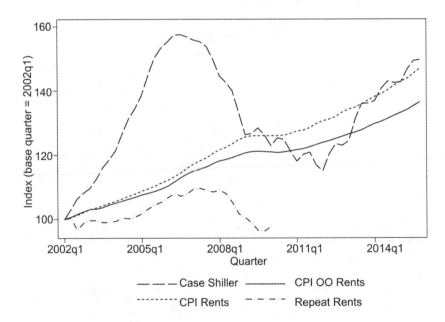

Fig. 12.2   Price and rent indexes of the US housing market

Sources: ACY; https://fred.stlouisfed.org/series/CSUSHPINSA; /CUUR0000SEHA; / CUSR0000SEHC.

matic in magnitude, was more consistent with the freefall in home prices as shown by the Case-Shiller National Home Price Index amid the (in)famous boom-bust-recovery in home prices over the broader period.

The divergence among these series stems from the underlying data and method.[4] Ambrose, Coulson, and Yoshida's (2015) finding, where market data and an alternative method paint a different picture of the rental market, motivates further research into other housing statistics and whether Big Data can find a similar pattern of divergence or whether this phenomenon is unique to the rental market they study.

The purpose of this paper is to explore the extent to which alternative data sources, namely Big Data from Zillow containing information on hundreds of millions of home transactions, can be used to construct an estimate of housing services. The data are suited to a user-cost approach, which we use to construct a time series and compare it to the BEA's current rental equivalence–based estimates since the early 2000s. The goal of this paper is not to construct an official account or argue for a particular method; rather, we investigate the implications of a new Big Data source and compare the results of associated methods to current nominal estimates.[5]

This paper also contributes to literature on user cost methods that are both well suited to Big Data sources and commonly used in academic literatures beyond national accounts. This is particularly true in cases where rental market data are inadequate (as in many countries).[6] For example, Himmelberg, Mayer, and Sinai (2005) employ a user cost approach to assess price fundamentals of the housing market, while others have used housing user costs in a number of applications from evaluating tax policy to interest deductions (e.g., Albouy and Hanson 2014; Poterba 1992; Poterba,

---

4. Critiques of the BLS's rental series, which fall outside the scope of our paper, are the subject of numerous papers, including Ambrose, Coulson, and Yoshida (2015). This topic is covered in an earlier review of this literature by Lebow and Rudd (2003). Ambrose, Coulson, and Yoshida (2015) argue that the CPI method and underlying data sources understated the extent to which rental market prices fell during the housing bust. See also Gordon and vanGoethem (2007), McCarthy and Peach (2010), and Ozimek (2014) for related critiques.

5. Constructing user cost estimates is also a prerequisite for a statistical agency to consider constructing a hybrid series that blends rental equivalence and user cost estimates like the opportunity cost approach proposed by Diewert (2009), as part of a comprehensive look at competing methods from the literature. A nominal series is also a necessary first step to take prior to constructing a real series based on these data, which we leave for future research.

6. A number of European and African countries have employed a user cost approach (or a variant thereof) for measuring housing services, often as a result of data limitations of thin unsubsidized rental markets (Katz 2009). A (nonexhaustive) list of such countries includes: Botswana, Central African Republic, Croatia, Estonia, Ghana, Hungary, Latvia, Lithuania, Malta, Montenegro, Nigeria, Poland, São Tomé, Serbia, Slovak Republic, Slovenia, Tunisia, Uganda, Zambia, Zimbabwe. According to Eurostat in 2016, nearly 70 percent of the population in EU28 countries own their own homes, with a sizable fraction of households living in subsidized or rent-free housing (e.g., over 80 percent in Lithuania, Malta, Bulgaria, and Croatia), limiting the representativeness of market rents in many countries (Komolafe 2018).

Weil, and Shiller 1991).[7] We provide a transparent method for constructing a nominal user cost-based series that can be built from the bottom up with similar microdata (e.g., data from vendors like CoreLogic) and could be replicated for a variety of uses in the literature.

12.2   Rental Equivalence versus User Cost

12.2.1   Background

A central problem for statistical agencies is finding the right data, and this is particularly true for imputing owner-occupied housing (OOH) statistics where the challenge emanates from accounting for transactions that are not *directly* measurable or observable. Statistical agencies like the BEA measure the value of housing services for OOH indirectly by using data that should closely approximate market rent that homeowners would expend. The two approaches briefly mentioned above are those recommended by the 2008 SNA statistical framework: rental-equivalence and user cost.[8] The former estimates what market rent would be for a given owner-occupied home if it were rented, while the latter focuses on the cost to the homeowner.[9] Conceptually, absent transaction costs and other market frictions, basic economic principles predict that market rents should approximately equal average cost (in the long run) if markets are competitive. The underpinning theory of this (approximate) equality can be derived from capital theory, which is based on Jorgenson's (1963, 1967) theory of capital and investment, where the rental cost of capital will equal its *ex ante* user cost (Katz 2009).[10] For example, if

7. Poterba and Sinai (2008) note: "the neoclassical investment model, which focuses on the user cost of capital, is a standard tool for studying housing demand and for analyzing the equilibrium value of the imputed rental income accruing to homeowners under various tax regimes" (p. 86).

8. Specifically, the SNA states that, "This approach can take either a user-cost formulation that attempts to measure the changes in the cost to owner-occupiers of using the dwelling, or a rental-equivalence formulation based on how much owner-occupiers would have to pay to rent their dwellings. The latter method is more generally adopted for CPIs" (United Nations et al. 2010, §15.141). However, some countries have adopted a variant of the user cost approach for their CPI measurement, including Canada, Estonia, Iceland, Slovakia, and Sweden (Baldwin, Nakamura, and Prud'homme 2009).

9. More generally, the OECD Manual "Measuring Capital," summarizes the broader concept for the user cost of capital as follows: "Suppose the owner of an asset wants to determine the minimum price (before adding on costs of associated labour and overheads) at which he is willing to rent the asset during one period of time. In the simplest case, three main cost elements have to be considered: *(i)* the cost of financing or the opportunity cost of the financial capital tied up through the purchase of the asset; *(ii)* depreciation, *i.e.* the value loss due to ageing; *(iii)* revaluation, *i.e.* the expected price change of the class of assets under consideration" (OECD 2009, 65).

10. As a thought experiment, one can think of user cost in this context as measuring the net expenditure associated with purchasing a home at the beginning of a period, incurring cost during the period, and selling the home at the end of the period, abstracting away from transaction costs and other market frictions. According to Jorgensonian capital theory, the rental rate for this home set at the beginning of the period would equal this expected cost, ex ante.

rent for an identical home was much higher than its user cost incurred by a homeowner, then more people would buy this preferred capital asset and fewer would rent, bidding down rents and bidding up home prices to the point where rents and costs are approximately equal.[11]

12.2.2   Current Approach of the BEA

The BEA's current approach, based on a rental-equivalence method, is the most common method used by national statistical agencies around the world (Katz 2017), in part due to the fact that countries collect high-quality data on rents from nationally representative, specifically designed surveys of tenants and other sources. Specifically, the BEA's current method uses the Residential Finance Survey (RFS, Census Bureau) to benchmark rent-to-value ratios for different value classes of properties, which are then used to impute average contract rent for owner-occupied properties across similar dimensions. This weighted rental imputation constitutes what is often referred to as "space rent," which is then multiplied by corresponding aggregate housing unit counts to obtain the aggregate estimate of the total imputed rent of owner-occupied housing.[12] During benchmark years, BEA used Decennial Census for quantity counts, while in nonbenchmark years either American Housing Survey (available biannually) or Current Population Survey data from the Census Bureau were used. The BEA last benchmarked the rent-to-value ratios used to derive space rent using the 2001 RFS, the last time the requisite data from this survey were available. Since then, the BEA has made quality adjustments and price adjustments, with the latter based on data from the BLS's CPI Owners' Equivalent Rent Index (which also relies on a rental-equivalence method).[13] This method is generally regarded as the

---

See also McFadyen and Hobart (1978) for an instructive cross-walk from Jorgenson (1967) to a user cost for housing.

11. Of course, this abstracts from risk, market imperfections, and transaction costs, which are particularly significant in housing (Bian, Waller, and Wentland 2016). Thus, some gap might persist, but generally rents and user costs should move together over longer periods of time. In fact, recent empirical work by Goeyvaerts and Buyst (2019) has found a "strong correspondence" between rents and user costs using detailed microdata.

12. For a more detailed discussion of the BEA's current method, refer to Mayerhauser and McBride (2007) and Katz (2017). To summarize, the 2001 method assumed OOH homes with comparable values as tenant-occupied homes also have comparable rent-to-value ratios, so the method takes weighted-average rent-to-value ratios by value class for tenant units from the RFS and applies the mid-point market value to owner-occupied units within the corresponding value classes reported in the American Housing Survey. This imputed total rental value is then weighted by the number of owner-occupied units reported in the American Housing Survey in each class to calculate an average annual rental value (AARV), which is then used to generate a total value of aggregate OONFP housing services by multiplying AARV by the number of owner-occupied housing units reported in the decennial Census.

13. BEA's weighting adjustment based on rent-to-value introduces a measure of home value into the imputation of owner-occupied space rent, as does the housing quality adjustment used since 2001. However, since 2001 the rent-to-value ratios have not changed due to the expiration of the underlying survey data, which is why the series has primarily moved with the CPI Owners' Equivalent Rent Index. Because the CPI for OOH is a constant-quality index, the purpose

preferred method for this imputation because most countries have relatively thick rental markets with substantial data on market rents. Indeed, more than one third of all housing units in the US are rented to tenants.

12.2.3   Methodology: A Comparison

The rental-equivalence approach, however, is not without its limitations due to the nature of the data. While a sizable fraction of homes are tenant occupied, rental data are not necessarily representative of the entire housing stock. Specifically, the distribution of rental units is not the same as owner-occupied units (Glaeser and Gyourko 2009); the share of detached single-family residences (SFRs) is higher for owner-occupied units as is the share of higher-value homes, as the market for rental units thins out and quality and home value increase.[14] Coulson and Li (2013) review the voluminous literature regarding these differences and provide additional evidence of homeowners taking better care of (and investing more in) their homes, resulting in difficult to measure qualitative differences between owner-occupied and tenant-occupied homes.[15] Also, because surveys record a snapshot of the market, rent surveys may overrepresent renewal rent for existing tenants and underrepresent new leases—a problem that may be exacerbated by business cycle fluctuations (Ambrose, Coulson, and Yoshida 2015). Verbrugge (2008) argues that this may oversmooth the series as someone surveyed in December may have signed their lease earlier in the year (in, say, February), reflecting lagged market conditions in the rental market.[16] While subject to its own limitations (as we discuss below), the user cost approach relies on different data than the rental-equivalence approach, which has led researchers and some statistical agencies to explore it as an alternative for estimating housing services. This approach instead utilizes data on the cost to the user of owning a home (e.g., interest, taxes, maintenance/depreciation),

---

of the additional quality adjustment is "to account for changes in the real value of housing per unit," which is the percent change in the "real dollar stocks of owner-occupied structures, of additions and alterations, and of major replacements" using values from BEA's fixed assets accounts divided by the number of owner-occupied units" (Mayerhauser and McBride 2007).

14. For additional discussion of this point and an illustration of these differences using recent Census data, see Aten (2018).

15. Crone, Nakamura, and Voith (2000) cite a number of reasons that complicate the BLS's attempts to compensate for the differences in owner-occupied versus tenant units by oversampling rental units that have characteristics like rentals: "First, these units are often temporary rentals that drop out of the sample in a short time, so that reporting is spotty. Second, the market for these units is very thin, so that the observed rents may not be good proxies for the implicit value of the unit's service flow if it were an owner-occupied unit. Third, rental units are subject to double-sided moral hazard, which leads to long-term contracts and price regulation. Fourth, rental units are professionally managed while owner-occupied units are not."

16. In addition, because the BEA has used the CPI Owners' Equivalent Rent Index to make adjustments to space rent, this also introduces potential measurement issues associated with the CPI. See Lebow and Rudd (2003) for a review of the literature on mismeasurement in the CPI, and Crone, Nakamura, and Voith (2000, 2009) for more on mismeasurement of CPI rents in particular.

which varies directly with the price of a home, rather than rents of different, possibly unrepresentative tenant-occupied homes.[17] Detailed microdata on home sales and corresponding home characteristics are primarily recorded by local municipalities; and because reporting often differs by locale, this has previously made a national effort to collect these data quite costly. Indeed, only in recent decades have most localities digitized these records, making rental survey data the most practical data source prior to the era of Big Data. But in the modern era, companies like Zillow have privately collected, compiled, and organized a massive database of public data from local tax assessors' offices across the US for the purposes of providing this information to users of their website. Zillow has recently provided much of their microdata to researchers free of charge, including those at BEA, which makes it feasible to implement a user cost approach based on fine-level price and home characteristic data to compare with current methods.

One benefit of the approach we are assessing is that it relies on directly observable data that cover a significant share of the housing market. While rents are not directly observable for owner-occupied homes, transaction prices, the backbone of the user cost method,[18] are readily available for virtually all strata of the housing market, both tenant-occupied and owner-occupied homes. As a result, given the differences in rental and owner-occupied housing units documented in the literature discussed above, the user cost method does not suffer from the same selection issues as rent-based approaches. Indeed, when rental markets are thin, the SNA recommends "other means of estimating the value of housing services," (United Nations et al. 2010, 109) like a user cost approach that does not rely on rent data.

There is, however, a sizable literature noting potential weaknesses of a user cost approach or conceptual departures that fundamentally differ from rental equivalence. For example, Gillingham (1983), Verbrugge (2008) and Diewert, Nakamura, and Nakamura (2009) and others have noted that the user cost approach often has greater volatility, sensitivity to interest rates, and introduces deeper conceptual issues with the role of asset prices in this estimate with ex ante and ex post measurement. For instance, the degree of volatility of Verbrugge's (2008) user cost estimates largely hinged on how he estimated expected (*ex ante*) appreciation/depreciation, which can vary

17. For an instructive review of this voluminous literature and novel examples of developing user cost estimates, see Diewert (2003, 2008), Katz (2009), Verbrugge (2008), Davis, Lehnert, and Martin (2008), Haffner and Heylen (2011), Hill and Syed (2016), Aten (2018), and numerous other papers on this topic.

18. Despite transaction costs and substantial frictions in the housing market, a thick literature has documented that home prices respond relatively quickly to a host of different types of shocks to demand, whether they are very local, neighborhood level shocks (e.g., Anenberg and Kung 2014; Linden and Rockoff 2008; Wentland, Waller, and Brastow (2014) or aggregate-level or informational shocks (e.g., Bernstein, Gustafson, and Lewis 2019; Bui and Mayer 2003; Moulton and Wentland 2018).

substantially depending on the assumptions used to construct this component. This literature also voices disagreements on precisely what parameter values should be used in the computation, including which interest rate is most appropriate or whether to include expected appreciation/depreciation at all. Small changes to these parameter values can change the estimates substantially, as we document in more detail below in our discussion of figure 12.7 and the alternative user cost estimates we produce by varying these parameters. Finally, as a more general conceptual point, by tying estimates of housing services more closely to the asset value of a home and interest rates, the user cost approach begs the question: to what extent should a measure of housing services vary with interest rates and asset prices? We return to this point in the Discussion section below.

12.3 Data

The novelty of this paper primarily arises from usage of new data, specifically residential housing microdata from Zillow's ZTRAX dataset. It contains transaction data as well as a large set of individual property characteristics for sales recorded from local tax assessors' data.[19] The data coverage is generally representative of the United States' national housing market, comprising 374 million detailed records of transactions across more than 2,750 counties.[20] This includes information regarding each home's sale price, sale date, mortgage information, foreclosure status, and other information commonly disclosed by a local tax assessor's office. We link each transaction to each home's property characteristics into a single dataset. The assessment data include an array of characteristics one would find on Zillow's website or a local tax assessor's office describing the home; namely, the size of the home (in square feet), number of bedrooms and bathrooms, year built, and a variety of other characteristics.[21] We received all these data in a somewhat raw form, requiring significant cleaning for research purposes.

19. Data are provided by Zillow through the Zillow Transaction and Assessment Dataset (ZTRAX). More information on accessing the data can be found at http://www.zillow.com /ztrax. The results and opinions are those of the authors and do not reflect the position of Zillow Group. Nonproprietary code used to generate the results for this paper is available upon request of the authors.

20. Because some states do not require mandatory disclosure of the sale price, we currently do not have price data for the following states: Idaho, Indiana, Kansas, Mississippi, Missouri, Montana, New Mexico, North Dakota, South Dakota, Texas, Utah, and Wyoming. In addition, Maine has a substantial share of missing data in our current sample and is accordingly omitted. Our method aggregates to the Census Division level by using housing unit counts from the ACS at the regional level. As a result, we assume that the states with data within a Census Division are reasonably representative of a state left out, which is an assumption we hope to explore in further research with supplemental data.

21. Zillow's ZTRAX dataset contains separate transaction and assessment files by state— that is, all transactions need to be linked to corresponding assessment records. With guidance from Zillow, we were able to merge the bulk of the data, but not without some data loss (which figures into the size of our final sample).

We carefully scrutinized missing data and extreme values as part of our initial culling of outliers and general cleaning. The initial dataset from Zillow contains sales of empty plots of land, some commercial property transactions, agricultural sales, and other types of properties that are outside the scope of the housing services estimates we aim to measure. Therefore, we limit the sample to single-family homes, townhouses, row-homes, apartments, condos, and properties that are most closely associated with the current estimates. While we estimate rural properties separately (properties with 1 to 100 acres), we drop homes that have greater than 100 acres (limiting the influence of large farms) and winsorize homes that are in the upper tail of the distribution (i.e., are larger than 10,000 square feet or have more than five bedrooms, more than three bathrooms). When we construct our final user cost estimates we also drop homes that sold for less than $30,000 for SFRs ($15,000 for non-SFRs), homes in the top percentile of predicted price, or that had a price 10 times higher than the county median.[22] We cull homes that report a negative age (i.e., sale year < year built). While the Zillow dataset contains a vast number of property characteristics, in our initial analysis we primarily rely on the variables above that have the most coverage nationally to limit how much data we would effectively discard.[23] We limit the results to the years from 2002 through 2015, when the data are most complete for the vast majority of the states in our sample.

To assess the quality of the final sample, we compared our cleaned Zillow sample to the ACS to ensure that these administrative data aligned with carefully collected (albeit more limited) survey data provided by the Census Bureau. Generally, there is only a limited set of home characteristics found in both the ZTRAX data and the ACS (e.g., number of bedrooms, year built, number of rooms, tax amount, and an indicator for whether the property has more than 10 acres). When we compare them in aggregate, we find that they are quite similar in terms of their summary statistics. In untabulated results, we found that these shared variables across datasets had median and mean values that fell within a few percentage points of one another.

22. To limit the influence of outliers or measurement error on model coefficients in our regressions, we drop homes that sold for less than $1,000 and extreme outliers at the top end (10 times the county median), and then the tails of the distribution for sale price at the 2.5 and 97.5 percentiles within each county within each quarter. This is a more restrictive culling at the regression stage because the main objective of the regressions is to obtain coefficients that provide the most reasonable price predictions, whereas when we construct the final user cost estimates we aim to exploit a somewhat less restrictive sample to maintain better representativeness (while still drawing a line to cull suspicious outliers).

23. In untabulated regressions, we conducted a sensitivity analysis for subsets of the sample that employed more property characteristics to determine whether the results are sensitive to omitted variables for which we can control. Our results were generally robust to omitting variables that have more limited coverage.

12.4   Methodology—An Idiosyncratic User Cost Approach

12.4.1   Overview

Generally, our approach using the Zillow microdata is motivated by constructing estimates from the bottom up, as we estimate a user cost for *each individual property* in our dataset *for each quarter* and then aggregate upward to produce a weighted national-level estimate. We begin by estimating a simplified user cost of housing services for each home in the dataset based on the formula

$$U_{it} = P_{it}(r_{it}^{rf} + \delta_i + \tau_{it} + \gamma_i - \varphi^m(r_{it}^m) - \varphi^\tau(\tau_{it}) - E[\pi_i]),$$

where for a given property (i) in quarter (t), P is the price of an individual home, r^{rf} is the owner's discount rate or financial opportunity cost for a long-term asset like a home (we use the nominal interest rate on a 10-year Treasury note for an appropriate risk-free rate in quarter t),[24] δ is a constant 3.5 percent representing depreciation and maintenance costs,[25] τ is the individual property's effective tax rate, and γ is a constant 2 percent risk premium associated with owning relative to renting.[26]

The latter three terms consist of potential offsetting benefits to homeownership, which are subtracted from the preceding costs such that user cost

---

24. While the dataset includes individual interest rates for transacted properties, the coverage is not as universal as other variables. However, it is customary for user cost estimates to use a single market interest rate to reflect the financial opportunity cost of the long-term asset (e.g., see Aten 2018 for a recent example, among numerous others). Conceptually, if a homeowner purchased a home when rates were at 4 percent, but rates have since risen to 7 percent, the latter rate more closely represents the opportunity cost in that time period, as the homeowner could alternatively be earning a return on that equity of a similar long-term asset. The time series dynamics are similar if we use average 30-year mortgage rates, which we show later in the paper for robustness.

25. A depreciation rate of 1.5 percent is common to the literature (e.g., Aten 2018, and Verbrugge 2008), and Gill and Haurin (1991) use a constant of (1.5% + 2% = 3.5%) for the combined maintenance and depreciation term. Conceptually, there is wear and tear on a home that would be similar to what a renter would incur in the analogous tenant-occupied counterfactual, but primarily this is structural depreciation due to the property itself aging. Because these costs (on average) would be priced into a tenant's rent, it is logical to factor this into the imputation for owner-occupied properties. Given that homes depreciate at different rates depending on age and other maintenance costs may vary by region and home type, we acknowledge that a constant rate is a simplification.

26. This risk premium was used by Himmelberg, Mayer, and Sinai (2005) "to compensate homeowners for the higher risk of owning versus renting" (p. 75). While a risk premium was used as early as Poterba (1992), the constant of 2 percent was used by Flavin and Yamashita (2002) and Poterba and Sinai (2008). The latter study argues that this accounts for the fact that, "homeowners bear both asset-class risk and idiosyncratic, house-specific risk" (p. 86). Himmelberg, Mayer, and Sinai (2005) also use a 2 percent constant but point out that a more sophisticated model would allow this premium to vary over time as the risk of owning relative to renting changes over time. This risk, however, is separate from rental risk which, as Sinai and Souleles (2005) point out, is hedged with homeownership. Sinai and Souleles (2005) find that this rental risk is directly capitalized in home prices.

represents the net cost to the homeowner. Mortgage interest and property taxes are tax deductible in the US (to a point), regardless of occupancy status. Himmelberg, Mayer, and Sinai (2005) use a constant average marginal tax rate (MTR) for all homes, which they multiply by the average 30-year mortgage rate (r_{it}^m) in period t. However, their approach assumes (1) all homeowners itemize their tax returns, (2) the interest is on the entire principal of the home, and (3) there is little variation in income across regions of the United States. Instead, we construct a multiplier, φ, to allow variation in our approximation of the average benefit to mortgage interest and property taxes, using the ACS to determine the average household income for homeowners by home type (SFR versus non-SFR) and home size (number of bedrooms) by each Census Division.[27] Based on average household income, we assign an MTR and a probability that the homeowner itemizes based on the percent of people who itemize in their income stratum. This allows a five-bedroom home in a high-income region like New England or the Pacific region to have a proportionately higher tax benefit than a two-bedroom home in a poorer region.

The φ^τ multiplier consists of this MTR and itemization probability, while the φ^m multiplier incorporates an additional product of the average loan-to-value (LTV) ratio by Census region to account for the fact that a homeowner can only write off interest on an outstanding loan amount (i.e., if the LTV ratio was zero for all homes, there would be no realized mortgage interest tax benefit).[28] Finally, $E[\pi]$ is expected appreciation (revaluation) for a given year. We set this to 2 percent, which assumes homeowners have a very long-term view of home prices appreciating approximately the same as overall inflation in the economy.[29] While approximately 2 percent is common

27. We use data from the IRS's Statistics of Income (Table 1.2) and the following adjusted gross income strata: under $30,000; $30,000–$49,999; $50,000–$99,999; $100,000–$499,999; above $500,000 (where the percent who itemize are: 7, 21, 44, 80, and 93, respectively).

28. We use data from the Federal Reserve's Survey of Consumer Finance (SCF), which contains information on the average mean value of mortgages and home equity/home value from 2002 to 2015 for each Census region.

29. Verbrugge (2008) rigorously considered a variety of measures of $E[\pi]$ using different forecast techniques, concluding that, "a very long horizon appreciation forecast (such as a long moving average), or an inflation forecast, should be used in the user cost formula" (p. 694). Preference for an *ex ante* long-horizon measure is consistent with Diewert's (2006) argument that, "it is unlikely that landlords use econometric forecasts of housing price appreciation one year away and adjust rents for their tenants every year based on these forecasts. Tenants do not like tremendous volatility in their rents and any landlord that attempted to set such volatile rents would soon have very high vacancy rates on his or her properties. It is, however, possible that landlords may have some idea of the long run average rate of property inflation for the type of property that they manage and this long run average annual rate of price appreciation could be inserted into the user cost formula." During the period we study, the Federal Reserve had maintained either an explicit or implicit target of 2 percent inflation over the long run (e.g., see their policy statements on their website regarding 2 percent: https://www.federalreserve.gov /faqs/money_12848.htm). Ex post, inflation, particularly in the housing market, departed from this target; but use as an *ex ante* measure of inflation may not be unreasonable. For robustness, we consider alternative expectations of price later in the paper.

to the user cost literature (e.g., Himmelberg, Mayer, and Sinai 2005; Poterba and Sinai 2008), we vary this assumption in a second user cost calculation we discuss later in the paper, where price expectations are based on recent home price appreciation/depreciation in one's local area. Overall, our primary contribution to the literature is estimating national property-level user costs using idiosyncratic price and property tax data, which we describe in more detail below. While we simplify this method using some constants in our calculation that follow the literature, we return to a discussion of these simplifications and ways to possibly create a more precise estimate in section 12.6.

12.4.2   Idiosyncratic P—Actual and Predicted

While Zillow already constructs property-level valuation estimates (Zestimates) using their propriety automated valuation model (AVM), for transparency we rely on a combination of actual transaction prices and, for homes that did not transact during our sample period, our own hedonic valuations based on the Zillow microdata. Because we have fine, transaction-level price data, we are able to first use actual market prices for P (when available and when it does not fail the outlier criteria discussed above). For example, if property i was purchased in the first quarter of 2010, then for that quarter the *actual* price was used for the transacted property (P in the formula above).[30] Turnover varies considerably by state and locality; approximately one third of properties in our dataset sold at least once within the window we study (2002–2015). For the value of the home in the following quarter, we posit that the price is simply the transacted price adjusted by the predicted price's appreciation/depreciation (discussed below). We use the same logic for the quarters following that sale until there is a new sale of that property.[31] Broadly, using more direct price data conforms most closely to the principles of valuation laid out by the SNA, where market prices are "the basic reference for valuation in the SNA" (United Nations et al. 2010, 22), and thus much of our aggregate calculation flows directly from millions of observed market prices underlying the housing stock.

As a more general principle of valuation, the SNA recommends that statistical agencies use market prices when market prices are available, but "in the absence of market transactions, valuation is made according to costs

---

30. The ACS has home price data with reasonably good coverage; however, these data come from asking survey respondents to place a value on their own home. An advantage of the Zillow data is that we have actual market transactions and predictions based on market data. Ideally, with linked microdata, eventually we would like to explore the differences between these datasets for use in the national accounts.

31. This method would likely be altered if it were implemented in national accounts over a longer time series because a single transaction price adjusted for inflation may be less predictive of the actual price in other years as the time series becomes much longer. For example, we may limit interpolations to a single five- or ten-year window; but because our time series here only covers fifteen years, we take this simplified approach.

incurred (for example, non-market services produced by government) or by reference to market prices for analogous goods or services (for example, services of owner-occupied dwellings)" (United Nations et al. 2010, 22). Hence, for homes that did not sell during our sample period, we predict their prices based on transactions of similar homes that sold in each quarter using a hedonic model.[32] Conceptually, most of a home's value can be explained by its physical characteristics, location, and time (Rosen 1974); hence, our hedonic model uses sale prices of similar homes along these dimensions to estimate an imputed market valuation for each home in our dataset.[33] While this approach is somewhat simplified compared to more complex machine learning techniques as used by Zillow's proprietary AVM, an advantage of this hedonic approach is transparency, an important pillar of national accounting methods, where the model can be fully described to the public or users of the accounts if an approach like this were to be formally adopted. Therefore, we impute a predicted sale price, $\hat{P}$, based on a hedonic model for each state by quarter separately for home i in quarter t in location j:

$$Sale\ Price_{ijt} = \alpha + \sum \beta X_{it} + \gamma LOCATION_{jt} + \sum \delta sqft_{it}$$

$$* LOCATION_{jt} + \sum \varphi acreage_{it} * LOCATION_{jt} + \varepsilon_{it},$$

where X is a set of physical characteristics (bedrooms, bathrooms, age of the structure, living area measured by square feet, lot size measured by the natural log of acreage, whether the home was a single story, whether it had a pool, whether the home had a basement, whether it had a porch, and whether the home was new construction), location fixed effects, and inter-action of location fixed effects with square footage and the natural log of acreage, respectively.[34] For practicality in estimation, we initially use Census tract fixed effects, although we obtain similar estimates using finer-level geo-

---

32. Within-quarter hedonic regressions allow for all coefficients in the model to change across quarters, accounting for changing tastes and preferences for location or for each housing attribute in the model.

33. Aside from the voluminous literature in real estate, hedonic valuation is not uncommon in the national accounts and price index literatures. For example, see Pakes (2003) or Benkard and Bajari (2005) for applications with personal computers.

34. While the Zillow ZTRAX data contain a lot more information about individual properties that would help with valuation, we chose the variables with extensive coverage across all states in the dataset. When compared to a fuller model that includes many more home characteristics, the marginal gain in precision was small compared to the potential loss in observations due to missing data in states/localities that do not regularly report certain variables. When one of the key characteristics (e.g., bedrooms, bathrooms) was missing, we imputed the number based on the size of the home, based on the rest of our sample. For SFRs with missing bedrooms, we replaced 1, 2, 3, 4, and 5 bedrooms for the following square footage buckets: < 500, 500–999, 1000–1999, 2000–3000, and 3000+. For non-SFRs and urban properties with missing bedrooms, we replaced 1, 2, and 3 bedrooms for the following square footage buckets: < 600, 600–999, 1000+. For all units, we replaced missing bathrooms with a full bathroom per each 1,000 square feet up to 3 bathrooms. Overall, the results are not sensitive to dropping these observations with missing characteristics entirely, but our coverage in some states/counties where this is more systematic would raise issues of representativeness if we drop them.

graphic fixed effects like Census block groups or blocks.[35] To avoid making predictions with thin cells, we specify that a given tract have at least 10 sales in the quarter of estimation. If this condition is not met within a given tract in a given quarter, we then estimate the same model only for observations that do not meet this threshold using county (FIPS) fixed effects.

While intensive for processing, allowing square footage and acreage to vary by location encapsulates the idea that valuation of these attributes varies widely across areas. For example, an additional 500 square feet in a home in New York City will be valued much differently than the same addition upstate in Syracuse.[36] For non-SFRs, which we estimate separately from detached SFRs, we omit acreage and other SFR-specific characteristics from the hedonic model.[37] In addition, we estimate price predictions for urban single-family homes with very small lots (less than one tenth of an acre) with non-SFRs; and, we separately estimate rural homes, which we define as having between 1 and 100 acres. In both cases, we do this only to generate better price predictions for these properties, as we eventually aggregate all SFRs together by number of bedrooms by Census Division, which we discuss more below in section 12.4.4.

12.4.3 Property Taxes

Property taxes vary widely across states and municipalities. As of 2017, the highest property tax state was New Jersey with an average effective tax rate of 2.31 percent, whereas Hawaii and Alabama have average rates of 0.32 percent and 0.48 percent, respectively.[38] Even within states there is con-

---

35. Smaller geographic units like block groups and blocks have fewer sales, which we found to be less ideal for quarterly predictions. In a previous draft, we had similar (albeit somewhat less precise) results to tracts using zip code fixed effects. We have also explored a variety of other specifications to improve model fit and predictions, including a semi-log specification, where sale price is logged.

36. This approach is used commonly in the hedonic valuation literature for housing and land. See, for example, Kuminoff and Pope (2013). For some of the larger states like California, this approach yields too many interaction terms that bump up against the limit for number of variables that can be used in a single regression for many statistical software packages, which required us to run substate samples (Northern CA versus Southern CA, for example). This allows noninteracted coefficients to vary within states.

37. Despite this relatively simple hedonic model construction, for most states and most quarters, the model fit (R^2) fell within 0.8 and 0.9 for our models using census tract fixed effects, producing errors that stack up quite reasonably compared to more sophisticated techniques. In order to assess the accuracy of our model's price predictions, we constructed a measure of error for each record for which we have an observed price as follows:

Average Percent Error (APE) = [(*Predicted Price − Actual Price*)/*Actual Price*] * 100

Then, to obtain an aggregate error, the median of all APEs in a state in a given time quarter is multiplied by the share of the observations in that state in the total observations. Overall, APE fell with ± 5 percent for the vast majority of quarters, with only a handful of quarters in the ± 5–10 range.

38. Variation in property taxes across states gained attention during the national coverage of the Tax Cuts and Jobs Act of 2017. For example, USA Today ran a story comparing effective property tax rates across the US: https://www.usatoday.com/story/money/personalfinance/2017/04/16/comparing-average-property-taxes-all-50-states-and-dc/100314754/.

siderable variation. Hence, for accurate estimates of user cost we attempt to account for the idiosyncratic nature of a property's taxes. Because the Zillow data are collected primarily from local tax assessor office databases, the coverage of property taxes is quite good. We use individual tax data to determine a property's effective tax rate based on a denominator of P (actual or predicted price) rather than the corresponding assessment value associated with each property in the data.[39]

We made this choice for a couple reasons. First, regarding the denominator, the assessment value is often much lower than the market value, so applying the rate based on the assessed value to the market value of P in the user cost calculation would overestimate the amount homeowners pay in our calculation. The degree of mis-assessment of value varies considerably by locale, and in some cases it is by design of local policies for states like California to have assessments tied to historical values for longer-tenured homeowners. Second, this approach better reflects the average effective tax rate, because like other elements of the tax code, homeowners do not all pay the same posted rate due to local property tax relief exemptions and relief for special groups (Moulton, Waller, and Wentland 2018).

Finally, in the present study we are unable to accurately determine the *net* tax bill for *each* homeowner or precisely consider the full range of offsetting tax benefits that come with homeownership (namely, mortgage interest deductions and state/local tax deductions); but, as we describe in section 12.4.1 above, we allow an estimated average benefit varying by home type, region, and home size, as household income (and therefore marginal tax rate and likelihood of itemization) varies tremendously across the US, which we capture to some extent with this approach.[40]

12.4.4 Quantity, Housing Counts, and Aggregation

Once we obtain user cost estimates for millions of individual properties across the United States, we then aggregate to a weighted national estimate of housing services based on the corresponding quantities of the housing stock by location/region, type of home (SFR versus non-SFR), and number of bedrooms. We use the weighted unit counts of the housing stock from the ACS for each year of our sample, which provides a yearly count

39. We currently have one year of tax amount data from Zillow but updating these data more often (preferably annually) may be required if this method is to be used for national accounts measurement. In rare cases where our computed tax rate estimates far exceeded the average tax rate of the state (by a factor of 3), we winsorized these observations to the state average. When they were much smaller (by a factor of 1/3), we also replaced them with the state average.

40. Our ambition is to eventually use linked administrative data to back out a more precise, idiosyncratic estimate of the tax benefits to owning a home. In addition, linkages to Census administrative data records, for example, would also allow us to better estimate maintenance and other costs for households (or at least regionally—where wear and tear from climate and other factors may contribute to households reporting systematically different levels of maintenance expenditures) and to better understand housing market dynamics of populations of homeowners versus renters. We return to this point in section 12.6.

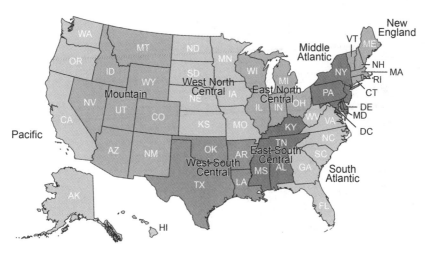

Fig. 12.3   Census divisions
Source: https://www.census.gov/geo/reference/webatlas/divisions.html.

of the aggregate number of residential housing units by Census Division, depicted in figure 12.3. Because the BEA's current method treats vacant homes differently than tenant- or owner-occupied homes, we omit these from our aggregation, reconstructing estimates according to the BEA's current method and using the same quantity of homes from the ACS such that the difference between the two series is independent of quantities used (labeling this "Quantity Adjusted PCE Housing" to reflect this difference from the official series). For illustrative purposes, refer to table 12.1 below, where we show the calculation of our national estimate for Q4 of 2015. For each Census Division or region of the US, we multiply the average user cost for each type of home (SFR versus non-SFR) for each bedroom category.[41]

This method of aggregation assumes that the nonmissing data are reasonably representative of the missing data. For example, Indiana's sale prices are missing from the ZTRAX dataset, as it is among the nondisclosure states that do not ordinarily record sale prices in public use tax assessor data. Hence, our final aggregate estimates must assume that the average user costs imputed from sales in its Census region (Illinois, Michigan, Ohio, and

41. We use bedrooms as a proxy for size of the home to create categorical differences that more accurately reflect the weighted total. The bins are numbered 1 through 5+ in table 12.1. However, for states that did not have good coverage of the number of bedrooms, we assumed that the distribution of user cost approximately aligned with the distribution of bedrooms and assigned homes to corresponding bins of bedrooms. In future work, we will explore using county-level quantity counts, as finer location averages could be more relevant than averages by physical characteristics.

Table 12.1   **User cost aggregation—Example quarter**

Total User Cost Calculation (Default Specification) for 2015 Quarter 4

		SFR			Non-SFR		
Division	Bedrooms	Avg. user cost	Q	P * Q (billions)	Avg. user cost	Q	P * Q (billions)
1	0 or 1	14,565	79,713	1	30,133	761,608	23
	2	16,669	491,998	8	32,612	1,006,532	33
	3	20,603	1,603,041	33	23,622	533,706	13
	4	29,814	838,816	25			
	5+	41,131	204,366	8			
2	0 or 1	11,749	142,736	2	17,386	2,599,754	45
	2	10,635	1,027,587	11	17,580	2,624,879	46
	3	15,848	3,614,253	57	28,243	2,174,197	61
	4	24,420	2,234,490	55			
	5+	38,896	579,746	23			
3	0 or 1	7,239	220,172	2	7,245	1,751,404	13
	2	6,887	1,946,805	13	10,839	2,480,621	27
	3	10,251	6,553,425	67	9,393	937,491	9
	4	16,547	2,979,940	49			
	5+	24,727	668,551	17			
4	0 or 1	9,682	143,659	1	10,554	769,223	8
	2	9,749	1,051,504	10	12,062	952,057	11
	3	12,754	2,678,916	34	14,576	351,747	5
	4	16,979	1,522,571	26			
	5+	20,061	470,828	9			
5	0 or 1	9,631	197,364	2	7,303	2,037,536	15
	2	8,813	1,922,406	17	9,670	3,258,601	31
	3	11,897	7,526,960	90	15,778	1,869,658	29
	4	20,120	3,739,500	75			
	5+	29,923	1,091,405	33			
6	0 or 1	7,300	94,430	1	6,881	443,190	3
	2	6,123	739,063	5	7,384	691,375	5
	3	7,685	2,895,377	22	10,281	246,935	3
	4	12,386	1,059,573	13			
	5+	18,240	243,589	4			
7	0 or 1	11,302	212,743	2	4,329	1,461,312	6
	2	5,616	1,315,520	7	7,323	1,449,698	11
	3	8,589	5,129,666	44	8,339	475,987	4
	4	13,350	2,283,730	30			
	5+	18,331	435,305	8			
8	0 or 1	15,553	127,213	2	10,601	779,253	8
	2	14,278	759,204	11	10,698	1,068,443	11
	3	14,736	2,597,256	38	13,958	428,687	6
	4	21,199	1,580,893	34			
	5+	28,338	623,233	18			

Table 12.1   **(cont.)**

Total User Cost Calculation (Default Specification) for 2015 Quarter 4

		SFR			Non-SFR		
Division	Bedrooms	Avg. user cost	Q	P * Q (billions)	Avg. user cost	Q	P * Q (billions)
9	0 or 1	17,924	314,491	6	23,344	2,515,810	59
	2	23,840	1,575,736	38	31,575	2,884,457	91
	3	25,817	5,077,243	131	36,109	1,132,319	41
	4	34,382	2,928,474	101			
	5+	43,812	755,755	33			
		Subtotal (SFR)		1,216		*Subtotal (non-SFR)*	618
						Total user cost: 1,216 + 618 = 1,834	

Wisconsin) reflect the Indiana market.[42] Missing data itself is not a prohibitive limitation for constructing national accounts (statistical agencies always have limited data); the issue is rather the representativeness of the data we do have. While many of these states are reasonably represented by their neighboring states' housing markets (e.g., Indiana), one exception might be Texas (the largest state for which we have missing price data).[43]

12.4.5   Varying Ex Ante Expected Price Appreciation/Depreciation

Finally, for robustness, we vary the $E[\pi]$ term of ex ante expected price appreciation. Our default specification assumes a very long-run view of home price inflation of a constant 2 percent per year, despite the fact that homeowners during this period may very well have perceived price appreciation quite differently, particularly for some regions that experienced steep price fluctuations. Rather than assuming that homeowners take a *constant long-run, national* view of price expectations, we can instead consider that that they take a *variable short-run, local* view of price expectations. Thus, our alternative specification supposes that homeowners expect ex ante price appreciation to be their local (county-level) average yearly price inflation from the prior two years (quarter $t - 8$ to $t - 5$ and $t - 4$ to $t - 1$). This is

42. Recall that one of the limitations of this dataset is that there are no price data from the following states: Idaho, Indiana, Kansas, Mississippi, Missouri, Montana, New Mexico, North Dakota, South Dakota, Texas, Utah, and Wyoming. Maine is also excluded due to limited data in a number of quarters of our sample period.

43. If this method (or similar) were to be adopted by the BEA or others, supplemental data would be required to verify these assumptions or to reweight the estimates to better represent the missing states' housing markets. The scope of this study, however, is to explore how far this particular Big Data set can go toward developing alternative housing estimates. The American Housing Survey (AHS) also has high-quality data on the unit counts of the housing stock, but the survey is only available every other year and is a significantly smaller sample.

calculated by taking the average percent change of the median predicted price by county over the previous eight quarters from our hedonic model estimates discussed above.[44]

In this alternative specification, we also limit appreciation (depreciation) expectations to 5 percent (−5 percent) to avoid substantially negative user costs and excessive volatility based on expectations. One can think of this specification as price appreciation being expected to cover or offset (approximately) the maintenance, physical deterioration of the property, and owner risk premium (which itself may fluctuate in proportion to price expectations). While this is somewhat simplistic, our goal is to provide a sense of a reasonable range of possible estimates, as a more moderate moving average (as in Verbrugge 2008) may produce an estimate somewhere in between this range of results, albeit closer to the long-run default specification.[45]

12.5   Results

Our full set of results for all years and quarters in our sample appears in table 12.2, which shows both the total and average user cost estimates of housing services as well as the corresponding estimates by housing type (SFR versus non-SFR) by quarter. A visual of these data is shown in figures 12.4 and 12.5. Specifically, figure 12.4 illustrates the default specification graphically over time, broken out by housing type using the default user cost specification, showing similar time series dynamics and that the total user costs of detached SFRs are consistently higher than non-SFRs, as one would expect.

The key figure of the paper is figure 12.5, where we compare our average yearly user cost measure of housing services with the BEA's yearly estimate of housing services from PCE, using the ACS to adjust the quantity of the stock of housing in each year to be equal across both series. Note that we compare the full estimates of aggregate housing services because we are

44. Note that this is not seasonally adjusted. Some of the volatility in prices will be from purely seasonal factors. This can be augmented by applying a standard seasonal adjustment. For now, we are reporting the raw, unadjusted nominal results.

45. Generally, countries that employ a user cost method for housing omit the $E[\pi]$ term entirely, simplifying the calculation (Diewert and Nakamura 2009). One way of thinking about this simplification involves referring back to the reason why the $E[\pi]$ term is factored into the calculation in the first place. As a thought experiment, the user cost method is often pitched as calculating the cost of an owner who purchases a home at the beginning of a period and sells it at the end (assuming away transactions costs). The $E[\pi]$ term in that case would simply be the capital gain/loss during a given period; but if the next period begins with repurchasing the same home at the price from the end of the last period, then the capital gain/loss is essentially erased immediately. For now, we remain somewhat agnostic to the different approaches by offering results for multiple ways of incorporating $E[\pi]$ into user cost; our default specification comes at the suggestion of feedback we received from the NBER-CRIW Pre-Conference in 2018 and is not uncommon in the academic literature.

Table 12.2   **Housing user costs by quarter from 2002 through 2015**

	Full Sample		SFR		Non-SFR	
	Total user cost ($B)	Avg. user cost	Total user cost ($B)	Avg. user cost	Total user cost ($B)	Avg. user cost
2002q1	1,489	14,876	1,051	15,773	438	13,088
2002q2	1,577	15,711	1,114	16,653	463	13,829
2002q3	1,498	14,884	1,051	15,665	447	13,322
2002q4	1,461	14,476	1,022	15,172	439	13,081
2003q1	1,481	14,638	1,032	15,261	450	13,383
2003q2	1,505	14,813	1,052	15,486	453	13,455
2003q3	1,677	16,445	1,169	17,119	508	15,080
2003q4	1,712	16,727	1,183	17,247	528	15,669
2004q1	1,711	16,657	1,184	17,177	526	15,595
2004q2	1,957	19,001	1,354	19,587	603	17,804
2004q3	1,947	18,848	1,340	19,345	606	17,833
2004q4	1,916	18,501	1,305	18,787	611	17,919
2005q1	1,961	18,885	1,322	18,980	640	18,692
2005q2	2,048	19,698	1,382	19,799	666	19,492
2005q3	2,139	20,545	1,446	20,655	693	20,319
2005q4	2,217	21,272	1,492	21,271	725	21,273
2006q1	2,280	21,848	1,533	21,800	747	21,948
2006q2	2,489	23,799	1,683	23,851	807	23,692
2006q3	2,458	23,440	1,659	23,451	798	23,417
2006q4	2,381	22,654	1,596	22,498	784	22,979
2007q1	2,415	22,922	1,624	22,821	791	23,131
2007q2	2,513	23,816	1,693	23,755	820	23,942
2007q3	2,460	23,263	1,662	23,277	797	23,234
2007q4	2,256	21,294	1,517	21,210	738	21,469
2008q1	2,051	19,326	1,378	19,235	673	19,517
2008q2	2,083	19,606	1,409	19,652	674	19,511
2008q3	2,027	19,051	1,374	19,153	653	18,841
2008q4	1,779	16,697	1,202	16,743	577	16,602
2009q1	1,591	14,912	1,078	15,006	513	14,719
2009q2	1,742	16,296	1,189	16,526	553	15,823
2009q3	1,786	16,666	1,221	16,942	565	16,100
2009q4	1,741	16,216	1,189	16,472	552	15,690
2010q1	1,771	16,461	1,209	16,720	562	15,931
2010q2	1,747	16,221	1,202	16,608	546	15,429
2010q3	1,572	14,578	1,083	14,956	490	13,808
2010q4	1,566	14,501	1,073	14,817	493	13,857
2011q1	1,651	15,278	1,132	15,631	519	14,558
2011q2	1,633	15,076	1,125	15,503	508	14,209
2011q3	1,461	13,455	1,006	13,832	455	12,691
2011q4	1,355	12,451	928	12,735	427	11,875
2012q1	1,344	12,318	922	12,627	422	11,693
2012q2	1,353	12,395	929	12,726	424	11,726
2012q3	1,332	12,189	916	12,542	416	11,477
2012q4	1,353	12,376	921	12,614	432	11,896
2013q1	1,407	12,853	956	13,086	451	12,385

(*continued*)

Table 12.2   (cont.)

	Full Sample		SFR		Non-SFR	
	Total user cost ($B)	Avg. user cost	Total user cost ($B)	Avg. user cost	Total user cost ($B)	Avg. user cost
2013q2	1,488	13,561	1,015	13,875	473	12,934
2013q3	1,687	15,339	1,146	15,632	541	14,755
2013q4	1,697	15,394	1,150	15,662	547	14,858
2014q1	1,729	15,656	1,162	15,813	567	15,343
2014q2	1,776	16,041	1,196	16,247	580	15,633
2014q3	1,773	15,979	1,190	16,149	583	15,643
2014q4	1,723	15,493	1,150	15,575	573	15,331
2015q1	1,675	15,030	1,111	15,027	564	15,036
2015q2	1,793	16,066	1,195	16,143	598	15,914
2015q3	1,832	16,390	1,220	16,456	612	16,259
2015q4	1,834	16,380	1,216	16,369	618	16,401

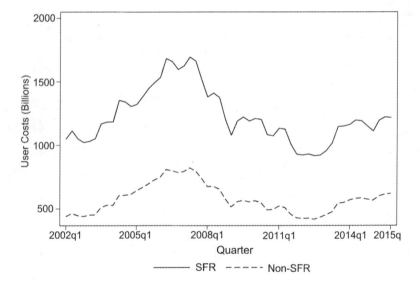

Fig. 12.4   Total quarterly user costs by SFR/non-SFR (default specification)

estimating the user cost for all residential homes in our sample, applying the same method to all homes whether they are owner-occupied or not.[46]

46. Also note that aside from methodology, there are other small differences that remain. For example, we do not include the imputed rent for farm dwellings, as we cull properties zoned for agriculture and we do not have separate estimates for group homes, nor do we include vacant dwellings. But these estimates are small and relatively constant over time, so they would not account for much of the differences in price dynamics over time in figure 12.5. Finally, some states and municipalities had limited data in the early few years of this sample, which may not

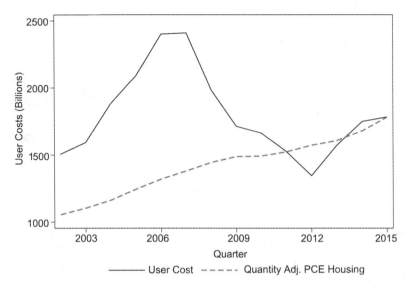

Fig. 12.5   Total yearly user cost (default) compared to PCE housing estimates

Our default aggregate measure of housing was initially much higher than the BEA's estimate in 2002, but this gap widened precisely when home prices throughout much of the US appreciated considerably during the run up to the financial crisis and Great Recession.

The more pronounced fluctuations in the path of the user cost-based estimate from 2002 through 2010, during the infamous bubble-bust years, bear a striking resemblance to national house price indices like Case-Shiller's, rising about $1 trillion from 2002 to the peak in 2006, with a similarly precipitous fall in the several years that followed. Broadly, this result is consistent with other recent work like Braga and Lerman (2019), who assess the divergence in CPI measures using a user cost versus rental-equivalence approach. Indeed, this result is consistent with Ambrose et al. (2015) in that a notable drop occurs in the latter part of the decade. However, beginning around 2010, the user cost-based estimate of housing services using Zillow data has tracked much more closely to the housing estimate based on the BEA's current rental-equivalence method, consistent with the time series dynamics of the price indices in the figure we discussed in the introduction (figure 12.2).

One alternative specification of the user cost method, factoring in recent (eight quarters) and very local (county-level) price expectations, depicts a more pronounced bubble and bust in its measurement of housing services of the same time period. Figure 12.6 shows a user cost closer to the rental-

---

have been random, as richer counties may have digitized these records earlier and more consistently, possibly explaining some of this difference in the first couple of years.

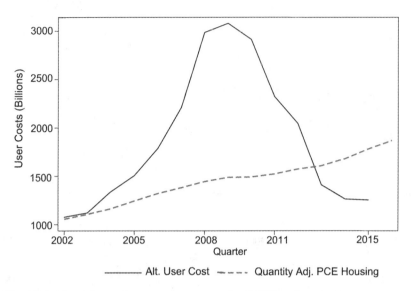

Fig. 12.6   Total alternative user cost compared to PCE housing

equivalence estimates early in the 2000s, but also shows price expectations producing a much sharper peak and trough with the alternative specification, with the level in recent years being considerably smaller than current BEA estimates of housing. However, given that this specification is more aggressive in its price expectations assumption, this result should be interpreted with care, as it incorporates greater volatility into the series based on a very simple model of price expectations. Indeed, this is one reason why most countries that actually employ the user cost method for housing in their national accounts or price indices often simplify this method further by omitting the price appreciation term in the user cost calculation (Diewert and Nakamura 2009).

For robustness, we vary some of the assumptions underlying the user cost formula, which we show in figure 12.7. First, rather than incorporate a fixed homeownership risk premium of 2 percent, one alternative would be to use the average 30-year fixed mortgage rate as a stand-in for the 10-year treasury rate and this 2 percent constant. The 30-year mortgage rate generally tracks the time-series dynamics of other long-term interest rates like the 10-year Treasury, but it contains this additional risk premium that can vary slightly over time due to market conditions. Not surprisingly, this specification produces very similar results to our default specification, due to the stability of this premium over our sample period. Second, if we omit the E[π] term entirely, a practice that some countries have elected to do when implementing a user cost approach, this shifts the series upward, effectively reflecting more costly housing services across the entire time series. Third, if we omit

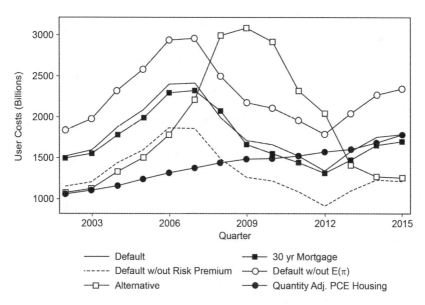

Fig. 12.7   Comparing different user cost methods with PCE

the risk premium entirely, we see an analogous downward shift in the series. Finally, note that because our E[π] term and risk premium term are both constants, one can also think of our default specification as simply including offsetting terms (where, even if one disagrees with the precise constant we use, if asset risk changes directly with price expectations, the choice of the constant becomes less relevant if they offset).

An important benefit to calculating user cost estimates with microdata is that there is greater scope for separating estimates geographically or by housing type. More generally, national statistical offices face increasing demands by users for finer partitions of the national accounts, which is a key advantage of Big Data over traditional designed survey data that suffer to a greater extent from a thin cell problem. As an example, figures 12.8 and 12.9 show average user cost by region (Census Division) for SFRs and non-SFRs respectively, although the data easily allow us to provide measures at the county or tract level (except, of course, for states with missing price data). The estimates produce the expected result—that the Pacific region and New England have the highest average user costs of housing, with several regions at the bottom experiencing mild, if any, bubble-bust market dynamics. This is consistent with numerous other regional metrics of the housing market over this same period.

Finally, while large aggregate estimates are often the focus of NIPA estimates, many users prefer per unit averages. Figure 12.10 depicts average user cost per residential unit for three different specifications and the cor-

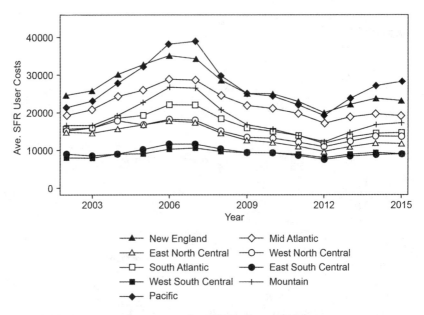

Fig. 12.8 Average yearly user costs for SFR by Census division

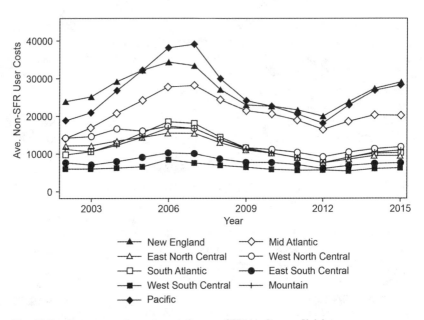

Fig. 12.9 Average yearly user costs for non-SFR by Census division

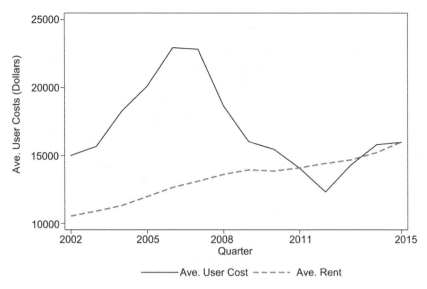

Fig. 12.10   Average user costs and PCE average rent

responding per unit space rent estimate (BEA). While the shape is identical to figure 12.7, the magnitudes may be helpful for assessing reasonability of the estimates, with the nominal average user cost and space rent both near $15,000 per year in the final couple of years in our sample period.

12.6   Discussion

Though for reasons discussed below the BEA is not adopting the user cost method, it is worth discussing a few caveats when comparing it to the current method and potential avenues for future research. We find that a user cost method using fine-microdata from Zillow can produce estimates of housing services comparable to the BEA's current method only for the most recent years we estimate, but the series behaves very differently over the bubble-bust period of the 2000s. Indeed, the departure from the rental-equivalence method during the first decade of this century (and extended periods prior to that, based on other studies using different data) shows that the theoretically predicted convergence of these estimates is far from guaranteed. And, if there are systematic divergences, particularly when the housing sector is experiencing a pronounced boom-bust cycle, a central question for national statistical offices will be: to what extent should housing estimates reflect underlying asset appreciation (that does not appear in rental data), which may or may not be temporary? And which conception of aggregate housing is more relevant to users of the data and to policy makers?[47] These are foundational conceptual questions in the economic measurement literature (e.g., Alchian and Klein 1973; Gilchrist and Leahy 2002; and Goodhart 2001), which this paper does not attempt to settle.

We made a number of methodological simplifications and assumptions which, if adopted by a national statistical office at some point, would need to be explored further because some (likely small portion) of the differences may be attributable to these choices. Additional precision gained from refining these estimates may, at least in part, help bridge the aforementioned gap between user cost and rental-equivalence estimates (particularly in the post-bubble/bust years when the gap was not as large). For example, the mortgage interest and property tax deductions are highly idiosyncratic depending on a number of factors such as income, where the probability of itemization and marginal tax rates could be higher during the boom (lowering user costs) and lower during the bust, potentially accounting for some of the cyclical departure of user cost from the rental-equivalence estimates. Or, insofar as maintenance and depreciation vary idiosyncratically or by region, a more sophisticated approach could exacerbate user cost differences if high-price areas experienced relatively higher costs during the boom period. In either case, linked administrative data could help us answer these questions by creating idiosyncratic, property-specific estimates of the tax benefits, maintenance and depreciation costs, and a host of other refinements that could generate even more precise estimates. Finally, linked administrative data may also help bridge the gap of our understanding of which user cost assumptions most directly compare to market rents, particularly for tenant-occupied homes for which we have rental data and user cost estimates based on Zillow data, as this would show the most direct apples-to-apples comparison of the two methodological approaches. These linked data could also help us test or even construct better sample weights to ensure the composition of the sample accurately represents the characteristics of the entire stock of housing in the United States.

After considering a number of options, the BEA does not plan to adopt the user cost approach because it plans to modify its rent-based approach by incorporating new source data (Census ACS data) and updating its method to include a new owner-premium adjustment (see Aten 2018). The proposed modified rental-equivalence approach would be less volatile and more incremental compared to user cost-based estimates. Nevertheless, this research demonstrates the potential upside to incorporating new data and exploring new methods in the national accounts more generally, and housing in particular. Statistical agencies are continuously seeking ways to lower response

---

47. There is evidence that the economic decisions of homeowners are, in fact, influenced by price appreciation/depreciation of their homes and housing wealth. See, for example, Mian and Sufi (2011), Mian, Rao, and Sufi (2013), Campbell and Cocco (2007), and Lowenstein (2018). Further, a related question would be: Which conception of aggregate housing would be the most useful to monetary policy makers? We leave this, however, to future research.

burden for survey respondents, which is of increasing concern in an era of falling response rates more generally, and to find more cost-effective means for delivering statistics to users. For example, survey respondents are asked to place a value on their own home. The kind of microdata used in this study could be used to update or even replace statistics that use these data (e.g., rent-to-value ratios or the housing stock quality measure used to adjust the BEA's current rental-equivalence method for owner-occupied housing). Linked Zillow-ACS data could provide an estimate for calculating an owner premium for owner-occupied housing, supplementing the (adapted) rental-equivalence method proposed by Aten (2018) by using market transaction values as opposed to survey-based values, which is currently being explored by BEA researchers. As another example, Big Data sources could also substantially improve precision for regional and type stratification, as linked data could provide additional details about individual homes (e.g., number of bathrooms, size of the home in square feet) that are not reported in a survey like the ACS, providing further potential for improving the economic measurement of housing services.

References

Albouy, D., and A. Hanson. 2014. "Are Houses Too Big or in the Wrong Place? Tax Benefits to Housing and Inefficiencies in Location and Consumption." *Tax Policy and the Economy* 28:63–96.

Alchian, A. A., and B. Klein. 1973. "On a Correct Measure of Inflation." *Journal of Money, Credit and Banking* 5 (1): 173–91.

Ambrose, B. W., N. E. Coulson, and J. Yoshida. 2015. "The Repeat Rent Index." *Review of Economics and Statistics* 97 (5): 939–50.

Anenberg, E., and E. Kung. 2014. "Estimates of the Size and Source of Price Declines due to Nearby Foreclosures." *American Economic Review* 104 (8): 2527–51.

Aten, Bettina. 2018. "Valuing Owner-Occupied Housing: An Empirical Exercise Using the American Community Survey (ACS) Housing Files." BEA Working Paper, Washington, DC. https://www.bea.gov/research/papers/2018/valuing -owner-occupied-housing-empirical-exercise-using-american-community.

Baldwin, A., A. O. Nakamura, and M. Prud'homme. 2009. "Different Concepts for Measuring Owner Occupied Housing Costs in a CPI: Statistics Canada's Analytical Series." In *Price and Productivity Measurement*, vol. 1, *Housing*, edited by W. E. Diewert, B. M. Balk, D. Fixler, K. J. Fox, and A. O. Nakamura, 151–60. Manchester, UK: Trafford Press.

Benkard, C. L., and P. Bajari. 2005. "Hedonic Price Indexes with Unobserved Product Characteristics, and Application to Personal Computers." *Journal of Business and Economic Statistics* 23 (1): 61–75.

Bernstein, A., M. T. Gustafson, and R. Lewis. 2019. "Disaster on the Horizon: The Price Effect of Sea Level Rise." *Journal of Financial Economics* 134 (2): 253–72.

Bian, X., B. D. Waller, and S. A. Wentland. 2016. "The Role of Transaction Costs in Impeding Market Exchange in Real Estate." *Journal of Housing Research* 25 (2): 115–35.

Braga, B., and R. I. Lerman. 2019. "Accounting for Homeownership in Estimating Real Income Growth." *Economics Letters* 174:9–12.

Bui, L. T., and C. J. Mayer. 2003. "Regulation and Capitalization of Environmental Amenities: Evidence from the Toxic Release Inventory in Massachusetts." *Review of Economics and Statistics* 85 (3): 693–708.

Bureau of Economic Analysis. 2018. Table 2.5.5: Personal Consumption Expenditures by Function. Accessed December 17, 2018. https://apps.bea.gov/iTable /iTable.cfm?reqid=19&step=2#reqid=19&step=2&isuri=1&1921=survey.

Campbell, J. Y., and J. F. Cocco. 2007. "How Do House Prices Affect Consumption? Evidence from Micro Data." *Journal of Monetary Economics* 54 (3): 591–621.

Coulson, N. E., and H. Li. 2013. "Measuring the External Benefits of Homeownership." *Journal of Urban Economics* 77:57–67.

Crone, T. M., L. I. Nakamura, and R. Voith. 2000. "Measuring Housing Services Inflation." *Journal of Economic and Social Measurement* 26 (3, 4): 153–71.

Crone, T. M., L. I. Nakamura, and R. P. Voith. 2009. "Hedonic Estimates of the Cost of Housing Services: Rental and Owner Occupied Units." In *Price and Productivity Measurement*, vol. 1, *Housing*, edited by W. E. Diewert, B. M. Balk, D. Fixler, K. J. Fox, and A. O. Nakamura, 51. Manchester, UK: Trafford Press.

Davis, M. A., A. Lehnert, and R. F. Martin. 2008. "The Rent-Price Ratio for the Aggregate Stock of Owner-Occupied Housing." *Review of Income and Wealth* 54 (2): 279–84.

Diewert, W. Erwin. 2003. "The Treatment of Owner Occupied Housing and Other Durables in a Consumer Price Index." Discussion Paper 03-08, Department of Economics, University of British Columbia, Vancouver, Canada. http://www .econ.ubc.ca/discpapers/dp0308.pdf.

———. 2006. "Conclusions and Future Directions." Summary paper of the OECD-IMF Workshop on Real Estate Price Indices, Paris. http://www.oecd.org/dataoecd /32/21/37848333.pdf.

———. 2008. "Conclusions and Future Directions." Paris OECD-IMF Workshop on Real Estate Price Indexes, Paris, November 6–7, 2006.

———. 2009. "Durables and Owner-Occupied Housing in a Consumer Price Index." In *Price Index Concepts and Measurement*, Studies in Income and Wealth, vol. 70, edited by W. E. Diewert, J. Greenlees, and C. Hulten, 445–500. Chicago: University of Chicago Press.

Diewert, W. E., and A. O. Nakamura. 2009. "Accounting for Housing in a CPI." In *Price and Productivity Measurement*, vol. 1, *Housing*, edited by W. E. Diewert, B. M. Balk, D. Fixler, K. J. Fox, and A. O. Nakamura, 7–32. Manchester, UK: Trafford Press. www.vancouvervolumes.com and www.indexmeasures.com.

Diewert, W. E., A. O. Nakamura, and L. I. Nakamura. 2009. "The Housing Bubble and a New Approach to Accounting for Housing in a CPI." *Journal of Housing Economics* 18 (3): 156–71.

Flavin, Marjorie, and Takashi Yamashita. 2002. "Owner-Occupied Housing and the Composition of the Household Portfolio." *American Economic Review* 92 (1): 345–62.

Garner, T. I., and R. Verbrugge. 2009. "Reconciling User Costs and Rental Equivalence: Evidence from the US Consumer Expenditure Survey." *Journal of Housing Economics* 18 (3): 172–92.

Gilchrist, S., and J. V. Leahy. 2002. "Monetary Policy and Asset Prices." *Journal of Monetary Economics* 49 (1): 75–97.

Gill, H. L., and D. R. Haurin. 1991. "User Cost and the Demand for Housing Attributes." *Real Estate Economics* 19 (3): 383–96.

Gillingham, Robert. 1983. "Measuring the Cost of Shelter for Homeowners: Theoretical and Empirical Considerations." *Review of Economics and Statistics* 65:254–65.

Glaeser, Edward L., and Joseph Gyourko. 2009. "Arbitrage in Housing Markets." In *Housing Markets and the Economy: Risk, Regulation, and Policy: Essays in Honor of Karl E. Case,* edited by E. L. Glaeser and John M. Quigley. Cambridge, MA: Lincoln Institute of Land Policy.

Goeyvaerts, G., and E. Buyst. 2019. "Do Market Rents Reflect User Costs?" *Journal of Housing Economics* 44 (June): 114–30.

Goodhart, C., 2001. "What Weight Should Be Given to Asset Prices in the Measurement of Inflation?" *Economic Journal* 111 (472): 335–56.

Gordon, R. J., and T. vanGoethem. 2007. "Downward Bias in the Most Important CPI Component: The Case of Rental Shelter, 1914–2003." In *Hard-to-Measure Goods and Services: Essays in Honor of Zvi Griliches,* Studies in Income and Wealth, vol. 67, edited by Ernst R. Berndt and Charles R. Hulten, 153–95. Chicago: University of Chicago Press.

Haffner, M., and K. Heylen. 2011. "User Costs and Housing Expenses: Towards a More Comprehensive Approach to Affordability." *Housing Studies* 26 (4): 593–614.

Hill, R. J., and I. A. Syed. 2016. "Hedonic Price–Rent Ratios, User Cost, and Departures from Equilibrium in the Housing Market." *Regional Science and Urban Economics* 56: 60–72.

Himmelberg, C., C. Mayer, and T. Sinai. 2005. "Assessing High House Prices: Bubbles, Fundamentals and Misperceptions." *Journal of Economic Perspectives* 19 (4): 67–92.

Jorgenson, D. 1963. "Capital Theory and Investment Behavior." *American Economic Review* 53 (2): 247–59.

———. 1967. "The Theory of Investment Behavior." In *Determinants of Investment Behavior,* edited by Robert Ferber, 129–75. New York: NBER.

Katz, Arnold J. 2009. "Estimating Dwelling Services in the Candidate Countries: Theoretical and Practical Considerations in Developing Methodologies Based on a User Cost of Capital Measure." In *Price and Productivity Measurement,* vol. 1, *Housing,* edited by W. E. Diewert, B. M. Balk, D. Fixler, K. J. Fox, and A. O. Nakamura, 33–50. Manchester, UK: Trafford Press. www.vancouvervolumes.com and www.indexmeasures.com.

———. 2017. "Imputing Rents to Owner-Occupied Housing by Directly Modelling Their Distribution." BEA Working Paper WP2017-7, Washington, DC.

Komolafe, M., 2018. "Dwelling Services, with an Emphasis on Imputed Rent in the European Union." *Regional Statistics* 8 (1): 168–86.

Kuminoff, N. V., and J. C. Pope. 2013. "The Value of Residential Land and Structures during the Great Housing Boom and Bust." *Land Economics* 89 (1): 1–29.

Lebow, D. E., and J. B. Rudd. 2003. "Measurement Error in the Consumer Price Index: Where Do We Stand?" *Journal of Economic Literature* 41 (1): 159–201.

Linden, L., and J. E. Rockoff. 2008. "Estimates of the Impact of Crime Risk on Property Values from Megan's Laws." *American Economic Review* 98 (3): 1103–27.

Lowenstein, Lara. 2018. "Consumption of Housing During the 2000s Boom: Evidence and Theory." Working Paper, Federal Reserve Bank of Cleveland, Cleveland, OH.

Mayerhauser, Nicole, and Denise McBride. 2007. "Treatment of Housing in the National Income and Product Accounts." BEA staff study presented before the Society of Government Economists at the Annual Convention of the Allied Social Science Associations, Chicago, December 2007.

McCarthy, J., and R. W. Peach. 2010. *The Measurement of Rent Inflation.* Staff Report No. 425, Federal Reserve Bank of New York, New York.

McFadyen, S., and R. Hobart. 1978. "An Alternative Measurement of Housing Costs and the Consumer Price Index." *Canadian Journal of Economics* 11 (1): 105–12.

Mian, A., K. Rao, and A. Sufi. 2013. "Household Balance Sheets, Consumption, and the Economic Slump." *Quarterly Journal of Economics* 128 (4): 1687–1726.

Mian, Atif, and Amir Sufi. 2011. "House Prices, Home Equity-Based Borrowing, and the US Household Leverage Crisis." *American Economic Review* 101 (5): 2132–56.

Moulton, J. G., B. D. Waller, and S. A. Wentland. 2018. "Who Benefits from Targeted Property Tax Relief? Evidence from Virginia Elections." *Journal of Policy Analysis and Management* 37 (2): 240–64.

Moulton, J. G., and S. A. Wentland. 2018. "Monetary Policy and the Housing Market." Working Paper, Washington, DC.

Organisation for Economic Co-operation and Development. 2009. *Measuring Capital: OECD Manual 2009.* 2nd ed. https://www.oecd.org/sdd/productivity-stats/43734711.pdf.

Ozimek, A. 2014. "Sticky Rents and the CPI for Owner-Occupied Housing." Working Paper. http://gradworks.umi.com/35/95/3595699.html.

Pakes, A. 2003. "A Reconsideration of Hedonic Price Indexes with an Application to PC's." *American Economic Review* 93 (5): 1578–96.

Poterba, J., and T. Sinai. 2008. "Tax Expenditures for Owner-Occupied Housing: Deductions for Property Taxes and Mortgage Interest and the Exclusion of Imputed Rental Income." *American Economic Review* 98 (2): 84–89.

Poterba, J. M. 1992. "Taxation and Housing: Old Questions, New Answers." *American Economic Review* 82 (2): 237–42.

Poterba, J. M., D. N. Weil, and R. Shiller. 1991. "House Price Dynamics: The Role of Tax Policy and Demography." *Brookings Papers on Economic Activity* 1991 (2): 143–203.

Rosen, S. 1974. "Hedonic Prices and Implicit Markets: Product Differentiation in Pure Competition." *Journal of Political Economy* 82 (1): 34–55.

Sinai, T., and N. S. Souleles. 2005. "Owner-Occupied Housing as a Hedge against Rent Risk." *Quarterly Journal of Economics* 120 (2): 763–89.

United Nations, Commission of the European Communities, International Monetary Fund, Organisation for Economic Co-operation and Development, and World Bank. 2010. System of National Accounts 2008. New York: United Nations. https://unstats.un.org/unsd/nationalaccount/sna2008.asp.

Verbrugge, R. 2008. "The Puzzling Divergence of Rents and User Costs, 1980–2004." *Review of Income and Wealth* 54 (4): 671–99.

Wentland, S., B. Waller, and R. Brastow. 2014. "Estimating the Effect of Crime Risk on Property Values and Time on Market: Evidence from Megan's Law in Virginia." *Real Estate Economics* 42 (1): 223–51.

IV

Methodological Challenges and Advances

13

Off to the Races
A Comparison of Machine Learning and Alternative Data for Predicting Economic Indicators

Jeffrey C. Chen, Abe Dunn, Kyle Hood,
Alexander Driessen, and Andrea Batch

13.1 Introduction

Gross Domestic Product (GDP) is one of the most widely used and cited measures of economic activity. Obtaining timely and accurate GDP estimates is essential for policy makers, the private sector, and individuals making a wide range of economic decisions. However, the Bureau of Economic Analysis (BEA), the agency responsible for producing GDP figures, must produce its initial estimates of GDP prior to when some critical source data are available. Thus, the reliability of advance estimates and the extent to which they capture news rather than noise hinges in part on successfully bridging data gaps.

One approach to bridging data gaps involves working with providers of source data to accelerate production of their estimates. For example, the US Census Bureau accelerated publication of the Monthly Retail Trade and Sales Survey (MRTS) as an advance publication, which has translated into marked reductions in GDP revisions. While effective, this solution can be costly, may place undue burden on respondents, and may reduce the rate of response.

Alternatively, the breadth of timely proprietary data sources has expanded significantly in recent decades. The financial sector has relied on such data (including credit card transactions, email receipts, search queries, etc.) to better forecast economic fundamentals and to anticipate financial performance of companies ahead of quarterly earnings reports. These data have the potential to do the same for official statistics. Nevertheless, these substitute data do suffer from some problems—nontraditional sampling, and large numbers of variables—that strain traditional statistical techniques. Instead, forecasters have developed sophisticated machine learning (ML) techniques in which nonparametric, nonlinear, or otherwise computationally intensive algorithms yield predictions in just this type of environment. This combination of alternative data sources and contemporary ML techniques provides a possible bridge for the data availability gaps that producers of official statistics face.

These advancements are not without challenges and the transparency of ML is often called into question. Some view ML as a black box, especially because the techniques may not lend themselves to traditional modes of linear interpretation and because modeling decisions in nonparametric models may be too voluminous to efficiently evaluate. They also represent a philosophical shift: ML is aimed at producing predictions $\hat{y}_i$ rather than parameter estimates $\hat{\beta}$ (Mullainathan and Spiess 2017). Without being able to understand or interpret coefficients, there are some who argue that we can never fully understand the predictions given by ML models. Nonetheless, it is not the case that studies that use ML are devoid of economic intuition. In our case, the prediction target is of economic significance, and economic intuition will be preserved through the application of national economic accounting principles.

On the data side, newer sources of data can be timelier, but the reliability and stability of alternative sources have yet to be proven for official statistical purposes as they are only a recent phenomenon.[1] The universe captured in alternative sources is not typically disclosed, making it challenging to evaluate the properties of the data.

In this paper, we explore how ML and alternative data sources can play a

---

1. Private sector data sources have been used for many components of the national accounts for decades. While the use of private sector data is not new, the availability and types of alternative data sources have changed dramatically (e.g., credit card data and search queries).

role in stabilizing official national statistics when faced with publication lags. We focus on Personal Consumption Expenditures Services (PCE Services) that account for more than \$9.8 trillion of the current dollar estimate in 2018 (> 45 percent of GDP). Approximately \$4.2 trillion of PCE Services is based on the Quarterly Service Survey (QSS), which is only fully available 75 days after the end of each quarter and informs the third estimate of GDP.[2] The current estimate revision to quarterly GDP has averaged \$27 billion since 2012, with an average revision of \$14 billion attributable to PCE.[3] QSS-based estimates contribute the largest share to PCE revisions, averaging \$11 billion. Thus, by predicting the QSS, estimates using ML and alternative indicators can deliver economic news earlier in the estimate cycle and improve data quality.

Our approach is not to apply an "off-the-shelf" ML algorithm, but rather to dedicate significant attention to the unique features of the problem at hand, while at the same time advocating broad principles that should apply to similar applications. For this purpose, forecasts must be both robust and stable, and we must carefully contemplate the way predictive accuracy should be defined in the national economic accounting context. More specifically, we evaluate potential revisions reductions, (a) for each PCE component across all modeling scenarios; (b) for each algorithm across all PCE components and other modeling choices (dataset, inclusion criteria, etc.); and (c) for combinations of these concepts.

Predicting these types of official statistics presents a unique challenge that guides the approach that we favor. Surveys or censuses are not conducted at high frequencies, and the intersection between their observations and the observations contained in alternative datasets to which we have access yields a rather short time series. The ML paradigm prescribes partitioning data into multiple parts: one for estimation, one for model selection, and one for testing. We do not have enough observations to subset the data into these multiple parts, so we propose a unique approach. Specifically, we estimate thousands of potential models for every series where each model applies distinct methods and data. Rather than selecting just the "best" model, which may overstate the improved prediction, we report and analyze the full distribution of predictions across model scenarios for a large cross-section of series. This approach has two distinct advantages. First, using the cross-section of series allows one to evaluate and identify which modeling decisions result in poor predictions across many series. For example, we find that the method of using a four-quarter moving average performs quite poorly across data series. A second advantage of this approach is that it avoids the overfitting that might occur by selecting only the best model. Instead, using

2. The Census Bureau also publishes an advance estimate of QSS at 45 days; however, it is a limited subset of all series.
3. The revision is calculated as the third estimate less the advance estimate.

a distribution of many models for each series, we can determine which series show consistent improvement across a sample of model scenarios.[4]

The paper is organized as follows. Section 13.2 places this work in the landscape of forecasting and nowcasting literature for macroeconomics. Section 13.3 describes the process of a prediction horse race and criteria for identifying PCE components that can be reliably improved. Section 13.4 examines prediction results, placing an emphasis on producing rules of thumb for modeling and estimating the effects of PCE revisions.

13.2   Literature Review

Traditional forecasting typically employs linear time-series models wherein theory dictates the appropriate estimators; based, for example, on asymptotics and an assumed class of data-generating processes. However, a major constraint—especially of linear models—is that the number of variables that can enter the forecast must be considerably less than the number of observations. This reduces the amount of data that can enter the models to help inform the prediction. The machine learning techniques applied in this paper are not bound by this constraint and allow for the consideration of a much larger number of variables.[5] The disadvantages associated with this approach are in the necessity to put one's faith in model validation and testing.

The popularity of Big Data and machine learning has been growing rapidly in the forecasting literature over the last decade. Our paper differs from many of these studies not so much in the techniques that are applied, but in the objects that we are forecasting. To our knowledge, forecasts using Big Data for incorporation into official statistics is a rather unique application. The closest application of these techniques in the recent literature has been to nowcast Macroeconomic aggregates.

A major benefit of writing a paper in a field that is growing in popularity is the existence of recent, high-quality review articles. Einav and Levin (2013) provide an overview of important concepts, data sources, and common fore-

---

4. This approach is in the spirit of Leamer (1983), who advocated reporting a broad distribution of models as he was concerned that researchers searching for the "correct" specification may cause a high degree of bias; and more recently Athey and Imbens (2015), who are concerned with misspecification uncertainty.

5. It is not impossible to approach problems with more predictors than observations using a more traditional paradigm, and many of the important conventions of ML, such as validation and testing, are not unique thereto. Frequentist approaches applicable to such problems include model selection (for a review see Kadane and Lazar 2004), model averaging (some recent examples include Hansen 2007, and Hansen and Racine 2012) and factor models (cf. Stock and Watson 2006). Bayesian model averaging may also be applied to "wide" data sets, using dimensionality-reduction techniques or stochastic searches (Fragoso, Bertoli, and Louzada 2018). ML is thus one among many approaches that could be applied. Nevertheless, it is particularly well-suited to this problem based on the sheer number of right-hand-side variable combinations that are possible.

casting techniques. They note that the larger scale, breadth of variables, and lack of structure present new opportunities, but also new problems that must be dealt with by the researcher. In addition, they note the need for cross-validation—a technique that is rarely used by economists but is essential in this context. Varian (2014) also offers an overview and a sort of how-to guide in applying machine learning techniques to big data, while identifying where these techniques originated in the broader scientific literature. Kapetanios and Papailias (2018) provide an extensive review of very recent studies that have used these techniques, organized by prediction target (unemployment, inflation, output, and financial variables), as well as a detailed discussion of many important techniques.

Because in this paper we focus on near-term forecasts of the recent past, what we are doing can be called nowcasting. Nowcasting is a portmanteau of "now" and "forecasting," and was defined by Giannone, Reichlin, and Small (2008) to comprise forecasting of the recent past, present, or near future. However, we are not exposed to several problems that are particular to nowcasting: "ragged edges" in which because of real-time data flow, the forecaster does not have access to all data series at all points in time, and mixed-frequency data. As such, our application has more of a forecasting flavor.[6]

The constellation of big data, machine learning, and nowcasting has spawned a literature that is somewhat distinct from the "traditional" nowcasting literature. This is precisely because these two approaches generally deal with a distinct collection of complications. Traditional approaches of regression and time series analysis have ready-made solutions to the ragged edge problem (that use, e.g., a Kalman filter), while the machine learning literature has generally ignored such considerations. As such, the types of Big Data that machine learning typically uses are somewhat different. Nevertheless, there is a recent and growing literature in this field summarized by Kapetanios and Papailias (2018). Biau and D'Elia (2012), for example, use survey data and a random forest algorithm to nowcast Euro-Area GDP; Nyman and Ormerod (2017) use a random forest algorithm to predict recessions; and Choi and Varian (2012) use Google Trends to nowcast several

6. Earlier nowcasting work relied on regression-based methods, which include what is termed "bridging" or "bridge equations" and MIDAS regressions (cf. Bańbura, Giannone, and Reichlin 2011 for a review). Bridging uses time aggregation of monthly data combined with regression analysis to produce a nowcast, while in MIDAS models (Ghysels, Santa-Clara, and Valkanov 2004), variables of different frequencies directly enter the regression equation. The ragged edge problem is solved with the application of "state-space" models in which variables that are used in the nowcast but are missing are themselves forecasted, a process typically implemented via a Kalman filter. Subsequent attempts to nowcast macroeconomic variables with large datasets involved the application of data-reduction techniques—for example, dynamic factor models (Bańbura et al. 2013). Bok et al. (2017) describe the New York Fed's nowcasting approach, which synthesizes many of these techniques. This summary does not cover the whole of the recent nowcasting literature, and so we refer the reader to Kapetanios and Papailias (2018) for a more detailed overview.

macroeconomic indicators such as auto sales and unemployment claims. Rajkumar (2017) compares various algorithms, including a random forest, to predict surprises in GDP growth.

Finally, the adoption of any type of nowcasting technique for "filling in" series that are not yet available to be used in official statistics has few examples in the literature. Cavallo et al. (2018) use the "billion prices project" data (Cavallo and Rigobon 2016) to produce high-frequency purchasing power parities (PPPs), which could be used to bridge the period between releases of the World Bank's Penn World Table's International Comparisons Program's PPPs. Similar price indices might also be used to replace certain headline numbers such as Argentina's CPI, which is believed to be unreliable (Cavallo and Rigobon 2016). B. Chen and Hood (2018) use traditional nowcasting techniques (bridge equations, bridging with factors) combined with model selection to nowcast detailed components of personal consumption expenditures on services that go into the calculation of GDP, showing the potential for significant reductions in revisions in many of these components.

13.3   Methods and Data

13.3.1   Modeling Considerations

The objective of this study is to reduce revisions to GDP by identifying predictive approaches that offer consistent improvements. There are challenges in this task, particularly in how we account for the properties of the data and in identifying where prediction can be reliably applied.

The properties of input data that are typically used for national economic accounts combined with the properties of alternative data present a unique forecasting challenge. Survey or census time series tend to be relatively coarse (e.g., monthly, quarterly, or annual). When used in conjunction with alternative data (which are a recent phenomenon, as mentioned above), the resulting time series tends to be short. The alternative data that we use, however, have a very broad cross-sectional dimension. As such, the number of variables, k, significantly exceeds the number of observations, n, a situation that is not a good fit for traditional statistical analysis. For this type of application, the problem with regression-based models is not that they are inaccurate (although they may be), but that they cannot even be estimated. One solution is to apply theory-driven methods that prune the input variables so that a model can be estimated, but this has proven to be ineffective for many applications (Stock and Watson 2014). Methods such as stepwise regression leave in inputs that are highly correlated with the series being predicted, but because pruning is based on in-sample correlations, estimation often results in overfitting and poor out-of-sample predictions.

In contrast, many ML techniques are designed for just this purpose, relying on a combination of model validation techniques and implicit variable selection. Traditional approaches often posit a "true model" that will obtain with enough observations, while ML focuses on producing generalizable predictions, using flexible nonlinear approaches such as bootstrap aggregation or shrinkage to overcome overfitting, and relying nearly exclusively on partitioning to assess fit and select models. As mentioned above, there are some trade-offs, but these types of models are needed to integrate into estimates the signal coming from these timely but high-dimensional datasets.

In this application, we are faced with a further problem that not only is the number of independent variables relatively large, but also the number of observations is small in absolute terms. Having a small sample size reduces power. Not only are a model's opportunities to learn economic patterns limited, but it is less likely to be resilient to structural instabilities that cause prediction accuracy to erode (Rossi 2013). Model selection also becomes challenging. When applying conventional forecast comparison techniques such as the Diebold-Mariano Test (Diebold and Mariano 1995), the lack of power prevents crowning a winning model. One can imagine a scenario in which a forecast model achieves lower error than its alternatives within the sample, but the relative performance may not persist as the sample grows. This is particularly problematic if researchers estimate many forecasting models and then choose to report only their best-fitting estimate, which results in overfitting problems and poor out-of-sample performance.

Small sample size is not a problem that ML is specifically designed for. Standard application of ML algorithms might involve splitting the data into three sets: One for training (estimation), one for validation (in this case, model selection), and one for testing (assessment of fit). Fit (i.e., accuracy) cannot be assessed using any part of the sample on which estimation or model selection is done, and model selection cannot be done using the sample from which the models were estimated. If we were to divide all 30-some quarters into three distinct sets, no inferences could be made with reasonable statistical power.

For this reason, we propose to run a prediction "horse-race," in which we estimate a large collection of models for each series. We vary these models along several dimensions: algorithm, data, and variable selection. By varying the conditions and comparing their results through a prediction horse race, we can determine which dimensions drive accuracy for each industry. If one modeling choice seems to produce inaccurate predictions in most series that are being forecasted, or if one modeling choice seems to do the best on average, we can decide as to which modeling choices can be included or excluded from the final ensemble. In our analysis, model performance is gauged by pooling the estimates of fit (root mean squared revision, or RMSR) of all models and series into a single dataset. A statistical analysis is then performed to assess the effect of each modeling choice on the expected revision.

In the subsequent subsections, we describe the process of constructing thousands of models that are trained under a multitude of modeling scenarios (e.g., combinations of algorithms, data, and variable selection procedures). We then construct measures of revision reductions and a simple framework to rate PCE components that are well suited for this prediction approach.

13.3.2 Prediction Models

We conduct a horse race between different algorithms, data, and variable selection procedures (each individual combination of the three we call a "model") the results of which are compared with current BEA methodologies to evaluate the improvement. Each model can be expressed as

$$y_{it} = f_m[g_k(X_t)],$$

where y_{it} is the not seasonally adjusted (NSA) quarterly growth in percentages of a QSS industry i in time t, f_m is any one of nine ML algorithms (see section 13.1.1), X_t is a matrix of input variables and dependent lags in the form of quarterly growths at time t, and g_k is the procedure k for variable selection that guides how input variables are included (see section 13.3.3).[7]

13.3.2.1   Algorithms

A diverse array of algorithms is selected that interact with the data in different ways. Some are commonly employed in the social sciences, whereas others are used in sectors that rely more heavily on data science techniques. We categorize these techniques into two broad buckets: *linear methods* and *nonparametric methods*.

To represent techniques that overlap with the traditional econometric toolkit, we consider four linear methods:

Four-Quarter Moving Average (4QMA). The simplest of the linear methods is the 4QMA that smooths the univariate series using a one-year sliding window:

$$\hat{y}_{it} = \frac{1}{4} \sum_{j=1}^{4} \frac{y_{i,t-j}}{y_{i,t-j-1}},$$

where j is an index of prior quarters. The effect is an extrapolation that appears to be seasonally adjusted. Its simplicity is also its weakness, producing predictions with the risk of carrying forward momentum from prior periods and ignoring contemporaneous information.

---

7. We model growth rates rather than trends or levels because growth rates in the QSS are applied to update PCE estimates, not the levels. Moreover, through the benchmarking and revision process, levels will eventually be replaced with data from more reliable sources.

Forward Stepwise Regression (Stepwise). Forward stepwise regression is an automated variable selection procedure built around linear regression. The process adds variables to a regression one at a time, doing so based on partial *F*-tests. Each step of the process is computationally intensive, starting by estimating a null model without predictors, then adding one variable at a time starting with the lowest partial *F*-test that is below a predefined threshold α. This requires that a set of candidate models is estimated prior to adding new variables (Efroymson 1960). We set $\alpha = 0.05$, requiring additional variables to yield partial *F*-test values below the threshold. In addition, given the small sample constraints, we place a cap on the number of parameters at $k = \sqrt{n}$. The technique has drawbacks, particularly that it conducts variable selection in-sample that results in predictions that are not generalizable (Copas 1983). In addition, the estimate is constructed on unconstrained least squares, so that ill-posed problems where $k > n$ are noninvertible.

Ridge Regression and Least Absolute Shrinkage and Selection Operator (LASSO). Several challenges with stepwise methods are addressed through regularized least squares methods, which introduce a constraint that forces sparse solutions in the regression coefficients. We consider two varieties: *Ridge Regression* (Hoerl and Kennard 1970) and *Least Absolute Shrinkage and Selection Operator (LASSO) regression* (Tibshirani 1996).

Ridge regression modifies least squares by adding a preselected constant λ into the coefficient estimator:

$$\hat{\beta} = (X'X + \lambda I)^{-1}X'Y.$$

The parameter estimates are obtained by minimizing the penalized sum of squares with a l_2 norm penalty:

$$PSS = \sum_{i=1}^{n}\left(y_i - \sum_{j=1}^{m}x_{ij}\beta_j\right)^2 + \lambda\sum_{j=1}^{m}\beta_j^2.$$

By adding the penalty, we can see that as coefficient β_j grows, the cost function is penalized and places greater preferences for smaller coefficients. The value of λ is tuned through *k*-fold cross-validation to minimize the cost function. A more recent innovation to this method is the LASSO model, that makes a simple modification to the penalty—replacing the *l2* norm with a *l*1 norm:

$$PSS = \sum_{i=1}^{n}\left(y_i - \sum_{j=1}^{m}x_{ij}\beta_j\right)^2 + \lambda\sum_{j=1}^{m}| \beta_j |.$$

Whereas the Ridge regression forces smaller parameter estimates, LASSO conducts variable selection by forcing some parameters to the edge case of exactly zero. While regularized least squares methods is an improvement on least squares, linear methods may not capture nonlinearities and interactions that nonparametric algorithms can. We thus also consider five non-parametric techniques that are more flexible.

Regression Trees (CART). The building block for a number of these nonparametric techniques is Classification and Regression Trees (CART), more specifically the *regression tree* (Breiman et al. 1984). The objective of CART is to recursively split a sample into smaller, more homogeneous partitions known as nodes. Each split yields two child nodes that are defined by a threshold θ along variable x_j:

$$I^- = \{i: x_j < \theta\}$$

$$I^+ = \{i: x_j \geq \theta\},$$

where I^- and I^+ are sets of observations that are below and above θ. As multiple values of θ are considered, the best θ minimizes the sum of squares:

$$SS = \sum_{i \in I^-}(y_i - \bar{y}^-)^2 + \sum_{i \in I^+}(y_i - \bar{y}^+)^2,$$

in which y^- and y^+ are the mean of y_i for candidate partitions above and below θ. Each resulting child node $(X_i, y_i)_{i \in I^-}$ and $(X_i, y_i)_{i \in I^+}$ is further partitioned until it cannot be split any further or when additional splits do not improve the model fit. Each terminal node is referred to as a *leaf c*. A fully-grown tree minimizes the sum of squares of tree f:

$$SS = \sum_{c=1}^{C}\sum_{i=1}^{n}(y_i - \hat{y}_c)^2,$$

where C are all leaves in the tree, n is the number of observations within a leaf c, and $\hat{y}_c = (1/n)\sum_{i=1}^{n} y_i$.

While we can see that CART implicitly conducts variable selection by selecting split thresholds along variables, each node could in theory be split until all leaves are $n = 1$. An overgrown, overly complex CART thus may overfit the data and introduce unnecessary variance into predictions. One remedy is to *prune* the tree to reduce the complexity, choosing a level of complexity that minimizes out-of-sample error. In small samples, however, these tuning strategies may have minimal effect on the quality of predictions as each leaf is an average of a small cell of observations that lend little statistically meaningful support.

Random Forests. Regression trees can be improved upon by an ensemble method known as random forests (Breiman 2001). The algorithm process is simple:

1. Construct B number of samples with replacement with n observations and m randomly drawn variables from X.

2. Train regression tree f_b on the sample b.
3. Average the predictions from each f_b to obtain $\hat{y}_i$,

$$\hat{y}_i = \frac{1}{B}\sum_{b=1}^{B} f_{bm}(x_i),$$

where $B = 500$ in this study and the number of variables m per tree is determined through tuning.

This technique offers a couple of gains over regression trees. First, constructing many trees under similar but randomly drawn conditions minimizes model variance while keeping bias uniform. Second, the bootstrapping builds in a natural validation sample to calculate the *out-of-bag* (OOB) error for evaluating generalizability of predictions.[8] Parameter tuning can also take advantage of the OOB error by training random forest algorithms under varying conditions such as variables per tree, then *comparing* the average OOB error between models.

Gradient Boosting (XG Boost). Another ensemble technique that has gained in popularity is *gradient boosting*. As developed in Friedman (2001), gradient boosting generates m-number of base learners $f_m(x)$ that are trained to correct errors made by prior iterations. Each base learner $f_m(x)$ is a *weak learner*—a model that may only have slightly better than random predictive power. In this case, we rely on a decision stump, which is a regression tree with only one split. Each base learner is generated sequentially and added to produce a prediction $F_M(x)$,

$$F_M(x) = \sum_{m=1}^{M} \eta f_m(x),$$

where η is a shrinkage parameter between 0 and 1 that controls the rate in which the boosting model converges and has been shown to be an effective way to mitigate overfitting. As η decreases, the number of iterations M required to converge needs to be increased—these parameters are tuned together.

At some iteration m, the loss will have effectively converged, meaning that the addition of subsequent base learners may add noise to estimates and use unnecessary computational resources. For simplicity, we set the $M = 300$ with a learning rate of $\eta = 0.05$, but specify an early stopping rule that ends training if 15 consecutive iterations fail to improve the model. We rely on XGBoost implementation of the technique as described in T. Chen and Guestrin (2016).

---

8. The out-of-bag error is the error based on the observations left out of the bootstrap draw, which is commonly applied in ML models.

Support Vector Regression (SVR). SVR fits a linear regression on input data that has been mapped using a nonlinear function. The nonlinear function can take on various functions $k(x_i, x_j)$, such as a Gaussian radial basis function kernel:

$$k(x_i,x_j) = \exp(|x_i - x_j|^2).$$

Here, $k(x_i, x_j)$ transforms the input variables x into a higher-dimensional space to better model patterns in the data. The linear regression yields a hyperplane in which each y_i resides within a hard margin of error ε: $(\hat{y}_i - \varepsilon) \leq y_i \leq (\hat{y}_i + \varepsilon)$. Each prediction $\hat{y}_i$ is found on this hyperplane. This constrained optimization problem can be infeasible as some observations may lie beyond the margin; thus, a cost parameter C can "soften" the margins. A soft margin of error allows some observations to reside beyond the margin but penalizes those observations by their distance from the margin (i.e., the amount of "slack" they are permitted), thereby regularizing the model to reduce the incidence of overfitting (Drucker et al. 1997).

SVR may require more time to train than other algorithms, thus for cost efficiency, we tune the cost parameter C along a grid for a sample of industry targets, then fix values of the parameters for all other industries based on the optimum.

Multiadaptive Regression Splines (MARS). MARS fits k-number of basis functions that are combined to produce a prediction (Friedman 1991):

$$\hat{f}(x) = \sum_{i=1}^{k}\alpha_i b_i(x),$$

where each basis function b_i is weighted by a coefficient α_i learned by minimizing the sum of squared errors. Each basis function $b_i(x)$ can take on one of three forms: a constant term—or intercept, a hinge function, or the interaction of hinge functions. Hinge functions fit splines to the data—allowing a regression line to bend at a threshold along x so that the slopes may vary on either side. By taking advantage of a potentially large number of splines, MARS molds to the nonlinearities and discontinuities in even highly dimensional datasets, but a potentially large number of basis functions may overfit the data. The technique thus unfolds as a two-step process: a forward stage and a backward stage. The forward stage fits and weights candidate pairs of hinge functions, choosing only to add the pair to the overall model if it reduces training error by the largest margin. The *backward pass* mitigates overfitting by removing least effective terms subject to generalized cross validation.

We apply MARS using an open-source implementation called *earth* (Milborrow 2018). The forward pass requires tuning the degree of interaction effects among basis functions. The backward pass is also tuned based on the number of terms to retain. We conduct a grid search by considering

Table 13.1   **Algorithms considered for the prediction horse race**

Technique	Training and tuning procedure
Linear Methods	
4-quarter moving average (4QMA)	Calculate 4-quarter moving average.
Forward stepwise regression	Set max number of parameters k to the square root of the sample size.
LASSO regression	Leave-one-out cross-validation to find value of lambda that minimizes mean squared error.
Ridge regression	Leave-one-out cross validation to find value of lambda that minimizes mean squared error.
Nonparametric Methods	
Regression trees	Grow tree to full depth and cross-validate error in each step, then select tree complexity that minimizes MSE.
Random forests (RF)	Number of trees set to 500. Select the number of variables per tree along a grid of possible values choosing the lowest OOB error.
Gradient boosting	Set maximum iterations to 300, $\eta\eta = 0.05$, early stopping if model error does not improve after 15 rounds.
Multiadaptive regression splines (MARS)	Tune over a search grid of degree of interaction effects (1 to 3) and number of terms to retain during pruning pass (5, 10, 15).
Support vector regression (SVR) with radial basis function (RBF)	Search hyperparameter CC along a grid for a sample of industry targets, then fix values of the parameters for all other industries based on the optimum.

all combinations of interaction effects for degrees 1 through 3 and number of retained terms (5, 10, 15).

A summary list of the different methods is shown in table 13.1 for reference.

13.3.2.2   Variable Selection

Models are only as good as their inputs. Too much information may lead to an overfitted model and highly variable predictions. Too little information places disproportionate weight on a few variables, thereby introducing bias into predictions. In machine learning, a happy medium involves conducting dimensionality reduction to reduce the number of variables considered, while still extracting the key information from the variables. Sample size constraints may limit the effectiveness of more sophisticated variable selection techniques.

We instead consider two contrasting approaches that represent the extremes of variable selection: *cherry picking* and *kitchen sink*. Economic intuition tends toward parsimonious specifications, including only variables that capture economic and behavioral forces. Thus, cherry picking in this context is defined as the inclusion of input variables that are conceptually like the left-hand-side variable. For example, if physician offices revenue (NAICS 6211) is the target, then only medical-related factors are included as input variables. However, if important information is omitted, then models are underfit and can miss the trend.

Alternatively, kitchen sink models include all available data, placing no assumption on which variables should be included. This implies that the algorithms have the capacity to conduct implicit variable selection and can incorporate information without introducing excess noise.

13.3.2.3 Data Sources

National accounts are an amalgam of public and private sources. In fact, private source data are incorporated in various areas of economic measurement such as motor vehicle production and Value Put In Place (VPIP) estimates for construction. Alternative private data offer the possibility of capturing news that may otherwise be overlooked by indicator series or projections, though recognizing that private administrative data are collected with a goal other than national statistics (e.g., profit maximization). Thus, our proposed machine learning–alternative data hybrid should not be viewed as a replacement for current projection methods, but rather a supplemental source that is run in parallel and assesses the validity of current projections.

The target series are 188 industry time series published in the QSS, available in time for the third estimate of GDP. To ensure predictions produce an output that is useful for estimate production, we target NSA percentage quarterly growths for both revenue and expenditure series for a 31-quarter period—between the second quarter of 2010 and the first quarter of 2018.

We assemble a variety of input data from traditional and alternative sources (for a summary see table 13.2). Among traditional sources are NSA aggregates from the Bureau of Labor Statistics' (BLS) Current Employment Survey (CES) and Consumer Price Indexes (CPI). These sources are currently used in estimating national indicators, are publicly available and constructed on probability samples—in other words, these are generalizable samples with known universes and quantifiable biases.

Two alternative data sources are considered. First, credit card transactions are acquired from First Data, which offers credit card processing services for a network of merchants across the United States. The data are available daily within the first 10 days after the end of a month and are processed by Palantir using a methodology developed by the Federal Reserve Board of Governors (Aladangady et al., forthcoming). To minimize the effect of churn, each monthly transaction estimate only includes merchants that have been First Data customers within the prior 13 months. These data provide a timely view into purchasing behavior, trading representativeness off with timeliness.

Table 13.2   **Data sources used for this prediction study**

Data	Description	Economic relevance
Census Bureau Quarterly Services Survey (QSS)	Longitudinal survey of 19,000 US businesses operating in the services sector.	Key input into BEA's Personal Consumption Expenditure (PCE) series.
BLS Current Employment Survey (CES)	Employment estimates released monthly, converted into quarterly average. CES is currently relied on for national accounting estimates. Contains 140 industry series.	Employment trends that coincide and trend with consumption.
BLS Consumer Price Indexes (CPI)	National-level price indices for products and are currently relied on for national accounting estimates. Each CPI is associated to NAICS code based on keyword similarity. Contains 600+ series	Price changes of items that are consumed alongside services.
First Data credit card transactions	Near real-time credit card transaction aggregates, converted from Merchant Class Codes (MCC) to NAICS. Contains 192 industry series.	Contemporaneous measure of consumption.
Google Trends	Monthly activity indices for search queries, Google News topics, and Froogle shopping activity. Converted from search terms to NAICS based on keyword similarity. Contains 240 industry series.	Gauge of interest and prospective buying behavior on the internet.

Google Trends is another source of timely, near-real-time data that covers a wide range of activity. In many respects, trends gauge public interest in various economically related issues, as captured through Google's online offerings, including Google Search, Google News, and Froogle. One hundred and sixty keywords were derived from QSS NAICS definitions and monthly estimates for the period 2003 through 2017 were requested via the Google Trends API. The API returned 240 volume indexes that were constructed from a simple random sample of search queries, aggregated into a time series of proportion of total Google search activity, and indexed to the maximum search volume share in the time series.

13.3.2.4   One-Step Ahead Validation

Of the $n = 31$ observations, $n = 12$ are set aside for validating performance. As our objective is to generalize and apply models, we simulate the PCE estimation process using a one-step-ahead model validation. The model validation technique is an iterative one, producing each $\hat{y}_{it}$ by training on all data $t < T$, then applying the prediction developed on data points $t < T$ to produce a prediction for the observation $t = T$. For each of the 12 validation quarters, we retrain each model by growing the data's time window (see

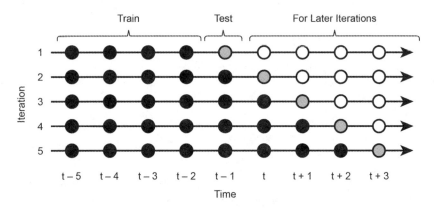

Fig. 13.1   One-step ahead model validation design

Note: The X axis represents both the training set (black) and test set (gray). The Y axis represents the prediction time periods.

figure 13.1), thereby producing predictions that are responsive to evolving economic patterns. In figure 13.1 we start with a prediction for $T = 0$ and use time periods $T = -1$ and less to form this prediction. We next move one step ahead to predict time $T = 1$ using information in time periods $T = 0$ and lower to form the prediction. The predictions in period $T = 2$ and future periods proceed accordingly. While the number of observations per prediction grows with time, we assume that the benefits of greater accuracy and stability among the predictions should affect all models in the same way.

In total, 73,884 model scenarios were trained and produced predictions for 12 consecutive validation quarters, resulting in 886,608 model runs and predictions.

13.4   Evaluating Performance and Revision Reduction

When a large sample is available, a robust model selection framework should include both a model validation step (e.g., one step ahead or k-fold cross-validation) to aid in selecting the most generalizable model and a test step to revalidate the chosen model's performance. The sample available for this study, however, is not sufficiently large to afford a test set, thus a model chosen from thousands of candidates may run the risk of overfitting the data. We instead take a conservative approach that evaluates performance by selecting ensembles of models developed under common conditions. For an industry i, for example, all models that were trained using a random forest would be considered one ensemble, whereas all models that rely on BLS CES would be considered another.

First, we train thousands of models for a cross-section of 188 QSS series covering many industries using one-step-ahead validation. QSS predictions $\hat{y}_{it}$ are converted into PCE component estimates $\hat{C}_m$ for a model m:

$$\hat{C}_m = g_c(\hat{y}_{it}),$$

where g_c is BEA's PCE estimation process that seasonally adjusts and converts available QSS data into components estimates. Note that some PCE components rely on only one QSS series while others rely on multiple.

A prediction model applied where revisions are unlikely to reduce revisions will likely add error to official estimates, so it is important to evaluate the reduction in revisions. From the perspective of data quality, an estimate should only be used if revision reductions are consistently expected across a broad distribution of models. We construct two measures to evaluate revision reduction potential: The *Mean Revision Reduction Probability (MRRP)* and the *Proportion of Improved Periods (PIP)*.

Proportion of Improved Periods (PIP). It is easy to imagine that an ensemble can reduce revisions on average, but masks generally poor individual quarter-to-quarter performance. The PIP is the proportion of the test period that would have had a revision reduction had a given model been applied. This measure captures the consistency of revision reductions over time, placing emphasis on cases where there is a net improvement over current BEA methodology:

$$\text{PIP}_m = \frac{1}{T} \sum_{i=1}^{T} (|\hat{C}_{m,t} - C_{third,t}| < |\hat{C}_{current,t} - C_{third,t}|).$$

To summarize proportion of improved periods for each component PIP_c, we calculate the proportion of models that yield improvements in the majority of historical quarters:

$$\text{PIP}_c = \frac{1}{M} \sum_{m=1}^{M} (\text{PIP}_m > 0.5).$$

In small samples, it may be challenging to distinguish models on their performance and to some extent can be viewed as an arbitrary decision. Thus, when PIP_c is high, we would have some surety that a model selected at random could improve component C at least a majority of the time. Conversely, a low PIP_c value indicates that a prediction strategy poses an increased risk of increasing quarterly revisions in component C.

Mean Revision Reduction Probability (MRRP). Whereas PIP captures revision reductions with respect to time, we also consider how often average dollar revision reductions yield improvements to PCE components in the long run. MRRP is based on the Root Mean Square Revision (RMSR) that compares PCE $\hat{C}_m$ to the actual third estimate of PCE, resulting in

$$\text{RMSR}_m = \sqrt{\frac{1}{n} \sum_{i=1}^{n} (\hat{C}_m - C_{third})^2}.$$

Similarly, RMSR is calculated for the current projection methodology:

$$RMSR_{current} = \sqrt{\frac{1}{n}\sum_{i=1}^{n}(\hat{C}_{current} - C_{third})^2}.$$

Relative revisions ($\Delta RMSR_m$) are expressed as the dollar difference between $RMSR_m$ and $RMSR_{current}$, where a negative value indicates a revision reduction:

$$\Delta RMSR_m = RMSR_m - RMSR_{current}.$$

Looking across a set of M models, we summarize their collective performance as the Mean Revision Reduction Probability (MRRP), defined as

$$MRRP_c = \frac{1}{M}\sum_{m=1}^{M}(\Delta RMSR_m < 0),$$

in which we are interested in the proportion of models that can achieve a net revision reduction. Like PIP, an arbitrary model selected to predict a component with a high MRRP value is more likely to yield revision reductions.

Together, PIP and MRRP can be summarized by taking the harmonic mean:

$$\mu_k = 2 \times \frac{MRRP \times PIP}{MRRP + PIP},$$

where larger values of μ_k indicate more revision reductions. In samples with little power, μ_k could be used as the basis for identifying the number of components that should be included to maximize revision reductions; However, in this study, we use μ_k to examine the revision impacts of applying a prediction strategy at a predefined cutoff, namely $\mu_k \geq 0.8$.

13.5   Results

13.5.1   QSS Predictions

We sift through the manifold of results to better understand which algorithms, datasets and modeling practices contribute to prediction performance. The process generates 393 sets of predictions for each of the 188 QSS series, representing possible growth paths under a broad set of assumptions.

Taking a closer look at key industries shown in figure 13.2, we see that the mass of the out-of-sample predictions tends to follow the variation in the target series. The center mass of the predictions over time also tends to have a central tendency, which suggests that prediction of the QSS growth is generally possible regardless of the modeling scenario.

Each algorithm reacts to data selection in a different way. The predictions for the physician offices category are a prime example, shown in figure 13.3.

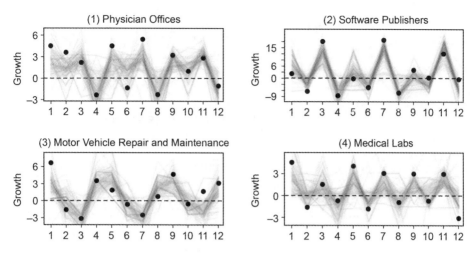

Fig. 13.2 Comparison of actual QSS quarterly growths (black dot) with 393 sets of out-of-sample predictions (gray lines)

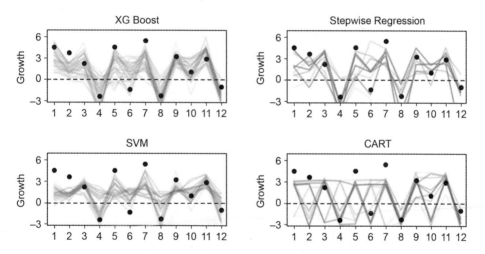

Fig. 13.3 Comparison of different modeling assumptions applied to physician services series

Stepwise and CART regressions are prone to overfitting the data and are sensitive to high-leverage data points. Rather than producing a diffuse cloud of predictions that have correlated movements, they produce a discrete set of predictions, many of which perform relatively poorly. In contrast, the XG Boost and SVM algorithms produce predictions that are more dispersed. However, none of the poorer prediction paths is particularly prominent; in some of these cases there are algorithms that seem to be flatter, but none that show highly variable fluctuations nowhere near the actual data like the CART algorithm does. Rather, the central tendency in these algorithms is toward the actual data.

Model selection for prediction use cases is guided by finding the model with the lowest error: given a series of models, we could choose the model that minimizes a squared loss function. This selection paradigm is effective when the sample size is large; however, as discussed previously, crowning a specific model champion is a foolhardy task with only $n = 12$, as the model selection process may overfit the data.

Instead, we take advantage of the sheer number of out-of-sample predictions to identify conditions that generally maximize predictive performance across a large cross-section of 188 series that we study. We estimate a simple fixed effect regression to extract the average contribution of each modeling dimension:

$$\text{RMSE}_{i,k,m} = \beta + \alpha_i + \gamma_m + \xi_k + \varepsilon_{i,k,m}.$$

As we would expect, some industries are more predictable than others due to sampling variability and volatility in the sector; thus, we control for industry fixed effects α_i. γ_m is a matrix of dummy variables for each model type (e.g., extreme gradient boost xg, random forests rf). ξ_k represents the data and variable selection procedures (e.g., cherry picking, CES, Google). From the resulting regressions reported in table 13.3, we can determine which modeling strategies tend to perform better in matching the QSS estimates.

13.5.1.1 Algorithms

Aside from the industry fixed effects, the choice of algorithm appears to have the greatest overall influence on RMSE. Among algorithms, we find that tree-based ensemble techniques offer the greatest improvements: relative to stepwise regression, random forests and gradient boosting reduce RMSEs on average -0.56 and -0.43 percentage points, respectively. LASSO regression offers an improvement over stepwise. In contrast, MARS and moving averages should be avoided due to their overwhelmingly poor performance. It is worth noting that prediction is a game of wins at the margins—if a technique does not perform well across industries, there is still a chance that it can offer consistent accuracy gains for individual industries. Nevertheless, because we lack the data to assess all of the series individually, we have to assess the performance of these models more generally.

13.5.1.2 Data and Variable Selection

The data and variable selection dimensions suggest three takeaways.

- There are diminishing returns to adding additional data sources. For example, the coefficients imply that if First Data is added as a data source instead of Google Trends, the reduction in error is -0.81. How-

Table 13.3   **Industry fixed-effect regression results with clustered standard errors**

	(1)	(2)	(3)
Constant	5.01 (0.06)***	6 (0.08)***	6.01 (0.09)***
Algorithms (Ref = stepwise regression)			
4Q moving average	1.97 (0.23)***		2.16 (0.25)***
Ridge regression	0.04 (0.07)		0.04 (0.07)
LASSO	–0.16 (0.04)***		–0.16 (0.04)***
CART	0.69 (0.11)***		0.69 (0.11)***
Random forest	–0.55 (0.05)***		–0.56 (0.06)***
Gradient boosting	–0.42 (0.05)***		–0.43 (0.05)***
SVM regression	0.25 (0.1)**		0.25 (0.1)**
MARS	1.47 (0.13)***		1.48 (0.13)***
Data (Ref = Google)			
CES		–0.86 (0.1)***	–0.97 (0.11)***
First Data		–0.72 (0.08)***	–0.81 (0.09)***
Consumer Price Indexes		–0.35 (0.06)***	–0.39 (0.07)***
Dependent lags		–0.83 (0.11)***	–0.87 (0.11)***
Variable selection (Ref = kitchen sink)			
. . .Cherry Picking		0.22 (0.05)***	0.28 (0.06)***
Number of data sets (Ref = 1)			
2 sets		0.36 (0.05)***	0.31 (0.05)***
3 sets		0.81 (0.1)***	0.8 (0.11)***
Fixed effects	Yes	Yes	Yes
N	73,884	73,884	73,884
R^2	0.64	0.62	0.65
Adjusted R^2	0.64	0.62	0.65
Residual standard error	2.75	2.83	2.72

ever, if First Data is added as a second data source, the reduction in RMSE is −0.5 (= −0.8 + 0.3). If First Data is added as a third data source, there is an even smaller reduction in RMSE (−0.3 = 0.8 + (0.8 − 0.3)). Moreover, more data are not necessarily better (e.g., adding Google as a second or third data source would increase RMSE).

• Second, models that are constructed on a purely conceptual basis may not necessarily translate into statistically accurate results. Cherry-picked specifications add an average of 0.28 percentage points to the RMSE, meaning that specifications motivated by conceptual assumptions may omit some useful information from predictions or introduce noise. Thus, relying on the implicit variable selection of the machine learning techniques to surface predictive variables offers some gains.

• Lastly, the Current Employment Survey and dependent lags of QSS, both of which have long been available publicly, on average have the greatest influence on prediction quality. The CES and CPIs are both currently used for the national economic accounts and if combined with machine learning could likely offer improvements in estimates.

The fixed effects from the above regression also provide estimates of the predictability of each QSS industry series. This is important because some series may be generally harder to predict than others, across all the methods that we consider. The difficulty in predicting a series could be related to a variety of factors, such as the volatility of an industry or the sampling error of the series that we are attempting to predict. To investigate the relationship with sampling error, we compare the average prediction error ($\beta_0 + \alpha_i$) and the Census Bureau–reported average sampling error for the QSS. If there were no prediction error, then all the error would come from sampling and our prediction error would be directly proportional to sampling error (dashed diagonal line), and for a few cases this is nearly the case—such as motor vehicle repair and maintenance, spectator sports, and insurance carriers. However, as shown in figure 13.4, we find that most prediction error is higher than the sampling error (as expected). Increases in sampling error are problematic for our model predictions; with a 1 percentage point increase in the target series' sampling error, prediction error increases at a rate of 0.56 percentage points. This serves as a reminder that predictions are only as strong as the targets they mimic.

While our goal is to identify the winner of the prediction horse race discussed above, we do not wish to pare the results down too much based only on this regression. We note, however, that algorithm is the single most important factor in determining RMSE, with a range of about 2.5 percentage points between the best- and the worst-performing algorithms. Because

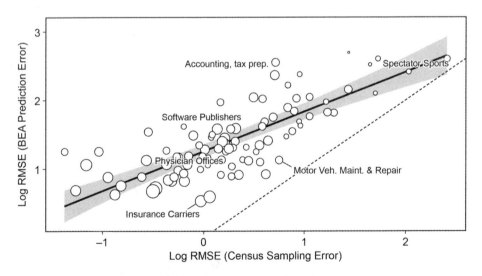

Fig. 13.4   Comparison of survey sampling error vs. prediction error
Note: Each point represents an industry, scaled by its total revenue or expenditure as of 2018-Q1. Transparency denotes statistical significance of fixed effect estimate—solid red indicates highly significant at the 1% level. Dashed diagonal line is the line of equality.

along this dimension, the performance is improved by the largest margin, we elect in the following exercise to retain all combinations of all other dimensions (dataset, scope), but retain only the most effective algorithm choice. The random forest algorithm generally seems to perform the best, and the second best (grading boosting) is a modification of the random forest algorithm. These two methods are both ensemble techniques, which form estimates based on averaging many nonlinear models. Nonlinear models that are not ensemble methods, such as CART and MARS, perform relatively poorly.

In subsequent sections, we evaluate the performance of the optimal modeling strategy based on a collection of 47 random forest models that were constructed under a variety of conditions.

13.5.2   Revision Reductions

Upon converting predictions of QSS to PCE estimates, each component of PCE can be evaluated on whether it may lead to revision reductions relative to current practice based on our measures of improved fit (PIP and MRRP). We consider 71 PCE services subcomponents—all of which incorporate one or more QSS series. We find that there is at least one prediction model for each of the 71 components that can improve upon current BEA methods. In large samples, this would be a reasonable finding. However, this is an overly optimistic conclusion for a small sample that lacks statistical power.

Instead, as we mentioned previously, we take a more conservative approach to evaluate models using measures of revision reductions (PIP and MRRP) to identify modeling strategies that on average yield improvements. In principle, one would place greater confidence in predicting a component in which 90 percent of models can reduce revisions rather than a component in which only 1 percent of models can meet the task. In low power samples, selecting a specific model from a pool of alternative models is like drawing a model at random. Thus, the chance of overfitting would arguably be less likely in the former case. Comparing across PCE components, the bubble chart (figure 13.5) shows significant heterogeneity in predictability—higher scores indicate greater surety that a model is not a random improvement. A component in the larger grey area indicates that one in two models can reduce revisions ($p \geq 50$) whereas the smaller box indicates that 8 in 10 models can reduce revisions ($p \geq 80$).

Based on these cutoffs, we find that 20 PCE components have at a least a coin flip's chance or better of seeing revision reductions—three of which have historically averaged at least $1 billion in revisions per quarter. This is not to say that other components are not predictable, but rather there is a far smaller margin of error for selecting a reliable model, especially given the limited sample size. When reviewing the less predictable components, we find evidence that evaluating components on only one loss function could reduce

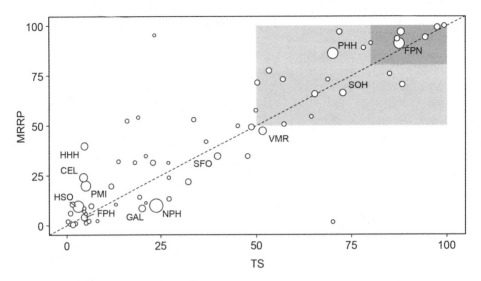

Fig. 13.5   Comparison of MRRP and TS for each PCE services component

Note: Circles are scaled based on average quarterly revisions under current BEA methodology and labeled when revisions exceed $1 billion.

data quality. MRRP alone would overstate the consistency of revision reductions because improvements could be concentrated in only a minority of time periods. For example, nearly half of the models predicting HHH (For-Profit Home Health Care Services) satisfy the condition ΔRMSR < 0, but less than 10 percent can improve estimates in at least a majority of test periods. Components like HHH have one or two large revision reductions that mask suboptimal performance in all other quarters.

The story becomes more nuanced as we evaluate among alternative modeling strategies for each PCE component. Figure 13.6 shows TS and MRRP across various modeling strategies for selected components. Generally, the consensus, or lack thereof, gives clues about what contributes to accuracy. Several components are predictable when applying almost any modeling strategy. Physician Services (PHH) and Specialty Outpatient Care (SOH) fall into this category, which translates as a need for fine-tuning toward optima rather that conducting an exhaustive search. Other components like Non-Profit Hospitals (NPH) have little chance of improvement regardless of the modeling strategy. These two scenarios may be due to a combination of the magnitude in sampling error of the underlying target series and availability of input variables. In contrast, modeling strategies for certain components fail to achieve consensus, such as in the case of motor vehicle repair and maintenance (MVR). However, two algorithms stand apart in their ability to reduce revisions. We can infer that accuracy in this case may be more likely a matter of identifying the appropriate functional form.

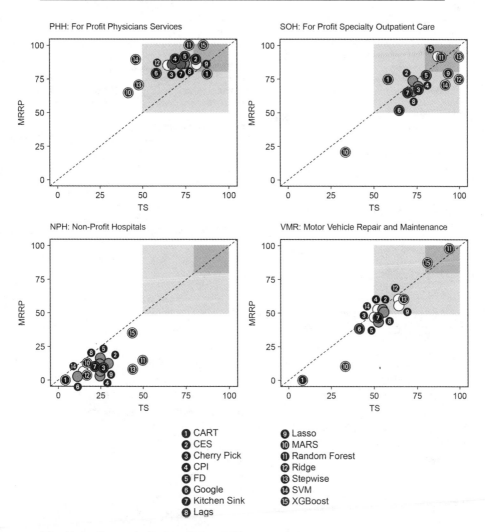

Fig. 13.6   **Comparison of MRRP and TS for four PCE services components by modeling component**

While revision reductions for individual subcomponents can be easily evaluated, the ability to achieve revision reductions among top line measures (e.g., overall PCE and PCE services) is more challenging due to *offsetting*. Given two subcomponents that are added together to estimate a more aggregate PCE component, one may have upward revision reductions and the other may have downward revision reductions. When added together, the revision reductions may partially offset one another, muting the magnitude of improvement to top-line measures. We estimate net revision reductions for the most versatile modeling strategy, random forest. Only PCE compo-

Table 13.4   Estimated revision reductions in historical test sample when only applying random forest to components that have at least an 80% chance of improvement

Component	Percent				Levels ($Mil)		Direction	
	10th	Mean	Median	90th	Mean	Median	ML	Current
PCE	5.59	12.17	13.11	18.33	2054.75	2213.61	100	100
PCE services	0.2	10.3	11.78	19.72	1552.69	1775.76	100	100
Health care	2.23	11.27	12.64	18.99	1442.62	1618	100	100
Transportation	2.91	25.57	26.7	43.86	1100.38	1149.29	75	67
Recreation	4.28	8.47	8.28	12.75	349.73	341.88	92	83
Education	1.74	3.25	3.11	5.16	17.6	16.83	100	100
Professional and other	1.38	4.2	3.72	7.02	77.84	68.89	75	67
Personal care and clothing	21.8	27.37	28.24	31.03	513.85	530.18	92	83
Social services and religious	10.29	14.21	14.7	17.82	155.06	160.42	83	83
Household maintenance	−24.25	10.94	16.71	34.38	45.49	69.49	100	92
GO NP social services	0.07	0.43	0.47	0.74	9.37	10.2	33	33
GO NP prof advocacy	26.24	36.99	41.03	47.8	235.12	260.79	100	100

Notes: Percent correct direction indicates if the ensemble mean's growth accurately anticipates the actual series' direction of growth (positive or negative). GO NP denotes Gross Output for Nonprofit.

nents where $\mu_k \geq 80$ are included in the calculations. The impact analysis in table 13.4 reflects the contributions of 20 PCE components, each of which has an ensemble of 50 models reflecting a broad range of assumptions.

Starting from the topline, we find that overall PCE revisions would have been reduced on average 12 percent with an ensemble median of 13 percent, translating to approximately $2 billion in net revision reductions. The ensemble's upper shoulder suggests that some of the better performing models within the ensemble could achieve as much as a 21.3 percent revision reduction ($3.6 billion); however, individual model selection would only be possible when statistical power is sufficiently large in the validation sample. Within PCE services, several components attain even larger revision reductions, with health care and transportation services leading (in absolute terms) with average 11.3 percent and 25.6 percent improvements, respectively.

While the shape of growth is matched by the models, the ability to correctly anticipate the direction of growth—whether it is positive or negative—has apparent effects on the levels. Anticipating a deceleration when growth is accelerating reduces estimate quality and magnifies revisions. We evaluate the performance of the ensemble average relative to current performance using the validation period. As would be expected, current BEA methods are able to anticipate direction of growth in most periods. While we do not find improvements among higher aggregate components of PCE, the prediction ensemble marginally improves subcomponents with one quarter improvement.

13.6   Conclusion

In this paper, we illustrate a suitable use of machine learning techniques for macroeconomic estimation. We focus on improving data quality by reducing revisions to PCE service components. Our proposed approach provides predictions of advanced estimates using machine learning techniques and identifies PCE components for which prediction-based improvements are likely.

In general, nonparametric techniques such as random forest and gradient boosting offer marked gains in prediction accuracy and are well adapted to conducting implicit variable selection at scale. Furthermore, these techniques can accommodate the typical ill-posed problem, sifting through quantities of data without significant loss in prediction quality.

One key evaluation point for macroeconomic prediction is its ability to detect economic downturns. As the current incarnation of the QSS does not span the 2008–2009 recession, it is not possible to test for downturns although it may be applied to anticipating other indicator series. Prior studies such Chauvet and Potter (2013) found that commonly used macroeconomic techniques for forecasting output, such as autoregressive models of a variety of builds, generally perform well during expansions but poorly in recessions. While we are unable to test the machine learning models in this context, we can foresee the likely performance of these nonparametric techniques during recessionary periods by taking note of the core assumptions. Like linear models, nonparametric algorithms are designed for stationary processes. Unlike linear models, the predicted values $\hat{y}_i$ are bounded by the range of y in the training sample. In small samples that do not span recessions, we can assume that the shape of economic growth can be predicted, but the depth of a contraction will likely be understated. A model switching mechanism such as a Markov switching model should be incorporated to provide greater flexibility to use both nonparametric and parametric extrapolators.

There are opportunities to improve the stability of predictions while increasing revision reductions. One extension is to train an additional model to marshal predictions and cut through the noise of less reliable models. Model averaging, as in the case of Hansen (2007), can improve predictions subject to a linear constraint. More generally, model stacking techniques offer a more flexible solution in which a supervised machine learning algorithm trains on values of $\hat{y}_i$ from the validation set to produce predictions. In either case, additional training observations would be required for the averaging and stacking model to learn which underlying models are in fact predictive. As the sample size is a constraint, we may adopt the leave-one-out model validation strategy as described in Cornwall et al. (2019) to expand the training sample while meeting Granger causality criteria.

This study also finds that prediction error will only grow with sampling error, as expected; therefore, industries with large sampling error limit the ability for the current strategy to predict highly variable PCE components.

One approach to overcome sampling error is to consider a top-down hierarchical forecasting model (Hyndman et al. 2016), predicting the top-line estimates of PCE, then sharing growth by component by modeling conditional probabilities. A benefit is that each component is logically consistent with parent series and has a decent degree of accuracy among low error series, but sampling error and noise may still pose a challenge. An alternative but more costly solution involves improving the underlying survey's sample design by oversampling strata with large sampling error. We recognize this would incur greater cost relative to a modeling strategy but may be a necessity for estimate quality.

This paper shows that using both traditional and alternative data sources can contribute to improved predictions. However, there are issues outside of the prediction methodology that should also be considered. For instance, while private data sources may lead to better predictions, the cost, quality, and availability of these data sources may change for external reasons (e.g., a company failing or a change in management). Users of alternative data sources should be mindful of the long-term availability and stability of these sources. Nevertheless, these concerns will be relevant irrespective of the methods that are applied, and it is worth noting that a benefit of the ML approach is that it reduces reliance on a single data source.

While the macroeconomic literature incorporating machine learning is in its nascent stages, we show that computationally intensive algorithms do in fact offer measurable improvements for estimates of the PCE Services component of GDP. There is considerable scope for future research to apply these techniques to other components of GDP, as well as other national statistics.

References

Aladangady, Aditya, Shifrah Aron-Dine, Wendy Dunn, Laura Feiveson, Paul Lengermann, and Claudia Sahm. Forthcoming. "From Transactions Data to Economic Statistics: Constructing Real-Time, High-Frequency, Geographic Measures of Consumer Spending." National Bureau of Economic Research. https://www.nber.org/books-and-chapters/big-data-twenty-first-century-economic-statistics/transactions-data-economic-statistics-constructing-real-time-high-frequency-geographic-measures.
Athey, Susan, and Guido Imbens. 2015. "A Measure of Robustness to Misspecification." *American Economic Review* 105 (5): 476–80.
Bańbura, Marta, Domenico Giannone, Michele Modugno, and Lucrezia Reichlin. 2013. "Now-Casting and the Real-Time Data Flow." In *Handbook of Economic Forecasting*, vol. 2a, edited by G. Elliott and A. Timmermann. Amsterdam: Elsevier.
Bańbura, Marta, Domenico Giannone, and Lucrezia Reichlin. 2011. "Nowcasting." In *The Oxford Handbook of Economic Forecasting*, edited by M. P. Clements and D. F. Hendry. Oxford: Oxford University Press.

Biau, Olivier, and Angela D'Elia. 2012. "Euro Area GDP Forecasting Using Large Survey Datasets: A Random Forest Approach." Euroindicators Working Papers EWP-2011-002. https://ec.europa.eu/eurostat/web/products-eurostat-news/-/EWP-2011-002.

Bok, Brandyn, Daniele Caratelli, Domenico Giannone, Argia Sbordone, and Andrea Tambalotti. 2017. "Macroeconomic Nowcasting and Forecasting with Big Data." *Federal Reserve Bank of New York Staff Reports.* https://www.newyorkfed.org/medialibrary/media/research/staff_reports/sr830.pdf.

Breiman, Leo. 2001. "Random Forests." *Machine Learning* 45 (1): 5–32.

Breiman, Leo, Jerome H. Friedman, R. A. Olshen, and Charles J. Stone. 1984. *Classification and Regression Trees.* Boca Raton, FL: Chapman and Hall/CRC.

Cavallo, Alberto, W. Erwin Diewert, Robert C. Feenstra, Robert Inklaar, and Marcel P. Timmer. 2018. "Using Online Prices for Measuring Real Consumption across Countries." *AEA Papers and Proceedings* 108:483–87.

Cavallo, Alberto, and Roberto Rigobon. 2016. "The Billion Prices Project: Using Online Prices for Measurement and Research." *Journal of Economic Perspectives* 30 (2): 151–78.

Chauvet, Marcelle, and Simon Potter. 2013. *Forecasting Output,* vol. 2. Amsterdam: Elsevier.

Chen, Baoline, and Kyle Hood. 2018. "Nowcasting Private Consumption of Services in the U.S. National Accounts with a Bridging with Factor Framework." Paper presented at Fifth Annual Conference of the Society for Economic Measurement, Xiamen, China, June 8–10, 2018.

Chen, Tianqi, and Carlos Guestrin. 2016. "XGBoost: A Scalable Tree Boosting System." *Proceedings of the 22nd ACM SIGKDD International Conference on Knowledge Discovery and Data Mining,* 785, 794. New York: Association for Computing Machinery. http://doi.acm.org/10.1145/2939672.2939785.

Choi, Hyunyoung, and Hal Varian. 2012. "Predicting the Present with Google Trends." *Economic Record* 88 (s1): 2–9.

Copas, J. B. 1983. "Regression, Prediction and Shrinkage." *Journal of the Royal Statistical Society, Series B* 45:311–54.

Cornwall, Gary, Jeffrey A. Mills, Beau A. Sauley, and Huibin Weng. 2019. "Predictive Testing for Granger Causality via Posterior Simulation and Cross Validation." In *Topics in Identification, Limited Dependent Variables, Partial Observability, Experimentation, and Flexible Modeling: Part A,* Advances in Econometrics Series, vol. 40A, edited by Ivan Jeliazkov and Justin L. Tobias, 275–92. Bingley, UK: Emerald Publishing Limited. https://doi.org/10.1108/S0731-905320190000040A012.

Diebold, Francis X., and Roberto S. Mariano. 1995. "Comparing Predictive Accuracy." *Journal of Business and Economic Statistics* 13 (3): 253–63.

Drucker, Harris, Christopher J. C. Burges, Linda Kaufman, Alexander J. Smola, and Vladimir N. Vapnik. 1997. "Support Vector Regression Machines." *Advances in Neural Information Processing Systems* 9:155–61.

Efroymson, M. A. 1960. "Multiple Regression Analysis." In *Mathematical Methods for Digital Computers,* edited by A. Ralston and H. S. Wilf. New York: John Wiley.

Einav, Liran, and Jonathan Levin. 2013. "The Data Revolution and Economic Analysis." *Innovation Policy and the Economy* 14: 1–24.

Fragoso, Tiago M., Wesley Bertoli, and Francisco Louzada. 2018. "Bayesian Model Averaging: A Systematic Review and Conceptual Classification." *International Statistical Review* 86 (1): 1–28.

Friedman, Jerome H. 1991. "Multivariate Adaptive Regression Splines." *Annals of Statistics* 19 (1): 1–141.

———. 2001. "Greedy Function Approximation: A Gradient Boosting Machine." *Annals of Statistics* 29 (5): 1189–1232.

Ghysels, Eric, Pedro Santa-Clara, and Rossen Valkanov. 2004. "The MIDAS Touch: Mixed Data Sampling Regression Models." *CIRANO Working Papers*. https:// EconPapers.repec.org/RePEc:cir:cirwor:2004s-20.

Giannone, Domenico, Lucrezia Reichlin, and David Small. 2008. "Nowcasting: The Real-Time Informational Content of Macroeconomic Data." *Journal of Monetary Economics* 55 (4): 665–76.

Hansen, Bruce E. 2007. "Least Squares Model Averaging." *Econometrica* 75 (4): 1175–89.

Hansen, Bruce E., and Jeffrey S. Racine. 2012. "Jackknife Model Averaging." *Journal of Econometrics* 167:38–46.

Hoerl, Arthur E., and Robert W. Kennard. 1970. "Ridge Regression: Biased Estimation for Nonorthogonal Problems." *Technometrics* 32 (1): 80–86.

Hyndman, Rob J., Roman A. Ahmed, George Athanasopoulos, and Han L. Shang. 2016. "Optimal Combination Forecasts for Hierarchical Time Series." *Computational Statistics and Data Analysis* 55 (9): 2579–89.

Kadane, Joseph B., and Nicole A. Lazar. 2004. "Methods and Criteria for Model Selection." *Journal of the American Statistical Association* 99 (465): 279–90.

Kapetanios, George, and Fotis Papailias. 2018. "Big Data and Macroeconomic Nowcasting: Methodological Review." ESCoE Discussion Papers 2018-12, Economic Statistics Centre of Excellence. https://EconPapers.repec.org/RePEc:nsr:escoed :escoe-dp-2018-12.

Leamer, E. 1983. "Let's Take the Con Out of Econometrics." *American Economic Review* 73 (1): 31–43.

Milborrow, Stephen. 2018. *Earth: Multivariate Adaptive Regression Splines*. https:// CRAN.R-project.org/package=earth.

Mullainathan, Sendhil, and Jann Spiess. 2017. "Machine Learning: An Applied Econometric Approach." *Journal of Economic Perspectives* 31 (2): 87–106. https:// doi.org/10.1257/jep.31.2.87.

Nyman, Rickard, and Paul Ormerod. 2017. "Predicting Economic Recessions Using Machine Learning Algorithms." https://arxiv.org/abs/1701.01428v1.

Rajkumar, Veg. 2017. "Predicting Surprises to GDP: A Comparison of Econometric and Machine Learning Techniques." Thesis, MIT Sloan School of Management, Cambridge, MA.

Rossi, Barbara. 2013. "Advances in Forecasting under Instability." In *Handbook of Economic Forecasting*, vol. 2, edited by G. Elliott, C. Granger, and A. Timmermann, 1203–324. Amsterdam: Elsevier.

Stock, James H., and Mark W. Watson. 2006. *Forecasting with Many Predictors*. Vol. 1. Amsterdam: Elsevier.

———. 2014. "Estimating Turning Points Using Large Data Sets." *Journal of Econometrics* 178 (Part 2): 368–81.

Tibshirani, Robert. 1996. "Regression Shrinkage and Selection via the Lasso." *Journal of the Royal Statistical Society, Series B* 58 (1): 267–88.

Varian, Hal. 2014. "Big Data: New Tricks for Econometrics." *Journal of Economic Perspectives* 28 (2): 3–28.

14

A Machine Learning Analysis of Seasonal and Cyclical Sales in Weekly Scanner Data

Rishab Guha and Serena Ng

14.1 Introduction

A mindboggling amount of data is now available for economists to analyze. This is made possible by improved technology in data collection and storage. Modern data differ from conventional data in at least two important ways: they tend not to be provided by government agencies, and they have what data scientists refer to as the "three V" characteristics: volume, variety, and velocity. Econometricians may think of them as short panels of big, often unbalanced, high-frequency, highly heterogeneous data. Such granular data can potentially allow new analyses of economic behavior. However, a full analysis of the data comes with unique challenges. A case in point is the weekly Nielsen Retail Scanner dataset, which has been collected since 2006 and has added roughly half a terabyte of data each year, reaching a size of about five terabytes in 2016.

Rishab Guha is a John M. Olin Fellow in Empirical Law and Finance, and a PhD candidate in business economics at Harvard University.

Serena Ng is the Edwin W. Rickert Professor of Economics at Columbia University, and a research associate at the National Bureau of Economic Research.

This analysis is based in part on data from The Nielsen Company (US), LLC and marketing databases provided through the Nielsen Datasets at the Kilts Center for Marketing Data Center at The University of Chicago Booth School of Business. The conclusions drawn from the Nielsen data are our own and do not reflect the views of Nielsen. Nielsen is not responsible for, had no role in, and was not involved in analyzing and preparing the results reported herein.

We thank Gary Cornwall at the BEA, the discussant Ramon Huerta, and seminar participants at the NBER Summer Institute and Amazon for helpful comments. All errors are our own. Finally, support from the National Science Foundation (Ng, SES-1558623) is gratefully acknowledged. For acknowledgments, sources of research support, and disclosure of the authors' material financial relationships, if any, please see https://www.nber.org/books-and -chapters/big-data-21st-century-economic-statistics/machine-learning-analysis-seasonal -and-cyclical-sales-weekly-scanner-data.

The Nielsen dataset has three features of interest. First, it consists of real-time sales and unit prices recorded at the store/UPC-code level. Such transactions data are distinctly different from official price indices that are survey based. Second, the data are not subject to revisions once a transaction is completed; they are also less susceptible to measurement errors because the data are digitally recorded. Third, the data are available for the major metropolitan areas and thus provide spatial information distinct from the official monthly retail sales data. The weekly data also provide higher frequency information than in quarterly and annual surveys. Fourth, many memorable events have occurred over the span of the sample: a big recession, destructive hurricanes, several elections, new tax initiatives, and a government shutdown. Though the weekly aspect of the data seems like it should appeal to researchers, work thus far has mostly aggregated the data to a monthly or quarterly frequency without taking advantage of the weekly information. With just a peek at the data, one understands why: the data exhibit strong seasonal patterns that are highly heterogeneous in the product and spatial dimensions. As will be shown below, this is true not only in our base case analysis for the four most populous states, but also in extended analyses that include more regions and states. The weekly data have limited use for business cycle analysis without a way to deconvolve the seasonal variations from the cyclical ones.[1]

The obvious solution is to seasonally adjust one series at a time. Unfortunately, there are few satisfactory methods for seasonally adjusting weekly data, let alone for a massive number of series. We argue below that the short span and the quasiperiodic nature of the Nielsen data make perfect adjustment of each series highly unlikely. This is problematic because in our data, counties within a state are likely to share common seasonal patterns. Even if the residual seasonal effects are negligible at the individual series level, they can become nontrivial when aggregated across counties.

This paper develops a framework for seasonally adjusting a large panel of data in which common and idiosyncratic seasonal variations coexist. We suggest complementing univariate seasonal adjustments with a second step that pools counties within a state to remove the within-year common seasonal variations, one year at a time. Our premise is that a good deal of the within-year variations are highly predictable *ex ante*. Hence, we treat within-year seasonal adjustment as a prediction problem. To find the prediction model of unknown functional form in the face of a large set of potential predictors, we use machine learning methods to perform estimation and variable selection. This bypasses the need to specify a single data-generating process, which is a difficult task when the data are so highly heterogeneous. Though our approach is rather model-agnostic, the adjusted data are no lon-

---

1. With some abuse of terminology, holiday effects will also be treated as seasonal variations.

ger dominated by seasonal effects so that insights about consumer behavior can be learned from analysis of demand systems.

In theory, Engel curves should be spanned by functions of prices and income that are common across product groups. Traditional demand analyses indirectly parameterize these latent processes by flexible functions. Consistent estimation of the underlying parameters is possible when T (the number of time periods) tend to infinity with N_g (the number of product groups) fixed. Given that $N_g = 108$ and $T = 469$ are reasonably large in our data, we can take advantage of results developed in large dimensional factor analysis to estimate the latent functions of prices and income directly. Big Data therefore provide a perspective of demand analysis that was not possible in the conventional small N_g large T setting.

Our demand analysis of the seasonally adjusted data leads to four conclusions. First, the demand systems are well described by three common factors relating to the trend, level, and curvature of Engel curves. Second, even though the data are primarily based on sales at grocery and mass merchandise stores, there is surprisingly clear evidence of cyclical spending patterns. The cyclical components move closely with measures of consumer sentiment and consumer confidence, indicating that the actions and "feelings" of consumers are aligned. Third, an analysis of the loadings on the cyclical factor yields a "distribution" of recession sensitivity across product groups. The budget share of a FOOD-IN basket, which collects goods related to home production of food, tends to be strongly countercyclical, while that of a LUXURY basket is procyclical, consistent with evidence from the monthly Consumer Price Index (CPI) weights. Fourth, recession sensitivity has a spatial dimension as cyclical changes in spending on the FOOD-IN basket are larger in metropolitan than rural areas. We use heatmaps to illustrate the changes in FOOD-IN as the economy moves through the business cycle. The data also reveal how consumers in the New York area adapted to changes in spending due to Hurricane Sandy. Overall, the business cycle information in the scanner data seems roughly consistent with the less granular official data. This is good news because it suggests that there is valuable higher-frequency information about consumer spending at the aggregate and local levels once the seasonal variations are removed. The proposed two-step procedure can be adapted to other panels so long as the variations to be removed are sufficiently pervasive for pooling to be effective.

The rest of the paper proceeds as follows. We begin in section 14.2 with a description of the data and highlight the presence of common seasonality. Section 14.3 discusses the challenges posed by cross-section dependence that seasonal adjustments must overcome. Section 14.4 presents our two-step approach and elaborates how the second step is formulated as a prediction problem. Section 14.5 analyzes the properties of the seasonally adjusted data and documents how the different products and regions react to changing economic conditions. Section 14.6 concludes.

14.2   The Data

The Nielsen Retail Scanner data are collected by the Nielsen marketing group and managed by the Kilts Center for Marketing at the University of Chicago. The data have over 1,000 products belonging to over 115 product groups (e.g., beer, wine, eggs) that can in turn be organized into 10 categories: dry groceries, frozen, dairy, deli meat, fresh food, nonfood, alcoholic beverage, general merchandise, health, and beauty. The data are heavily weighted toward groceries and mass-merchandise goods, with limited coverage of consumer durables. Specifically, the products cover over 3 million universal product codes (UPCs) collected from over 35,000 participating stores in 55 MSAs (Metropolitan Statistical Areas) across the United States. Each store reports weekly data for every UPC code that had any sales volume during the week. Nielsen uses a Saturday week-ending label to identify the week in which the data are reported. We have information about the location of the retailer (but not the name), the units sold, and the volume weighted average of the product for that week. Following Nielsen's documentation, a week's total dollar sales is calculated as

$$\text{sales} = \frac{\text{price}}{\text{prmult}} \times \text{units.}$$

The *movement files* of the database provide data for UNITS (the number of units sold), PRICE (the volume weighted average price of the product for the week), PRMULT (a price multiplier to indicate deals such as three for $1).

We analyze the total sales of products within a product group (hereafter simply referred to as "groups"). The sales data are constructed as follows. For each state, s, we first compile a list of stores that report a sale in at least one of the 115 groups in each of the 469 weeks between Saturday, January 7, 2006, and Saturday, December 27, 2014. Restricting attention to groups with data in every week reduces the number of groups from 115 to $N_g = 108$. This gives a balanced panel of stores. Throughout, we will use "county" to reference a specific geographic county (e.g., New York County, New York). We let $s(i)$ denote the state containing county i.

The variables are indexed as shown in table 14.1.

Group by group, we construct a measure of weekly total sales at the county level by aggregating over all stores located in each county within the compiled list. The variable of interest is $\log(sales_{gct})$, the log sales of group g

Table 14.1   Index variables

	County	Group	Week	Year
Index	cc	gg	tt	$\tau\tau$
Total	NN_{cc}	$NN_{gg} = 108$	$TT = 469$	$NN_{yr} = 9$

Table 14.2   **Budget shares (%): Most-purchased product groups**

CA: NN_{cc} = 53		FL: NN_{cc} = 58		NY: NN_{cc} = 58		TX: NN_{cc} = 161	
Share	Description	Share	Description	Share	Description	Share	Description
3.4	bread	4.5	medications	4.2	medications	3.8	carbon. bev.
3.4	beer	4.3	tobacco	3.3	fresh produce	3.7	medications
3.3	juice	3.1	carbon. bev.	3.2	bread	3.4	snacks
3.2	wine	2.9	liquor	3.1	candy	3.0	bread
3.1	fresh produce	2.8	beer	2.9	snacks	2.8	tobacco
3.1	carbon. bev.	2.7	juice	2.8	juice	2.7	packaged meat
3.0	snacks	2.7	candy	2.6	tobacco	2.6	candy
2.8	packaged meat	2.5	snacks	2.6	beer	2.6	fresh produce
2.7	salad dressing	2.3	milk	2.4	carbon. bev.	2.6	juice
2.7	medication	2.3	bread	2.3	milk	2.5	beer

in county $c(s)$ in week t. Since a county is state-specific, the state index s will be suppressed when the context is clear. At each week t, the budget share of an arbitrary group $g \in [1, N_g]$ is

$$\text{share}_{gt}^s = \frac{\sum_{c(s)} sales_{gc(s)t}^s}{\sum_g \sum_{c(s)} sales_{gc(s)t}^s} = \frac{\text{sales of group } g \text{ in state } s \text{ at week } t}{\text{total sales in state } s \text{ at week } t}.$$

Our base case analysis uses data from the four most populated states in the US: California (CA), Florida (FL), New York (NY), and Texas (TX). We also construct a measure of total sales, labeled FOUR, that aggregates sales over the four states. Our extended case adds states from the Midwest (Illinois, Indiana, Iowa, Kansas, Michigan, Minnesota, Missouri, Nebraska, North Dakota, South Dakota, Ohio, Wisconsin), Mid-Atlantic (Delaware, Maryland, New Jersey, Pennsylvania, Virginia, and Washington DC), and Southwest (Arizona, Nevada, and New Mexico). This sample encompasses a total of 24 states (plus DC) covering about 70 percent of the population in the US with sales in 15,631 stores in 1,147 counties. Results that pool over all states in this extended dataset will be labeled SEVEN. The most comprehensive analysis groups the remaining states into MOUNTAIN, PACIFIC NORTHWEST, NEW ENGLAND, and SOUTH for a total of nine regions. The pooled results will be labeled ALL and cover 24,280 stores in 2,095 counties.

The 10 product groups with the largest sales in FOUR are listed in table 14.2 below. The relative importance of the groups is reasonably similar across states, with bread, beer, juice, carbonated beverages, medication, and snacks making the list in each of the four states.[2]

A more systematic analysis of the data requires a framework. We appeal to demand theory, which also forms the basis of price indexes and measures

2. We work with shares instead of sales, which tend to have even stronger seasonal effects.

of cost of living. A (product group based) demand system expresses N_g budget shares in terms of r functions of prices $p = (p_1, \ldots, p_{N_g})'$, and income Y. Hence, we may write $\text{share}_g^s = \sum_{k=1}^r \lambda_{gk}^s(\log p)F_k^s(\log p, \log Y)$. Importantly, the functions $F = (F_1, \ldots, F_r)$ are common across groups. The adding-up constraint requires that F_1^s is a constant.[3] The value r is the dimension of the space spanned by Engel curves and is known in the literature as the rank of a demand system. A rank-one system occurs when budget shares are independent of the level of income, in which case all income elasticities equal one. Rank-two demand systems are linear in log prices but not in log income. Examples include the translog and the linear expenditure system. Many rank-two systems belong to the PIGLOG class discussed in Muellbauer (1975). Quadratic Engel curves can be rank two or rank three. Gorman (1981) shows that exactly aggregable demand systems must have rank no larger than three.

Product-based demand systems were commonly estimated in the 1970s and 1980s to obtain price elasticities and to understand substitutability across products until characteristic-based demand systems became popular. A demand analysis typically proceeds by using flexible functions to approximate the expenditure function. Imposing the axioms of demand theory then allows the shares or sales to be expressed as linear functions of prices, income, and a theoretical price index, say P. Under two-stage budgeting, income can be replaced by total expenditure on the N_g groups. In empirical work, a proxy variable P^* that can be constructed prior to estimation is often used to bypass the cross-equation restrictions imposed by the ideal price index P. For example, the Almost Ideal Demand System (AIDS) of Deaton and Muellbauer (1980) uses Stone's price index defined by $\log P_t^* = \sum_{g=1}^{N_g} \text{share}_{gt} \log(p_{gt})$. Given data for N_g shares and prices, the AIDS regression model is

$$\text{share}_{gt}^s = \lambda_{0g}^s + \sum_{j=1}^{N_g} \lambda_{jg}^s \log p_{gt}^s + \beta_g^s \log(Y_t^s / P_t^{s*}) + e_{gt}^s, \quad t = 1, \ldots, T.$$

The term e_g^s can be due to measurement error or anything that shifts spending for reasons other than changes in prices and income, such as omitted time variation in preferences. In cross-section analysis, T would be the number of households whose spending patterns are recorded. In time series analysis, T would be the number of observations on aggregate spending over long periods of time. With panel data, the same household may be observed more than once. Using data with N_g small and T large, the rank of demand systems is typically estimated to be two or three, and at most four.[4]

We are interested in analyzing all product groups in the Nielsen data available, which is well over 100 in number, not five or six. A large N_g may

---

3. For a discussion on the rank of demand systems, see Lewbel (1991).
4. See, for example, Lewbel (1997, 2003); Banks, Blundell, and Lewbel (1997).

appear to hinder analysis at first glance because the number of parameters in a demand system is quadratic in N_g. But because N_g and T are both large, we may deviate from traditional demand analysis and let the shares data identify the space spanned by the latent functions and its dimensionality without directly using data on prices or of P^*, or make approximations of the expenditure function. To do so, consider the factor representation of the budget shares:

$$\text{share}^s_{gt} = \Lambda^s_g{}' F^s_t + e^s_{gt},$$

where F^s_t is a $r \times 1$ vector of latent factors and Λ^s_g is the corresponding vector of factor loadings. Appealing to theoretical results in the literature for large dimensional factor analysis, we estimate the factors and the loadings by applying the method of principal components to the shares data alone. For a survey of the literature, see Bai and Ng (2008).

In implementation, we take a three-week rolling average of budget shares to smooth out the variations due to temporary promotional sales. Principal components are then estimated from the standardized data.[5] In $s=$ (NY, TX, and FOUR), the largest factor $\hat{F}^s_1$ explains over 0.9 of the variations of PACKAGED-MILK. As eggnog is one of the products in the group, we may think of $\hat{F}^s_1$ as a *Christmas* factor. Other product groups also exhibit recurring patterns toward the end of the year. In California, for example, the share of juice takes a big dip in week 51, while in Florida, the share of haircare products bottoms around week 51.

Figure 14.1 plots the first four factors from the pooled data FOUR. The factors are only identified up to sign, so they are plotted to be procyclical. Recalling that the factors are mutually orthogonal by construction, figure 14.1 indicates the presence of a multitude of seasonal effects. Though all four factors have spikes around week 48, the exact week of the spike is different over years and across factors. Indeed, the spectrum of these factors peaks around but not exactly at the seasonal frequency of $(2\pi j / 52) 208j$ for $j \geq 1$. Though the first two factors are strongly periodic, $\hat{F}_3$ and $\hat{F}_4$ appear somewhat cyclical. Evidently, cyclical and seasonal common factors coexist.

The criterion of Bai and Ng (2019)[6] finds five factors in CA, FL, NY, four factors in TX, and five factors in FOUR. In all cases, the first factor explains about one third of the variations in the data, the first two factors together explain just under 60 percent, while four factors explain around 75 percent of the variations in budget shares. Taking into account that we demeaned the data before estimation by principal components, the actual rank is one

---

5. Since our data are demeaned, the constant factor is controlled for prior to estimation.

6. The criterion is defined as $\bar{r}^s = \min_{k=0, \dots, rmax} \log(1 - \sum^k_{j=1}(\sigma^s_j - \gamma)^2_+) + k \cdot penalty\,(N, T)$, where $penalty\,(\underline{N, T}) = (N + T)/NT \log[NT/(N + T)]$ and σ_j is the j-largest eigenvalue in a $T \times N$ panel $Z = X/\sqrt{NT}$, where X is the given panel of standardized budget shares. A regularization parameter of $\gamma = 0.05$ is used to penalize common variations due to outliers. The maximum number of factors is set to 10.

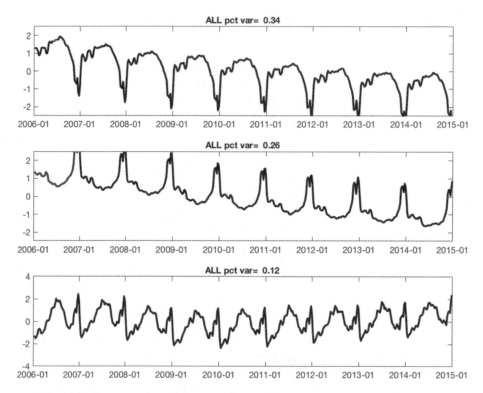

Fig. 14.1   Factors estimated from raw shares: FOUR states

larger than reported above, making the rank of the demand systems in the Nielsen data about twice as large as the estimates typically reported in the literature. In the next section, we show that this finding can be attributed to seasonality.

14.3   Seasonality and Cross-Section Dependence

Consumer theory suggests that it is desirable to smooth consumption over time. But in reality, spending is uneven over the course of a year. It tends to be concentrated around holidays, special events, and toward the last six weeks of the year. In addition to eggnog sales that peak around Christmas, sales of stationery and school supplies peak around week 36. Sales of "cough and cold" products are higher during the winter months, while ice-cream sales are higher in the summer months. Flower sales are higher around Valentine's Day and Mother's Day than the rest of the year. Beer sales tend to be highest around July 4th, while wine sales are higher around Thanksgiving and Christmas. The point to highlight is that such seasonal sales tend to recur every year, though not necessarily on the same day or even the same week. Furthermore, for many of the product groups, the seasonal pattern is similar irrespective of location.

The challenge that seasonality poses for factor analysis is that principal components can identify pervasive variations but are blind to the source of pervasiveness. Hence in the presence of strong common seasonality across product groups, the dominant principal components can be unrelated to cyclical economic conditions. This being the case in our data, a natural approach would be to seasonally adjust each series prior to demand estimation. A variety of univariate methods are available to de-seasonalize monthly and quarterly data, the most notable being X13ARIMA-SEATS and TRAMO-SEATS. However, these methods do not seem appropriate for data with the three V features. For one thing, although we have 469 weekly observations, they only span nine years, meaning that we only have nine data points from a seasonal perspective. Time series seasonal adjustment methods typically assume that we have a large number of observations at the seasonal frequency of interest. Even if an ideal seasonal filter were available, finite sample bias is unavoidable because the span of our data is reasonably short.

Weekly data pose an additional challenge because weekly variations are not exactly periodic. For example, Thanksgiving and Christmas do not always fall on the same numbered week of the year, and July 4th is sometimes in week 26 and sometimes 27. This is a consequence of the fact that we are on a Gregorian calendar. We cannot "difference away" the seasonal effects like we could with monthly and quarterly data. Week-of-year and day-of-year differencing mitigate the problem to some extent, but it cannot capture events that occur on different days of the year, the most difficult to handle being Easter. In our sample, Easter was as late as April 24 in 2011, and as early as March 23 in 2008. Further complicating the problem is that these events have differential impact depending on the product in question and location of the sale. A "one size fits all" seasonal filter is unlikely to ever exist.

The literature for adjusting weekly data is quite sparse. Notable exceptions are the fully parametric state-space analysis of Harvey, Koopman, and Riana (1997) and the nonparametric approach of Pierce, Grupe, and Cleveland (1984), Cleveland and Scott (2007), and Cleveland, Evans, and Scott (2014). Structural time series modeling requires careful specification of the model for the series under investigation. The nonparametric approach is to approximate the seasonal component by basis functions such as trigonometric series. Cleveland, Evans, and Scott (2014) suggest to control for weekly effects, holiday effects, and outliers using locally weighted regressions and apply the method to unemployment income claims and steel production data. But our data have several features that are distinct from these series.

First, the Nielsen sales data tend to be "spiky." For many groups, the spikes only occur once per year, usually around Black Friday. For other series, the spikes can be observed a few times a year and can be attributed to temporary sales. Spikes are problematic because they tend not to be well approximated by nonparametric regressions that are smooth by design. As noted above, we use a three-week rolling average of the data in demand estimation, but this may not be enough to annihilate the problem. Second, some variations do not repeat over the course of the year. Instead, they repeat in reference to a date t's position within the *month*. As an example, consider sales increases around food stamp distributions, or end-of-month price changes. Strictly periodic functions based on fixed positions within the year may be too restrictive for these variations.

A third characteristic of our data is the volume. We have not one, but a large number of heterogeneous and short time series that need to be adjusted. It seems unrealistic to expect any statistical procedure to be able to completely de-seasonalize every series in the panel.

The possibility that a conventionally adjusted series will likely have some residual seasonality has implications for any analysis that involves aggregation of the individually adjusted series. Consider an arbitrary variable Z that has a seasonal and a nonseasonal component:

$$Z_{gct} = Z_{gct}^{nseas} + Z_{gct}^{seas}.$$

In our case, Z_{gct} is normalized sales of product group g in county c at t. Let $\hat{Z}_{gct}^{seas}$ be some $\sqrt{T}$ consistent univariate estimate of the seasonal component of Z_{gct}. The seasonal adjustment error can be decomposed into a term $\hat{e}_{gct}^{seas}$ that is uncorrelated across counties c, and a term $\hat{\Phi}_{gct}$ that is correlated across c; namely,

$$\hat{Z}_{gct}^{seas} - Z_{gct}^{seas} = \hat{\Phi}_{gct}^{seas} + \hat{e}_{gct}^{seas}.$$

Aggregating the data over counties, we have

$$\hat{Z}_{gt}^{nseas} = \sum_{c=1}^{N_c} Z_{gct}^{nseas} + \sum_{c=1}^{N_c} \hat{\Phi}_{gct}^{seas} + \sum_{c=1}^{N_c} \hat{e}_{gct}^{seas}.$$

While $\sum_{c=1}^{N_c} \hat{e}_{gct}^{seas}$ tends to zero as $N_c \to \infty$, the sum of $\hat{\Phi}_{gct}^{seas}$ over c may not be mean zero. Chamberlain (1984) pointed out that Euler equation errors that are mean zero over time need not be mean zero in the cross-section dimension if the units face common shocks. For a similar reason, the seasonal variations left over from an imperfect univariate adjustment can survive aggregation in the presence of common seasonality. This is relevant because we aggregate over counties to obtain total sales for the product group in the state. Since sales in neighboring counties will likely have similar seasonal patterns, aggregation will likely preserve the common seasonal component. Univariate seasonal adjustments yield group-level sales data that may be better characterized by a model with two distinct types of common factors, seasonal and nonseasonal. Figure 14.1 suggests that the seasonal factors dominate.

This is also consistent with the finding in Ng (2017) that the principal components of budget shares constructed from data adjusted from the bottom up continue to exhibit seasonal variations.

14.4   Seasonal Adjustment as a Prediction Problem

Aggregation of the seasonally adjusted data will not, in general, be the same as seasonal adjustment of the aggregate data. If we are only interested in the aggregate series, direct seasonal adjustment of the aggregate series might well be the simplest approach. But when the county- and group-level seasonally adjusted information are both of interest, as is the case here, there is no choice but to perform seasonal adjustment from the bottom up, one (county, group) pair at a time. But the foregoing discussion suggests that existing filters will likely leave residual seasonal variations in the adjusted data. Our proposed approach is to complement the univariate adjustments with an additional step to "mob up" the residual seasonality prior to aggregate analysis.

To motivate our approach, note first that if there is commonality in seasonal patterns, it would seem inefficient to seasonally adjust each series in isolation. Seasonality is in fact a common feature in the sense of Engle and Kozicki (1993), but there is little work in this dimension. Geweke (1978) suggests that a multivariate adjustment might dominate a univariate adjustment in a mean-squared error sense, but the population analysis assumes that the model is correctly specified and abstracts from model and sampling uncertainty. McElroy (2017) considers a multivariate procedure in a large T, small N_g setting. Fok, Franses, and Paap (2007) consider a large T, large N_g panel of data and use a hierarchical Bayes method to avoid the proliferation of dummy variables needed to control for seasonal fixed effects. Like Fok, Franses, and Paap (2007), we also pool information across counties and over time. But instead of treating all dummy predictors as relevant, we train machine learning algorithms to determine which ones to use, and how they are to be used. In other words, we treat a large N_g as a big data blessing. Furthermore, we pool the data across counties and perform adjustment year by year while allowing the prediction model to differ every year.

14.4.1   A Two-Step Panel Approach

In time series analysis, seasonal variations are those that recur with seasonal periodicities. For example, monthly variations are those that recur every twelve months. However, as discussed above, weekly variations are not strictly periodic. This motivates us to use a definition of seasonality that does not depend on periodicity.

Recall that for each state s, we have county-level data over 469 weeks, and group-level sales is the sum over sales in the counties. Our maintained assumption is that sales in the same group g collected in different counties c share common seasonal patterns over the course of a year. In other words, two neighboring counties share seasonal patterns even if one county has 10 times as many sales as the other. As some counties are much larger than others, we demean the data year by year to remove the size effect. We further standardize the data to ensure scale independence across years and locations. Normalized sales within each year and each county are defined as:

$$y_{gct} = \frac{\log(Z_{gct}) - \mu_{pc\tau}}{\sigma_{gc\tau}}, \ \tau = \text{yr}(t),$$

where $\mu_{pc\tau}$ denotes the mean of log sales of group g in county c over the year τ containing week t, and $\mu_{pc\tau}$ is the corresponding standard deviation. The within-year normalization isolates within-year seasonal patterns while preserving long-term trends in aggregate sales and volatility, which the econometrician can model separately. The normalization also allows us to pool observations across counties in subsequent estimation. Pooling county-level data compensates for the relatively short time span of data for each county.

Next, we posit that y_{gct} has three components: a group-specific seasonal component, a common seasonal component, and a cyclical component:

$$y_{gct} = (\text{countyspecificseasonalsales}) + (\text{commonseasonalsales})$$

$$+ (\text{non} - \text{seasonalsales})$$

$$= d_{gct} + q_{gct} + u_{gct}.$$

In this decomposition, the seasonal component of sales is $d_{gct} + q_{gct}$. The goal is to extract u_{gct} when only y_{gct} is observed. An overview of the estimation methodology is as follows:

Step 1: Estimation of d_{gct}: For each (g, c) pair, perform time series estimation of

$$y_{gct} = \alpha_{gc}^0 + \text{Fourier}_{gct}(\beta_{gc}, \psi_{gc}) + \varepsilon_{gct},$$

where using strictly periodic predictors $\delta_{tj} = 2\pi j (\text{dayofyear}_t / \text{daysinyear})$ and $m_{tj} = 2\pi j (\text{Dayofmonth}_t / \text{daysinmount})$,

$$\text{Fourier}_{gct} = \sum_{j=1}^{P_d} \beta_{1,gcj} \sin(\delta_{tj}) + \beta_{2,gcj} \cos(\delta_{tj}) + \sum_{j=1}^{P_m} \psi_{1,gcj} \sin(m_{tj})$$

$$+ \psi_{2,gcj} \cos(m_{tj}).$$

The regression only includes an intercept and will preserve any trends in sales that might be in the data. Hereafter, we will refer to step 1 as the Fourier regression.

We use a simple Fourier regression to fit the seasonal variations at the (g, c) level in step 1 because least squares regression is simple to implement, especially when the predictors are the same across (g, c) pairs. Furthermore, there is a history in using Fourier regressions to first remove deterministic weekly seasonality, followed by ARMA modeling or local regressions to remove the stochastic seasonality one series at a time. But this approach is not practical when the number of series to fit is large. We use machine learning methods in the second step, and we pool information in the spatial dimension.[7]

Step 2: Estimation of q_{gct} from $\hat{\varepsilon}_{gct}$: Let $\hat{\varepsilon}_{gct} = \widehat{q_{gct} + u_{gct}}$ be the least squares residuals from step 1. Because this step is based on estimation of a smooth regression, these residuals will have spikes and can be cross-sectionally correlated. To proceed, we assume that (i) d_{gct} and q_{gct} are partially predictable *over the course of a year*, and (ii) q_{gct} has variations that are common across counties. This allows us to exploit cross-section dependence among counties to remove the within-year seasonal variation. In a nutshell, we pool information across counties to predict the common seasonal component q_{gct} using a large number of predictors, which are mostly dummy variables. To alleviate the problem of overfitting, we use machine learning algorithms to pick out the most important predictors, leaving the functional form of the model unspecified. Details will be explained in the next subsection.

To complete the seasonal adjustment, let $\hat{q}_{gct}$ be the prediction of the common seasonality in $\hat{\varepsilon}_{gct}$ obtained from step 2. From these, we can obtain $\hat{u}_{gct}$, an estimate of u_{gct}. A seasonally adjusted value of log sales is obtained by plugging the estimated residual $\hat{u}_{gct}$ into

(1) $$\widehat{y_{gct}^{sa}} \equiv \hat{u}_{gct} \cdot \sigma_{g\tau} + \mu_{g\tau}.$$

The log seasonally adjusted series has the intuitive interpretation of being the unpredictable part of the series' variation around its overall mean for the year. An estimate of seasonally adjusted sales is $\exp(\widehat{y_{gct}^{sa}} + \text{adj}_{gc})$ where $\text{adj}_{gc} = \sigma_{g\tau}/2$ is a Jensen's inequality adjustment for going from log-levels to levels.

An optional step that we use in the application is to let the relative importance of $\hat{q}_{gct}$ and $\hat{d}_{gct}$ vary across products, using the method of least squares to determine the weights of the two predictable components on y_{gct}:

(2) $$y_{gct} = \alpha_{g0} + \alpha_{g1} \cdot \hat{d}_{gct} + \alpha_{g2} \cdot \hat{q}_{gct} + u_{gct}.$$

Inserting $\hat{u}_{gct}$ into (1) and inverting gives an alternative estimate of log-adjusted sales. We now elaborate on step 2.

14.4.1.1   Predictors $\mathbb{Z}_{gct}$

Regardless of the method used in step 1, we are limited to nine seasonal observations for both training and validation, so the seasonal adjustment is likely imperfect. To more thoroughly remove the seasonal effects, we need to first understand the nature of the seasonal variations in the data. Con-

7. Cleveland and Devlin (1980) suggest using the spectrum to detect preidentified calendar and holiday effects in monthly data. For use of Fourier regressions in seasonal adjustment of weekly data, see Pierce, Grupe, and Cleveland (1984), Cleveland and Scott (2007), and Cleveland, Evans, and Scott (2014).

sider the event Cinco de Mayo. It occurs on a fixed calendar date, and so is not strictly periodic with respect to the weeks within a year. The seasonal effects of Cinco de Mayo may be more important for counties with a higher Hispanic population. Another example is the event of Thanksgiving, which is always on the fourth Thursday in November and is celebrated across the country. The day in the year on which Thanksgiving falls shifts over time.

We need a flexible methodology to capture not just the week of the year and location effects, but also the day-of-the-year effects. The last consideration may seem surprising because our data are weekly. But a major challenge is precisely that many of our seasonal events occur at different days of the year that cannot be parametrically modeled. With this in mind, we consider date- and week-specific dummies as well as demographic and spatial predictors collected into Z_{gct}. These are defined as follows: let $start_t$ denote the date on which week t starts, and end_t denote the date on which week t ends.

A. Date-specific predictors: a dummy variable for each potential calendar date (MM-DD) which is 1 if that date is contained in $[start_t, end_t]$ and 0 otherwise. As an example, if $t =$ Feb 4, 2006, the date-specific predictors Z_{gct}^A is as follows:

01/01	⋯	01/29	⋯	02/04	⋯	12/31
0	⋯	1	⋯	1	⋯	0

B. Week specific predictors.
   (i) $start_t$ and end_t's positions within the year (out of 366)
   (ii) $start_t$ and end_t's position within the months (out of 31)
   (iii) $start_t$'s position within the month containing end_t (this will be a negative number, and differ from the previous column, if and only if the week ending on t crosses two different months)
   (iv) A dummy variable that is 1 if Easter is in the week ending on t, and 0 otherwise
   (v) A dummy variable encoding the month in which end_t falls
   For example, for $t =$ Feb 4, 2006, the week -based predictors Z_{gct}^B will be

(i)	(i)	(ii)	(ii)	(iii)	(iv)	(v) Jan	(v) Feb	⋯	(v) Dec
28	34	29	4	–2	0	0	1	⋯	0

C. Demographic predictors depend only on county c. These variables are drawn from the 2013 American Community Survey, and held constant across time:
   (i) the percentage of the county that is Black, Hispanic, White, and Asian
   (ii) the percentage of the county on SNAP, in poverty, and median household income
   (iii) the percentage of the county c over 60 and under 18

(iv) Centroid latitude, and centroid longitude for the county
(v) NOAA's 30-year estimates of average rainfall and temperature for county c during the week of t (which depend on c and t)

The predictors in list A are day-of-the-year dummies. As distinct from list A, the predictors in list B capture the Gregorian calendar effects at the week level. For example, some months have four Saturdays but other months may have five; a week may begin in one month and end in the other. The interaction of the three sets of predictors generates as many as 400 potentially relevant predictors. Ex-post, the 366 date-based predictors are the most important. Results will be reported treating these predictors as the base case.

14.4.1.2   The Prediction Model

Generically denote data with N cases by $\mathcal{D} = (\mathbb{Y}, \mathbb{Z})$ where $\mathbb{Y}$ is the response variable and $\mathbb{Z}$ is a set of observed predictors. To make predictions for all weeks in year τ, we partition $\mathcal{D}$ into $\mathcal{D} = (\mathcal{D}_{1\tau}, \mathcal{D}_{2\tau})$ where $\mathcal{D}_{1\tau}$ collects data for all weeks $t \in \mathrm{yr}(\tau)$, and $\mathcal{D}_{2\tau}$ collects all data not in year τ. The $N_{1\tau}$ cases in $\mathcal{D}_{1\tau}$ will be used for training, and the $N_{2\tau}$ cases in $\mathcal{D}_{2\tau}$ will be used for validation, with $N = N_{1\tau} + N_{2\tau}$. The goal is prediction of points z^* in $\mathcal{D}_{2\tau}$.

Since we are interested in predicting the common seasonal variations in the composite error that emerges from the Fourier regression in step 1, the mapping into $\mathcal{D}$ notation is

$$\mathcal{D} = (\{\hat{\varepsilon}_{gct}\}, \{\mathbb{Z}_{gct}\}) = (\hat{\varepsilon}^s_{g\tau}, \mathbb{Z}^s_{g\tau}), \ \forall t : \mathrm{yr}(t) = \tau$$

$$\mathcal{D}_{1\tau} = (\{\hat{\varepsilon}_{gct}\}, \{\mathbb{Z}_{gct}\}) = (\hat{\varepsilon}^s_{g\tau}, \mathbb{Z}^s_{g\tau}), \ \forall t : \mathrm{yr}(t) \neq \tau,$$

where $\hat{\varepsilon}^s_{gt}$ is a stacked vector of $\hat{\varepsilon}_{gct}$ for all c in state s, and $\mathbb{Z}^s_{gt}$ is similarly defined. In words, the training data $\mathcal{D}_{1\tau}$ consist of observations for all counties in state s over all 469 weeks, less those weeks in year τ (which is 52 except in a leap year). Thus, the training data are indexed by the triplet (g, s, τ).

State by state, we train algorithms to fit a prediction model for each product group in each of the nine years. Thus, for each state the exercise involves training $N_g \times N_{yr}$ models. For a given predictor set $\mathbb{Z}$, we use training data $\mathcal{D}_1$ to estimate several models:

1. Linear panel model using all predictors by POOLED OLS.
2. Linear panel model using LARS-type methods to perform variable selection.
3. Regression trees using RANDOM FOREST-type methods to determine the tree size.

We have close to 400 potential predictors, but we also have $(469 - 52)$ weeks of data for each county. Though a pooled least-squares regression that uses all predictors (method 1) is possible, it will unlikely be efficient. Hence, we consider two machine learning procedures.

Introduced in Efron et al. (2004), the *least angle regression* estimator LARS is a functional gradient descent method that repeatedly fits a model to the residuals of the previous step. LASSO, forward stagewise regressions, and boosting can be obtained as special cases of LARS. Under the boosting view, each model (also known as learner) is individually weak but is "boosted" to produce a strong learner via averaging. Averaging in this case reduces bias. Our implementation of LARS-type methods is actually based on LASSO because it requires fewer choices of tuning parameters. The base learner is thus a linear model rather than a regression tree. The LARS perspective helps understand the difference with random forests.

The random forest (RF), attributable to Breiman (2001), is an ensemble method that builds a prediction from a collection of regression trees. Each tree is fitted to a randomly selected subset of predictors in a bootstrapped sample. Like LARS-type estimators, the final model is also an average over trees. But unlike LARS, these trees are built either separately or in parallel rather than sequentially. Regression trees can uncover complex relations and are strong learners, but they tend to have high variance. Averaging in the case of random forests reduces the variance of models that have low bias. One advantage of regression trees over nonparametric regressions is that the smoothness condition on the regression function can be relaxed. Random forest is an extension of BAGGING, which averages over trees grown on bootstrapped samples using all predictors.

The prediction provided by LARS or random forest is implicitly formed by averaging over the predictions of models that use only a subset of available predictors. Hence, they are more resistant to overfitting. Though these methods have been widely applied to i.i.d data, applications to time series data are more limited. Success of these algorithms in the present setting is very much an empirical matter. Of the three methods, the random forest is the most flexible because it does not impose linearity or smoothness. We use it as a benchmark in the discussion of results. We implement random forests using the R package RANGER with default parameter settings.[8] We find that the LARS-type methods do not uncover sparse models as our trained estimators have nonzero loadings on over 80 percent of the included variables, with worse performance than the random forest. By contrast, variable-importance tests for the random forest show that a small number of predictors (mostly having to do with a week's position within the year) are being used in highly nonlinear ways. This suggests that the underlying seasonal process is highly nonlinear, and a better fit for the random forest algorithm than the LARS algorithm.

---

8. The default size of forest is ntree = 500 trees, and the default value of mtry (the number of independent variables considered for each split) is the square root of the total number of independent variables. The min node size parameter, which controls the depth of each tree grown, is set to 5 by default. It is possible that fine-tuning the parameters can yield improved results.

14.5   The Seasonally Adjusted Data

The crux of our two-step procedure is to first remove deterministic seasonal effects using univariate Fourier regressions, and then exploit cross-section dependence to remove the residual common seasonal/holiday effects. Once this is accomplished, the seasonally adjusted budget shares can be computed as the ratio of seasonally adjusted sales for the group to total adjusted sales summed across groups. The largest differences between the unadjusted and adjusted shares are in groups like floral, insecticides, canning, ice, fragrances, toys, stationery, and candies. These results make sense because effects due to seasonal holiday events are precisely what we want to remove.

Table 14.3 uses two products to contrast the seasonal patterns in the raw and adjusted data. Consider first beer sales, which tend to be higher in the summer and peak around July 4th. In 2009, July 4th (week 183) fell on a Saturday when the Nielsen data were collected. As July 4th is a common event, high beer sales likely occurred across counties. Our step 2 should smooth out this holiday effect. As shown at the top of table 14.3, the adjusted data are indeed smoother and exhibit a smaller spike than the raw data. Take the case of New York as an example. The share of beer computed from the raw data is 3.8 for the week ending July 4 but is 2.4 for the week ending February 7. The adjusted data exhibit smaller differences, being 2.5 and 2.7 for the two weeks in question. Beer sales nonetheless spike each winter around the first week of February because of the Superbowl. This is illustrated for 2009, when the Superbowl took place on Sunday, February 1. The adjusted shares are smoother within and between months.

It is also important that the second step adjustment does not remove

Table 14.3	Effects of seasonal adjustment on selected series' share (%)							
	Adjusted data				Raw data			
Week Ending	CA	FL	NY	TX	CA	FL	NY	TX
The 2009 July 4th effect on beer spending								
June 27	3.5	2.9	2.5	2.6	4.1	3.3	3.2	3.0
July 4	3.5	2.8	2.5	2.7	4.9	3.2	3.8	3.6
July 11	3.2	2.8	2.4	2.2	3.8	3.5	3.3	2.8
The 2009 Superbowl effect on beer spending								
Jan 31	3.3	2.6	2.6	2.5	3.3	2.4	2.2	2.1
Feb 7	3.7	2.7	2.7	2.6	3.3	2.7	2.4	2.3
Feb 14	3.0	2.5	2.3	2.3	2.5	2.2	1.9	1.9
The April 1, 2009 cigarette tax hike								
April 4	1.2	4.4	2.7	3.2	1.2	4.8	2.6	3.2
April 11	1.1	4.1	2.4	2.7	1.0	4.1	2.3	2.7
April 18	1.3	4.4	2.8	3.3	1.3	4.3	2.8	3.3

Table 14.4   **Importance of the seasonal component**

		Average of R^2 in equation (2)					
Sample	Method	Mean	Median	Max	q75	q25	Min
FOUR	Fourier	0.52	0.53	0.95	0.63	0.40	0.14
	RF	0.58	0.59	0.95	0.70	0.44	0.14
SEVEN	Fourier	0.52	0.51	0.95	0.62	0.40	0.14
	RF	0.57	0.57	0.95	0.70	0.44	0.14
ALL	Fourier	0.53	0.52	0.96	0.63	0.41	0.14
	RF	0.57	0.57	0.96	0.70	0.44	0.14

spikes and variations that are nonseasonal. To check this, we consider the 62-cent federal tax hike on cigarettes on April 1, 2009, which corresponds to week 171 in our data. Recall that the data for 2009 are adjusted using training data for all years except 2009. Since the tax hike is a one-time event, nothing in the training data should predict the tax hike specific to 2009. The bottom panel of table 14.3 reports the share of tobacco for the week before, during, and after the tax hike. According to the raw data, the tax hike led to a temporary decline in sales and hence in the budget share of tobacco. The seasonal adjustment preserves this feature. In results not reported, we find that as in the raw data, the average share of tobacco is generally higher in the 170 weeks after the tax hike than the 170 weeks before the tax hike, suggesting that the tax did little to discourage cigarette consumption.

The premise of our analysis is that the residuals from the univariate Fourier regressions in step 1 have comovements that are predictable. To evaluate the incremental predictive power provided by different adjustment methods, we consider the R^2 corresponding to (2), which is a regression of log sales y_{gct} on the two estimated seasonal components: $\hat{d}_{gct}$ and $\hat{q}_{gct}$. Table 14.4 summarizes the distribution of R^2 over all groups and states. A little over 50 percent of the variations in log sales are seasonal and predictable. The degree of predictability varies across groups, ranging from 14 percent to over 90 percent. Notably, step 2 improves upon the univariate Fourier regressions implemented in step 1 alone. The highest and lowest quantiles of the R^2 do not depend on the procedure. This suggests that the improvements apply not to a few groups with extreme seasonality, but to a large number of groups.

Figure 14.2 illustrates the difference between using step 1 alone and the two-step procedure by plotting the R^2 of random forest results against those based on the Fourier method. If the random forest estimator provides relatively little additional information, the optional step regression after step 2 will push λ_g toward zero. In such cases, the R^2 values will be bunched along the 45-degree line. Figure 14.2 indicates such groups do exist. However, many other groups have values in the scatterplot located above the 45-degree

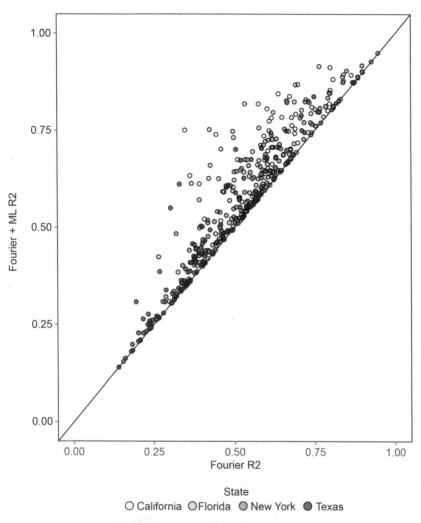

Fourier + ML R2

0.00   0.25   0.50   0.75   1.00
Fourier R2

State
○ California ◑ Florida ◐ New York ● Texas

Fig. 14.2 Incremental predictive power of random forests

line. For some of these groups, the improvement in fit from adding the panel data step is quite significant. A quarter of groups see increases in R^2 of 13 percent or greater.

At face value, it may seem that the improvement of a few percentage points in predictability over the univariate Fourier regression is trivial. However, the adjusted data have far fewer spikes than those adjusted using the Fourier regressions alone. This difference has direct implications for demand estimation.

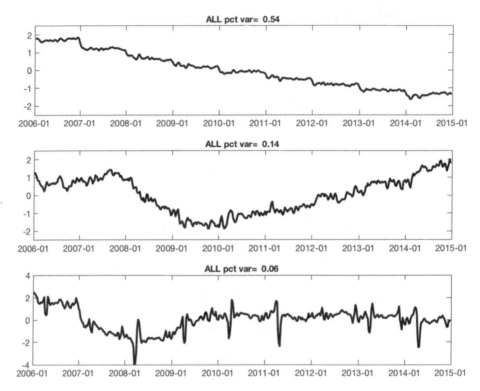

Fig. 14.3   Factors estimated from seasonally adjusted shares: FOUR states

14.5.1   The Factor Estimates

A main finding in the demand analysis of the raw data is that the first few factors exhibit strong seasonal patterns. We now explore features of the common factors obtained from the first step alone, and from the two-step procedure. We find four factors in the data adjusted by the Fourier step alone. The first two factors explain over 68 percent of the variation in the data and consist of a trend and a cyclical component. However, factors three and four remain spiky and quasiperiodic, indicating that the Fourier regressions by themselves leave nontrivial seasonal variations unexplained. In contrast, we find either three or four factors depending on the state in the shares data adjusted by our two-step procedure, whether it is based on LASSO or RANDOM FOREST. Compared to factors estimated from no adjustment and step 1 alone, the most notable difference is the absence of large spikes.

Figure 14.3 plots the three factors in FOUR using data adjusted by random forests. These factors, denoted $\hat{F}_{RF}$, are to be distinguished from the ones estimated from the unadjusted data, now denoted $\tilde{F}_{NSA}$. Though not immediately evident, $\hat{F}_{2,RF}$ is strongly correlated with $\hat{F}_{4,NSA}$. A regression of

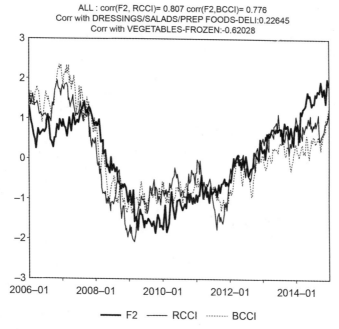

Fig. 14.4   The level factor: $\hat{F}_{2,RF}$

$\hat{F}_{4,\text{NSA}}$ on $\hat{F}_{2,RF}$ yields an R^2 of 0.6. The largest residuals of that regression are precisely spikes between weeks 46 and 50, indicating that step 2 is picking up the spikes not accounted for in step 1.

The first three factors together explain about 80 percent of the variations of the adjusted shares, with $\hat{F}_{1,RF}$ explaining 56 percent, and $\hat{F}_{2,RF}$ explaining 15 percent. As can be seen from figure 14.3, $\hat{F}_{1,RF}$ has a trend component. An investigation into the factor loadings finds that $\hat{F}_{1,RF}$ always loads heavily on books and magazines, ethnic hair treatment, and photographic supplies. These product groups appear to have experienced secular trends during our sample.

Even though the Nielsen data are concentrated on grocery store sales with few consumer durables that are traditionally known to be cyclical, $\hat{F}_{2,RF}$ is visually cyclical and warrants further investigation. We use two measures of consumer confidence as benchmarks of cyclicality: the Rasmussen RCCI index and the Bloomberg index of consumer confidence. The former is a daily national survey collected by the Rasmussen group that tracks 1,500 consumers concerning their confidence, expectations, and sentiment about the US economy. The latter started as the ABC News consumer comfort index and has been under the control of the Bloomberg Corporation since 2011. Figure 14.4 plots $\hat{F}_{2,RF}$ (thick solid line), RCCI (thin solid line), along with BLOOMBERG (dotted line). It is evident that spending moves posi-

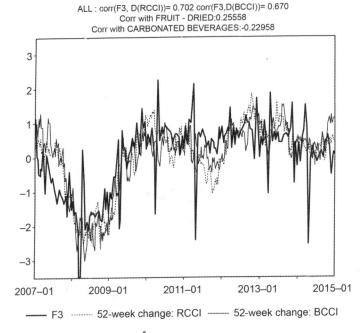

Fig. 14.5   The curvature factor: $\hat{F}_{3,RF}$

tively with consumer sentiment. These confidence measures have absolute correlation with $\hat{F}_{2,RF}$ of about 0.8. In this regard, consumers' actions are aligned with how they feel. Because our data cover a very large sample of stores, which is distinct from the much smaller set of consumers surveyed by Bloomberg and Rasmussen, we are able to correlate beliefs with purchasing actions without worrying about the confounding influence of "meremeasurement" effects studied in Morwitz and Fitzsimons (2004), by which asking consumers about their beliefs might affect their ensuing purchasing decisions.

Turning now to $\hat{F}_{3,RF}$, it takes a big dip in the week ending March 22, 2008. As a point of reference, JP Morgan purchased Bear Stearns on March 17, 2008. Furthermore, oil prices spiked up to nearly \$110 per barrel a few days earlier. Upon examination, the factor is actually highly correlated with the 52-week change in consumer confidence. Figure 14.5 plots $\hat{F}_{3,RF}$ estimated using data for four states along with the 52-week change in RCCI and BLOOMBERG. Their correlation with $\hat{F}_{3,RF}$ are 0.74 and 0.68, respectively. If $\hat{F}_{2,RF}$ indicates the level of economic activity, $\hat{F}_{3,RF}$ indicates direction of change. We may think of the three factors in the seasonally adjusted demand system as characterizing the trend, level, and curvature of Engel curves. These estimates of the latent functions are interesting in their own

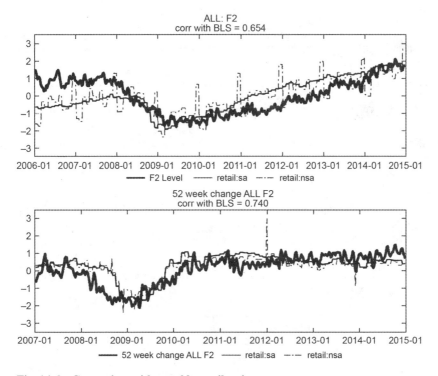

Fig. 14.6   Comparison with monthly retail series

right because the classical estimation of demand system cannot consistently estimate the latent functions of prices and income.

It remains to check how our aggregate weekly adjusted sales data compare to the official monthly retail sales. The US Census Bureau releases both the raw and seasonally adjusted data for retail sales each month.[9] To compare with our weekly series, we interpolate values for the weeks in a month to the officially released sales for the month. Figure 14.6 plots both series along with $\hat{F}_{2,RF}$. The top panel shows that our $\hat{F}_{2,RF}$ has a correlation of 0.65 with the officially adjusted series. The bottom panel plots the 52-week change in the series. The correlation of the adjusted series is 0.74. The most notable difference is seen around the 2008 financial crisis, during which the $\hat{F}_{2,RF}$ shows a steeper decline than the official data. But the weekly series generally tracks the monthly series reasonably well. Some discrepancy is to be expected because our weekly data do not cleanly line up with the monthly calendar.

The results so far have focused on four states: CA, FL, NY, TX. How-

---

9. The series are RETAILSMNSA and RETAILSMSA in FRED.

ever, similar results are obtained in an extended analysis that groups additional states into three regions: the Midwest (IL, IN, MI, OH, WI), the Mid-Atlantic (DC, DE, MD, VA), and the Southwest (AZ, NM, NV). In each of the three regions, $\hat{F}_1$ is a trend, $\hat{F}_2$ is correlated with the level of consumer confidence, while $\hat{F}_3$ is correlated with the 52-week change in consumer confidence. Not surprisingly, pooling data for the four states and three regions also gives three factors with very similar properties. Hereafter, we use the extended data when appropriate. These results will be labeled SEVEN and ALL.

14.6   Cyclical Sensitivity

A unique feature of the Nielsen scanner data is the availability of weekly information at the spatial and product group levels. This presents an opportunity to study the timing of the response of spending to economic conditions at a disaggregated level. Subsection 14.6.1 considers cyclical sensitivity of product groups, while subsection 14.6.2 considers spatial variations in spending.

14.6.1   Variation across Product Groups

We first turn to the sensitivity of the product groups to business cycle conditions. Since $\hat{F}_{2,RF}^s$ is positively correlated with RCCI, a positive loading indicates that the share of product j is procyclical, while a negative value means that the share of product j is high when $\hat{F}_{2,RF}^s$ is low. The dispersion of sensitivity to aggregate conditions across product groups is best seen from the distribution of $SGNR_{sj}^2$. This is defined as the signed fraction of variance of $SHARE_j^s$ explained by $\hat{F}_{2,RF}^s$, where SGN is the sign of the loading of $\hat{F}_{2,RF}^s$ on $SHARE_j^s$. Though there are some minor differences across states and regions, the pattern across states is broadly similar. Figure 14.7 presents results for SEVEN. The distribution is noticeably asymmetric because there are more countercyclical product groups and the magnitude of the absolute loadings are larger (top) than procyclical ones (bottom). Product groups little affected by $\hat{F}_{2,RF}^s$, plotted in the middle of figure 14.7, are disposable diapers, shaving products, cold and cough remedies, and somewhat surprisingly, beer.

The effect of the cyclical factors on the shares is highly heterogeneous. According to the factor loadings, a decrease in $\hat{F}_{2,RF}$ has the largest marginal impact on the share of frozen vegetables, canned vegetables, and pasta. The impact of an increase in $\hat{F}_{3,RF}$ is most adverse (i.e., most negative) on eggs and most positive on dried fruit, which is often marketed as a snack. These results suggest less eating out during downturns in favor of preparing meals at home. There is increasing evidence for adaptive changes in the pattern of food consumption during the Great Recession. The USDA finds not only that total food spending fell during the Great Recession, but also that

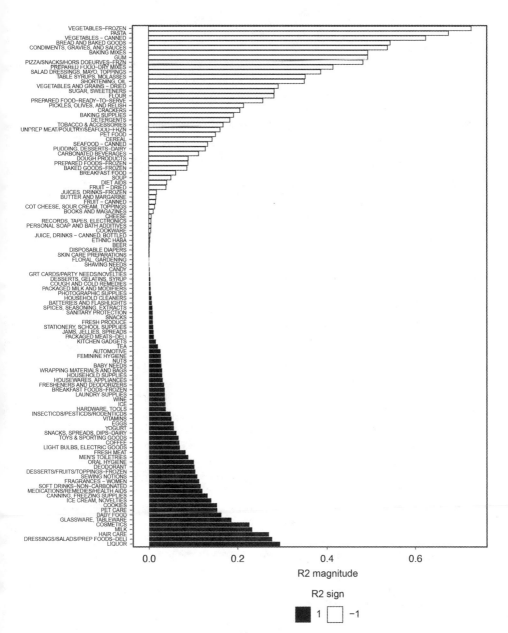

Fig. 14.7 R^2 from regression of adjusted shares on $\hat{F}_2$: FOUR states

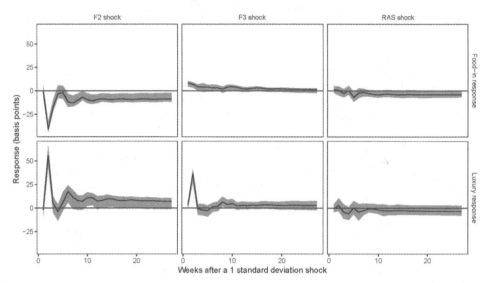

Fig. 14.8   Response of FOOD-IN to shock in $\hat{F}_2$

recovery was slow.[10] Cha, Chintagunta, and Dar (2015) aggregate the weekly Homescan data to annual level and find that food consumed at home is countercyclical. Grittith, O'Connell, and Smith (2015) find that households also adjusted food spending in the UK. Our results reinforce these findings using a completely different approach.

To further explore this phenomenon at a more granular level, state by state we aggregate spending on the five product groups with large negative loadings. These are frozen vegetables, canned vegetables, pasta, bread, and condiments/sauces. Because these products all seem related to home cooking, we designate them the FOOD-IN group. We also identify the five products with large positive loadings on $\hat{F}_{2,RF}^s$: liquor, prepared food, milk, hair care, and cosmetics. These five products are then aggregated to form a LUXURY good basket, one for each state. Note that because our data are restricted to grocery-store goods, our LUXURY goods are relatively less "luxurious" than conventionally defined.

Next, we use a five-variable VAR to evaluate the dynamic response of FOOD-IN and LUXURY to an unanticipated increase in the two cyclical factors $\hat{F}_{2,RF}$, $\hat{F}_{3,RF}$, and to RCCI. We report results for FOUR, but results for SEVEN and ALL are similar. The dynamic responses to one-standard-deviation shocks are shown in figure 14.8. A positive $F_{2,RF}$ shock, which is an increase in economic activity, has a negative effect on FOOD-IN that peaks after two weeks and nearly recovers after five weeks. This negative effect on

10. See https://ageconsearch.umn.edu/bitstream/120969/2/10FoodSpending.pdf.

FOOD-IN is mirrored by an opposite effect on LUXURY. The absolute impact on LUXURY is actually larger than that on FOOD-IN. The effect of a $\hat{F}_{3,RF}$ shock is mainly on LUXURY; the impact on FOOD-IN is negligible. In terms of decomposition of variance, about 55 percent of the variations in FOOD-IN are explained by its own lag, 35 percent explained by $\hat{F}_{2,RF}$, 7 percent by $\hat{F}_{3,RF}$, with little attributed to RCCI. About 37 percent of the variations in LUXURY are explained by its own lag, 28 percent by $\hat{F}_{2,RF}$ and 32 percent by $\hat{F}_{3,RF}$. It thus appears that FOOD-IN is primarily affected by the level factor, while LUXURY is affected by both the level and the curvature factors (i.e., where the economy is and where it is going). The results are robust to whether RCCI is ordered second or last. Interestingly, even though the correlation between RCCI and FOOD-IN is well over 0.75, shocks to RCCI account for little of the variations in FOOD-IN and LUXURY once conditioned on $\hat{F}_{2,RF}$ and $\hat{F}_{3,RF}$.

14.6.2   Variation across Regions

According to the NBER's business cycle chronology, the downturn in economic activity leading to the Great Recession began in December 2007 when the last business cycle peaked, and continued to decline until it reached a trough in June 2009. This subsection looks at the spatial aspect of the change in food spending before, during, and after the Great Recession.

The CPI is based on a comprehensive consumer expenditure survey conducted by the Bureau of Labor Statistics (BLS) every two years. The CPI weights reflect the relative importance of the particular good in the consumption basket. The top panel of table 14.5 reports the CPI weights for *food consumed at home* and *luxury* as defined by the BLS. In their own study

Table 14.5   **Spending over the business cycle**

	Dec 2007	Dec 2009	Dec 2011	Dec 2013
CPI weights (%)				
FOOD-IN	7.6	—	8.6	8.1
FOOD-OUT	6.1	—	5.6	5.7
Seasonally adjusted Nielsen shares (%)				
FOOD-IN:FOUR	5.6	6.0	5.8	5.6
FOOD-IN:SEVEN	6.0	6.5	6.2	6.1
FOOD-IN:ALL	6.3	6.7	6.6	6.4
FOOD-IN:FLORIDA	4.3	5.0	4.7	4.6
FOOD-IN:MIDATL	6.9	7.4	7.2	7.0
LUXURY:FOUR	8.3	8.6	8.8	9.0
LUXURY:SEVEN	7.9	8.2	8.3	8.5
LUXURY:ALL	7.8	8.2	8.1	8.3
LUXURY:MIDATL	6.6	6.5	6.5	6.6
LUXURY:NY	7.3	7.3	8.1	8.1

on how consumer spending changes during boom, recession, and recovery, 2007 was used as a boom year, 2011 as recession, and 2013 a year of recovery.[11] The CPI weights indicate an increased importance of FOOD-IN and a reduced importance of LUXURY items during recessions.

How well do our adjusted shares corroborate with the CPI weights? The bottom panel of table 14.5 reports the shares of FOOD-IN and LUXURY averaged over the weeks in December for four years that represent different stages of the business cycle. Notably, FOOD-IN is much higher in 2009 and 2011 than in 2007 and 2013, while LUXURY is lower in 2009 than in 2013. Even though our definitions of FOOD-IN and LUXURY are data driven, factor based, and restricted to grocery-store nondurables, the Nielsen data also indicate an increased importance of FOOD-IN and reduced importance of LUXURY items during recessions, similar to the more comprehensive CPI weights.

An appeal of the Nielsen data is that they provide granular information in both the time series and cross-section dimensions. The share of FOOD-IN ranges between 5 percent in Florida to 7.8 percent in the Mid-Atlantic regions, with an average of 6.6 percent over the entire sample. The series is most persistent in California and least persistent in the Midwest, with first order autocorrelation coefficients of 0.83 and 0.50, respectively. The share of LUXURY ranges between 6.6 percent in the Mid-Atlantic regions to 12 percent in Florida, with an average of 8.9 percent over the full sample. The series is most persistent for the Midwest and least persistent in the Southwest, with autocorrelation coefficients of 0.86 and 0.5, respectively. The contemporaneous correlation between FOOD-IN and LUXURY is strongly negative in California, New York, and the Midwest, with cross-correlations in excess of 0.6 in absolute value. The correlation is much weaker in the Southwest and even positive in Florida. The heterogeneity across states in spending behavior underscores the difficulty in designing policies that would satisfy all consumers.

To analyze local sensitivity to (aggregate) business cycle fluctuations, we also estimate for each county in each state, the regression

$$(3) \qquad \text{food-in}_{ct} = a_{c1} + a_2 \hat{F}_{2,RF,t} + a_{3c} \hat{F}_{3,RF,t} + \text{error}_{ct}.$$

The R^2 provides a measure exposure of county c to the two common factors. Upon ranking the R^2s, the urban and densely populated counties are found to be more exposed to aggregate shocks. Take the state of New York as an example. The counties of Rockland, Nassau, and Kings have a combined population of over 4 million according to the 2010 census. Each of these counties has an R^2 above 0.45. In contrast, the counties Seneca, Lewis, and Broome, with a combined population of under 300,000, each have an R^2s of at most 0.01.

11. See https://www.bls.gov/opub/btn/volume-3/how-does-consumer-spending-change-during-boom-recession-and-recovery.htm.

Change in food in share from Dec 2006 to Dec 2007 (bps)

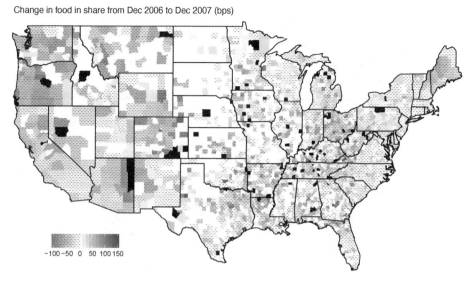

Change in food–in share from Sep 2008 to Sep 2009 (bps)

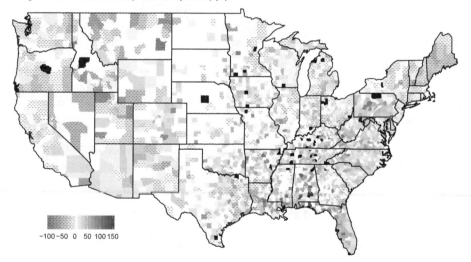

Fig. 14.9   Regional changes in FOOD-IN

Heatmaps provide a more compact way to see how different regions are affected by economic conditions. The top panel of figure 14.9 plots the change in FOOD-IN between 2006 and 2007. Regions with dotted gray shading indicate larger reductions in FOOD-IN. With the exception of isolated regions in Michigan, this boom episode was associated with reductions in FOOD-IN. The reductions were largest in Nevada and Arizona, one possible explanation being the housing boom in those regions. The bottom panel presents the change in FOOD-IN from 2008 to 2009, an episode of economic downturn. Darker solid gray indicates larger increases in FOOD-IN share. Now there are more regions shaded solid gray than dotted gray, with Arizona and Florida witnessing the largest increase in FOOD-IN. This shows that the Great Recession differentially affected regional purchasing behavior of FOOD-IN goods.

14.6.3   Sandy Regression

The regressions based on equation (3) help understand the impact of aggregate economic conditions on weekly spending. It is also of interest to learn about the impact of local rather than aggregate economic conditions. To illustrate, we take advantage of the weekly and spatial information in the Nielsen data to examine purchasing behavior in New York around landfall of Hurricane Sandy on Monday, October 29, 2012.

In hindsight, Sandy was a much bigger storm than expected and consumers were caught somewhat unprepared. Figure 14.10 shows little evidence of stocking up during the week prior to Sandy, but that there was a distinct increase in FOOD-IN share during the week containing the storm. One might be concerned that the increase in the raw data shown in the top panel is an artifact of seasonality as the week ending November 3rd was close to the beginning of the Thanksgiving and Christmas shopping season. But the bottom panel shows that when using the seasonally adjusted data, there is a clear post-Sandy spike in 2012, which brings the seasonally adjusted FOOD-IN share to its highest value for the year.

To quantify the impact of Sandy, we estimate a simple panel data model. Let $y_{i,t}$ be the share of FOOD-IN in county i and week t, normalized to have standard-deviation 1 within each county. Let *sandy – county$_i$* be a dummy variable that indicates if i is a coastal county that was hit by Hurricane Sandy. Let *landfall$_t$* be a dummy variable that indicates if t is the week containing the landfall of Hurricane Sandy, which is the week ending November 3, 2012. We estimate the regression

$$y_{it} = \alpha_i + \lambda_t + \sum_{j=0}^{5} \beta_j \cdot sandy - county_i \times landfall_{t-j} + \text{error}.$$

Our results show that FOOD-IN consumption increases by about 2.5 standard deviations during the week that Sandy made landfall. The effects of Sandy on FOOD-IN purchases persisted for about one month. Figure 14.11 shows that the effects of Sandy were localized to the counties near New York City and Long Island, which were most exposed to the hurricane. Other counties in the state of New York were nearly unaffected by the storm.

14.7   Conclusion

Large volumes of highly heterogeneous data are increasingly available, but they are often not immediately useful for economic analysis without remov-

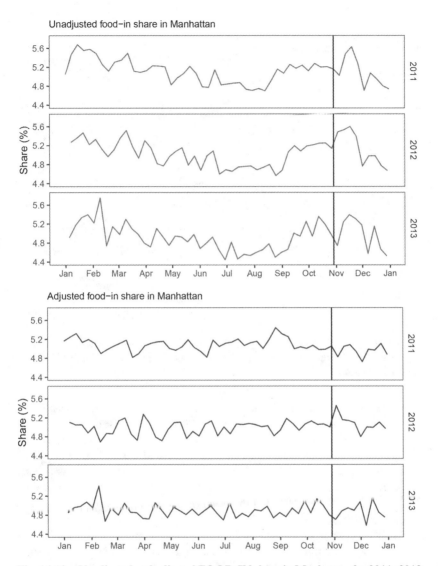

Fig. 14.10 Unadjusted and adjusted FOOD-IN share in Manhattan for 2011–2013
Note: Vertical line denotes October 29 (the date of Hurricane Sandy's landfall).

Table 14.6   **Consumption increases**

j	0	1	2	3	4	5
$\hat{\beta}_j$	2.541***	0.318	0.152	0.323**	−0.606***	−0.123
	(0.242)	(0.203)	(0.202)	(0.153)	(0.166)	(0.197)

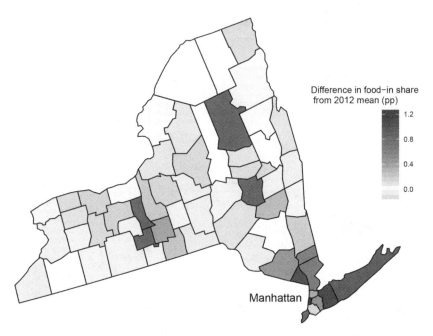

Fig. 14.11   Difference between $y_{i,landfall}$ **the FOOD-IN share for the week containing Hurricane Sandy's landfall, and** $\bar{y}_{i,2012}$, **the average FOOD-IN share for 2012, by county in New York state**

ing some nuisance variations and performing some form of aggregation. In this paper, the nuisance variations in question are the seasonal and holiday effects. As they cannot be adequately removed by conventional procedures, the adjusted data continue to exhibit seasonal patterns when aggregated over counties. We propose to augment univariate seasonal adjustments with a machine learning step that pools information across counties. The validity of this second step relies on the presence of common seasonal patterns across counties.

There is no shortage of examples in which common seasonality would be a feature of the raw data. For example, employment and output of firms in a given sector will likely be correlated. Unless we can perfectly remove seasonality at the firm level, the sectoral data obtained by aggregating over firms will likely exhibit seasonality. Informal discussions with staff researchers at the Bureau of Economic Analysis confirm such experiences. Our analysis provides an explanation for why a bottom-up approach to seasonality might be inadequate. In a Big Data setting, it is possible to improve upon the conventional way of removing nuisance variations one series at a time by taking advantage of cross-sectional dependence. Though our focus has been on handling seasonal effects, the procedure can be adapted to remove other nuisance variations. A limitation of our analysis is the lack of a way to assess sampling uncertainty of the two-step procedure. This is left for future research.

References

Bai, J., and S. Ng. 2008. "Large Dimensional Factor Analysis." *Foundations and Trends in Econometrics* 3 (2): 89–163.
———. 2019. "Rank Regularized Estimation of Approximate Factor Models." *Journal of Econometrics* 212 (1): 78–96.
Banks, J., R. Blundell, and A. Lewbel. 1997. "Quadratic Engel Curves and Consumer Demand." *Review of Economics and Statistics* 79:527–39.
Breiman, L. 2001. "Random Forests." *Machine Learning* 45 (1): 5–32.
Cha, W., P. Chintagunta, and S. Dhar. 2015. "Food Purchases during the Great Recession." Kilts Booth Marketing Series, Paper 1-008. https://papers.ssrn.com /sol3/papers.cfm?abstract_id=2548758.
Chamberlain, G. 1984. "Panel Data." In *Handbook of Econometrics*, vol. 2, 1247–1318. Amsterdam: North Holland.
Cleveland, W., and S. Devlin. 1980. "Calendar Effects in Monthly Time Series: Detection by Spectrum Analysis and Graphical Models." *Journal of the American Statistical Association* 75 (371): 487–96.
Cleveland, W., T. Evans, and S. Scott. 2014. "Weekly Seasonal Adjustment— A Locally Weighted Regression Approach." Working Paper No. 473, US Bureau of Labor Statistics, Washington, DC.
Cleveland, W., and S. Scott. 2007. "Seasonal Adjustment of Weekly Time Series with Application to Unemployment Insurance Claims and Steel Production." *Journal of Official Statistics* 23 (2): 209–21.
Deaton, A. S., and J. Muellbauer. 1980. "An Almost Ideal Demand System." *American Economic Review* 70:312–26.
Efron, B., T. Hastie, I. Johnstone, and R. Tibshirani. 2004. "Least Angle Regression." *Annals of Statistics* 32 (2): 407–99.
Engle, R. F., and S. Kozicki. 1993. "Testing for Common Features." *Journal of Business and Economic Statistics* 11:369–79.
Fok, D., P. Franses, and R. Paap. 2007. "Seasonality and Non-Linear Price Effects in Scanner Data Based Market Response Models." *Journal of Econometrics* 138:231–51.
Geweke, J. 1978. "The Temporal and Sectoral Aggregation of Seasonally Adjusted Time Series." In *Seasonal Analysis of Economic Time Series*, edited by A. Zellner, 411–32. Washington, DC: National Bureau of Economic Research.
Gorman, W. M. 1981. "Some Engel Curves." In *Essays in the Theory and Measurement of Consumer Behavior in Honor of Sir Richard Stone*, edited by A. Deaton. Cambridge: Cambridge University Press.
Grittith, R., M. O'Connell, and K. Smith. 2015. "Shopping Around: How Households Adjusted Food Spending over the Great Recession." *Economica* 83 (330): 247–280. https://onlinelibrary.wiley.com/doi/abs/10.1111/ecca.12166.
Harvey, A., S. Koopman, and M. Riana. 1997. "The Modeling and Seasonal Adjustment of Weekly Observations." *Journal of Business and Economic Statistics* 15:354–68.
Lewbel, A. 1991. "The Rank of Demand Systems: Theory and Nonparametric Estimation." *Econometrica* 59 (1): 711–30.

————. 1997. "Consumer Demand Systems and Household Equivalence Scales." In *Handbook of Applied Econometrics*, vol. 2, edited by M. H. Pesaran and P. Schmidt, 167–201. Oxford: Blackwell.

————. 2003. "A Rational Rank Four Demand System." *Journal of Applied Econometrics* 18:127–35.

McElroy, T. 2017. "Multivariate Seasonal Adjustment, Economic Identities, and Seasonal Taxonomy." *Journal of Business and Economic Statistics* 35:511–25.

Morwitz, V., and G. Fitzsimons. 2004. "The Mere-Measurement Effect: Why Does Measuring Intentions Change Actual Behavior?" *Journal of Consumer Psychology* 14 (1–2): 64–71.

Muellbauer, J. 1975. "Aggregation, Income Distribution, and Consumer Demand." *Review of Economic Studies* 62:269–83.

Ng, S. 2017. "Opportunities and Challenges: Lessons from Analyzing Terabytes of Scanner Data." In *Advances in Economics and Econometrics*, Eleventh World Congress of the Econometric Society, vol. 2, edited by B. Honoré, A. Pakes, M. Piazzesi, and L. Samuelson, 1–34. Cambridge: Cambridge University Press.

Pierce, D., M. Grupe, and W. Cleveland. 1984. "Seasonal Adjustment of the Weekly Monetary Aggregate: A Model Based Approach." *Journal of Business and Economic Statistics* 2:260–70.

Estimating the Benefits of New Products

W. Erwin Diewert and Robert C. Feenstra

15.1. Introduction

One of the more pressing problems facing statistical agencies and economic analysts is the new goods (and services) problem—that is, how should the introduction of new products and the disappearance of (possibly) obsolete products be treated in the context of forming a consumer price index? Hicks (1940) suggested a general approach to this measurement problem in the context of the economic approach to index number theory. His approach was to apply normal index number theory but estimate hypothetical prices that would induce utility-maximizing purchasers of a related group of products to demand 0 units of unavailable products.[1] With these reservation (or

W. Erwin Diewert is professor emeritus of the Vancouver School of Economics at the University of British Columbia, and a research associate of the National Bureau of Economic Research.

Robert C. Feenstra holds the C. Bryan Cameron Distinguished Chair in International Economics and is a professor of economics and director of the Center for International Data at the University of California–Davis, and a research associate of the National Bureau of Economic Research.

We thank the organizers and participants at the *Big Data for 21st Century Economic Statistics* conference, and especially Marshall Reinsdorf and Matthew Shapiro, for their helpful comments. We also thank Ninghui Li for her excellent research assistance. Financial support was received from a Digging into Data multi-country grant, provided by the United States NSF and the Canadian SSHRC. We acknowledge the James A. Kilts Center, University of Chicago Booth School of Business, https://www.chicagobooth.edu/research/kilts/datasets/dominicks, for the use of the Dominick's Dataset. For acknowledgments, sources of research support, and disclosure of the authors' material financial relationships, if any, please see https://www.nber.org/books-and-chapters/big-data-21st-century-economic-statistics/estimating-benefits-new-products.

1. "The same kind of device can be used in another difficult case, that in which new sorts of goods are introduced in the interval between the two situations we are comparing. If certain goods are available in the II situation which were not available in the I situation, the p_1's cor-

virtual[2]) prices in hand, one can just apply normal index number theory using the augmented price data and the observed quantity data. The practical problem facing statistical agencies is: *how exactly are these reservation prices to be estimated*?

Following up on the contribution of Hicks, many authors developed bounds or rough approximations to the bias that might result from omitting the contribution of new goods in the consumer price index context. Thus Rothbarth (1941) attempted to find some bounds for the bias while Hofsten (1952, 47–50) discussed a variety of approximate methods to adjust for quality change in products, which is essentially the same problem as adjusting an index for the contribution of a new product. Additional bias formulae were developed by Diewert (1980, 498–501; 1987, 779; 1998, 51–54) and Hausman (2003, 26–28). Hausman proposes taking a *linear approximation to the demand curve* at the point of consumption and computing the consumer surplus gain to a new product under this linear demand curve. Provided that the demand curve is convex, then this linear approximation will be a *lower bound* to the consumer surplus gain. We will compare that proposal to other methods of dealing with new goods.

Researchers have also relied on some form of econometric estimation in order to form estimates of the welfare cost (or changes in the true cost of living index) of changes in product availability. The two main contributors in this area are Feenstra (1994) and Hausman (1996).[3] Feenstra assumes a *constant elasticity of substitution* (CES) utility or cost function, while Hausman assumes an *almost ideal demand system* (AIDS). The CES functional form is not fully flexible (in contrast to the AIDS), so that is one drawback of Feenstra's approach.[4] He adopts that case because it has a particularly simple form of the reservation prices: in the CES case, the demand curve never touches the price axis and so the reservation price is *infinity*. As we will show in the following sections, however, the area under the demand curve is bounded, provided that the elasticity of substitution is greater than unity, and it can be computed with information on the expenditure

---

responding to these goods become indeterminate. The p_2's and q_2's are given by the data and the q_1's are zero. Nevertheless, although the p_1's cannot be determined from the data, since the goods are not sold in the I situation, it is apparent from the preceding argument what p_1's ought to be introduced in order to make the index-number tests hold. They are those prices which, in the I situation, would *just* make the demands for these commodities (from the whole community) equal to zero." (Hicks 1940, 114). Hofsten (1952, 95–97) extended Hicks's methodology to cover the case of disappearing goods as well.

2. Rothbarth introduced the term "virtual prices" to describe these hypothetical prices in the rationing context: "I shall call the price system which makes the quantities actually consumed under rationing an optimum the 'virtual price system'" (Rothbarth 1941, 100).

3. See also Hausman (1999, 2003) and Hausman and Leonard (2002).

4. See Diewert (1974, 1976) for the definition of a flexible functional form. Feenstra (2010) shows that the CES methodology discussed here to measure the gains from new goods can be extended to the AIDS case.

on the new goods and the elasticity. So Feenstra's methodology sidesteps the issue of estimating the reservation prices, but instead requires that we estimate the elasticity of substitution. Feenstra (1994) provides a robust double-differencing method to estimate that elasticity that can be applied to a dataset with many new and disappearing goods, as typically occur with scanner data.

To summarize, there are two problems with Feenstra's CES methodology for measuring the net benefits of changes in the availability of products: (i) the CES functional form is not fully flexible; and (ii) the reservation price that induces a potential consumer to *not* purchase a product is equal to plus infinity, which seems high. Thus, the CES methodology may overstate the benefits of increases in product availability. Against these drawbacks, a benefit is that the elasticity of substitution can be estimated quite easily using the double-differencing method, and the elasticity along with the expenditure share on the items is sufficient information to compute the consumer benefits from new products.

In section 15.2, we begin with the simple example of a partial equilibrium, constant-elasticity demand curve, which has a reservation price of infinity. We show that the consumer surplus under a constant-elasticity demand curve is at least twice the consumer surplus under a linear approximation to the demand curve. This result is our first illustration of the extent to which a constant-elasticity case will lead to greater gains than a linear demand curve—that is, by about a factor of at least two when the elasticity of demand is the *same* for the two demand curves and reasonably high. While these results in section 15.2 are suggestive, they are not rigorous because they rely on a partial equilibrium demand curve with a single new good. Our general goal is to measure total consumer utility (not just consumer surplus) when there are potentially many new and disappearing goods. Accordingly, in section 15.3 we examine a constant elasticity of substitution (CES) utility function and show that the exact gains from new goods are still at least twice as high as those obtained from a linear approximation to that demand curve. In addition to the CES utility function, we also examine the *quadratic flexible functional form* that was initially due to Konüs and Byushgens (1926, 171). That utility function can be used to justify the Fisher (1922) price index, and so we will also call it the *KBF functional form*. The demand curves for both the CES and KBF demand curves are convex under weak conditions, but the CES demand is *more* convex.

In section 15.4, we turn to the econometric estimation of the demand system for the CES and KBF utility functions, using scanner data for frozen juice in one grocery store, as described in section 15.4.1. The estimation of the CES demand curves can be simplified using a double-differencing method due to Feenstra (1994), which eliminates all unknown parameters except the elasticity of substitution. In sections 15.4.2–15.4.3, we show that this method performs very well on the scanner data. In comparison, estimation of the demand curves corresponding to the quadratic utility function is more difficult because it inherently has more free parameters; that is, $N(N+1)/2$ free parameters in a symmetric matrix with N goods. We solve this degrees of freedom problem by introducing a *semiflexible version* of the flexible quadratic functional form.[5] This new methodology is explained and implemented in sections 15.4.4–15.4.5.

In section 15.4.6, we compare the results obtained from the CES and KBF utility functions for the consumer benefits from new goods. According to our theoretical results in section 15.3, we would expect that the CES gains should be not much more than twice as high as the KBF gains (because the KBF gains exceed those from a linear approximation), provided that those demand curves have the same elasticity at the point of consumption. In fact, that is not what we find: the CES gains are about *six times the size* of the KBF gains, and their 95 percent confidence intervals do not overlap. The reason for this result is that the implied elasticities of demand for the two preferences systems, evaluated at the same point of consumption for the new goods, are actually quite different: the KBF preferences give *demand that is about three times as elastic* as the CES demand for the new varieties of frozen juice. This finding highlights an important difference between the CES and KBF utility functions: because the former has a single estimation parameter, and the latter has a whole matrix of parameters, it will not in general be the case that they have the same elasticity of demand when estimated. Indeed, this result is implied by the limitation that the CES utility function is not fully flexible.

That theoretical limitation becomes an important simplification for estimation, however. We believe that it is practical for statistical agencies to implement the double-differenced estimation of the CES system, but it would be much more challenging for statistical agencies to implement the estimation of the KBF system, at least for most datasets. In the end, we are left with a trade-off between the practicality of using the CES system against the challenge of estimating a more flexible utility function to obtain a more general measure of gains. Further conclusions are provided in section 15.5.[6]

15.2   Constant-Elasticity Demand Curve

Consider a constant-elasticity demand curve of the form $q_1 = kp_1^{-\sigma}$, where q_1 denotes quantity of good 1, p_1 denotes its price, and $k > 0$ is parameter. In

---

5. Our new semiflexible functional form has properties that are similar to the semiflexible generalization of the normalized quadratic functional form introduced by Diewert and Wales (1987, 1988). In section 15.4.4 below, we also show how the correct curvature conditions can be imposed on our semiflexible quadratic functional form.

6. The dataset on frozen juice products is listed in appendix A of our working papers (Diewert and Feenstra 2019a, 2019b). Certain results presented here are proved in appendixes B and C of Diewert and Feenstra (2019b).

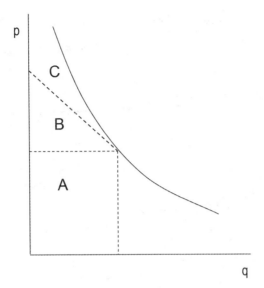

Fig. 15.1   Constant-elasticity demand

period t this good is newly available at the price of p_{1t} and the chosen quantity q_{1t}. The demand curve is illustrated in figure 15.1 and it approaches the vertical axis as the price approaches infinity, which means that the reservation price of the good is *infinite*. But provided that the elasticity of demand σ is greater than unity, the area under the demand curve, as shown by the regions $A + B + C$ in figure 15.1, is bounded above. Region A is the expenditure on the good, while $B + C$ is the consumer surplus. The consumer surplus is calculated as the area to the left of the demand curve between its price of p_{1t} and infinity, and relative to total expenditure E_t on all goods it equals

$$(1) \qquad \frac{B+C}{E_t} = \frac{1}{E_t} \int_{p_{1t}}^{\infty} kp^{-\sigma}dp = \frac{p_{1t}q_{1t}}{E_t(\sigma - 1)} = \frac{s_{1t}}{(\sigma - 1)}, \sigma > 1,$$

where $s_{1t} \equiv p_{1t}q_{1t}/E_t$ denotes the share of spending on good 1. We see that this expression for the consumer gains from the new good shrinks as the elasticity of substitution is higher, indicating that the new good is a closer substitute for an existing good.

One might worry that calculating the consumer gains this way, with a reservation price of infinity, results in gains that are too large. A suggestion given by Hausman (2003) is to use a linear approximation to the demand curve, as shown by the dashed line in figure 15.1. The linear approximation to the demand function goes through the price axis at the reservation price p_1^*, where $p_1^* \equiv p_{1t} + \alpha q_{1t}$ and $\alpha \equiv (p_1^* - p_{1t})/q_{1t} > 0$ is the absolute value of the slope of the inverse constant-elasticity demand curve evaluated at $q_1 = q_{1t}$. Hausman took the area of the triangle below the linear approximation to the

Table 15.1   Consumer gains from a new product with share = 0.1 (% of expenditure)

	$(B+C)/E_t$	B/E_t	Ratio	G_{CES}	$G_{H,CES}$	Ratio
2	10.0	2.50	0.25	11.1	2.78	0.25
3	5.00	1.67	0.33	5.40	1.85	0.34
4	3.33	1.25	0.37	3.58	1.39	0.39
5	2.50	1.00	0.40	2.66	1.11	0.42
6	2.00	0.83	0.42	2.12	0.93	0.44
10	1.12	0.50	0.45	1.18	0.56	0.47

Notes: Column two computes the constant-demand-elasticity gain in (1); column three computes the Hausman gain (2) as a lower bound to the constant-demand-elasticity case; column four computes the ratio of the previous two columns; column five computes the CES gain (15); column six computes the Hausman gain (18) as a lower bound to the CES case; and column seven computes the ratio of the previous two columns.

true demand curve but above the line $p_1 = p_{1t}$ as his lower-bound measure of the gain in consumer surplus that would occur due to the new product. That consumer surplus area is region B in figure 15.1, which is less than the area under the constant elasticity demand curve, $B + C$. Indeed, we now show that the consumer surplus B following Hausman's method is less than one half of the true consumer surplus region $B + C$.

The consumer surplus B relative to total expenditure on the product E_t is obtained by computing the area of that triangle,

$$(2) \qquad \frac{B}{E_t} = \frac{(p_1^* - p_{1t})q_{1t}}{2E_t} = \frac{\alpha(q_{1t})^2}{2E_t} = \frac{\alpha(q_{1t}/p_{1t})p_{1t}q_{1t}}{2E_t} = \frac{s_{1t}}{2\sigma},$$

where the second equality follows from the definition of the slope $\alpha \equiv (p_1^* - p_{1t})/q_{1t}$ of the inverse demand curve; the third equality from algebra; and the fourth equality because we have assumed the slope of the constant-elasticity demand curve and its linear approximation are equal at the point of consumption, so it follows that the inverse elasticity of demand must also be equal, $\alpha(q_{1t}/p_{1t}) = 1/\sigma$. Comparing equations (1) and (2), the ratio of the consumer surplus from the linear approximation to that from the constant-elasticity demand curve is *less than one half*, $B/(B + C) = (\sigma - 1)/2\sigma < 1/2$. Those two measures of gain are summarized in table 15.1 for $s_{1t} = 0.1$ and various values of σ.

Column two in table 15.1 consists of the constant-demand elasticity gain in (1) and column three shows the Hausman approximate gain in (2), while column four takes their ratio. While these results give us a first illustration of the gains in the constant-demand-elasticity case, they lack rigor by dealing with consumer surplus for a partial equilibrium demand curve with only one new good. Accordingly, in the next section we extend our results to many new (and disappearing) goods while using a constant-elasticity-of-substitution (CES) utility function. We will find that the constant-demand-elasticity and CES cases give quite similar results.

15.3   Utility-Based Approach

15.3.1   Utility Function Approach

We begin with a CES utility function for the consumer,[7] defined by

$$(3) \qquad U_t = U(q_t, I_t) = \left[\sum_{i \in I_t} a_i q_{it}^{(\sigma-1)/\sigma} \right]^{\sigma/(\sigma-1)}, \sigma > 1, \ t = 1 \dots, T,$$

where $a_i > 0$ are parameters and $I_t \subseteq \{1, \dots, N\}$ denotes the set of goods or varieties that are available in period $t = 1, \dots, T$ at the prices p_{it}. We will treat this set of goods as changing over time due to new or disappearing varieties. The unit-expenditure function is defined as the minimum expenditure to obtain utility of one. For the CES utility function, the unit-expenditure function is

$$(4) \qquad e(p_t, I_t) = \left[\sum_{i \in I_t} b_i p_{it}^{1-\sigma} \right]^{1/(1-\sigma)}, \sigma > 1, \ b_i \equiv a_i^{\sigma}, \ t = 1, \dots, T.$$

It follows that total expenditure needed to obtain utility of U_t is $E_t = U_t e(p_t, I_t)$.

From Shephard's Lemma, we can differentiate the expenditure function with respect to p_{it} to obtain the Hicksian demand q_{it} for that good:

$$(5) \qquad q_{it}(p_t, U_t) = U_t \left[\sum_{i \in I_t} b_i p_{it}^{1-\sigma} \right]^{\sigma/(1-\sigma)} b_i p_{it}^{-\sigma}, \ t = 1, \dots, T; i \in I_t.$$

Multiplying by p_{it} and dividing by expenditure E_t to obtain expenditure shares,

$$(6) \qquad s_{it} \equiv \frac{p_{it} q_{it}}{E_t} = \frac{b_i p_{it}^{1-\sigma}}{\sum_{n \in I_t} b_n p_{nt}^{1-\sigma}}, \ t = 1, \dots, T; i \in I_t.$$

Notice that the quantity q_{it} approaches zero as $p_{it} \to \infty$, in which case the share in (5) also approaches zero provided that $\sigma > 1$. Differentiating $-\ln q_{it}$ from (5) with respect to $\ln p_{it}$, we obtain the (positive) Hicksian own-price elasticity corresponding to the CES utility function,

$$(7) \qquad \eta_{it}|_U \equiv -\left. \frac{\partial \ln q_{it}}{\partial \ln p_{it}} \right|_U = \sigma(1 - s_{it}).$$

This elasticity is not constant as was assumed for the partial equilibrium, constant-elasticity demand curve in the previous section. Rather, the elasticity in (7) varies between an upper-bound of σ when $p_{it} \to \infty$ and the share

7. The CES function was introduced into the economics literature by Arrow et al. (1961), and in the mathematics literature it is known as a mean of order $r \equiv 1 - \sigma$; see Hardy, Littlewood, and Polyá (1934, 12–13). Rather than being a utility function for a consumer, equation (1) could instead be a production function for a firm. In that case, we would replace utility U_t by output Y_t.

in (6) approaches zero, and a lower-bound of zero when the share of this product approaches one.[8]

Initially, we consider the case where there is no change in the set of goods over time, so $I_{t-1} = I_t \equiv I$. Our goal is to measure the ratio of the unit-expenditure functions with a formula depending only on observed prices and quantities, which will then correspond to an "exact" price index (Diewert 1976). We maintain throughout the assumption that the observed quantities are optimally chosen for the prices; that is, that they correspond to the shares given in (6). When these shares are computed over the goods $i \in I$, we denote them as

$$(8) \qquad s_{i\tau}(I) \equiv \frac{p_{i\tau} q_{i\tau}}{\sum_{n \in I} p_{n\tau} q_{n\tau}}, \quad \tau = t-1, t; \, i \in I.$$

Then dividing $s_{it}(I)$ by $s_{it-1}(I)$ from (6), raising this expression to the power $1/(\sigma - 1)$, making use of (4) and rearranging terms slightly, we obtain:

$$(9) \qquad \left(\frac{s_{it}(I)}{s_{it-1}(I)} \right)^{1/(1-\sigma)} \frac{e(p_t, I)}{e(p_{t-1}, I)} = \left(\frac{p_{it}}{p_{it-1}} \right), \quad i \in I.$$

To simplify (9) further, we make use of the weights $w_i(I)$ defined by,

$$(10) \qquad w_i(I) \equiv \frac{[s_{it}(I) - s_{it-1}(I)] / [\ln s_{it}(I) - \ln s_{it-1}(I)]}{\sum_{n \in I} \{[s_{nt}(I) - s_{nt-1}(I)] / [\ln s_{nt}(I) - \ln s_{nt-1}(I)]\}}, \, i \in I.$$

The numerator in (10) is the logarithmic mean of the shares $s_{it}(I)$ and $s_{it-1}(I)$, and lies in between these two shares,[9] while the denominator ensures that the weights $w_i(I)$ sum to unity.

Then we take the geometric mean of both sides of (9), using the weights $w_i(I)$ to obtain:

$$(11) \qquad \frac{e(p_t, I)}{e(p_{t-1}, I)} \prod_{i \in I} \left(\frac{s_{it}(I)}{s_{it-1}(I)} \right)^{w_i(I)} = \frac{e(p_t, I)}{e(p_{t-1}, I)}, \text{since } \prod_{i \in I} \left(\frac{s_{it}(I)}{s_{it-1}(I)} \right)^{w_i(I)} = 1,$$

$$= P_{SV}(I) \equiv \prod_{i \in I} \left(\frac{p_{it}}{p_{it-1}} \right)^{w_i(I)}, \text{ using (9).}$$

The result on the first line of (11) that the product shown equals unity follows from taking the log of this expression and using the weights defined in (10), along with the fact that $\sum_{i \in I} s_{it-1}(I) = \sum_{i \in I} s_{it}(I) = 1$ from (8). Then it

8. The fact that the elasticity is close to zero for shares approaching unity suggests that the Hicksian CES demand curve cannot be globally convex for all shares: very inelastic demand must be concave in a region as prices rise and the demand curve bends toward the price axis. Nevertheless, it is shown in appendix C of Diewert and Feenstra (2019b) that the Hicksian demand curve in (5) is strictly convex provided $s_{it} \leq 0.5$.

9. Treating $s_{it-1}(I)$ as a fixed number, it is straightforward to show using L'Hôpital's rule that as $s_{it}(I) \to s_{it-1}(I)$ then the numerator of (10) also approaches $s_{it-1}(I)$. So, the Sato-Vartia weights are well defined even as the shares approach each other. The concavity of the natural log function can be used to show that the numerator of the Sato-Vartia weights lies in between $s_{it}(I)$ and $s_{it-1}(I)$ for all goods $i \in I$.

follows from (11) that the ratio of the unit-expenditure functions equals the term $P_{SV}(I)$ defined as shown, which is the price index due to Sato (1967) and Vartia (1967) constructed over the (constant) set of goods I.

With this result in hand, let us now consider the case where the set of goods is changing over time but some of the goods are available in both periods, so that $I_{t-1} \cap I_t \neq \emptyset$. We again let $e(p_\tau, I)$, for $\tau = t - 1$, t, denote the expenditure function defined over the goods within the set I, which is the set of goods available in both periods, $I \equiv I_{t-1} \cap I_t$. We refer to the set I as the "common" set of goods because they are available in both periods.[10] The ratio $e(p_t,I)/e(p_{t-1},I)$ is still measured by the Sato-Vartia index as in expression (11). Our interest, however, is in the ratio $e(p_t,I_t)/e(p_{t-1},I_{t-1})$ that incorporates new and disappearing goods. To measure this ratio, we return to the share equation (6), which applies for all goods $i \in I_t$. Notice that these shares can be rewritten as

(12) $$s_{i\tau} \equiv \frac{p_{i\tau}q_{i\tau}}{\sum_{n \in I_\tau} p_{n\tau}q_{n\tau}} = s_{i\tau}(I)\lambda_\tau, \quad \tau = t - 1, t; \ i \in I_t,$$

$$\text{with } \lambda_\tau \equiv \frac{\sum_{n \in I} p_{n\tau}q_{n\tau}}{\sum_{n \in I_\tau} p_{n\tau}q_{n\tau}}.$$

Now we can proceed in the same fashion as (9), using (4), (6) and (12) to form the ratio,

(13) $$\left(\frac{s_{it}(I)\lambda_t}{s_{it-1}(I)\lambda_{t-1}}\right)^{1/(1-\sigma)} \frac{e(p_t,I)}{e(p_{t-1},I)} = \left(\frac{p_{it}}{p_{it-1}}\right), \quad i \in I.$$

Once again, we take the geometric mean of both sides of (13) using the weights $w_i(I)$, and shifting the terms λ_t and λ_{t-1} to the right, we obtain in the same manner as equation (11):

(14) $$\frac{e(p_t,I_t)}{e(p_{t-1},I_{t-1})} = P_{SV}(I)\left(\frac{\lambda_t}{\lambda_{t-1}}\right)^{1/(\sigma-1)}.$$

This result shows that the exact price index for the CES utility and expenditure function is obtained by modifying the Sato-Vartia index, constructed over the common set of goods, by the ratio of the terms $\lambda_\tau(I) < 1$. Each of these terms can be interpreted as the *period τ expenditure on the goods in the common set I, relative to the period τ total expenditure.* Alternatively, $\lambda_\tau(I)$ is interpreted as *one minus the period t expenditure on new goods (not in the set I), relative to the period t total expenditure,* while $\lambda_{t-1}(I)$ is interpreted as *one minus the period t − 1 expenditure on disappearing goods (not in the set I), relative to the period t − 1 total expenditure.* When there is a greater

10. Feenstra (1994) shows that we can instead define I as a nonempty subset of the goods available in both periods, and obtain the same results as shown below, but we do not pursue that generalization here. Later in the paper, we will refer to the price index constructed with these common goods as the *maximum overlap* index.

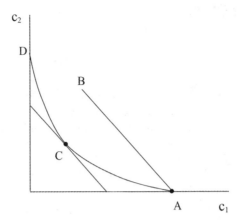

Fig. 15.2   CES indifference curve

expenditure share on new goods in period t than on disappearing goods in period $t-1$, then the ratio $\lambda_t(I)/\lambda_{t-1}(I)$ will be less than unity, which leads to a *fall* in the exact price index in (14) by an amount that depends on the elasticity of substitution.

The importance of the elasticity of substitution can be seen from figure 15.2, where we suppose that the consumer minimizes the expenditure needed to obtain utility along the indifference curve AD. If initially only good 1 is available, then the consumer chooses point A with the budget line AB. When good 2 becomes available, the same level of utility can be obtained with consumption at point C. Then the drop in the cost of living is measured by the inward movement of the budget line from AB to the line through C, and this shift depends on the convexity of the indifference curve, or the elasticity of substitution.

To relate the CES result in (14) back to equation (1), suppose that only good 1 is newly available in period t so that $\lambda_t(I) = 1 - s_{1t}$; there are no disappearing goods so that $\lambda_{t-1}(I) = 1$; and the prices of all other goods do not change so that $P_{SV} = 1$. We follow Hausman (2003) in constructing the expenditure that would be needed to give the consumer the same utility level U_t even if good 1 is not available. That expenditure level is $E_t^* \equiv U_t e(p_t, I_{t-1})$. Then taking the difference between E_t^* and E_t, we have the compensating variation for the loss of good 1:

$$(15) \qquad G_{CES} \equiv \frac{E_t^* - E_t}{E_t} = \frac{e(p_t, I_{t-1}) - e(p_t, I_t)}{e(p_t, I_t)} = (1 - s_{1t})^{-1/(\sigma - 1)} - 1,$$

using the formula for $e(p_t, I_{t-1})/e(p_t, I_t)$ from (14). Taking a second-order Taylor series expansion around $s_{1t} = 0$, this gain can be expressed as

(16) $G_{CES} = (1 - s_{1t})^{-1/(\sigma-1)} - 1 = \dfrac{s_{1t}}{(\sigma-1)} + \dfrac{\sigma \tilde{s}_{1t}^2}{2(\sigma-1)^2}, \text{for } 0 \leq \tilde{s}_{1t} \leq s_{1t},$

$\geq \dfrac{s_{1t}}{(\sigma-1)}, \quad \text{since } \tilde{s}_{1t}^2 \geq 0.$

We see that the second line of (16) is identical to (1), which is therefore a lower bound to the CES gains. In the fifth column of table 15.1, we show the CES gains from (15), which are slightly above the constant-demand-elasticity gains from (1). Our results in this section show that the CES gains with many new (and disappearing) goods give a generalization of the simple, *consumer surplus* calculation of section 15.2. In the next section we compare these CES gains to an approximation of the measure of *total consumer utility* gain due to Hausman (2003).

15.3.2   Hausman Lower Bound to the Welfare Gain

Hausman (1999, 191; 2003, 27) proposed a very simple methodology for calculating a lower bound to the gain from the appearance of a new good. We illustrated that approach for a demand curve with elasticity of σ in section 15.2, but Hausman argues that it holds more generally for any Hicksian demand curves with constant utility. Letting $\eta_{1t}|_U$ denote the (positive) compensated demand derivative for good 1 when it first appears, we obtain the generalization of (2) by replacing σ with the Hicksian elasticity:

(17) $$G_H = \dfrac{s_{1t}}{2\eta_{1t}|_U}.$$

For the CES demand curve, we can calculate the lower bound to the welfare gain using the elasticity of demand for the CES system, as calculated in (7), and we obtain

(18) $$G_{H,CES} = \dfrac{s_{1t}}{2\sigma(1 - s_{1t})}.$$

In column six of table 15.1 we calculate the Hausman lower-bound gains in (18) using the Hicksian elasticities for CES demand, and in column seven we show the ratio of the CES gain in (15) and the Hausman lower bound in (18). Similar to what we found for the constant-demand-elasticity case in the previous section, the Hausman lower-bound calculation in (18) is less than one half of the CES gains in (15) and approaches one half of those gains for elasticities of substitution that are reasonably high.

We next derive the formula for the Hausman lower-bound formula in (17) for a *general form* of utility even when the Hicksian demand curves are not well behaved and differentiable. That will turn out to be the case for the quadratic utility that we consider in the next section, which will give rise to well-behaved inverse demand curves (prices as a function of quantities), but not necessarily well-behaved direct demand curves (quantities as a function of prices). So, this derivation focusing on inverse demand curves will be important for the rest of the paper.

Denote the utility function by $U = f(q) \geq 0$, where $f(q)$ is nondecreasing, concave and homogeneous of degree one for $q \equiv (q_1, \ldots, q_N) \geq 0_N$, and twice continuously differentiable for $q \gg 0_N$. We suppose that the consumer faces positive prices $p_t \equiv (p_{1t}, \ldots, p_{Nt}) \gg 0_N$ in period t and maximizes utility:

$$(19) \qquad \max_{q \geq 0}\{f(q): p_t \cdot q \leq E_t\},$$

where $p_t \cdot q$ is the inner product. The first-order necessary conditions for an *interior maximum*[11] with the period t quantity vector $q_t \gg 0_N$ solving (19) are

$$(20) \qquad \nabla f(q_t) = \lambda_t p_t,$$

$$(21) \qquad p_t \cdot q_t = E_t,$$

where $\nabla f(q_t)$ is the vector of partial derivatives $f_i(q_t) \equiv \partial f(q_t)/\partial q_i$ evaluated at q_t, and λ_t is the Lagrange multiplier on the budget constraint. Take the inner product of both sides of (21) with q_t and solve the resulting equation for $\lambda_t = q_t \cdot \nabla f(q_t)/p_t \cdot q_t = q_t \cdot \nabla f(q_t)/E_t$ where we have used (21). Euler's Theorem on homogeneous functions implies that $q_t \cdot \nabla f(q_t) = f(q_t)$ and so $\lambda_t = f(q_t)/E_t$. Using this result in equation (21), we obtain the first-order condition:

$$(22) \qquad \nabla f(q_t)/f(q_t) = p_t/E_t.$$

To simplify the notation in the rest of this section, we consider only $N = 2$ commodities: good 1 is potentially new in period t, and good 2 represents all other expenditure. In addition, for this section we also scale the utility level so that it equals expenditure for period t:

$$(23) \qquad f(q_{1t}, q_{2t}) = E_t.$$

It follows that the first-order condition (22) becomes $\nabla f(q_t) = p_t$, and specializing to the case of two goods these conditions become:

$$(24) \qquad p_{it} = f_i(q_{1t}, q_{2t}) \equiv \partial f(q_{1t}, q_{2t})/\partial q_i, \quad i = 1, 2.$$

We will derive a second-order Taylor series approximation to the utility loss if good 1 were removed and compare that approximation to the Hausman measure defined by (17).

To make this calculation we reduce purchases of q_1 down to 0 in a linear fashion, holding prices fixed at their initial levels, p_{1t}, p_{2t}. Thus, we travel along the budget constraint until it intersects the q_2 axis. Hence q_2 is an

---

11. Since $f(q)$ is a concave function of q over the feasible region, these conditions are also sufficient for an interior maximum. In the following sections we will characterize the conditions for a maximum on the boundary of the feasible region, with some quantities equal to zero.

endogenous variable; it is the following function of q_1 where q_1 starts at $q_1 = q_{1t}$ and ends up at $q_1 = 0$:

$$(25) \qquad q_2(q_1) \equiv (E_t - p_{1t}q_1)/p_{2t}.$$

The derivative of $q_2(q_1)$ evaluated at q_{1t} is $q_2'(q_{1t}) \equiv \partial q_2(q_{1t})/\partial q_1 = -(p_{1t}/p_{2t})$, a fact which we will use later. Define utility as a function of q_1 for $0 \le q_1 \le q_{1t}$, holding expenditures on the two commodities constant at E_t, as follows:

$$(26) \qquad U = u(q_1) \equiv f(q_1, q_2(q_1)) = f(q_1, [E_t - p_{1t}q_1]/p_{2t}).$$

We use the function $u(q_1)$ to measure the consumer loss of utility as we move q_1 from its original equilibrium level of q_{1t} to 0. Alternatively, the difference between the utility levels $u(q_{1t})$ and $u(0)$ is the *gain of utility due to the appearance of product 1*, defined as a share of expenditure:

$$(27) \qquad G_U \equiv [u(q_{1t}) - u(0)]/E_t.$$

We express $u(0)$ by a second-order Taylor series expansion around the point q_{1t}:

$$(28) \qquad u(0) = u(q_1) + u'(q_1)(0 - q_1) + \frac{1}{2}u''(q_{1t})(0 - q_{1t})^2.$$

The term $u'(q_{1t})$ is computed as

$$(29) \qquad u'(q_{1t}) = f_1(q_{1t}, q_{2t}) + f_2(q_{1t}, q_{2t})\partial q_2(q_{1t})/\partial q_1, \quad \text{differentiating (26)}$$

$$= f_1(q_{1t}, q_{2t}) + f_2(q_{1t}, q_{2t})(-p_{1t}/p_{2t}), \quad \text{differentiating (25)}$$

$$= 0, \quad \text{using (24),}$$

so this term vanishes as an envelope theorem result. It follows from (28) and (29) that a second-order approximation to the consumer gain from good 1 in (27) is

$$(30) \qquad G_H = -\frac{1}{2}u''(q_{1t})q_{1t}^2/E_t.$$

In appendix B of Diewert and Feenstra (2019b), we calculate the second derivative $u''(q_{1t})$ and we show that it is nonpositive, so that the first term on the right of (30) is a nonnegative gain. Furthermore, we define an inverse demand function, $p_1 = D_1(q_1)$ that is consistent with our model; that is, holding other variables constant. The variables that Hausman holds constant are the utility level U_t and the price of product 2, p_{2t}. Endogenous variables are q_1, q_2 and E while the driving variable is p_1, which goes from p_{1t} to the reservation price $p_1^* = D_1(0)$ when q_1 goes from q_{1t} to 0. Because utility is held constant, we regard this derived inverse demand curve as a Hicksian demand curve. We show that the slope of this inverse demand curve at q_{1t} equals $D'(q_{1t}) = u''(q_{1t})$ and so the inverse demand curve is convex if and only if $u'''(\tilde{q}_1) \ge 0$. Convexity of the demand curve implies that the Hausman approximation in (30) is a *lower bound* to the consumer gain from the introduction of good 1.

Substituting the result that $D'(q_{1t}) = u''(q_{1t})$ in (30), we have therefore established that the Hausman gain G_H due to the availability of good 1 is

$$(31) \qquad G_H = -\frac{1}{2} q_{1t}^2 D'(q_{1t}) / E_t.$$

$$= -\frac{1}{2} s_{1t}[D'(q_{1t})(q_{1t}/p_{1t})],$$

where the final term appearing in brackets in (31) is the *elasticity of the constant-utility inverse demand curve*. In appendix B of Diewert and Feenstra (2019b), we solve for this elasticity for particular utility functions, and in the CES case we find that it is precisely the inverse of the price elasticity of the Hicksian demand curve $\eta_{1t}|_U$, as shown in (7). More generally, we likewise expect that $[D'(q_{1t}(q_{1t}/p_{1t}))]$ equals the inverse of $\eta_{1t}|_U$ whenever the Hicksian demand is well behaved and differentiable. Our results in this section are therefore an alternative proof of the Hausman approximation in (17), but we have obtained these results even in cases where the Hicksian demand elasticity does not exist and instead the *inverse* demand functions are well behaved and differentiable. This result will be very useful as we explore a quadratic utility function in the next section.

15.3.3 Konüs-Byushgens-Fisher (KBF) Utility Function

The functional form for the consumer's utility function $f(q)$ that we will consider next is the following quadratic form:[12]

$$(32) \qquad U = f(q) = (q^T A q)^{1/2},$$

where the N by N matrix $A \equiv [a_{ik}]$ is symmetric (so that $A^T = A$) and thus has $N(N+1)/2$ unknown a_{ik} elements. We also assume that A has one positive eigenvalue with a corresponding strictly positive eigenvector and the remaining $N-1$ eigenvalues are negative or zero.[13] These conditions ensure that the utility function has indifference curves with the correct curvature.

Konüs and Byushgens (1926) showed that the Fisher (1922) "ideal" quantity index $Q_F(p_{t-1}, p_t, q_{t-1}, q_t) \equiv [(p_{t-1} \cdot q_t / p_{t-1} \cdot q_{t-1})(p_t \cdot q_t / p_t \cdot q_{t-1})]^{1/2}$ is exactly equal to the aggregate utility ratio $f(q_1)/f(q_0)$, provided that the consumer maximizes the utility function defined by (32) in periods $t-1$ and t, where p_{t-1} and p_t are the price vectors with chosen quantities q_{t-1} and q_t. Diewert (1976) elaborated on this result by proving that the utility function defined by (32)

---

12. We assume that vectors are column vectors when matrix algebra is used. Thus q^T denotes the row vector which is the transpose of q.

13. Diewert and Hill (2010) show that these conditions are sufficient to imply that the utility function defined by (32) is positive, increasing, linearly homogeneous and concave over the regularity region $S \equiv \{q: q \gg 0_N \text{ and } Aq \gg 0_N\}$.

was a *flexible functional form*; that is, it can approximate an arbitrary twice continuously differentiable linearly homogeneous function to the accuracy of a second-order Taylor series approximation around an arbitrary positive quantity vector q^*. Since the Fisher quantity index gives exactly the correct utility ratio for the quadratic functional form defined by (32), he labeled the Fisher quantity index as a *superlative index* and we shall call (32) the *KBF functional form*.

Assume that all products are available in period t and consumers face the positive prices $p_t \gg 0_N$. The first order conditions (22) to maximize the utility function in (32) become

$$(33) \qquad p_t = E_t A q_t / (q_t^T A q_t).$$

While these are the conditions for an interior maximum with $q_t \gg 0_N$, we can obtain the condition for a zero optimal quantity $q_{it} = 0$ if we impose that value on the right of (33) and then define the left-hand side for good i as the reservation price p_{it}^*. Then for all prices $p_{it} \geq p_{it}^*$, the consumer will optimally choose $q_{it} = 0$. We see that an advantage of the quadratic functional form is that the corresponding reservation price can be calculated very easily from (33), for any good where the quantity happens to equal 0 in the period under consideration.

In order to characterize demand, it is useful to work with the expenditure function. Assume for the moment that the matrix is of full rank and denote $A^* = A^{-1}$. Then the minimum expenditure to obtain one unit of utility when the optimal $q_t \gg 0_N$ is

$$(34) \qquad e(p_t) = (p_t^T A^* p_t)^{1/2},$$

The total expenditure function is then $E_t = U_t e(p_t)$, and Hicksian demand is obtained by differentiating with respect to p_{it},

$$(35) \qquad q_{it}(p_t, U_t) = U_t \left[\frac{\sum_{n=1}^{N} a_{in}^* p_{nt}}{(p_t^T A^* p_t)^{1/2}} \right], \quad i = 1, \ldots, N,$$

where a_{in}^* are the elements of A^*. Differentiating $-\ln q_{it}$ with respect to $\ln p_{it}$, we obtain the (positive) Hicksian elasticity,

$$(36) \quad \eta_{it}|_U \equiv -\frac{\partial \ln q_{it}}{\partial \ln p_{it}}\bigg|_U = \frac{-a_{ii}^* p_{it}}{\sum_{n=1}^{N} a_{in}^* p_{nt}} + \frac{p_{it} \sum_{n=1}^{N} a_{in}^* p_{nt}}{p_t^T A^* p_t} = \frac{-a_{ii}^* p_{it}}{\sum_{n=1}^{N} a_{in}^* p_{nt}} + s_{it},$$

where s_{it} is the share of expenditure on good i. Notice that the denominator of the first ratio on the right of (36) must be positive to obtain positive demand in (35), but it approaches zero as the quantity q_{it} approaches zero in a neighborhood of the reservation price as $p_{it} \to p_{it}^*$ and $q_{it} \to 0$. Because the share then approaches zero, it follows that the Hicksian elasticity of demand in (36) remains positive if and only if $a_{ii}^* < 0$, $i = 1, \ldots, N$, which we assume is the case.

The fact that the KBF utility function has finite reservation prices suggests that it lies in between the demand curves for the CES utility function (which have infinite reservation prices) and the linear approximation illustrated in figure 15.1. That conjecture can be established more formally, as we show in appendix C of Diewert and Feenstra (2019b). We compute the second derivatives of the Hicksian demand curves for the quadratic utility function and show that so long as the demand curve is downward sloping, then it will be convex. In appendix C of Diewert and Feenstra (2019b) we also compare the second derivative of the demand curve in the KBF case with that obtained in the CES case. Provided that the first derivatives of the demand curves are equal at the point of consumption (p_{it}, q_{it}), and that the expenditure share satisfies $s_{it} < 0.5$, then the second derivative of the CES Hicksian demand curves will *exceed* the second derivatives of those quadratic demand curves. This means that the demand curves for the quadratic utility function lie *in between* the constant-elasticity demand curves considered in the previous section and the straight-line Hausman approximation.[14]

Using the expenditure function (34) with coefficients $A^* = A^{-1}$, where A is the matrix of coefficients for the direct utility function in (32), requires that the matrix A has full rank so that it is invertible. It is quite possible that A can have less than full rank, however, which means that there are certain goods in the utility function (or linear combinations of goods) that are perfect substitutes with other goods (or their combinations). In that case, at certain prices the demand for goods will not be uniquely determined, so we cannot work with demand as a function of prices or with the expenditure function. Instead, it makes sense to go back to the utility function in (32) and work with the *inverse demand functions* which are defined by (33), where prices (on the left) are a function of quantities and expenditure (on the right). The matrix of coefficients A will be of less than full rank in our empirical application of the KBF utility function, as we shall explain in section 15.4, so we shall use the inverse demand functions in (33) for estimation. Fortunately, even in this case we can define a constant-utility Hicksian inverse demand curve, as we denoted by $p_{1t} = D(q_{1t})$ in section 15.3.2. Then our analysis of the Hausman approximation in that section continues to hold. Indeed, we show in appendix B of Diewert and Feenstra (2019b) that in this case the elasticity of the inverse demand curve is:

$$(37) \qquad \frac{\partial \ln D_1(q_{1t})}{\partial \ln q_{1t}} = \frac{s_{1t}}{(1 - s_{1t})^2}\left(\frac{a_{11}}{p_1^2} - 1\right),$$

which can be used in (31) to obtain the Hausman approximation to the gain from good 1 in the KBF case:

14. While we formally establish this result in appendix C of Diewert and Feenstra (2019b) in a neighborhood of the consumption point, we expect that it will hold for all prices up to the reservation price, which is finite for the quadratic demand curves but infinite for the CES demand curve.

$$(38) \qquad G_{H,KBF} = -\frac{1}{2}\left(\frac{s_{1t}}{1-s_{1t}}\right)^2\left(\frac{a_{11}}{p_1^2}-1\right).$$

15.4   Empirical Illustration Using CES and KBF Utility Functions

15.4.1   Scanner Data for Sales of Frozen Juice

We use the data from store number 5^{15} in the Dominick's Finer Foods Chain of 100 stores in the Greater Chicago area on 19 varieties of frozen orange juice for three years in the period 1989–1994 in order to test out the CES and quadratic utility functions explained in the previous two sections. The micro data from the University of Chicago (2013) are weekly quantities sold of each product and the corresponding unit value price. However, our focus is on calculating a monthly index and so the weekly price and quantity data need to be aggregated into monthly data. Since months contain varying amounts of days, we are immediately confronted with the problem of converting the weekly data into monthly data. We decided to sidestep the problems associated with this conversion by aggregating the weekly data into *pseudo-months*—which we simply refer to as "months"—that consist of four consecutive weeks.

Expenditure or sales shares, $s_{it} \equiv p_{it}q_{it}/\sum_{n=1}^{19}p_{nt}q_{nt}$, were computed for products $i=1,\ldots,19$ and months $t=1,\ldots,39$. We computed the sample average expenditure shares for each product. The bestselling products were products 1, 5, 11, 13, 14, 15, 16, 18, and 19. These products had a sample average share that exceeded 4 percent or a sample maximum share that exceeded 10 percent. There is tremendous volatility in product prices, quantities, and sales shares for both the bestselling and least popular products. There were no sales of products 2 and 4 for months 1–8 and there were no sales of product 12 in month 10 and in months 20–22. *Thus, there is a new and disappearing product problem for 20 observations in this dataset.*

In the following sections, we will use this dataset to estimate the elasticity of substitution σ for the CES utility and unit-expenditure functions, making differing assumptions on the errors underlying the price and expenditure share data.

15.4.2. Estimation of the CES Utility Function with Error in Prices

In this section and the next, we will use the *double differencing approach* that was introduced by Feenstra (1994) to estimate the elasticity of substitution. His method requires that product shares be positive in all periods. In order to implement his method, we drop the products that are not present in all periods. Thus, we drop products 2, 4, and 12 from our list of 19 frozen

---

15. This store is located in a northeast suburb of Chicago.

juice products because products 2 and 4 were not present in months 1–8 and product 12 was not present in months 20–22. Thus, in our particular application the number of always present products in our sample will equal 16. We also renumber our products so that the original product 13 becomes the Nth product in this section. This product had the largest average sales share. If we assume that purchasers are choosing all 19 products by maximizing CES preferences over the 19 products, then this assumption implies that they are also maximizing CES preferences restricted to the always present 16 products.

There are 3 sets of variables in the model ($i = 1, ..., N; t = 1, ..., T$):

- q_{it} is the observed amount of product i sold in period t;
- p_{it} is the observed unit value price of product i sold in period t and
- s_{it} is the observed share of sales of product i in period t that is constructed using the quantities q_{it} and the corresponding observed unit value prices p_{it}.

In our particular application, $N = 16$ and $T = 39$. We aggregated over weekly unit values to construct pseudo-monthly unit value prices. Since there was price change within the monthly time period, the observed monthly unit value prices will have some time aggregation errors in them. Any time aggregation error will carry over into the observed sales shares. Interestingly, as we aggregate over time, the aggregated monthly quantities sold during the period do not suffer from this time aggregation bias. We therefore allow for measurement error in the log shares due to the measurement error in prices, treating the quantities as accurate.[16]

Our goal is to estimate the elasticity of substitution for a CES direct utility function (3) that was discussed in section 15.3.1 above. The system of share equations that corresponds to this consumer utility function was shown as (6) when expressed as a function of prices. An alternative expression for the shares as a function of quantities can be obtained by denoting the CES utility function by $f(q_t)$ and using the first-order condition (22) for good i multiplied by q_{it} to obtain the share equations:

$$(39) \qquad s_{it} \equiv \frac{p_{it} q_{it}}{E_t} = \frac{a_i q_{it}^{(\sigma-1)/\sigma}}{\sum_{n \in I_t} a_n q_{nt}^{(\sigma-1)/\sigma}}, \quad i = 1, ..., N; t - 1, ..., T,$$

where $T = 39$ and $N = 16$. This system of share equations corresponds to the consumers' system of inverse demand equations for always present products, which give monthly unit value prices as functions of quantities purchased. We take natural logarithms of both sides of the equations in (39) and add error terms u_{it} to reflect the measurement error in prices and therefore in shares,

---

16. See our working paper, Diewert and Feenstra (2019b), for other methods. We discuss there the more general technique from Feenstra (1994) that corrects for errors in prices, quantities, and expenditure shares.

$$(40) \qquad \ln s_{it} = \ln a_i + \frac{(\sigma - 1)}{\sigma} \ln q_{it} - \ln\left(\sum_{n=1}^{N} a_n q_{nt}^{(\sigma-1)/\sigma}\right)$$

$$+ u_{it}, \quad i = 1, \ldots, N; t = 1, \ldots, T,$$

where by assumption the q_{it} are measured without error and the error terms u_{it} have 0 means and a classical (singular) covariance matrix for the shares within each time period and the error terms are uncorrelated across time periods. The unknown parameters in (40) are the positive parameters a_i and the elasticity of substitution $\sigma > 1$.

The Feenstra double-differenced variables are defined in two stages. First, for any variable x_{it} we difference the *logarithms* of x_{it} with respect to time; that is, define $\Delta \ln x_{it}$ as follows:

$$(41) \qquad \Delta \ln x_{it} \equiv \ln(x_{it}) - \ln(x_{it-1}), \quad i = 1, \ldots, N; t = 2, 3, \ldots, T.$$

Now pick product N as the numeraire product and difference the $\Delta \ln x_{it}$ with respect to product N, giving rise to the following *double differenced log variable*, $\Delta^2 \ln x_{it}$:

$$(42) \qquad \Delta^2 \ln x_{it} \equiv \Delta \ln x_{it} - \Delta \ln x_{Nt}, \quad i = 1, \ldots, N-1; t = 2, 3, \ldots, T$$

$$= \ln(x_{nt}) - \ln(x_{nt-1}) - \ln(x_{Nt}) + \ln(x_{Nt-1}).$$

We apply this technique to obtain the *double-differenced log share* $\Delta^2 \ln s_{it}$, the *double-differenced log quantity* $\Delta^2 \ln q_{it}$, and the *double-differenced error variables* $\Delta^2 u_{it}$. Then using equation (40), it can be verified that the double-differenced log shares $\Delta^2 \ln s_{it}$ satisfy the following system of $(N-1)(T-1)$ estimating equations:

$$(43) \quad \Delta^2 \ln s_{it} = \frac{(\sigma - 1)}{\sigma} \Delta^2 \ln q_{it} + \Delta^2 u_{it}, \quad i = 1, \ldots, N-1; t = 2, 3, \ldots, T,$$

where the new residuals, $\Delta^2 u_{it}$, have means 0 and a constant covariance matrix with 0 covariances for observations that are separated by two or more time periods. Thus, we have a system of linear estimating equations with only one unknown parameter across all equations—namely, σ. This is almost[17] the simplest possible system of estimating equations that one could imagine.

We have 15 product estimating equations of the form (43) that are estimated with STATA.[18] The resulting estimate for $(\sigma - 1)/\sigma$ was 0.849 (with a standard error of 0.006) and thus the corresponding estimated σ is equal to 6.62. The standard error on $(\sigma - 1)/\sigma$ was tiny using the present regression results so σ was very accurately determined using this method. The

17. The variance covariance structure is not quite classical due to the correlation of residuals between adjacent time periods. We did not take this correlation into account in our estimation of this system of equations; that is, we just used a standard systems nonlinear regression package that assumed intertemporal independence of the error terms.
18. The STATA code to obtain the results in this paper is available on request.

equation-by-equation R^2 for the 15 products $i = 1, ..., N - 1$ were as follows: 0.998, 0.996, 0.997, 0.990, 0.995, 0.994, 0993, 0.993, 0.990, 0.997, 0.991, 0.995, 0.997, 0.991, and 0.995. The average R^2 is 0.994, which is very high for share equations or for transformations of share equations. The results are all the more remarkable considering that *we have only one unknown parameter* in the entire system of $(N - 1)(T - 1) = 570$ observations.[19] This double differencing method for estimating the elasticity of substitution worked much better than any other method that we tried.

15.4.3   Estimation of the Changes in the CES CPI Due to Changing Product Availability

Recall that the Feenstra methodology to measure the exact CES price index used the Sato-Vartia $P_{SV}(I)$ in (11), expressed over the common products, and multiplied that index by the terms $(\lambda_t / \lambda_{t-1})^{1/(\sigma-1)}$ in (14) that captures new and disappearing products. This term will differ from unity if the available products change from the previous period. For our dataset, the term λ_t is less than unity for months 9 (products 2 and 4 become available), 11 (product 12 becomes available), and 23 (product 12 again becomes available). The term λ_{t-1} is greater than unity for months 10 (product 12 becomes unavailable) and 20 (product 12 again becomes unavailable). Computing $(\lambda_t / \lambda_{t-1})^{1/(\sigma-1)}$ using our estimate of $\sigma = 6.62$ gives the results shown in the third column of table 15.2. In the final column, we can *invert* this term to obtain the gain in CES utility (or loss if less than one) due to the availability of goods, which is reported along with its bootstrapped 95 percent confidence interval:[20]

$$(44) \qquad\qquad G_{CES} = (\lambda_t / \lambda_{t-1})^{-1/(\sigma-1)}.$$

Recall that in month 9, products 2 and 4 make their appearance, and table 15.2 tells us that the effect of this increase in variety is to lower the price level and increase utility for month 9 by 0.83 percentage points. In month 10, when product 12 disappears from the store, this has the effect of increasing the price level and lowering utility by 0.40 percentage points. That product comes in and out of the dataset, and the overall effect on the price level of the changes in the availability of products is equal to 0.9918 × 1.0040 × 0.9951 × 1.0044 × 0.9965 = 0.9918, for a decrease in the price level and increase in utility over the sample period of 0.83 percentage points. Notice that this overall effect just reflects the introduction of products 2 and 4 in month 9, since the net impact of the disappearance and reappearance of product 12 *cancels out* when cumulated. That canceling of the impact of availability of product 12 is a highly desirable feature of these CES

19. The results are dependent on the choice of the numeraire product. Ideally, we want to choose the product that has the largest sales share and the lowest share variance.
20. In our bootstrap, we resample with replacement the monthly observations across all products 500 times.

Table 15.2   **Changes in the price level and CES gains due to the availability of products, $\sigma = 6.62$**

	Availability	$(\lambda t/\lambda t - 1)1/(\sigma - 1)$	GCES
9	2 and 4 new	0.9918	1.0083
			[1.0075, 1.0091]
10	12 disappears	1.0040	0.9960
			[0.9955, 0 .9963]
11	12 reappears	0.9951	1.0049
			[1.0045, 1.0054]
20	12 disappears	1.0044	0.9956
			[0.9952, 0.9960]
23	12 reappears	0.9965	1.0035
			[1.0032, 1.0039]
Cumulative Gain		0.9918	1.0083
			[1.0075, 1.0091]

results, but it is not a necessary outcome because it depends on the shares of product 12: it just so happens that these shares are nearly equal when it exits and reenters, leading to zero net impact. We will explore in later sections whether this desirable result continues to hold with other functional forms for utility.

These results in table 15.2 are our first estimates of the gains from increased product availability in our frozen juice data. While they are promising results, as we mentioned in section 15.1, there are two potential problems with the Feenstra methodology: (i) the CES functional form is not fully flexible; and (ii) the reservation prices that induce consumers to demand 0 units of products that are not available in a period are infinite, which *a priori* seems implausible. Thus, in the following section, we will introduce a flexible functional form that will generate finite reservation prices for unavailable products, and hence will provide an alternative methodology for measuring the net benefits of new and disappearing products.

15.4.4   Estimation of the KBF Utility Function

The quadratic or KBF utility function was introduced in section 15.3.3 above. Multiplying both sides of equation i in (33) by q_{it} and dividing by $p_t - q_t = E_t$, we obtain the following *system of inverse demand share equations*:

$$(45) \qquad s_{it} \equiv \frac{p_{it}q_{it}}{p_t \cdot q_t} = \frac{q_{it}\sum_{n=1}^{N}a_{in}q_{nt}}{q_t^T A q_t}, \quad i = 1, \ldots, N,$$

where a_{in} is the element of A that is in row i and column n for $i, n = 1, \ldots, N$. These equations will form the basis for our system of estimating equations in this and the following section. Note that they are nonlinear equations in the unknown parameters a_{ik}. It turns out to be useful to reparameterize the A matrix as follows:

(46) $A = bb^T + B; b \gg 0_N; B = B^T; B$ is negative semidefinite; $Bq^* = 0_N,$

where q^* is a positive vector. The vector $b^T \equiv [b_1, ..., b_N]$ is a row vector of positive constants and so bb^T is a rank 1 positive semidefinite N by N matrix. The symmetric matrix B has $N(N + 1)/2$ independent elements b_{nk} but the N constraints Bq^* reduce this number of independent parameters by N. Thus, there are N independent parameters in the b vector and $N(N - 1)/2$ independent parameters in the B matrix so that $bb^T + B$ has the same number of independent parameters as the A matrix. Diewert and Hill (2010) showed that replacing A by $bb^T + B$ still leads to a flexible functional form.

The reparameterization of A by $bb^T + B$ is useful in our present context because we can use this reparameterization to estimate the unknown parameters in stages. Thus, we will initially set $B = 0_{N \times N}$, a matrix of 0's. The resulting utility function becomes $f(q) = (q^T bb^T q)^{1/2} = (b^T q b^T q)^{1/2} = b^T q$, a linear utility function. Thus, this special case of (32) boils down to the *linear utility function* model, which means that the goods are perfect substitutes for each other. We will add the matrix B into our estimation as described below but restrict it to be of less than full rank, so the matrix A will also be of less than full rank. As anticipated earlier (see the end of section 15.3.3), this means that A cannot be inverted and it will be necessary to work with the inverse demand curves of the KBF system, rather than the expenditure function or the associated Hicksian or Marshallian demand curves.

The matrix B is required to be negative semidefinite. We can follow the procedure used by Wiley, Schmidt, and Bramble (1973) and Diewert and Wales (1987) and impose negative semidefiniteness on B by setting B equal to $-CC^T$ where C is a lower triangular matrix.[21] Write C as $[c^1, c^2, ..., c^N]$ where c^k is a column vector for $k = 1, ..., N$. If C is lower triangular, then the first $k - 1$ elements of c^k are equal to 0, $k = 2, 3, ..., N$. Thus, we have the following representation for B:

(47) $$B = -CC^T = -\sum_{k=1}^{19} C^k C^{kT},$$

where we impose the following restrictions on the vectors c^k in order to impose the restrictions $Bq^* = 0_N$ on B:[22]

(48) $$c^{kT} q^* = 0; k = 1, ..., N.$$

If the number of products N in the commodity group under consideration is not small, then typically, it will not be possible to estimate all the

---

21. $C = [c_{nk}]$ is a lower triangular matrix if $c_{nk} = 0$ for $k > n$; that is, there are 0's in the upper triangle. Wiley, Schmidt, and Bramble (1973) showed that setting $B = -CC^T$ where C was lower triangular was sufficient to impose negative semidefiniteness while Diewert and Wales showed that any negative semidefinite matrix could be represented in this fashion.

22. The restriction that C be lower triangular means that c^N will have at most one nonzero element, namely c_N^N. However, the positivity of q^* and the restriction $c^{NT} q^* = 0$ will imply that $c^N = 0_N$. Thus, the maximal rank of B is $N - 1$. For additional materials on the properties of the KBF functional form, see Diewert (2018).

parameters in the C matrix. Furthermore, typically nonlinear estimation is not successful if one attempts to estimate all the parameters at once. Thus, we estimated the parameters in the utility function $f(q) = (q^T A q)^{1/2}$ in stages. In the first stage, we estimated the linear utility function $f(q) = b^T q$. In the second stage, we estimate $f(q) = (q^T[bb^T - c^1 c^{1T}]q)^{1/2}$ where $c^{1T} \equiv [c_1^1, c_2^1, ..., c_N^1]$ and $c^{1T}q^* = 0$. For starting coefficient values in the second nonlinear regression, we use the final estimates for b from the first nonlinear regression and set the starting $c^1 \equiv 0_N$.[23] In the third stage, we estimate $f(q) = (q^T[bb^T - c^1 c^{1T} - c^2 c^{2T}]q)^{1/2}$ where $c^{1T} \equiv [c_1^1, c_2^1, ..., c_N^1]$, $c^{1T}q^* = 0$, $c^{2T} \equiv [0, c_2^2, ..., c_N^2]$ and $c^{2T}q^* = 0$. The starting coefficient values are the final values from the second stage with $c^2 \equiv 0_N$. In the fourth stage, we estimate $f(q) = (q^T[bb^T - c^1 c^{1T} - c^2 c^{2T} - c^3 c^{3T}]q)^{1/2}$ where $c^{1T} \equiv [c_1^1, c_2^1, ..., c_N^1]$, $c^{1T}q^* = 0$, $c^{2T} \equiv [0, c_2^2, ..., c_N^2]$, $c^{2T}q^* = 0$, $c^{3T} \equiv [0, 0, c_3^3, ..., c_N^3]$ and $c^{3T}q^* = 0$. At each stage, the log likelihood will generally increase.[24] We stop adding columns to the C matrix when the increase in the log likelihood becomes small (or the number of degrees of freedom becomes small). At stage k of this procedure, it turns out that we are estimating the substitution matrices of rank $k-1$ that is the most negative semidefinite that the data will support. This is the same type of procedure that Diewert and Wales (1988) used to estimate normalized quadratic preferences and they termed the final functional form a *semiflexible functional form*. The above treatment of the KBF functional form also generates a semiflexible functional form.

15.4.5 The Estimation of KBF Preferences Using Price Equations

We considered two methods for estimating the KBF utility function. The first used a stochastic version of the share equations (45).[25] When we applied that method to predict prices for products that were actually available, it performed rather poorly, giving us little confidence that the reservation prices for products *not* available would be reliable. Accordingly, we switched from estimating share equations to the estimation of price equations. We considered the system of estimating equations using prices as the dependent variables, as was shown in (33):

(49) $p_{it} \equiv E_t \sum_{j=1}^{19} a_{ij} q_{jt} / [\sum_{n=1}^{19} \sum_{m=1}^{19} a_{nm} q_{nt} q_{mt}] + \varepsilon_{it}, t = 1,...,39; i = 1,...,18,$

where the A matrix was defined as $A = bb^T - c^1 c^{1T} - c^2 c^{2T} - c^3 c^{3T} - c^4 c^{4T}$ and the vectors b and c^1 to c^4 satisfy the same restrictions as the last model in the previous section. We stack up the estimating equations defined by (49) into a single nonlinear regression and we drop the observations that correspond to products i that were not available in period t.

23. We also use the constraint $c^{1T}q^*$ to eliminate one of the c_n^1 from the nonlinear regression.
24. If it does not increase, then the data do not support the estimation of a higher rank substitution matrix and we stop adding columns to the C matrix. The log likelihood cannot decrease because the successive models are nested.
25. See our working paper, Diewert and Feenstra (2019b).

We used the final estimates for the components of the b, c^1, c^2, c^3 and c^4 vectors from the previous model as starting coefficient values for the present model. The initial log likelihood of our new model using these starting values for the coefficients was 415.6. The final log likelihood for this model was 518.9, an increase of 103.5 as compared to using shares as the dependent variable. Thus, switching from having shares to having prices as the dependent variables did significantly change our estimates. The single equation R^2 was 0.945. We used our estimated coefficients to form predicted prices p_{it}^* using equations (49) evaluated at our new parameter estimates. The equation-by-equation R^2 comparing the predicted prices for the 19 products with the actual prices were as follows: 0.830, 0.862, 0.900, 0.916, 0.899, 0.832, 0.913, 0.035, 0.244, 0.275, 0.024, 0.007, 0.870, 0.695, 0.421, 0.808, 0.618, 0.852, and 0.287. The average R^2 was 0.594. Of particular concern is product 12, which comes in and out of the sample and has a very low R^2 of only 0.007.

Since the predicted prices are still not very close to the actual prices, we decided to press on and estimate a new model, which added another rank 1 substitution matrix to the substitution matrix; that is, we set $A = bb^T - c^1c^{1T} - c^2c^{2T} - c^3c^{3T} - c^4c^{4T} - c^5c^{5T}$, where $c^{5T} = [0, 0, 0, 0, c_5^5, ..., c_{19}^5]$ and the additional normalization $c_{19}^5 = -\sum_{n=5}^{18} c_n^5$. We used the final estimates for the components of the b, c^1, c^2, c^3 and c^4 vectors from the previous model as starting coefficient values for the present model, along with $c_n^5 = 0.001$ for $n = 5, 6, ..., 18$. The initial log likelihood of our new model using these starting values for the coefficients was 518.9. The final log likelihood for this model was 550.3, an increase of 31.4. The single equation R^2 was 0.950.

Since the increase in log likelihood for the rank 5 substitution matrix over the previous rank 4 substitution matrix was fairly large, we decided to add another rank 1 matrix to the A matrix. Thus, for our next model, we set $A = bb^T - c^1c^{1T} - c^2c^{2T} - c^3c^{3T} - c^4c^{4T} - c^5c^{5T} - c^6c^{6T}$ where $c^{6T} = [0, 0, 0, 0, c_6^6, ..., c_{19}^6]$ with the additional normalization $c_{19}^6 = -\sum_{n=6}^{18} c_n^6$. We used the final estimates for the components of the b, c^1, c^2, c^3, c^4 and c^5 vectors from the previous model as starting coefficient values for the new model along with $c_n^6 = 0.001$ for $n = 6, 7, ..., 18$. The final log likelihood for this model was 568.9, an increase of 18.5. The single equation R^2 was 0.953. The present model had 111 unknown parameters that were estimated (plus a variance parameter). We had only 680 observations and it was becoming increasingly difficult to converge to the maximum likelihood estimates. Thus, we stopped our sequential estimation process at this point.

The parameter estimates for the rank 6 substitution matrix are listed below in table 15.3.

The estimated b_n in table 15.3 for $n = 1, ..., 18$ plus $b_{19} = 1$ are proportional to the vector of first order partial derivatives of the KBF utility function $f(q)$ evaluated at the vector of ones, $\nabla_q f(1_{19})$. Thus, the b_n can be interpreted as estimates of the relative quality of the 19 products. Viewing table 15.3, it can be seen that the highest-quality products were products 6, 17, and 4

Table 15.3   **Estimated parameters for KBF preferences**

Coef	Estimate	t Stat	Coef	Estimate	t Stat	Coef	Estimate	t Stat
b_1	1.35	11.39	c_3^2	-0.08	-0.11	c_9^4	0.16	0.26
b_2	1.31	10.77	c_4^2	-0.71	-0.72	c_{10}^4	-0.03	-0.05
b_3	1.43	11.31	c_5^2	-0.10	-0.24	c_{11}^4	-0.61	-0.81
b_4	1.57	11.54	c_6^2	-0.64	-1.28	c_{12}^4	-1.59	-1.13
b_5	1.37	11.23	c_7^2	-0.61	-1.38	c_{13}^4	-0.23	-0.31
b_6	2.09	11.89	c_8^2	1.15	1.81	c_{14}^4	-0.16	-0.24
b_7	1.42	11.40	c_9^2	-0.39	-1.35	c_{15}^4	-0.67	-1.69
b_8	0.82	9.02	c_{10}^2	-0.54	-1.73	c_{16}^4	-0.22	-0.30
b_9	0.57	9.67	c_{11}^2	1.00	2.14	c_{17}^4	3.27	3.55
h_{10}	0.59	9.40	c_{12}^2	1.90	1.67	c_{18}^4	-0.35	-0.44
b_{11}	0.80	10.01	c_{13}^2	-0.46	-1.48	c_5^5	-0.06	-0.11
b_{12}	1.10	9.16	c_{14}^2	-0.73	-1.46	c_6^5	-0.04	-0.12
b_{13}	1.24	11.14	c_{15}^2	-0.32	-0.80	c_7^5	-0.10	-0.06
b_{14}	1.61	11.12	c_{16}^2	0.26	0.84	c_8^5	-0.25	-0.04
b_{15}	0.71	10.12	c_{17}^2	0.02	0.01	c_9^5	-0.62	-0.89
b_{16}	1.34	11.47	c_{18}^2	-0.50	-1.13	c_{10}^5	-0.56	-0.80
b_{17}	1.58	7.97	c_3^3	1.36	5.41	c_{11}^5	-0.11	-0.03
b_{18}	1.37	11.40	c_4^3	1.72	4.41	c_{12}^5	-0.31	-0.04
c_1^1	1.98	10.03	c_5^3	1.03	5.10	c_{13}^5	0.63	0.12
c_2^1	1.66	6.65	c_6^3	-0.43	-1.09	c_{14}^5	0.05	0.01
c_3^1	-0.25	-1.19	c_7^3	0.90	2.43	c_{15}^5	-0.08	-0.02
c_4^1	0.13	0.55	c_8^3	-0.46	-0.81	c_{16}^5	0.76	0.13
c_5^1	0.013	0.09	c_9^3	-0.01	-0.04	c_{17}^5	0.61	0.23
c_6^1	-0.01	-0.05	c_{10}^3	-0.08	-0.28	c_{18}^5	0.48	0.05
c_7^1	-0.38	-1.92	c_{11}^3	-0.59	-1.06	c_6^6	-0.01	-0.03
c_8^1	-0.43	-1.86	c_{12}^3	-0.14	-0.14	c_7^6	0.18	0.38
c_9^1	-0.02	-0.11	c_{13}^3	-0.02	-0.09	c_8^6	-0.76	-0.30
r_{10}^1	-0.28	-1.58	c_{14}^3	-0.45	-1.18	c_9^6	-0.08	-0.02
c_{11}^1	-0.96	-4.48	c_{15}^3	-0.46	-2.03	c_{10}^6	0.08	0.02
c_{12}^1	-0.88	-2.69	c_{16}^3	-0.01	-0.06	c_{11}^6	-0.44	-0.27
c_{13}^1	0.11	1.52	c_{17}^3	-2.16	-2.38	c_{12}^6	-0.95	-0.23
c_{14}^1	-0.22	-1.02	c_{18}^3	0.01	0.03	c_{13}^6	-0.60	-0.11
c_{15}^1	-0.13	-0.85	c_4^4	-0.50	-0.71	c_{14}^6	0.47	0.98
c_{16}^1	0.14	1.25	c_5^4	0.49	1.34	c_{15}^6	0.39	0.34
c_{17}^1	-0.68	-1.54	c_6^4	0.27	0.47	c_{16}^6	0.66	0.10
c_{18}^1	0.08	0.45	c_7^4	0.38	0.63	c_{17}^6	0.12	0.00
c_2^2	0.72	1.58	c_8^4	-0.11	-0.12	c_{18}^6	1.02	0.26

($b_6 = 2.09$, $b_{17} = 1.58$, $b_4 = 1.57$) and the lowest quality products were products 9, 10, and 15 ($b_9 = 0.57$, $b_{10} = 0.59$, $b_{15} = 0.71$).

With the estimated b and c vectors in hand (denote them as $\hat{b}$ and $\hat{c}^k$ for $k = 1$, ..., 6), form the estimated A matrix as $\hat{A} \equiv \hat{b}\hat{b}^T - \hat{c}^1\hat{c}^{1T} - \hat{c}^2\hat{c}^{2T} - \hat{c}^3\hat{c}^{3T} - \hat{c}^4\hat{c}^{4T} - \hat{c}^5\hat{c}^{5T} - \hat{c}^6\hat{c}^{6T}$, and again denote the ij element of $\hat{A}$ as $\hat{a}_{ij}$ for $i, j = 1, ..., 19$. The *predicted price* for product i in month t is calculated using the new $\hat{a}_{ij}$ estimates. The equation-by-equation R^2 that compares the predicted prices for the 19 products with the actual prices were as follows: 0.827, 0.868, 0.900, 0.917, 0.896, 0.854, 0.905, 0.034, 0.328, 0.424, 0.052, 0.284, 0.865, 0.7280,

0.487, 0.814, 0.854, 0.848, and 0.321. The average R^2 was 0.642, which is a noticeable increase from the rank 4 model (average $R^2 = 0.594$), and now 12 of the 19 equations had an R^2 greater than 0.70, while five of the equations had an R^2 less than 0.40 (product 12 had $R^2 = 0.284$).[26]

15.4.6   The Gains and Losses Due to Changes in Product Availability

In this section, we consider a framework for measuring the gains or losses in utility due to changes in the availability of products that can be applied to the KBF (or any other) utility function. We suppose that we have data on prices and quantities on the sales of N products for T periods. The vectors of observed period t prices and quantities sold are $p_t = (p_{1t}, ..., p_{Nt}) \geq 0_N$ and $q_t = (q_{1t}, ..., q_{Nt}) \geq 0_N$, respectively, for $t = 1, ..., T$. Sales or expenditures on the N products during period t are $E_t \equiv p_t \cdot q_t$ for $t = 1, ..., T$.[27] We assume that a linearly homogeneous utility function, $f(q_1, ..., q_N) = f(q)$, has been estimated where $q \geq 0_N$.[28] If product i is not available (or not sold) during period t, the corresponding price and quantity, p_{it} and q_{it}, are set equal to zeros.

We calculate *reservation prices* for the unavailable products. We refer to these as *predicted prices* for the available commodities, where the predicted prices are consistent with our econometrically estimated utility function and the observed quantity data, q_t. The period t *reservation or predicted price* for product i, p_{it}^*, is defined as the prices satisfying the first-order conditions (22) using partial derivatives of the estimated utility function $f(q)$:

(50) $p_{it}^* \equiv E_t[\partial f(q_t)/\partial q_i]/f(q_t), \quad i = 1, ..., N; t = 1, ..., T.$

The prices defined by (50) are also Rothbarth's (1941) *virtual prices*; they are the prices that rationalize the observed period t quantity vector as a solution to the period t utility maximization problem. Since $f(q)$ is nondecreasing in its arguments and $E_t > 0$, we see that $p_{it}^* \geq 0$ for all i and t. If the estimated utility function fits the observed data exactly (so that all errors in the estimating equations are equal to 0),[29] then the predicted prices, p_{it}^*, for the available products will be equal to the corresponding actual prices, p_{it}.

Imputed expenditures on product i during period t are defined as $p_{it}^* q_{it}$ for $i = 1, ..., N$. Note that if product n is not sold during period t, $q_{it} = 0$ and hence $p_{it}^* q_{it} = 0$ as well. *Total imputed expenditures* for all products sold during period t, E_t^*, are defined as the sum of the individual product imputed expenditures:

26. The sample average expenditure shares of these low R^2 products were 0.026, 0.026, 0.043, 0.025, and 0.050, respectively. Thus, these low R^2 products are relatively unimportant compared to the high expenditure share products.
27. We also assume that $\Sigma_{i=2}^{19} p_{it} q_{it} > 0$ for $t = 1, ..., T$.
28. We assume that $f(q)$ is a differentiable, positive, linearly homogeneous, nondecreasing and concave function of q over a cone contained in the positive orthant. The domain of definition of the function f is extended to the closure of this cone by continuity and we assume that observed quantity vectors q_t are contained in the closure of this cone.
29. This assumes that observed prices are the dependent variables in the estimating equations.

(51) $E_t^* \equiv \sum_{i=1}^N p_{it}^* q_{it}, t = 1, \ldots, T$

$\qquad = \sum_{i=1}^N q_{it} E_t[\partial f(q_t)/\partial q_i]/f(q_t),$ using definition (50)

$\qquad = E_t,$

where the last equality follows using the linear homogeneity of $f(q)$ since by Euler's Theorem on homogeneous functions, we have $f(q) = \sum_{i=1}^N q_i \partial f(q)/\partial q_i$. Thus, period t imputed expenditures, E_t^*, are equal to period t actual expenditures, E_t.

The above material sets the stage for the main acts: namely, how to measure the welfare gain if product availability increases and how to measure the welfare loss if product availability decreases. Suppose that in period $t-1$, product 1 was not available (so that $q_{1t-1} = 0$), but in period t it becomes available, and a positive amount is purchased (so that $q_{1t} > 0$). Our task is to define a measure of the increase in consumer welfare that can be attributed to the increase in commodity availability.

Define the vector of purchases of products during period t, excluding purchases of product 1 as $q_{\sim 1t} \equiv [q_{2t}, q_{3t}, \ldots, q_{Nt}]$. Thus $q_t = [q_{1t}, q_{\sim 1t}]$. Since by assumption, an estimated utility function $f(q)$ is available, we can use this utility function in order to define the *aggregate level of consumer utility during period t*, U_t, as follows:

(52) $\qquad\qquad\qquad U_t \equiv f(q_t) = f(q_{1t}, q_{\sim 1t}).$

Now exclude the purchases of product 1 and define the (diminished) utility, $U_{\sim 1t}$, the utility generated by the remaining vector of purchases, $q_{\sim 1t}$, as follows:

(53) $U_{\sim 1t} \equiv f(0, q_{\sim 1t})$

$\qquad \leq f(q_{1t}, q_{\sim 1t})$ since $f(q)$ is nondecreasing in the components of q

$\qquad = U_t$ using definition (52).

Define the *period t imputed expenditures on products excluding product 1*, $E_{\sim 1t}^*$, as follows:

(54) $\qquad\qquad\qquad E_{\sim 1t}^* \equiv \sum_{i=2}^N p_{it}^* q_{it}$

$\qquad\qquad = E_t - p_{1t}^* q_{1t}$ using (51)

$\qquad\qquad \leq E_t$ since $p_{1t}^* \geq 0$ and $q_{1t} > 0$.

It will be useful to work with the ratio of $E_{\sim 1t}^*$ to E_t, defined as

(55) $\qquad\qquad\qquad \lambda_1 \equiv E_{\sim 1t}^*/E_t \leq 1$ using (54).

Notice that the scalar λ_1 is exactly the same as the term λ_t defined in (12), provided that we use the "common" set of goods $I \equiv \{2, \ldots, N\}$ in (12). In other words, this is the period t expenditure on the set of goods $\{2, ..., N\}$ that were also available in period $t - 1$, relative to total expenditure. Then divide the vector of period t purchases excluding product 1, q_{1t}, by the scalar λ_1, and calculate the resulting imputed expenditures on the vector $q_{\sim 1t}/\lambda_1$ as equal to E_t:

$$
(56) \qquad \sum_{i=2}^{N} p_{it}^* q_{it} / \lambda_1 = (1/\lambda_1) \sum_{i=2}^{N} p_{it}^* q_{it}
$$

$$
= (1/\lambda_1) E_{1t}^* \quad \text{using definition (54)}
$$

$$
= (E_t / E_{\sim 1t}^*) E_{\sim 1t}^* \quad \text{using definition (55)}
$$

$$
= E_t.
$$

Using the linear homogeneity of $f(q)$ in the components of q, we are able to calculate the utility level, U_{A1t}, that is generated by the vector $q_{\sim 1t}/\lambda_1$ as follows:

$$
(57) \qquad U_{A1t} \equiv f(0, q_{\sim 1t}/\lambda_1)
$$

$$
= (1/\lambda_1) f(0, q_{\sim 1t}) \quad \text{using the linear homogeneity of } f
$$

$$
= (1/\lambda_1) U_{\sim 1t} \quad \text{using definition (53).}
$$

Note that λ_1 can be calculated using definition (55) and $U_{\sim 1t}$ can be calculated using definition (53). Thus, U_{A1t} can also be readily calculated.

Consider the following (hypothetical) consumer's period t aggregate *utility maximization problem where product 1 is not available* and consumers face the imputed prices p_{it}^* for products $2, ..., N$ and the maximum expenditure on the $N-1$ products is restricted to be equal to or less than actual expenditures on all N products during period t, which is E_t:

$$
(58) \qquad \max_{q's} \{ f(0, q_2, q_3, ..., q_N) : \sum_{i=2}^{N} p_{it}^* q_{it} \le E_t \} \equiv U_{1t}
$$

$$
\ge U_{A1t},
$$

where U_{A1t} is defined by (57). The inequality in (58) follows because (56) shows that $q_{\sim 1t}/\lambda_1$ is a feasible solution for the utility maximization problem defined by (58). We also know that the actual utility level in period t, U_t exceeds the maximized utility level U_{1t} when good 1 is not available, so that we have

$$
(59) \qquad U_t \ge U_{1t} \ge U_{A1t}.
$$

We regard U_{A1t} as an approximation (and lower bound) to U_{1t}. Given that an estimated utility function $f(q)$ is in hand, it is easy to compute the *approximate* utility level U_{A1t} when product 1 is not available. The *actual* constrained utility level, U_{1t}, will in general involve solving numerically the nonlinear programming problem defined by (58). For the KBF functional form, instead of maximizing $(q^T A q)^{1/2}$, we could maximize its square, $q^T A q$, and thus solving (58) would be equivalent to solving a quadratic programming problem with a single linear constraint. For the CES functional form, it turns out that there is no need to solve (58) because the strong separability of the CES functional form will imply that $U_{1t} = U_{A1t}$. In other words, for the CES utility function, when good 1 is not available, then the consumer will *optimally choose* to inflate the purchases $q_{\sim1t}$ by $(1 / \lambda_1)$ in order to exhaust the budget E_t.

A reasonable measure of the gain in utility due to the new availability of product 1 in period t, G_{1t}, is the ratio of the completely unconstrained level of utility U_t to the product 1 constrained level U_{1t}—that is, define *the product 1 utility gain in period t* as

$$(60) \qquad G_{1t} \equiv U_t / U_{1t} \geq 1,$$

where the inequality follows from (59). The corresponding *product 1 approximate utility gain* is defined as

$$(61) \qquad G_{A1t} \equiv U_t / U_{A1t} \geq G_{1t} \geq 1,$$

where the inequalities follow again from (59). Thus, in general the approximate gain is an upper bound to the true gain in utility due to the new availability of product 1 in period t.

Note that for the CES utility function we have $G_{A1t} = G_{1t}$ since $U_{1t} = U_{A1t}$. Furthermore, using the shares in (39) assumed no measurement error in prices, so that $p_{it} = p_{it}^*$, and we have

$$(62) \quad G_{A1t} = \frac{U_t}{U_{A1t}} = \lambda_{1t} \frac{U_t}{U_{\sim1t}} \qquad \text{from definitions (57) and (61)}$$

$$= \frac{\sum_{i=2}^{N} p_{it}^* q_{it}}{E_t} \frac{U_t}{U_{\sim1t}} \qquad \text{from definition (55)}$$

$$= \frac{\sum_{i=2}^{N} a_i q_{it}^{(\sigma-1)/\sigma}}{\sum_{i=1}^{N} a_i q_{it}^{(\sigma-1)/\sigma}} \frac{U_t}{U_{\sim1t}} \qquad \text{from (39) with } p_{it} = p_{it}^*$$

$$= \left[\frac{\sum_{i=1}^{N} a_i q_{it}^{(\sigma-1)/\sigma}}{\sum_{i=2}^{N} a_i q_{it}^{(\sigma-1)/\sigma}} \right]^{1/(\sigma-1)} \qquad \text{from (3) with } \frac{\sigma}{\sigma-1} - 1 = \frac{1}{\sigma-1}$$

$$= \left(1 - \sum_{i=2}^{N} s_{it} \right)^{-1/(\sigma-1)} \qquad \text{from (39) once again.}$$

So, for the CES case, the *approximate* measure of gain G_{A1t} equals the *true* gain G_{1t}, and these are exactly equal to the CES gain we defined earlier in (44) when applied to the case of new product 1. In other words, the earlier CES gain is identical to the approximate measure of gain that we have proposed in this section when applied to that functional form. But our definitions in this section also apply to *any other* functional form for utility, including the KBF form, while recognizing that we are using the approximation (and upper bound) G_{A1t} rather than G_{1t}.

Now consider the case where product 1 is available in period t but it becomes unavailable in period $t + 1$. In this case, we want to calculate an approximation to the loss of utility in period $t + 1$ due to the unavailability of product 1. It turns out, however, that our methodology will not provide an answer to this measurement problem using the price and quantity data for period $t + 1$; we have to approximate the loss of utility that will occur in period t due to the unavailability of product 1 in period $t + 1$ by instead looking at the loss of utility that would occur in period t if product 1 became unavailable. Once we redefine our measurement problem in this way, we can simply adapt the inequalities that we have already established for period t utility to the *loss* of utility from the unavailability of product 1 from the previous analysis for the *gain* in utility.

A reasonable measure of the hypothetical loss of utility due to the unavailability of product 1 in period t is the ratio of the product 1 constrained level of utility U_{1t} to the completely unconstrained level of utility U_t to the product 1. We apply this hypothetical loss measure to period $t + 1$ when product 1 becomes unavailable—that is, define *the product 1 utility loss that can be attributed to the disappearance of product 1 in period $t + 1$* as

(63) $L_{1,t+1} \equiv U_{1t} / U_t \leq 1,$

where the inequality follows from (59). The corresponding *product 1 approximate utility loss* is defined as

(64) $L_{A1,t+1} \equiv U_{A1t} / U_t \leq L_{1,t+1} \leq 1,$

where the inequalities again follow from (59). Thus, in general the approximate loss is a lower bound to the "true" loss $L_{1,t+1}$ in utility that can be attributed to the disappearance of product 1 in period $t + 1$. As was the case with our approximate gain measure, if $f(q)$ is a CES utility function, then $L_{A1,t+1} = L_{1,t+1}$.

It is straightforward to adapt the above analysis from product 1 to product 12 and compute the approximate gains and losses in utility that occur due to the disappearance of product 12 in period 10, its reappearance in period 11, its disappearance in period 20, and its final reappearance in period 23. These approximate losses and gains for the KBF utility function are listed in the third column of table 15.4. It is also straightforward to adapt the above analysis to situations where two new products appear in a period, which is the case for our products 2 and 4, which were missing in periods 1–8 and make their appearance in period 9. The approximate utility gain due to the new availability of these products in the KBF case is also listed in the third column of table 15.4. In the fourth column of table 15.4 we repeat the CES gain in utility from table 15.2 for period 9 due to the introduction of products

Table 15.4   **The gains and losses of utility due to changes in product availability**

Month	Availability	$\dfrac{G_{A,KBF}}{L_{A,KBF}}$	G_{CES} ($\sigma = 6.62$)
9	2 and 4 new	1.0013	1.0083
		[1.0009, 1.0040]	[1.0075, 1.0091]
10	12 disappears	0.9975	0.9959
		[0.9935, 0.9996]	[0.9955, 0.9963]
11	12 reappears	1.0030	1.0049
		[1.0005, 1.0088]	[1.0045, 1.0054]
20	12 disappears	0 .9988	0.9956
		[0.9968, 0.9998]	[0.9952, 0.9960]
23	12 reappears	1.0008	1.0035
		[1.0001, 1.0020]	[1.0032, 1.0039]
Cumulative Gain		1.0014	1.0083
		[1.0011, 1.0047]	[1.0075, 1.0091]

2 and 4, and the various impacts of the exit and entry of product 12. Thus, table 15.4 compares the gains and losses in utility for the KBF and CES models for the five months in which there was a change in product availability.

In month 9, when products 2 and 4 become available, the CES model implies that the enhanced product availability increases consumers' utility by 0.83 percentage points, while the KBF model implies a much smaller increase of 0.13 percentage points. Following that product introduction, we have the disappearance and reappearance of product 12 over all several months.

Recall that in our earlier calculation of the CES gain (see table 15.2), the net effect on utility of the entry and exit of product 12 canceled out, so that the overall utility gains came only from the initial entry or products 2 and 4. That result roughly holds in the KBF case, too, where product 12 now has only a very small impact on overall utility, increasing the utility gain from 1.0013 (first row of the third column in table 15.4) to 1.0014 (final row of the third column).

So, product 12 has only a very minor effect on utility, and the principal impact comes from the month 9 introduction of products 2 and 4, *where the CES gains are six times higher than the KBF gains* in table 15.4 (and their bootstrapped 95 percent confidence intervals do not overlap). That is a surprising result because our argument throughout this paper has been that the CES gains are at least twice as high as the Hausman gains obtained from a linear approximation to the demand curve. We have noted in section 15.3.3 that the demand curves of the KBF utility function are convex, and since these convex demand curves lie above their linear approximation, the utility gain from a new product with KBF utility should *exceed* the utility gain along linear approximation. It follows that CES gains should be *not much more than twice as high as the KBF gains, provided that those demand curves have the same elasticity at the point of consumption.* Instead, we are finding in our estimation that we must divide the CES gain by about *six* to get the estimated KBF gain.

The resolution to these surprising empirical results is that the *KBF and CES demand curves must have different slopes at the point of consumption.* But there is nothing in our estimation that will guarantee that result, and in fact our KBF utility function has *more elastic* demand on average for any products—including products 2 and 4 when they are introduced—than the estimated CES utility function. To illustrate the more elastic demand for the KBF function, we compute the Hausman approximation to the KBF gain as shown in (38) and to the CES gain as shown in (18). To be more specific, we single out each product and regard it as a product 1 in the approximate formulae (18) and (38). The remaining products are aggregated into product 2. The share of this aggregate product 2 is simply $s_{2t} \equiv 1 - s_{1t}$.[30] With these modifications, we can calculate $G_{H,KBF}$ and $G_{H,CES}$ for each product and time period. That is, we pretend that each product is newly introduced in each time period and calculate the corresponding gains. Then we take the mean of these measures for each product over the 39 time periods for our estimated KBF and CES functional forms, as reported in table 15.5, together with the bootstrapped 95 percent confidence intervals.[31]

From table 15.5, it can be seen that averaging over all products and all time periods, the approximate gain in utility from the introduction of a product is about 0.17 percentage points using our estimated KBF utility function and about 0.46 percentage points using our estimated CES utility function. So, the CES functional form gives a high estimate of the welfare gain by nearly a factor of three. The difference between them is explained *entirely* by the differing estimates of the inverse demand elasticities, as can be seen from equation (31). In order to have the Hausman approximation to the CES gains that are about three times as high on average as the Hausman approximation to the KBF gains, it must be that the elasticity of demand for the KBF function is about three times as high as for the CES.[32] With the results shown in table 15.5, it is not surprising that the CES gains (from products 2 and 4) *are six times higher than the KBF gains* in table 15.4: about three times

30. The KBF shares that we use for this exercise are fitted shares; that is, we use the actual quantities that are observed in period t, q_{it}, and the estimated prices $p_{it}^* \equiv f_1(q_t)E_t / f(q_t)$ where $f(q)$ is the estimated utility function. In the CES case, we use the observed shares for simplicity.

31. The bootstrap uses 500 draws with replication. In some cases, the estimated coefficient was below the 95 percent confidence interval obtained by dropping the top and bottom 2.5 percent of observations. In those cases, we dropped fewer observations at the bottom and more at the top (still dropping 5 percent in total), so that the coefficient was within the confidence interval.

32. In appendix B of Diewert and Feenstra (2019b), table B1, we report some average elasticities for each product that are quite similar to the elasticities of inverse demand.

Table 15.5   **Gains from the appearance of each product for the estimated KBF and CES utility functions**

Product	$G_{H,KBF}$	$G_{H,CES}$	Product	$G_{H,KBF}$	$G_{H,CES}$
1	0.0041	0.0042	11	0.0034	0.0034
	[0.0029, 0.0139]	[0.0039, 0.0046]		[0.0011, 0.0129]	[0.0031, 0.0037]
2	0.0008	0.0017	12	0.0021	0.0019
	[0.0006, 0.0052]	[0.0015, 0.0018]		[0.0004, 0.0057]	[0.0018, 0.0021]
3	0.0006	0.0026	13	0.0056	0.0221
	[0.0004, 0.0038]	[0.0024, 0.0029]		[0.0039, 0.0108]	[0.02037, 0.0239]
4	0.0008	0.0021	14	0.0009	0.0057
	[0.0004, 0.0020]	[0.0020, 0.0023]		[0.0004, 0.0108]	[0.0053, 0.0062]
5	0.0033	0.0095	15	0.0009	0.0017
	[0.0026, 0.0091]	[0.0088, 0.0103]		[0.0003, 0.0075]	[0.0016, 0018]
6	0.0001	0.0027	16	0.0031	0.01012
	[0.0001, 0.0013]	[0.0025, 0.0029]		[0.0016, 0.0121]	[0.0093, 0.0110]
7	0.0005	0.0030	17	0.0019	0.0021
	[0.0005, 0.0040]	[0.0028, 0.0033]		[0.0003, 0.0034]	[0.0020, 0.0024]
8	0.0010	0.0020	18	0.0011	0.0039
	[0.0002, 0.0069]	[0.0018, 0.0022]		[0.0007, 0.0047]	[0.0036, 0.0042]
9	0.0008	0.0020	19	0.0004	0.0041
	[0.0006, 0.0038]	[0.0019, 0.0022]		[0.0004, 0.0165]	[0.0037, 0.0044]
10	0.0005	0.0014	Mean	0.0017	0.0046
	[0.0003, 0.0031]	[0.0013, 0.0016]		[0.0017, 0.0041]	[0.0042, 0.0049]

within this difference comes from having more elastic demand for the KBF than for the CES utility functions (so that the Hausman linear approximation to the gains in the CES case are nearly three times as high as in the KBF case), while the other two times comes from CES demand curves being more convex (with gains about twice higher) than KBF demand.

15.5   Conclusions

Determining how to incorporate new goods into the calculation of price indexes is an important, unresolved issue for statistical agencies. That issue becomes particularly important with the increased availability of scanner data to measure prices and quantities, because new and disappearing products at the barcode level occur frequently in such data. Our goal in this paper has been to compare several empirical methods to deal with new and disappearing products: the proposal by Hausman (1999, 191; 2003, 27) to use a linear approximation to the demand curve to compute a lower bound to the consumer surplus, assuming that the true demand curve is convex; and with the estimation of two utility functions, the CES case and a quadratic utility function that we refer to as the KBF case. We have extended the approach of Hausman to apply to the analysis of inverse demand curve (prices as functions of quantities) rather than direct demand curves (quantities as functions of prices), as needed in the KBF case.[33] Then we have illustrated our results using the barcode data for frozen juice from one grocery store. While obviously limited in its scope, there are several tentative conclusions that can be drawn from the computations undertaken in this paper:

- The Feenstra CES methodology for dealing with changes in product availability is dependent on having accurate estimates for the elasticity of substitution. The gains from increasing product availability are very large if the elasticity of substitution σ is close to one and fall rapidly as the elasticity increases, as discussed in section 15.3.1.
- It is not a trivial matter to obtain an accurate estimate for σ. Section 15.4.2 developed one methodological approach to the estimation of the elasticity of substitution if purchasers of products have CES preferences. These methods adapt Feenstra's (1994) double log-differencing technique to the estimation of σ in a systems approach, where only one parameter needs to be estimated for an entire system of transformed CES demand functions.
- A major purpose of the present paper was the estimation of Hicksian reservation prices for products that were not available in a period. In the CES framework, these reservation prices turn out to be infinite. But typically, it does not require an infinite reservation price to deter a consumer from purchasing a product. Thus, in section 15.3.3 we discussed the utility function $f(q) \equiv (q^T A q)^{1/2}$, which was originally introduced by Konüs and Byushgens (1926). They showed that this functional form was exactly consistent with the use of Fisher (1922) price and quantity indexes, so we called this the KBF functional form. The use of this functional form leads to finite reservation prices, which can be readily calculated once the utility function has been estimated.
- We indicated how the correct curvature conditions on this functional form could be imposed and we showed that it is a semiflexible functional form that is similar to the normalized quadratic semiflexible form introduced by Diewert and Wales (1987, 1988).
- In section 15.4.5 we estimated the unknown parameters in the A matrix using prices as the dependent variables. This approach generated satisfactory point estimates for the KBF functional form, but because of

---

33. Generally, it is challenging to estimate direct demand functions when there are new goods because the reservation prices for goods not available—which will influence the demand for available goods—are unknown. In some cases, the reservation prices can be solved as a function of observed prices and quantities for available goods, and therefore included in the estimation (see Feenstra and Weinstein (2017) for an application to a symmetric translog expenditure function). This problem does not arise when the inverse demand functions are estimated instead, because then the quantity for goods that are not available is simply zero, which can be used in the inverse demand equations for all goods that are available.

the large number of parameters, many of the individual estimates are insignificantly different from zero.

- The results presented in section 15.4.6 indicate that the Feenstra CES methodology for measuring the benefits of increases in product variety may overstate these benefits as compared to our semiflexible methodology. We find that the CES gains *are about six times greater than the KBF gains*: in rough terms, about three times within this difference comes from having more elastic demand for the KBF than for the CES utility functions (so that the Hausman linear approximation to the gains in the CES case are three times as high as in the KBF case), while the other two times comes from CES demand curves being more convex (with gains about twice higher) than KBF demand. Furthermore, the confidence intervals for these estimates of gains in the KBF and CES cases do not overlap.

There is one other functional form that we have not explored in this paper, but which deserves more attention when examining new goods, and that is the translog expenditure function. In its most general form this function is flexible, and under additional conditions the demand curves are convex with finite reservation prices for new goods. Feenstra and Shiells (1997) have examined the case of a single new good, and assuming that the translog and CES demand curves are tangent at the point of consumption, they argue that the gains from the new good in the translog case is *one half* as large as the CES gains. Feenstra and Weinstein (2017) have examined a simplified *symmetric* translog expenditure function that has the same number of free parameters as the CES; that is, it is not a fully flexible functional form. With that simplification, they confirm that the translog case is about one half as large as the CES gains on a large dataset involving new imported products into the United States: they find that the gains from new imports are about one half as large in the translog case as what Broda and Weinstein (2006) find in the CES case.[34] Applying the translog functional form to scanner datasets would be a valuable exercise to see whether that method might be an alternative to the CES functional form, and we expect that the adjustment for new and disappearing goods will be about one half as large in the translog case as for the CES.

Our approach can be compared to the recent work of Redding and Weinstein (2020), who also use a CES utility function. They assume that this functional form represents the "true" preferences, so that any observed deviation

---

34. Note, however, that Feenstra and Weinstein (2017) find another source of gains from new goods in the translog case, and that is a procompetitive effect on lowering the markups on existing goods. This procompetitive effect does not occur under a CES utility function because then markups are fixed. When this procompetitive effect is added to the gains from new products in the translog case, the *total* gains are comparable in size to what Broda and Weinstein (2006) estimate as the gains from new products in the CES case,

from the CES demand curves must represent a shift in tastes. For example, a good with a falling price and a very large increase in demand—a greater increase than what would be implied by the elasticity of substitution—must have a shift in tastes toward that good. They argue that the consumer gain from that price reduction is *greater* than what we would compute using constant tastes (which is the usual assumption of exact price indexes). So, *in addition* to the CES correction for new goods, they would propose a further correction to allow for taste change. Our results in this paper show, in contrast, that once we move away from the CES case and consider alternative utility functions such as the KBF (or the translog case just mentioned), then the gains from new products will be less than that found for the CES utility function.

References

Arrow, K. J., H. B. Chenery, B. S. Minhas, and R. M. Solow. 1961. "Capital-Labor Substitution and Economic Efficiency." *Review of Economics and Statistics* 63:225–50.

Broda, Christian, and David E. Weinstein. 2006. "Globalization and the Gains from Variety." *Quarterly Journal of Economics* 121 (2): 541–85.

Diewert, W. E. 1974. "Applications of Duality Theory." In *Frontiers of Quantitative Economics*, vol. 2, edited by M. D. Intriligator and D. A. Kendrick, 106–71. Amsterdam: North-Holland.

———. 1976. "Exact and Superlative Index Numbers." *Journal of Econometrics* 4:114–45.

———. 1980. "Capital and the Theory of Productivity Measurement." *American Economic Review* 70 (2): 260–67.

———. 1987. "Index Numbers." In *The New Palgrave: A Dictionary of Economics*, vol. 2, edited by J. Eatwell, M. Milgate, and P. Newman, 767–80. London: Macmillan.

———. 1998. "Index Number Issues in the Consumer Price Index." *Journal of Economic Perspectives* 12 (1): 47–58.

———. 1999. "Index Number Approaches to Seasonal Adjustment." *Macroeconomic Dynamics* 3:48–67.

———. 2018. "Duality in Production." Discussion Paper 18-02, Vancouver School of Economics, University of British Columbia, Vancouver, Canada.

Diewert, W. E., and R. Feenstra. 2019a. "Estimating the Benefits of New Products: Some Approximations." Discussion Paper 19-02, Vancouver School of Economics, University of British Columbia, Vancouver, Canada.

———. 2019b. "Estimating the Benefits of New Products." NBER Working Paper No. 25991, National Bureau of Economic Research, Cambridge, MA.

Diewert, W. E., and K. J. Fox. 2017. "Substitution Bias in Multilateral Methods for CPI Construction Using Scanner Data." Discussion Paper 17-02, Vancouver School of Economics, University of British Columbia, Vancouver, Canada.

Diewert, W. E., and R. J. Hill. 2010. "Alternative Approaches to Index Number Theory." In *Price and Productivity Measurement*, edited by W. E. Diewert, Bert M. Balk, Dennis Fixler, Kevin J. Fox, and Alice O. Nakamura, 263–78. Victoria, Canada: Trafford Press.

Diewert, W. E., and T. J. Wales. 1987. "Flexible Functional Forms and Global Curvature Conditions." *Econometrica* 55:43–68.

———. 1988. "A Normalized Quadratic Semiflexible Functional Form." *Journal of Econometrics* 37:327–42.

Feenstra, R. C. 1994. "New Product Varieties and the Measurement of International Prices." *American Economic Review* 84 (1): 157–77.

———. 2010. "New Products with a Symmetric AIDS Expenditure Function." *Economic Letters* 2:108–11.

Feenstra, R. C., and M. D. Shapiro. 2003. "High Frequency Substitution and the Measurement of Price Indexes." In *Scanner Data and Price Indexes*, Studies in Income and Wealth, vol. 64, edited by R. C. Feenstra and M. D. Shapiro, 123–49. Chicago: University of Chicago Press.

Feenstra, Robert C., and Clinton Shiells. 1997. "Bias in U.S. Import Prices and Demand." In *The Economics of New Goods*, edited by Timothy Bresnahan and Robert Gordon, 249–76. Chicago: University of Chicago Press.

Feenstra, Robert C., and David E. Weinstein. 2017. "Globalization, Markups, and U.S. Welfare." *Journal of Political Economy* 125 (4): 1041–74.

Fisher, Irving. 1922. *The Making of Index Numbers*. Boston: Houghton-Mifflin.

Hardy, G. H., J. E. Littlewood, and G. Polyá. 1934. *Inequalities*. Cambridge: Cambridge University Press.

Hausman, J. 2003. "Sources of Bias and Solutions to Bias in the Consumer Price Index." *Journal of Economic Perspectives* 17 (1): 23–44.

Hausman, J. A. 1996. "Valuation of New Goods under Perfect and Imperfect Competition." In *The Economics of New Goods*, edited by T. F. Bresnahan and R. J. Gordon, 209–37. Chicago: University of Chicago Press.

———. 1999. "Cellular Telephone, New Products and the CPI." *Journal of Business and Economic Statistics* 17(2): 188–94.

Hausman, J. A., and G. K. Leonard. 2002. "The Competitive Effects of a New Product Introduction: A Case Study." *Journal of Industrial Economics* 50 (3): 237–63.

Hicks, J. R. 1940. "The Valuation of the Social Income." *Economica* 7:105–24.

Hofsten, E. von. 1952. *Price Indexes and Quality Change*. London: George Allen and Unwin.

Konüs, A. A. 1924. "The Problem of the True Index of the Cost of Living." Translated in 1939 in *Econometrica* 7:10–29.

Konüs, A. A., and S. S. Byushgens. 1926. "K probleme pokupatelnoi cili deneg." *Voprosi Konyunkturi* 2:151–72.

Marshall, A. 1887. "Remedies for Fluctuations of General Prices." *Contemporary Review* 51:355–75.

Redding, Stephen, and David E. Weinstein. 2020. "Measuring Aggregate Price Indices with Taste Shocks: Theory and Evidence for CES Preferences." *Quarterly Journal of Economics* 135 (1): 503–60.

Rothbarth, E. 1941. "The Measurement of Changes in Real Income under Conditions of Rationing." *Review of Economic Studies* 8:100–107.

Sato, K. 1976. "The Ideal Log-Change Index Number." *Review of Economics and Statistics* 58:223–28.

Shephard, R. W. 1953. *Cost and Production Functions*. Princeton, NJ: Princeton University Press.

University of Chicago. 2013. *Dominick's Data Manual*. Chicago: James M. Kilts Center, University of Chicago Booth School of Business.

Vartia, Y. O. 1976. "Ideal Log-Change Index Numbers." *Scandinavian Journal of Statistics* 3:121–26.

Wiley, D. E., W. H. Schmidt, and W. J. Bramble. 1973. "Studies of a Class of Covariance Structure Models." *Journal of the American Statistical Association* 68:317–23.

Contributors

Katharine G. Abraham
Department of Economics and
Joint Program in Survey Methodology
University of Maryland
College Park, MD 20742

Aditya Aladangady
Federal Reserve Board
20th Street and Constitution Avenue,
  NW
Washington, DC 20551

Shifrah Aron-Dine
Department of Economics
Stanford University
Stanford, CA 94305

Andrew Baer
International Monetary Fund
700 19th Street NW
Washington, DC 20431

Nevada Basdeo
US Census Bureau
4600 Silver Hill Road
Washington, DC 20233

Andrea Batch
Bureau of Economic Analysis
4600 Silver Hill Road
Washington, DC 20233

Sudip Bhattacharjee
School of Business
University of Connecticut
Storrs, CT 06269

Nathaniel Burbank
Wayfair
4 Copley Place, 7th Floor
Boston, MA 02116

Tomaz Cajner
Federal Reserve Board
20th Street and Constitution Avenue,
  NW
Washington, DC 20551

Jeffrey C. Chen
Nordic Entertainment Group
Ringvägen 52
118 67 Stockholm Sweden

David Copple
Bank of England
Threadneedle Street
London EC2R 8AH United Kingdom

Leland D. Crane
Federal Reserve Board
20th Street and Constitution Avenue,
  NW
Washington, DC 20551

John Cuffe
US Census Bureau
4600 Silver Hill Road
Washington, DC 20233

Ryan A. Decker
Federal Reserve Board
20th Street and Constitution Avenue,
    NW
Washington, DC 20551

W. Erwin Diewert
Vancouver School of Economics
University of British Columbia
Vancouver, BC V6T 1L4 Canada

Jyldyz Djumalieva
Nesta
58 Victoria Embankment
London EC4Y 0DS United Kingdom

Alexander Driessen
Bureau of Economic Analysis
4600 Silver Hill Road
Washington, DC 20233

Abe Dunn
Bureau of Economic Analysis
4600 Silver Hill Road
Washington, DC 20233

Wendy Dunn
Federal Reserve Board
20th Street and Constitution Avenue,
    NW
Washington, DC 20551

Gabriel Ehrlich
Department of Economics
University of Michigan
Ann Arbor, MI 48109

Ugochukwu Etudo
School of Business
University of Connecticut
Stamford, CT 06269

Don A. Fast
Bureau of Labor Statistics
2 Massachusetts Avenue, NE
Washington, DC 20212

Robert C. Feenstra
Department of Economics
University of California–Davis
Davis, CA 95616

Laura Feiveson
Federal Reserve Board
20th Street and Constitution Avenue,
    NW
Washington, DC 20551

Susan E. Fleck
Bureau of Labor Statistics
2 Massachusetts Avenue, NE
Washington, DC 20212

David M. Friedman
Bureau of Labor Statistics
2 Massachusetts Avenue, NE
Washington, DC 20212

Marina Gindelsky
Bureau of Economic Analysis
4600 Silver Hill Road
Washington, DC 20233

Edward L. Glaeser
Department of Economics
Harvard University
Cambridge, MA 02138

Dana Goldman
Leonard D. Schaeffer Center for
    Health Policy and Economics
University of Southern California
Los Angeles, CA 90089

Rishab Guha
Department of Economics
Harvard University
Cambridge, MA 02138

John Haltiwanger
Department of Economics
University of Maryland
College Park, MD 20742

Adrian Hamins-Puertolas
Federal Reserve Board
20th Street and Constitution Avenue,
    NW
Washington, DC 20551

Kyle Hood
Bureau of Economic Analysis
4600 Silver Hill Road
Washington, DC 20233

Rebecca J. Hutchinson
US Census Bureau
4600 Silver Hill Road
Washington, DC 20233

Ron S. Jarmin
US Census Bureau
4600 Silver Hill Road
Washington, DC 20233

J. Bradford Jensen
McDonough School of Business
Georgetown University
Washington, DC 20057

David Johnson
Institute for Social Research
University of Michigan
Ann Arbor, MI 48106

Hyunjin Kim
INSEAD
1 Ayer Rajah Avenue
Singapore 138676

Shawn Klimek
US Census Bureau
4600 Silver Hill Road
Washington, DC 20233

Crystal G. Konny
Bureau of Labor Statistics
2 Massachusetts Avenue, NE
Washington, DC 20212

Christopher Kurz
Federal Reserve Board
20th Street and Constitution Avenue,
  NW
Washington, DC 20551

Paul Lengermann
Federal Reserve Board
20th Street and Constitution Avenue,
  NW
Washington, DC 20551

Michael Luca
Harvard Business School
Harvard University
Boston, MA 02163

Jeremy G. Moulton
Department of Public Policy
University of North Carolina, Chapel
  Hill
Chapel Hill, NC 27599

Brian C. Moyer
National Center for Health Statistics
Centers for Disease Control and
  Prevention
3311 Toledo Road
Hyattsville, MD 20782

Serena Ng
Department of Economics
Columbia University
New York, NY 10027

Shawn R. Roberts
Akari Technologies

John A. Romley
Leonard D. Schaeffer Center for
  Health Policy and Economics
University of Southern California
Los Angeles, CA 90089-7273

Claudia Sahm
Jain Family Institute
568 Broadway, Suite 601
New York, NY, 10012

Matthew D. Shapiro
Department of Economics
University of Michigan
Ann Arbor, MI 48109

Lisa Singh
Department of Computer Science
Georgetown University
Washington, DC 20057

Justin C. Smith
Optum
3501 S. Harbor Blvd.
Santa Ana, CA 92704

Neeraj Sood
Leonard D. Schaeffer Center for
   Health Policy and Economics
University of Southern California
Los Angeles, CA 90089

Bradley Speigner
Bank of England
Threadneedle Street
London EC2R 8AH United Kingdom

Joseph Staudt
US Census Bureau
4600 Silver Hill Road
Washington, DC 20233

James Thurgood
Royal Bank of Scotland
175 Glasgow Road
Edinburgh EH12 9BH Scotland

Arthur Turrell
Bank of England
Threadneedle Street
London EC2R 8AH United Kingdom

Yifang Wei
Department of Computer Science
Georgetown University
Washington, DC 20057

Scott A. Wentland
Bureau of Economic Analysis
4600 Silver Hill Road
Washington, DC 20233

Brendan K. Williams
Bureau of Labor Statistics
2 Massachusetts Avenue, NE
Washington, DC 20212

Author Index

Subject Index

Note: Page numbers followed by "f" or "t" refer to figures or tables, respectively.